Preface.

This book is not about h~~~~~~~~~~~
is not yet fit to speak of them.
Nor is it about battles, ~~and glory~~ deeds or land
~~nor~~ about glory honour, ~~any~~ myght~~~~, mycty, dominion or power
~~whatsoever~~, ~~any~~ except War.

Above all ~~this~~ ~~Poets~~ book is ~~not~~ concerned with Poetry.
~~My this~~ the subject of it is War. and the pity of War.

The Poetry is in the pity.

~~I have no hesitation in making public~~
Yet these ~~& really publishing~~ such
Elegies are ~~not~~ ~~this~~ ~~consolation~~
~~Poe~~ it is ~~a beaeaved~~ in no sense ~~consolatory~~
to ~~this~~ generation. They may be to the
next. ~~If I thought the letter of this~~
~~book would last,~~ All a 'poet can do today is warn.
~~used proper names;~~ That is why the True War Poet must be truthful.
(If I thought the letter of this book would last, I
might have used proper names; but if the spirit of
it survives ~~Prussia~~ my ambition and those names will
be content; ~~prettily~~ have achieved themselves fresher fields than Flanders,
ourselves.

MECHANICS--
MERCANTILE
LIBRARY.

Wilfred Owen

Wilfred Owen

A NEW BIOGRAPHY

Dominic Hibberd

IVAN R. DEE
Chicago 2003

WILFRED OWEN. Copyright © 2002 by Dominic Hibberd. All rights reserved, including the right to reproduce this book or portions thereof in any form. For information, address: Ivan R. Dee, Publisher, 1332 North Halsted Street, Chicago 60622.

First published in Great Britain in 2002 by Weidenfeld & Nicolson. First American edition published 2003 by Ivan R. Dee.

ISBN 1-56663-487-3

A CIP catalog record for this book is available from the Library of Congress.

Contents

Illustrations

Artists' Rifles officers and cadets, Hare Hall camp (*Imperial War Museum*)

The Poetry Bookshop, Bloomsbury (*from* The Bookman, *1913*)

Lt-Col. William Shirley (*from the* Artists' Rifles Journal)

Sentry duty, Hare Hall camp (*Danny Wigley*)

Wilfred's hut and its inmates, Hare Hall camp, 1915 (*OEF*)

Balgores House, Romford (*Danny Wigley*)

Second Lieutenant W.E.S. Owen, July 1916 (*author*)

Officers of the 5th (Reserve) Battalion, Manchester Regiment, 1916 (*Michael Thompson*)

Tom and Susan Owen, with Harold, Colin and Mary (*Shropshire Records and Research*)

Practice trenches, near Romford, 1916 (*Imperial War Museum*)

Troops in captured enemy trenches at Serre, March 1917 (*Imperial War Museum*)

Between pages 268 and 269

Members of a 2nd Manchesters working party near Serre, January 1917 (*Imperial War Museum*)

Troops clearing a mined road in Nesle, March 1917 (*Imperial War Museum*)

St Quentin Cathedral seen from the new front line, April 1917 (*Imperial War Museum*)

Craiglockhart War Hospital from the air (*Napier University*)

Captain Arthur Brock at Craiglockhart (*Mrs Sydney Brock*)

Front cover of *The Hydra* (*OEF*)

Siegfried Sassoon (*Hulton Getty Picture Library*)

Nancy Nicholson and Robert Graves (*Richard Perceval Graves*)

Wilfred with Arthur Newboult, Edinburgh, 1917 (*Owen Estate*)

Charles Scott Moncrieff (*from* C.K. Scott Moncrieff, Memories and Letters, *1931*)

Robert Ross (*Robert Robertson*)

Osbert Sitwell (*from* The Bookman)

Harold Monro (*British Library*)

North Bay, Scarborough (*postcard, 1918*)

The parade ground, Burniston barracks, Scarborough (*author*)

The last photograph of Wilfred, August 1918 (*Owen Estate*)

Second Lieutenant John Foulkes (*Patricia Denny*)

The unfinished German front trench, Beaurevoir-Fonsomme line, October 1918 (*Imperial War Museum*)

'Swiss Cottage' (Moulin Grison Farm), Joncourt, October 1918 (*Imperial War Museum*)

The Sambre-Oise canal near Ors (*from* The Story of the Fourth Army, *1920*)

Endpapers: Wilfred Owen's draft list of contents and Preface for a projected book, spring 1918 (*Owen Estate*)

Maps

Drawings

The Owen family

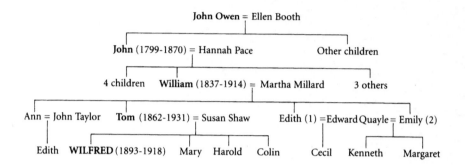

The Salter family

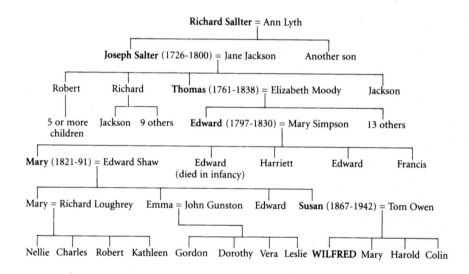

Acknowledgements

I have made innumerable enquiries in the course of writing this book, and almost all of them have been answered with warm enthusiasm, often with more information than I have been able to use. My first debt is to Peter and Elizabeth Owen, and other members of Wilfred's family. Peter, Wilfred's eldest nephew and next of kin, has been always encouraging and helpful, telling me at the outset to write what I believe to be true and to write it as well as possible for Wilfred's sake. Elizabeth's family researches and insights have been invaluable, and her drawings of Owen-associated houses are a most welcome addition to the book. June Calder (daughter of Wilfred's cousin Leslie Gunston) has told me much about the Gunstons and Alpenrose. I am also indebted to Marjorie Gunston (daughter of Leslie's elder brother, Gordon), Joan James (granddaughter of William Hewison Gunston, the Cambridge don) and Colin Dymott (grandson of Wilfred's uncle and aunt, Ann and John Taylor).

I renew my thanks to the many people acknowledged in my previous Owen publications. I am as grateful as ever to Dennis Welland, doyen of Owen scholars, for his research and his encouragement of my early interest in Wilfred; to John Bell for his editing of Wilfred's letters and Harold Owen's memoirs; and to Jon Stallworthy for his work as Wilfred's editor and first biographer. As the two executors of Harold Owen's literary estate, John Bell and Jon Stallworthy asked to read my chapters, kindly giving advice and information but not insisting on changes. I am also grateful to Douglas Kerr for his counsel and his illuminating study, *Wilfred Owen's Voices.*

Many members of the Wilfred Owen Association have given me assistance and information, especially the former chairman, Helen McPhail, and the former treasurer, Philip Guest. Among other kindnesses, Helen and Philip invited me to join them on several of the 'recces' they made in preparation for the Association's battlefield tours. I shall never forget the day when the three of us, guided by friendly villagers, climbed Joncourt ridge in a blizzard and stood on a German pillbox, possibly the very one Wilfred captured in 1918. Philip has done more than anyone to identify the places where Wilfred fought, and this book owes much to his researches. Helen's fluent French has been a great help in France, and her hospitality a great

ACKNOWLEDGEMENTS

pleasure in Shrewsbury, where she has done much to further my own and other people's knowledge of Wilfred. I am also grateful to Vanessa Davis, Caroline Thewles, William Mostyn-Owen, Laurence Le Quesne and other WOA members.

Several people have generously shared their local researches. I owe warm thanks to John Baxter (Birkenhead), Jean Eastwood (Dunsden), Ken Simcox (Shrewsbury), Danny Wigley (Romford) and Roland Bouyssou and the late Michel Roucoux (France). Thanks, too, to Arthur Smith and others (Birkenhead); Vera Lee and Ian Watson (Romford); Christine Bland, Mr and Mrs Raymond Williams and the late Mrs Robins, formerly house-keeper to Herbert Wigan (Dunsden); and the owners of seven houses Wilfred stayed in for willingly showing me round.

Years ago I talked about Wilfred with three people who had known him, Leslie Gunston, Canon Roland Bate and Sir Sacheverell Sitwell. More recently I have had invaluable help from the next generation, not only from the Owens and Gunstons already mentioned but also from Patricia Denny (daughter of John Foulkes), Mary Knight (niece of Ray Williams, the Hornchurch Scout), Barbara La Touche (daughter of Charles de la Touche), Mary Townsend (daughter of Vivian Rampton) and Rachel White (daughter of Mary Gray).

For advice on Wilfred's army career and related military matters, I am grateful to Captain Robert Bonner (Museum of the Manchesters), John Gavin (Artists' Rifles) and Martin Middlebrook. Gary Sheffield, one of the leading 'revisionist' historians of the Great War, has kindly read my 1916–17 chapters and made many helpful comments, and my last chapter has been read with similar care by Vince Connolly, author of a perceptive, detailed study of the Fourth Army's operations on the Sambre Canal. Some years ago the late T.H.A. Potts wrote to me about his father, Captain G.A. Potts, and more recently Malcolm Brown, another well-known historian of the war, very kindly drew my attention to Captain Potts's papers in the Imperial War Museum, with their story of Colonel Marshall's work and death on the canal.

Tony Carr and his colleagues at the Shropshire Records and Research Centre have been unfailingly helpful. I am also grateful to Neil Cobbett (Public Record Office), Tony Richards (Imperial War Museum) and to many local librarians and archivists, including Diane Backhouse (Cheshire), Alan Cater (Tameside), M. Copley (Hereford), Carol Greenwood (Bradford), David Preston (Town Clerk, Oswestry), J.L. Revill (Wigan), Hilary Ritchie (Surrey), R.J. Trayburn (Swindon) and Derek Williams (Oswestry).

Sue Usher (English Faculty Library, University of Oxford) has readily given me access to the Owen Collection and made me feel always welcome in her domain, as did her predecessors, Margaret Weedon and Gwen Hampshire. Other university librarians and archivists to whom I owe thanks include Adrian Allan (Liverpool), Michael Bott (Reading), Kathleen

XIV

Cann (Cambridge), Irene Ferguson (Edinburgh), Clare Hopkins (Trinity College, Oxford), Sue Howard (University College of Ripon St Mark and St John), Nicholas Jeffs (London), Roger Norris (Durham) and Mark Shipway (Leeds). Thanks also to Simon Blundell (Reform Club), Estela Dukan (Royal College of Physicians), Penelope Hatfield (Eton College), David Knight (Stonyhurst College), Shaw McCloghry (Bloxham School), Tony Money (Radley College), Richard Mortimer (Westminster Abbey), Edward Pinsent (Church of England Records Centre) and Jeremy Ward (Manchester Grammar School).

Other people who have kindly given me help include Clifford Askew, Pat Barker, Pam Blevins, Mark Bostridge, Pamela Bowen, Robert Christoforides, Brian Cooke, Max Egremont, Adrian Goodman, Edith Gunston, Marjorie Hall, Linda Hart, Stephen MacDonald, John Onions, Ann Park, Dez Quarrell, Sally Roberton, Rhys Robinson, Miranda Seymour, Tony Verity, Loretta Williams, Jean Moorcroft Wilson and Simon Wormleighton.

For permission to reproduce illustrations, I am grateful to June Calder for Leslie Gunston's drawing of Alpenrose; D.S.W. Jones, former art master at the Birkenhead Institute, for three drawings; Elizabeth Owen for five drawings; the English Faculty Library, Oxford (OEF); and other owners shown in the list of illustrations, especially to Michael Thompson for the photograph of (capless) 5th (Res.) Manchester Regiment officers.

Unless otherwise stated in my endnotes, extracts from poems by Wilfred Owen are quoted as they appear in *Wilfred Owen The Complete Poems and Fragments*, edited by Jon Stallworthy © The Executors of Harold Owen's Estate 1963 and 1983 published by Chatto & Windus, used by permission of The Random House Group; and prose extracts, © Oxford University Press, are reprinted from *Wilfred Owen: Collected Letters* edited by Harold Owen and John Bell (1967) and *Journey from Obscurity: Wilfred Owen 1893–1918*, Volumes I–III by Harold Owen (1963–1965) by permission of Oxford University Press. In verse quotations, words cancelled in manuscript by Wilfred Owen are shown in square brackets.

On a more personal note, I record my thanks to the kind friends – in addition to those already mentioned – who have between them read and commented on all my chapters: John Baxter, Roland Bouyssou, June Calder, Tim Clarke, Jean Eastwood, Philip Guest, Douglas Kerr, Helen McPhail, Peter and Elizabeth Owen, Ken Simcox and Danny Wigley. I am most grateful to all of them, and to my agent, Bruce Hunter, and editor, Benjamin Buchan, for suggesting many improvements and saving me from howlers. The faults that remain are all my own work. Finally, my thanks to my co-researcher, old friend and shrewdest critic, Tom Coulthard, who has shared my interest in Wilfred since we studied the poems together more than thirty years ago and to whom I dedicate this book.

Introduction

'I can see no excuse for deceiving you,' Wilfred Owen wrote to his mother on first coming out of the front line. 'I have suffered seventh hell.' His testimony to 'the truth untold' has had an ever-growing influence on modern attitudes to the First World War and to war in general. For many young people he is now the archetypal voice of 1914–18, even though historians point out – sometimes with exasperation – that it is highly misleading to see him as representative. He was a unique, extraordinary figure, unlike any other poet or soldier of his time.

Most of Owen's war poems are based on his experiences in the first five months of 1917. During that time he was in hospital for six weeks, on a course in the base area for four weeks and in action for only about thirty days. His front-line service was unusually concentrated and varied. It took place in what was said to be the worst winter France had known for forty years, first in mud and heavy rain, then in the intense frost that clamped down on the battle zone in mid-January. After helping to defend shattered positions that had hardly moved for over a year, he took part in a few days of fast-moving, open warfare, virtually the only such moment anywhere on the British front between October 1914 and March 1918. He was never wounded, and he endured very little of what is thought of as the standard Western Front experience, the ghastly monotony of routine trench duty. Nevertheless he endured and witnessed 'unnameable tortures', and he was almost buried alive, half-frozen to death and nearly blown to pieces.

Out of it all, months later, came poem after poem, including 'Strange Meeting' and 'The Sentry' with their subterranean settings, 'Futility' and 'Exposure' with their deadly snow, 'Spring Offensive', where the green earth explodes under a hurricane barrage, and hospital studies such as 'A Terre' and 'Mental Cases'. Even so, the Great War did not turn Owen into a poet, although critics sometimes say that it did. Short though his life was, it was remarkably complete, and almost everything in it contributed to his final success as soldier and poet, leader and pleader. He was fascinated by the lives of other poets, and he is himself an outstanding example of a poet caught up in, but never overwhelmed by, enormous historical events.

Among my many sources for this biography, *Wilfred Owen: Collected Letters* has been constantly on my desk, although I have used that irreplaceable volume with a little caution. The great majority of Owen's surviving letters were written to his mother, and there was much he did not tell her. Some of the things he did tell her were later removed by his brother Harold, who cut or painted out many passages and sometimes burned whole letters. A friend of Harold's once remarked to me that he destroyed more papers than he kept, and while that may be an overstatement there can be no doubt that the loss was very severe, much more so than is generally realised. Again and again there are gaps in the record, often at crucial points in the story. It was not only letters that disappeared. One of Harold's many lists of documents, for instance, includes a notebook and diary used by Wilfred in 1918, the only clue that Wilfred ever did use a diary. The late Patric Dickinson saw the notebook and several fragments of early verse, referring to them in a 1953 broadcast, but now only two pages of the notebook survive, and the fragments quoted by Dickinson, like the diary and many letters, are 'missing'.[1]

Harold left another difficulty for Owen biographers. His three-volume autobiography, *Journey from Obscurity*, has sometimes been regarded as an objective, accurate record, but when one looks closely at his stories they frequently turn out to contain a good deal of fiction. He was convinced he was writing the truth, and his defenders insist, no doubt rightly, that he was a most honest, honourable man. But he was also a talented artist, and his memoirs are best understood as a series of vivid, imaginative paintings, full of strong colours and contrasts. They illustrate the past as he wanted to remember it, but not necessarily as it really was.

I have used many other sources, including the vast collections of military archives in the Public Record Office. A battalion's movements on the Western Front, and the reasons for them, can often be worked out in detail, and I have tried to reconstruct each of the engagements Owen took part in. The recent release of thousands of officers' personal files has also made it possible to identify many of his colleagues.

I have also drawn on some of my previous publications about Owen, referring to them in endnotes rather than repeating academic details. My *Owen the Poet* (1986) is a critical study, and *Wilfred Owen: The Last Year* (1992) is an illustrated account of Owen's life in 1917–18. I have almost completely rewritten my 1917–18 chapters, adding new material and correcting errors.

Owen has often been enrolled by partisan critics as one of their own, sometimes on the flimsiest evidence. Pacifists have regarded him as a pacifist, socialists as a socialist; feminists, improbably, have assumed he was a feminist; Christians, including his mother, have insisted he was always a

Christian. He has been described as a practising sado-masochist, apparently on the grounds that one of his war poems mentions belts and straps; and his ready affection for children has even allowed paedophiles to claim him. The truth is that he was avowedly not a pacifist, nor was he a socialist, although like Keats he was inclined to 'take the liberal side of the question'. He was no misogynist, but he was scornful of women in wartime. He did not regain his early religious belief, even though he might never have described himself as an atheist. His imaginative processes undoubtedly contained strong sado-masochistic elements, but there is nothing to suggest that he ever voluntarily gave them physical expression. As for children, it was perfectly acceptable in his day for young men to make friends with them. Owen delighted in young company, but with his strict moral upbringing he would never have sexually interfered with a child.

One claim often made about Owen is undoubtedly true, although there are still people who prefer not to believe it. He was gay – not that there was an accepted adjective in his time for the love that dared not speak its name. There is abundant evidence in his writing of a strong homoerotic impulse, something that he seems to have recognised and accepted without much difficulty. Evidence for sexual relationships is necessarily less obvious, but there are a good many clues that he was neither ignorant nor completely inexperienced. Caution was essential in an age when gay men were always at risk from blackmailers and the law, and secrecy became a continuing theme in his poetry.

～

Owen would have survived the war if the attempted canal crossing at Ors had been called off earlier. Ten minutes might have been enough. Writing about his death was an ordeal that I put off for many weeks, but his daily companionship during the last five years has been an immense pleasure. He lived his life to the full: everything interested him, and he was never bored. He had a wicked sense of humour, an ironic eye for social pretension and an ear for comic voices. He loved words and language; even if he had written no poems he would deserve to be remembered as one of the finest letter writers of his century. He knew that his capacity for pleasure made him vulnerable to pain, and he experienced both, making poetry out of them with enormous skill and courage. The endearing, sometimes pretentious young versifier, self-absorbed, class-conscious and pedantic, grew into a fiercely compassionate, deeply impressive man. His achievement testifies to the enduring strength of poetry and of the human spirit.

Dominic Hibberd
Kingham
April 2002

From Plas Wilmot to
Wilmot House

'Sir Wilfred Edward Salter-Owen.' So Susan Owen wrote her son's name early in March 1894, as she wrapped up a lock of his baby hair and hid the little package in her jewel-box. He was almost a year old. His carefully chosen names would allow him to have a hyphen like the local gentry when he became famous.[1] Three Christian names were unheard-of even on her side of the family until now, and her husband had been christened plain 'Tom'. Sir Wilfred Edward Salter-Owen of Plas Wilmot, Oswestry, Shropshire. It is usually said that she wanted her eldest son to become a clergyman, but her first ambitions for him were more worldly. The house would be his one day, with its paddocks and fields, and the garden and specimen trees she could see from the bedroom window. He bore the name of the man who had built it, her mother's father, Edward Salter, and Edward's ambition to raise the family up in the world was going to be fulfilled by his great-grandson.[2]

Susan would have been appalled to know that within three years Plas Wilmot would be lost, and her children would grow up knowing little or nothing about their Salter relations. The Salters are never mentioned in Wilfred's letters, nor in his brother Harold's memoirs, *Journey from Obscurity*. Harold suspected the two families might be connected, but when in 1964 he wrote to a distant cousin, Emma Salter, asking if she knew why Wilfred had been christened Salter, she replied that there was no blood relationship whatever. She could remember playing with Wilfred at Plas Wilmot, and could only suppose he had been given his third name because her mother and Susan had been friends.[3] Harold's ignorance and Miss Salter's denial suggest that the two families had lost touch many years before. Susan may have found it hard to make contact with her relations or talk about them to her children after the ancestral home was sold.

There had been numerous Salters in the Oswestry area since the early Middle Ages, and Susan's direct ancestry can easily be traced back to the late seventeenth century. Among her Georgian and Victorian relatives were several printer-booksellers, two clockmakers and at least two mayors. One wrote a book on angling, and another, unusually for a Salter, became an officer in the militia, so Wilfred was not the tribe's first author or soldier. Susan would have been brought up to think of the Salters as a long-established, highly respectable family, and of her own branch as the most respectable of all, owning the best house and the most land.

~

The Edward Salter who built Plas Wilmot was a joiner, born in 1797, son of an Oswestry timber merchant. In 1829 he began building a villa on the edge of his native town, hoping to live there as a country gentleman. The house is charming and unpretentious, built well but not for show. The largest of the five original bedrooms is only fourteen foot square, although Edward's high standards are evident in the room's handsome coved ceiling and sturdy panelled door. French windows open from the parlour into the garden, where the gabled front quietly echoes the pediments of grander houses. The long boundary wall to the lane and the little cottage for servants imply a prosperous estate, but the formal lawns soon give way to fields and a large kitchen garden, and the big stable yard next to the house seems almost a farmyard.

Plas Wilmot, Oswestry

Edward never lived at Plas Wilmot. He died aged thirty-two, while the builders were still at work. At least his new status was recognised, and he was officially recorded as a 'gentleman', not as a joiner. His young widow and their four children moved into the new house. She had to run the property as a business, farming more than four acres of arable land, four of meadow and one of pasture, as well as the kitchen garden, responsibilities that must have been a heavy burden. She died of heart failure in

2

1842, and Plas Wilmot passed to the eldest of the children, Mary, who was only twenty-one. All four of the young Salters were able to maintain the social level won for them by their father: Mary was a landed proprietress, one of her two brothers became a clergyman, the other a surgeon, and her sister married a doctor. They were probably sustained by Evangelical religion, like many Victorians of their generation. Mary was well known locally in later life for her church and charitable work, and her children were brought up to be strictly Evangelical.

Mary Salter of Plas Wilmot was a desirable match, but she did not marry until she was thirty-five. Her husband, Edward Shaw, two months her junior, was a farmer's son, born at Shobdon, Herefordshire, in 1821. He had moved to Oswestry in his late twenties, buying an ironmongery business at 16 Bailey Street and soon becoming influential in the town. He and Mary had four children: Mary ('May') Salter in 1860,[4] Emma Yeld in the following year, Edward Gough in 1863 and Harriett Susan, Wilfred's mother, who was born at Plas Wilmot on 17 March 1867. The two youngest children were christened at the town's second Anglican church, Holy Trinity, in preference to the great parish church of St Oswald. Edward Shaw seems to have transferred his allegiance to the smaller church, and in due course two of his grandchildren, Wilfred and Mary Owen, were also to be christened there.

Under Shaw's pious but far from parsimonious rule, Plas Wilmot came into its own at last as a family home. It was probably in his time that the house was considerably enlarged and altered. The 1871 census shows him and Mary living there with their four children, a governess, a cook and a housemaid. Had the census listed animals as well, it might have recorded a parrot and a cat or two, sheep and a few cattle, pigs, geese, ducks, a horse for the carriage, and a collection of prize fowls, Shaw being a well-known poultry fancier often called on to judge shows. Described in the census as magistrate and ironmonger, he was also a town councillor and had just served a year as mayor. He was strongly conservative in politics, holding office in the anti-radical Primrose League and chairing the local Tories for at least one election, and he was equally conservative in religion, a dedicated Evangelical. When he resigned in 1872 as Superintendent of the St Oswald's Sunday School after sixteen years' service, the congregation presented him with an inkstand, acknowledging the inadequacy of the gift but declaring that 'in prayerful love we point you onward for your full reward to the Bright Day of our Coming Lord'.[5] The Shaw children grew up amid this kind of language, the three girls becoming almost as devout as their parents. Edward junior, however, was inclined to rebel.

It may be that public duties and worries about his increasingly wayward son distracted the elder Shaw's attention from his main source of income. It would have been easy for him to leave the running of the ironmongery business to his employees, of whom there were probably a dozen or more.[6] Men in his workshops made nails, tools and tinware for sale in the Bailey Street premises, where there were many other items in stock: ranges, grates and chimney-pieces, bedsteads, farm machinery and corrugated iron, cutlery, brooms, paint and sometimes even groceries. Despite the outward prosperity of the shop, its proprietor's finances were apparently less sound than they should have been.

In 1884 the eldest of the Shaw girls, May, married Richard Loughrey, an Irish-born doctor with a practice in the East End of London. The lane outside the house was decorated with flags and an arch of evergreens, bearing the motto 'Long Life and Happiness to Mr and Mrs Loughrey', and cannon were fired at intervals during the day.[7] The transition from Plas Wilmot to the Mile End Road in Stepney must have been hard for May, but her decision to share her husband's labours among the poor had no doubt been made with much prayer.

Less than two years later it was Emma Shaw's turn to be married. Like her sister, she chose a man who worked for the London poor, although John Gunston was a trader rather than a doctor.[8] He ran a chain of pork shops in Bermondsey and Southwark, in partnership with his father Robert. Pork was the cheapest meat in those days. 'The poorer the district, the more money I make,' Robert Gunston used to say, and he made a good deal. Every Saturday he would go round his shops in a hansom cab to collect the takings. The Gunstons were not 'carriage folk', but they had money and time for civilised living at their house in Brixton, and Robert's three children had been brought up to enjoy literature and the arts. The eldest son was a brilliant maths don at Cambridge, the daughter a talented painter, and John a keen pianist and photographer. The bride's parents must have been pleased, especially as there was every chance that John Gunston would eventually inherit a share of his father's wealth and be free to retire.

The third of the Shaw sisters, Susan, fell in love with a railway clerk named Tom Owen. Tom and Susan are always said to have been introduced by young Edward Shaw before Tom went to India in 1880, but the only source for that story, as for so many others, is *Journey from Obscurity*, the memoirs of Tom's second son, Harold, whose chronology is often unreliable. If Harold is right that Tom arrived in Oswestry at the age of fifteen, that is to say in 1877–8, the bride-to-be was only ten or eleven. Tom may well have got to know her brother, but he is unlikely to have promised to marry Susan or even to have seen much of her before he went abroad. It was no doubt assumed in the Shaw family that Susan's lot in life, like that of many other youngest daughters, was to devote herself to looking after her parents.

Quiet and affectionate, with dark blue eyes, fine skin and a pleasant, shy face that some people thought beautiful, Susan busied herself with household affairs and practised some of the accomplishments proper to a young lady, playing the harp with modest skill and winning a prize or two for her competent little sketches and paintings. When she read novels she was inclined to skip to the happy endings.[9] Her version of religion, which she clung to all her life, was that one should trust in God unquestioningly, in complete confidence that He had prepared a 'Home' for His children, a kind of celestial Plas Wilmot where everyone would be reunited. The Bible assured her this would be so, and she read it dutifully, memorising the so-called 'promise texts' and sometimes writing in a date. Yet her apparent passivity was misleading: in some ways she was strong-willed, expecting other people to behave and think as she did and firmly closing her mind to alien ideas.

Her faith and strength were soon tested. Her brother Edward, an only son with three sisters to make a fuss of him, may have been spoiled from childhood. He had become a skilled footballer, good enough to play for Wales for several seasons, but in 1884 the Welsh selectors decided he was English and dropped him.[10] That year, aged twenty-one, he came into some money left to him by a Salter great-uncle, and perhaps as a result he got into bad company and started drinking.[11] Sometimes he would return late at night, firing a shotgun in the yard, and Susan would have to calm him down and get him to bed. Here again the only source for the story is Harold Owen, who blames the 'excessively morbid' religion of the elder Shaws and their 'unbending and wilfully blind attitude to life', but as he never knew his grandparents and was heavily biased against the religiosity which his mother inherited from them, he may not be entirely accurate. Susan herself blamed drink, and she later trained her children to regard alcohol as a hideous evil: hence Wilfred's reference years later to 'the Tragedy of Uncle Edward Shaw, torn up by the roots by a perverted appetite'.[12] Harold may well be right, though, in saying that the more the son rioted, the more the father reprimanded and quoted scripture. In the end the young man disappeared, sending a message that he was going to America. He was later reported to be in Colorado, and that was the last the family heard of Edward Gough Shaw.

The parents must have taken the loss of their only son as something almost worse than a bereavement. They had been shamed, and a soul had been lost for the Lord. Susan probably felt more strongly than ever that her place was at their side, although by now she had met Tom Owen, who was back from India and working in Shrewsbury. Maybe he had helped to get her brother away from sessions in the pub and taken him home, earning the family's gratitude. By 1890 Tom and Susan seem to have been engaged. In 1891 Edward and Mary Shaw, both now seventy, contracted influenza, Mary becoming seriously ill. They cannot have been too keen on their daughter's marrying a railway clerk from a humble background, but they must have decided it was time for Susan to be settled, and the wedding was arranged for 8 December. On 22 November Susan went to church twice, noting the texts of the lessons in the back of her Bible and adding two lines from the devotional poetry she was fond of reading: 'Not a single shaft can hit / Until the God of love sees fit'. Her mother died seven days later. The wedding went ahead in St Oswald's as planned, but the bride was dressed in black.

~

It would not have escaped the notice of the Oswestry guests at the wedding that the groom's family was less genteel than the Shaws and Salters. The Owens were natives of Nantwich in Cheshire, where their forefathers had lived for generations, though their surname implied a Welsh origin. Several of the men were shoemakers. Tom's mother Martha had spent much of her life working as a clothier and small shopkeeper. His father William, a thin kindly man with an enormous moustache and piercing blue eyes, had been a tailor among other things, and was now a commercial traveller in drapery.

In later years Tom Owen could make his ancestry sound romantic. His son Harold remembered how he would talk of 'good stock', possibly descended from one Baron Lewis Owen, a famous Sheriff of Merionethshire in Tudor times, and of gradual slippage into the yeoman class, with the 'occasional flurry of more exalted station' and a few adventurous sailors. Tom loved to tell a good story, especially to Harold his favourite son, and if he could bring the sea into it so much the better. The Baron, who had certainly existed, was claimed by several noble families in their pedigrees, but his connection with Tom's family seems a trifle unlikely. Harold was Tom's loyal ally, and like Wilfred he was taught to be intensely class-conscious, so in his memoirs he makes the Owens sound as impressive as he can. The reality was more awkward. He is almost cruelly dismissive of the only senior Owen he knew, his grandfather William, half-confessing that he had thought of the old man as an embarrassment.

It was presumably as a result of Tom's stories and the family surname that both Harold and Wilfred Owen believed themselves to be Welsh by distant descent. Wilfred shared the common Victorian view that Celts had poetry and fighting in their veins. When he was on the Hindenburg Line in 1918 he thought of 'my forefathers the agile Welshmen of the Mountains', and Harold echoes that in *Journey from Obscurity* by claiming to have heard 'the succouring cry from the mountains' at moments of danger. On the other hand, in border towns such as Oswestry and Shrewsbury it was socially more desirable to be English. When Wilfred was described as a Welsh poet in a 1944 radio broadcast, his sister wrote to *The*

Listener to say that 'we are an English family'. 'Wilfred … would, I feel sure, have mildly resented the suggestion that he was Welsh.'[13] Mary's letter, her only known public utterance, was actually written for her by Harold. By the time he came to write his memoirs some twenty years later, attitudes were changing and he was happy to claim Welsh descent for both his parents.

The Nantwich church registers trace Tom Owen's ancestry as far back as 1799, when one John Owen, a currier, married Ellen Booth. A currier's job was to scrape the fat off raw animal hides to prepare them for tanning. John's son, another John, born in the year of the marriage, followed his father into the leather trade, becoming a cordwainer or shoemaker. Shoemaking was a major cottage industry in the town, the 'Nantwich boot' being popular among Lancashire and Yorkshire workers. In 1832 John junior married Hannah Pace, probably the daughter of the local butcher, and husband and wife began working as a team like many of their neighbours, Hannah putting the finishing touches to John's boots and shoes. The couple lived in a series of houses in Welsh Row, the ancient street that leads westwards out of Nantwich. By the time of the 1851 census John could describe himself proudly as a 'master employing four men', but Hannah was still a bootbinder and their current home – 1 Nixson's Row, the end house of a terrace recently built by a friend – was tiny and crowded with children. When John died in 1870 his death certificate recorded him as a taxidermist. He had evidently developed his skills into a more specialised business. One of his sons followed his example: there is no evidence that either Wilfred or Harold Owen was ever aware of their great-uncle Edward, but well into their lifetimes he was still working in Nantwich, advertising himself as a 'professor of taxidermy – birds, beasts and reptiles preserved'.

William Owen, the second son of John and Hannah, was born in 1837. In 1859 he married Martha Millard, a grocer's daughter from Wiltshire, and set up home at 86 Welsh Row.[14] He had started out as an apprentice shoemaker, but by the time of the 1861 census he was a garment cutter and Martha was a waistcoat maker. Two of his brothers are listed as shoemakers, two more as a painter and a labourer. Clearly there were no 'flurries of more exalted station' in these generations of the Owen family. William and Martha were as enterprising as their circumstances allowed, and while she put her experience to good use by opening a grocery and clothes shop, he took up provisions dealing as well as tailoring. At times he also worked as a commercial traveller, perhaps for one of the town's cloth mills.

Tom, the second of William and Martha's four children, was born on 30 May 1862 in Welsh Row. Like his contemporary the young Edward Shaw, Tom grew up as the only brother of three sisters – Ann born in 1859, Edith in 1864 and Emily in 1869 – and he too longed for escape and adventure.[15]

The houses in Welsh Row backed on to fields between the River Weaver and the steep embankment of Telford's Shropshire Union Canal, where the barges went slowly past, high above roof level, and the boy developed a lifelong passion for boats and water. He also became an enthusiastic observer of plants, animals and the night sky, in due course doing his best to pass these interests on to his children.[16] According to Harold, Tom was 'quite heartlessly' sent away from home at fifteen to earn his living after a brief basic education, but the education must have been a little more than basic and the parents less than heartless in an age when many working-class boys had to leave school at twelve. Tom learned enough to do clerical work, and he was taken on by Cambrian Railways, an Oswestry-based company.[17] He seems to have been an agreeable young man, short but sturdy, energetic, a good cricketer, with a fine singing voice and ready smile, but he had neither money nor connections. If he did indeed become acquainted with the ten-year-old Susan Shaw, he would have known he was aiming too high. In any case he wanted to see the world before settling down.

On 23 September 1880 Tom set out on the one great adventure of his life, working his passage to India. Long afterwards he would tell Harold enthralling tales of this voyage, sometimes, as a great treat and in a meticulous, secret ritual, showing him the certificate of discharge which proved that Tom Owen, aged eighteen, had served as a 'Boy' aboard the SS *Benalder* from Liverpool to Bombay, earning the captain's commendation 'V.G.' for ability and conduct. He had got himself a clerkship with the Great Indian and Peninsula Railway, in the company's head offices in Bombay. That much of the India story is certainly true, for the certificate survives and Tom is listed as a GIPR clerk in the 1884 Bombay directory, but what follows comes from Harold, who seems to have misremembered a good deal of it. According to Harold, Tom joined the 'Indian Militia Volunteers' and a sailing club, and did so well at his job that he had every chance of a 'spectacular' career. He remained in India for four years, corresponding with Susan several times a week, hoping she would join him as soon as they could afford to get married. Then he fell seriously ill, and the doctors advised home leave. He was reluctant to go, until Susan wrote that her mother was dying, her brother drinking and her father in financial trouble, whereupon Tom returned to Oswestry like a knight to the rescue. By the time he got back, old Mrs Shaw was dead, but the wedding was held as soon as possible. The young husband moved into Plas Wilmot and joined 'an English railway ... with a salary of only seventy-five pounds a year'.

It may be that Harold is simply repeating the story his father had told him, but he enjoyed romancing as much as Tom did. His memoirs are strongly influenced by guilt about his father, whom he thought the family had always undervalued, and by resentment against his mother. The rescue story not only makes Tom seem chivalrous, but also implies that Susan had been to blame for her husband's thwarted prospects. Harold remembered how bitterly his father regretted having been unable to pursue a sea career, how often he revealed – apparently only to Harold – his nostalgia for ships and distant places, and how furious he would sometimes be at the restrictions of domestic and office life. Nevertheless, however much Harold may have wanted to believe otherwise, Tom did not give up India for Susan's sake. It is true that the young clerk came home after four years, but the wedding did not take place until 1891, seven years later. In December 1884 Tom started work as a clerk with the London & North Western and Great Western Joint Railways on an annual salary of sixty-five pounds, working in the Superintendent's office at Shrewsbury station. His parents, William and Martha, moved to Shrewsbury from Nantwich, and until his marriage Tom seems to have lived with them.[18]

William Owen had got a job with Maddox & Company, Shrewsbury's leading clothiers and drapers, probably earning more than he had ever done before. Martha no longer needed to keep a shop, and their new house, 2 Hawthorn Villas in Underdale Road, was small but modern and well-built, with a long garden. Two of their daughters were soon off their hands. In 1888 Edith was married in the Abbey, the family's parish church in Shrewsbury, to Edward Quayle, a commercial clerk from Liverpool, and two years later, again in the Abbey, her sister Annie was married to John Taylor, a widower with several children. *Journey from Obscurity* does not reveal that Taylor was a newsagent, stationer and bookseller, with a shop in the suburbs of Manchester.[19] Similarly, Harold never mentions Martha's shop, nor Edward Shaw's ironmongery business, while William Owen is merely said to have had 'some connection with the wool trade and mills' and John Gunston is described as 'a successful London businessman' rather than an owner of pork shops. Harold eventually reconciled himself to the idea of being Welsh, but he was never able to admit that one of his family's principal occupations had been shopkeeping.

For Tom, as for his parents, Shrewsbury was an improvement on Nantwich. There was plenty of music to hear and take part in, and the Abbey Foregate Literary Society held regular meetings in winter to hear talks from writers and travellers.[20] His parents' house was close to the River Severn, and in the early mornings he could be a boy again, swimming, fishing and looking for birds' nests. He either made or renewed his friendship with Edward Shaw junior, probably encountering him at games and admiring his prowess. Oswestry was only a brief train ride away, and a railway employee could get privilege tickets, so Plas Wilmot was easy to visit. By 1888 if not earlier Tom had met Susan Shaw, soon introducing her to his family, and in 1890 she was a witness, perhaps even a bridesmaid, at

Annie Owen's wedding.[21] That Susan was willing to be courted shows that her suitor must have been able to share in her Evangelical faith. She and her parents would not have compromised on that, and Harold's later efforts to present his father as a sceptic are not to be relied on. Tom's political views would also have earned approval; such evidence as there is suggests that he was almost as right-wing as old Edward Shaw.

Tom no doubt moved into Plas Wilmot as soon as he was married, commuting daily between Oswestry and Shrewsbury, where he continued to work in the Superintendent's office. His salary was now ninety pounds a year. Susan had never lived anywhere but Plas Wilmot; she adored the place, but her husband must have been conscious of the contrast between it and the cramped little houses in which he had grown up. He cannot have been entirely at ease amid the immaculate table linen and gleaming silver, and the visitors who made polite conversation while trying not to hint that poor 'Suzie' had married beneath her.

Scarcely had Susan come out of mourning for her mother than she and Tom had another death to grieve over when his sister, Edith Quayle, died after a miscarriage in February 1892. Susan herself became pregnant in the summer. The burden on Tom was increased by Edward Shaw's retirement in that year. The old man had been in partnership for some time at new premises in Cross Street, and he now sold his share to his colleague, Edwin Gardner. The shop remained in business for a decade or more under the name of Shaw & Gardner, but Mr Shaw ceased to receive income from it, and his capital was not enough to meet his expenses. If Tom saw his father-in-law's accounts, he would have known that ruin could not be staved off for long.

$\sim$

The young couple's first child, Wilfred Edward Salter Owen, was born at Plas Wilmot on 18 March 1893. It may only be modern legend that says he was born under the coved ceiling in the main bedroom, probably his grandfather's room. The birth was perhaps supervised by Dr Roderick, the local physician, whose daughter Nelly was an old friend of Susan's. The new baby no doubt absorbed his mother's attention to the exclusion of most other matters, including financial worries, and he was swaddled in the elaborate shawls and caps of the period to be marvelled over by visiting friends and relations.

Susan's sister Emma Gunston would have been among the first visitors. The two sisters were close, and Emma already had three children of her own, so she could give advice. No doubt the eldest sister, May Loughrey, came too, but Wilfred was to have no memories of her. May died of sudden peritonitis three years after he was born, leaving her husband with three small children. Susan kept in touch with Richard Loughrey, and Wilfred could remember being taken to see him in the East End at the age of five, but the doctor married again in 1899 and had more children, whom Wilfred was to meet rarely, if at all.[22] May's death, which must have caused great distress at Plas Wilmot, probably increased the intimacy between the two surviving sisters, and in due course Wilfred was to get to know the young Gunstons much better than any of his other cousins.

When Aunt Emma and her family came on a visit in about 1895, Uncle John assembled everyone in the house to pose for a photograph on the terrace: Susan and Wilfred, Emma and her children, Grandfather Shaw in his stovepipe hat, the two Welsh maids and the gardener's boy, even the cat and Jubilee the parrot. Wilfred sits on his mother's knee, deep in his own thoughts, his doll lying forgotten at his feet. Many of the early pictures of him show this 'small dark look', as Harold calls it, a slightly mysterious look, intelligent, secret and detached.[23] Wilfred was going to go his own way.

~

Family memory later gave the last five years at Plas Wilmot a mythic status, representing them as a final summer in the Garden of Eden, but in reality they began with the death of Susan's mother and ended with that of her father, and in between came the final loss of contact with her brother, the deaths of Edith Quayle and May Loughrey, the slow decline of old Mr Shaw, and what must have been severe financial worries for Tom. Even the birth of Wilfred's sister, Mary Millard Owen, on 30 May 1896,[24] was not an entirely joyful event; she was a frail, tiny baby, and for months her life was in danger. Tom must have foreseen that he and Susan would soon have to sell Plas Wilmot: already in 1896 the Shrewsbury directory shows his name in place of his father's at Hawthorn Villas in Underdale Road. It was a sad irony that Susan's family had originally seemed far superior to Tom's, yet now he had to fall back on his own parents, who had never had any money to spare. If that pained him, it must have galled Susan.

Tom distracted himself, as he was often to do when things got difficult, by building a model boat. The SS *Susan* was his finest creation, an exquisitely detailed working steamer, and he sailed her on the little lake at Plas Wilmot. Once she caught fire, but he rescued her, and for many years afterwards she was kept in a glass case to be admired by children and visitors. Despite the *Susan*, though, the young Wilfred was never attracted to seagoing as his father hoped he might be. The child was photographed in a sailor suit, holding a toy boat Tom had made for him, but Susan made him military uniforms and he was just as happy to pose for the camera as a soldier, looking appropriately stern.

On 14 January 1897 Edward Shaw went into the garden as usual to inspect his birds. Next morning he was found to have suffered a stroke, and by the evening he was dead. The funeral was held at Holy Trinity, with John Gunston, Tom Owen and Edwin Gardner as chief mourners. A posse of police and several councillors also attended, for the old man had been eminent in Oswestry for many years. His house and possessions had to be disposed of immediately. Susan kept some of the silver, china and linen, but apart from these and a few other treasures everything that could be moved was auctioned on 16 March, from the drawing-room walnut furniture and the fine piano to the stair-rods and doormats. The pony carriage went, with the cob that pulled it, and old Edward's dozen Brahma fowls; even the iron railings round the paddock were rooted up. Many books went too, including an old 'breeches' bible and volumes of Shakespeare, Milton, Pope, Byron and Burns.[25] When all the creditors were paid, the residue of the estate, little more than a hundred pounds, was divided between Susan, Emma Gunston and, presumably, the Loughrey children. Harold says most of Susan's share had to be spent on medical care for Mary.

The loss of the family home and so many heirlooms was a bitter, very public humiliation. Whether Tom and Susan were blamed or merely pitied, they must have dreaded having to face Salter relations, many of whom still lived locally. There could be no future for the Owens in Oswestry.

~

According to Harold, Tom was given a job in Birkenhead after leaving Oswestry, but he could find nowhere for the family to live. He applied for another transfer and was appointed to a temporary post at Shrewsbury, where Harold was born. Then another job came up in Birkenhead, and this time the family was able to join him there. This move is always said to have taken place early in 1898, but railway and other records show that Tom did not in fact leave Shrewsbury until 1900. Not long after the sale of Plas Wilmot the Owens were at 'Wilmot House' in Canon Street, Shrewsbury, the last house at the newest end of a very new street. They were probably the first tenants, and they must have chosen the name, arranging for it to be boldly inscribed over the door, where it can still be seen. Their third child, William Harold Owen, was born in the house on 5 September 1897. Tom is described on the birth certificate as a 'Relief Clerk' at the railway station, and his name is in the Shrewsbury street directory for 1899, both in Canon Street and at 2 Hawthorn Villas.

If myth has exaggerated the delights of Plas Wilmot, it has also exaggerated the miseries that followed. Harold describes the house in Canon Street as 'rather shabby ... in a long street of other mean little houses – all exactly the same'. As so often, he instinctively colours his narrative, highlighting the contrast between his own birthplace and Wilfred's. Wilmot House was certainly no Plas Wilmot, but it was neither mean nor particularly small and the street was far from uniform. Tom had known the area well for years, becoming very fond of it. Underdale Road, only a few streets away, was an old lane that still led into fields, and some of the houses on the opposite side to Hawthorn Villas were quite grand, their gardens sloping down to the River Severn. The grandparents' upper windows looked past a large, elaborately ornamented villa to river meadows and the spires and castle battlements of the old town. Nevertheless Harold reserves the district's attractions for a later stage in his story. In the immediate post-Oswestry period he wants to emphasise the depths to which the family has fallen, so his memoirs depict the Owens' part of Shrewsbury as a near-slum: the old people live in a 'horrid little house', and when the young Harold looks out of one of their upstairs windows he sees urban litter and the line of 'mean' little houses that appears in most of the remembered streets of his childhood.[26] Plas Wilmot has already become the lost paradise.

The Owens lived at Wilmot House for three years, until Wilfred was almost seven. He probably went to an infants' school, unless Susan chose to teach him at home, and he could certainly read and write quite competently by the age of five. After his mother's death an envelope was found in her jewel-box marked 'Wilfie's first letter, 1898':

> my dear mother
> i no that you have got there safely. We are making huts. I have got a lantern, and we are lighting them up to-night.
> With love from Wilfred I remain your loving son Wilfred[27]

2

Schoolboy

Birkenhead

1900–1907

On 1 February 1900 Tom Owen was appointed stationmaster at Woodside, the Joint Railways' main terminus in Birkenhead. Susan and the children must have waited in Shrewsbury until he could find a house: the Birkenhead Institute register shows that Wilfred Owen of 7 Elm Grove did not start in the school's Preparatory Department until 11 June, although term had begun in April.[1] Wilfred's youngest brother, Colin Shaw Owen, was born at Elm Grove on 24 July. It must have been an exhausting year for Susan, and she began to be a chronic invalid, taking to her bed with un-identified ailments or going away for weeks at a time. The family's troubles in Birkenhead have often been overstated, however, mainly because accounts of their life in the town have been taken from Harold Owen, who had painful memories of his childhood. It is easy to miss Harold's comment that the Birkenhead years were the most tranquil in Wilfred's life.[2]

Harold says the new house was in a smelly slum, occupied by dockers, stevedores and their unwashed children and 'slatternly' wives ('slatternly' is one of his favourite adjectives), and his description of the family's arrival is one of the most vivid scenes in his memoirs.[3] Aged about two-and-a-half, he had developed a high fever and was only intermittently aware of his surroundings:

I was being unloaded from a dark and dripping cab on to a black wet pavement in a dank and evil-smelling street outside one of a long line of small, squalid, and near-slum dwellings. Our cab driver, who was terribly drunk, threw off our boxes and bags, somehow regained his seat and drove away, cursing and singing very loudly. When we had groped our way into the house, and my father had made a light, the floor and walls of the passage and the small room leading from it appeared to surge and lift as if covered with a simmering treacle. We had been welcomed to our new home by armies of black beetles. The disgusting crunching as our feet pressed down on these horrible insects, the loathsome smell of the air in the house … was more than my small body could withstand. I was immediately and very violently sick, and the last impression I had before consciousness once again drifted away from me, was of Wilfred's protective rush towards me, the feel of his arms around me, and the fearful sight of the racing heaving black mass of beetles converging upon what I had thrown up.

No. 7 had stood empty for a while, and there was a patch of open ground – now and probably then a bowling green – beyond the back garden, so perhaps the house had indeed become infested, but the thickly-applied adjectives reveal the painter at work. Harold establishes his loathing of Birkenhead, the shame of having to live there, and his role as the most

7 Elm Grove, Birkenhead (centre)

pitiable member of a close family group, and he ends with one of his first images of Wilfred, the elder brother who could show affection in a crisis – though not at other times, as Harold soon reveals.

Elm Grove, a street of detached and semi-detached villas and one small terrace, was by no means a slum. In fact it was one of the best locations on the upper slopes of Higher Tranmere, a steep hill well secluded from industry and the town centre. At the top end there were tall piers and a gate for privacy, made more imposing by the adjacent stone walls of a convent. Occupants of the smaller houses included an engine driver and even one stevedore, but among the more typical residents were a former parliamentary candidate, the secretary of the local Conservative Association and, just before the Owens came, the assistant curator of the Walker Art Gallery in Liverpool. No. 7 itself was semi-detached, with a garden and an elm tree, four bedrooms, an attic room for a maid and an array of nine bells to summon her from anywhere in the house. If Susan complained that her new home was far inferior to Plas Wilmot, Tom might have been tempted to reply that it was very much better than anything *he* had known as a child.

It may be, indeed, that Tom was too ambitious in choosing such a good area, although he was not as badly off as Harold repeatedly suggests. His annual salary had gone up to £150, a respectable figure but only twenty pounds more than he had reached in Shrewsbury.[4] Elm Grove may have proved too expensive, or perhaps he had taken the house cheaply at the end of a lease. By November 1902 the family was at 14 Willmer Road, a street of harsh red-brick terraces at the bottom of the hill and much nearer the bottom of Higher Tranmere's social scale.[5] This may have been the house with the cockroaches, and it certainly had the gloomy little yard behind high walls that Harold mentions. Even here, though, the neighbours were not the dockers' wives who figure in his descriptions, foul-mouthed harridans shouting insults at the respectably-dressed Owen children. Contemporary directories record no dockers or stevedores in Willmer Road. It was an unhappy time all the same, and Wilfred later referred to the 'old dark days' there. He kept his spirits up by lavishing affection on baby Colin, teaching him a few first words.[6] Tom took a better house as soon as possible, and by November 1903 the Owens had moved to 51 Milton Road, halfway up the hill.

Birkenhead was not such a bad place to live. It had begun as a rural dormitory for commuters from Liverpool on the opposite bank of the Mersey, and there were parks, hills and views of the great river. World-class industry had followed, spawning grim areas of poor housing but also leafy suburbs and many amenities, including one of the first cinemas outside London, theatres, new swimming baths and a magnificent central square. The Mersey was full of shipping. The Joint Railways' trains from Chester and London arrived at Woodside on the edge of the river, next to the ferry terminal in the heart of the town, and the nearby Mersey Railway could take passengers to the Wirral resorts and under the river to Liverpool. One regular commuter was Tom's brother-in-law, Edward Quayle, who was working as a tinplate broker and doing well. He had actually become Tom's brother-in-law twice over: some years after the death of his first wife Edith, he had married her sister Emily. Uncle Ted and Aunt Emmie, as the Owen children knew them, lived in Wallasey, one of the seaside towns at the top end of the Wirral. There was one child by the first marriage and would soon be two by the second, so the young Owens were to have cousins within easy reach, and the dunes, beaches and marine lakes of the peninsula were to become familiar territory.

~

One of the advantages of living in Higher Tranmere was that Wilfred, and later Harold, were near the only independent middle-class school in Birkenhead. Parents wanting secondary education for their children had been obliged to send them to Liverpool until 1889, when a local philanthropist, George Atkin, had founded the Birkenhead Institute Limited. He established the school as a commercial company with shareholders, directors and – in theory and occasionally in practice – dividends, on the principle that parents should take responsibility for their children's education if they could afford to do so. A long stone building had been constructed in Whetstone Lane near Elm Grove, and the Institute had been opened by the Duke of Westminster, Cheshire's biggest landowner. The motto was *Doctor in se semper divitias habet* ('A learned man always has riches in himself'), but actual finances were always to be difficult. The Duke helped a little: when one of the founding directors undertook to pay for an annual scholarship of twenty pounds, the Duke promised another, admitting he was rumoured to be not altogether impecunious.

Every chance was taken for favourable publicity, and enamel advertisements for the school were placed at the Wirral stations, including two at Woodside. Parents must often have heard the argument urged on them at Speech Day ten years after the opening: now that the working classes were being well educated by the state, the middle classes would be left behind unless parents were willing to make sacrifices. By 1900, Wilfred's first year, a new building for science and art was being planned, and the directors risked going into debt to pay for it, hoping the Institute would qualify for a grant as a 'School of Science'. When the new laboratory was opened in 1902, the guest list included the names of Mr and Mrs Owen.

Wilfred was just under seven years and three months old when he entered the Preparatory Department in 1900. The Prep shared the same congested site as the Junior and Senior Schools, an unsatisfactory arrangement that meant mingling with much older boys. Harold found this difficult a few years later, but Wilfred, self-reliant and hard-working, made a few quiet friends and stood aside from the crowd in the playground. He did well in class, earning the regard of Miss Martha Farrell, the mistress who had been in charge of the Prep since the school's foundation. Harold tells a story of being invited home for the night by Miss Farrell and being required to share a bed with her, much to his horror. If Wilfred had to undergo a similar ordeal he must have been less shocked by it. He was happy to visit Miss Farrell in 1908 after the family had left Birkenhead, writing unconcernedly to Harold that she sent her love.[7] After two terms at the Prep he was awarded a prize for coming second in his form, and his parents may have seen him collect it at the 1901 Speech Day in the Town Hall.[8] He became an avid reader and developed a clear, steady handwriting, illustrating his letters with little sketches of people and animals. His second

The Birkenhead Institute

surviving letter, dated April 1902 by Harold long afterwards, was written from Shrewsbury, where he was staying with his grandparents and doing some gardening. William Owen apparently liked to give visiting grand-children a piece of ground to look after. In September of that year Wilfred met a new pupil at the Institute, Alec Paton, who became his closest school friend, a tall, lanky boy, slow of speech and serious of mind. They both went up into the Junior School in the following January and started Latin.

In November 1902 Wilfred enrolled in the Sunday School at Christ Church, just across the valley from Higher Tranmere. If the Birkenhead Institute had been one factor in the Owens' choice of a place to live, Christ Church, Evangelical and in a highly respectable district, must have been another. The Owens would have rented a pew, as there were no free seats except where the servants sat in the galleries, and they would have thought the money well spent. Evangelicals attached great importance to membership of a church committed to the Ministry of the Word. The best preachers became well known, and few Birkenhead ministers were more famous than the Vicar of Christ Church, Canon W.H.F. Robson, a superb speaker with a saintly, magnetic personality. His death in 1914 was a major local event, with crowds lining the streets and at least fifty clergymen attending the funeral. Every Sunday he would address his large congregation (the church held a thousand or more) with such power that his words touched every listener personally, yet he believed in action more than in talking and spent his weekdays in tireless parish work. Comments about 'the Canon' in Wilfred's letters show that he and his mother held Robson in very high regard.[9] Outside the family there was perhaps no one who influenced the young Wilfred more profoundly.

The Sunday School movement was still strong. In Birkenhead alone there were forty-six such schools, catering for over eleven thousand children, and Wilfred joined one of the most active. On three Sundays a month some two or three hundred children crowded into the big hall below the church, sitting in groups according to age and sex. 'Redeeming the time', said the motto round the clock on the tower, and at Christ Church time was never allowed to be wasted. Under the watchful eye of a Superintendent, the teachers introduced children to the Bible's stories and promises. 'To neglect the study of God's Word is a deadly sin,' Robson told confirmation candidates, and he would have said the same thing from the pulpit on the first Sunday of each month, 'Church Sunday', when the children attended a service instead of class.[10]

Parents would have been encouraged to help, and for several months after Wilfred started Sunday School there are dates in Susan's Bible. The earliest of these marked passages, apparently chosen by the Vicar, suggests the reassuring role mothers were expected to take: 'Run now, I pray thee, to meet her, and say unto her, Is it well with thee? is it well with thy husband? is it well with the child? And she answered, It is well. *Canon Robson Nov 2nd 1902*'. Other verses include: 'Fear not: for I have redeemed thee, I have called thee by thy name; thou art mine. *Motto 1903*'; 'If we suffer, we shall also reign with him: *Wilfred Sunday Feb 8th 1903*'; 'As one whom his mother comforteth, so I will comfort you; *Wilfred Feb 16th 03 Promise text*'.[11] The family had recently moved to Willmer Road, so morale was low. Mother and son studied the Bible together until Wilfred was able to continue on his own, and for years afterwards he kept up the discipline of a daily 'walk with the Lord', reading a prescribed passage with the aid of Scripture Union notes in the approved, prayerful fashion. There must have been times when he felt himself to be in the very presence of Jesus, but the exercise was literary as well as religious, a regular, intense exposure of the imagination to a book. He learned the language of the Authorised Version, storing up words and phrases.

Private devotion was reinforced by public worship on Church Sundays, when the Canon's preaching brought the Bible's messages to life. Years later, when Wilfred had to give talks himself as a parish assistant at Dunsden, he asked his mother to send him old copies of the Christ Church magazine so that he could glean ideas from Robson's sermons, and when he listened to a visiting preacher there he was vividly reminded of the Canon: 'When he compresses his lips; droops the eyebrows, takes in a deep breath, and pats nervously with his hand upon the table – then the scene changes; I am in Christchurch!'[12] The urgency in the Canon's delivery reflected his passionate desire that waverers and non-believers should be saved before it was too late. Souls would face immediate judgement after death, and the only guarantee of salvation was faith in Christ. Such doctrines were no cause for anxiety to the true Christian, although they were an incentive to go out into the world and win souls for the Kingdom, but the Devil was always on the watch for signs of doubt. Hell was a reality. It was essential to keep one's faith alive through worship, prayer and Bible study.

Wilfred probably had no doubts at Birkenhead, but Harold claims to have been unconvinced even as a child, and the descriptions of Susan's religion in *Journey from Obscurity* are witheringly sarcastic. When Harold is about ten or eleven, for example, at the first of his schools in Shrewsbury, he is shocked to see some older boys exposing themselves in the latrines. He tries to tell Wilfred about it and Wilfred tells Susan, who earnestly advises Harold to put his trust in God.

> In a reverently lowered voice she told me with frightening solemnity that if I went on like this – speaking of these things that were not nice – as I had done to Wilfred, then my feet would be set on a road which could only lead to eternal hellfire … good little boys did not see or hear these things … and then God saw to it that no harm came to them … If I did not try harder to be nicer I should not only displease God but break her own heart as well – so I must promise to stop speaking of these things even to Wilfred … and of course none of these things could possibly be true … I must stop making things up.[13]

The young Harold is unlikely to have been as sceptical as his adult self more than half a century later, but his portrait of Susan may have a good deal of truth in it. Wilfred also knew how she chose to shut her mind to anything unpleasant. Like the rest of the family he felt obliged to protect her, needing her steadfastness though subconsciously already longing to be free. Once during a childhood holiday he buried her in flowers while she pretended to be asleep. Her love towards them all never wavered, nor did her faith in divine providence. Writing to Alec Paton soon after Wilfred's death, she repeated her conviction that a childlike trust in God would be rewarded with a place in heaven, where families and friends would be reunited.[14] What seemed mere feebleness to Harold, at least in retrospect, was 'waiting on the Lord' to her, and the Canon would not have regarded her as inactive; there could be no greater service than rearing children to rely on God, read the Bible and pray.

Evangelicals prayed frequently, not only in private and in what Robson called 'the great congregation' but also as families and in groups, where anyone could pray aloud extempore as the Spirit moved. The Owens apparently never held daily prayers, but Wilfred's early letters refer to 'our service' on Sundays and 'our reading' after weekday tea. The service developed into what Harold remembers as 'Wilfred's Church', a Sunday evening event at which Wilfred officiated and preached, dressed in robes and mitre beautifully made for him by Susan. Victorian children, including Ruskin and Browning, had often preached to their families, though perhaps not in mitres. Harold says the services were conducted with perfect decorum, but he comments elsewhere that Wilfred could sometimes induce an 'unnatural religious fervour' in the other Owen children.[15] Wilfred loved dressing up, and Susan would have enjoyed arraying him as a bishop, secretly hoping he might become one, but Harold thinks she may have become uneasy, fearing that Wilfred might be tempted into popery. The services eventually lapsed. With or without services, however, Susan must often have prayed with the children, their father attending when he could.

51 Milton Road, Birkenhead (left)

It may be that Tom's commitment flagged in 1903 during the dismal months at Willmer Road. Susan would have been at her most miserable and pious, a state of mind that would have communicated itself to the children. She kept them aloof from other youngsters in the street, so the family was no doubt considered snobbish, a reputation enhanced by frequent visits from clergymen. The move to Milton Road must have been a great relief. Number 51 was semi-detached, with a tiny garden, and the view down the street was closed by the reassuring bulk of Christ Church looming on the opposite slope. Records identify the next-door neighbour as John Cannell, clerk, although Harold only remembers a sea-captain's widow. If Mr Cannell had indeed been a Merchant Navy officer, Tom would have been delighted to have a nautical man next door. Susan became friendly with Mrs Cannell, an elderly lady who expected children to behave. It may have been in accordance with a New Year resolution that Tom started teaching in the Sunday School at the beginning of 1904. In March of that year he gave Susan *Pilgrim's Progress* as a birthday present, perhaps as a pledge of renewed faith.

Harold claims that Tom joined the Sunday School before any of the children did, that the two eldest boys followed him only under protest, and that Tom soon gave up. The Superintendent's log shows that it was actually Wilfred who joined first, followed by Harold a year later in November 1903, then their father (as a teacher) in January 1904 and Mary in the following May.[16] Harold has Tom causing disapproval among the other teachers by telling his boys' classes about ships rather than the Bible, an appropriate subject because the boys were mostly sons of stevedores or seamen. Not many parishioners in Claughton, Oxton and Higher Tranmere can really have been so employed, and in any case it would have been difficult for Tom to ignore the prevailing ethos of Christ Church. Nor did he give up, even though he was one of only half-a-dozen men in a team that otherwise consisted of some thirty maiden ladies (one of whom was Miss Farrell). He continued teaching for the rest of his time in Birkenhead, and the fact that he was willing to be seen as a committed Christian must have added weight to Susan's displays of faith at home.

The adult Wilfred cannot be understood as man or poet unless his youthful experience of Evangelical religion is remembered. It was a religion based on the Word, on words, on language. He grew up in a family and congregation where there was frequent spoken contact, real or imagined, between individuals and God, who answered through scriptural texts. Wearing the armour of faith, Wilfred could feel himself to be a Christian soldier, marching as to war under Robson's inspiring general-ship. He was taught that his first task was to train himself spiritually, and when his faith was mature enough he would have to play his part in the great campaign of soul-winning. Perhaps it was testimony from him that persuaded his friend Alec Paton to join the Sunday School in May 1905. No one could be a true Christian without being filled with longing to reach out to people still lost in the darkness of unbelief. The Christian was special, belonging to a select fellowship, in the world yet not of it, sharing secret mysteries yet charged with the supreme public duty of being a messenger, warning and guiding, basing all his thinking on a thorough command of scripture. 'Mystery' and 'mastery': the future war poet began to learn his role at Christ Church.

~

The close, devout relationship between Susan and Wilfred set up a barrier between them and the rest of the family. He was her first-born, the object of her hopes and dreams. None of the other three children was as intelligent and articulate, solemn and self-absorbed though he often was. She bound him to her with religion and talk of sacrifice, and on the whole it suited him to be compliant, enjoying his privileged position, although there must have been times when even he found her trying. He later apologised to her for 'all the abominable rudenesses, ingratitudes, huffs, grumps, snaps, and sulks' he had aimed at her.[17] One of her sister's grandchildren, June Calder, remembers how cloyingly affectionate 'Auntie Sue' always was, with a 'mimsy' way of talking and a habit of fussing over guests. She was 'continually fluffing out her metaphorical feathers around you', according to another of Emma's grandchildren, David Gunston, so much so that visiting children would wriggle away and even hide in the garden.

> Basically, her nature was an undemanding one: she found unending pleasure in simple things, little things – babies, children, flowers, birds, fish, pot-plants, ornaments, butterflies, teacups. Her front drawing room was an untouched Victorian sanctum, almost full of green things which she treated as children, tenderly and admiringly. Time and again she gave me roots and cuttings and seeds of the things that filled her ebony jardinière and stood in leafy rows on her shelves and sills.[18]

Wilfred's huffs and grumps do not emerge in his letters to Susan, but he occasionally reveals impatience with her hypochondria, telling her to get out of the house more often, to go abroad, to take a course of physical exercises, and in 1918 even to drink claret. On the other hand her temperament made her an ideal listener; she was his audience throughout his life, and he sometimes wrote to her with little thought for her feelings, knowing that all he had to do by way of repayment was to enquire after her health and express fervent devotion. He discovered from an early age how tempting it was to luxuriate in her love, and the delight was near-erotic, so that even in some of his adult letters he writes to her almost as a lover. Sometimes he felt her arms could shield him for ever from the dangers of the world outside, yet her all-enveloping love was itself dangerous. Images of suffocation and (s)mothering were often to appear in his poems. The pleasure of passivity – the 'unhoping happiness' of being 'a Mother's boy', as he was to call it in the first poem he wrote after coming out of the trenches – would have stifled his growing-up if he had not resisted.

Susan's ill-health seems to have been the result of child-bearing, and she may have developed some chronic trouble that could not be talked about. She had given birth to Mary in the last, anxious year at Plas Wilmot, and Harold had arrived only fifteen months later, following the miseries of the house sale and its aftermath. With equally unfortunate timing, her fourth and last pregnancy had coincided with the move to Birkenhead. Both

Mary and Colin were sickly babies, Colin suffering from rickets in his early years, and Susan must have had to devote whatever energy she had to looking after them. Perhaps there was an element of guilt and compensation in the affection she lavished on Wilfred.[19]

Wilfred was often put in charge of the other three children, and because Mary's smallness made her seem young for her years he tended to be isolated in an adult role. One result of that was the schoolmasterly attitude he often took towards his brothers and sister, loftily correcting their spelling (his own was none too good) and using long words they could not understand. Even in 1914 he could demand an assurance from Colin that 'you continue to feel my affection and respect my influence'.[20] Colin was a semi-invalid at Birkenhead, wearing heavy leg supports, and as the baby of the family, sweet-natured, shy and quiet, he was an obvious target for affection and 'influence'. Wilfred adored him, behaving as elder brothers often did by making a pet of the child, tweaking his nose and ears (hence 'Tweak', his name for Colin) and no doubt often hugging and kissing him, but Colin was expected to be a pupil, too, even in infancy. Susan may have been equally prone to petting Colin, and it was her ready affection for children that gave Wilfred his later habit of making friends with any 'Colinesque' small boy he happened to meet, friendships he readily told her about in letters.

Unlike Colin, Harold was hard to deal with. Wilfred said later he had never had a sense of humour, which was probably true: Harold took everything seriously, including teasing. Wilfred pulled his ears and tweaked his nose as though he were as young as Colin, but showed him much less affection, complaining when he knocked furniture over and lecturing him, sometimes angrily, for not being grown-up and sensible.[21] Harold protected himself with a show of bravado and maybe occasionally with his fists (he evidently had a violent temper when goaded too far), but he suffered inwardly from being endlessly criticised and laughed at. At best the elder brother seemed insensitive, at worst downright cruel, as when he shut the children up in dark cupboards or pretended to be a ghost to frighten them. Harold thought him insufferably aloof and unsympathetic, and was deeply puzzled in later years that the famous poet of 'pity' should have been so pitiless at home. *Journey from Obscurity* suggests – more generously than convincingly – that the future poet was experimenting with drama and emotion, using the children as necessary guinea-pigs.

No one understood why Harold was a difficult child. In a later age he would almost certainly have been diagnosed as dyslexic and dyspraxic, two related conditions that seem to explain a good deal about him.[22] He could not cope with academic work and was often called stupid, yet like many dyslexics he was exceptionally good at art. His spelling and handwriting were highly eccentric, even late in life, and as a child he was clumsy and prone to getting lost, all symptoms of dyspraxia. Knowing nothing of later psychological theory, his family despaired of him. Afterwards he blamed his mother more than anyone, remembering her pious complacency, her refusal to believe his stories, and her lack of practical ambition for him. That lack, which Harold mentions several times with bitter incredulity, was less incomprehensible than he thought: in the new age of universal education, a child with his handicaps seemed to have no future. Susan could only say that God would provide, a phrase Harold came to detest.

The child most affected by Susan's passivity was neither Wilfred nor Harold but Mary, who probably owed her life to her mother's nursing and who in return had to become her lifelong slave. Wilfred was devoted to his sister, though he sometimes upset her by being too critical, complaining that she rarely spoke and had no interests of her own. He even remarks in a 1912 letter to their mother that Mary might benefit from Japanese wrestling, keel-hauling or being dropped from a balloon, suggestions all the more heartless because by then everyone must have realised that Mary was physically retarded. Harold loyally mentions her 'perfection of proportion', but people who knew her in later life remember her as a tiny, 'frail', 'quaint' figure, with an adult head on a child's body. Visiting children were warned not to make comments. There is something curiously symbolic in Mary's lack of growth. She sacrificed her adult life to her mother.[23]

Symbolism seems to run through the story of the Owens, although some of it may be the creation of the family's two artist-recorders, Harold and Wilfred. Harold's story of Colin's scarlet fever, apparently at Willmer Road, is a typical example. The disease being highly infectious, Susan hangs a carbolic-soaked sheet across the bedroom doorway, isolating herself and her patient from the rest of the family. For six weeks her love is concentrated on the little boy, and for all that time Wilfred is in charge of the other two children. He keeps control on walks by attaching Mary and Harold to lengths of clothes-line, but on one occasion he ties a knot too tightly on Harold's arm, stopping the blood supply (a stranger cuts the knot just in time, heaping abuse on Wilfred). When the three Owens get home, Susan only allows Harold to put his damaged arm past the sheet for inspection; bandages have to wait until Tom's return in the evening. Perhaps these events did happen as Harold describes them, but the story is a microcosm of the way he saw his own past: once again he is damaged by Wilfred's unthinking lordliness, excluded from his mother's affection, and treated kindly by his father.[24]

The most symbolic event in the Birkenhead years happened in about 1904. Susan took Wilfred to the scattered Cheshire hamlet of Broxton, where she had been lent a cottage by a friend. The woods sloped up behind the house to a high sandstone ridge, facing west over miles of rich fields and hedgerows to the long blue line of the Welsh mountains. On a clear day one could see the towers of Chester and Liverpool, and far to the south the spires of Shrewsbury. This was Wilfred's home country, and he seems to have become aware of its beauty for the first time at Broxton. 'It was in Broxton,' Harold says, 'among the ferns and bracken and the little hills, secure in the safety and understanding love that my mother wrapped about him with such tender ministration, that the poetry in Wilfred, with gentle pushings, without hurt, began to bud, and not on the battlefields of France.' Wilfred himself certainly looked back to Broxton as the start of his life as a poet – 'was there not Broxton Hill for my uplifting, whose bluebells, it may be, … fitted me for my job' – but his memory of the holiday seems to have been quite unlike Harold's later version. In a strange, fragmentary poem drafted in 1914 Wilfred wrote that his 'poet-hood' had been born at Broxton in darkness and disobedience, 'Suckled' by the moon, his poetic mother. The eleven-year-old had perhaps slipped out of the cottage at night to see the landscape by moonlight, an enthralling experience for an imaginative little boy. The key elements of his poetic environment, then as later, were darkness, secrecy and breaking the rules.[25]

~

According to *Journey from Obscurity*, Wilfred's early rebellions were almost always directed against his father. Harold represents Tom as often at odds with Susan about Wilfred, and often in a fury with Wilfred himself. The intimacy between mother and son was hard to bear, as was Wilfred's reluctance to take any interest in seafaring and sport. Tom believed in fresh air and exercise, and he was a stickler for punctuality, unlike Wilfred, who was inclined to leave everything until the last minute, a characteristic that may have developed as a means of resisting paternal authority. They could never even agree on musical matters, Harold says, although music was a passion for both of them, and Wilfred's habit of monopolising the family piano led to frequent rows.[26] Harold has some splendid descriptions of Tom in a rage, a stocky little man glaring and snorting like 'a small but uncertain bull', a comparison confirmed by several references to glares and snorts in Wilfred's early letters. There can be no doubt that Tom's short temper was often on display and that it was sometimes aimed at Wilfred, who must have been exasperating on occasions, but not all the evidence supports the accepted picture of relationships within the family. An old friend who wrote to Harold after the publication of his memoirs remembered Tom as a jovial man who often had to pour oil on troubled waters, whereas Susan had been a tremendously strong, determined personality and, by implication, the cause of whatever disturbances there were.[27] In Wilfred's long struggle for independence, quarrels with his father may only have been sideshows.

Over five hundred and fifty of Wilfred's known letters are addressed to Susan, some of them marked private; one is addressed to her and Tom together, and only four to Tom alone. However, it would be easy to exaggerate the significance of these figures. Sons often wrote exclusively to mothers in those days, consulting fathers only on practical matters, and letters to a mother, being more personal, were more likely to be kept. Susan was a hoarder, Tom was not, but there is no reason to think he was any less devoted to Wilfred than she was. Wilfred's letters to him are written in an open and – to use a standard adjective of the time – manly style, as custom required, but they are affectionate and loyal, with no sign of awkwardness. Most mentions of Tom in the letters to Susan are similarly affectionate, although there are occasional shared jokes at his expense (once Susan earns a rebuke for saying Father was 'just shuffling off to bed').[28] One of the letters to Tom accompanied a copy of Siegfried Sassoon's war poems in 1917, asking for his comments. Father and son may well have exchanged letters about books before, since Tom seems to have encouraged the children to read, making sure the household had plenty of Scott, Stevenson and other adventure stories, and he was excellent at reading aloud, holding his listeners spellbound with the Uncle Remus stories. He must deserve some credit for Wilfred's early interest in literature.

If Harold is right that Tom often grumbled about Wilfred's lack of sporting ability, the grumbles were not entirely fair. Wilfred was a small, slight boy, quite unsuited to rough team games, but he was as lithe and agile as his supposed Welsh forefathers, blessed with a straight back and natural balance. Tom had no difficulty in teaching him to swim in the town baths, and Wilfred became a lifelong enthusiast, never missing a chance of getting into the water. He loved skating and was fearless on horseback, galloping along the New Brighton sands on a beach pony with Alec Paton, and he enjoyed tennis and cricket, not only as a boy but also in the army. The family had many games of its own, too, some of them invented by Tom, and Wilfred would hurl himself into them with noisy hilarity. He and his father were both good actors, excelling at charades.

Sometimes Tom took the boys down to Woodside station. The adult Harold preferred not to admit that his father had been a stationmaster, describing him instead as a head of department at Birkenhead, but the young Wilfred enjoyed being connected to an important official. The Chief Clerk to the Superintendent called in at Tom's office one day and found it empty except for a small, upright figure. 'Well, my boy,' said Mr Williams, 'are you the Stationmaster?' He never forgot the promptness with which Wilfred replied, 'No sir, but I'm his son!'[29] Hardly a trace of the station remains today, but Wilfred must have known it well, the noisy, soot-blackened train shed, the grand quayside entrance that nobody ever used, and the bustling side gate leading to the trams and the ferry. Tom was in charge of it all, and he must have been good at the job, remaining in post for seven years until he was promoted again, so perhaps he enjoyed his responsibilities rather more than Harold later believed.

Tom's hopes of having a mariner son had to focus on Harold, who became his companion on expeditions to the Birkenhead docks. They must often have seen the ships of the 'Birkenhead Navy', the Pacific Steam Navigation Company, one of the largest shipping lines in the world. Every Sunday the PSNC cadets would be lined up for church parade, and Tom may well have said that being one of those smart young men would be a fine thing to aim for. He could be in his imagined element on the riverside, striding along purposefully like the captain he longed to be, revelling in rough weather, caring nothing for the hazards of cables, slippery gangplanks and sheer dock walls. With his broad shoulders, long-sighted blue-grey eyes and abrupt manner he looked convincing, and he thought himself into the part so well that when people in a dockland café addressed him deferentially as 'Captain' he became a regular customer, in due course taking Harold there after instructing him not to give the game away. Susan may never have known about this deception, which apparently continued for years, but Wilfred probably knew: some years later he presented his father to friends in Bordeaux as a baronet, and Sir Thomas acted up to the part with pleasure.

Tom managed to get himself aboard ships by helping with the Mersey Mission to Seamen, going out on the Mission's launch *Good Cheer* to deliver tracts. Harold says his father regarded the religious side of this as an embarrassment, but the Mission chaplain, Henry Grindon, seems to have been friendly with the family, on one occasion showing Wilfred round the docks at Liverpool. The Mission ran an Asiatic Institute where Indian sailors could spend their evenings, and Tom once invited four of these men to supper with the family. He could still speak some Hindustani, so Wilfred asked to be taught a few words. The guests kept their embroidered caps on for the meal but took off their shoes, much to the children's fascination. This was perhaps the only opportunity Susan ever had to gain some insight into her husband's experience of India. Harold says she was not enthusiastic, and the experiment was not repeated.

~

Every year there were holidays. In about 1902 the family went to Ireland, where Harold caught an enormous shark that refused to die, and Tom nearly drowned himself in a gallant attempt to save Colin, who wasn't actually in the water at all. Harold also tells a story of the family walking into a sinister, tunnel-like fog and encountering a ghostly figure which threatens them with a stick when spoken to. Sven Bäckman has seen parallels between this vision and the poem 'Strange Meeting', and some of the similarities are indeed striking, although it has to be remembered that Harold had mulled over Wilfred's poems for years; the poem may have influenced his description rather than the other way about.[30] The Owens also spent at least one holiday in Scarborough, the home of Susan's first cousin, May Susan Davies.[31] The boys and Tom played cricket on the North Bay beach, just below a large hotel called the Clarence Gardens, a building Wilfred was later to know well. A photograph taken near the little harbour on the South Bay shows the three youngest children on tiny ponies, Wilfred and his father on larger mounts and Susan bravely standing beside them, clutching her hat in the sea wind. May Davies owned a girls' school in Pavilion Square, though it is hard to imagine her as a headmistress if Harold's portrait of her is accurate. She painted her face, as Susan warned the children in hushed tones, and she wanted to take the two eldest boys to the theatre. The young Owens, like their Gunston cousins, were not allowed to visit theatres, places regarded by Susan and her sister as dangerously immoral. The children adored Cousin May, delighting in her stories and her readiness for adventure.

Wilfred had several holidays in Wales, twice going with the Patons to Rhewl, where Alec's uncle was a farmer. As Harold notes, one of the letters Wilfred wrote from the farm in 1905 shows its twelve-year-old author's fondness for long words ('Indeed I fare very sumptuously') and his grown-up attitude to his siblings ('the children'). When Alec and Wilfred found two little streams Alec called one of them 'Wiswos', but his guest gave the other the ostentatiously literary name of 'Fontibel'. Wilfred learned a little Welsh to add to his Hindustani, but he also learned to milk cows, and he accompanied the Patons on a strenuous walk up Moel Fammau. On the Sunday they all went to a tiny candle-lit church, where he was astonished to see that the full congregation was only about forty people. He was used to much larger numbers at Christ Church.

At Christmas or New Year, and again in spring or summer, Susan took her children to stay with the Gunstons, who lived in a large house named Alpina at 3 Clement Road in the wealthy London suburb of Wimbledon. Uncle John's pork shops were still prospering, so it may be that he and Aunt Emma felt morally obliged to help the Owens by giving them hospitality. Emma maintained her parents' style of religion more strictly than her sister did, forbidding alcohol and tobacco and ensuring that prayers were read daily. (The ban on tobacco may be one reason why Tom was not a regular visitor: he was fond of a good cigar.) On Sundays family and visitors attended Emmanuel church, an Evangelical stronghold where the minister, E.W. Moore, was a much-revered preacher, as important to the Gunstons as Robson was to the Owens. Alpina was by no means an austere house, however, and the four Gunston children had more books and useful toys than could be found at 51 Milton Road. Wilfred got on especially well with the youngest cousin, Leslie, two years younger than himself, a lively, stuttering boy, full of schemes and enthusiasms. When they played on Wimbledon Common they sometimes saw the diminutive figure of Algernon Swinburne, the last of the great Victorian poets, taking his regular walk. Occasionally there were visits to Grandfather Robert Gunston in his fine residence at Brixton with its greenhouse and elaborate garden.

～

The tone of the Birkenhead Institute was raised in 1903 when James Smallpage was appointed headmaster. Numbers began to go up, and in 1904 the directors felt able to pay a small dividend, the first for some years. Smallpage's son Eric entered the school, soon becoming friendly with Wilfred. In September 1904 Wilfred went up into Senior School, starting a course that could have taken him, as it was to take Alec Paton, to university entrance. The role of serious student suited him well. He liked to advertise the burden of homework by loading his pockets and satchel with books and staying up late to write his essays. He kept his hair as long and untidy as his parents would allow, and made a point of being as late as possible in the mornings, Susan often having to hurry him out of the door. The grey Institute uniforms must have been a familiar sight throughout Higher Tranmere, perhaps occasionally drawing jeers from less privileged children, and the crest on the cap, a closed helmet, seemed to symbolise the defensive solidarity of the middle classes. Harold claims to have been often attacked when he came home from the school, but he says he was in the habit of taking long detours.

Wilfred was not the sort to get into trouble. *Journey from Obscurity* portrays him as a model pupil, carrying himself with an air of 'assured diffidence', as Harold memorably describes it. 'This gravity of approach, which remained always in advance of his years, coupled as it was with his attractive appearance (not to be confused with good looks), his thick dark brown hair and small delicacy of build – perhaps a lack of robustness even – gave him an air of over-adultness.'[32] Wilfred worked hard, anxiously aware that he was not in the very top rank intellectually. Perhaps he was driven, as his brother later believed, by some deep inner sense of being destined for poetry, or perhaps his motives were more mundane. His parents must often have told him that academic success would give him the best chance of avoiding the economic trap they felt themselves to be in, and he grew up to be very conscious of the need to earn money.

He loved words, and his strongest subjects were English and French. His weakest was probably maths, in which he sometimes needed help from his father, but he was keen on science, taking Senior School courses in the new laboratory at a cost to Tom of five shillings a term. The science master,

William Watts, was an expert astronomer and must have been responsible with Tom for Wilfred's knowledge of the stars, a knowledge that was to be life-saving for a company of soldiers in 1918. Wilfred was taught English by Harry Bennett, a formidable disciplinarian, and Latin by the more genial Henry Wood, but the only Birkenhead teacher named in his letters, apart from Miss Farrell, is Miss Taylor, who was not on the Institute staff. Miss Taylor came to Milton Road to give piano lessons, apparently believing in Wilfred's ability enough to continue teaching him for reduced fees when Tom could not afford her usual rate. By contrast, an Institute master who was asked about the famous poet years later could only say, 'A very ordinary boy, *I* thought. *I* could see nothing like this about him.'[33]

Harold Owen joined the Institute in April 1904. The account of his Birkenhead schooldays in *Journey from Obscurity* is moving but far from accurate. He remembers the Prep as being in a private house, but it soon closes down. He transfers to the Junior School on the main site, where his elder brother takes as little notice of him as possible. After a short time he is taken away, his parents having decided he's not worth the expense. They send him to a free church school, where Wilfred leaves him on the first day with a wave and a typical 'little dark half-smile'. 'I think he was sorry at that moment for the forlorn little creature that was me, with my hands and face blue with cold, and standing so alone in the pools of scummy rain-water.'[34] The new school is appalling, and Harold is soon taken away again. After being taught at home for a while he goes to a larger free school, about which he can remember almost nothing.

Some sixty pages later Harold makes an admission that fatally undermines his story: 'I cannot now remember whether I survived at the Birkenhead Institute until we left the town or if I was taken away before we went.'[35] If he survived, he cannot have been to the other two schools. He did in fact survive at the Institute, and the Prep did not close down. Part of the confusion in his narrative stems from the fact that he was only on the main site for his first term. Smallpage was arranging a merger with a little private school run by Robert Galloway, and in September 1904 Galloway became Second Master at the Institute (there is a cartoon of him in one of Wilfred's letters, a comical figure in top hat and long black coat), while the Prep and Junior School moved into his former premises, a large house in Clifton Road, a few minutes down the hill from the Whetstone Lane site.[36] This was the building Harold remembers, and he went there for the rest of his time in Birkenhead. When he joined the Prep in 1904 he was one of the two youngest pupils (at six years and seven months he was some eight months younger than Wilfred had been).[37] The register shows beyond doubt that he attended the school every term thereafter until the family left the town in 1907.[38] In Birkenhead, as in Shrewsbury later, Tom Owen ensured that both Wilfred and Harold went to the best possible school at the earliest possible age.

At the March 1905 Speech Day Alec Paton and Wilfred shared most of the prizes for their own form, Wilfred being awarded a copy of Macaulay's *Essays and Lays* for 'excellence in languages'. One of the three Prep prizes went to Harold, who soon went up into the Junior School and did rather well, his talents for narrative and drawing perhaps compensating for early signs of probable dyslexia. He won the under-eights hundred yards at the school sports in June 1905 and another prize on Speech Day in 1906. Eric Smallpage and Alec were also prizewinners that year, but Wilfred outshone them all by winning one of the four five-pound Duke of Westminster scholarships, a prestigious award that saved his father fees for almost two terms.[39]

One of Wilfred's contemporaries at the Institute, P.N. Williams, remembered him as a very congenial companion.[40] Wilfred clearly had a small circle of friends in Birkenhead, and Harold's nickname for him of 'Lone Wolf' is misleading if it suggests he was a solitary child. (Harold soon alters the name without comment to 'Old Wolf'. If the family used either version, it probably derived from the baby name, 'Wulfie', without any implication of lone-wolfishness. Wilfred himself only mentions having been called 'Philosopher' and 'Judge'.[41]) Wilfred often walked home with Alec, whose route was the same to the top of Milton Road. They amused themselves on the way by inventing names for passers-by, and one man with almost black eyes whom they labelled 'Nig-oc' was so annoyed by their giggles that he slapped Wilfred round the head. That was probably the nearest Wilfred ever got to being attacked in the street. He sometimes took Alec home for tea, Alec later remembering how they had played battles of 'attrition' with toy soldiers. Perhaps they also played with Wilfred's model theatre, for which, according to Harold, its owner wrote and acted miniature dramas.[42]

In 1906 Wilfred went to Wales again, this time for a fortnight with the Smallpages at Waenfawr, near Caernarvon. He and Eric shared a room and told one another what were supposed to be original stories, 'but when Wilfred began "You have often wondered how I came to lose the top of my left ear", Eric recognised one of the tales of Brigadier Gerard and the ensuing pillow-fight had to be quelled by Mr Smallpage'.[43] It may be a measure of Wilfred's standing at the Institute that he was a chosen companion for the headmaster's son: Mrs Smallpage had been careful to check that the Owens were entirely respectable, as Eric later recalled, and Mr Smallpage regarded Wilfred as a very promising scholar.

The headmaster had much on his mind that summer. He had gained some good publicity by starting a rifle club and taking it to compete at

Bisley, where, as the only northern head present, he had been sought out by Field Marshal Lord Roberts. Roberts was convinced the country needed to arm itself against the growing power of Germany, so he was keen to get boys involved in military exercises. Smallpage made sure the Birkenhead newspapers reported this encounter with the nation's most famous soldier, but unfortunately the papers also had to report that the Institute was in financial crisis. Behind the scenes the directors were facing the possibility of closure. The Board of Education had refused their application for a School of Science grant on the grounds that the school was a commercial business, so the loan on the new laboratory could not be paid off. The building itself had been put up on the cheap and was already starting to give trouble, with a leaking roof and inadequate drains. The only hope was for the school to be taken over by the local education authority, but some councillors were hostile to the idea of rescuing a blatantly middle-class establishment that had always made a show of its independence.

Towards the end of 1906 Tom Owen applied for a senior job in Shrewsbury. The chance was too good to be missed, and it was a good time to move, with the Institute apparently on the brink of collapse and Wilfred nearing fourteen, the normal school-leaving age. Tom became increasingly flustered and ill-tempered as the final interview approached, but when he got home after it he announced to the family that life was going to be much better for them all – they would soon be leaving Birkenhead, and he was going to be almost the top man in the Joint Railways, assistant or Chief Clerk to the Superintendent. The current assistant, John Williams, was to be Superintendent, so there was a good chance that one day Tom might in turn succeed him. No doubt Smallpage wanted Wilfred to remain at the Institute, but Harold says that a plan for Wilfred to stay with the Patons during term-time was rejected by Susan, who could not bear the thought of being parted from her son. So the two Owen brothers were taken away from the school soon after term began in January 1907, Tom being charged only token fees. The headmaster expressed regret in assembly at Wilfred's leaving, according to P.N. Williams long afterwards. Williams could not recall any other leaver being paid a similar public tribute, and he thought Smallpage must have seen more in Wilfred than the boys had done.

Even Smallpage could not have guessed that one day Wilfred would be the Institute's most famous pupil. The school was saved from closure by being municipalised in 1908, and Wilfred's name was remembered, though not accurately at first. He was listed on the war memorial as 'Wilfred T. Owen, M.C.'. During the nineteen-thirties and forties several numbers of the school magazine contained a history of the Institute which said that the name of one Old Instonian would always live, that of the poet 'Wilfrid T. Owen, M.C.'. In the sixties, when Wilfred's poems at last began to be widely known, the school established a 'Wilfred Owen Library' and Harold donated the prize copy of Macaulay won by his brother in 1905.[44] The library did not last long. In the educational upheavals of the seventies the buildings in Whetstone Lane were demolished, and the Institute's name was transferred to a comprehensive school elsewhere in the town. Twenty years later that school too was demolished, and a housing estate was built on its site with an access road labelled 'Wilfred Owen Way'.

3

Pupil-Teacher

Shrewsbury

1907–1911

Writing to Siegfried Sassoon while on leave in 1917, Wilfred said, 'I can't get sociable with my Father without going back on myself over ten years of thought.'[1] He seems to be remembering 1907 as a turning point. The year perhaps started with a row between father and son, for the children were given no warning of the move to Shrewsbury. Wilfred and Harold began a new term at the Birkenhead Institute as usual, and within a week or two they were suddenly taken away. The thirteen-year-old Wilfred may well have been upset, while Tom was on edge, trying to cope with the move and a new job. It was an unsettling time in the wider world, too, with a new Liberal government promising radical reforms and the trades unions becoming powerful. Tom – patriotic, conservative, just promoted to senior management – would have been alarmed at the threat to the established order. The tranquillity Wilfred had known in Birkenhead was not going to repeat itself in Shrewsbury.

According to Harold, the family stayed briefly with Tom's parents at 2 Hawthorn Villas, but they soon had a home of their own a few doors down Underdale Road at 1 Cleveland Place. Despite its number, the new house was the middle one in a corner block of three: the first house was in Cleveland Street at the side, the other two were in Underdale Road, and that was all there was of Cleveland Place. No. 1 was tall and narrow, but it was slightly bigger than 51 Milton Road and, like Hawthorn Villas, it had a top-floor view over meadows to the old town. Better still, there was open country nearby, quiet fields enclosed in a great loop of the river. Harold's narrative reflects the change, the gloom of Merseyside giving way to strong sunlight and richly coloured summer days on the banks of the Severn, a 'calm, gracious river', as Wilfred sententiously described it in a school essay, 'bearing strength on its tide and plenty in its bosom'.[2]

The local countryside was a delight. Harold remembers Wilfred as reluctant to accompany him and their father on early-morning river expeditions, but Wilfred's letters often mention boating and fishing with brothers and friends, and occasionally with Tom. Perhaps no one in the family enjoyed their new home more than Tom. If he missed the Mersey, he had the familiar Severn again with its birds and fish and otters. A railway halt near the house allowed him to get to work easily, but in fine weather he could cross the river from Underdale Road by ferry, an open boat propelled by a ferryman hauling hand over hand on a fixed cable, and from the landing stage opposite there was a pleasant stroll to the grand Gothic station at the foot of the castle walls.

The ancient fortress town of Shrewsbury stands on a hill almost encircled by the river. Picturesque streets wind up to a cluster of churches, then down again to Welsh Bridge on the west side and English Bridge on the east. English Bridge was the only road link between the town centre and the Owens' suburb, an area dominated by the huge church of a vanished abbey. To the north of the church, behind Abbey Foregate with its old houses, lay some handsome Regency terraces, a tangle of railway lines, and an assortment of recent speculative housing, including Underdale Road and Canon Street. It was very different from Birkenhead, but Harold remembers that there were still distasteful neighbours to cope with. Cleveland and Tankerville Streets, connecting Underdale and Monkmoor Roads, consisted of long terraces occupied in daytime, he says, by 'idle, blowsy, dirty and vindictively resentful' women and their 'visibly unclean, always scabrous and dirty' children. Harold says that Wilfred preferred to avoid these areas, but several of Wilfred's letters casually mention going to Teece's 'shed', an ugly little grocery shop in Cleveland Street.

It was the railway age that had added such streets to a once-beautiful district, and the Owens would have been constantly aware of railway activity. The main line crossed Underdale Road on a bridge not far from the house, before curving past engine sheds into the station. There was an appalling accident just beyond the station in October 1907, when the night mail from Crewe jumped the tracks in darkness and heavy rain, killing twelve people and injuring many more. Tom seems to have been given the task of raising staff morale: the local newspaper reports him chairing a newly-instituted dinner for over fifty Joint Railways officers in January 1908, when he took part in a musical entertainment he had helped to devise, telling his new colleagues how happy he was to be among them. In June he presided over another morale-boosting event, making a presentation to a meritorious inspector.[3] His family made frequent use of the free tickets and reserved compartments he could get for them. Wilfred was now old enough to travel on his own; when he went to stay with the Gunstons, Susan and Mary would stand at the garden gate to wave at his train, and when they made the same journey he would wave to theirs from a window at the back of his school.

～

Wilfred entered the Shrewsbury Borough Technical School in the spring term of 1907. Little has been known about his education there except that he began at 'the Technical' in that year and worked as a pupil-teacher at Wyle Cop School in the summer of 1911. The Wyle Cop term was first mentioned in a *Collected Letters* footnote, the information coming from Harold, whose memory of Wilfred's teaching career was remarkably vague. Pupil-teachers were in fact required to pursue a two-year probationer course, followed by another two years of combined teaching and study, and Wilfred actually joined the system for his entire school career in Shrewsbury, thirteen-and-a-half terms altogether. The Technical doubled as the local Pupil-Teacher Centre (PTC), and a minute of the town's higher education sub-committee on 19 March 1907, the day after Wilfred's fourteenth birthday, confirms his admission to the PTC's probationer course, subject to his passing an entrance exam.[4]

Fourteen was the minimum age for a probationer. Harold says Tom and Susan delayed before settling on a school, but they must in fact have applied to the PTC soon after arriving in Shrewsbury. They may well have considered other possibilities, but secondary schools were expensive.[5] The pupil-teacher route might have been the only realistic option for Wilfred even had he remained at the Birkenhead Institute, which had itself recently become a PTC. The delay, such as it was, was caused not by indecision but by his age. Harold is wrong, too, in claiming that Tom had to find 'considerable' fees. No doubt Harold felt sure about this, convinced as he always was that his own education had been kept to a minimum for Wilfred's benefit, but PTC courses were actually free. Not only that, but Wilfred earned a small salary in 1909–11, his two years as a qualified pupil-teacher.

The pupil-teacher system had been producing staff for elementary schools for over fifty years. It had the advantage of being a means to free secondary education for intelligent children, and the corresponding disadvantage that pupil-teachers tended to be looked down on because they were thought to come from poor backgrounds. They were expected to be deferential, and schools often gave them heavy workloads. The year 1907 brought a painful drop in Wilfred's social status. A pupil-teacher from the Birkenhead Institute might have carried some prestige, at least locally, but the Shrewsbury Technical was a more lowly establishment, drawing many of its students from working-class homes. The long-term prospect was no better. Wilfred's likely fate was to be an elementary school teacher, a dead-end job with low esteem and worse pay, unless he could do well enough to get to university. A degree would qualify him to teach in the secondary sector. Harold says he worked desperately hard.

Most towns had designated an existing secondary school as the local Pupil-Teacher Centre, and in Shrewsbury, conveniently for Wilfred, the chosen school was the Technical at 1 Abbey Foregate, next to English Bridge. The pleasant stone building actually housed three more or less separate institutions, the Technical School and the PTC, both under Harold Timpany, and the School of Art under Herbert Weaver. All three had links with the elementary school in Wyle Cop, the old street leading up from the bridge into the town. The PTC had advertised its Preparatory Class in the previous summer, and some twenty-six children had passed the entrance exam (one of them was Fred Hartop, whom Wilfred was to meet again in the army in 1917). That Wilfred was allowed to join in mid-course was apparently thanks to his father, who, according to Harold, went to see the headmaster. The Timpanys lived in Underdale Road and the Owens were soon on neighbourly terms with them, as they had been with the Smallpages in Birkenhead.

Timpany was probably only too pleased to take on an extra probationer. The Council had been uneasy for some time about finances and pupil numbers in his two establishments. Officially he was the town's 'Master for Science', and advertisements for the Technical offered courses in his own specialisms, practical maths and science, as well as in subjects such as typing, cookery and building. Wilfred and everyone else seem to have called the school 'the Technical' rather than 'the Centre', and outsiders might well have imagined that he was studying some sort of vocational subject. In practice, however, the PTC seems to have taken up more than its fair share of the school's resources, so much so that inspectors complained in 1906 that the Technical itself was not technical enough, being mainly concerned with training teachers.

Wilfred missed out on the scholarly teaching he would have received in the upper forms at Birkenhead, and he was unable to continue Latin, a loss that was to cause him trouble later. On the other hand he learned more science than he would have done at most independent schools. Only a few weeks after starting at the Technical he asked for a geological hammer. He was also taught botany, chemistry and maths, as well as French, history, geography and English, and he did well, as much by hard grind as by innate ability, coming top in French in his first round of exams in April 1907 and scoring in the nineties three years later in French and history. His fellow pupils sometimes found him alarmingly earnest. One of them, Minnie Williams (girls and boys were taught together, a new experience for him), remembered how she was so flustered by his intensity in a Shakespeare reading that she muddled her lines. According to her, he sought the company of older boys. Another pupil, A.J. Wright, who was in the year below, remembered Wilfred as aloof and snobbish, wandering about by himself at break-times and never joining in games. He was a good actor according to Wright, with a deep, expressive voice, and he occasionally wrote humorous literary verses for entertainments. Wright could still remember an example, an epigram on Miss Strachan, Timpany's deputy in 1910:

> *In age above, in size below the middle,*
> *Howe'er she came o'er us to crow, a riddle.*[6]

Wilfred disliked Miss Strachan and thought Timpany a tyrant, but he got on well with some of the younger teachers.

Exercise books Wilfred used for English during the probationer course show him composing essays on such subjects as 'The Sponge', 'The Force of Example' and 'My Native Country' ('England is the greatest and best among all countries … each generation has been better than the one before it, and it is for us to make the generation in which we live better than the last'). In October 1907, the month of the rail accident, he writes on a subject of intense public concern, 'The Imagined Effects on the Country of a Strike Among Railway Workers', putting the management case, no doubt with his father's help, but also showing understanding of the workers' grievances. Another essay a year later sounds cribbed from Joint Railways propaganda: 'Every year we see the speed record increased, more safeguards made, another luxury provided, while the fares still remain at the minimum.' Other essays are just as obviously second-hand, often with high-flown Victorian phrasing. 'Use simple words,' his teacher comments testily, and 'Write as you would speak', sound advice that Wilfred often ignored, perhaps fortunately. His delight in what he later called 'Fine Language' was to be crucial to his poetry in 1917–18.

Most of his work on English literature consists of paraphrases and plot summaries, exercises that made him read attentively. If he worked through the complete original texts, his reading in 1907–9 included the first book of *The Faerie Queene*, poems by Scott and Macaulay, *The Vicar of Wakefield*, *Hiawatha* and no fewer than eleven Shakespeare plays. One of his first essays to show any personal feeling, written in the autumn of 1907, discusses the murder of the boy prince in *King John*. He had perhaps seen the play on stage, for Susan was finally prevailed upon – by Tom, Harold says – to let him go to the theatre. When the travelling Benson Company came to Shrewsbury he had the chance to see a different Shakespeare play every night for a week, and the experience was a revelation, making him a devotee of the company for the rest of his life. He studied several late-medieval and Elizabethan poets, as well as Milton, Gray and Collins. Literary criticism in the modern sense scarcely existed, but he eventually owned over twenty biographies of authors. He bought more books by Shakespeare, Dickens, Scott and Keats than by any other writers, though Keats was a comparatively late discovery. Writing on 'Autumn' in September 1907 he said that 'we will remember with Scott how pleasant has been this

"Season of mists and mellow fruitfulness" ', but he got the name right a few lines later in quoting what 'Keats has beautifully said' about the season. That was perhaps his first mention of the poet who was soon to become his ideal.

By 1908, aged fifteen, he had encountered Wordsworth, and it was Wordsworth who aroused his first strong expressions of literary enthusiasm. An essay on 'The Return to Nature', written in the spring of that year, dismisses eighteenth-century poetry as 'entirely lacking in imagination and moral nature' ('Too strong,' the teacher remonstrates), but towards the end of the century 'a new sympathy with man especially the poor' had arisen, exemplified in the work of Burns and Wordsworth. Poets were now inspired 'with high objects, with enduring things', Wordsworth always being the leader, though himself led by nature. A few months later Wilfred noted that the value of poetry lay in its power to elevate the mind above the common sphere, and he continued his quotation from Wordsworth's invocation to the 'Wisdom and Spirit of the universe', the power that teaches the child through nature, purifying

> The elements of feeling and of thought,
> And sanctifying, by such discipline,
> Both pain and fear, until we recognise
> A grandeur in the beatings of the heart.

In his first thoughts about the function of poetry and the relationship between poet and environment, Wilfred looked to Wordsworth and not, as is still often believed, to Keats.

The teacher who influenced him most was Miss Elizabeth Wright. Originally from Sunderland, she had gained a science degree at Durham in 1903 and had been appointed to the PTC three years later, apparently to teach biology. She was promoted to deputy head in 1910, when Miss Strachan resigned after less than a year in the post. Miss Wright was popular and capable though diminutive, reminding Wilfred of Little Dorritt, and A.J. Wright reckoned later that most of the boys had been in love with her. Literature was her recreation, according to Wilfred. She directed the trial scene from *Pickwick* for a Christmas 'social' in 1908, giving by far the most important part to Wilfred, who played the sanctimonious lawyer, Serjeant Buzfuz.[7] A small-statured fifteen-year-old could not have acted that role convincingly, thundering Dickensian oratory at the jury, without a powerful voice, an infectious delight in language and irony, and a strong stage presence. The local newspaper said the scene was 'remarkably well performed'. It seems almost certain that Miss Wright taught English as well as biology, geology and botany, and that it was she who led Wilfred to Wordsworth, the poet of rocks and stones and lesser celandines, and to

Ruskin, the great advocate of education through practical nature study as well as through books and art. Harold says she gave Wilfred extra coaching in his weaker subjects, doing much to strengthen his confidence.

A new teacher arrived in January 1908, Miss Mary Jones, a Liverpool graduate from Llangollen.[8] Wilfred liked her immediately, saying later that a fee of fifty guineas would not have been enough to repay her for her geography lessons. She and Miss Wright both got to know his family. These two young women seem to have done more than anyone else to develop his interest in literature and nature, and it may well be that it was in 1907–8 that he felt the first stirrings of an ambition to become a poet in the Wordsworthian tradition.

$\sim$

No. 1 Cleveland Place was only just big enough for the Owens. Wilfred and Harold had to share a top-floor room, although it was recognised that only Wilfred was entitled to work there, the table and chair by the window soon becoming known as his 'study'. Even in his earliest letters from Shrewsbury, he talks of going to bed late and of having masses of homework. Harold had to be quiet when climbing into the bed they both slept in, or risk being tetchily rebuked. The room had no electricity or heating, so Wilfred would wrap himself in blankets and read at his table by candlelight. A boy who lived across the road, Roy Denville Jones, remembered seeing him there every night. Harold would lie awake hardly daring to move, until Wilfred finally got into bed shivering with cold, and in the mornings Jones would see Wilfred leave for school, staggering under a loaded satchel.

Wilfred's ally and confidante in everything was Susan. When she took the three youngest children to her sister's in April 1907, needing a rest after the strain of the move, Wilfred wrote to her frequently. 'My own dear Mother,' he began, in a letter that was later partly obliterated by Harold,

In the last letter I didn't tell you all I wanted to. We went to Grandpa's to tea on Saturday. They were talking about you, how you didn't take enough fresh air [*several words illegible*] & denouncing your habits of staying in! They don't know that its your self-sacrifice for us, I do though. I haven't asked you how you are, for three letters, I don't think, Mother dear, but you know I never forget to do something that is of more avail then 'wishing' and 'hoping'. On Sunday they came here for [*one word illegible*]. Father has suddenly decided to get me a new suit! He says I ought to have long trousers & a collar!! And when Grandpa said 'When shall I send it up?' I fairly choked with wrath!! The idea! of not asking *you*! Well father did say then 'Oh! We'll wait till Mother comes home.'[9]

Old William Owen meant well. As a tailor for years, and now a manager at

Maddox's, he naturally took an interest in his eldest grandson's clothes, but Wilfred – and Tom – knew Susan would have to be consulted first. Wilfred's letter is designed to please its recipient, while reinforcing his special status. He alone appreciates his mother's self-sacrifice, understanding she needs rest rather than exercise. He assures her he never forgets to pray for her, and he remembers, albeit belatedly, to be anxious about her health. His annoyance at his grandfather perhaps reflects the way she talked to him about the old Owens. The only other story about them in his letters is of his playing the piano for the edification of some visitors and his grandfather chuckling, 'He! He! But you'll make your livin' at it yet', a comment instantly snubbed by Grandmother Owen and pooh-poohed by the guests.[10] Susan may not have been altogether sorry when William retired in 1908[11] and moved with Martha to Torquay, to be near Tom's sister and brother-in-law, Ann and John Taylor, who had themselves moved there from Stockport some two years earlier.

Wilfred's reference to prayer is typical of his early Shrewsbury letters. He reports hymn numbers and sermon texts from church services and twice ends with a scriptural blessing.[12] He was doubtful when the local curate suggested he should attend confirmation classes in 1908, but he must have been confirmed. The depth of his commitment can be judged from his devotions one Sunday in 1909 while on holiday with the Taylors. He went to church in the morning with his relations and again in the evening on his own, when everyone else went to the seaside, and before the others returned he also attended an open-air service held by Plymouth Brethren. 'It was so like our own. The same hymn book and the same Gospel messages.' In Shrewsbury, however, the family never found substitutes for Canon Robson and Christ Church. On Sunday mornings they probably all went to the Abbey, where Tom became a sidesman in 1908, but when Susan was away he was often unsure which church to go to, making up his mind at the last minute. It may be that his and his wife's religious tastes were now diverging a little; if so, that would have made for tension. There is no sign that he ever accompanied her and Wilfred to St Julian's at the top of Wyle Cop, the church she liked to attend on Sunday evenings.

St Julian's was the centre for Shrewsbury's keenest Evangelicals. The steep climb up Wyle Cop was an effort for Susan, but she made it whenever she felt well enough. 'I can imagine you seated in the Pew,' Wilfred wrote to her one Sunday in 1913, 'recovering from your exertions on the Cop', and he thought of those exertions again on another Sunday four years later as he scrambled up the stairs of a German dugout.[13] His letters imply that he regarded St Julian's as his own church in Shrewsbury, and when he had to get someone to sign a certificate of good character in 1916 he went to the Vicar, Norton Duncan. Duncan was a strong opponent of Romish tendencies in the Church of England, openly criticising his High Church colleague, William Pennyman, Vicar of nearby St Mary's ('Preserve me from Pennyman', Wilfred wrote in 1917). Duncan gave some lectures in 1908–9 on the claims of Rome, and his strong views may be reflected in one of Wilfred's essays, where the Messina earthquake seems to be blamed on the fact that the local people were Roman Catholics. St Julian's was not noted for its tolerance.

~

Wilfred's aunts and uncles were well placed for holidays, especially after 1908, when the Gunstons moved from Wimbledon to the Oxfordshire countryside, the Quayles moved from Wallasey to a bigger house at Meols, still on the Wirral, and the Owen grandparents joined the Taylors at Torquay. The happiest destination was the Gunstons' new home, Alpenrose, and Wilfred continued to stay with them for Christmas or New Year and again each spring, doing his best not to feel like a poor relation from the provinces. He remarked in April 1908 that their Wimbledon house made 1 Cleveland Place seem tiny, and he was conscious of their southern accents, as they were of his northern one: he was used to the flat northern 'a', but his cousins said '*arf*ternoon' and when they mentioned 'Auntie Sue' among themselves they often pronounced the first word to rhyme with 'shanty' in imitation of her speech.[14] The contrasts between the two families increased when John Gunston's father sold the jointly-owned pork business and retired. Family legend says that Emma Gunston, still a Salter and Shaw at heart, told her husband he should retire, too, and live as a country gentleman. John bought some land from a cousin at Kidmore End, near Reading, and by the spring of 1908 the walls of Alpenrose were rising. John, Emma and their four children moved in some months later, and Wilfred came on a first visit for the New Year.

The family at last had a replacement for Plas Wilmot. The new house was similar to the old one in many ways, with six bedrooms and a little estate of about five acres. Once again there were paddocks, a kitchen garden and a stable yard. Prayers were read daily as before, although life was generally less formal than it had been at Plas Wilmot and there was no carriage (Uncle John rode a tricycle, until he bought a Model T Ford in 1916). 'Are you gentry or do you stack?' a new maid asked as she cleared away the plates in the dining room, according to a family story. The Gunstons stacked. Perhaps that was Uncle John's influence, and he was certainly responsible for the alpine souvenirs that gave the place a holiday atmosphere, the Alps being a passion of his. The stained glass round the front door depicted alpenroses, and a huge Swiss cowbell hung in the hall instead of a gong. Everyone who knew the house loved it, all except Harold, who loathed its religious atmosphere, at least in retrospect. He

Alpenrose, Kidmore End, as it was before John Gunston's studio was added to the end of the house. (Apprentice architectural drawing by Leslie Gunston.)

insists that Wilfred loathed it, too, but Wilfred's letters record nothing stronger than occasional impatience at Aunt Emma's dogmatism.

John Gunston, though a Londoner, knew how to run a smallholding. Wilfred mentions cows, a calf, chickens and turkeys, while John's grandchildren remember a pigsty and an orchard, as well as quantities of Gunston fruit and vegetables going to Reading market. When Wilfred arrived for Christmas 1909 there were two pheasants and a hare in the larder, and several fattened chickens were about to join them. Alpenrose was a wonderful place for children. Beyond the big garden lay an old chalk-pit, full of cowslips in spring, and in front of the house was a wood where nightingales and the occasional poacher could be heard at night. Uncle John sometimes arranged shooting matches, Wilfred proving himself a good marksman. In summer, family and friends played tennis in the garden, and winter brought skating on the village pond and tobogganing on the slopes of the Chilterns. The house was full of treasures, with curio cabinets in the drawing room, ornaments crowded on every shelf, and plenty of books. Wilfred spent hours browsing through bound sets of *Royal Academy Pictures*, Cassell's *Popular Science* and *Punch*, the last of which attuned him to notice the comic incidents and voices that often figure in his letters.

It was as well to laugh noisily while reading *Punch* because Uncle John was always astonished by anyone who could read it in silence. He was a slightly awesome figure to children, but he enjoyed silly jokes: Kidmore End was 'Knickers Bottom' in his vocabulary, and Susan's children were 'Souza's Band'. He loved music, singing in London choirs and performing solos at local recitals. On summer evenings after the children had gone to bed he would play the piano, and the sound would drift through the house, enchanting his sleepy audience. His greatest talent was as a photographer. Every summer he took his family to Switzerland, where they had to trail round after him, Emma riding a mule with the tripod. He became so interested in his hobby when he retired that a large studio and darkroom soon had to be added at one end of the house. He no doubt regarded his mountain photographs as his greatest achievement, and they are preserved by the Royal Photographic Society, but he is remembered now for his portraits of the family. His haunting photographs of Wilfred as a newly-commissioned officer in 1916, taken in the studio, have become icons as famous as that celebrated image by Sherril Schell of the bare-shouldered Rupert Brooke.

Emma Gunston's practical competence seems to have matched her husband's, although she may have lacked his sense of humour. She looks deeply serious in his portraits of her, except for one taken in her old age, when she laughs happily at the camera. Wilfred thought her much more argumentative than her sister, but her granddaughter, June Calder, remembers her as a charming character, as kindly as Susan but less fussy and far more energetic. Emma knew how to cope with Susan, who would arrive with numerous medicines and sometimes even her own chamber-pot. Mary was always in attendance, and occasionally Harold and Colin came too, although Wilfred usually came on his own.

The eldest of the Gunston children, Gordon, was perhaps a trifle bored by these frequent visitors. Six years older than Wilfred, with whom he seems to have had little in common, he was more interested in trains and ships than in literature. Once when the two cousins arrived together at Reading station and found no transport, Gordon set out for the five-mile walk home so fast, making no concessions to Wilfred's smaller frame, that Wilfred feared a heart attack and regarded the offer of a lift from a passing trap as nothing less than divine intervention. Gordon's two sisters were more congenial companions, Dorothy fiery and warm-hearted, Vera placid and easy-going. But it was their younger brother Leslie who most enjoyed Wilfred's company, looking forward excitedly to his visits and scarcely allowing him a moment's peace once he had arrived. Throughout their adolescence, Leslie was Wilfred's closest friend and perhaps his only disciple. He liked to plan activities that would appeal to Wilfred's interests, putting his chemistry set and telescope at the visitor's disposal, and organising cycle rides in search of plants and fossils, or visits to the museum at Reading with its collection of finds from the Roman site of Silchester.

In 1907 Wilfred, Leslie and Vera founded an 'Astronomical, Geological and Botanical Society', with the Ruskinian motto, 'To observe the world'. Wilfred proposed the Society's aims, which were to promote the study and exploration of mountain regions with special reference to 'Art' (he meant photography) and plants, and to work for the Christian education of the inhabitants. 'It is hoped,' he wrote with airy authority, 'that you, V., will become the Photographic Representative,' adding that he wanted pictures of geological formations for his own school work. Clearly he had no scruples in exploiting his cousins' efforts, even though he had never even seen the Alps. He treated his sister and brothers in much the same way, asking them to make notes on interesting features they might see from the train between Shrewsbury and Reading, because he sometimes had to write essays on local topography. The young Gunstons were more tolerant of this kind of thing than Harold was, Leslie following Wilfred loyally in every enterprise.

The other two families of cousins were less useful, although they lived in agreeable places. Dorfold, the Quayles' house at Meols not far from Birkenhead, was semi-detached but newly built and much larger than 1 Cleveland Place, with spacious rooms on three floors and a large garden.[15] There was a magnificent view over miles of uninterrupted fields, stretching round to the Dee estuary and the Welsh mountains, as Wilfred saw with pleasure on his first visit in September 1908. The sea was only a few minutes away, with a public swimming pool on the shore and plenty of amenities nearby, so there was no shortage of things to do, and Cecil Quayle, the eldest of the three children, was a pleasant enough companion. Nevertheless Wilfred's letters have far less to say about his Meols relations than about the Gunstons. He could not forget that Uncle Ted Quayle was becoming a rich man by Owen standards. A small subsidy from him would give his nephew the chance of a university education, or so Wilfred believed, and Susan seems to have thought the same, although her husband was probably too proud to ask his brother-in-law for a loan. As the years went by, Wilfred felt bitter towards 'Edward Quayle Esquire' (perhaps unfairly: if Quayle had been a really rich man he would have lived in a grander house than Dorfold).

Tom's other sister and brother-in-law, Annie and John Taylor, and their daughter Edith, some two years younger than Wilfred, now lived in Torquay at 264 Union Street, a big, handsome house between a bank and a pub in the old main street. The ground floor was a shop, and John was still selling newspapers, stationery and books. Visiting the Taylors in the summer of 1909, Wilfred described himself as being 'in the house with hundreds of books to choose from' (the word 'house' has actually been written into the manuscript by Harold over an erasure: Wilfred probably wrote 'shop'). By that stage Wilfred knew the town quite well, having stayed with his aunt and uncle there several times. The whole clan had gathered in January 1909 to celebrate the grandparents' Golden Wedding, and a group photograph shows William and Martha Owen with their three surviving children, Tom, Annie and Emily, all with spouses, and the eight grandchildren, Wilfred wearing the suit his father had bought him.

It was now a comparatively rare event for all six Owens to be away together. When Susan went for one of her frequent breaks, she arranged for someone to take charge of the household. Harold recalls a series of irresponsible 'slatterns' who maltreated the children. Wilfred's letters merely complain of occasional inefficiency and record that Susan's replacement was sometimes Mrs Cannell, the family's former neighbour in Milton Road. Mrs Cannell was neither slatternly nor inefficient; in fact she was stricter than Susan, refusing to allow Wilfred to read during meals or leave the table before everyone had finished. He dared not disobey, admitting later that Mrs Cannell's countenance always had a Medusa-like effect on him. Neither she nor Susan could have run the house without help, so there was a succession of maids, some of whom may have been Harold's slatterns (one servant, an older woman, apparently stole the Plas Wilmot silver). Tom occasionally felt obliged to undertake chores himself, much to his annoyance. Wilfred reported in 1908 that his father was cleaning the bath with paraffin, glaring and snorting indignantly and filling the house with the smell.[16]

Tom was a kindly father, in spite of the glares and snorts. It is at least possible that his wife's absences were partly the result of difficulties in their relationship, and Harold reckons she was responsible for whatever lack of understanding there was between Tom and Wilfred. Left to themselves, father and eldest son seem to have got on happily enough. In 1908 and again in the following year, Tom found time to take Wilfred to Brittany, and Wilfred was delighted, unworried by the rough crossings and writing cheerfully to Susan. Harold tends to suggest that Tom was unsympathetic to Wilfred's academic ambitions, but the main purpose of these trips was apparently to let the boy practise his French, an opportunity Wilfred gladly seized, chatting to anyone who would listen. Bathing at Morgat was an added pleasure. Wilfred collected shells for Colin, and during a walk on the cliffs Tom killed an adder, nearly falling over the edge in his eagerness, so that was kept for Colin too.

~

One of the French people Wilfred talked to in 1908 was a charming girl he met on the boat, possibly the 'Annik' who is mentioned a month later: 'another post card from Annik nearly turned my head, *perhaps* she is going to a school in London.' Now that he was fifteen, he was expected to start taking an interest in girls, and his contemporaries at the Technical were no doubt pairing off for social occasions. A few of his letters hint at an interest in Bernice Cornwall, whose father, a friend of the Gunstons, was Sir Edwin Cornwall, MP, Chairman of the London County Council and later a government minister. Whether Wilfred was really attracted to Bernice herself or to her social position is not clear; probably he hardly knew himself. Mary Ragge, a local girl who sometimes went out for walks with the Owen brothers, recalled later how honourable they were and how safe she felt with them.[17] Susan was no doubt jealous of anyone who seemed to threaten her own supremacy in her eldest son's affections, and she teased him whenever he tried to make friends with girls. Later he felt she had let him down, advising her in an obscurely-worded 1918 letter not to make the same mistake with Colin.

> Deny him not the thing he craves, as I was denied; for I was denied, and the appeal which, if you watched, you must have seen in my eyes, you ignored. And because I knew you resisted, I stretched no hand to take the Doll that would have made my contentment.
>
> And my nights were terrible to be borne.
>
> For I was a child, and you laughed at my Toys, so that I loved them beyond measure; but never looked at them.[18]

Maybe it was not only his mother's laughter that held him back. He felt he ought to be reaching out to a girl, but the impulse was somehow lacking.

Wilfred often complained that Shrewsbury was boring. He joined the YMCA and met earnest young men who went for cycle rides and held prayer meetings, but his mother's attitudes made casual socialising difficult, even with his own sex. In a revealing comment in 1909 he tells her he had dared to talk to a stranger at the swimming baths, but only after he had 'first heard the aspiration of the H'. Making friends higher up the social scale was scarcely easier: plenty of local families were grander than the Owens, but they were also richer and their children went to better schools. He got to know several boys of his own age, including Stanley Webb, the eldest son of a large, lively family in Abbey Foregate. Like Harold and Colin, and Leslie when he came to stay, Stanley was sometimes recruited for one of Wilfred's favourite recreations, digging at the enormous Roman site of Uriconium, several miles south-east of Shrewsbury. Wilfred would cycle energetically along the dusty roads, dreaming of making a great find, and patient searching in the fields was often rewarded with shards and bones. He brooded over the collection in the museum, building up such a vivid picture of the ancient city that he wished he was in the fourth century, when life seemed to have been so much more exciting than in peaceful, oppressively conventional Shrewsbury.

'The museum & Haughmond are my only consolations,' he said in 1909.

He may have found Haughmond before Harold and Colin did, although it is Harold's lyrical description of discovering the hill and the nearby village of Uffington that has justly enshrined the area in Owen mythology. Some two miles east of Shrewsbury, Haughmond could be reached by a little ferry like the one below Underdale Road. The ferryman lived in Uffington on the far bank and had to be summoned by shouts, so the expedition had a sense of adventure from the start. The steep, grassy slope of the hill, rising abruptly from woods behind the village and ending equally suddenly at an 'open stretch of herb and heather', was typical of Shropshire and very similar to the Cheshire ridge at Broxton.

Wilfred's response to nature was Ruskinian as well as Wordsworthian. It was in the spirit of Ruskin that he looked for plants, rocks and fossils, seeking to understand his environment as evidence of a benevolent, divinely-ordered universe. Walking with Leslie on Caer Caradoc, he said the curled bracken shoots looked like croziers blessing the passer-by, an image Leslie borrowed for a poem some years later. A more famous, though unfortunately less reliable story comes from Harold, who remembers a walk home with the family from Uffington through fields full of buttercups. His young self exclaims he has feet of gold, but no one takes any notice until Wilfred poeticises the idea by describing Harold's boots as 'blessed with gold', an image that reappears in the 1918 poem 'Spring Offensive'. However, Harold's story probably quotes from the poem rather than from any childhood incident.[19] Well before writing *Journey from Obscurity* he added a note to 'Spring Offensive' in his 'Working Copy' of the 1931 edition of the poems: 'The family walk home from Uffington on early summer evenings through the water-meadows when we would look with delighted wonder on our shoes and stockings flushed with gold – unconscious recollection?' That suggestion seems more convincing than the later, carefully crafted story, and it is perceptive in its awareness of the parallel between the Shropshire landscape and the setting of the poem.

Early in 1910 the Owens moved to Wilfred's fifth family home, a semi-detached house in Monkmoor Road. They rented it for a pound a week from a neighbour, Mr Knight, who had recently built it and several others. Tom called it 'Mahim' (which he and the family pronounced '*May*him', not '*Maheem*'). He would never explain why he chose the name, but he must have had secret memories of Mahim in India, a coastal district of Bombay. The house was larger than any since Plas Wilmot, with a long garden at the back, and the situation was excellent, facing the vast green expanse of a former racecourse, five miles round and used only for grazing and occasional special events. Monkmoor Road petered out into fields beyond the racecourse gates, so there was no through traffic. Wilfred took over the tiny attic room, where a mattress was squeezed in for him under the slope of the roof and a desk under the gable of the dormer window. From this

Mahim, Monkmoor Road, Shrewsbury

eyrie he could see Haughmond and, in the distance, the Wrekin, Shropshire's most famous hill. The countryside he had got to know during the previous three years was now within his daily view, and he had the room and the view to himself, as Harold was now sharing with Colin. He hid himself away to work, growling at any interruption except when his mother came up with cake and cups of tea. Some of the new neighbours thought she spoiled him, making him selfish and rather conceited.

In the summer of 1910 Wilfred and Harold went to stay with the Taylors in Torquay for several weeks. Their uncle was by then very ill with the cancer that was to kill him two years later, so the two brothers were left to amuse themselves. On 27 July they sat on a cliff-top to watch the King and Queen reviewing the fleet in Torbay, the Royal Yacht moving slowly through the long lines of warships while gun salutes boomed across the water. The most exciting moment came when an aeroplane took off from the grounds of Torre Abbey, piloted by the famous aviator, Claude Grahame-White, who wanted to demonstrate that the greatest navy in history had no guns that could be aimed at a target in the sky. Neither Their Majesties nor the Owens had ever seen a plane in flight before. The two brothers dreamed for years afterwards of becoming airmen, and in Wilfred's mind the tiny aircraft defying the vast armaments below became an image of the hero-poet soaring above the world's destructiveness. Full of poetic thoughts, he discovered that a granddaughter of Coleridge lived in Torquay, so he made his first literary pilgrimage, tracking down the house with Harold's help and nervously knocking on the door. Harold says no one was in, but if that was so the pilgrim must have tried again, for on 10 August Miss Coleridge and her brother signed their names in Wilfred's copy of their grandfather's poems.

Wilfred and Harold sometimes had the company of their cousin Edith and of other Taylors, presumably the children of John's first marriage, and they met an attractive, rich American boy named Russell Tarr, who impressed them with his prowess as a diver.[20] Wilfred seems to have been happy to have Harold around, even in the company of this glamorous new friend, although Harold represents himself as taking part in the Coleridge expedition only on sufferance. 'The whole day to Harold & me centres round the *bathing*,' Wilfred reported to Susan. 'The most enjoyable we have ever had, *I* think.' Another, less pleasant thing to share with Harold was realising that the sort of spending and freedom Tarr took for granted was hopelessly out of their reach. In Harold's story Wilfred stares enviously at a newspaper office, dreaming of being a journalist, while Harold gazes at an expensive paintbox in a shop window.

~

By the time of the move to Mahim in 1910, Wilfred was into his last two years at the Technical and his parents were beginning to worry about his future. During one of his periodic visits to Alpenrose, Susan wrote to him at length to review the options. She favoured the Church, and he agreed she should consult their old mentor Canon Robson about a theological college in Birkenhead. Study there might lead to a degree, but Wilfred and Susan both knew that Robson would say no one should become a minister without being certain of a call from God. Wilfred felt no such certainty, and Susan wisely refrained from pressing him. She suggested he might be able to make use of his French in some way, and he thought that was an interesting idea. Almost anything seemed better than a career in elementary education. The usual route for pupil-teachers was to spend two years in a training college, if possible with a King's Scholarship, a government award that would pay the fees. The snag was what Wilfred later called the 'Obligations': he would be required to serve for at least seven years in an elementary school or repay all grants. 'And really,' he told his mother in August 1910, 'I have no desire to be chained to an *elementary* school for the best years of my life by the King's scholarship.'[21]

He could speak with some experience by this stage, having just completed a year as a fully-fledged pupil-teacher. His letters say very little about his teaching, since he rarely had occasion to write to Susan in term-time, but they contain a few clues. An August 1909 letter mentions seeking advice about 'curriculum, way in, kind of children, etc.' from somebody called Davies. Wilfred was in fact preparing for his two-year stint as a pupil-teacher at Wyle Cop School, having passed exams at the end of the preparatory course and reached the minimum age of sixteen. Lewis Davies, a PTC student, had started as a pupil-teacher at the school the year before.[22] For the next two years, from August 1909 to July 1911, Wilfred's time was divided equally between PTC classes and teaching. The classes continued to be free, and the teaching was paid for, probably at the usual rate of fifteen pounds a year, a contribution to family finances his father must have welcomed.[23]

While Wilfred was on the staff at Wyle Cop, Harold seems to have been a pupil there. *Journey from Obscurity* describes the place vividly, but never mentions that Wilfred had worked at the school, nor even that he had been a pupil-teacher. Perhaps Harold's memory failed him, or perhaps he preferred not to reveal that his brother had occupied such a humble role. Silence on the matter certainly helps the contrasts in his story. While Wilfred is enjoying a supposedly privileged education in Shrewsbury, Harold fares no better than in Birkenhead. At his first school he has to fight the bully, as he had done at the Institute, and once again his parents and elder brother are hopelessly unsympathetic. Convalescing after a serious illness, he temporarily joins Mary and Colin in their infants' class, run by a Miss Goodwin in a private house. 'Goody', who lived in one of the bigger houses in Underdale Road, became a family friend, according to Harold, helping Wilfred with his French and giving piano lessons to all the children except Harold himself, who was not considered worth teaching. She sees he has learned nothing at his first school, so he is transferred to another, a small charitable foundation which he much prefers, but here again he gets into a fight, this time with no less an opponent than the headmaster, and is again taken away.

Harold's third and last school, reached by an alleyway off a main street, is undoubtedly Wyle Cop, and his description of it aches with disgust and shame.[24] He remembers that the alley, which stank horribly in summer, was inhabited by 'filthy slatternly women' who made lewd suggestions to him as he passed, and that the boys were foul in mind and body, products of the worst slums in the town. There certainly were very poor, overcrowded areas of central Shrewsbury at the time. However, Harold's account of his leaving the school is unlikely to be accurate. According to him, he escaped on his own initiative: discovering that evening classes were available at the Art School, he asked to see the Principal, Mr Weaver, who agreed to let him attend. Wilfred was annoyed at first, but eventually had to recognise that the budding artist should be taken seriously. Harold then resolved to leave the Cop altogether, knowing he might soon be expelled as usual. He was still in short trousers (his narrative implies that the year was 1910), but Weaver bent the rules to take him on as a full-time art student.

Actual events were probably more straightforward. The 1906 inspectors had recommended that the Cop should act as a feeder school for the Technical, and there was much coming and going between the two establishments. Promising pupils from the school must often have been sent on to Timpany and Weaver (a clue as to the social background of some of Wilfred's fellow students), and Harold was showing real talent as an artist. Moreover Harold finished at Wyle Cop not because he chose to, but because he had reached the normal leaving age.[25] He was not quite as young as he later imagined. The year was actually 1911, and on 29 September, three weeks after his fourteenth birthday, the authorities approved an application from 'Mr T. Owen as to his son Harold age fourteen being allowed to attend the Art Classes free of fees on the understanding that he becomes an Art Pupil Teacher'. There seems to be no similar minute in the official records for any other applicant, except Wilfred and one other in 1907. Tom Owen made exactly the same arrangements for the younger brother as for the elder: both became probationer pupil-teachers as soon as they reached the minimum age, even though term had already started.

Wilfred's letters give no hint that he himself ever found the Wyle Cop children disgusting, and he later referred to the school as 'the "Cop" of amiable memory'. An obscure pun about bamboo and 'the palmy ... Edwardian days ... of blessed memory' in another letter seems to imply that he maintained discipline in the usual way by caning his pupils on the hand, not without enjoyment. His only mention of them is a specimen of 'Wyle-Copic' in May 1910: 'Hall the skule his 'aving er oliday, so Mist' Howin wunna ave is sums & stuff what 'e learns us wiv hon Fursdee same as hother times'.[26] Unlike Harold, Wilfred was able to find the children amusing, perhaps even endearing, although A.J. Wright, who joined him as a pupil-teacher at the Cop in 1910, thought he was far too snobbish to have had any real sympathy with them. Whatever the truth of that, Wilfred certainly had to work with children from poor homes over a period of two years, so he must have learned a good deal about social deprivation. His letters make no complaint on that score. The objection to being a pupil-teacher as far as he was concerned was the sheer volume of work. He was servant to two exacting headmasters, S.J. Lightbown at the Cop and Timpany at the Technical. He said later that Lightbown had been a dictatorial bully, and that no one had understood the strain of doing a job quite unsuited to an inexperienced teenager while trying to keep up his own studies. He sometimes felt faint from weariness. Teaching 'sums & stuff' could be done by rote, but he also had to prepare Victorian-style 'object lessons' on general topics: 'did not get out till 5.25 yesterday', he told Susan in April 1911, 'took an object lesson requiring preparation today, and so on'.[27] Harold remembers how exhausted he used to look, white-faced and hollow-eyed.

Wilfred's labours were well rewarded in the final exams for the course in April 1911, when he was the only Shrewsbury candidate to gain two distinctions, in English and French. He was now qualified either to start work at once as an Uncertificated Teacher, with no chance of promotion even within the elementary school system, or to proceed to training college. He was determined to avoid even the second option if he could. Instead of resting from his studies and concentrating on teaching for his last term, he entered himself for London University Matriculation, the first step towards a London external degree. Some 'Difficulty Papers' slipped into one of his botany textbooks show that he signed up with the Cambridge-based University Correspondence College for postal tuition. (One of these papers asks for the floral diagram of the lesser celandine, and the college duly supplies a model answer.) He may have taken UCC courses in other subjects as well, sending regular essays and test papers to be marked and commented on. All this had to be done in such spare time as he had.

~

It was in this period of stress and uncertainty that Wilfred discovered Keats. He had read some of the poems before, but not with the passionate feeling that appears for the first time in a letter of 2 April 1911. Susan was at Alpenrose, where she had heard a nightingale. 'I crave to hear it,' Wilfred told her, 'and yet I should almost be afraid lest it should not be as fine as I imagine it. At present my soul is in a ferment, and the "leafy month of June" promises as many terrors as leaves.' He quoted some lines from Keats, then urged Susan to find the Gunstons' copy of the poems and read the 'Ode to a Nightingale', although he warned her not to believe the editor's condemnation of Keats's attitude to knowledge.[28] Having often been told that the Christian believer could hear the voice of God speaking through the Bible, he was now reading and hearing Keats in that same Evangelical spirit, and the poet who had longed for a life of sensations rather than of thoughts spoke to the heart of the adolescent schoolboy more powerfully than the Bible ever had. Even so, Wilfred's new-found enthusiasm did not overwhelm his other interests, and he closes his letter with a request for geological specimens from the chalk-pit and botanical ones from the wood where the nightingale sang.

Wilfred's April letter marks the beginning of a fundamental change. From now on his literary vocabulary, previously little more than an affectation, gradually becomes his own language, and poetry begins to replace scripture as a guide to life. Later that April he went to Torquay, where he bought a copy of Sidney Colvin's life of Keats and piously began a sonnet, 'Before reading a biography of Keats for the first time'. This sort of exercise was to be typical. Whenever he found a new poet he would look for things to imitate so that he could learn by practice. Without any lessening of reverence he could examine a Keats sonnet as he examined a plant, noting its structure and special characteristics. The most frequent marks in his books are underlinings of rhyme schemes and unusual words and images, although in biographies he was also inclined to mark passages relating to his own life.

Unable to finish his first Keatsian sonnet, he nervously settled down to read Colvin in detail, marking comments that Keats's mind was 'unapt for dogma', that Keats and Leigh Hunt were given to 'luxuriating' over 'deliciousness', and that Keats's friend Reynolds came from Shrewsbury and lacked health and energy. When he found that Keats had stayed at Teignmouth not far away, he wrote home for a railway pass and was soon standing transfixed outside the house, the bewildered occupants peering at him through the window. He walked to the end of the beach where the Teign flows into the sea, noticing how the river's current momentarily checked the incoming waves, and he thought that with a bit of ingenuity the image could be worked into a sonnet about Keats resisting death, 'like a new dating on his doom' (a phrase echoed from *The Fall of Hyperion*). The idea got no further than a prose outline, but he managed to complete several other sonnets based on Keatsian models, including one 'written at Teignmouth, on a Pilgrimage to Keats's House'.[29]

Longing for more than practice in craftsmanship, he wrote a rhetorical invocation 'To Poesy', imploring the goddess to grant him companionship with the great poets. Inside the dust-jacket of his copy of *A Midsummer Night's Dream,* he roughed out some lines which show the young botanist-poet hoping for a May morning vision like those granted to the bards of old.

> *When glossy celandine forgets to flower,*
> *And bugle blooms where hyacinth hath been ...*
> *I went in quest of healing for a body tired,*
> *[And new] enthusiasm for a soul*
> *Grown faint in love of beauty and of truth*
> *And furthermore I half-foreknew,*
> *Some vision waited me, even me*
> *As [unto] those old dreamers on May Morn*
> *When England's muse was young.*[30]

One element in all this pent-up desire was undoubtedly repressed sexuality, and he later described himself as 'in love' with Keats. Buying a five-volume edition of the poems and letters, he busily marked exotic words and lush passages. A bookmarker he left in *Endymion*, embroidered with the text 'Create in me a clean heart O God', seems to have prayed in vain, but perhaps guilt overcame him after reading 'Lamia', where four pages of sensuous description have been carefully stuck together. His remark in April that his soul was in a ferment is a quotation from the preface to *Endymion*, and he quoted more from it in September. Keats had said there is a stage between boyhood and maturity when 'the soul is in a ferment, the character undecided, the way of life uncertain, the ambition thick-sighted': 'yes indeed!' Wilfred sighed, and Keats's poem remained with him as a source of words and inspiration. He marked the portrait of the sleeping boy-hero Adonis as especially memorable.

He was back at Shrewsbury by the end of April, obsessed with Keats and more undecided than ever about his future. His mother, still at Alpenrose, sought advice from the Vicar of Kidmore End, Herbert Robson (not to be confused with Canon Robson of Birkenhead). Wilfred tried to seek it from a higher source, as Susan had no doubt often urged him to do, but he told her he could not distinguish between drifting and waiting for God to answer. Two American preachers were holding a mission in Shrewsbury, so he went to a few of their crowded meetings, but he was revolted by their melodramatic gestures and bellowing oratory.[31] Mrs Timpany, the head-master's wife, called in one evening to warn him against elementary teaching, saying with remarkable honesty how wicked it was that pupil-teachers were not told of the miseries awaiting them. She suggested Wilfred should talk to her husband out of school, and she recommended trying for the civil service, an idea that left Wilfred more gloomy than grateful, dismayed at the thought of having to exchange literature for office routine. There seemed to be no attractive way of earning a living, yet he admitted that holidays at Dorfold and Alpenrose had shown him the importance of money.

He went to see the headmaster and told him he wanted to write, so Timpany suggested journalism. That thought had already occurred to Wilfred, but what he really wanted to do was to write like Keats, and as he said in 'To Poesy', echoing Keats, years of study and thought would be needed before such a high ambition could be realised. When Miss Wright took the pupil-teachers on a field excursion, he discovered that her sister, who came too, was keen on literature, and he spent so much of the day discussing books that the rest of the party suspected a romance. A brief school holiday in June for George V's coronation gave him the chance to visit Alpenrose and call on the Vicar of Kidmore End, who had been making enquiries on his behalf.

~

Mr Robson said that if Wilfred wanted to get a degree, there were several ways of going about it. Ideally he should raise a loan from a rich relation, if any, in order to study full-time at university. Failing that, a pass at Matric would qualify him to read for an external London degree, either while teaching in a secondary school, though that would be murderously hard work, or – and here the Vicar came up with an idea none of the Owens had thought of – while acting as an 'assistant' to a parson, perhaps a solitary bachelor in a rural parish, in return for board and lodging and probably an allowance of some twenty pounds a year. It so happened that Herbert Wigan, the Vicar of Dunsden just down the road, was going to be in need of help during the coming winter. Robson suggested applying to him, Wilfred told Susan, 'especially as his views coincide with ours'. When Wilfred asked about elementary teaching, Robson raised his hands in horror.

Wilfred reported all this to Mahim, asking his parents' opinion, and they can have had little hesitation in favouring the Dunsden plan. Wilfred himself seemed to like it, it would save him from having to study and teach at the same time, and living in a country vicarage would be both civilised and healthy. The Gunstons would be able to keep an eye on him, and there would be no need to beg from the Quayles. Most important of all from Susan's point of view, the Vicar of Dunsden was an Evangelical, as Robson had been careful to point out. She answered Wilfred's letter promptly, giving her own and Tom's approval, and on 23 June 1911 Wilfred went over to Dunsden with Leslie to meet Mr Wigan, whom he thought charming. The two cousins were invited to 'lunch'. Writing home afterwards Wilfred put the word in inverted commas: used to the midday meal being called 'dinner', even in the official rules of the Birkenhead Institute, he was already pleasantly aware that life at the Vicarage was at a higher social level than at home. Wigan for his part must have seen that the visitor would be a useful young man to have in the parish. Wilfred's religious beliefs were sound, as was to be expected of a nephew of Mrs Gunston, and he was clearly well versed in doctrine and scripture. He could play the piano and sing, and he was an experienced teacher, used to dealing with working-class children. There would be no lack of jobs for him, nor any lack of space in the house, even though the current assistant, Alfred Saxelby-Kemp, was likely to stay on until the spring.

Wilfred explained that what he wanted for himself was time and space in which to prepare for exams, and Wigan made him an offer, though what the terms were can more safely be guessed at from Wilfred's subsequent letters than from Harold's confident account. Nothing in the letters suggests Susan took any direct part in the negotiations, nor that Wigan promised tuition, and Harold's claim that Wilfred confessed to serious religious doubts is simply not credible.[32] If the would-be assistant's faith had really been in such a poor state he could hardly have contemplated working in an Evangelical parish, and Wigan would certainly not have contemplated employing him. Wilfred had never had any occasion to question his basic commitment to religion, even though his new-found devotion to Keats was starting to overlay his youthful piety. Both he and the Vicar would have taken it for granted that a right relationship with God was the one essential qualification. Wilfred had told Susan a year before that he was unsure about taking holy orders, adding that it was possible 'to serve Him, as *you* say, in any station just as well', and he probably said much the same to the Vicar.[33] As far as Wigan was concerned, though, the justification for taking on an assistant was not only that the parish would benefit, but also that a candidate for the ministry would get some worthwhile experience. He seems to have stipulated that Wilfred could have two years in which to decide for or against a life of full-time service to the Church. It was probably understood that Wilfred would inherit Kemp's study and small allowance in due course. Harold says Wigan promised an allowance of five shillings a week from the start. No final agreement was to be made until Matric results were known, but Wilfred went back to Shrewsbury feeling happier about his future than he had done for some time.

His days as a schoolboy and pupil-teacher ended in mid-July 1911, and it was just as well they did. The *Shrewsbury Chronicle* had been publishing letters from a 'Dissatisfied Parent' highly critical of the PTC, and on 28 July the paper suddenly reported that the Centre had been closed and the services of Mr Timpany 'dispensed with'. The Technical had been in debt for seven years, its accounts were in confusion and student numbers had fallen. The terse reference to Timpany implies that he was leaving in disgrace, after eight years as head. The other PTC teachers had to leave with him, including Miss Wright and Miss Jones. The latter soon got a job at a secondary school in Finchley. When Wilfred visited her later in the year, she spent most of the evening telling him about Timpany's misdeeds, although what they were Wilfred's letter does not say.

The *Chronicle* soon had more momentous topics to deal with. The long-expected crisis in labour relations came to a head that summer, the big trades unions – seamen, dockers, miners, railwaymen – coming out on strike one after the other. The country was unused to troubles on such a scale, many people fearing that society itself was in danger, and the authorities overreacted. Troops killed two demonstrators in Liverpool and two in Wales. Warships were sent to the Mersey and cavalry to Chester. Tom Owen and his colleagues must have struggled to keep their section of the railways going, apparently with some success. Amid talk of famine and revolution, visitors came by the usual special trains to the annual Shrewsbury Flower Show, where they inspected the flowers, took balloon rides and gasped at the lavish fireworks, which included set pieces of aeroplanes and the new King. Strings of electric lights glittered in the trees, an innovation Wilfred was to remember when he came to write 'Disabled' six years later.

About this time Town used to swing so gay
When glow-lamps budded in the light blue trees,
And girls glanced lovelier as the air grew dim ...

～

Matric was held in September. Gordon Gunston had to be in London then, so he and Wilfred met at Paddington and went to Wimbledon, where they stayed at 38 Worple Road, a private school the Gunstons knew from their years in the neighbourhood. On Monday 11 September in stifling weather, Wilfred reported to Imperial College in Kensington, cramming himself into a stuffy entrance hall with more than six hundred other candidates. He thought it was like the Black Hole of Calcutta, especially as there were plenty of Indian faces and a rajah-like examiner, enviably splendid in hood and gown. When the doors were opened, everyone rushed in to find their seats and fall to work. Wilfred was amused to see an elderly clergyman scribbling away under the stern eye of a young female invigilator.

Several people who saw his question papers afterwards said they were exceptionally difficult. Even the Correspondence College commented that some of the English essay topics were over-ambitious: 'Social Life in the Reign of Queen Anne', 'The Romance of Astronomy', 'A Dialogue between Two Visitors from the Colonies on the Subject of the Coronation Ceremony'. Like most other candidates Wilfred chose another coronation title, 'The English Ideal of a King', though if he misread it as 'The Ideal English King', as he quoted it on a postcard home that evening, his essay may have been slightly off target. The second English paper was also demanding, but he must have been pleased to be asked for examples of the narrative poem, the ode and the historical novel, gift questions for an admirer of Scott and Keats. Candidates were required to pass two papers in English, two in elementary mathematics and any three others, including either Latin or a science. He had chosen French, history and botany as his options.[34] He thought the first two went well, but a gladiolus corm puzzled him and when he finally identified it he forgot to write down the answer. In general, though, he enjoyed the three-day challenge, feeling almost nostalgic when a pompous invigilator called for the last time, 'Laydeezanjenulmun, You have abow-oot Five Minutes Maw!' and then, 'Cease Writing Please'.[35] Susan sent him a New Testament in case he needed reassurance.

He stayed on in Wimbledon for more than a week to tread sacred ground, armed with rail tickets from his father. The Keats manuscripts on display at the British Museum held him in silent ecstasy for several hours. He thought the handwriting was rather like his own. At the National Portrait Gallery he gazed entranced at the Keats portraits and death-mask, at one point stepping backwards on to a lady's toe, much to his and her confusion. He went to Hampstead, walked on the Heath, stared at Keats's house and found a collection of Keats relics in the public library, including a lock of hair. More poems resulted. 'Written in a Wood, September 1910' seems to refer to the Heath, despite the date in the title (1910 was ninety years after Keats's death, as the poem says: 'ninety-one' would have ruined the metre). An unfinished sketch for another poem describes hearing long-dead poets on Hampstead Heath,[36] and an attempt at a sonnet, 'On Seeing a Lock of Keats's Hair', apparently drafted a year later, again declares that believers can hear Keats's voice:

> *Turn ye to Adonais; his great spirit seek.*
> *O hear him; he will speak!*

In addition to these pilgrimages, Wilfred spent a morning at Hampton Court and a whole day at Kew, as well as visiting the Tate Gallery, where an unfortunate lady fell on the polished floor and was asked for her name and address. 'Yes'm,' the attendant said, like some character in a *Punch* cartoon. 'We takes the nimes of all lidies as slips dahn in the gelries.' Wilfred remembered that Harold had just started as a full-time art student and sent him good wishes. He spent at least two evenings at the theatre, seeing a disappointing *Macbeth* and his beloved Benson Company in *The Tempest*. On the Saturday he accompanied Gordon to call on an old friend of both their mothers, a former maid at Plas Wilmot, and on the Sunday he twice attended Emmanuel Church, listening with pleasure to the Gunstons' former minister, E.W. Moore. After this strenuous London fortnight Wilfred returned to Alpenrose, where he was invited over to Dunsden for tea and croquet in the idyllic garden, and the Vicar renewed the offer of an assistantship. The prospect of living at the Vicarage seemed more attractive than ever.

Wilfred told Susan he intended to stay on at Alpenrose until he heard his Matric result, which was due on 2 October. Letters normally only took a day to arrive, and as he was still at the Gunstons' on the 3rd the description in *Journey from Obscurity* of the news arriving in Shrewsbury may be misplaced. That memory of Wilfred's tension and bitter disappointment may belong to 1913, when he failed a scholarship to Reading. Getting through Matric in 1911 was actually a fine achievement, as Herbert Robson said afterwards. Wilfred was one of the comparatively few candidates noted on the pass list as working from 'Private Study' rather than a school. The top quarter or so of the successful candidates were placed in a 'First Division', and he had hoped to be in it, but the honour would have had little effect on his future academic chances.[37] He was now technically an undergraduate of London University, so he bought the cap and gown to which he was entitled, apparently even wearing them in the street when opportunity offered.[38] The way was now open to the next stage, the second-year undergraduate exam known as Intermediate Arts. On 20 October 1911 he took up residence at Dunsden Vicarage.

4

Parish Assistant

Dunsden

OCTOBER 1911–JULY 1912

Wilfred wrote home from Dunsden on 23 October 1911, three days after his arrival, that everything at the Vicarage was on the scale of a fine manor house. Susan must have been pleased to think that at the age of eighteen he was already beginning to live as a gentleman. He had equipped himself with the necessary clothes – bowler hat, dark suit, dinner jacket – but he was nervous about having to behave correctly. He was also worried about the time available for work, and about the Vicar's apparent lack of interest in books. It was a relief to discover that 'dear Mr Wigan' had heard Ruskin lecture and met Holman Hunt and was even distantly related to William Morris.

The Reverend Herbert Wigan, Vicar of Dunsden from 1904 until his death in 1947, has had a bad press. He is usually portrayed as he emerges from a cursory reading of Wilfred's letters: snobbish, selfish, extravagant, painfully dull, a man of 'very *de*cided and *one*sided religious beliefs',[1] often absent from duty, and apparently devoid of sympathy for the sick and the poor. A very different memory of him survives in the parish he served for so long, and a group of elderly villagers in 1997 described him with warm affection as 'a lovely man', 'a real gentleman', 'a saint'.[2] He mellowed in later life, as his nephew recalled, and perhaps marriage in 1915 made him less withdrawn, but even Wilfred's letters allow him some good qualities. Wigan was cheerful and kindly, welcoming Owens and Gunstons whenever they came to the Vicarage, and he clearly liked Wilfred, treating him well and giving him special responsibilities. Happening to speak of the Vicar of Kidmore End one day in 1912 he said, 'I shall ever be grateful to him for having sent me you.' But Wigan was not at all the sort of man to understand the hopes of a would-be poet. He watched the new assistant's progress with warm approval, confident that the ministry stood to gain an excellent recruit.

It was hardly Wigan's fault that Dunsden Vicarage was far too large for a bachelor. It was a family house, late Victorian and complicated, with three storeys, a cellar, two staircases and twelve bedrooms, and his predecessor had lived there with a wife, seven children and five servants. The ground floor had a study for the Vicar, a dining room and a large drawing room, and at the back, with access from the yard, the kitchen and services and two rooms intended for parish use (the 'Den' and the 'Boudoir' in Wilfred's letters). Parishioners attending meetings could thus come and go through the yard without disturbing the private side. The coach-house had stabling for three horses, and there was a beautiful one-and-a-half-acre garden overlooking fields. The place would have been impossible to run without servants, and the staff of four – housekeeper, maid, gardener, boy – was probably the minimum needed. They kept everything in immaculate condition, inside and out, but not just for Wigan's benefit; hospitality often had to be provided for meetings and visiting preachers.

The Vicar would have been astonished if anyone had accused him of living grandly. The house was well furnished, but the only occupant of the stables was a necessary pony that spent its days plodding round a well in the garden, pumping water to a tank in the roof. Wigan rode about on a bicycle, sometimes in old clothes. Nevertheless, in a rural and largely working-class parish he was inevitably the grandee, and being tall, dignified and bearded he looked the part. The villagers addressed him as 'Your Riverence', the older women curtseying to him in the traditional way. He took such things for granted, having been brought up in a country parsonage. Yet he was not autocratic in his ministry, believing strongly that members of his congregation should be free to express their views. When they asked him to make changes to church services in 1912, he complied, even though the new arrangements conflicted with his principles.[3]

Dunsden Vicarage

Wigan's family, well-connected and proud of its coat of arms, owned the patronage of Luddesdown parish in Kent, where his father had been Rector. Alfred Wigan, evidently a man of High Church views, had sent Herbert to Radley, a High Church school, and Oriel, the Oxford college that had been at the heart of the Tractarian movement. The young Wigan became one of the many admirers of Edward King, a notoriously Romish professor, later attending King's controversial enthronement as Bishop of Lincoln. He scraped a pass degree in classics and philosophy, went on to Cuddesdon, the Oxford theological college, was ordained in 1888 and after a curacy in London became chaplain of Bloxham School, an Anglo-Catholic foundation. His eldest brother had meanwhile become Rector of Luddesdown on their father's death. When the brother died prematurely Herbert did not succeed to the family living, instead remaining at Bloxham until 1899, when he was advised to give up work for a while and take a sea voyage for the sake of his health. The school magazine reported in the following year that he had taken a curacy, but he was soon travelling again, this time round the world, and by early 1902 he was back at Bloxham, helping out for a few months. There is no clue as to what was wrong with his health, but he may have been going through a crisis of faith. In 1903 he was appointed curate at Sonning, the mother church of Dunsden, and a year later he moved up the hill as, at last, a vicar.[4]

At some stage before or soon after arriving in Dunsden, Herbert Wigan saw the light. He renounced his Tractarian past, hid away his biretta and his signed portrait of Pope Leo XIII, and became a committed Evangelical. The change took him from one extreme of Anglicanism to the other, and it must have been a painful process, costing him friends and maybe damaging his career. His family seems to have forgiven him, and two of his sisters came to live in the Vicarage during his early years there to help with what he often called 'the work', meaning the Lord's work. After they returned home in 1909, he was sometimes assisted by a parson from Bournemouth, Trevor Lingley, who may have played some part in his change of faith. Lingley is frequently mentioned in the parish magazine as a well-known figure among the Dunsden 'workers', as is a friend of his, the Reverend Walter Lewty. Lewty in turn introduced Alfred Saxelby-Kemp, who became Wigan's first full-time assistant in June 1911. This was the team Wilfred joined.[5]

'We have been cheered lately by visits from both Mr Lingley and Mr Lewty, the latter preaching on Sunday October 15 and giving an address to the mothers on the following Thursday, and now we have Mr Owen at the Vicarage to help for a while in the work,' Wigan wrote in the November 1911 magazine. The Vicar seems to have been somewhat isolated from the local clergy, few of whom are likely to have shared his strict views. He was now forty-nine, a lonely and perhaps unhappy man, disguising his inner feelings and innate shyness under a combination of affability and deep reserve. Cut off in an obscure parish with no close companions, he held to his Evangelicalism with a convert's determination, praying earnestly that God would use him as a channel of the Spirit.

∼

The daily routine at the Vicarage was an entirely new experience for Wilfred. His large bedroom, handsomely furnished with soft carpet, bureau and enormous wardrobe, was kept in perfect order by invisible servants. Every night he found his pyjamas neatly laid out on the bed, and punctually at seven each morning a respectful maid tapped on his door to tell him his shaving water was waiting outside. The bathroom was inaccessible, being connected to the Vicar's room, so ablutions had to be conducted in an absurdly small bowl on the washstand. Wilfred washed and shaved as best he could, uncomfortably aware of spots and occasional boils, but at least the water was hot and the huge white towels were luxurious. When the gong went, he descended to sit next to Kemp by the dining-room fire while the Vicar read the day's passage from scripture, the servants sitting meekly at the back of the room. Prayers followed, after which the staff withdrew and the three gentlemen helped themselves to breakfast, Wilfred as the junior wielding the bread-knife. As soon as the servants had cleared away the meal, the dining room was his study until they returned to lay up for lunch. This arrangement limited his working hours and prevented him from strewing books and papers about in his usual way; on the other hand his bedroom had no fire, and he could hardly sit there swathed in blankets as though still in Shrewsbury. Envying Kemp, who had been allowed to take over the Den, he installed himself at a bureau-bookcase by the long dining-room windows and started reading for the next round of exams nearly two years away.

His plan at this stage was to take Intermediate Arts in July 1913, for which he would have to offer five subjects: Latin combined with Roman history, English, and three options, to include a science and another language. He chose French, botany and history, feeling reasonably confident about all of them, although botany would require supervised practical work. The big obstacle was Latin, and it was dismaying to watch poor Kemp struggling with irregular verbs at the age of twenty-four. Wilfred made a start by translating a Latin hymn for a Bible Society competition, and was gratified to win a prize. Three second-hand bookshops in Reading yielded up plenty of textbooks, and guidance was available in University Correspondence College publications.[6] He would need to take some UCC courses, reinforcing them with classes at University College, Reading (the college was not yet a university in its own right, but it prepared students for London degrees).

Alfred Kemp was hoping to get to theological college, but had twice failed his exams. Wilfred had to help him with his Latin, thinking him endearingly simple though very agreeable. When they walked the choirboys down to Reading to see an entertainment put on by the Church Missionary Society, Kemp was delighted by the performance, whereas Wilfred was secretly unimpressed, telling Susan how an 'Indian' boy had been flung to the Ganges crocodiles while 'tipsily smirking at mamma somewhere at the back of the audience'. The junior assistant, who had just been reading Dickens and George Eliot, already had an ironic eye, trained by *Punch* and the Victorian novelists.

At first the most important duty seemed to be talking at meals. Dinner – 'late dinner' as Wilfred called it for his mother's benefit – was a formal occasion at which he was sometimes called upon to carve, a task he was unused to, but the main difficulty was not how to deal with a pheasant but how to deal with Wigan, who was an embarrassingly poor conversation-alist. Kemp's most vivid memory of the Vicarage was 'the awful evening silences', and he told Wilfred that Lewty had sometimes talked nonsense just to fill the gaps. The awkwardness contrasted oddly with a certain professional camaraderie. Wigan observed the Evangelical custom of addressing male colleagues as 'Brother', so Wilfred had to get used to being Brother Owen and to speaking of 'the other Brother' as Brother Kemp. When Lewty came on a visit in December he, too, called Wilfred Brother, and Wilfred felt honoured because Brother Lewty was an MA and 'is or was a reader of Modern Poetry' (the 'was' is significant: once one became a clergyman, time might have to be spent on more important things than poetry). Wigan was also an MA, but he told Wilfred that literature was 'an alternative to life or an artificialized life', a distraction from true spirituality.[7]

After dinner the Vicar and his two assistants retired to his study, where they sat round the fire and did nothing, according to Wilfred, unless the Vicar read aloud from some improving book. In October 1911 the book was a history of the 1859 Irish Revival. Wilfred told Susan the Vicar had 'the hope of a Revival in the place much on his mind, during these times'. Wigan probably thought of these evening sessions as important periods of meditation and fellowship, and they usually ended in extempore prayer, in which the two younger Brothers would have been expected to join. Some-times the proceedings did not close until half past eleven or later, seeming interminable to Wilfred, who longed to get back to work, and he could see Kemp was similarly restive. The two young men exchanged sighs as they lit their candles before going upstairs to bed. As the winter drew on, the maid's knock in the mornings came all too early, and Wilfred was still half asleep as he shaved by candlelight over his inconvenient pot of a basin.

'The Vicar has the hope of a Revival in the place much on his mind, during these times.' That sentence is crucial to an understanding of what happened to Wilfred at Dunsden. The labour troubles of the previous summer may well have convinced Wigan, a strong Tory, that there was a real danger of revolution, and from his point of view the cure was religion. As a first step, the life of the parish had to be renewed by the phenomenon known to Evangelicals as Revival, a spiritual reawakening that could fill a Christian community with fresh conviction, bringing a flood of new conversions and facing lukewarm believers with the ultimate choice between faith and denial. Wigan was uncompromising on the reality of that choice. 'The acceptance of the Gospel means *Life*,' he wrote grimly in the magazine in 1914, 'the failure to accept means *Death*, and there is no intermediate position.' Christ's challenge must often have been pondered on during those long evenings, while the study fire burned down to embers: 'Verily, verily, I say unto thee, Except a man be born again, he cannot see the kingdom of God.'

Most of Wilfred's early letters from Dunsden are optimistic, scarcely hinting to his mother that even in his first few weeks there he was gripped by intense depression. He was homesick, anxious about exams and already feeling the strain of having to appear better educated and more pious than he really was. In a poem apparently written during the winter of 1911-12, 'Supposed Confessions of a Secondrate Sensitive Mind in Dejection', he records being visited on autumn nights and even in daylight by Despondency, a Gorgon-like figure, pale, beautiful and horrifying:

> ... *face to face, she fixed on me her stare:*
> *Woe, woe, my blood has never moved since then;*
> *Down-dragged like corpse in sucking, slimy fen,*
> *I sank to feel the breath of that Despair.*
>
> *With Autumn mists, and hand in hand with Night,*
> *She came to me. But at the break of day,*
> *Went not again, but stayed, and yet doth stay.*
> *' – O Horror, doth not Pain take note of light*
> *And darkness, – doth he not hold off betimes,*
> *And yield his victim for an hour to Sleep?*
> *Then why dost thou, O Curst, the long night steep*
> *In bloodiness and stains of shadowy crimes?'*

Even in 1911 Wilfred's dreams and fantasies apparently involved a good deal of blood and violence. 'Supposed Confessions' is a very literary piece, with its archaic language and Tennysonian title, but it seems to represent real experience. The image of the terrifying face with fixed eyes paralysing its victim was to become a recurrent feature of his later work, culminating in poems such as 'Dulce et Decorum Est' and 'Strange Meeting'. It is one of the key images of Romanticism, deriving from many sources but above all, for Wilfred, from Keats's description of the goddess Moneta, whose blind gaze makes poets see. Wilfred was working his way towards poetic vision years before he knew anything about the 'bloodiness and stains of shadowy crimes' of war.

~

Dunsden was a tiny community of fewer than six hundred people, many of them living in cottages scattered among the fields. Cut off from Reading less than three miles away by the Thames and the Chiltern escarpment, the area felt remote, an idyllic landscape of farms, little lanes that were scarcely more than cart tracks, and occasional long views over the river valley below. Wilfred was delighted to find local associations with Tennyson, Shelley, Gray and Arnold. The parish contained two villages, Binfield Heath, where a small brickworks provided local employment, and Dunsden Green, where the road up from the valley divided at a triangle of common land. In so far as the area had a centre it was at the green, and the well at the point of the triangle was a daily meeting place. The shaft went down a hundred and fifty feet to river level, and anyone could have a key to the windlass for a shilling a year. Wilfred was probably remembering the approach to Dunsden in 1918 when he imagined soldiers in 'The Send-Off' returning 'silent, to village wells, / Up half-known roads'.[8]

Dunsden had been regarded as a wild, inaccessible place for centuries until philanthropic Victorian landowners had made improvements, building a chapel-of-ease and a school in the 1840s, and in the 1870s converting the chapel into a parish church, enlarging the school, and building the well and the Vicarage. The most recent addition was the parish hall next to the green, a functional structure of terracotta blocks. It had been built in 1909, largely at the expense of Wigan himself, who had seen that a hall was essential for Evangelical outreach.[9] Wilfred was to become very familiar with it, and with the little school nearby.

School, hall and church were all controlled by the Vicar. The parish had no other public buildings except three pubs and a Congregational chapel. Religion dominated local life, especially for the children, providing education, entertainment, culture and welfare, even though most adult villagers rarely attended church services. As it happened, Wilfred arrived just as an era was ending. He had to keep accounts for the simple insurance schemes run by the parish, clubs for Coal and Clothing, and Sickness and Benefit, but the Church was about to lose its ancient role as social provider. He attended a meeting in the hall in 1912, one of many held up and down the country, to hear about the new Insurance Act, one of the measures the Liberals were bringing in to provide pensions, healthcare and other benefits.

An obvious sign of change in the village was that water mains were being laid, bringing redundancy for the well and the Vicarage pony. Nevertheless the old ways were to continue at Dunsden for a while yet, and the Vicarage was a centre of temporal as well as spiritual power.

The house was half a mile away from the green, with All Saints Church and a farm as its only neighbours. Wilfred unkindly described the church as a shanty in 'depraved Gothic', but it was a pleasant, tranquil little building among trees and fields. The interior mirrored the two poles of Anglicanism that Wigan knew so well, the aisleless nave of 1842 a plain Evangelical preaching hall, and the east end of 1872 a monument to Tractarianism, with a carved stone reredos, choir stalls, stained glass and gaily painted organ pipes. Wilfred was inclined to be scornful, being used to much bigger churches, but there were times when he thought the gentle village services far preferable to noisier worship at St Julian's in Shrewsbury. Oil lamps and candles were the only lighting, and on summer nights the ivy in the churchyard shone with glow-worms.

He was soon drawn into the weekly parish routine. Afternoons were often taken up with visiting, 'sitting on uncomfortable chairs talking to uncomfortable folk in uncomfortable cottages' – and learning uncomfortable lessons. He had to spend hours in the foul-smelling, tumbledown homes of the poorest parishioners, as he told Mary in November 1911. Many of the old people were illiterate, their minds scarcely moving beyond the 'stone box with a straw lid' where they had spent all their lives. Those who believed in the Christian hope had faces 'bright with the white radiance of eternity'; the rest seemed dead to all pleasures. One old woman, living off nothing but bread and tea, was blind, deaf, unable to speak and in constant pain. 'Why am I telling you these dreadful things?' Wilfred exclaimed to Mary. 'Simply to let them educate you, as they are educating me, in the Book of Life ...' His sister and brothers were accustomed to his inflicting his bookishness on them, but readings from the Book of Life were something new.

He told Mary he had accompanied the Vicar to a meeting at a grand house, where the address was by Ernest Ingham, a former bishop of Sierra Leone and a leading Evangelical. Mary admired Ingham, having heard him in Shrewsbury, and Wilfred agreed he was a fine speaker, but the contrast between making conversation with the Bishop and other clerics over afternoon tea in an enormous billiard room and talking to parishioners in their hovels was impossible to ignore. Wilfred's use of Shelley's phrase, 'the white radiance of eternity', shows he was already thinking of that great atheist and rebel. Nevertheless he assured his sister that in speaking to the parish children he gave them 'the Messages, with one Purpose'. Occasionally there were practical good works to be done, such as cycling down to Reading to fetch medicine, but the chief Purpose in all his parish work was, or was supposed to be, to strengthen the faithful and win over the unbelievers.

The first regular meeting of the week was the Sowers' Band, a dozen or so girls aged ten to fourteen who gathered in the Boudoir for Bible study on Monday afternoons, sowing the seed of the Word so that they could be a band of reapers in later life. Discussions were led by Mrs Lott, the Vicarage housekeeper, who was also the parish clerk. Wilfred sometimes had to give a talk, and Mrs Lott asked him to teach the girls a carol for the Sunday School Christmas Treat. He wrote the carol himself, a simple 'chorus' of the kind often used at Evangelical gatherings, and thoroughly enjoyed training his little choir, encouraging 'the rosy mouths to ope a trifle widah!'.[10] Then at seven in the evening on Mondays, Tuesdays and Thursdays he had to be in charge of the boys' club in the hall, where the amenities included a piano, bagatelle tables and the latest acquisition, gym equipment bought from funds collected for the coronation celebrations. He sometimes found time to write letters during these evenings, saying on one occasion that he had ten youths under his eye and on another that he was timing boxers. He told Susan how happy he was to be with intelligent, if ill-educated youngsters. Evening duties had the further advantage of allowing him to escape dinner and the tedium of the study. He came back late, had supper in solitary contentment and retired to his room.

Wigan had inaugurated the hall two years earlier by holding a three-week mission there, saying that although the building was often to be used for entertainment, its true purpose was to serve the spiritual welfare of the parish. He continued the work by holding a 'Mission Service' in the hall every winter Wednesday evening, when a visiting speaker would give a Gospel address, or a missionary would talk about life in far-away places. Sometimes these Wednesday meetings were advertised as hybrid 'Lantern Services', at which readings were supplemented with illustrations. Wilfred had to feed slides into the acetylene-lit projector, while the Vicar kept a nervous eye on the controls. At the end of 1912 a 'cinematograph' was acquired, the first ever seen in Dunsden. Films and sets of slides on Christian themes could be hired from London, and Wilfred sometimes had to collect them from the station.

Thursday was the busiest weekday. Wilfred was occasionally asked to address the two-fifteen Mothers' Meeting in the hall, although the speakers were usually women. Emma Gunston gave at least two talks, one of which was on temperance, and she brought her daughters with her to help with tea, Wigan valuing her assistance so highly that he wished the Gunstons would move into the parish ('I *don't* think!' said Wilfred). Another speaker, more surprisingly, was Susan Owen, though the magazine does not record the date or subject of her talk. She came to stay at Alpenrose in November 1911 and several times in 1912, attending meetings and services, no doubt often accompanied by her sister, so that Wilfred was seen by everyone to belong to an impeccably Evangelical family. His special Thursday responsibility was the four-fifteen children's Scripture Union, a Bible study group started by Lewty and continued by Kemp. Wilfred enjoyed these events more than any of his other duties. Having been to many similar classes in his own childhood, he knew the form: one chose a Message, a biblical verse, expounding it in a simple talk, then turned to the piano and got the children to sing and learn a little chorus based on the text. The Vicarage had a stock of choruses, but the class had seen most of them already and they were not difficult to write; Wilfred composed several new ones himself.[11] When the children dispersed he probably lingered in the hall, reading or playing the piano until the boys' club at seven.

Friday evenings brought choir practice in the church. Wilfred sang bass, well enough to be entrusted with the occasional solo, and the rest of the choir seems to have consisted of about a dozen boys and five or six men, including Kemp, a ploughman, a blacksmith's assistant and William Hullcoop, the village schoolmaster, whom Wilfred thought a self-important windbag.[12] Saturday evenings were a time of quiet inner preparation for the Lord's day on the morrow. Wilfred had to be in the hall before seven for the 'PM', the weekly prayer meeting, an engagement that could never be missed because Wigan regarded it as vital to the spiritual health of the parish. Wilfred's very first job at Dunsden was to read the day's 'Portion' of scripture to one of these meetings. Fewer than a dozen people were present, but they would have been the keenest local Christians, and the Vicar would have wanted them to give a prayerful welcome to the new assistant. If Revival ever got under way they would be the shock troops, so their morale and training were important.

Sundays began with a communion service, then Morning Prayer (not called Matins in an Evangelical parish), at which the Vicar preached. His sermons were 'horrifyingly dismal', according to Wilfred, but he greeted his parishioners jovially in the porch afterwards. Sunday School was held in the afternoon, alternating with a monthly Children's Service in the usual way, and Wilfred was nearly always called on to teach a class or give a talk. Eventually he succeeded Kemp as Superintendent and enjoyed acting the role, speaking in solemn tones as he moved about the hall, overseeing the six teachers and keeping order among their charges. Susan occasionally sat at the back, no doubt rejoicing to watch him as she remembered her father's work as Superintendent in Oswestry long before. After Sunday School there was sometimes more visiting, followed by Evening Prayer and another sermon, often by a minister from another parish, and when the Vicar was preaching elsewhere Brothers Kemp and Owen had to be hosts at dinner. Some of the Wednesday and Sunday visitors were leading figures in the Evangelical world, including Canon

Arthur Barnes-Lawrence, well known for his Gospel tracts, and George Clarke, a long-serving missioner and regular author of Scripture Union notes (he wrote some at Wilfred's desk). Brother Owen took some pleasure in being treated as a colleague by published authors.

～

Yet the more Wilfred read Dickens, Ruskin and Shelley, the more shallow seemed the little exhortations produced by these visiting preachers. Evangelicalism had a pat scriptural answer to every problem, too easily learned and repeated, so that after a while every talk and meeting seemed the same. Listening to the regulars at the PM, he could soon predict every formula before it was uttered. His veneration for books set him apart. None of these people knew what he knew, or so he must have thought as he sat in the hall on Saturday evenings, head bowed, nerving himself to make his weekly contribution.

In November 1911 he came across a handsomely produced, almost new book of poems in one of the Reading shops. It was a complimentary copy, but the recipient had got rid of it, and at sixpence it was irresistible. He explained to Susan that he wanted to find out what the latest modern poetry was like, and when she replied that it was likely to be rubbish he told her she was wrong, but he said no more. By a chance that Wigan, had he known of it, would have seen as the Devil's work, Wilfred had discovered one of the most subversive books of the year. New poetry by John Masefield, Rupert Brooke and others was at last challenging the supremacy of Victorian themes and rhetoric, and Wilfred's find was the most uncompromising manifesto of them all, *Before Dawn* by Harold Monro. The contrast between Monro's poems and everything the Vicarage stood for could hardly have been greater.

Monro had started as an imitator of Keats and Wordsworth, much like Wilfred, but his book was dedicated to 'those who, with me, are gazing in delight towards where on the horizon there shall be dawn. / Henceforth, together, humble though fearless, we must praise, worship, and obey the beautiful Future, which alone we may call God.' The coming dawn was to be of a new society, in which people would be responsible for their own destiny, living close to nature without notions of any supernatural God or paradise. Sexuality would be open and free, and restrictions such as formal marriage would be abolished. One of the poems rejected Tolstoyan chastity, another glorified Don Juan, and there was an astonishing portrait of a woman longing for the end of her virginity. The beautiful Future would sweep away Christianity, with its burdens of guilt and sin, and if Christ came again he would come as a man-hero, proclaiming beauty and social justice. The angriest denunciations in *Before Dawn* were of priests and the Church.

Monro's zeal for the future made him discard the tired imagery of late Romanticism, but he had not fully succeeded in finding a new language. His most modern-sounding poems were a set of 'Impressions', brief, often satirical portraits of contemporary figures. Having bought the book to find out what modern poets were writing, Wilfred tried his hand at an 'Impression' of his own, just as he had imitated Keats's sonnets earlier in the year, roughing out some lines on the back of a chorus he had been working on. His subject, unidentified, was someone who valued 'every man at market price' and regarded parks and 'neat cemeteries' as perfect natural landscapes.[13] He had not written anything like that before, but he had seen that Monro was aiming to be unromantic, sincere and true to the earth, using plain language. Wilfred had in fact stumbled across the modern style that was soon to be known as 'Georgian'. He kept *Before Dawn* by him, quoting from it two months later and drawing on its ideas long after that.

His faith was further undermined in December by news that his first cousin, Kathleen Loughrey, had died of rheumatic fever. Typically, instead of expressing sorrow for Kathleen and her family, he commented that he was the same age and had recently feared he might develop the disease himself because his socks had got wet. Attending a funeral for the first time in his life a few days later, he wore a black suit and solemn face, but his mourning was secretly for his own mortality, as he told Susan with his usual disarming candour. Yet he had to recognise that plenty of other people were less fortunate than he was, and when he grumbled at having to get up in the dark he reminded himself that the local carters had to get up at four every day of the year.

He spent Christmas week in Shrewsbury at the Vicar's good-natured suggestion, but all too soon he was back again, trying to get used to 'the Silence, the State, and the Stiffness'. Fortunately parish activities were far from silent, and he had to be on duty at a series of annual junketings, probably with the concertina he was learning to play. His bowler hat came in useful at the Day School Treat, when a conjuror commandeered it to prove, in its owner's ironic phrase, 'the truth of miracles'. The well-rehearsed Sowers' Band sang their carol fairly well at the Sunday School Treat in the hall on 2 January 1912, and at the same event, after noisy games in which Wilfred took a leading part, the Vicar announced that Mr Owen would hold a Bible Class in the Boudoir on Sunday afternoons for 'lads' who had left school. The same Mr Owen amused the choirboys at their annual supper by pretending to read their thoughts, and sat through an excruciatingly boring tea for the Sunday School teachers, at which the company looked at innumerable postcards the Vicar had collected during his world tour. At the Mothers' Evening on the 15th Kemp sang 'The Lost Chord', and Wilfred recited some of Tennyson's little 'bijoux' and sang 'The

Arrow and the Song' with satisfying lack of nerves, receiving compliments on his voice 'when it matures (!)'.[14]

The institution of the lads' Bible Class was a public accolade from the Vicar, a sign that he now had complete confidence in his assistant. Boys were liable to drift away from church once they left school, so the new class must have been the subject of much prayer and planning. Wigan went up to London to buy a miniature organ for the Boudoir, and Wilfred wrote home for Canon Robson's sermons.[15] Wilfred had been proud to receive a New Year letter from the Canon, and could tell himself that he looked forward to being with the boys for spiritual reasons. 'It will be hard to part with the boys and others if I stay much longer. Surprising how my opinions of ploughmen's sons have changed now I know some. Thought they had round vacant eyes and mouths and intellects to correspond – Find them possessed of (sometimes) fine features, and (somehow) nice manners ...'

The Reading Free Churches organised a Young People's Campaign in January 1912, led by two professional evangelists, Fritz and Arthur Wood (their publicity took care to point out that they were Irish, not German). Wilfred attended one of their Bible studies, being now a teacher of scripture himself. Kemp and Mrs and Miss Fordham, two devout parishioners, went with him, Wigan joining them for a further meeting. The Woods' technique was much like that of the Shrewsbury missioners in 1911, with much arm-waving, clapping and smiling, and there were embarrassing moments when Fritz singled out individuals, including the Vicar, to compliment them on their singing.

~

Wilfred was beginning to lead a double life. Outwardly he was the successful assistant, no longer a probationer and, as he was very much aware, no longer a boy. His parents approved of his parish work, sending him money for a new Bible and a new bicycle, necessary equipment for his job. His Sunday classes went well, attended by a dozen or so regulars. Inwardly, though, he was under increasing stress. Susan seems to have visited him in February, her anxious fussing probably doing nothing for his confidence, and he soon began complaining of lassitude, skin trouble, a painful eye and indigestion. He was also afraid there was something wrong with his heart – he seems to have been suffering from harmless tachycardia, a rapid pulse perhaps made worse by heavy dinners and the heat of the study fire during what he called the 'Wasted Hours'.[16] He had always been able to share health concerns with his mother, but for the time being he confined his religious doubts to verse. Apart from his choruses, the few attempts at poetry that survive from early 1912 are entirely at odds with the sort of views he was supposed to be propagating. He muses on the incessant war between sea and rock, or (having seen the Vicar's postcards) on the miseries of great American cities where his uncle, Edward Shaw, had been swallowed up; he wonders why humans breed, when they are trapped by death like snakes in a pit; and he vows never to marry and introduce a child into 'that bitterness which we call consciousness', closing his will like an iron door against intimacy with another person.

The two big difficulties were the obvious ones, sex and death. He could say almost nothing about the former to his parents, and perhaps not much to himself, having apparently never had any guidance from them or anyone else beyond a few vague pieties and the Church's one clear instruction, that sex was sinful unless it was for the purpose of producing children within marriage. In vowing never to marry and father a child he was trying to turn away from the whole subject. Death was much easier to talk about, being a frequent topic at the Vicarage, and it soon became a pressing theme in his verse. His letters mention cases of chicken-pox, scarlet fever, diphtheria and consumption in the village, and some of the invalids were on his visiting list. Attending funerals and consoling bereaved families gave him more food for thought than would have come the way of most young men of his age. Fourteen people, with an average age of thirty-seven, were buried in the churchyard while he was living in the parish. Two fifteen-year-old boys had died of diphtheria in March 1911: 'what a warning to us all to be *ready* for the Master's coming,' Wigan had said in the magazine.

The Vicar unwittingly contributed to Wilfred's eventual undoing by entrusting him with the Bible Class. Wilfred now had to cope with the questions and doubts of some of the most intelligent youths in the parish, and he was apparently expected to counsel them in private if necessary. One Sunday in March he had a young farmhand to tea at the Vicarage because the boy could not believe in immortality. 'How shall I answer?' Wilfred asked himself and his mother, admitting he was already spending most of his time 'reading, analysing, collecting, sifting, and classifying Evidence'. The boy confessed to using bad language, a habit he hated but could not break, and Wilfred reflected that he was himself enslaved by language, '*Fine* Language, to yield wholly to the glamours of which would be accounted "of this world" by those who aver they are not of this world' (the biblical injunction that Christians should be 'in' the world yet not 'of' it was no doubt often quoted in the Vicarage). This letter is Wilfred's first clear admission to his mother that his faith was in trouble. He told her he dared say no more.

March and April 1912 were a crucial period in his life at Dunsden.[17] The Vicar went away for a few days on Monday 11 March, so the two Brothers could relax a little. Kemp read from Bunyan at the Wednesday Lantern Service, one of a series for Lent on *The Pilgrim's Progress*, while Wilfred worked the projector, telling Susan afterwards he had allowed one of his favourite boys to help with the slides. He had apparently already told her about Vivian Rampton (part of a letter he had written on the 11th is 'missing'). Other letters reveal that he had agreed to give Vivian four free piano lessons in the hall after the children's meetings on Thursday afternoons, an arrangement he kept secret in the Vicarage. The first lesson may have been on Thursday 14 March, and after it Wilfred managed to 'smuggle' Vivian into the Den for tea, having somehow induced Kemp to visit the Fordhams. Host and youthful guest, two happy conspirators, sat by the open window, enjoying the scents of spring and the elegance of the Vicarage's silver teapot. The servants would think that the boy had come for spiritual counselling.

Vivian Rampton, aged twelve, was the eldest of five children. His father Charles was a skilled though uneducated bricklayer, who is said to have taken up the trade as a boy after watching builders at work on Dunsden church. Brought up in a poor cottage near the well, Charles had prospered enough to build a pair of small, semi-detached houses at Binfield Heath, one of them – Vivian Cottage – for his own family.[18] The family next door were named Montague (two Montagues figure in Wilfred's letters, Willie, a fifteen-year-old stable boy, and Milly, a pupil at the school; Milly and Vivian were roughly the same age and great friends). Vivian's mother Edith was Charles's second wife and some twenty years his junior. Having worked as a lady's maid, she had seen how the gentry lived and knew the importance of education, and she must have been delighted when Mr Owen started taking an interest in her son. Wilfred would soon have discovered that he and Vivian had things in common. The boy was the cleverest child in the family and his mother's health was poor, so he was mature beyond his years, accustomed to being in charge of his brothers and sisters and regularly helping in the house. He did all the family's baking, and walked a mile or more every morning before school to fetch milk. His mother knew, and perhaps he did too, that with a little help he could cross the borderline from working to middle class. He had the open, eager look of a highly intelligent child on the edge of adolescence, and his striking brown eyes, deep and strangely melancholy, seemed hungry for knowledge. Wilfred could be of real use; he resolved to teach Vivian how to speak properly and how to enjoy books, as well as how to play the piano.[19]

On the day after the tea party, still elated by splendid weather and the Vicar's absence, and perhaps still in pursuit of Vivian, Wilfred spent the afternoon at the village school. Mrs Hullcoop, the headmaster's wife, who was taking the infants for physical drill outside, was pleased when the visitor asked to take over for a moment. Remembering many similar sessions at Wyle Cop, he put the children through 'the old familiar Hips – FIRM! Neck – RESST!' thinking how enchanting some of them were. That evening the Vicar returned, and the brief holiday was over.

Top left: Tom and Susan Owen at the time of their marriage, Oswestry, 1891. Susan is in mourning for her mother. *Top right:* Wilfred, their first child, born in 1893. *Bottom:* At Plas Wilmot, *c.* 1895. Front row: Jubilee the parrot, Gordon Gunston, Grandfather Edward Shaw, Susan with Wilfred on her knee, Dorothy and Vera Gunston. Back row: Emma Gunston and three servants.

Above: Susan with Mary, a nursemaid with Harold, and Wilfred standing between them, *c.* 1898.
Below left: Wilfred as a soldier, with sword.
Below right: Wilfred as a sailor, with a toy boat made for him by his father.

Above: Colin (left, wearing leg supports), Mary, Harold, Wilfred and Susan.
Below left: Wilfred, aged about eleven. *Below right:* Leslie Gunston.

Above: Wilfred (left), Mary, Tom, Colin, Harold and Susan. South Bay, Scarborough.
Below: The Owen grandparents' Golden Wedding, 24 January 1909. Back row: Wilfred and Tom Owen; Emily, Edward and Cecil Quayle; William Owen; John Taylor. Middle row: Susan Owen, Kenneth Quayle, Martha Owen, Margaret Quayle (with arm raised), Anne Taylor; Edith Taylor. Front row: Mary, Harold and Colin Owen.

Above: Wilfred in his pupil-teacher days, *c.* 1910. *Right:* St Julian's church (right foreground), Shrewsbury. *Below:* Shrewsbury Borough Technical School (also the Pupil-Teacher Centre and School of Art).

Above left: Herbert Wigan, Vicar of Dunsden. *Above right:* Vivian Rampton in private's uniform, *c.* 1918.
Below: The well and village school, Dunsden, *c.* 1900. The field later became the village green.
Opposite: Brother Owen in the Vicarage garden, Dunsden, probably photographed by
Brother Kemp, 1912.

The Gunston family: John (left), Emma, Gordon, Dorothy, Vera and Leslie.

The Scottish holiday, Kelso, 1912: Nelly Bulman (left), a guest, Blanche Bulman, Walter Forrest (standing); Harold, Colin (sitting in front), Susan, Tom (standing) and Mary Owen; Bill Bulman and another guest. Wilfred had not arrived when John Bulman took this photograph.

~

Wigan's reappearance was a depressing reminder of the life his assistant ought to be leading. The fine weather gave way to sleet and rain as if to reinforce the message. Wilfred took part in the usual weekend duties, but on the evening of Sunday 17 March, his mother's birthday and the eve of his own, his mind and body rebelled at the prospect of dinner and yet another evening in the study, his insides starting to hurt so much that he lay down on the dining-room floor, much to the alarm of the household. Mrs Lott provided a light supper of chicken and ginger wine, put a bottle of brandy in his room and ordered him to bed. Next day the servants set up a couch for him, and he lay on it all day, though 'finding relief' (presumably from constipation) soon after breakfast. As he half admits in his letter to Susan, his aim in all this melodrama was to oblige the Vicarage inhabitants to behave like her and make a fuss of him. He thoroughly enjoyed his day as an invalid, relaxing luxuriously on the red velvet couch and drafting a poem, 'Lines written on my Nineteenth Birthday'.

'Two Spirits woke me from my sleep this morn', the 'Lines' begin, with an echo of Harold Monro (the first poem in *Before Dawn* describes two visions seen at sunrise). The first spirit reminds Wilfred that a quarter of his allotted span has gone, and wasted time cannot be regained. The second, formless and silent, is Pain, but it brings a reward: people who had been unsympathetic before are now taking notice. His mother's photograph and letter bring him comfort, and he reflects that the melting '*of Torture's needles in the flesh*' and the return to 'the placid plains of *normal ease*' are greater joys than whatever delights might be found by ascending 'Into the dangerous air where actual Bliss doth thrill'. Wilfred knew by now that pain could lead to pleasure. When things got difficult he was inclined to long for mothering, the easiest way of avoiding 'actual Bliss' (by which he presumably meant either sexual love or what he was to describe later in 1912 as the 'madness-giving air' of religious fervour).

He made sure he was well enough on the Thursday to take the children for their weekly Scripture Union meeting, Vivian probably staying on afterwards for another piano lesson before the older boys arrived for the club. The Vicarage was in turmoil, Wigan having suddenly decided to change the furniture, and Mrs Lott was frantic, besieged by upholsterers and deliveries.[20] Wilfred lost his bureau from the dining room and had to make do with a Chippendale one instead, much more valuable but far less convenient. He was appalled by the disappearance of a roll-top desk from the Den, having set his heart on inheriting the Den when Kemp left. It all seemed pointless extravagance. 'Shall I enjoy tomorrow's denunciation of things temporal,' he fumed to Susan on the Saturday; 'oh no doubt! "Let us pray" – "Certainly, by all means!"'.

His secret fury spilled over into thoughts about life and death in the parish, especially death. He resolved to give some of the shortbread Susan had sent him for his birthday to five-year-old Violet Franklin, who seemed to be dying of consumption. Her father was out of work, and her mother was going without food for the sake of the children. 'This, I suppose, is only a typical *case*; one of many *Cases*! O hard word! How it savours of rigid, frigid professionalism! How it suggests smooth and polished, formal, labelled, mechanical callousness!' These passionate exclamations are recognisably Dickensian, reminders that literature was not an alternative to life for Wilfred as it was for Wigan, but a guide to living and feeling. He had to sympathise with human suffering because that was what true poets did. He was delighted to find from a biography of Shelley, who had lived for a while not far away in Marlow, that the poet had visited the local poor. 'I *knew* the lives of men who produced such marvellous verse could not be otherwise than lovely.' He must have been reading the verse Shelley had produced in the region, *The Revolt of Islam*, a long revolutionary poem condemning war and social injustice.[21] The ways of feeling and expression that Wilfred learned at Dunsden were to persist into his later writing. His reaction to the word 'Cases' in 1912 is precisely the reaction he intends to evoke in his reader with the 'formal, labelled, mechanical' title of his 1918 poem, 'Mental Cases'.

E.W. Moore spoke to a large audience in the hall on Wednesday 27 March, giving 'a most uplifting and inspiring message on the Power of the Indwelling Spirit to free the soul from every yoke', according to Wigan. Wilfred was less convinced. He was fascinated by the saintly old man's style of oratory, which was very like Canon Robson's, but he saw through it now, feeling veneration for the messenger rather than the message and noticing how the boys were smothering giggles. The entire Gunston clan came over from Alpenrose to hear their former pastor, who was shocked to be told by them afterwards that Dorothy was in a state of what Wilfred described as apostasy. She had probably just announced that she had made Wigan's spiritual journey in reverse by moving from Evangelicalism to the High Church beliefs she was to hold for the rest of her life. Moore pleaded with her for a quarter of an hour in front of her family and cousin, but she was not to be moved. Wilfred did not risk a public confession of his own much more perilous state, merely asking Moore a few tentative questions after supper, 'but gained nothing conclusive; where shall I?' Next day he cycled down to Reading for a secret meeting with Mrs Rampton, who had asked him to inspect a piano she was hoping to buy for Vivian.

~

Easter brought further spiritual tasks and worldly distractions, as well as more fine weather. The Vicar began to talk about croquet. 'Every hoop will be a gallows for my minutes,' Wilfred said gloomily, preferring to sit in the garden and read Tennyson. He sang a solo, 'O come and mourn', at the Good Friday service, but next day, a holiday, he felt far from mournful as he strolled off down the lane, trying to look as though he were going nowhere in particular. He had arranged a secret outing with Vivian. They met at a stile and went for a 'delicious ramble', then lay under hawthorn bushes in Crowsley Park watching the deer, while Wilfred began to educate his companion in the pleasure of books, telling him tales and getting him to read aloud. The tales were probably from the *Arabian Nights* and Hans Christian Andersen, Wilfred having recently asked for both books from home in the hope of turning a few of the stories into verse. The Vicar would have been appalled if he had known his assistant was introducing young Rampton to such unchristian literature, and the secret expedition itself might have appalled him even more. He had been chaplain at a boys' boarding school, and the sexual implications of the friendship would have been obvious to him. They were less obvious to Wilfred himself, who told Susan about the ramble without embarrassment, reminding her that 'Vivian' was a boy's name. Even so, his letters from Dunsden make no further mention of his young protégé, although the friendship continued. Perhaps Wilfred became more circumspect, or perhaps some of his remarks fell victim to his brother's censoring.

Fifty-three people came to communion on Easter Sunday, more than usual, and the church was bright with flowers. Next day the Vicar trapped Wilfred in the study for the entire afternoon to discuss a stack of pictures that had come with the new furniture. 'Ha! Hum! Well! I'm puzzled. Very puzzled. Try *this* frame! Now that. Now this. Hum! well, I'm puzzled! Perfectly GHASTLY, isn't it? Rather smitten with *that*, I must confess.' So it went on, until they went for tea at the Fordhams, where the talk briefly became literary. Wigan thoughtlessly remarked that Wordsworth '*may* have been a nice old man and a lover of "Nacher", but he was *not* a poet', at which point he caught Wilfred's eye and hastily changed the subject. Wilfred resolved not to forget that moment. Later in the week he had to spend a whole evening with the Vicar in Reading, looking at prints to fill the empty picture frames. He was given a print as a reward, but reluctant gratitude gave way to alarm when Wigan hinted that the Den might not be available after Kemp's departure, apparently on the grounds that with only two people in such a large house it would not be right for one of them to occupy a room that was really meant for parish meetings. Such scruples earned no credit with Wilfred, who was longing to escape from the dining room. It would be possible to work undisturbed in the Den, and perhaps to have visitors without the Vicar's knowledge, as had already happened at least once with Vivian. Sensing Wilfred's strength of feeling, Wigan put off making a decision.

Wigan had come to esteem his assistant as both friend and colleague, and at a meeting of the school managers on 15 April he proposed that Wilfred should be appointed the school's Correspondent. This was a clerical job which involved taking minutes, writing letters and checking accounts, but it was a responsible one and until now it had been done by the Vicar himself. Wilfred saw that it would be an interruption to work, but he couldn't help feeling rather pleased at gaining a little power and prestige, telling his mother he could 'pull the strings, and set five teachers and a hundred scholars chattering'. In a good mood again he went down to Reading that evening to the annual prize-giving at Kendrick School, where Leslie was a pupil.[22] Leslie won a history prize and played the Duke in extracts from *The Merchant of Venice*. Ernie Hullcoop, the Dunsden headmaster's son, played Bassanio in absurdly baggy tights. 'Dunston [*sic*] was full of dignity as the Duke', the local newspaper said afterwards.

Wilfred was in Reading again on 17 April, having decided to register for botany classes at University College.[23] He had been to see the Principal in February to explain his plans, at that time thinking of taking courses in Latin and French as well, but botany alone required six hours a week, which seemed as much as he would be able to cope with now that parish work was multiplying. He sent home for his gown, pleased to be a student again, although he was beginning to realise he had little chance of being ready for Intermediate in 1913 unless he could find more working time. A secluded room and free evenings would help, but he knew he could not put all the blame on other people. He was letting the days slip by and his motivation was slackening, as can be seen in many of his books, where again and again his underlinings and marginal notes thin out and disappear after the first few chapters. He could not even make up his mind to enrol for courses with the University Correspondence College. Uncertain about himself as much as about his future, he retreated into Keats's letters, which he was reading with rapt attention.

He came across a comment in a history of literature that the ideals of the French Revolution had 'inspired the British School of revolt and reconstruction in Burns, Shelley, Byron, Wordsworth, Coleridge and Tennyson, till its fires have died down today', and that made him declare to Susan that the fires were still burning in his own breast. He was steadily 'liberalising and liberating' his own ideas in spite of Wigan's reactionary opinions. 'From what I hear straight from the tight-pursed lips of wolfish ploughmen in their cottages, I might say there is material ready for another revolution ... Am I for or against upheaval? I know not; I am not happy in these thoughts; yet they press upon me.'[24] His outburst, reinforced by allusions to Dickens, Keats and Tennyson, was actually prompted not by selfless pity for the villagers but by news from home that Stanley Webb had borrowed a tent with Tom's permission. The Webbs were better off than the Owens, and Wilfred thought they could perfectly well afford to buy their own tent. He himself had no money even for a new pair of flannels, he said, and his father was unable to send him the three-pound fee for botany classes. He ended his diatribe by saying that in response to urgings from Susan, and what seemed to be worrying symptoms, he had consulted the Gunstons' doctor about his heart, and Dr Gandy had advised him not to play tennis or cycle up hills. The advice was by no means unwelcome: if true poets were revolutionaries, they were also often invalids.

All this perhaps caused anxiety at Mahim, and Tom Owen paid a rare visit to Alpenrose in late April, walking over with Leslie for Morning Prayer and lunch at Dunsden. Wilfred was pleased to see him, despite the tent affair. They went for a stroll in Crowsley Park, where Tom may have taken the chance to urge the need for hard work and definite decisions. Wilfred went to Dr Gandy again next day and allowed himself to believe that the doctor thought it would be 'dangerous madness' for him to play tennis. He then spent the rest of the day at Alpenrose with his father, the Gunstons and Kemp, pointedly refusing to join everyone else on the court, despite Tom's insistence that a little healthy exercise could do no harm.

~

A week later Wilfred felt very much alone. Kemp left the Vicarage on 6 May, at a moment when the Vicar was in bed with a variety of complaints, including the arthritis he often suffered from. The other Brother had been a cheerful companion during the previous few weeks, having passed his exams and raised enough money for a place at the London College of Divinity. He had taught Wilfred how to develop photographs, and they had amused themselves by taking numerous pictures of each other and the children. Wilfred inherited Kemp's allowance as well as the Superintendentship of the Sunday School, but when he enquired about the Den the Vicar responded with embarrassed hums and ha's, making it obvious that the room was indeed going to go back to parish use. Bitterly disappointed and angry, Wilfred cleared his books out of the dining room and decamped to his bedroom, where he could at least be sure of privacy.

Kemp's departure and the loss of the Den were a turning point. From now on Wilfred felt himself to be an alien in the Vicarage, and the strain of living there slowly became intolerable. His letters began to complain of bad dreams as his troubles started to find their way out in nocturnal visions of illicit desire and violence. In his poem of the previous autumn, 'Supposed Confessions', he had admitted that Dejection had drenched his nights in 'bloodiness and stains of shadowy crimes'. Now he drafted a poem about the torment of lying awake on summer nights: the sunset forces fire under his eyelids, and he watches the dying light as a murderer has to watch the last gleam fading from a victim's eyes, while the flushed and guilty Sun gazes incestuously at its sister, Night.[25]

'Did jew notice Mister Owin?' Wilfred overheard Mrs Lott saying one Saturday in May. 'Wern't 'e whoite!' He had just taken the weekly Prayer Meeting after a strenuous geological excursion with the botany class, and it may have been the PM as much as the excursion that had made him feel ill. He was starting to get bouts of giddiness, with whirling dots and spirals in front of his eyes, and his nightmares were invading the day. Happening to read George Borrow's extraordinary autobiography, *Lavengro*, he was upset by Borrow's sudden fits of manic despair, terrors that may have seemed unpleasantly familiar. *Lavengro* was fascinating, all the same, the story of an independent-minded youth whose father is appalled to have a son with opinions of his own, and whose mother adores him and wants him to study the Bible. The young man reads widely in search of truth, just as Wilfred was doing, but he concludes that everything is an enigma. Wilfred seems to have passed on some of Borrow's many tales to Vivian, who retained a lifelong enthusiasm for the book.

Susan was worried, writing frequently. 'O Blessed art thou among women!' Wilfred wrote back on 20 May, as though she were the Virgin Mary, and he continued in language more appropriate to a lover. 'Oh how do I stand (yes and sit, lie, kneel & walk, too,) in need of some tangible caress from you. / Ink-slung ones are all very well in their way, and no one appreciates them more than I do; but my affections are physical as well as abstract – intensely so – and confound 'em for that, it shouldn't be so.' 'Adieu, sweet Mother. Give me particulars of your pulse, when next you write. I think about it, oftener than mine own,' he ended another letter. He busied himself with rendering one of Hans Andersen's grisly stories, 'Little Claus and Big Claus', into blank verse, not without pangs of guilt at its lack of moral correctness.

Botany classes made a welcome change from parish duties, though he thought some of the students were regrettably common. The lecturer, Miss Rayner, was interested to discover his enthusiasm for literature. She must have thought his tastes rather old-fashioned, as he seemed to know little about any poets after Tennyson (he probably preferred not to mention Monro), so she lent him Meredith's *Modern Love*, later inviting him and a colleague for an evening of poetry reading, when Wilfred read Keats and she read Swinburne. While Meredith failed to impress, Swinburne became a powerful influence, his hypnotic rhythms and often masochistic imagery leaving many traces in Wilfred's poems. The botany course ended on 2 June, but Wilfred remained in touch with Dr Rayner at least until 1917.[26]

Parish work slackened with the onset of summer. Wigan had learned from experience that there was no point in keeping most of the meetings going during the warm weather, and in any case he liked to take long holidays himself, so the Mothers dispersed and the Sowers' Band held a party on the Vicarage lawn, playing Owen family games under Wilfred's direction. On a river trip for the old folk and several of the children, organised by Mrs Lott, Wilfred enjoyed being the object of rivalry between Milly Montague, his favourite among the girls, and a small boy nicknamed Knowledge, likening the contest to an allegory of beauty and knowledge competing for him. He hoped the outcome was not prophetic when beauty won, Milly capturing the coveted place next to him. The Vicar teased him afterwards on looking immensely happy, apparently thinking he was interested in one of the older girls.

The first of July brought the choir's annual outing to the seaside, an ordeal Wigan loathed. He chose Bournemouth as usual, probably because he could escape for most of the day by taking refuge with his friend Trevor Lingley, but it meant getting up at three in the morning and sharing a reserved compartment with the choirboys. Adult villagers may have treated the Vicar with deference but the boys were not so respectful, making the journey a torment for His Riverence by sticking pins into him, firing pellets with rubber bands, stealing his hat, interfering with his newspaper and generally causing trouble. Every now and then his patience gave way, as Wilfred gleefully told Susan afterwards, and the outraged man of God would 'grasp an urchin, and thwack, lam, hide, beat, belabour, whack, smack, flog, flail, thump, lick, and kick the creature till the tears swam round its eyes'. Wigan visited Lingley in the afternoon, leaving Wilfred to take the party to Swanage. They got back to Reading long after dark, enjoying the last leg of the journey, a sleepy return in horse-drawn vans along the moonlit lanes. The school managers met in the infants' classroom next day, with the new Correspondent taking the minutes.[27] After that there was little more to do except attend services on the Sunday. On Monday 8 July Wilfred left for a much-needed break, and the Vicar departed next day, leaving the house in the care of the servants and the parish in the care of a Reading vicar.

Apostate

Dunsden

JULY 1912–FEBRUARY 1913

The summer break started with a holiday. All six Owens had been invited to stay with Susan's old friend, Nelly Bulman, formerly Nelly Roderick, daughter of the Oswestry doctor. Now a widow, Mrs Bulman lived in Scotland, in a handsome old house at Kelso. She had discovered that the Owens' circumstances were less prosperous than her own, so she and her grown-up children, John, Bill and Blanche, had planned a perfect holiday for them. Wilfred arrived some days after the rest of his family, delayed by parish duties. Having sent his trunk in advance before realising he would have to set out early on a Monday morning, he had to travel in his Sunday suit, and he seems to have made his journey even more uncomfortable, not only by taking his bicycle on the train, but also by pausing in Shrewsbury to collect a box of books. He could not contemplate going north without plenty of Scott and Wordsworth. He looked exhausted and ill when he reached Kelso, as Harold remembered years later.[1]

Some of the holiday was spent at Mrs Bulman's country cottage at Yetholm. While her two sons and Blanche's fiancé, Walter Forrest, took Harold and Colin fishing, and Blanche played golf with Tom, Wilfred sat alone with a book, thinking of Dr Gandy's advice and the strain of the last few months. He risked competing with the Bulmans and Forrest at rifle shooting, and they were impressed with his skill, but he was acutely aware of how unlike him they were. John Bulman was a cheery medical student, fond of telling stories about riotous parties, and his brother and Forrest were powerfully built rugby players. The contrast between them and Wilfred must have pained Tom, who had already been put out by having to arrange different railway passes for the journey from Reading after several changes of plan. So Tom grumbled, and his son withdrew further into books, an isolated, almost pathetic little figure according to Harold.

The fourteen-year-old Harold enjoyed himself enormously, flattered to be taught masculine pursuits by his hosts instead of being patronised by Wilfred. He remembers the Scottish holiday in his autobiography with gratitude and delight, painting it in glowing colours, especially one after-noon when he meets a beautiful girl and senses the attraction of the opposite sex for the first time. This event is not lost on Wilfred, who moralises and asks insistent questions afterwards, admitting Harold is now 'one up' on him. In writing about this and other early encounters with girls, Harold gives the strong impression, not without a hint of triumph, that in these matters at least he was well ahead of his elder brother. It may not have occurred to him that in drawing attention to his own sexual awakening, he was likely to leave readers wondering why he had nothing to say about Wilfred's.

The Bulmans did all they could to make Wilfred feel at home. John gave up a day to showing him round Edinburgh. Wilfred admired the city's splendours, but was shocked, perhaps visibly, by his guide's swearing and drinking. When he said he wanted to go to university, John told him that what he really needed was a course in the university of life. Wilfred was not entirely convinced, remarking to Susan later that there was something to be said for having an eccentric son like himself rather than a 'normal, manly fellow' like John or Bill. He stayed on to complete his fortnight after the rest of the family left, making a pilgrimage to Scott's house at Abbotsford and cycling twenty-eight miles with Blanche to Flodden, where he spent four or five hours reconstructing the battle with the aid of *Marmion* and a guidebook. He became so absorbed that he forgot the cold wind and Dr Gandy, while poor Blanche, who had hoped to show him more places, nobly endured the weather and his lengthy explanations. He refused to feel guilty afterwards, saying that he couldn't let himself be led about by a Scots girl.

~

If Wilfred still looked strained after these excursions, that was partly because of what was coming next. On Saturday 20 July he had to revert to his role as a servant of the Gospel by travelling down to the Lake District to attend the Keswick Convention. This annual gathering, one of the great events in the Evangelical calendar, had grown out of a conference nearly forty years earlier, when a group of clerics, including E.W. Moore, had decided to start a 'Convention for the Promotion of Practical Holiness'. The Convention's slogan, 'All One in Christ Jesus', proclaimed it to be non-sectarian, although many of its leading figures were in fact Anglicans. Wilfred had already met at least three of them, Canon Barnes-Lawrence, Bishop Ingham and Moore himself, while Wigan knew several others, including the London preacher, Stuart Holden, and the editor of the Convention's unofficial periodical, *The Life of Faith*, Evan Hopkins, who had helped to inaugurate the new hall at Dunsden in 1909.

Keswick Christianity was Wigan's sort, not the arm-waving, foot-stamping variety that had been on display at the Shrewsbury Mission and the Woods' meetings in Reading. The 'platform members' of the Convention were mostly public school, university men whose reason and instincts put them on their guard against emotional excesses and the risks inherent in dealing with large numbers of excited people. Conventionists were advised that going to three meetings a day would be quite enough. Early bed and plenty of air and exercise were recommended, and late-night prayer sessions strongly discouraged. There were two huge marquees for meetings, each holding audiences of well over two thousand, and numerous little bell-tents for hardy folk who chose not to stay in guest-houses. Full advantage was taken of the local landscape, and Wilfred climbed the fells and swam in Derwentwater like everybody else, again forgetting Gandy. Yet the fundamental purpose of Keswick was never for a moment lost sight of. Everyone was assumed to have come in search of Revival. 'Before we can be right and do right, we must get right,' one speaker said. That was the aim of Keswick: to get right with God.[2]

Wilfred must have arrived in a state of nerves, especially as his luggage had gone temporarily astray. Spotting Dorothy and Vera Gunston and Miss Fordham at the station, he embarrassed himself by greeting them over-effusively, but it would have been a relief to see Dorothy, whose attitude to the Convention was presumably rather sceptical. He had to share a tent with three Durham undergraduates, perhaps feeling a little awkward in such company. There was just room for his green trunk when it arrived, although his bicycle had to stay outside in the rain. The camp was unpleasantly spartan after the comforts of Kelso and Yetholm. His primitive bed was on a slope, only one coarse blanket was provided, the food was unappealing and the tea revolting, and some of the conventionists were 'absolute boors'. A violent wind blew all the first night, making sleep impossible, and by the morning the tent reeked of damp clothes. Each day began with a prayer meeting at seven, after which the camp was noisy all day with piano music and singing, the rattle of crockery and the drone of talks and prayers. There were special meetings for young men, but the psychological pressure was at its most intense at the evening prayer meetings, when everyone knelt except those who felt touched by the Spirit to stand as a sign of total consecration.

Wilfred's letters give little indication of how he coped with all this. When he wrote home on the 24th, within earshot of a prayer meeting and a family service, he said the best thing about the camp was the enormous variety of people, boors and all, from every part of the country and every level of society. He was deeply impressed by a Northumberland 'mining lad', whose faith seemed the real thing. 'The watching of his conduct, conversation, expression of countenance during meetings, bids fair to speak louder to my soul than the thunderings of twenty latter-day Prophets from their rostra upon these everlasting hills.' The lad never used bad language, 'tho' pricked with piercing pain and surrounded by the grossest human mud that ever sank to a pit's bottom'. He was 'scar-backed' from having to run bent double along underground galleries, and had forfeited a week's pay to be at the Convention. Furthermore, he was teaching himself physics and taking a correspondence course in mining. Here was a true example of 'practical holiness', a Christian who witnessed by living instead of by preaching.

However, the Convention was not the place to dream about interesting young men, even on a high moral plane. Wilfred probably attended as few meetings as possible, and he absented himself for nearly twenty-four hours to make a pilgrimage to Ruskin's house at Coniston, cycling well over forty miles there and back, perhaps taking the chance to look at Wordsworth's cottage at Grasmere on the way. He told Leslie Gunston afterwards in a verse letter that he was twice soaked in heavy rain and had to dry out in hotels. Miss Rayner had given him an introduction to W.G. Collingwood, Ruskin's friend and biographer, who still lived on the edge of Coniston Water. Wilfred had been reading the biography at the camp. According to a rough note among his papers, he reached the Collingwoods' house late in the evening, warmed himself in the geniality of their welcome, and soon set out again in a violent storm, spending all night on the hills 'a little drunk on Ruskin' (and perhaps on Collingwood's whisky). The long ride back to Keswick over Dunmail Raise would have been extremely strenuous in such weather, but it seems to have done him no harm.[3]

The Convention closed on Sunday 28 July with a praise meeting, when many people got to their feet to testify. Groups rose, with a spokesman or repeating a text together, then all newcomers were asked to stand. Finally the platform members gave witness, Holden declaring that every hour henceforth should be 'filled with obedient, self-surrendered service to Christ ... with a child's simple, living, loving faith'. Susan Owen would have said amen to that, had she been present, but her son may have found it more difficult. For some conventionists, according to *The Christian* afterwards, the week was a 'dark, hidden tragedy, secret sin strangling the soul'.

Wilfred went to Shrewsbury for a fortnight, probably making little attempt to hide his state of mind from his mother, who would have been as patient and comforting as ever. He did some more photography and went digging at Uriconium again with Stanley Webb. Discussions at Mahim probably centred on his academic future. As he had feared from the beginning, he had not been able to keep up with work at the Vicarage. His mother had already suggested that he should aim for Intermediate in 1914 rather than 1913, and his father must have agreed. Wilfred could hardly expect Wigan to keep him for another two years, but Susan had heard of another parson who might be willing to help, and the extra time would make it possible to take some papers at Honours level. Tom apparently undertook to pay for a UCC course in Anglo-Saxon, a subject required for Honours English.[4] When the time came to return to Dunsden, Wilfred said goodbye to his mother on the station and fought back tears throughout the journey, haunted by a strange sense of insecurity. It was a relief to leave the train and cycle back through the familiar lanes, although he was still close to weeping ('*not* altogether an unpleasant feeling') when he wrote to Susan that evening ('Alack the day!') from ('Alas!') the Vicarage. He tried in vain to put his emotions into a poem.

~

The lanes were less safe than he thought. A few days after his return he visited an old man, comforting him in the Evangelical way by reading from the famous Victorian preacher, Charles Spurgeon, about human lives being as frail as flowers, as fleeting as meteors. Afterwards, riding back past the village well with his mind on Spurgeon's ominous message, he skidded and crashed to the ground. The only damage seemed to be a few grazes, so he picked himself up and rode back to the Vicarage. The Vicar was still away, Mrs Lott was away as well and the maid had gone out, but the temporary housekeeper hurried to fetch bandages. Wilfred was washing his left hand, which had lost more skin than he had realised, when, as he told Susan afterwards, 'sudden twilight seemed to fall upon the world, an horror of great darkness closed around me', and although he did not actually faint the blood roared in his ears and he felt as though he were swimming underwater. The housekeeper, turning as white as he was, brought brandy in answer to his barely audible request and sent the kitchen boy for the doctor.

Wilfred soon recovered, finding himself in a cold sweat, gasping at a window without knowing how he had got there. Looking at himself in a mirror, he couldn't help admiring his 'really beautiful and romantic pallor'. After the doctor had cleaned up the wound, and kind-hearted Dorothy, who had also been summoned, had cycled over to check her cousin's bandages, the invalid settled down in the most comfortable chair in the Vicar's study and began to luxuriate in the drama. He had caused a satisfying panic among the servants and even alarm at Alpenrose, and he could now write to his mother with some fine literary flourishes, knowing she would be more worried than anybody.[5] It had been a very minor accident, yet he was clearly fascinated by wounds, darkness and horror, and it was the prelude to a much more serious ordeal that was to unfold during the next few months.

When the Vicar returned on 17 August, he was concerned enough about the injury to write to Susan, suggesting she should visit her son to reassure herself, a kindly intervention that Wilfred only discovered when Edith the maid let slip a mention of it during her daily task of renewing the dressing. Wilfred and Edith both enjoyed these opportunities for gossip, and bandages had the extra advantage of excusing him from croquet. Other duties could not be avoided so easily. When he was asked to give his impressions of Keswick to the Saturday prayer meeting he told Susan he would not be able to talk honestly, either about his personal experiences, which had been more like wounds than impressions, or about his current religious beliefs. Some weeks later he referred to the weekly PM as 'Pious Moments, 'Plainful mumblry, Pish-tush Muggery, or what-you-will'. It was safe, if unkind, to say such things to his mother, but a correct attitude had to be maintained in public.

When Wigan's newly-married brother and sister-in-law came to stay at the end of August, the gentlemen wore dinner jackets in the evenings, and that at least was a formality Wilfred could enjoy, thinking he had never looked smarter. Cuthbert Wigan was younger than the Vicar and more easy-going, but he, too, was a parson, with a curacy in Bexhill, so mealtime conversation was probably mostly to do with church and family. The Vicar remained as stiff as ever, continuing to address Wilfred – but never Cuthbert – as 'Brother', to Wilfred's secret amusement. Brother Kemp came to stay for a few days in September and was delighted to be back, until he had to endure a meal alone with the Vicar.

In Kemp's absence, Wilfred's closest companion had become Leslie Gunston. 'Leslie the invaluable', now seventeen, was as keen to share his cousin's literary interests as he had been to swap fossils in earlier years. Visiting the Gunstons was always a pleasure. Uncle John was talking of organising Shakespeare readings and glee-singing. Wilfred cycled back from an evening at Alpenrose in September, carolling at the top of his voice under a violet sky and yellow moon, revelling in the peace of the countryside. Watching swifts flying round the high gables of the Vicarage one day, he and Leslie each agreed to write a poem on 'The Swift', Wilfred soon producing a Shelleyan ode in praise of the bird's enviable freedom. With his passion for Keats and Shelley rekindled by Leslie's enthusiasm, he read William Rossetti's biography of Keats and was overwhelmed by the death scene, responding to it almost as though he were St Thomas reaching into Christ's side: 'Rossetti guided my groping hand right into the wound, and I touched, for one moment the incandescent Heart of Keats.'

Perhaps remembering Keats's remark that composing a long poem is a good test of invention, Wilfred worked on another Hans Andersen story, giving it far more of his time than he should have done. At over six hundred lines, 'The Little Mermaid' is by far his longest surviving poem, and it was certainly good practice, its Keatsian language and stanzas flowing with remarkable assurance. His favourite passage, describing a statue the mermaid finds on the seabed, is one of the first in his poetry to foreshadow his later concerns:

> ... *a marble statue, – some boy-king's,*
> *Or youthful hero's. Its cold face in vain*
> *She gazed at, kissed, and tried with sighs to thaw,*
> *For still the wide eyes stared, and nothing saw.*
>
> *Thereby she set a weeping-willow tree*
> *To droop and mourn. Full dolefully it clung*
> *About the form, and moved continually,*
> *As if it sighed; as if it sometimes wrung*
> *Convulsive fingers in sad reverie.*
> *And ever o'er the light blue sand it hung*
> *A purple shade, ...*

Fixed eyes, convulsive fingers, an unchanging underworld, twilight, purple, a statuesque youthful hero: similar images were to reappear in work for his 1915–16 project, 'Perseus', and in 1918 poems such as 'Mental Cases' and 'Strange Meeting'.

Wilfred told Harold he was struggling as never before with the question of evolution by making his own enquiries into botany.[6] Staring into the garden and watching the leaves fall when he should have been working, he wrote a poem, 'The Dread of Falling into Naught', saying that spring would return but human life would not. 'Before my time I bear a hoary head,' and it was true his hair was showing the first signs of grey. His eyesight was giving trouble, too, so he went up to London to get his eyes tested at Watson's in Holborn, where Gordon Gunston was now working, and reading glasses were prescribed. When his bedroom became too cold, he was driven down to the dining room again, like a grumbling bear from the mountains, as he told Mary. Mary and Susan were due to visit Alpenrose in the second week of October. Harvest Festival was held on the 6th, the church decorated with 'fowsty apples and fag-ends of the stubble fields', and he spoke to the children and his Bible class in appropriate platitudes about the bounty of nature, even though his imagination was still running on thoughts of sudden accident, death and darkness.

⁓

On Friday 11 October Wilfred rode over to Alpenrose to take part in a reading of *The Tempest*, which happened to be one of his set texts for Intermediate in 1914. He had to be content with finding different voices for Sebastian, Stephano, Francisco and Iris, because Uncle John bagged

Prospero and Caliban, but it was a memorable occasion, and everyone present signed copies of the play as souvenirs.[7] Afterwards he probably cut choir practice and stayed on to supper, as his mother and sister seem to have been due that evening, so he may not have been at the Vicarage when news arrived of one of the worst accidents Dunsden had ever known. His letters say nothing about the event simply because his mother heard about it at first hand, but it had a profound impact on him, as on many people in the parish.

A local carter, John Allen, was due to move from Binfield Heath to a job at Maidenhead that day. His new employer had sent transport, a flat cart drawn by two horses harnessed in tandem. Allen and his young wife Alice piled their few bits of furniture on the cart and put an old sofa on the top, Alice installing herself on it with their baby son and two small daughters. The horses ambled along the lane to the green, Allen walking beside them, but as they started downhill at the well they broke into an ever faster trot. The sofa slipped forward on to the rear horse, and both horses bolted, forcing Allen to let go after a desperate struggle. The lurching cart hit a bank, careering on down the hill out of sight, and the two girls were thrown out by the impact, one of them dying instantly as a wheel passed over her, the other suffering severe injuries. Their mother, still clutching the baby, fell through the shafts on to the road, where her husband found her lying in agony, bleeding to death from a thigh wound. She asked after the children, and he told her they were safe. Villagers placed her on the sofa at the side of the road, but by the time the doctor arrived nothing more could be done for her. The baby was picked up alive and well, apart from a few scratches. The bodies of the mother and child were taken to the parish hall to await an inquest the following evening.

Records do not say whether the Saturday prayer meeting, which Susan had planned to attend, was in fact held at the usual time in the hall, just before the inquest and in the presence of the dead, but the Vicar would hardly have cancelled it. Then, as in church next day, he would have taken the opportunity to repeat his urgent message: 'May we all learn anew the much-needed lesson of the absolute uncertainty of life.' That would also have been his theme at the funeral on the 15th, when he had never seen the church and churchyard so crowded. Here were hearts ready for the Lord, and in the charged atmosphere of the next few weeks he must have made his appeal again and again. Death might come at any time, followed inexorably by judgement, when no soul would be able to plead excuses or ask for delay. The decision for life or death had to be made *now*. As the programme of winter meetings got under way, attendances rose to unprecedented levels.[8]

On the evening of the 15th Wilfred attended a school managers' meeting, taking notes about routine matters that must have seemed unreal after the funeral. Watching the mother and child being buried had been one of the most moving experiences of his life so far, and his thoughts about it were very unlike the Vicar's. No sooner had the decorations been removed from the church than masses of flowers from autumn gardens had been heaped round the new-dug grave, as though in mockery of the harvest celebrations. He wrote a poem, 'Deep under turfy grass and heavy clay', admitting that instead of weeping like everybody else, he had

> *... rebelled, scorning and mocking such*
> *As had the ignorant callousness to wed*
> *On altar steps long frozen by the touch*
> *Of stretcher after stretcher of our dead.*
> *Love's blindness is too terrible, I said;*
> *I will go counsel men, and show what bin*
> *The harvest of their homes is gathered in.*

As he had tried to say in verse at the beginning of the year, marriage and procreation could only lead to death. But his new poem moves on to a different conclusion: as he stands by the grave, the village children come to look at it, too, wondering what the half-buried flowers mean, and the sight of one little girl whose 'pale brows / Wore beauty like our mother Eve's' is enough to persuade him that birth and life must continue.

In 'Deep under turfy grass' the voice of the mature Wilfred Owen begins to be audible for the first time. Like the best of his 1917–18 work the poem is based on strongly felt experience, and it takes a passionate stand against majority opinion. Understanding – as others do not – the true meaning of harvest, as well as the irony and in the end the appropriateness of placing coffins on the steps where marriages take place, he feels driven to 'go counsel men', an impulse he had learned from Evangelicalism. What fires him, and what changes his mind, is pity for the beauty and brevity of young life. As in 'The Little Mermaid' he uses images that were to become familiar: blind Love, pale brows, ambiguous flowers. Many of the later poems had their roots in the accident at Dunsden Green in 1912. Or perhaps the two accidents, for Wilfred would not have missed the thought that he had fallen off his bicycle at the spot where the horses had got out of control. In 'Deep under turfy grass' one can begin to hear the poet of the famous question, 'Was it for this the clay grew tall?'

~

A parish assistant named Clyde Black had recently been recruited, and his help was clearly going to be needed.[9] Wigan described him in the magazine as a Christian worker and a friend of Lingley's, recommendation enough. Black was very unlike Kemp, much older and more serious, and he set about making reforms in Vicarage routine (one of them was going to bed early, a change Wilfred must have welcomed). He also took over Wilfred's Sunday Bible Class, perhaps because Wigan felt it needed a more mature leader, and the class became what it had always been intended to be, a means of winning souls. If Wilfred regretted losing the boys, he was probably relieved to shed his most awkward responsibility at a time of such religious excitement. The conflict between his private doubts and public role was becoming almost unendurable, although for economic and academic reasons he had to keep going. Unable to confide fully even in his mother, he could only relax in the company of the children, yet even they were a source of sadness, for their innocence could not last and in the end death would claim them, too. He must have had to listen every day while Wigan and Black talked about saving souls for the joys of heaven, and most of the poems he wrote in this second winter at Dunsden, 1912–13, are his secret response, a bitter commentary on the impossibility of an afterlife. On 6 November he wrote a furious little poem about men like Black who inflict absurd sufferings and denials on themselves in order to reach God.

> *Unto what pinnacles of desperate heights*
> *Do good men climb to seize their good! …*
> *And their sole mission is to drag, entice*
> *And push mankind to those same cloudy crags*
> *Where they first breathed the madness-giving air*
> *That made them feel as angels, that are less than men.*

He wrote several poems about a girl, possibly Milly, saying she alone could bring him rest and calm, now that his heaven was empty and his family and spiritual teachers had all failed him. He spares her 'even imagined' kisses, but he dreams of her hands on his face, quenching the fires that rage behind his eyes. In 'The Two Reflections', a sonnet probably written in autumn 1912, he looks into a child's brown eyes and sees 'June's late light through long lanes, beechen-aisled', a melancholy reminder of walks in summer woods.[10] Vivian Rampton had deep brown eyes, and the sonnet implies that rambles with him had continued at least until June (or, as Wilfred originally wrote, August). The secret piano lessons may well have continued into autumn and winter, although the tutor's conscience was not entirely easy. In a fragmentary 1914 poem Wilfred was to recall sharing many of his ideas with an unnamed boy during a short year or two, while the boy underwent the 'secret change' into manhood, the fragment concluding that it might have been better if Wilfred had never seen him or touched his hand.[11]

Academic work was a less complicated refuge than being with the children, but Wilfred had to struggle to concentrate as the pace of life quickened in the Vicarage. Another difficulty arose from studying Old English by correspondence course, without ever hearing the language spoken. When he mentioned this to one of the botany lecturers, she sent him to the Professor of English, Edith Morley. Miss Morley, burly and deep-voiced, was a formidable character, devoted to her students though often tiresome to her colleagues. A few years earlier the college had made its heads of department professors, all except herself, it being unthinkable that a woman should occupy a chair, but she had fought back and won, in 1908 becoming the first female professor in the country. Sizing Wilfred up as an 'unhappy adolescent, suffering badly from lack of understanding … and in need of encouragement and praise',[12] she invited him to attend some of her classes, suggesting he might try for a scholarship to Wantage Hall, the college's new hall of residence. She also asked him if he wrote poetry, and for at least the next two years Wilfred occasionally sent her poems for comment, although her standards seem to have been very old-fashioned.

For six weeks or more after his mother and sister left Alpenrose in the third week of October, Wilfred's letters say little about events in the parish. He concentrated on other matters, writing at length about a local girl, Vera Bint, whom Susan was considering taking on as a maid. There were now meetings every night of the week. Early in November he assured Mary she was mistaken in thinking he often had giddy fits, but on the 16th he told her he had suffered a violent bout of vertigo, and to illustrate it drew a cartoon of himself in his new glasses, sitting at the dining-room bureau with the room whirling round him. He blamed the attack on an indigestible lunch, but mentioned that he had been due to accompany the Vicar to yet another meeting, a missionary reception at the big house where he had met Bishop Ingham a year before.

His next letter, addressed to Susan, is dated 10 December, an unusually long gap. By now he could no longer conceal what was going on. For over a year the Vicar had been praying, 'now hotly, now coldly, for *Revival*', and it was coming at last. Regular churchgoers were committing themselves anew to Christ. Backsliders were beginning to return. The organist had been converted, and the man who worked the bellows was about to follow. A woman seeking help at the prayer meeting had been 'prayed through'. Willie Montague had made a second declaration of faith when 'cornered' by Black after the Bible Class that had been Wilfred's. Vera Bint and her father had both accepted Christ as their saviour at meetings led by Black. Mrs Montague had 'yielded herself to God' at a Mothers' Meeting, to the delight of her daughter Milly. Women were weeping at the Sunday-evening sermons. And Wilfred, outwardly helping with the work and inwardly desperate, was 'halting between two, aye, more than two opinions, till sense deserts my mind, and strength my body'. He told Susan his nerves were in a bad state, and his chest felt full as though he were choking in foul air, but he was horrified when she said she would write to the Vicar. He could not leave until there was somewhere else to go.

A present to Wilfred of a new book about Elizabeth Barrett Browning, 'with affectionate Christmas wishes from his friend Clyde Black', was no doubt intended to demonstrate that Black was interested in poetry as well as religion. Wilfred went home for five days over the holiday. On the return journey, with his mother's encouragement, he paused in Birmingham to see a clergyman named Morgan, a friend of the Vicar of St Julian's.[13] Morgan needed an assistant and was willing to coach for theological college, but Wilfred saw at once that an Evangelical front would still be necessary, so he explained his doubts, and that was the end of Susan Owen's last effort to coax her son towards a church career. He returned to Dunsden, where the seasonal round of entertainments was in full swing, as was the Revival. The Wednesday mission services were attracting up to seventy people each week, and the Saturday prayer meetings now had thirty or so regulars.

~

And here Harold Owen interrupts the story, scissors in hand. A crucial page in one of Wilfred's January letters has been cut away, leaving only one fragmentary sentence: 'The furor [*several words missing*] now abated in the Vicarage, thank Mnemosyne; but I hope that I, who "discovered" him something over a year ago, may [*half page missing*]'.[14] The 'furor' may have had something to do with the Revival and Vivian Rampton, Wilfred's principal 'discovery' in the village. If Black had also 'discovered' the boy, cornering him as he had cornered Willie Montague, Wilfred would have felt driven to intervene, unable to bear the thought that his pupil might become a captive. Questions would have been asked, the Vicar would have found out about the piano lessons and the secret educational enterprise that had been going on under his nose for months, and Wilfred would have had to explain why he had done so much for Vivian without making any attempt to save the boy's soul. Whatever the furor was about, the rest of Wilfred's letter implies that it led to the inevitable moment when he finally had to reveal his spiritual state to Wigan, and after that the horrified Vicar would have forgotten everything else in the desperate task of urging the straying assistant to get right with God. In the middle of the longed-for Revival, an infinitely precious soul was falling towards hell-fire.

Wigan must have been deeply distressed to find that his confidence in Brother Owen had been so badly misplaced, and his usually cheery manner gave way to worried silence as he reflected on what to do. The apostate was solemnly interviewed in the study and given tracts to read, and when that failed he was sent up to London to see Stuart Holden.[15] It was all to no avail. 'Murder will out, and I have murdered my false creed,' Wilfred told

Susan. 'To leave Dunsden will mean a terrible bust-up; but I have no intention of sneaking away by smuggling my reasons down the back-stairs. I will vanish in thunder and lightning, if I go at all.'

The family tried to help. Susan, or perhaps her sister, sent a pamphlet by E.W. Moore, but Wilfred's questionings had gone too far for him to be impressed by arguments that assumed belief in 'Adam's getting outside some fruit or other'. One evening at Alpenrose he had a long talk with Dorothy, whose High Church outlook enabled her to be relaxed about scriptural authority, but he thought her position illogical. If there had been no Adam and no fall, he said, where was the need for atonement and redemption? As far as he could see, reason, science and literature all seemed to contradict Christian doctrine. Susan came down to Alpenrose, although she could do nothing except pray and sympathise. Mary made an effort too, writing to her brother about her own religious experience, but he advised her not to look to him for advice on such things, and he made it clear to her and Susan that there was much he preferred not to say, for he had no wish to damage their own beliefs or anyone else's.

He felt sure now that Revivalist religion was largely a matter of language and social pressures. Among the children especially, the new-found piety was caused by environment. 'Alter the environment and it will go. For already I grieve to say (though *why I grieve* is not very patent, considering) that "impressions" are "wearing off" in some cases, already. In fact I am convinced that I hold under my tongue, powers which would shake the foundations of many a spiritual life.' The powers were those of words and poetry. He promised he would not use them, unlike Shelley, who had unleashed them on his own young friends. It was possible, after all, that Shelley and many others like him had never met true Christianity. 'It exists none the less, you say,' Wilfred continued in this frank letter to Susan. 'Only I haven't met it – to know it – yet.' Sowing doubts among the children would be an unforgivable sin. His feelings for them seemed a combination of 'fraternity, paternity, and amativeness all in one', and his affection for his favourites even made the doctrine of election almost credible. He grieved at the prospect of leaving them, feeling he knew every detail of their lives, but he would have to leave them one way or the other. The Vicar seems to have told him that if he remained an assistant he would have to devote his time to other work. 'All my pretty ones?' Wilfred lamented, quoting *Macbeth*, '… all my pretty chickens / At one fell swoop?' Writing poetry would also have to be given up, a sacrifice all the more painful because he felt his poetic talents had lately been increasing.

If Wigan really made it a condition that poetry-writing should cease, he decided the issue. Left with no real choice, Wilfred encouraged himself with the thought that leaving the Vicarage would be equivalent to Shelley and Coleridge leaving university, and his letters filled with quotations from Keats and others. As the crisis grew, he found that turning his predicament into verse was good therapy, a discovery he put into a sonnet, 'On my Songs': poets had often spoken for him, but now he had to find his own words like a motherless child singing himself to sleep. Perhaps his poems would help others, just as earlier poets had helped him. 'Tonight, if Thou should'st lie in this same Room, / Dreading the Dark ... / ... my songs may haply give thee ease.'

On Tuesday 4 February 1913 he nerved himself to talk to the Vicar about leaving, and Wigan, who had only been waiting for him to broach the subject, agreed he should go that same week unless he could 'get right'. Wilfred wrote at once to Susan: 'My allegiance to you and my Father is never to be shaken. For the rest, I have not the slightest feeling of humility for anything in existence, but the Eternal Being, the Principle of Beauty, and the Memory of Great Men.' And with that ringing declaration, quoted from Keats without the least acknowledgement, he made his decision. By the Friday evening he was back at Shrewsbury.

~

Wilfred's departure from Dunsden has sometimes been misrepresented. It was probably explained at the time as being due to a breakdown in health, and there was certainly no sort of scandal. Later in 1913 he considered returning as a teacher at the school, an idea neither he nor anyone else could have contemplated if he had been in disgrace at the Vicarage. He revisited the parish at least twice and was warmly greeted by local people, including Mrs Rampton, Mrs Montague, Mrs Lott and the Vicar himself. Nor was the break with religion by any means absolute. He attended church on one of his visits, and there is plenty of evidence that he went to services elsewhere on occasions, remaining, in Thomas Hardy's useful word, 'churchy', attuned to the music, stories and splendid language that had helped to shape his imagination since childhood. But he never retrieved his early faith. The framework of Evangelical religion seemed a flimsy structure once he had moved beyond it, and he soon found more interesting things to think about.

One of his manuscripts vividly records his state of mind soon after leaving Dunsden. On one side there are a few clumsy lines about romance, some quotations from Keats and a scrawled first draft of a sonnet about the finality of death. The sonnet was to be revised several times during the next four years, eventually becoming 'The Unreturning'. With its opening echo of the 'sudden twilight' of the 1912 bicycle accident ('Suddenly night crushed out the day'), and its despair of a meaningful afterlife ('I dreaded even a heaven with doors so chained'), the final version of the poem is an example of how much Wilfred's later poetry owed to Dunsden experience. Finished in 1917–18 and often assumed to be wartime work, it is in fact a statement of the position he had reached by early 1913, and it is clearly influenced by a poem about God in Harold Monro's *Before Dawn*.[16]

The other side of the manuscript bears a very rough outline of a letter to the Vicar, written 'solely on the grounds of affection'. Wilfred says he had been a boy when he went to the Vicarage, regarding the Vicar much as a boy might look up to a headmaster, but by the time he left he had felt like an old man. He now thinks Christianity is no more than one system of ideas among many, and by no means the best because it allows no room for 'imagination, physical sensation, aesthetic philosophy'. These three phrases are worth noting. Physical sensation had been a central concern of late nineteenth-century Aestheticism, when beauty had been considered art's only goal. Since beauty could only be apprehended through bodily senses, the artist had to have a highly developed capacity for sensation. Wilfred had discussed his own nerves in a November letter while the Revival was beginning, telling Susan that in his philosophy 'those mortals who have nerves exquisitely responsive to painful sensation, have a perfect right to use them ... *to respond equally keenly to enjoyment*'. He said he was willing to suffer pain, because that meant he could also experience pleasure to the full. These and other comments in his Dunsden letters suggest he had been reading the Aesthetes, perhaps even the French Decadents, in his search for ideas that would break the confines of Evangelicalism and give him space to grow as a poet. Terms such as 'exquisite' and 'sensation' were part of the Aesthetic vocabulary. It was entirely appropriate that his next destination after recovering from Dunsden should be France.

6

Escape

Shrewsbury

FEBRUARY–AUGUST 1913

Leaving Dunsden in February 1913 was by far the most traumatic event in Wilfred's life until he saw the trenches in 1917. He fell seriously ill soon after he got home. Susan is said to have been convinced he had tuberculosis, although he himself called it pneumonia and the doctor preferred the ambiguous term 'congestion of the lungs'. But the most alarming symptom was not difficulty in breathing. When his health gave trouble again in November 1913, he assured his mother that this time he had no 'phantasies' or 'horrors', and in February 1914 he wrote that 'a YEAR ago the pneumonia definitely appeared. It was "to-night" I had the first phantasms.'[1] That sounds like nightmares or even hallucinations. The doctor probably explained in 1913 that a high fever can trigger such symptoms, and that they can become recurrent. Wilfred had suffered from bad dreams at Dunsden, as well as reacting strongly to the waking 'horrors' described in *Lavengro*. His collapse in 1913, like his shellshock in 1917, attacked him at his weakest point. The 1913 'phantasies' seem to have been vivid and terrifying, some of them probably manifesting themselves as intense versions of his Dunsden dreams, visions of 'bloodiness and stains of shadowy crimes' and of the Gorgon-face of Despondency.

He had thrown away his best chances for the future, the possibility of good exam results and a church career, and he had turned against the most treasured element in his Shaw-Salter inheritance, the religion of his mother and aunt, calling it a 'false creed'. Ever since childhood he had heard Evangelical preachers describe the dreadful penalty awaiting those who hear the Gospel and turn away from it. Wigan would have told him bluntly that he was risking damnation, and if Susan asked for help from Canon Robson of Birkenhead the advice would have been the same. Faced with Wilfred's demand for 'imagination, physical sensation, aesthetic philosophy', Wigan perhaps quoted a text from St Jude about traitors from within the Church, 'filthy dreamers' who defile 'the flesh', 'wandering stars, to whom is reserved the blackness of darkness for ever', words that lodged in Wilfred's mind.[2] Guilt and fear took visible shapes as 'phantasms', tormenting his nights and perhaps his days as well.

He sought refuge in the maternal love he had been longing for, letting Susan's affection close round him, although it was no longer a safe haven. He knew he would not be able to stay at home for long. She would never give up her own faith. Even while she nursed him she must have been thinking what to do when he recovered, what tracts to leave in his way, which clergymen to invite in for a friendly chat. The religion that permeated Mahim was more kindly than its counterpart at the Vicarage, but no less demanding. He had not even escaped from meetings. His mother had taken over an infants' class from Miss Goodwin, so the house was noisy with small children in the mornings (many years later one of the pupils recalled the devotion with which Susan used to read the daily prayers).[3] One way and another the household was under strain, for space and cash were limited and Tom could hardly afford to provide board and lodging for all four of his offspring. Wilfred must have been painfully aware of having become a sudden burden on the family, and he was not his parents' only worry: Harold, now aged fifteen, was also at home and earning nothing.

Harold's plans for the future, like Wilfred's, had collapsed. After prospering at the Art School and doing well in his first-year exams in the summer of 1912, he had been forced to abandon his studies. His memoirs put the blame partly on a new government regulation raising the minimum age for art teachers to twenty-one, and partly on his parents, whom he remembers as unwilling to contemplate so long a wait. In fact the new rules only raised the minimum age to nineteen, but they also required would-be art teachers to pass Matric or its equivalent, an obstacle Harold had no chance of overcoming.[4] Giving up the Art School and the hope of qualifying as a pupil-teacher, he tried in vain to find local employment. It cannot have been coincidence that barely a month after Wilfred's unexpected return Harold finally decided to leave home, fulfilling his father's dream by going to sea. He sailed from Liverpool on 14 March 1913 as a cadet (apprentice officer) in a cargo steamer bound for Calcutta. His autobiography sets this first voyage in 1912, while his brother was still at Dunsden, but he nevertheless remembers Wilfred as ill in bed at Mahim when they said goodbye. Wilfred turns away, whispering, 'If I can't please Father and I never seem to be able to – at least I should think you must be doing so, now.' Then he sits up to pontificate enviously about the educational value of travel, without saying anything affectionate or encouraging.[5]

Wilfred may still have been in bed for his mother's birthday on 17 March, and for his own next day, but he must have been on his feet again not long after that, and by early April Susan felt able to go away for one of her rests. He wrote to her that he was sleeping and eating very well and feeling almost back to normal, and he had even been to St Julian's, although he could no longer take the service entirely seriously, telling her the psalms had been chanted 'in the original Hebrew': 'My strethfaileth me cos miniquity'nbones acusume. I came proof-gall-anemonies; bushspeshly 'mongmnayb, 'n they've mine quaintswere afrayme uncoveyselves frummy.' He had recovered his sense of humour, and had no wish to start questioning himself about religion all over again.

Later in the month he and Colin went to Torquay for a few weeks to see their grandparents and stay with Aunt Annie Taylor, now a widow.[6] No doubt they were made a fuss of, and the sea air and a daily swim soon completed Wilfred's return to health. He told his mother he was fit again, in mind as well as body. Ending a light-hearted letter, he wrote that 'too much compoes gives me the beleak in my Chump but I hopes this little letter what I have erected in the gardain which is so nice will be a preciate'. And a few days later: 'I scarcely *think* of anything but what I see before me, and not more than superficially about that.' He made another pilgrimage to Teignmouth in search of Keats, for whom he was feeling more devotion than ever. 'I fear domestic criticism when I am in love with a real live woman. What now I am in love with a youth, and a dead 'un!'[7] Here, too, he was avoiding serious thought about the future. Superficially he still assumed he would follow the conventional route of falling in love with a girl and in due course marrying her. But the Dunsden crisis had not only been about religious orthodoxy. Apprehensively, perhaps still only half-aware, he was preparing himself – and his mother – for the possibility that when he fell in love it might be with a real live youth.

Professor Morley was still keen for him to sit for a scholarship to University College, Reading, so he sent in application forms, albeit without much hope of passing. Meanwhile, since his only qualification was as a teacher, he wrote for advice to his former headmasters, Timpany and Lightbown, and started looking through advertisements in *The Schoolmaster*. Tom enquired about temporary clerical work at the station and may well have found some, as he did for Harold later in the year. Whatever the outcome, Wilfred would not have been content to idle away the summer living off his parents, even if Tom had allowed it; he must have earned his keep somehow, by working in his father's office or perhaps by rejoining the staff at Wyle Cop.

There would have been time for verse-making again. He had already set out his new ideas in two remarkable manifesto-poems, 'O World of many worlds' and 'The time was aeon', both apparently written in his last months at Dunsden.[8] In the first, he imagines himself qualifying as a poet by crossing a cosmic 'floor', much as Keats had crossed the floor of Moneta's temple in *The Fall of Hyperion*. Looking down on the millions of men whose lives follow fixed orbits, he resolves not to 'keep step with such a band'.

> *To be a meteor, fast, eccentric, lone,*
> *Lawless; in passage through all spheres,*
> *Warning the earth of wider ways unknown*
> *And rousing men with heavenly fears …*
>
> *This is the track reserved for my endeavour;*
> *Spanless the erring way I wend;*
> *Blackness of darkness is my meed for ever?*
> *And barren plunging without end?*
>
> *O glorious fear! Those other wandering souls*
> *High burning through that outer bourne*
> *Are lights unto themselves.*

As though in defiance of Evangelical orthodoxy and St Jude, 'blackness of darkness' is welcomed as a meteor's proper environment. And the lawlessness of the poet would include sexual liberty. In that outer bourne where free spirits could ignore conventions and false creeds, it would be possible, even glorious, to be one's true self. Wilfred never forgot the imagery of 'O World of many worlds'. He seems to have shown the poem to Siegfried Sassoon in 1917, describing himself soon afterwards as Sassoon's 'satellite', 'always a mad comet', soon to be an independent star. 'Oh! world you are making for me, Sassoon!' His freedom was completed by Sassoon, who not only showed him how to 'warn the earth' in poetry, but also introduced him to gay friends in London.

'The time was aeon' uses scripture in a similarly defiant way. In a vision, a 'true resumption of experienced things', the poet sees the world beautified by 'a strange, regnant Presence' named 'the Flesh'. This spirit bears 'the naked likeness of a boy', supremely beautiful like a living statue:

> *Mere portraiture were fond futility*
> *For even thought is not long possible,*
> *Becoming too soon passion: and meseemed*
> *His outline changed, from beauty unto beauty,*
> *As change the contours of slim, sleeping clouds.*
> *His skin, too, glowed, pale scarlet like the clouds*
> *Lit from the eastern underworld;*

but even as the Flesh seems to overcome the world's disorder like 'a strong music', a 'small Jew' leads in a mob crying 'Crucify him!' The obvious allusion here is to St Paul, the small Jew who preached the need to 'crucify

the flesh', but there is also an echo of Harold Monro's *Before Dawn*, the
book Wilfred had found in October 1911, where the opening poem
personifies the humanity of the future as 'the Titan of the dawn':

> *Colossal as the silences that brood*
> *Over the deep, he filled the tranquil sky; …*
>
> *His visionary eyes looked out afar*
> *Beyond the transient semblances of death.*
> *No sound of supplication came to mar*
>
> *The rhythm of his calmly-taken breath.*
> *No ripple of a thin or faint delight*
> *Moved round his crimson lips; and underneath*
>
> *His bright skin aureoled by the rose twilight*
> *Rolled the vast torrent of majestic thews.*
> *Master of his strong passion …*
>
> *Beautiful human body cool and strong …*

Wilfred had clearly been impressed by Monro's vision of humanity
triumphing over religious delusion, even though he was probably unaware
of the advanced ideas that lay behind the image. Monro was an admirer of
H.G. Wells, Edward Carpenter and other modern prophets, and above all
of Nietzsche, and his Titan is a version of Nietzsche's *Übermensch* or
Superman, the new breed of human who will accept destiny without
thought of God or heaven. The image also reflects Wells's dream of the
'Samurai', the ideal leaders of the future, and Carpenter's descriptions of
beautiful worker-heroes. Carpenter was one of the very few contemporary
writers who was willing to speak out in defence of 'Uranianism', love
between men. *Before Dawn* had put Wilfred in touch with some radical
thinking, albeit indirectly. In echoing Monro he was associating himself
with a meteor-poet who had broken away from the fixed laws of religion
and social convention in the belief that life in the modern world should be
lived to the full without guilt or fear. He was also responding to the
homoerotic element in Monro's poem. Ancient tradition allowed poets to
represent the god of love, Eros or Cupid, as a naked boy, but Wilfred's
passionate language goes beyond tradition. He must have been aware of
that, because he added 'maid' as an alternative to 'boy' in 'The time was
aeon', presumably with the idea of making his poem seem more respectable. The three elements he considered to be lacking in Christianity,
'imagination, physical sensation, aesthetic philosophy', were all personified
in his image of the Flesh, the beautiful body Evangelicals wanted to crucify.
It would be his duty as a poet to declare the truth, 'warning the earth of

wider ways unknown', as a meteor gives light in darkness. His experiences at Dunsden had convinced him that poets had to speak out against repression and oppression, as Shelley, Monro and many others had done. He foresaw that the task might involve suffering. In an undated sonnet that belongs stylistically to late Dunsden, 'The Poet in Pain', he said he would accept pain if that gave authority to his work. If pain were necessary to 'proof-test' his thoughts and teach him how to speak for 'speechless sufferers' in 'words bleeding-fresh', he would not try to quench it. He would speak for the speechless, whatever the cost. But he was not yet free. Unless he could find some way of ceasing to be dependent on his parents, he would never be able to put his new principles into practice.

He went to stay with the Gunstons in mid-June, then spent a few days in lodgings at Reading to take the scholarship. He sat the exams in pessimistic mood and summer heat, and although the botanists soon assured him he had passed in their subject, he felt sure he was not going to win an award. When it was all over he returned to Alpenrose, where Leslie was developing a talent for sketching, having inherited his father's skill with a pencil. Uncle John took the family and Wilfred up to London one afternoon to see the summer exhibition at the Royal Academy. This was the sort of art Leslie and his father liked, new but still in the Victorian tradition and not at all 'modern', and Wilfred seems to have shared their tastes, enjoying browsing with his cousin through the annual *Royal Academy Pictures*. Leslie also seems to have been a regular reader of *The Bookman*, a popular literary monthly. The January 1913 number reported that Harold Monro had just opened the Poetry Bookshop in Bloomsbury, a venture that may well have resulted in the cousins' making another trip to London. The Bookshop is not mentioned in Wilfred's letters until 1915, but by then he seems to have been familiar with it.

He cycled over to Dunsden from Alpenrose one weekday afternoon. Mrs Lott welcomed him into the dining room, where he had spent so many tedious hours, but the Vicar was out. After some polite conversation, during which Mrs Lott perhaps mentioned that Vivian Rampton was away, Wilfred went on to Binfield Heath and called on Mrs Montague and Milly. As he was leaving, Mrs Rampton hurried to her gate at Vivian Cottage next door, full of reproaches that he had not given her the chance to invite him for a meal. 'I shall be glad to see you on Monday, O Mother mine,' he wrote afterwards. 'Objectionable men, and delusive, drive me back upon myself and Keats; unlovable women, and girls incapable of sympathy, drive me back to You.' Perhaps meeting Milly again had been a disappointment.

On 6 July, back in Shrewsbury, he learned he had failed the scholarship. His parents were away, but Harold had recently got home from India, so this was probably the occasion described in *Journey from Obscurity* when

Harold takes the envelope upstairs and Wilfred opens it in trembling excitement, only to slump back under the bedclothes with a sigh of bitter disappointment. The news was what Wilfred had been expecting, yet failure was hard to bear after the hopes that had been pinned on him as the one likely scholar in the family. He did his best to hide his feelings later that day when he wrote to Susan (sections of the letter were later painted out by Harold, but some passages can be partly restored):

> [*two or three words illegible*] this mng. that I am not [*one or two words illegible*] the Scholarship. I am piqued at this but not [?distracted or] dejected. I feel sure that the Latin [?Boggle is to blame for] that and the fact that Miss Morley was not examining this year.
>
> So things are as they were six weeks ago, unless a windfall of £80. saves me. I must therefore take Philosophy (in two senses) and Education, and wear out the seven-years sentence as best I may.
>
> It will be a [?trifle] humiliating [?to work] with Hullcoop, (long Leslie's detestation) who used to [?bow] and scrape to me. But all this must be talked over when Father and you are back.[9]

It must have been agreed that if Wilfred failed the Reading exam he would have to become an elementary teacher after all, as there was no possibility of his parents being able to pay university fees. He would need to pass Matric in geography, and get through an undemanding entrance exam to Reading or some other college, thereby qualifying for a free place as a 'primary student', taking a course that would include philosophy (actually logic) and education. The rules would then require him to teach for a minimum of seven years. William Hullcoop, the Dunsden head-master, whom Wilfred disliked as much as Leslie did, was apparently prepared to take him on as a junior colleague, a plan that must have had Wigan's approval although it was hardly realistic. A return to the necessary appearances of religious correctness would have been impossible, and the former Correspondent naturally hated the thought of having to bow and scrape to Hullcoop. The only way out seemed to be that primary students could read for a London degree concurrently with their education studies, but Wilfred was not at all sure he would be able to cope with such a taxing double course.

Contemplating this dismal quandary cannot have been made any easier by having Harold in the house. Harold was the centre of attention for once, having returned from India as a temporary invalid after nearly dying from heat exposure in Calcutta, and his adventures had given him a significant advantage over his elder brother. He may well have taken a mischievous pleasure in telling Wilfred about dockside bars, and a brothel he had been taken to on his first night in London, although he had never really misbehaved in such places, according to his memoirs. Wilfred was in no mood to be tolerant, and in an effort to conceal shame at the exam result and envy of his brother's supposed experiences, he put on a show of moral outrage and schoolmasterly superiority. Even so, he knew he had to emulate Harold by getting away from home. Deeply reluctant to trap himself in the elementary system, let alone work for Hullcoop, he revived an idea his mother had first suggested in 1910: he could not hope to rival his brother's travels, but he might be able to find a teaching job in France for the winter.[10] That would give him the opportunity to become fluent in the language, and he could come back in the spring to prepare for a second attempt at the Reading scholarship. Privately he must also have thought that six months abroad would allow him to be independent at last. A London agency was regularly advertising in *The Schoolmaster* for young teachers interested in working on the Continent, so he made enquiries.

He went to see some new excavations at Uriconium, meeting some of the archaeologists and feeling miserably jealous of two of them, who were from Oxford.[11] The Roman city had been large and prosperous, but it was believed to have been destroyed in a ferocious Saxon attack, many of the Romano-Celtic inhabitants allegedly dying in the blazing buildings. Wilfred had read in the guidebook that the disaster had been the inspiration for an ancient Welsh lament, so he decided to write a poem of his own, the ruins being an eminently suitable subject for a poet who thought of himself as both a Saxon and a Celt. 'Uriconium: an Ode' is written in painfully stilted language, and its list of ancient objects, added for realism, is based on displays in the site museum, but some of the key elements in Wilfred's later work are beginning to emerge. He sees the 'secret things' of Hades in the 'riven ground', and then, always the teacher, he draws the moralising conclusion that England should treasure its Celtic inheritance, the blood that 'makes poets sing and prophets see'. The Welsh tradition in poetry was musical and elegiac, as much of Wilfred's poetry was to be. He would write as a prophet, conscious of his Celtic blood, warning the earth of wider ways unknown, a task that might well involve uncovering the secrets of the underworld.

In August he went to stay with the Quayles at Meols on the Wirral. The weather was perfect and the house stuffy, so he spent most of his time out of doors with his cousins, bathing, walking, or rowing on the marine lake at West Kirby. He wrote to Susan, who was at Torquay, that he was eating well, drinking two glasses of milk a day and getting plenty of exercise, while his two small cousins, Kenneth and Margaret, were taking up hours of his time. 'Eros is not wholly forgotten either,' he added, evidently meaning he had been socialising with girls of his own age.[12] He told Leslie he had been to a tennis party with the eldest cousin, Cecil, then 'promenaded, and met the Set'. Later in the month he went to the Shrewsbury Flower Show, reporting to Leslie that the roses had been so impressive that he had noted down some of their names. He enclosed a sonnet, 'When late I viewed the gardens of rich men': he had been content merely to see the flowers and 'bear away sweet names', the poem says, but in 'more spacious pleasances' he had felt envy at seeing a thousand buds he might not kiss, though 'loving like a lover, sire, and God'. The rich man might give a flower to a parting guest, but 'God hath vouchsafed my meek longing – whom?' Wilfred said the sonnet had been written before his visit to the Quayles, but its allusions to the Flower Show and his uncle's garden seem to prove that it was in fact written afterwards.

His next surviving letter, actually a postcard to Leslie, has a Bordeaux postmark and the date 21 September 1913. He had left home again, this time for good.

Professor of English

Bordeaux

SEPTEMBER 1913–JULY 1914

Except for one brief visit to England in the summer of 1915, Wilfred remained in France for two years. Leaving home in September 1913 proved to be a final break. He seems to have had little inclination to return to his mother, despite many declarations to the contrary in his letters, and he never stayed at Mahim again for more than a few weeks at a time. In France there was no one to object when he drank wine with meals like a local, or when he attended social events on Sundays in preference to going to church. He took up smoking, developing a passion for Egyptian cigarettes. Susan remonstrated from Shrewsbury in vain. Within a week or two of his arrival he exercised his new-found liberty by agreeing to take part in a music-hall act, despite her horror of theatres. Opportunities to earn extra money could not be ignored; his pay from the Berlitz School during the first winter was barely enough to live on, and he was determined to be independent.

The record of Wilfred's life in 1913–15 will always be incomplete, partly because his Bordeaux letters have suffered exceptionally badly from his brother's work as self-appointed censor. Harold Owen was especially ruthless with letters that mention himself, and he removed comments about money and other topics that may have revealed more than he wanted to be known about the family's social position. But he did not stop there. Wilfred was now mature enough to speak more openly than before about himself and his ambitions, and all too often readers of the *Collected Letters* come up against this sort of thing:

I have no long confessional to make [*seven lines illegible*] (March 1914)
You may ask me what friend I ever made among the living of this world; [*eight lines illegible*] (May 1914)

My late letters have been writ for the *object* thereof; for *subjects* I lacked. But today I have subject enough [*nine lines missing*] (March 1915)[1]

This last example is one of several where the gap is larger than it seems: Harold not only cut away about nine lines from the first page of the letter, but also destroyed the whole of the second page and most of the third. Nevertheless, the surviving letters are full of lively information.

By the time Wilfred sent his first surviving postcard from Bordeaux in the third week of September 1913, he had found a room in the Rue Castelmoron, a grimy back-street near the cathedral, and had begun to adjust to a new country and long working hours. The Berlitz School occupied offices not far away above smart shops at 46 Cours de l'Intendance, the city's principal thoroughfare.[2] Wilfred's classroom gave on to a balcony, so he could take the air between lessons and watch for the approach of his next pupils, but apart from these breaks and an hour off for lunch he had little free time. The Director, Maurice Aumont, who owned Berlitz franchises in Nantes and Angers, as well as in Bordeaux, worked the tutors ruthlessly hard. The school was open from seven in the morning until nine at night, and Wilfred often had to be there by eight, ready to teach for seven or eight hours a day, six days a week. Sometimes his daily load went up to ten or even eleven hours. Not surprisingly, he developed a lasting hatred for Aumont.

The rest of the staff consisted of the sub-director, M. Langholz, who taught German; a friendly Spaniard with the splendid name of Sr Fernando Ruiz de Toledo; a shrivelled little Russian woman, Mlle Markowski; an Italian; and an Englishman named Tofield, a tall, gawky figure, two years older than Wilfred. Tofield had been a student at Nottingham, but had failed his Intermediate exams and was now failing to earn his living as a teacher. He seems to have been away for some of the winter, working at Nantes or Angers, his place at Bordeaux being taken in November by a recruit from Merseyside, a Miss Hewitt, with whom Wilfred got on well. All the staff were known as *professeurs* (teachers), a title Wilfred un-hesitatingly translated as 'Professor' for the benefit of Leslie, Alec Paton and others at home.

In the mornings and afternoons the new Professor of English could feel quite grand. His pupils were ushered into his room by a servant, and he taught most of them singly for an hour. They were cultivated people, sometimes wealthy: doctors, lawyers, businessmen, a countess whose daughter was married to a duke, five army officers who occasionally turned up resplendent in uniform, a lady with rings on nine fingers, and students from the university. Wilfred thought lessons were more like a doctor's consultation than normal teaching. He was rapidly converted to the Berlitz Direct Method, which did away with grammar books and compelled both teacher and pupil to speak exclusively in English, the more advanced pupils also being required to compose business letters or study literature. It was hard work, though, and it prevented him from practising his own French. Mealtimes gave him little chance, either; he often retreated to his lodgings for a hasty lunch, and in the evenings ate alone in the cheapest restaurants he could find.

~

His French was already proficient enough to earn him his music-hall engagement. Langholz introduced him to a young engineer named William Perry, who was looking for an interpreter. On the afternoon of Wednesday 17 September Wilfred and Perry appeared on the stage of one of the largest theatres in Bordeaux, the Apollo, before an audience of journalists and invited guests. Perry had invented a *ballon dirigeable à distance*, a miniature radio-controlled airship fitted with several propellers, billed as the 'the beginning of a new epoch in aerial navigation'. The preview was a great success, and the *ballon* became the star attraction in a ten-day gala programme.[3]

Perry and Wilfred were not on stage until eleven o'clock at the evening performances, but the large audiences watched fascinated for another hour as the little craft flew around the theatre. While Perry worked the controls and explained what was happening, his English was converted into passable French by Wilfred, who had hastily learned a new vocabulary of technical phrases. Miss Wright and her former colleagues at the Technical would have been proud of their actor-pupil as he made himself heard and understood above the roar of the airship's motors. Perry was delighted. Relaxing in a café after a show, he suggested Wilfred might like to accompany him to Paris and Mexico ('of all marvellous places!') with expenses paid and a salary better than Berlitz rates. Wilfred wrote home for advice. Knowing Susan would be shocked to hear that he had been appearing in a theatre, he made the event sound thoroughly respectable, saying it was attended almost exclusively by high-class people and even by the Mayor ('a great personage I assure you'). He did not reveal that there were cowboy dancers and acrobats in the programme, nor that there were Sunday performances; and for some reason he avoided mentioning Perry's name, though telling Susan that 'the Inventor' neither smoked nor drank and that their late-night refreshments in the café were only 'syrops'. The response from home must have been discouraging, although Tom and Susan probably never knew that if their son had gone to Paris with Perry his next stage appearance would have been at the Folies Bergères.

The music-hall show was part of the city's celebrations in honour of a brief visit by the President of France, Raymond Poincaré, who arrived by river on Friday 19 September and drove in a carriage to the Prefect's mansion, very near Wilfred's lodgings. Wilfred got a good view of him, probably from the school balcony. In the afternoon Poincaré unveiled a monument to the dead of 1870–1, those terrible years when the provinces of Alsace and Lorraine had been lost, Prussian soldiers had marched in triumph through Paris, and the King of Prussia had been declared Kaiser of a united Germany at Versailles. The memory of those humiliations still burned in the national consciousness. The sculpture showed France personified and defiant, bearing a dying soldier in her arms. 'Victi sed in Gloria': conquered, but in glory. The country was longing for revenge.

~

On about 27 September Wilfred moved to cheaper lodgings at 95 Rue Porte-Dijeaux, above a soft-furnishings shop. The landlady, Mme Dubo, who ran the house as a business, was not inclined to be maternal. He apparently had the use of a gas ring, but if he wanted a bath he had to take soap and towel to a wash-house a few streets away. His first-floor room was small and spartan, but it had a fireplace and was blessedly quiet, except for noise from the room next door and sometimes an out-of-tune piano, badly played. The large window overlooked a walled yard with a shrub or two, an urn on a pedestal and, at the far end, an elegant little eighteenth-century house occupied by a midwife, whose patients came and went discreetly through the passage underneath Wilfred's room.

The Rue Porte-Dijeaux is the ancient main street of Bordeaux. Wilfred's end, near the *porte* itself, a classical arch replacing a medieval gate, was lined with smart little shops and cafés, but the street changed its character entirely as it approached the river, becoming a red-light area. As Wilfred walked past the seedy houses and along the crowded quays, he thought of Harold, for Bordeaux was an international port and the Garonne was lined with ships from many nations. Everywhere, even in the shabbiest alleys, stone façades and classical proportions testified to a long history of civic pride and prosperity. He was living in the heart of one of the great cities of Europe, an enormous change from Monkmoor Road. When people asked about his home, he answered evasively, reluctant to admit that his father was a railway official. Nor did he much want to talk about his own likely future as a schoolteacher. No one knew anything about him, and no one was likely to check. So he hinted quietly that his father had a title, perhaps a hereditary one – not a peerage, of course, only a baronetcy – and that he himself was waiting to go up to Oxford. His mother had long hoped he would one day be Sir Wilfred Salter-Owen, and he could play the part, having learned gentlemanly ways at the Vicarage. As time went on he began to make friends in France at higher social levels than he might ever have reached in Shrewsbury.

He was delighted, if a trifle apprehensive, when his father offered to visit him in early October. Mme Dubo had a room to let, so Tom duly arrived, and according to Harold there was a mutually embarrassing conversation, when Wilfred struggled to come clean about the title and Tom thought he was trying to confess to a relationship with a girl. But Wilfred must have been pretty confident that the one-time Captain Owen of Birkenhead would enjoy acting the part of Sir Thomas Owen of Shrewsbury, and so it proved. Having been introduced to his son's new acquaintances, Sir Thomas was a baronet for a week, much to his and everyone else's satisfaction. The two Owens promenaded in the park, listening to the band, and took a boat trip up the river.[4] When Tom left on 15 October, Wilfred saw him off at the railway station with real regret.

Wilfred still expected to return to England in the spring to make another attempt at the Reading scholarship, although he was beginning to say he might need more time to perfect his French. In the weeks following his father's visit he wrote about the prospect of university with some enthusiasm, but after a while his intentions began to waver. Aumont made vague promises of advanced lessons in French for the *professeurs*, but not until the summer when more time would be available. Wilfred wondered whether it might be worth staying for another year, postponing a second attempt at the scholarship until 1915. On the other hand there was no chance of doing any academic work in his present job, which was clearly going to be drudgery throughout the winter.

Winter evening classes began on 25 October 1913, the Saturday after Tom left. They were intended for less prosperous people than the 'private pupils' who came singly in the daytime, so Wilfred had to cope with groups of tired workmen and shop assistants. Sometimes he had to become a schoolteacher again, shouting to make himself heard. It was no longer possible to earn extra money in the evenings or sit up late in cafés; except for Sundays the whole week was taken up by lessons. He complained of loneliness to Alec Paton, and asked for letters. Perhaps acting on admonitions from his parents, he sought out the English church one Sunday, but it was closed. The familiar language of Bible and Prayer Book would have been comforting. He was beginning to feel painfully homesick.

Rowdy classes left him with a sore throat, but more talking cured it, so when Susan said her own throat was giving trouble he advised her to become a suffragette or a strike-leader, or even a teacher. She saw through his bravado, sensing that his health would soon give way, and wrote to him lovingly and often, sending him parcels: apples, gingerbread, toffee, chocolate, Horlicks, Bovril. Her instincts were accurate. At the beginning of November he wrote to her in confidence to say he was indeed ill. He had been living off milk for several days and teaching wrapped in an overcoat, sitting in an armchair. On All Saints' Day, 1 November, the school was closed and he felt too weak to go out, although Mme Dubo was very reluctant to get food for him. What might have been a restful afternoon was horribly disturbed when a band of veterans struck up in the street with drums and bugles, honouring comrades who had fallen in 1870. Salutes to the dead became universal next day, the day of All Souls, and Madame went off to the cemetery to decorate family graves, as was the French custom. Wilfred had managed to get a fire going, so he made himself tea and toast and boiled an egg, thinking of his own family having supper at Mahim while the twilight faded over Haughmond. His lonely evening was measured by the tolling of every bell in the city, an irregular, relentless clangour quite unlike English change-ringing, the notes coming singly or in clusters, punctuated by a deep, sinister boom from the cathedral, all speaking of death. He was never to forget that sound, using it in several poems and eventually making it an image of gunfire in the 'passing bells' of 'Anthem for Doomed Youth'.

For a while his resolution failed him as he gazed at his mother's photograph and remembered her devoted nursing earlier in the year. He told her his ailments: constipation, discoloured urine, stomach pains, night fevers, headaches, a nosebleed. At one point he feared he was developing pneumonia, but he had none of the hallucinations that had plagued him in February. A kindly Dr Aumont, father or brother of the Berlitz Director, came to see him, diagnosed mild influenza and sent him some wine.[5] Wilfred taught for another week until the doctor and a colleague concurred in ordering him to bed, having persuaded Mme Dubo to be a little more humane. Susan sent copies of *Punch* and *The Life of Faith*, as well as a stream of letters giving news of anything she thought might be of interest: her plants and kittens, the infants' class, the piano (still in tune despite Wilfred's absence) and an unwelcome house that had just been built on the racecourse. He asked her not to tell the neighbours he was ill, perhaps knowing he had something of a reputation as a hypochondriac. She seems to have written to the Anglican chaplain in Bordeaux, asking him to help. The Reverend J.W. Lurton Burke, a charming old gentleman, duly called round and did what he could to cheer the patient, taking the opportunity to warn him against prostitutes.

Wilfred stayed in bed for a week, until the doctors finally agreed on a diagnosis. 'I must not conceal from you my malady,' he wrote on 16 November in typically dramatic tones. 'It is Enteritis – Gastro-Enteritis.' The Spanish *professeur* came to see the invalid, making him laugh by advising sagely, but in erratic English, that if he worked 'hardly' he 'must hardly eat'. Wilfred's infection was genuine enough, but it was closely associated with exhaustion, loneliness and insecurity, and it sounds remarkably like his digestive troubles during the Dunsden Revival. If anyone can be said to have cured him, it was perhaps Mme Dubo, whose lack of sympathy reminded him that he could never again rely on being mothered. The school treated him surprisingly well, paying him for his week's absence and starting him off with a light teaching load when he returned. By 5 December 1913 he was able to tell Susan he was feeling better than he had done a year earlier at Dunsden. He translated a business letter for his father, writing to him affectionately, and was sent a pound in return. There seemed to be no chance of finding better digs at an affordable rent, but he discovered the Protestant *Union Chrétienne*, the French version of the YMCA, very near the school. The food was inexpensive and reliable, and there was a warm common room, open all day, where one could read, play the piano and get some practice in French conversation.

He had no more mysterious illnesses in Bordeaux. His collapse in November 1913 was a brief reversion to the old self he was leaving behind, and within a few weeks he was cheerfully coping with up to ten hours' teaching a day. Ignoring the cold, wet weather, he spent every available hour out of doors. His mother enquired about his heart, but he had nothing to report except a dream of struggling to help her up Wyle Cop, no doubt on her way to St Julian's. He thought this might be a reminder of weak heart muscles, although it perhaps had more to do with guilt at not going to church and not sympathising enough with Susan's endless worries about her own health. His conscience drove him into making further efforts to find a church, and in mid-December he went to a crowded chapel in the grounds of a Protestant hospital, staying for a cup of tea and a tour of the wards after the service. There is no sign that he ever went again, however, although Susan must have urged him to do so. She raised objections when he said he had been to a social gathering at the *Union* on a Sunday, but he was able to tell her it had ended with prayer and Bible reading. Occasionally he even attended a *Union* Bible class.

Teaching took up so much of his time and energy that his reading was limited to the magazines he was sent from England. The only verse he is known to have worked on during his first few months in Bordeaux is 'The Imbecile', a little poem about a mad girl. There are three manuscripts of this, two in English and one in French; one has a note of some pupils' names on the back, and another a calculation of the salary Perry had offered him. And there is another note, a list of curious rhymes in which the first and last consonants are identical and only the vowels are changed: 'land / learned / leaned' and so on. 'The Imbecile' was first published in C. Day Lewis's 1963 edition of Wilfred's poems, with an editorial note that it had perhaps been written at Dunsden. Wilfred was becoming established as the national poet of pity in the early 1960s, and his admirers were keen to read even his most minor verse as proof of his compassion for real people. One of his Dunsden letters happens to mention a mad girl in the village, so 'The Imbecile' had to be about her. The truth is, though, that the poem is a literary exercise. The English version is an unfinished translation, and the French version is not by Wilfred at all but by a Swiss poet,

Henri Spiess. Wilfred had found 'La Folle' in the *Saturday Westminster Gazette*, where it had appeared on 30 August with the offer of a prize for the best translation. As a first attempt at capturing the subtleties of French Symbolist poetry, his two stanzas are interesting for their technical competence rather than for their compassion. There is no knowing when he added the list of pararhymes: the handwriting looks later than September 1913, but perhaps the system of rhyming for which he was to become famous did occur to him then, suggested by the elaborate sound effects in contemporary French poetry.

Christmas approached. He sent cards to Vivian Rampton and Milly Montague, getting no response. Alec Paton wrote with news of Birkenhead, and Leslie with news of Alpenrose and Dunsden. Leslie also sent a miniature suede-bound copy of Tennyson's *Elaine*. A big parcel came from Shrewsbury, less welcome than it might have been because it incurred two francs in customs duty, more than the cost of a meal. Among other things it contained a sprig of mistletoe, which Wilfred hung on the gas bracket in his room. Two members of the *Union* took him to midnight mass at the cathedral, although this first experience of a Roman Catholic service was not improved by an icy draught and his companions' tiresome giggling. He ate alone next day.[6] It was the most solitary Christmas of his life, but he had survived his first three months abroad and was beginning to find his feet.

~

Like most other British families the Owens entered 1914 expecting it to be much like any other year. Wilfred saw it in at the *Union*, where a party adjourned just in time for prayers at midnight. The *Union* regulars included a number of Germans, who emerge in his letters as the stereotypes he must often have seen in French and British cartoons: noisy, soup-slurping, bullet-headed, bull-necked, sausage-fingered barbarians, monopolising the common-room piano. When one of them commandeered his sheet music and murdered one of his favourite pieces, he felt he would welcome a war with Germany. He had heard talk of war, like everyone else, and he knew the British public was becoming alarmed about spies and invasion rumours.[7] French and British newspapers were familiarising readers with some of the more alarming ideas coming from Germany, such as prophecies by Nietzsche and Treitschke that the Teutonic 'blond beast' and German *Kultur* would dominate the world, and General Bernhardi's notorious theory that war was a biological necessity. But Wilfred seems to have felt little anxiety. Every year since 1895 had brought either a war or a war scare, international crises that had come and gone without affecting ordinary people. On New Year's Day he put on his black suit and a new waistcoat, and went out into the snow to call on his employer, M. Aumont, as French etiquette required.

In Shrewsbury, Tom Owen was anxious about his father, who had been failing in mind and body for some time, and Susan was complaining of exhaustion as usual. Colin was about to enter the Boys' High School, better known as Thompson's, a small private school which trained boys for the professions. Harold was still living at Mahim, apparently to the family's annoyance. He had decided to go to sea again and was waiting for a berth, a wait that was to continue for several months more. News of the delay made Wilfred 'furious … quite like being at home'. He thought Harold ought to be thrown out of the house.[8]

The first weeks of 1914 were horribly cold in Bordeaux. Wilfred was told it was the worst winter for thirty years.[9] The water froze in the jug on his washstand, and he spent his spare time in the *Union*, wishing he could join the skaters in the park. He had never felt so completely a town dweller in his life, as he told Susan, even in the bad times at Willmer Road, but he was beginning to enjoy himself. Most of his original pupils had completed their courses and left, so the New Year brought a fresh intake, making him feel an old hand. He was starting to get offers of French tuition in exchange for lessons in English. In the middle of January the sub-director, Langholz, astonished him by suggesting in confidence that he might actually buy the franchise of a small Berlitz school. Wilfred wrote to Tom in some excitement, giving him the details.

The school was the one at Angers, which Aumont was finding difficult to manage at a distance. Langholz reckoned it ought to produce an annual profit of at least £160, if Wilfred were to become resident director and English *professeur*. Wilfred was tempted, knowing he would never be able to earn much more than sixty pounds a year in his present position, but he readily admitted to his father that he was very young to run a business, his exams would have to wait, and the capital could only come from Uncle Ted Quayle. This last objection probably weighed most heavily with Tom. His own annual salary had just been raised to £275, and the thought of Wilfred on £160 or more was attractive; on the other hand, the venture would look dangerously speculative to a hard-headed businessman like Quayle. In February Wilfred reported that the Angers school had been sold to someone else. He was not altogether sorry, having realised he would have had to commit himself to it for at least five years. Susan told him to stick to his original intention of entering for the Reading scholarship, which he promised to do.

～

Another parcel arrived, but Wilfred's new-found health and confidence was making Susan's solicitude less welcome than it had been: 'if you must include fresh eggs, cabbages, half a pair of old socks,' he said, 'pack them in hermetically-sealed lead coffins, because of the smell'. He must have enjoyed casually mentioning that he had been given a ticket for the Students' Ball and intended to go in cloak and mask. Susan was at Alpenrose for her usual New Year visit, so he sent good wishes to any Dunsden folk she might meet, including the Vicar. The *Bal des Étudiants*, one of the great events of the Bordeaux year, was held on 31 January 1914 in *le Skating Palace* amid magnificent decorations and 'le ran-plan-plan et le zim-boum-boum' of rag-time music, with much flirtation and merriment. Dunsden Vicarage must have seemed very far away.

On the day after the ball Wilfred walked miles into the suburbs with a new friend to watch a display by the celebrated aviator, Roland Garros, who had recently made headlines by flying over the Mediterranean. Half Bordeaux seemed to be walking in the same direction. Huge crowds, including Wilfred, had watched Garros perform a week earlier, and now the hero had returned to compete against another pilot. For several hours the two planes swooped about the sky, sometimes diving low over the spectators, until in the end the judges nullified the match because both men had shown equal skill and courage. Wilfred was deeply impressed. Ever since seeing Grahame-White flying over the fleet in Torbay, he had been conscious of aviation as the newest science, a spectacular promise of things to come. For the first time in human history it was possible to look down on the earth like a god, not in visions but in reality. Here, surely, was a subject fit for the poetry of the new century, if only he could find time to work on it. He ached to be free like the airmen, or the swifts he and Leslie had admired in 1912. He complained about his workload to Aumont, who gave him slightly fewer hours for a while, but that only meant that poor Miss Hewitt had more than ever, churning out lessons 'as a Mangler mangles'.

Susan kept up her efforts to control her son, remarking lightly that she and Mary would have to become fluent in French because he was probably going to come home married to a countess. Seeing what she really meant, he said he had never been 'so absolutely free of "heart trouble" within these ten years past':

> This will no doubt give you immense satisfaction. But it *should* not …
>   You ought not to discourage too hard.
>   If you knew what hands have been laid on my arm, in the night, along the Bordeaux streets, or what eyes play upon me in the restaurant where I daily eat, methinks you would wish that the star and adoration of my life had risen; or would quickly rise.

She should rejoice, he said, that a calmer time had come for him, thanks to home and poetry:

All women, without exception, *annoy* me, and the mercenaries (which the innocent old pastor thought might allure) I utterly detest …

But I should not like to have seen myself in this town, two years earlier. And if you have not already spoken to Harold, I do implore you to muster courage and tell him a [?something] or two more than you told me, which was nothing.

Still, if you never had any revelations to make to me, at 14, I shall have no confessions now I am 21.

At least none such as must make me blush and weep and you [?grow] pale.[10]

As in other such passages in Wilfred's letters, some of the implications seem obvious, some cryptic. If all women without exception annoyed him, his mother must have been one of them. She had told him nothing about sex and had laughed him out of his early friendships with girls. If he felt more sure of himself now, it was no thanks to her. When late February brought the anniversary of his 1913 pneumonia, he remembered her nursing with gratitude but took part in the Carnival, Bordeaux being once again *en fête*. Some student friends had invited him to join them on the streets, so he wore the mask he had made for the ball, adding to it by dressing up as a Poet with laurel crown, palm sceptre and his academic gown (he had brought that treasured garment from home, presumably in the hope of being required to wear it for teaching; it had come in useful as a blanket in the cold weather). The others applauded his costume, and he happily jostled through the crowds, trying not to swallow confetti.

The 18th of March 1914 was his twenty-first birthday.[11] His mother had asked him what presents he wanted, and had duly sent a Waverley fountain pen from herself and Tom, and a collected Shelley from Mary, Harold and Colin. Wilfred needed the book because an advanced pupil wanted to read Shelley with him. His grandmother and aunt wrote from Torquay, but otherwise the 18th was a normal teaching day until the evening, when he was excused classes, the parents of one of his pupils having asked him out to dinner. M. and Mme Berthaud, both primary-school teachers, lived in a charming little house not far from the park. Their fourteen-year-old son Pierre was exceptionally good at languages, and Wilfred had begun to take an interest in him. It is impossible to know whether Pierre Berthaud was another Vivian Rampton. Both boys were seven years younger than Wilfred, and both were promising pupils who worked hard and wanted to learn. Like Mrs Rampton, Pierre's parents knew the value of education and kept their son at his books. Like her, too, Mme Berthaud had a high opinion of Wilfred. Pierre told Susan after the war that Wilfred had been his dearest friend, and that his mother had loved him as 'a fine, a charming, a perfect fellow'.[12] Wilfred and Pierre were still corresponding in

1918, but there is no sign in Wilfred's letters and poems that the French boy ever meant as much to him as Vivian had done.

One ostensible reason for getting to know youngsters was that a pen-friend was wanted for Colin, who was now almost fourteen. After some consideration Wilfred chose Jean Thouverez, a schoolboy footballer who could share his brother's interests rather better than Pierre might have done. Colin's French would benefit even more if someone could be found to go and stay at Mahim for a while, but here Wilfred had to be careful. It would never do to send a boy from a wealthier or better-educated family than the Owens, nor a Roman Catholic, nor anyone who had heard about Sir Thomas. The best choice seemed to be Raoul Lem, although he was about three years older than Colin. Raoul was a spoilt only child, emotional and inclined to be silly, but his big doe-like eyes may have made him attractive to Wilfred, who had probably met him at the *Union*.[13] His parents lived in a dingy area well away from the districts Wilfred usually visited, and they were Protestants.[14] M. Lem was a commercial traveller, as old William Owen had been. He and his wife seem to have been delighted to make Wilfred's acquaintance, and it was agreed that their son should spend part of the summer in Shrewsbury if he could get a grant to cover his expenses.

Soon everyone was talking of summer holidays, warning Wilfred that July and August in Bordeaux were unpleasantly hot. He applied for Berlitz jobs on the Riviera with no result, and dreamed of getting to Italy or Spain. His parents asked him about his future, but his reply, very unusually addressed to them both, has been so heavily censored by Harold that not much sense can be made of it. The last chance of returning home for the Reading exam in 1914 was slipping away. It would be better to wait for another year, but Wilfred said that if his parents objected to that on financial or other grounds he would return in the coming autumn to become a trainee elementary teacher. They knew how much he disliked that idea, so they seem to have agreed to a postponement. In his heart of hearts he wanted to stay abroad for as long as possible. The more he talked to people in Bordeaux, the more he heard of opportunities to travel while earning enough money to keep alive. There were more interesting things to do in the world than slave over Latin grammar or chain oneself to some dreary job in an elementary school.

Easter brought the chance for a brief escape from town life. He had hoped to spend a day at La Rochelle with Harold, who had at last pleased the family by being taken on as a cadet by the great line they would all have remembered as the 'Birkenhead Navy', the Pacific Steam Navigation Company.[15] However, Harold wired that his ship, the *Esmeraldas*, had been delayed, and Wilfred, sadly disappointed, fell back on an invitation from the Lems to join them on what he imagined would be a rather dull visit to friends in the country. Good Friday was a normal working day (he thought Bordeaux was remarkably godless one way and another) and so was the Saturday, but early on Easter Sunday, 12 April 1914, he met the three Lems at the station and set out for Castelnau-en-Médoc, a little town among the vineyards and forests just north of Bordeaux. The excursion turned out to be anything but dull, and afterwards he longed to tell someone about it, but as it was not the kind of story he could easily tell Susan he wrote about it to Mary, who must have been surprised to get a much longer letter than usual.

Expecting rustic informality, he had put on an old suit, not bothering with the refinements of gloves, stiff cuffs or a hair parting, so he was alarmed to notice that Raoul was wearing best clothes and a starched shirt. The visitors were met by an ancient man in equally ancient coat and trousers and wooden *sabots*, but old M. Poitou was followed by two fashionably dressed granddaughters. Wilfred had already met the elder sister at the Lems', thinking her large, pleasant and uninteresting. The younger sister proved to be very different: Henriette Poitou, aged sixteen, was stunningly beautiful. The reason for Raoul's attire was now obvious. Wilfred felt 'mighty queer' as the young ladies led him to their parents' farm, where the guests were welcomed by Mme Poitou and the grandmother, the latter weeping incessantly as she told Wilfred how her beloved grandson was serving as a conscript in Algeria. M. Poitou arrived with dog and gun, fortunately in workaday clothes. Etiquette demanded a session in the parlour, looking at family photographs, after which everyone except the mother and grandmother went for a walk in the forest. Wilfred and the grandfather talked about 'France, and her past', while a little peasant boy trotted along behind them gathering huge bunches of spring flowers for the foreign visitor. The child was unwittingly playing the part of Eros, for when the party got back to the house Mme Poitou indicated that Wilfred should present the bouquet to Henriette. That made Raoul jealous, and the more he tried to be charming over lunch the more his involuntary rival sat 'like an Egyptian piece of Statuary', watching how often 'the marvellous eyes looked in my direction, which was exactly four times per minute'. Eventually Raoul's attempts to win attention became so absurd that Henriette fled the room.

The afternoon was spent in the woods. At first Raoul sulked, while Wilfred 'paced along, stiff as a frightened cat', and M. Lem capered about and sang. When they had all calmed down, an impromptu dance was held under the trees, Wilfred rather spoiling the effect by not knowing the steps. Despite his awkwardness and his old clothes, it was his arm, not Raoul's, that Henriette took as they walked on through the forest. She confided to him that she was 'watched and warded everywhere', though longing to be free. 'I could scarcely have been happier,' he told Mary. 'And the memory of those moments will remain sweet to me, chiefly, my dear Sister, chiefly because I took no *advantage* of that young and ardent nature.' At dinner M. Poitou brought out bottles of old wine, going back as far as that never-forgotten year, 1870. His wife read a letter from their soldier-son, describing an English girl he had met in Algeria, so Wilfred copied Susan's joke about the imaginary countess and warned the girls to learn English. He shared a bedroom with Raoul and lay awake, listening to the nightingales and breathing the pine-scented air.

On the Monday morning, after the men had been shown the vineyards, there was a typically slow French lunch and just enough time for a game of hide-and-seek before the visitors had to leave. Castelnau being at the end of the line, the train was already in the station, so for twenty minutes the Poitous exchanged farewells with their guests, passing masses of sweet-scented lilac in through the carriage window, a gift Wilfred perhaps remembered four years later in 'The Send-Off'.[16] Back in his little room in the Rue Porte-Dijeaux, he looked at the wilting flowers and 'underwent a sad reaction', but he worked off his feelings by writing '50 lines of poetry in as many minutes', after which he went round to the *Union* to hammer away on the piano.

So the long winter had ended in a spring idyll, a more romantic episode than he could ever have hoped for. For the first time since his stay at Meols in the previous August he had escorted a girl, and for the first time ever, maybe, he had experienced the excitement of being in sexual competition with another male. His victory over the unfortunate Raoul had been complete and gratifying. Yet it had also been deeply unsettling. He knew very well he had done nothing whatever to bring it about, behaving instead like 'a frightened cat', nervous, passive, taking 'no advantage' of Henriette. Her marvellous eyes had made him as immobile as a statue, almost as though she had turned him into stone. That experience, at least, was far from new: he had felt paralysed by the beautiful, terrible eyes of Despondency in his first months at Dunsden.

Wilfred's reaction to the Henriette episode set him writing poetry again after six months' silence. There is only one manuscript among his papers that could be the fifty lines he poured out on that Easter Monday in 1914. It consists of just over fifty lines of verse, rapidly jotted down on a large double sheet. Unfinished, incoherent, chaotic, yet obviously written under pressure of strong feeling, the lines begin with a despairing question, 'What have I done, O God, what have I done?'[17] The speaker, Wilfred or some imaginary character, hears the wings of Eros beating as though in a furnace, and knows that love has come at last. He pauses to renounce the world, rejecting the sun's sweetness and the moon's comfort, turning away friends and 'all youth': he has 'touched the god; [and] touch me not' (Wilfred later added 'ess' to 'god').

> *On all that had been sweet to me, I laughed.*
> *I trampled on the flowers I so much loved*
>
> …
>
> *[And the dear books I blotted out and tore]*
> *Let music [be my terror] a jar [to all] my peace*
> *I would no more remember my old home*
> *Nor the old days or people or the places*
> *And turned adrift even my helpless hopes*
> *And bade the flame of this love burn them down.*

That sounds like Wilfred speaking in his own voice, listing the things he most treasured: flowers (botany), books, music, home, family, ambitions. The sacrifice is presumably to the god of love, as in the later sonnet, 'To Eros', which uses very similar imagery. The next section of the fragment, passionate though it is, may in fact be describing Eros, a beautiful male figure, pure as mountains, his brow like a cloud and his feet white as snowdrifts. The 'flower of all flesh' seems open, and between his 'shining shoulders' there are 'valleys for my rest for ever'. But the sacrifice is in vain. On 'the [second] day' (a hint of the two-day Poitou visit?) the speaker is himself rejected by whoever it is he has fallen in love with. Realising Eros has used a poisoned arrow, he enters 'hell's low sorrowful secrecy', smiling a skull-smile, his eye-sockets empty, his arms 'wrenched with inexplicable weakness' and his heart beating violently as though in the first moment of death. He meets Age, an ancient hag who tells him she will be his lover from now on. Again the imagery seems to be drawn from Wilfred's own experience of what he had called 'horrors', the onset of sudden acute depression, marked by physical weakness, tachycardia and 'phantasms'.

Whether or not this strange manuscript has anything to do with Henriette Poitou or Raoul Lem, it certainly has a great deal to do with Wilfred. It reads like a first, tentative sketch for some of the leading themes and images of his subsequent work, including the beauty and treachery of Eros ('To Eros' and several other sonnets), the rejection of the sun's blessing ('Spring Offensive', 'Futility'), the climax of agonised death and the prohibition of touch ('Greater Love'), and the skull-smile and the descent into hell ('Mental Cases', 'Strange Meeting'). 'What have I done, O God, what have I done?' The fragment seems to contain a possible answer: 'I have touched the god.' Was he remembering touching a boy's hand during another spring idyll two years earlier? Had it really been Henriette who had excited him at Castelnau? Or had it been Raoul? When he tried to personify love, the image insisted on being male. The marvellous eyes of a girl were a Gorgon's eyes, making him feel as helpless as a cold statue. So he would be in love only with love, with Eros as the ideal, pure and distant as mountains, but Eros was actually a hot and notoriously fickle god. In the end there would only be solitude, old age and despair.

Some such notions may lie behind the fragment. Wilfred was probably none too sure what it meant himself, although he seems to have been aware that it was more revealing than was prudent, especially in the matter of gender. He made some half-hearted efforts to change the pronouns from masculine to feminine. It was still fashionable to disguise confessional poetry under a veneer of classical myth, so he tried out two extra lines in the margin about Persephone, the goddess of spring, and added a few more overleaf about her husband Pluto, miserably alone in the winter of hell. These first attempts at turning what seems to be a personal statement into myth may actually be clues that the fragment did indeed begin as his response to the Castelnau visit. He had been trapped in Bordeaux for six winter months, just as Persephone had been forced to spend half of each year in the underworld, and Henriette seemed the embodiment of spring. He kept his manuscript, perhaps knowing it was somehow important and wondering how it could be developed.

His letters only mention Henriette once more. He met her again at the end of April, when the Lems asked him to a Sunday dance, and in the company of other pretty girls she was less interesting than she had been. Some weeks later, on another outing with the Lems, he and Raoul found themselves alone with four girls and were at once required to kiss them all. Wilfred thought the ritual rather silly, remarking to Mary that if this was the way French girls behaved they deserved to be 'watched and warded'. Susan – who usually read his letters to Mary – must have been relieved, although it had been worrying to hear of him dancing on a Sunday. She reproached him for that and for spending his money on wine and cigarettes. He promised her he was not a regular smoker and that ordinary wine was no temptation, but he cheerfully admitted that French convention worked on the conscience, melting away the last traces of 'Keswick Convention'.

~

Grandfather William Owen died at Torquay on 3 May 1914, with his son at his bedside.[18] A week later Wilfred spent an afternoon with a pupil named Bizardel, a law student, son of a newly appointed judge. The two young men sat under the chestnut trees in the Bizardels' garden, reading English literature (Bizardel may have been the pupil who wanted to read Shelley), and on the way home Wilfred passed an old church where a funeral was in progress. With his grandfather's death still in mind, he was in receptive mood, so he went in.[19] Amid the gloom and incense and 'the shine of many candles', the 'melancholy of a bass voice, mourning, now alone, now in company with other voices or with music, was altogether fine; as fine as the Nightingale – (bird or poem)'. 'I hope you will at least try to understand me,' Wilfred added when he described the experience to Mary, aware that she would be alarmed to find him speaking favourably of Roman Catholic ritual. Like the bells on All Souls' Night, the chanting and candles were to provide imagery for 'Anthem for Doomed Youth' in 1917.

His family's bereavement made him think wistfully of home, but he admitted to Mary that whenever he dreamed of being back in Shrewsbury he always felt sorry to have left France too soon. His speech was not quite fluent yet, although his pupils and Aumont now often complimented him on his pronunciation. There was to be a two-month course at the university in the autumn, leading to a diploma in the teaching of French. If he could give up his Berlitz job and become *Diplomé de l'Université de Bordeaux*, paying his way by private tutoring (he had some business cards printed), he might be able to earn his keep at home during the winter, and that would buy him time to work for the scholarship or even for Intermediate itself. Meanwhile he encouraged his father to revisit Bordeaux, knowing Tom needed a break.

On 24 May he wrote a long, ruminative letter to Susan about his future. She still assumed – as he did in theory – that he would one day marry, but he defined his ideal wife in impossibly demanding terms. As for a job, he said he would much rather run a Berlitz school than take an ordinary teaching post in England, but first he had to study. He was no longer concerned with getting through exams. An inner longing was now driving him, nagging at him all day 'like the call of an Art'. What sort of art he was not yet sure, but he felt certain he had the strong feelings necessary for artistic achievement; that at least was in his blood, as was proved by the examples of Susan's brother, Edward the drunkard, and Tom's sister, Emily Quayle, who 'literally palpitates with excess of physical sensation' (proof or not, such evidence was hardly likely to encourage Susan). The art might be music, but he admitted he had not shown much sign of original talent, any more than he had ever felt an urge to cover Teece's shop with frescoes or carve the staircase knob at Mahim into a 'serene Apollo'. 'Yet wait, wait, O impatient world, give me two years, give me two *free months*, before it be said that I have Nothing to Show for my temperament. Let me now, seriously and shamelessly, work out a Poem. Then shall be seen whether the *Executive Power* needful for at least one Fine Art, be present in me, or be missing.' Having scarcely mentioned his poetic ambitions in previous letters from Bordeaux, he recognised that his mother might be disappointed to hear of them again, but his dedication was evidently renewing itself in the wake of the Castelnau expedition. Perhaps it was now that he added the names of Persephone and Pluto to his scribbled manuscript, as a first step towards 'seriously and shamelessly' working out a poem.

The start of summer heat was not accompanied by much reduction in teaching hours after all. Miss Hewitt had left to take over a Berlitz school elsewhere, and Tofield had apparently been brought back to replace her, but in mid-June he was mysteriously dismissed, leaving Wilfred as the only English *professeur*. Little Mlle Markowski was drafted in to take some of his classes. He felt ever more frustrated, grumbling that if he only had time he could amuse himself 'admirably' by accepting pupils' invitations to watch operations at the hospitals or listen to trials at the law courts. Eventually he did at least find time to start attending lessons in Spanish, with the aim of making himself more versatile as a language teacher. Langholz invited him to join him at a school in Nice for November, and there was apparently some talk of going to Austria for August, but several letters discussing these plans seem to be missing.

Everything changed in June. A pupil, Mme Léger, 'Parisian lady, *distinguée*', invited him to be her tutor during August. She and her husband and small daughter were going to spend the month in a delightful little villa among the foothills of the Pyrenees, near Bagnères-de-Bigorre. The offer was all the more attractive because M. Léger was a highly-regarded *professeur* of elocution (he had been chosen to read a welcoming ode during the President's visit), so Wilfred would be able to learn as well as teach. Madame intended to take two maids to the villa, and several cultured friends were expected as guests. M. Léger came to the school to persuade Aumont that the sole remaining English teacher should be given leave, but Wilfred probably gave notice anyway. Aumont can scarcely have been pleased.

Towards the end of the month Raoul Lem heard that he had won the scholarship he needed to visit England. Tom and Susan were willing for him to stay at Mahim, although Wilfred was a little uneasy at the prospect, now that he had seen how silly the boy could be about girls. Raoul's slurred lower-middle-class speech was not the ideal model for Mary and Colin, either. However, it was too late now to have second thoughts. At least the Lem parents could be relied on for help and hospitality, should any be needed.

On 28 June an Austrian archduke was shot in Sarajevo. The Bordeaux newspapers ran the incident as an interesting news item for a few days, then more or less forgot it.

King George V drove down Monkmoor Road in a carriage on 3 July. He had come to see the Royal Agricultural Show, which was being held that year on the old Shrewsbury racecourse. He must have looked preoccupied: the newspapers commented on the brevity of his visit, and officials explained that he was very busy. He inspected some old soldiers and toured the show for an hour, followed by thousands of his cheering subjects, among whom were Colin and Mary Owen and Mary Ragge, and then he hurried back to London. Tom must have been on duty at the station, looking important in top hat and morning dress. Susan no doubt stood outside Mahim to watch the King go by. She had been able to make a little money by letting a room or two to visitors.

On 14 July all France commemorated the fall of the Bastille as usual. In Bordeaux crowds poured into the huge Esplanade des Quinconces in stifling heat to watch a big parade of troops, heavy artillery and machine guns, raising a special cheer for a detachment of sweating army cyclists. Bands played in the squares and each district held its own festivities, although many people could do little more than sit at café tables trying to cool down. In the evening everyone streamed back to the Quinconces for the fireworks. Wilfred had never seen such a vast mass of people, or such an impressive display. As huge letters of fire along the river promenade spelled out 'Vive la République', and the sky filled with golden rain, flashes of real lightning mingled ominously with the bursting rockets. The sound of many thousands of feet and voices surging back into the city put him in mind of *A Tale of Two Cities*, appropriately enough. The storm soon broke with great violence, flooding out the open-air dances and parties.

About four days later Wilfred took the chance to economise by paying his final rent to Mme Dubo and moving himself and his belongings to the Lems'. On 21 July Raoul left for Shrewsbury, where Susan, instinctively motherly as ever, felt an urge to lick him because he had so recently touched her son. Wilfred taught a last class at the school on Saturday the 25th, ending almost eleven months of hard labour, and on the same day the leading Bordeaux paper suddenly broke with its usual conventions by putting international news into its main headline, reporting that war between Austria and Serbia seemed frighteningly close. The Légers left for Bagnères two days later, while Wilfred made one more visit to the school to attend a Spanish class. The language might come in unexpectedly useful: Spain was the safest place in Europe, as he commented on a postcard home, and he was going to be near the border. On Thursday 30 July he got up at half past five to go to the station, leaving some of his possessions with the Lems. The train ran south for several hours through the immense pine forests of the Landes, then emerged into open country, and for the first time in his life Wilfred saw real mountains.

Très-joli garçon

Bagnères-de-Bigorre

JULY–SEPTEMBER 1914

Charles Léger[1] and his eleven-year-old daughter were waiting at Bagnères station when Wilfred's train pulled in. The green trunk that had been to Dunsden, Keswick and Bordeaux was hoisted on to the donkey cart. No one of any status in Bagnères-de-Bigorre would have dreamed of keeping a donkey *charrette*, but the Légers were much too Parisian to worry. Little Albine, always called Nénette, gazed with shy suspicion at the visitor and he smiled back, pleased to have the company of a child again. M. Léger explained that the villa was a mile or so outside the town, up the narrow Gailleste valley. Some weeks earlier the unusually hot weather had melted the mountain snows so fast that a stream behind the house had flooded the ground floor, but now the water was back to its usual summer level and the house was dry again. A track signposted 'Castel Lorenzo' led up from the valley road through hayfields to a little copse. The villa, 'secret, 'mid hills', as Wilfred later described it, was hidden behind the trees, standing above a steeply sloping garden. It was not at all a *castel* but an enchanting French *bijou*, a miniature baroque mansion with urns, statues, white-painted balustrades and an upper storey like a little pavilion. The Légers were renting the house from a local doctor, who had built it as a holiday retreat but was now too old to use it. Dr Cazalas had prospered by treating the rich and famous, Bagnères being a renowned health resort, and he had occasionally accepted antiques and works of art in payment. Some of the villa's furnishings were of high quality, but the place had clearly been neglected for years.

The main room of the house, divided into three sections by decorative iron columns, occupied the entire front of the ground floor. One end was the dining area, with a handsome round table, one of the doctor's antiques. At the other end was a decrepit piano – 'absolutely untouchable,' Madame said, 'O la! la!' The central section of the room had what was in effect a glass wall, big windows and doors framing a superb view over the garden to steep hills that reminded Wilfred of Shropshire. Higher still, gleaming against the sky, rose the great snow-peaks of Mont Aigu and the Pic du Midi. His own room at the back had a bed and table, and in one corner a *cabinet de toilette* with a basin where the tap never stopped running. He was told someone might come to fit a new washer, but he was used to French plumbing and soon worked out a method of deadening the noise with rags. French windows opened to the side of the garden, where the stream flowed away down a precipitous hillside with a pleasanter sound of water, singing 'to the sleeping woods all night … a gentle song', as Wilfred said, misquoting Coleridge. The garden at night was magical, with bamboo leaves stirring faintly in the cool air from the mountains, and the stars more brilliant and numerous than he had ever seen them.

M. Léger took Wilfred for a walk to show him the lie of the land and they soon became good friends, exchanging ideas about art and life in general. Charles Léger was fifty-two, but he sometimes seemed almost boyish. There was something rather impressive about him, despite his baldness and small stature. He moved gracefully, holding his head high and looking about him with fine dark eyes. It was pleasing to discover that as a child he had met with kindness from Elizabeth Barrett Browning.[2] Léger had studied engineering in Paris, but had given it up to devote himself to acting and the arts. He was well known in Bordeaux, holding Tuesday recitations in the *salons* of his large town house and apparently producing plays.[3] His many friends were happy to perform for him, but none of his enterprises made any money. Luckily he had inherited an interior design firm, which was being profitably managed for him by his wife. She was much younger than he was, and more businesslike.

~

Each morning after a leisurely breakfast at eight, the tutor had to earn his keep for an hour or two by giving Mme Léger conversation practice, often in some shady corner out of doors and usually with interruptions from Nénette. Madame was keen to get her English up to scratch by October, when she was due to visit customers in Canada. She took Wilfred into the town to buy *espadrilles* to wear around the house and garden, telling him to consider himself one of the family. He probably resolved to be in for every meal to save expense: the holiday was costing him nothing, but he was not being paid. It rapidly became obvious that Madame's motives in inviting him to Bagnères had not been exclusively professional. She said the day after he arrived that she detested plain people and was not much in love with her husband. She had married at the age of seventeen and was still only thirty-one. Wilfred felt a little apprehensive. When she said she could do whatever she liked with her men friends, he answered like a character from a novel that if she found him compliant she should remember his position in her household. But she insisted he should speak and behave exactly as he wished. She was strikingly elegant, her clothes and *coiffure* always impeccable, even for drives in the donkey cart. When he first saw her fully made-up for a social event in the town, he thought she looked 'a surpassingly fair and dangerous woman', and she was well aware of the impression she created.

If Madame, ten years older than Wilfred, made little attempt to hide her interest in him, her daughter, ten years younger, had no need to. Nénette soon realised he was an excellent playmate, and from his point of view she was a useful buffer between himself and her mother, even though she was ill-disciplined and demanding. She was also very intelligent and had already started writing plays, some of which Wilfred thought astonishing. She pestered him to draw, act, tell stories, and make boats to sail on the pond. Trying out the untouchable piano in a moment of inspiration, he played discords and harmonies to represent people they both knew. He had brought some music with him, and when Nénette asked him to turn her own personality into music, he played Sinding's 'Rustle of Spring' for its 'pretty rippling triviality' and occasional earnestness. Before long it seemed to her mother that Nénette was in love with Wilfred, talking about him incessantly, choosing clothes that would please him and asking, 'Monsieur Owen est très-joli garçon, n'est-ce-pas?'

So for the second time in 1914 Wilfred found himself the object of female admiration. The Henriette episode had lasted barely two days, but his stay at the villa was likely to be for six or seven weeks, and all that time mother and daughter would be competing for his attention. Their compliments made him realise that he was indeed an attractive young man. His winter illness had long since given way to exuberant health, and the mountain sun was turning his old pallor into the tan he was to keep for the rest of his life. While still in Bordeaux he had grown a little moustache (Nénette hated it) and bought himself some bow ties, a straw hat and a walking stick. With his dark hair fashionably parted in the middle and his boots gleaming, dressed in his best clothes to accompany Monsieur and Madame to a concert or to take Nénette to church on a Sunday, he looked as *chic* as anyone in Bagnères. He wrote to his mother that his life was 'a lived-out book', but he seems not to have posted the letter; Susan would not have enjoyed the thought of his living as though in a French novel.[4] In fact the more he told her about his circumstances, the more alarmed she became about Madame, whom she mistakenly suspected of having been an actress. By contrast, when Wilfred produced a photograph of Susan, Madame said, 'Oh, but she must be good, your Mother.'

Once the morning lesson was over he could spend his time as he liked, and the little town of Bagnères-de-Bigorre, full of summer visitors, was only about twenty minutes' walk away. The celebrated poet Laurent Tailhade, a former resident, had written in praise of Bagnères as a place of kisses, its white-painted houses sleeping at the foot of the mountains like a swan. A statue by the distinguished sculptor, Jean Escoula, of *La Muse Bagnéraise*, with lines from Tailhade's poem carved on the plinth, symbolised the town's connections with the arts. Natives of the area included Escoula, Tailhade, Théophile Gautier the poet of 'l'art pour l'art', and other famous names. Bagnères was by no means a backwater, despite its rural setting.

Wilfred went into the town on most days, but sometimes when the air was clear enough he scrambled up a hill, with the aid of a borrowed alpenstock, to see the long chain of the Pyrenees. He shocked the Légers one day by saying he wished he could find somewhere to bathe. They thought that would be unhealthy, but he went out one morning pretending to botanise and found a secret pool where the chill mountain water was deep enough. He took to going there daily, coming back refreshed and smug to the envy of his hosts. But when the sun was at its height there was nothing to do but sit in the garden, smoking cigarettes and contemplating the distant peaks. Looking at the pretty but not altogether convenient villa and its overgrown surroundings, he discussed the ideal country house with Madame, afterwards sketching out a poem about it, imagining the statues, fountains and children he would people it with. As he relaxed in the shade of the birch trees and read the newspapers, he thought he was one of the most enviable young men in France.

~

War had been brewing when Wilfred arrived on Thursday 30 July. One of the local weeklies, *L'Avenir*, reported on the Sunday that the tocsin was sounding and the young men departing for their regiments. Germany declared war against France on Monday 3 August, and Britain joined in next day. Within less than a week of Wilfred's leaving Bordeaux, the world had changed for ever. Sometimes at night, under a red harvest moon, he climbed to his hilltop and gazed south to neutral Spain, wondering if he should go there.[5] The distant crisis in the north made his present life seem even more like a lived-out book. He played the opening bars of Chopin's funeral march to Nénette, and the slow, solemn music enthralled her so that every day she forced him to play it again. 'It is a torture to me,' he said, 'but I do it for the sake of her expression.' When they walked into Bagnères together they talked about armaments and what Britain was doing for France.

Neither he nor the French public were aware of the appalling losses on the frontiers. M. Léger went into Bagnères for news every day, but it was all propaganda. The next number of *L'Avenir* was full of 'la Guerre Sacrée': Belgian machine guns mowing down the enemy, two German cruisers sunk by *les Anglais*, American sympathy with France, German atrocities, the divisive work of pacifists. Daily concerts on the main promenade continued, to keep up people's spirits. Nevertheless there was great distress in Bagnères, as elsewhere in France. Wilfred saw women weeping in the streets, business came to a temporary halt as the conscripts left, and the farm next to the villa lost its labourers, M. Léger remarking that he and Wilfred would have to bring in the hay. When the shops opened again, food prices soared and even bread was in short supply. There was much talk of spies, so that aliens became objects of suspicion. Wilfred had to get a police permit to stay, and the Légers advised him to stop wearing his glasses because they made him look foreign. He was glad of the warning, having seen someone almost lynched for claiming to be German, but without glasses he looked French and women glared at him, assuming he was a shirker. When people knew he was English, he was treated with great respect.[6]

Military service being compulsory in France, the authorities had no need to drum up volunteers, so Wilfred experienced none of the recruiting propaganda that was sweeping Britain, nor much of the idealism and guilt that would have affected him had he been in Shrewsbury. He told Madame he ought to be doing something, but she said there was nothing he could do except perhaps become a stretcher-bearer. When French troops made their ill-fated entry into Alsace, Bagnères held a celebratory concert which he and his hosts seem to have attended, hearing the town band play patriotic songs and the anthems of the Allies. He remembered the games of soldiers he had played with Alec Paton in Birkenhead and confessed in a letter to Colin that he longed to be on France's eastern front, helping to regain the lost provinces, but that was mere romancing. He said he knew he could not go because he would never get permission from home, conveniently forgetting that now he was twenty-one he could make his own decisions.

It seemed pointless to plan for the future, although he still hoped to take some autumn courses at the university. The Légers intended to return to Bordeaux in mid-September, about a month before Madame was due to leave for Canada, so they invited him to stay with them in their town house until she left. He was delighted: it would cost him nothing and the house was in a grand area. Writing home about this on 24 August, he thought it wise to say that while Madame was undoubtedly attracted to him both physically and intellectually, he had made it clear that her physical interest was not reciprocated. He was sure she had got the message. 'If it were not so, – I should hop it, immejit.' He was simply a friend of the family. But next day he added an excited postscript that she had just said she wanted him to go to Canada with her, all expenses paid. It was too late to include him in her October visit, but she was due to go again in the spring. He admitted this would interfere with his half-forgotten plan to try for the

Reading scholarship. 'But what a go!' If Susan had been unhappy about Perry's suggestion of a trip to Mexico, she must have been horrified to hear of Madame's invitation. Wilfred seemed to have become entangled in the wiles of a painted Frenchwoman, and he was quite beyond reach: Tom had hoped to visit Bordeaux again, but the war had made that impossible.

Susan could do little but pray and write anxious letters. She offered to send a copy of *The Christian* and Wilfred said yes, he would like to read reports of the latest Keswick Convention and what the prophets were saying about 'Armageddon'. The magazine was less concerned with current events than he might have expected, the prophets concentrating almost as much as ever on saving souls and 'opening the Word'. The first wartime number wondered whether the spiritual upsurge in the nation might be a sign of coming Revival, but later numbers were less hopeful. One article sternly pointed out that it was an incorrect use of a biblical term to describe the current war as Armageddon.

~

Wilfred was soon preoccupied with a new friendship that was to prove far more important to him than his awkward relationship with Madame. The distinguished visitors who had been expected at the villa were all unable to come, but on Saturday 22 August and again next day Laurent Tailhade lectured at the Casino in Bagnères. He was an old friend of Léger and Dr Cazalas, so M. Owen was introduced. The meeting was momentous for Wilfred, one of his three crucial encounters with living poets (the other two were with Monro in 1915–16 and Sassoon in 1917), although all that has usually been said about it is that Tailhade was a committed pacifist who influenced Wilfred against war. Harold Owen denied any influence, however, maintaining that after the first flush of enthusiasm his brother neither liked the French poet nor admired his work. Harold may have had his own motives here, having discovered at least two letters implying that Tailhade had made sexual overtures to Wilfred. The truth is that the French poet was a very important influence, though not towards pacifism.

Tailhade read two of his stock lectures at the Casino. On the Saturday he spoke about the tales of Mother Goose, 'a poetic promenade through the legends of all lands and times', as *L'Avenir* described it. On both days there was a supporting programme organised by Charles Léger, who recited poems. A quartet played Beethoven and Schumann, and a local *divette* sang – exquisitely according to the newspaper, infamously badly according to Wilfred, who sat in the front row between Mmes Léger and Cazalas. The Sunday lecture was on Gautier, but Tailhade must have realised the audience was expecting him to say something about the war, so he prefaced his talk with a magnificent display of Gallic eloquence. He declared that the war obliged France to fight for the 'Roman-ness of our spirit' against the modern descendants of the 'blond barbarians' who had destroyed decadent Rome. Heroic French youth was ready for 'sublime gestures' in defence of Latin civilisation. Talking about poetry at such a time might seem futile, Tailhade said, but listening to the voices of the poets and the sublime language of France was in fact one of the most patriotic things French people could do.

> Among the sacred treasures the great-hearted soldiers of France are defending today there is nothing more dear than this language of crystal and gold, ... nothing more rich and glorious than this language without equal, this vehicle of reason and intellectual liberation, this tongue of Rabelais and Voltaire, Bossuet and Montesquieu, Michelet and Renan, ... this language, unbroken by disasters and the flight of days, which even on the ruins of a world will yet guard the soul of France, the eternal tradition, ... the very essence, the best of *la patrie*: to glorify the poets, that is still to serve France and share in her honours!

For at least the next year Wilfred's thoughts about the war were to be based on Tailhade's ideals. He said in December 1914 that the only thing that would keep him going in battle would be the thought that he was fighting for the language 'Keats and the rest of them wrote'; and his repeated excuse for not enlisting was that a live poet was worth more than a dead soldier.[7] A few days after the lecture he said his attitude to the war was like the English way of dealing with an offender: 'a Frenchman duels with him: an Englishman ignores him.'

> I feel my own life all the more precious and more dear in the presence of this deflowering of Europe. While it is true that the guns will effect a little useful weeding, I am furious with chagrin to think that the Minds which were to have excelled the civilization of ten thousand years, are being annihilated – and bodies, the product of aeons of Natural Selection, melted down to pay for political statues.

He added that he regretted the losses in the conscripted European armies more than British casualties because the British soldiers were 'all Tommy Atkins, poor fellows'. Wilfred often drafted his more thoughtful letters several times, and this one sounds carefully composed. It was written soon after an intimate conversation with Tailhade, and the unsympathetic, patrician ideas in it are precisely what the older man might have said, even to the aside about duelling and the reference to Tommies. Tailhade was no pacifist, but for much of his life he had been a passionate anarchist, mistrusting all governments and authorities. He also loathed democracy and all forms of vulgarity. Spirited, charming and elegant, he was described as having the air of a landless aristocrat. He had picked many quarrels with political and literary opponents and had fought seventeen duels, as Wilfred knew. He thought Germany was destroying what he loved most: intellectual and physical beauty, and youth, made manifest in the finest minds and bodies of France.[8]

~

The Légers invited Tailhade to lunch at the villa on 27 August. Aged sixty, he was in a poor state of health after many years of over-indulgence in drugs and absinthe, and he seemed an old man to Wilfred. He suffered from palpitations during the meal, so all the windows had to be flung open. Nevertheless he accepted Madame's invitation, made for Wilfred's sake, to come and stay. He loved the local landscape, which had inspired his earliest attempts at poetry, and he no doubt welcomed the prospect of saving himself hotel bills, being always short of money, but another reason for agreeing to stay at the villa was that he had taken a fancy to the young Englishman. They had no opportunity for conversation that day, but next morning Wilfred called at the hotel to fix a date for Tailhade's move.

'He received me like a lover,' Wilfred told Susan later on the 28th. 'To use an expression of the Rev. H. Wigan's, he quite slobbered over me. I know not how many times he squeezed my hand; and, sitting me down on a sofa, pressed my head against his shoulder. [*two lines illegible*]' The illegible lines have been crossed out very thoroughly. At least one other letter written from the villa has disappeared, but a passage from it happens to survive because Susan quoted it to Edmund Blunden in 1930: 'The poet Tailhade calls my eyes "so very lovely!!!" etc and my neck "The neck of a statue!!!! etc" – because he is a poet, and unconsciously appreciates in me, *not* the appearance of beauty but the Spirit and temperament of beauty, Tailhade says he is going to write a Sonnet on me.'[9] Wilfred may have succeeded in convincing Susan there was nothing erotic in Tailhade's behaviour, but his own illusions must have been short-lived, if they ever really existed. Tailhade had been married twice, but he was almost certainly bisexual or gay, and plenty of his poems imply first-hand knowledge of the world of *éphèbes*, rent-boys and the *Troisième Sexe*, the title of one of his sonnets. 'Ton col surgit du sein comme une tour d'ivoire / Jeune homme!' another of his sonnets begins, in words he might have quoted to Wilfred if it hadn't been for the suntan. There is no sign that Wilfred responded positively, but he was clearly not repelled. To receive such warm admiration from an eminent man of letters was an experience to be treasured.

Tailhade was a celebrated talker. Like Wilfred he had broken away from home, religion and an adoring mother to become a poet. He had married in 1879, living in Bagnères and working for *L'Avenir*, which was monarchist-Catholic in its sympathies, but the deaths of his wife and baby after a few years seem to have changed him into a rebel and bitter atheist. He went to Paris, becoming a well-known dandy in the *salons,* acquainted with many distinguished writers. He married again, later describing his second wife as a turkey, but a turkey well stuffed with banknotes; she soon divorced him, complaining of his 'eccentricities'. One of his eccentricities was his commitment to anarchism, a commitment so extreme that when a bomb was thrown into the French Parliament in 1893 he made himself notorious by remarking that the victims were of no importance as long as the 'gesture' was beautiful. Soon afterwards another bomb deprived him of his right eye, much to the amusement of Paris. Tailhade was undeterred. His right hand was mutilated in a duel with Maurice Barrès, a leader of right-wing opinion. In 1901 he was imprisoned for six months for advocating the assassination of the Czar and all the Russian Government and clergy. Two pamphlets he published some years later, calling on French soldiers not to fight, are the source of his undeserved reputation as a pacifist, but the pamphlets were written in protest at France's alliance with Russia. He was quite willing to contemplate mass slaughter as a means of overpowering tyranny, or for that matter of overcoming a German invasion of France.

Tailhade probably saw a good deal of his new friend during the next few weeks. Writing to 'Mon cher Wilfred' six months later, he said he had not forgotten their afternoons together, nor the Gailleste road and the Casino, nor Beaudéan, a picturesque village near Bagnères that they must have visited. He added he was still getting daily pleasure from using Wilfred's old pen, imagining how often it had been in its former owner's hand.[10] He made several attempts to settle at the villa in September 1914, but retreated each time to his hotel, complaining of a neuralgic abscess. 'No end of a fuss,' Wilfred reported on the 4th. Tailhade asked him to dine at the hotel that evening and next day gave him a copy of Flaubert's *La Tentation de Saint-Antoine,* signing the book again three days later and adding a copy of Ernest Renan's *Souvenirs d'Enfance et de Jeunesse,* inscribed 'amical souvenir des beaux après-midi de La Gailleste'. In Tailhade's opinion these were two of the greatest French classics of the nineteenth century, and they seemed appropriate gifts for his young friend. He and Wilfred marked this symbolic moment by posing together for a photograph in the villa garden, reverentially holding the *Tentation* between them. Tailhade turns away from the camera a little to conceal his missing eye and damaged hand, resting his arm round Wilfred's shoulders, while Wilfred seems to lean gently against him, acting the new disciple, dapper, respectful, honoured to be introduced to French literature.

Wilfred read the two books with care, marking difficult words and interesting passages, including a remark by Renan that Celts can reach into a man's entrails and bring out secrets of the infinite. Like Wilfred and Tailhade, Renan had been of Celtic descent and brought up by a devout mother. While training as a priest he had come to the conclusion that the Bible could not be literally true. This discovery, famous among French intellectuals, made Renan lament in a letter to a friend: 'Goodbye for ever to my mother, my little room, my books, my peaceful studies … Goodbye to the pure and tranquil joys which seemed to bring me so near to God … Farewell for me to pure happiness.'[11] Some of Wilfred's later sonnets, such as 'Happiness' and 'To Eros', seem to echo this farewell. In giving him the *Souvenirs*, Tailhade was showing him that one of France's great philosophers had made the same painful journey they had both made from religious orthodoxy to freedom.

Wilfred's copy of Flaubert's *Tentation* has an introduction by a well-known critic, Émile Faguet, who tries to present the book as essentially Christian. Tailhade wrote 'crétin!' against a comment by Faguet that the novel had great defects, and altered the title page to read 'le stupide Émile Faguet … qui déshonore ce chef d'oeuvre'. Flaubert's extraordinary book, mysterious, exquisitely written, the inspiration for work by Symbolist painters and poets, was like a catalogue of the themes and imagery of French late-Romantic literature and art. Wilfred could have had no better introduction to Aestheticism and its offshoots, Decadence and Symbolism.

Tailhade had been a disciple of the leading Symbolist, Mallarmé, and a close friend of the leading Decadent, Verlaine, whom he regarded as the greatest poet of his time. He was also a fervent admirer of Baudelaire and Gautier. These poets and their associates had turned art away from bourgeois reality into a secret, autonomous world of the imagination, where the supreme task was to capture beauty in pure form, in a language of crystal and gold. Mallarmé had sought to 'purify the dialect of the tribe', a phrase borrowed by Tailhade in at least one essay, and Verlaine had called for 'de la musique avant toute chose', music being the purest of the arts. Tailhade had been one of a group of young Aesthetes in the 1880s who had declared themselves 'Decadents', claiming that civilisation had reached a cultural autumn, a ripeness verging on decay. The modern artist should be concerned only with the refinement of sensation and the pursuit of beauty, even if that meant exploring the darkest recesses of the human mind. Morality and ideals were out of date. Hence, in the 1890s, Tailhade's description of the anarchist bomb as a 'beautiful gesture', or Oscar Wilde's equally notorious comment that there is 'no such thing as a moral or an immoral book. Books are well written, or badly written.'

Years later Tailhade said the Decadent movement had been a mere publicity stunt. There had certainly been an element of that in it, but at the time the Decadents regarded themselves as the last Romans, clad in purple and gold, feasting on beauty in a final twilight, the sun setting blood-red even as the Teutonic barbarians broke down the gates. Themes of passive suffering and smiling martyrdom constantly recur in Decadent art, pain and death being welcome as supreme sensations. The barbarian enemy included bourgeois respectability, so that shocking the middle classes was a laudable aim, and the Decadents liked to associate themselves with anything that might cause outrage, notably homosexuality and sado-masochism. But another enemy was Prussia. Familiar imagery of the Roman decadence and language pure as jewels is given an immediate political significance in Tailhade's Casino lecture. His words illustrate the way in which established poetic conventions were not overthrown by the Great War, but adapted to new circumstances. Wilfred's own poetic language was to go through just such an adaptation: his war poems are in the tradition of the English Romantics and the French Decadents, and his passionate onslaught on the civilian conscience is a wartime version of the Decadent urge to shock.

~

Wilfred had perhaps not been altogether ignorant of Decadent conventions even at Dunsden, where he had affected a purple tie and purple slippers. Purple was the cult colour of Decadence, just as Chopin was one of its cult composers. When Wilfred made what was perhaps his first artistic response to the war, by playing Chopin's *Marche Funèbre* to Nénette and delighting in the child's soulful expression, he was making a 'beautiful gesture' that any Decadent might have approved of. He had rejected Evangelical religion on the grounds that it lacked 'imagination, physical sensation, aesthetic philosophy', and his knowledge of French late-Romantic principles was enormously extended by listening to Tailhade and reading the old poet's favourite authors. Wilfred seems to have written a good deal of poetry during the next twelve months, and enough of it survives to show that he became a more ambitious poet than he had been, in technique as well as in subject matter.

Tailhade's poems were available in two collected volumes, *Poèmes Élégiaques* and the satirical *Poèmes Aristophanesques*, the *élégiaque* lyrics being easier to understand than the satires. Wilfred started to rough out a translation of one of the lyrics, a 'Ballade élégiaque pour le morose après-midi', in which the poet resolves to escape from the 'common crowd' by retiring into the woods, his 'moon-white hair' decked with flowers, while music brings back memories, 'the roses of former times'.[12] *Ennui*, nostalgia, symbolic flowers, contempt for the crowd: all this is typical Decadent material. Even 'moon-white' is characteristic of the Decadent fondness for subtle variations of pallor and moonlight. 'Morose' is one of many stock words; others, such as 'sweet', 'strange', 'mystery', 'smile', 'exquisite', become conspicuous in Wilfred's later work. Decadent poets, their nerves exquisitely attuned to pleasure and pain, saw themselves as masters of strange, secret mysteries known only to the few. Wilfred became an initiate by studying Tailhade's work, finding the conventions thoroughly congenial, for they were, after all, only an extreme development of Romanticism.

Tailhade's lyrics tend to be derivative, but they were highly admired for their technical skill. Like other Decadents he was a fine craftsman, fascinated by the subtleties of language and adept at creating elaborate patterns of assonance, alliteration and internal rhyme. According to *L'Avenir*, he upset a local audience later in 1914 by arguing for disharmony in verse. Some of Wilfred's 1915 work shows a new interest in sound effects. Tailhade must deserve some credit for that, and perhaps for Wilfred's later experiments with disharmony, although pararhyme itself does not seem to have been used as a regular pattern by French poets. Tailhade would certainly have recommended Verlaine and the need for music above everything. Wilfred copied out Verlaine's well-known sonnet, 'Mon rêve familier', using it during the next few years as the model for more than a score of sonnets in the French style.

Avant-garde writers, including Ezra Pound and Richard Aldington in England, valued Tailhade as a satirist rather than a lyricist. Some of his *aristophanesques* poems were not unlike Harold Monro's 'Impressions', albeit much sharper and more explicit. The characters in Tailhade's *pays du mufle*, the land of the boor, range from middle-class suburbanites in their gardens to whores in vomit-stained bars; priests pass by on smelly feet, ancient actresses dream of the past and an old magistrate makes dirty suggestions to little girls; Jews sing praises to the deity that has deprived them of their foreskins; small boys go to church, 'dirai-je masturbés'; a respectable old lady longs for soldiers, rent-boys loiter in the dark and pious believers make themselves constipated with Good Friday food. The Légers urged Tailhade to satirise polite society at Bagnères, as perhaps he did. When a fund was set up for a local memorial to him after his death in 1919, Dr Cazalas is said to have been the only contributor.

With his sharp tongue and fiery, mercurial opinions, Tailhade was prone to making enemies. His memoirs attack old friends and deplore the excesses of the Decadents. Aggressively modern in some of his literary tastes, he was also a devoted champion of the great writers of the past, and in some ways he was thoroughly traditional. He believed poets should not try to create new kinds of feeling, as some of his contemporaries had wanted to do, but act as spokesmen for their age, working as hero-missionaries – and if necessary martyrs – in the undying cause of art and beauty. As for the war, he was as noisily patriotic, *cocoriquiste*, as anyone, writing articles in praise of France, even though he detested unthinking jingoism almost as much as German barbarism. He made an audience's flesh creep in 1914 by describing the horrors of the battlefield, yet in November of that year, with typical inconsistency and showmanship, he presented himself at a recruiting office alongside another elderly author,

Anatole France, to show support for the national effort, a 'beautiful gesture' that impressed Wilfred.

Tailhade probably spent little time talking about the war in Wilfred's company. The subject that most interested both of them was literature. Wilfred later made a rough attempt at a war poem in French on the back of his copy of Verlaine's sonnet, but its sentiments were conventional and he soon abandoned it. On the back of his translation of Tailhade's 'Ballade' there is a far more significant fragment, the lines about a boy that were perhaps a memory of Vivian Rampton.

> We two were friends while two short years outran
> The while he suffered that grand, crucial change
> The inalterable change, from boy to man …
>   … or would it after all
> Be better if I had not [touched] … [hand] seen his face?

Another rough draft almost certainly written at Bagnères recalls the birth of Wilfred's 'poethood' at Broxton, a memory revived by a walk on the Shropshire-like hills above the villa.

> Over the boscage of the foreign hills
> Floated the fullness of the [ruddy] moon
> There, for [an hour the memories of ten years]
> I so repassed into my life's arrears
> Even the weeks at Broxton by the Hill
>   … There was born
> [Out of a dark and disobedient] moon so sweet and [so forlorn]
> [My poethood][13]

These two fragments look back to two key experiences in his poetic career, his discoveries of love at Dunsden and natural beauty at Broxton. Meeting Tailhade seems to have prompted him to explore his identity and origins as a poet. The hints of illicit love in the first piece and disobedience in the second are appropriate – Tailhade would have thought nothing of a poet who remained within the bounds of respectable behaviour.

~

One more poem probably begun at the villa was the first of Wilfred's sonnets in Verlaine's style, 'The Sleeping Beauty'. The first draft recalls 'a [fair] house, secret 'mid hills / Where bode a marvellous Beauty'.[14] The Beauty is undoubtedly Nénette, sleeping though 'lithe of limb, and keen of glance'. '[She stirred not when I kissed her, flesh to flesh]', so he drew back, knowing it was not his part to 'light in her the fires of Consciousness'. The idea probably came from Tailhade's poems, several of which describe young girls whose virginity has not yet been touched by love, their lips knowing no kisses and their souls guarding 'le doux trésor' of a woman's secrets.[15] Wilfred was in an extraordinary position, caught between three admirers, Nénette, her mother and Tailhade. As at Dunsden, thinking about the child was a way of avoiding adult problems. Nénette never reappears in his letters after Bagnères, but it would have pleased him to know she was destined to become a writer herself, publishing three novels as well as translations of *Middlemarch*, *The Rainbow* and other English classics. At her early death she left an unfinished novel that opens with a description of herself and her parents visiting Bagnères in about 1909. Later chapters might well have introduced her mother's young tutor. She always remembered Wilfred with affection and was distressed when she heard he had been killed.[16]

Wilfred had been writing home from the villa at approximately weekly intervals, but no letters remain from the fortnight between 4 September, the day he dined at Tailhade's hotel, and the 18th, his first full day back at Bordeaux. A postcard he sent on the 18th refers to the 'momentous affair treated in my last letter'. He promised to write at more length in the evening, but that letter too has disappeared, so the 'momentous affair' at Bagnères, like the 'furor' at Dunsden in 1913, remains a mystery, except that on the 30th he told his mother not to worry because the 'Affair Léger' had been settled. Whatever the trouble was, it did not prevent him from staying with the Légers for almost another month, as had been agreed. The affair may not have involved him directly. It could have been a row between husband and wife, for instance: the 1913–14 Bordeaux directories list M. and Mme Léger alongside each other, but in 1915 Charles's name appears alone. Or perhaps Madame's flirtation with Wilfred came to some sort of crisis. He had toyed with the idea of returning home in October, and Madame had asked him to go with her as far as Le Havre, but in the event she travelled alone and there was no further talk of his accompanying her to Canada in the spring. One or two comments in his letters during the winter suggest he eventually decided to have nothing more to do with her, possibly on the grounds that she was neglecting Nénette.

It was a painful wrench to leave the villa on the 17th. Wilfred took his last farewell of the sunlit garden where he had spent some of the happiest hours of his life, and soon the mountains were dwindling into the distance as the train crawled north. The railway was clogged with military traffic, including numerous 'cages', as he called them, full of wounded Germans, so the journey took twelve hours. He and his hosts arrived at midnight in a city that had been transformed since he had left it seven weeks earlier in the last days of peace. Bordeaux was now the capital of France.

Freelance

Bordeaux

The French Government had moved to Bordeaux on 3 September, fleeing the German advance on Paris. President Poincaré was once again in residence at the *Préfecture*, while the Apollo Theatre, where Wilfred and Perry had demonstrated the *ballon dirigeable*, was now the senate chamber. The city's population had swollen by some fifty thousand, and the streets were full of smart Parisians, busy officials and important-looking people in uniform. Some locals were indignant at the expensive *toilettes* of the newly arrived ladies, but Wilfred remarked in a letter to Harold, adopting a suitably man-to-man tone, that beautiful women were what the fighting was all about.

Wilfred made some worrying discoveries on his first morning. The university had been taken over by the War Ministry, so he would not be able to take courses there as he had hoped. The Berlitz School had closed for want of custom. He called on the Lems, who said he would be welcome to stay with them when he left the Légers, but only for a week or so because after that their only spare room was to be occupied by a lodger. There seemed to be only two options: either to give up and go home, or to find enough freelance work to pay for food and rent, at a time when pupils seemed to be in short supply. It was too soon to admit defeat. Wilfred made enquiries, called on old acquaintances and introduced himself at the British Consulate, which happened to be only a few doors away from the Légers.

The Légers' imposing house at 12 Rue Blanc-Dutrouilh was an excellent base, being in an exclusive district near the Place des Quinconces. Nénette had gone back to her rural boarding school, and Wilfred was given her 'charming' room. There were images of the child everywhere in the house, photographs and sculptures, as well as a pretty statuette of her mother in the drawing room and a fine bust by Escoula of M. Léger. Wilfred was not invited to visit Madame's workrooms, where her team of three designers and several assistants made *broderies d'art* and other decorative items, but the finished products convinced him that she had a 'genius for Design'. He had expected to 'have the run' of M. Léger's theatre, the only one in Bordeaux where good classical and modern plays could be seen, but the war had put an end to most cultural activities, at least for the time being.

Life in the temporary French capital was exciting. Wilfred's friend Bizardel, who had written to him at least once in Bagnères, had access to confidential information, having been attached to the Prefect's Cabinet. He had the use of a chauffeur-driven car, sometimes taking Wilfred with him on his rounds. Once they dressed themselves up *en grand chic* and called on all the government ministers, giving themselves the air of 'tremendous diplomats', although all they really did was to leave the Prefect's card at each address. Occasionally they went to antique shops, when the Prefect, a keen collector, sent Bizardel out to inspect possible purchases.

Another former pupil, Dr Sauvaître, fulfilled a long-standing promise by taking Wilfred to watch surgical operations. Volunteer surgeons in the military hospital, a hastily converted school, were working on wounded soldiers, French and German alike, in a classroom where blood mingled with ink stains on floor, walls and ceiling. There were no anaesthetics and only one water tap. Wilfred sent Harold a detailed description of some of the more gruesome wounds, complete with diagrams, saying in his most elder-brotherly way, 'I deliberately tell you all this to educate you to the actualities of the war.'[1] He thought his steady nerves amid the ghastly sights and sounds were proof of his good health. They were also proof that he could cope with blood and horrors, finding them strangely educative and fascinating. The future war poet might be expected to have said something about the pity of war, but his letter gives no sign that such thoughts even crossed his mind.

Only one pupil had volunteered for lessons, and Wilfred glumly started looking through advertisements in *The Schoolmaster* again, noticing that temporary French teachers were wanted in Birkenhead and Chester. Determined to make full use of whatever time was left to him in France, he read and talked as much as he could, meeting 'dozens' of interesting people. He had recently been given a collection of poems by Carlos Larronde, considered to be one of the most promising young writers in the city, Larronde inscribing the book to 'M. Wilfred Owen avec ma cordiale sympathie et l'espoir que ces vers lui en feront aimer d'autres – plus beaux – des Poètes que j'aime'. No doubt Larronde recommended books, as Tailhade and others must have done, and Wilfred busied himself 'studying French Literature', as he told Susan on 30 September. On 11 October Mme Léger left for Le Havre on her way to Canada. Her departure brought her tutor's job to an end after ten marvellously rewarding weeks, and he moved himself to the Lems'. Summer weather continued for another week, then broke in miserable rain as though there had never been an autumn.

Wilfred made a strenuous effort to find work, soon telling his mother that he had raised just enough pupils to carry on until Christmas. He had in fact only recruited two, but more seemed likely to follow. Delaying his return meant missing Harold, who had got home safely from his first South American voyage and was now about to embark on another. As before, the brothers hoped to meet in La Rochelle, but at the end of October Harold once again wired that the *Esmeraldas* would not be calling there.[2] Wilfred was sad not to see him, but at least there was direct news of him and the rest of the family from Raoul Lem, who had just come back from Shrewsbury. Harold was apparently strong and quite grown up (a 'hard-case officer', as he describes himself, although he was in fact still a cadet). Mary had become a voluntary nurse, Colin, still at school, was in the Scouts and Tom had joined a part-time volunteer force.[3]

Journey from Obscurity caricatures Raoul at Mahim as a stereotypical Latin, effeminate, boastful, hysterical, fawning and dishonest, though oddly likeable. Harold's chronology is as erratic as ever and he places the story well before August 1914, thereby missing the fact that poor Raoul had been in England during the first terrible weeks of the war, when France had seemed on the edge of defeat. Fortunately Susan seems to have been her usual motherly yet determined self, eventually taming her young guest so that he became 'her adoring slave'.[4] Harold says that in the end Raoul was sent home because he kept eating poisonous toadstools, but a more likely reason is that his college term was about to start. He and his parents were grateful to Susan, even suggesting she should come and stay with them.

The Lems' house was very unlike the Légers'. It was scrupulously clean and tidy, but small and sparsely furnished, Wilfred's room containing little more than a bed and chair. He described the district as 'poor but not low'. At six o'clock every morning lorries started thundering over the *pavé* below his window, while a neighbouring cooper rolled barrels about and stacked iron strips, and the donkey in the yard brayed loudly for its breakfast. Things were quieter in the afternoons, when Wilfred could watch children going home from school, a sight that always made him feel 'tender and poetical', but he was not sorry his stay had to be brief. His ever-helpful hosts found him a cheap attic room behind the docks, with a view over thousands of roofs and chimneys, and he was attracted by the romance of living in a proper garret.

Then a message came from the Consul that a lady, wife to one of France's most senior generals, wanted a tutor for her nephew, the Viscount de Maud'huy. A garret would hardly do as a classroom for a titled pupil, so Wilfred hastily chose more respectable lodgings at 31 Rue Desfourniel, in a quiet corner near the temporary Ministry of Justice, usually the law courts. He moved on 19 October, M. Lem bringing his possessions, which now filled three trunks, on the donkey cart. The new room was delightful, with a big window overlooking a little square. The ample furnishings included four armchairs, a genuine Louis XV bureau, no fewer than thirty pictures and even a piano. There was also a little dressing room with another big window, facing east so that he could wash and dress in sunlight when there was any. The landlady, Mme Martin, a widow with a son at the war, was as kindly as Susan could have wished.

Sitting at the bureau to write a letter home, Wilfred surveyed his new surroundings with some satisfaction. The room was far pleasanter than the one he had occupied all the previous winter. Ten or eleven pupils had come forward, so his income looked likely to be adequate. He had even found a course in French after all, at Raoul's college, so he had started going there for free evening lectures. He thought the students and teachers had deplorable accents, but that was a measure of how good his own had become after conversations with M. Léger. Above all, he was his own master for the first time in his life.

> And the feeling that I am under obligations to no man, is as sweet as it is new. For the moment I have neither schoolmaster nor taskmaster, neither patron nor boss. I have slain … four tyrants: first, Timpany, who taxed his subjects with grievous work; next Lightbown, a bullying boss; next Wigan, who essayed to dominate one's entire being; next Aumont, unmercifully grinding, being goaded by avarice.

The new room turned out to be not really necessary because he was required to teach the Viscount and probably most of the other pupils in their own homes. He went to the Viscount twice a week for two hours each session. The young man was nineteen and about to spend several months in England. His aunt had wanted a moral guide for him, explaining that he was worryingly 'flighty', but Wilfred had declined the role, being obviously too young for it. It was enjoyable to be teaching an aristocrat, but after barely three weeks, just as a friendship was developing, the Viscount left for England, saying he looked forward to meeting Wilfred there in due course.

The other pupils included two agreeable girls, working for exams; another girl, pretty but less agreeable; two charming little boys; a Russian professor of mathematics, who lasted no longer than the Viscount; the Lems' new lodger, accompanied by Raoul, who annoyed Wilfred by fooling about; young Pierre Berthaud, whom Wilfred had taught at the Berlitz School; and Auguste Peyronnet, a manufacturer of perfumes. Wilfred had been to M. Peyronnet's house in July, enjoying the garden and the scents from the laboratory, and had almost certainly translated letters for him. He probably went there again, and he often visited the Berthauds, who were as hospitable as ever. Pierre was still expected to work hard, but Wilfred sometimes connived at his playing truant, on one occasion letting him down badly when the boy passed him a secret message to expect an afternoon visit. The trusted tutor went off to buy soda water and liquorice for a French version of the tea party with Vivian in 1912, only to realise with horror that he had left Pierre's note on the Berthauds' table, where the parents inevitably found it.

Of the other people Wilfred had been looking up in the town, his letters mention only one, a fifteen-year-old named André Martin who had got talking to him at the *Union Chrétienne* in the summer. Remembering André's eyes and face as the 'most romantically beautiful' he had ever seen, Wilfred sought out the Martins' house in a shabby district and found the family in great distress, with the father dying. The mother implored their English visitor to be a friend and counsellor to her sons. André appears only once more in the letters, ten months later in August 1915, but he clearly became a devoted friend. Wilfred's first mention of him is emotional, partly because of the father's death, and the second is unconvincingly casual. It is unlikely that there was any overtly sexual element in the friendship, especially after the mother's trusting appeal, but Wilfred's long silence about the family is curious.[5] He seems to have been more interested in André than he liked to admit to Susan. He told her the Léger 'episodes' had not taken the bloom off his innocence, but it was not quite true. After Madame's compliments and Tailhade's caresses, Wilfred was more self-aware than he had been, watching himself and others with a knowing, *aristophanesque* eye, able to see sexual implications in behaviour that might have seemed innocent before. Robert Graves said many years later that Wilfred had picked up young men in Bordeaux, but had felt too guilty to form any lasting relationships. Graves's stories are often unreliable, but he claimed to have had this one from Wilfred himself in 1918.[6] Wilfred's letters give no evidence one way or the other, but he was undoubtedly longing for intimacy in the autumn of 1914. 'I ought to be in love and am not … I lack any touch of tenderness. I ache in soul, as my bones might ache after a night spent on a cold, stone floor.'

Wilfred occupied himself with lessons and the evening lectures, 'visits on & by friends', 'my interesting books' and suppers in restaurants with a group of talkative students from several countries. His activities were a good excuse for not writing home as often as in less sociable times. On 31 October he called on M. Léger, who reported that Madame had arrived safely at Montreal. Wilfred told Susan that French people such as Léger, Tailhade and their friends were wonderfully intelligent in their conversation, and he lamented the intellectual poverty of her own circle in Shrewsbury with its endless church gossip. Susan stepped up her complaints about her health and sent him more religious magazines, but her world was too small for him now. He began hinting that he might return to Bordeaux after Christmas.

One of his strangest poems is dated 31 October 1914, the day he visited Léger. Only one manuscript survives, a fair copy written in a curiously childish hand with some deliberate spelling mistakes; he gave it to Osbert Sitwell in 1918, perhaps meaning Sitwell to read it as mere juvenilia. Critics have said it shows the influence of Wilde and Swinburne, but the more direct influence is French. 'Long ages past' is Wilfred's first exercise in the Decadent manner, and it shows how much he had learned in the two months since he had met Tailhade.

> *Long ages past in Egypt thou wert worshipped …*
> *Thy feet were dark with blood of sacrifice.*
> *From dawn to midnight, O my painted idol,*
> *Thou satest smiling, and the noise of killing*
> *Was harp and timbrel in thy pale jade ears.*

The idol is at first imagined as a statue, perhaps a sphinx, made of ivory and precious stones. Then it becomes a king's mad slave in ancient Persia:

> *Thou slewest women and thy pining lovers,*
> *And on thy lips the stain of crimson blood,*
> *And on thy brow the pallor of their death.*

Finally the image is generalised into a beautiful, terrible face reflected in a mirror, the face of 'wild desire, of pain, of bitter pleasure'. 'Long ages past' has sometimes been regarded as a war poem, but only because it is by Wilfred Owen and dated 1914. It is about what Mario Praz called the 'Romantic Agony', the persistent theme of Romanticism from Keats and Shelley to Flaubert and Verlaine: the mysterious power of erotic desire, combining pain and pleasure, often symbolised as a face that attracts and destroys, the face of a fatal lover, a Gorgon, deathly white, with blood-red lips and terrible eyes. Wilfred knew about these things in himself, as well as from books, but he may have been imitating or even translating a French poem, or deliberately experimenting with Decadent imagery. He was learning a poetic language that was to continue into his later work: *femmes fatales* sending men to death, the 'pallor of girls' brows', bleeding mouths, mass sacrifice – these and similar images in the 1917–18 poems have some of their origins in the 'interesting books' he read in France.

All Souls' Day came again, and again the bells tolled for the dead, but this time he was untroubled by the noise, thinking how much better off he was now than in 1913. He had found a few more pupils to fill the gaps left by the Viscount and the professor, and he told his mother, perhaps rather optimistically, that his earnings were now about the same as his Berlitz salary. Nevertheless, November brought an ominous change. On the 6th he said he had heard that 'Tailhade, together with Anatole France, is shouldering a rifle! Now I *may* be led into enlisting when I get home: so familiarise yourself with the idea! It is a sad sign if I *do*: for it means that I shall consider the continuation of my life of no use to England.' He would not hesitate to join up, he said, if he thought the war was threatening the 'perpetuity and supremacy' of his mother-tongue. This letter marks a crucial moment, the first stage in the long process of decision that was to take him into the British Army almost a year later. He had not talked seriously about enlisting before – what had made him change his mind was the news about Tailhade. As Wilfred well knew, the only possible reason for the veteran anarchist's joining the ranks was that French language and culture seemed to be in peril. Far from influencing Wilfred against volunteering, Tailhade was indirectly responsible for turning his mind towards it.

Had Wilfred kept to his plan of returning to England for good at the end of 1914, he would probably have joined up within a few months under pressure from recruiting propaganda. He nearly did return. His financial position was precarious, the supply of pupils unpredictable and his former employer, Maurice Aumont, now also freelance, was a potentially hostile rival. The two men passed in the street one day, Aumont looking as ruthless as ever, but fortunately Wilfred was unrecognisable behind suntan, moustache and new winter cloak. Staying in Bordeaux would have its risks, but in late November going home began to seem much riskier, following reports of German submarines sinking merchant shipping. The French mainland, by contrast, seemed safer than before, and the Government was about to return to Paris. Wilfred was still dithering, reluctant to hurt his mother's feelings, when the Vice-Consul's sister, Miss Patterson, sent a message that a lady was looking for a tutor. Wilfred went to see Miss Patterson and the prospective employer, Mlle Anne de la Touche, and on 8 December he wrote to Susan that he had decided to stay for another month.

~

Anne de la Touche, charming, grey-haired, in her early fifties, lived at Mérignac, a village just outside the city. She was indeed a lady, being a member of a distinguished old Huguenot family that had settled in Ireland and maintained links with France. She had been in the service of the Belgian royal family as governess to some of the young princesses, and Wilfred was pleased to find she was distantly related to Ruskin's adored Rose La Touche. Mademoiselle's sister, the Baronne de Bock, lived in

Bordeaux – the Baron had an insurance office in the Place des Quinconces – but their brother was working for the British customs service in China, where he had married an Englishwoman and produced four sons and four daughters. The two eldest boys were to be Wilfred's charges.

The youngest boys, ten-year-old twins, David and Charles de la Touche, were living with their 'Aunt Nanny' at Mérignac. Their elder brothers, Johnny and Bobbie, aged fourteen and twelve, had come over for the summer from England, where they were boarders at Downside School, and the outbreak of war had prevented them from getting back. They had spent the autumn term at an unsatisfactory school in Bordeaux. Mademoiselle was nervous of having to cope with all four boys during the Christmas holidays; there had been a disaster in the summer, when Charles had broken his pelvis during a rowdy game, and the ensuing operation had been horribly expensive. Wilfred's duties would be to help the two eldest boys catch up on work for Downside and escort them back there in January. He would also supervise all four brothers during some of their free time. The twins were being taught by governesses, including Miss Patterson.

That His Majesty's Consul in Bordeaux, Arthur Langford Sholto Rowley, heir to a barony, and the Vice-Consul, James Patterson, were happy to recommend Wilfred to the Viscountess de Maud'huy and to Mlle de la Touche shows how readily they accepted him as a gentleman, even though there may have been lingering traces of Birkenhead in his English accent. Wilfred himself was as conscious as ever of his true social back-ground. The de la Touche boys impressed him as 'English thoroughbreds', with their 'delicious' public-school slang and 'elegant' vowels ('get off the grahss, silly ahss!'). He must have been careful not to revive the Sir Thomas story, which could easily have been checked in the Consulate's reference books, but Mademoiselle was given to understand that he was 'preparing for Oxford'.[7] Privately he was still hoping to try for Reading if he had to go home, and he told Susan on 14 December that when he returned he would discuss his future with her and then with either a professor or a recruiting sergeant. Teaching the boys Latin would be useful revision for the scholar-ship exam. As for the army, he was moved by attacks in the *Daily Mail* on young men who were playing football instead of volunteering, but he concluded that 'while those ten thousand lusty louts go on playing football I shall go on playing with my little axiom:- that my life is worth more than my death to Englishmen'.

Mademoiselle had at first thought of taking lodgings for him and his two pupils, but she decided to pack them and an invalid friend of hers, Mlle de Puységur, into her own small house, Le Châlet. There were only five rooms altogether, four on the ground floor and a tiny bedroom in the roof. The four boys fitted themselves into one of the ground-floor bedrooms, and Wilfred gladly agreed to occupy the attic, having always had a taste for eyries. On Saturday 19 December he vacated his lodgings at Rue Desfourniel, and hired a four-wheeler to take him and his luggage out to Mérignac. It had been agreed that he would have free board and lodging, but no pay. He would give morning lessons to his regular pupils in the city as usual, returning at lunchtime to supervise the boys and teach Johnny and Bobbie. This was a gratifying bargain, saving him virtually all expenses except tram fares. Cramped though the house was, life there was very civilised, with a manservant, two maids and an excellent cook living in a cottage in the big garden. Wilfred said he was more comfortable than he had been even at Dunsden. Mademoiselle was very kind to him and clearly devoted to her nephews, although having lived in a royal palace she was 'a stickler for correctness', especially at table.

Wilfred soon settled into the routine he was to keep for the next four months. Hot water was delivered to his door each morning, and after a two-egg breakfast he made the twenty-minute tram journey into Bordeaux in time to start lessons at nine. He taught as many pupils as he could manage, even having to turn some away. On the busiest days he remained in town for lunch, but the food at the house was 'smashin'', as the boys said, and it cost him nothing, so whenever possible he ate there. In the afternoons he often took the boys and their local playmates on expeditions. They had the freedom of several big estates in the vicinity, Mérignac being still largely rural, with woods, orchards and châteaux. The boys were friendly with the children of Admiral Castéjas at the Château du Parc with its candle-snuffer towers and orangery, the largest private house Wilfred had ever seen.

Returning to the Châlet by five, everyone had tea and toast before Wilfred set to work for two hours with his pupils, teaching them English grammar, Shakespeare, Roman history, maths and Latin, although he could not add Greek, a subject they needed practice in. Mademoiselle approved of his methods, reporting to the headmaster of Downside that Mr Owen 'teaches ... in a most interesting way'. The two boys were attentive, intelligent and virtually bilingual, though not very well informed (Miss Patterson had unfairly described them as 'thick'), and their tutor enjoyed being able to use the knowledge he had acquired for Matric. Dinner was at seven. Prayers were held at about nine, Wilfred standing respectfully in the background, for the de la Touches were Roman Catholics, the family having returned to the old religion in the 1860s. After the boys had gone to bed, he sat for half an hour with Mademoiselle, smoking and chatting, then read for a while and went to bed.

At Christmas 1914, instead of going to St Julian's with his family as he might have done if the Mérignac job had not been offered to him, he accompanied his 'kindest of hostesses – *employers* is not the word', to midnight mass with her nephews. They took Mlle Puységur with them, wheeling her carriage into the sanctuary, so that Wilfred found himself 'all mixed up with candles, incense, acolytes, chasuble and such like'. Some people at home would have been scandalised to see him there, he remarked to Susan, but 'candlegrease and embroidery' were not likely to Romanise him. 'The question is to un-Greekize me.' What most caught his attention were 'the dear, darling little acolytes' trying to keep awake.

A British battleship, the *Formidable*, was sunk in the Channel on 1 January 1915.[8] The news alarmed Mademoiselle, and there was much debate about whether Johnny and Bobby should be sent back to Downside or not. The headmaster and their father wrote that they should go, but neighbours and a marine insurance agent, one of Wilfred's pupils, said the sea was too dangerous. The Consul would not commit himself, and Wilfred followed his example, feeling coolly English. The boys themselves being keen to stay, it was finally decided they should do so until the spring, provided Wilfred would stay too. He was happy to agree, flattered to be preferred to Downside.

The war sometimes nagged at his conscience. He took the boys out shooting in the woods, where the sound of their erratic firing mingled with the boom of artillery from nearby training grounds and the buzz of a spotter plane. 'And I thought of the thousand redeemers by whose blood my life is being redeemed.' Reading the casualty lists was like reading Christ's lament over Jerusalem or Severn's account of Keats's death, 'neither readable without tears'. When Wilfred heard that German ships had attacked Scarborough, one shell blowing up a group of schoolboys, he 'raved'. Biblical and literary phrases about war, redeemers and 'the end' kept coming into his mind. In what was perhaps his first poem about the war, the sonnet '1914', he used Shakespearian language to express a typically Decadent view of modern history as a slow, inevitable autumn, 'rich with all increase', leading now to winter and 'the need / Of sowings for new Spring, and blood for seed'. News of his Shrewsbury and Birkenhead contemporaries made him feel guilty at the contrast between his current life and their discomforts in the army, but then he thought of 'certain happenings' in his past, presumably his ordeal at Dunsden, and decided he was entitled to enjoy himself for a while yet.[9]

Every now and then someone urged him to think about his future. Peyronnet the scent manufacturer, 'a very "business" businessman', was keen for him to go into trade. When Wilfred mentioned Uncle Ted Quayle, Peyronnet was enthusiastic: the army had no use for scent, alas, but his friends the bootmaker and the bicycle maker were making fortunes from government contracts, and no doubt the English tin merchant could do the same. Wilfred was excited too, thinking Bizardel might be able to get him interviews with War Ministry officials, some of whom were still in

Bordeaux. But either Tom Owen declined to approach Quayle, or Quayle himself showed no interest, so the dream of profiteering was short-lived. Peyronnet then started talking of sending Wilfred to Egypt as a commercial traveller, a scheme that seemed a possibility for some months.[10] A trip to Egypt would be a great adventure, but commerce had no attraction, as Wilfred told Susan in mid-January. He reckoned he might make plenty of money, but only at the cost of his soul. Rowley startled him one day by recommending a career in the consular service, but the only attraction about that was that it would involve living in Spain to learn a second foreign language. Wilfred concluded that one thing at least was certain: the profession of 'Assistant Elementary Certificated or Uncertificated Schoolmaster' was no longer to be considered. One of the wisest steps in his life was the one he had not taken, to proceed to training college in 1911. John Bulman had told him he needed a course in the university of life. 'I have taken that Course,' Wilfred said, 'and my diplomas are sealed with many secret seals.'

Several other early 1915 letters hint at secret knowledge. When his father wrote, probably in response to the tin scheme, advising him to think of making a 'comfortable future' for himself because his current way of life seemed to be leading nowhere, Wilfred replied – to Susan, but knowing she usually passed his thoughts on to Tom – with unusual care, asking her to preserve the letter because he kept no diary. Harold later destroyed nearly three pages of the final letter and probably some of the draft, but enough remains of both to show that Wilfred was bitter at what he regarded as Quayle's selfishness. All he wanted, he said, was capital to get himself started. The years since 1911 had not been wasted. '[In Dunsden] I have made soundings in Deep waters, and I have looked out from many observation towers: and I found the deep waters terrible, and nearly lost my breath there.'[11] He might seem aimless, but he had in fact had a single aim for years. Even as a boy he had guessed that 'the fullest, largest liveable life was that of a Poet. I *know* it now …'. He had grown out of 'the B.A. Craze' and 'the "Reverend" pretension' (though here he prudently assured his mother he had not stopped his ears to a call from above). He had no desire to run a school or a business. 'There is *one* title I prize, one clear call audible, one Sphere where I may influence for Truth, one workshop whence I may send forth Beauty, one mode of living entirely congenial to me.' And in order to be a poet he would have to study: hence the need for money. 'Shall Poverty leave me unlaunched? Shall my Timidity bar me? Shall my Indolence moor me to the mud?'

He was no longer unsure which art to follow. The time had come to start work on a big poem, something to justify his long period of silence. He said in mid-February that he had not 'thought poetically' for over a year, 'at least not by act of will'. He had sown his 'wild oats' by being idle as a poet, and poppies might now be growing among them, 'poppies where-with many dreams may be fed, and many sores be medicined …'. He also said he had not read any poetry; he had in fact read some, but much of his reading in French may have been prose. Now all he wanted was 'pure strong poetry' – and here again a page is 'missing', perhaps because it contained comments on some of his interesting French books (in this instance, very unusually, the censor seems to have been Susan, who has added a date to the next page). 'All that novelists have to tell has been told me, and by the best of them. I have even found out more. And that *more* which I had not been told I feel I ought to tell.' As he was to say in 'Strange Meeting' later, the poet's task was to tell 'the truth untold' and act as a social healer. Once again he was determined to 'seriously and shamelessly work out a Poem', as he had tried to do in the spring. He looked out the fifty-odd lines he had scribbled 'not by act of will', maybe after the Henriette episode, and wrote at the top, 'For Perseus'.

So little remains of Wilfred's long poem about Perseus that no one will ever know what the finished work might have looked like. Maybe he never knew himself, although he must have thought of it as some kind of epic. All that survives are a few fragments, three of them written on a type of paper he used for letters from the Châlet in March–April 1915. Another seems to date from 1917 and even in 1918 he was still hoping to finish the project. All the fragments are unfinished and unpromising, but they contain the seeds of much of his later work. He aimed to put his secret knowledge into 'Perseus', and for the rest of his life he drew on the ideas and images he had stored up for the poem.[12]

One of the 1915 manuscripts is about Perseus's mother, Danae. In the original story she was locked up in a tower to keep her from men, but Zeus fell in love with her and entered the tower window as a ray of sunlight or shower of gold. The fragment describes her intense longing, using imagery of trees that 'shook and were bowed' in the embrace of a storm; 'then the whole sky fell / In vortices of flashings and showering gold', and from this 'sprang the infant Perseus, / Fair from the moment of his birth'. From this also sprang Wilfred's mysterious later sonnet, 'Storm', with its image of the poet as a tree, 'tremulous, bowed', attracting lightning from a beautiful face in a moment of ravishment that will result in the birth of poetry. One element in 'Perseus' would probably have been the familiar Romantic theme of poetic creation and the poet's agony. Another would have been frustrated sexual desire. Several of the fragments use imagery of dark woods to suggest strong feelings, the 'horrors of an obscene mind … afraid of self'. Wilfred hoped to use the myth as a means of exploring his own concerns, much as Keats had used the stories of Endymion and Hyperion. Private experiences could be projected into classical characters. The fiery descent of Eros and the lover's hellish torments in the fifty lines Wilfred had marked as raw material 'For Perseus' now become the descent of Zeus and the suffering of Danae. Later the imagery shed its classical trappings and culminated in such poems as 'Spring Offensive', where the 'whole sky' burns against the soldiers, and 'Mental Cases', where the victims shake incessantly in the tortures of a wartime underworld.

One of the 'Perseus' manuscripts has no connection with the traditional legend, except that it is marked 'Danae speaks'. The subject is a youth in the grip of helpless passion, his eyes dark 'with gloom of death and hell' and his mouth red 'like fresh, uncovered blood'. His eyes and fingers tremble unceasingly, and his scalp sweats (the madmen in 'Mental Cases' have these same symptoms, typical signs of shellshock). Wilfred then tries to make the sketch more literary by describing the boy as a hermaphrodite, a favourite Decadent subject, and adding a classical veneer with the title, 'The cultivated Rose (From the Greek)'. 'The question is to un-Greekize me': the manuscript was probably written in the months after Bagnères, when Wilfred was studying Decadent literature, with its frequent references to Greek statues and Greek love.

'Perseus' was not only going to be about poetry and sexuality. It was also going to be a war poem. One of the 1915 fragments introduces a huge, iron-throated 'Beast' and an Emperor frowning 'imperially', clearly the German Army and the Kaiser. Allied propagandists held the Kaiser personally responsible for the war and often referred to his nation as 'the Beast', calling up echoes of Nietzsche's 'blond beast' and the Beast in the Book of Revelation. Like the great majority of people in France and Britain, Wilfred saw no reason to disagree with such views. He went on to draft a line about ministers smiling 'ministerially' – a direct link to his later war poems, where the frowning emperor and smiling ministers turn up again in preliminary work for 'The Dead-Beat'. The link to Greek legend is the beast: Perseus rescued Andromeda by killing a sea monster, attacking it from the air.

One reason for Wilfred's choice of Perseus as a subject must have been that the Greek hero could fly. The poem was probably started in rivalry with Leslie Gunston, who was certainly writing a long poem on another Greek hero, Icarus, in July 1915. Leslie was a great admirer of the British pilot, Gustav Hamel, who had crashed into the sea, a modern Icarus, in May 1914, and Wilfred had marvelled at Roland Garros, now an ace in France's fledgeling air force. Garros could be seen as a new Perseus, swooping down out of the sky to rescue Andromeda-France from the German monster. Unfortunately he was soon shot down and captured, which rather spoiled the story. Another problem would have been giving a contemporary slant to Perseus's ultimate weapon, the Gorgon's head, which turned anyone who looked at it into stone.[13] Wilfred may never have got as far as solving such difficulties, but the Gorgon's paralysing stare had haunted his poetry since 1911, in the end proving more important to him than anything else in the ancient legend.

There was little time for sustained writing. The de la Touche boys were energetic, often filling the little house with the noise of their boots and voices, giving their aunt severe migraines. Wilfred was a strict disciplinarian, sometimes giving lines or sending a boy to bed. Once he caned Johnny for not getting down from a tree when told to, and on the same day he beat David with a ruler for touching an orange at the Château. On the whole, though, his charges were well-behaved and friendly, in due course becoming affectionate. When he threatened to give David five strokes one day in July, he felt his hair being caressed ('not an unusual procedure') and heard David saying, 'I'm giving *you* the *strokes* instead.' Afternoon activities were sometimes hilarious, Wilfred drawing on his store of family games. As at Dunsden he had a favourite among the boys: when the time came to leave Mérignac he admitted that he would part more sorrowfully with one of them than with the others. He could have meant Johnny ('pretty rather than handsome') or David, the most mischievous and entertaining of the four, or Bobbie, who wrote to him several times later. Outwardly, no doubt, the tutor tried to be impartial. He took his job seriously, sending lengthy reports to the boys' father in China. The father wrote to Mademoiselle that M. Owen's comments were clear-sighted and fair, but so young a man naturally lacked the experience that would enable him to distinguish between childishness and signs of promise.[14]

The plan was still for Wilfred to take the boys to England in time for the summer term at Downside. Another reason for him to return at that time emerged in March, when the local paper published a letter from the British Consulate advertising a British Industries Fair to be held in London from 10 to 21 May. This was to be a trade exhibition by manufacturers of domestic goods, aimed at finding new export markets to replace those lost in Germany and Austria. Peyronnet seems to have taken notice. The opening of the Gallipoli campaign had made Wilfred's projected trip to Egypt look unlikely, but it would be worth sending a representative to the fair.

In mid-March Wilfred developed what he thought was influenza. He spent a few days in bed, in his 'little pill-box of a room', unable to read, talk or swallow, while Mademoiselle hurried up and down the stairs with 'gargles, inhalations, paintings, poultices, pastilles, hot drinks, and cold drinks, eau-de-Cologne, Bandage, Thermometer, and such like, not forgetting the country doctor'. She was anxious, as her patient later discovered, because the doctor diagnosed 'Diphtheric Throat', but the boys were unaffected and Wilfred was soon well again. Lengthy illnesses and slow convalescence were of no interest to him any more.

He accompanied the de la Touches to church in Holy Week for the annual rite of the Veneration of the Cross, when the congregation filed up to kiss a silver crucifix. He went again on Easter Sunday, 4 April 1915, for 'real, genuine Mass, with candle, with book, and with bell, and all like abominations of desolation'. He promised Susan he had emerged from these services 'an hour and a half older: *otherwise unchanged'*. No doubt he observed the 'dear, darling little acolytes', as he had done at Christmas.[15] The ritual of the Veneration later became the subject of his sonnet 'Maundy Thursday', in which the crucifix is held in the brown hands of an acolyte. The men kiss the crucifix as an emblem, the women as the true body of Christ, and the children as a silver doll. Then the poet kneels in his turn, seeing the Christ as 'thin, and cold, and very dead', yet he bows his head and kisses, too, ' – my lips did cling. / (I kissed the warm live hand that held the thing.)' 'Maundy Thursday' is Wilfred's wittiest, most accomplished effort in Tailhade's satirical style. Its polished insouciance suggests it was written well after the event it describes, perhaps in 1916.

Plans for travel were once again interrupted. Admiral Castéjas, the Baronne de Bock and others advised Mademoiselle that the Channel was more dangerous than ever, so after another flurry of enquiries she decided not to send the boys back to Downside after all. She wanted Wilfred to stay on, feeling sure Johnny and Bobbie had made great strides under his tuition, but Peyronnet wanted him to be in London by the end of April, ready for the trade fair, and Wilfred agreed to go. Mademoiselle dreaded the prospect of having sole responsibility for the boys, but perhaps a temporary tutor could be found. Wilfred himself half-hoped to find a permanent substitute, telling Susan he would like a month at Shrewsbury in which to devote himself to 'certain writings'. He explained that a poem could not 'grow by jerks'. It had to develop 'naturally as leaves to a tree', as Keats had said. 'And as trees in Spring produce a new ring of tissue, so does every poet put forth a fresh, and lasting outlay of stuff at the same season.'

The spring at Mérignac was magnificent. Wilfred's companion on woodland walks, successor to Vivian and Henriette, was the 'seraphic-faced', eight-year-old heir to the Castéjas estate.

> Into his woods we go in the hot afternoons; into the woods we go; and the floor of the coppice surges with verdure; the meadows heave with new grass as the sea with a great tide; the violets are not shy as in England but push openly and thickly; the anemones are dense like weeds, and the primroses like the yellow sands of the sea. And there the nightingale ever sings; but I had rather she did not, for she sings a minor key. And the idyll becomes an ode-elegiac.

This passage, with its sense of pressing fecundity, might almost be by D.H. Lawrence, although the last two words are an allusion to Tailhade, and the description may owe something to Tailhade's poem, 'Lundi de Pâques', a celebration of nature's spring urge to generation, in which children gather lilac and narcissi while the sun impregnates the earth. As the plants grow towards fruition and the boy towards his inheritance, so the poet is driven by the same natural imperative towards his new outlay of writing. Wilfred was brooding on the Perseus legend and how it might be developed. In response to some news from home, apparently that his brother had failed to get promotion, he wrote that Perseus had been a sailor lad and had never worn 'epaulets on his brown shoulders or gold-braid on his bare chest; but his name is written in stars'.[16]

On 13 April Wilfred attended a lecture at the Alhambra Theatre in Bordeaux by the well-known poet, Jean Richepin. The large audience greeted the speaker with thunderous applause, and was rewarded with an uplifting patriotic sermon on 'The three miracles of France': Joan of Arc, the soldiers of the Revolution, and the 'passionate, tranquil heroism' of the troops now at the front. All France was united, Richepin declared, and even women could not hate a war that was being fought for the mother-land. After more applause, there were patriotic songs and recitations about Alsace, then the Marseillaise and a final storm of cheering. Wilfred thought it was a 'glorious' finish to his stay in France. Earlier in the day he had met a Welshman named Bonsall, 'public school man', who was willing to teach the boys in his absence and perhaps even to replace him for good.

A few days later everything seemed to be disrupted yet again. Wilfred developed what appeared to be measles, his eyes and face swelling alarmingly. He worked as usual for a day, though feeling far from well. Next morning the boys took the unheard-of liberty of bursting into his room, exclaiming that he had given his spots to Bobbie, and within an hour or two Johnny began showing symptoms, too. Luckily the infection turned out to be much less serious than everyone expected, disappearing within a few days.[17] Mademoiselle was still anxious for Wilfred to return after his London expedition, although at the last minute she heard that some relations of Mlle Puységur wanted to come and stay, so his room would be needed. He seems to have bargained for an absence of about six weeks, as well as for payment towards the cost of alternative accommodation and his return fare, and it was finally agreed that he would come back for the summer on those terms.

On Monday 3 May he took the night train to Paris, where he put up at a hotel for at least one night, having forewarned Tailhade of his arrival. The old poet signed a copy of *Poèmes Élégiaques*, 'en souvenir de nos belles causeries et des beaux soirs à La Gailleste / Paris, le 4 mai 1915', and gave him a taste of cultural life in the capital, apparently taking him to a concert and introducing him to a composer, Xavier Leroux.[18] After a little sight-seeing Wilfred went on to Calais, where the station must have been full of

British troops, and where he himself would return within two years, bound for the trenches. He probably paused in London to start his mission for Peyronnet. It may have been during his onward journey to Shrewsbury that he shared his train compartment with the young sailor described in his undated ballad, 'It was a navy boy'.[19] According to the poem, the sailor, a golden-haired, silken-muscled hero, had just returned from Hong Kong on a ship laden with explosives, a cargo that would win another mile for France. His courage, and his devotion to his mother, cleanse the poet from 'a cowardice', presumably a lingering reluctance to enlist. It was uncomfortable to be a young male civilian in England, even if one did look French. Even at Mahim, perhaps, there was a slight sense of awkwardness.

Wilfred was back in London by 19 May, staying at Cranston's Waverley Hotel,[20] not far from Harold Monro's Poetry Bookshop, which he may well have visited. He spent a happy time at the Royal Academy summer show, and found a gold purse, a good omen he thought, in the Brompton Road, where he may have gone to see the museums. After much travelling in lifts and buses, he got himself a ticket as a bona fide trader and gained entry to the fair, which was being held at the Royal Agricultural Hall in Islington. He worked busily, presumably arranging a display of Peyronnet's scents, maybe for the Peace Pillow Company, a firm listed in the catalogue as exhibiting perfumes with warlike names such as 'Esprit de Liège'. He may also have been in search of bottles; several of the six hundred stands were displaying specialised glass, a field which Germany had dominated before the war. Among the many other exhibits were toys, including some clockwork Allies who could be made to toss the Kaiser in a blanket.

Wilfred said he had a 'prime object' in London other than the fair. He may have meant finding an agent for Peyronnet, which was certainly part of his commission. Or perhaps he had decided to enquire about enlisting. It was a dramatic time to be in the capital. The sinking of the *Lusitania* on 9 May had intensified public demands that the war effort should be made more effective. On the 18th sensational news had broken that the Liberal Government had fallen, and that a coalition was to be formed, still with H.H. Asquith as Prime Minister. Lloyd George was expected to become 'organiser of the war'. In the House of Lords that afternoon the current Minister for War, Lord Kitchener, who looked likely to lose his job, made a call for another 300,000 men, an appeal that appeared as a full-page newspaper advertisement next morning. Recruiting posters were everywhere. 'Are YOU in this?' 'Why aren't YOU in khaki?' 'Have you a Reason or only an Excuse ... ?' 'Will they never come?' 'The Only Way.' On the afternoon of the 19th Wilfred managed to get into a patriotic meeting at the Guildhall, to hear Asquith and other politicians. Bonar Law, soon to become a cabinet minister, said to cheers that when a venomous reptile was loose the only thing to be done was to kill the 'monster'. Wilfred must have appreciated that. Scanning the assembly on the platform, he spotted the Archbishop of Canterbury and Rudyard Kipling. 'I feel intensely happy in dear London!' he told Susan, later remarking that he found the bustle, noise and smells of the city 'the very best strengthener of nerves'.[21]

He went back to Shrewsbury after the fair and probably worked on his epic for a week or two, taking advantage of the 'idle, protected, loving, wholesome, hidden, intimate, sequestered' life that was always available at Mahim. Then he went to Alpenrose, no doubt keen to discuss the new poem with Leslie and hear about Leslie's plans for 'Icarus'. Professor Morley still had some of Wilfred's old poems, so he retrieved them from her at the college, telling Leslie afterwards that she thought he had managed to 'slip into *Poetry*' here and there in 'The Little Mermaid'. The main news at Alpenrose was that Herbert Wigan had got married on 20 April. The loyal congregation at Dunsden, knowing their Vicar's tastes, had presented him with a silver salver engraved with his coat of arms. Wilfred apparently revisited the village, where he must have been amused at the contrast between the tall, dignified husband, so long a bachelor, and the little, bird-like wife.[22]

Wilfred returned to London for a final three days, sending postcards to his mother and Johnny de la Touche from the Imperial Hotel in Russell Square.[23] He found an agent for Peyronnet and finished the complicated process of getting ticket, visa and wartime passport for the journey to France. Then he had his eyes tested at Watson's in Holborn, where Gordon Gunston was still working, and had an enjoyable lunch with Leslie. It must have occurred to him that the Gunston brothers, like himself, were among the young men who were still being attacked in the press for not joining up. Leslie was believed to have a 'mitral murmur', a minor heart defect (no doubt diagnosed by the same Dr Gandy who had been doubtful about Wilfred's heart in 1912), but both brothers seemed perfectly fit. The recruiting campaign had been easy to ignore in Mérignac, but in London it was inescapable. 'There are three types of men. Those who hear the call and obey. Those who delay. And – the Others. To which do you belong?' The Gunstons had apparently chosen to be among the Others. At least Wilfred was delaying rather than refusing, and on the hotel noticeboard he saw an announcement that any 'gentleman returning from abroad' could obtain a commission by joining the Artists' Rifles, subject to age and fitness. The Only Way. The process that had begun with Tailhade's symbolic shouldering of a rifle in the previous autumn was almost complete.

By the Friday evening Wilfred had almost run out of British money, so for some free entertainment he followed an impulse to revisit the East End, remembering being taken there at the age of five to see his uncle, Dr Loughrey. The old house in the Mile End Road still had Loughrey's name painted above the door. Fascinated by the area, Wilfred went again next evening, wandering through the Jewish district in Whitechapel. He told Susan he had expected ugliness, but had never seen 'so much beauty' in two hours. Jews at home on the Sabbath seemed delightful, and back at the hotel he re-read some of the Old Testament with warm sympathy. His feelings were not just aesthetic or spiritual, however. Two years afterwards, recovering from shellshock, he drafted a poem entitled 'A Vision in Whitechapel' or 'Lines to a Beauty seen in Limehouse'. The vision was of a godlike youth, another statuesque idol with blood-red lips, whom he had admired but not dared to approach.

These two evenings in the East End seem to have prompted Wilfred's mysterious poem, 'A Palinode', in which he declares a new preference for the 'City' rather than nature. Not long before, according to the poem, he had decided to live without human contact, delighting in the woods and seasons, content to watch the 'sovereign sun … blessing all the field and air with gold'. This mood had intensified until, crazed by the staring moon, he had felt actual hatred for humanity. However, men had not allowed him to bask in his moonbeams, and he had taken 'antidotes; though what they be / Unless yourself be poisoned, do not ask'. Now he is overdosed, and all his pleasure is in town life: crowds, traffic, bridges echoing under wheels, the 'pacific lamentation of a bell',[24] old men, children, ships leaving for far-off lands. Many of these details seem to belong to the spring of 1915, alluding not only to the countryside at Mérignac, the din of London and the Thames bridges and docks, but also to the descent of Zeus as sunlight and other imagery from 'Perseus'. The secret antidotes were perhaps taken in the East End.

Wilfred left London on the morning of 13 June 1915. It was against his mother's principles to travel on a Sunday, but he explained that his penniless state had left him no alternative. He took the Folkestone–Boulogne route this time, and had enough francs for dinner on the train. An evening stroll in Paris was a disappointment after London. His patriotism had been strongly revived, and he was aware at last of the immense, still voluntary effort that was going on in his own country. He could only be a temporary visitor in Bordeaux now. Dawn over France revealed a beautiful land worth defending. He reached his destination at seven in the morning, feeling grubby and short of sleep, but three hours of searching led him to lodgings at 18 Rue Beaubedat in the old city, with a balcony overlooking the cathedral.[25] The room was clean and well furnished, despite wallpaper like 'ten thousand cabbages, over-boiled, and partly digested'. After unpacking books and a new suit from Shrewsbury, he had a much-needed bath and went to see the Lems.

Within a few days he had settled happily back into French life. His commuting was now in reverse, to Mérignac for lunch and afternoon lessons, and back in the evenings. Bonsall taught the boys Latin and Greek on several mornings a week. Wilfred was delighted to be warmly welcomed at the Châlet and to start work again with the 'dear, clever lads', Johnny and Bobbie. The boys secretly preferred Bonsall, but Mademoiselle disapproved of his casual discipline and manners. Wilfred's morning lessons in Bordeaux continued as before, with no lack of pupils, and he again joined a French language course. His hard work in London was applauded by Peyronnet, who reimbursed his expenses and renewed the suggestion of a trip to the eastern Mediterranean, perhaps in September if the Gallipoli campaign was over by then.

Wilfred felt pretty sure the war would go on into 1916, and he told Peyronnet that if the Dardanelles were still closed in September he would return to England and enlist. 'I don't want the bore of training,' he wrote to Susan. 'I don't want to wear khaki; nor yet to save my honour before inquisitive grand-children fifty years hence. But I *now do* most *intensely want to fight.*' His work in France was a perfectly good reason for delaying, but he felt 'full of peace – and of war' at the thought of returning home. Early drafts of the 'The Ballad of Peace and War', a project he was to tinker with for the next three years, reflect his mood after his six weeks in England: it is sweet and meet, the poem says, to be at peace with other people, but it is 'sweeter still and far more meet' to die in war 'with brothers'. *Dulce et decorum est pro patria mori*: it is sweet and meet to die for one's country. The Latin tag seemed entirely appropriate – not until 1917 would it become 'the old lie'. Reading one of Hilaire Belloc's travel books, Wilfred came across a quotation from de Vigny: 'If any man despairs of becoming a Poet, let him carry his pack and march in the ranks.' He asked his mother to send him the address of the Artists' Rifles.

'Gentlemen returning from abroad' had to be fit. He resolved to play tennis regularly and took to walking into town from Mérignac, sometimes with the boys. He had said little about the war at home, but among his French friends it was an obsessive topic of conversation. By early July he was feeling '*traitorously* idle: if not to England then to France'. Pressure for conscription was growing in England, but he noticed a statement by Asquith that the Government had no intention of introducing compulsory service. Susan failed to come up with the Artists' Rifles address, so he wrote to them without one and duly had a reply. Had he been a public school man, he would have been eligible for a rapid commission, but with his background he would have to serve as a cadet for months: the army had grudgingly decided to accept time spent abroad as the equivalent of a gentlemanly education, but a long training was still considered necessary. Always inclined to romance, Wilfred thought he might do better to join the Italian cavalry, 'for reasons both aesthetic and practical', an idea Susan refused to contemplate. She said one of his uncles thought he should try for a job in the War Office.[26] That would be safe, but not heroic.

His romantic notions of war were not in the least dimmed by his knowledge of its horrors. He had already seen wounded soldiers being operated on without anaesthetic. He read Flaubert's *Salammbô*, one of the most gruesome war books ever written, and thought it enthralling. 'Flaubert has my vote for novel writing!' He also seems to have read the *Song of Roland*, another tale of slaughter, and he wanted to take the boys to Castillon, the battlefield where the English had finally lost the Hundred Years War. Looking at his 'Perseus' manuscripts, he added a few lines about a Zeppelin he had apparently seen over the Thames during his East End walks. A Zeppelin would be a monster worth slaying.[27] But it was no good being too romantic, as he remarked to Susan, when he might become nothing more than 'National Hero, number million, grade Private, allowance one bob'.

When Leslie wrote in July that there were 'wars and rumours of wars', biblical phrasing of the sort Wilfred himself had used in earlier letters, he got a sharp response. '*Vous en êtes là seulement?* You hear Rumours? The rumours, over here, make the ears of the gunners bleed …'. Wilfred admitted to having spent a year of 'fine-contemptuous nonchalance', but now that he was getting fit after plenty of exercise with the boys he could see only one honourable course of action, 'the best way – The Only Way'. Leslie was about to take an architectural course in Oxford, and it was difficult not to be annoyed at his easy conscience. Wilfred said 'Oxford' should be a banned word between them, because it represented one of his bitterest regrets. He had never had a chance to go there, and now he probably never would.

All the same, it was good to be able to correspond with Leslie. Seeing him again had revived the old companionship. 'I thank God for the intercourse you and I have set up between us,' Wilfred told him, asking to see the latest instalment of 'Icarus' and sending him a lyric entitled 'Impromptu', apparently pretending it was a translation from Gautier. 'Impromptu' had homoerotic implications – 'Now, let me feel the feeling of thy hand – / For it is softer than the breasts of girls' – and typically French elements, with imagery of pale flowers, jewels, moonlight and dawn. During the next few years Wilfred used several fashionable Chopinesque titles: 'Impromptu', 'Rhapsody', 'Sonata', 'Nocturne'. 'De la musique avant toute chose': the new poem had some careful patterns of sound ('And kiss across it, as the sea the sand') and even a touch of pararhyme ('bless me with a bliss unguessed of God').[28] Leslie, who was keen to see his own and his cousin's work in print, had discovered a series of 'Little Books of Georgian Verse' by young, unknown writers. Wilfred wanted to know more, so Leslie sent him a specimen volume.[29]

Wilfred's daily routine gave him free evenings in the city. He often met the Viscount de Maud'huy, who was now back from England. The motley assortment of foreigners at the *Union* included a Norwegian who could read German and knew what was being said in German newspapers. (The Norwegian married a girl from Swansea in July, but Wilfred felt unable to introduce her into local English society because her speech was too common.) The Lems' lodger, Philippe, took Wilfred and Raoul upriver one Sunday to Philippe's house at Preignac, where they danced with the village girls and tried some table-turning. Once Wilfred attempted to call on M. Léger (his letter makes no mention of Madame), but the house was shuttered and the brass doorplate tarnished. In August an 'oddish' new friend, an eighteen-year-old radio operator named Thuret, began coming round to the Rue Beaubedat as soon as Wilfred got back at seven, often staying until one in the morning. One Sunday they went to hear an open-air opera about a tramp, *Le Chemineau*, based on a play by Richepin. Rain and umbrellas muffled the music by Leroux, whom Wilfred had met in Paris, but the composer himself conducted with gusto, and the proceedings closed with the inevitable patriotic songs and great applause. A week later Wilfred went to the seaside with Thuret and a group of Boy Scouts from the *Union*.

Peyronnet was expecting to have some more work for Wilfred in London before long. Meanwhile Mademoiselle decided Johnny and Bobbie needed a holiday, so she asked Wilfred to end their lessons on 1 August and stay on for a fortnight after that, a proposal he happily agreed to, foreseeing that much of the time would be spent in 'Ragging'. She suggested he might take lodgings in the village, but he preferred his freedom. One of her acquaintances had offered to take the boys back to England in September, so he would not need to wait until then. He told his landlady he would soon be leaving, and enquired at the docks whether he could hitch a lift home on a cargo boat, but a friendly young English sailor, speaking in an accent that stirred memories of Birkenhead, explained that such journeys were not allowed. Thuret proposed a route via Rouen, his home town, and wanted to accompany Wilfred there, but this scheme, too, proved impracticable.

The last weeks were as happy as Wilfred expected, with picnics, games and walks. Mademoiselle said she wished he would stay to tutor the two youngest boys, and there were plenty of people wanting English lessons in town, but he was not to be tempted. The countryside was hot and luxuriant after a period of heavy rain. He said the heat 'stuns one pleasantly, like strong music'; every day he received a new 'nature-shock'. He worked at getting fit, noticing how steady his heart was. 'This aft. I ran, with the boys, almost a mile – significant!' He delighted in the power of the noonday sun, feeling strengthened by it, 'a sure sign of being Right with Nature'. The purple heather reminded him of his dual training as poet and naturalist, and he thought of Broxton and botanising with Dr Rayner.

Meanwhile the muscle and pulse of France remained as strong as his own, he said, and although the 'Emperor yet frowns imperially', 'our ministers yet wear a ministerial smile'. He was clearly still working on 'Perseus'.

M. de la Touche sent instructions that his two eldest sons must not delay their English education any longer. The person who had been willing to take them back to Downside was not available after all, so Mademoiselle once again had to call on Wilfred and pay him to stay until the school term was due to begin. Having given notice to his landlady, he was obliged to move at the end of August, but he turned the chore into an amusement by finding three small boys to carry his belongings down the street to a room at 1 Place St Christoly. He made farewell visits to friends, many of whom begged him not to enlist. When he went to see the beautiful André Martin, the widowed mother wept and her sons demonstrated the horrors of war by producing sharp bits of shrapnel. André took out his wallet to reveal that among his most treasured keepsakes was a postcard Wilfred had sent him from Shrewsbury. Wilfred remained resolute. Even an afternoon in the Châlet garden entertaining ten wounded soldiers could not alter his decision, although he admitted their injuries 'played the devil' with his patriotism.

He left Bordeaux with Johnny and Bobbie and nine heavy pieces of luggage, including his own trunks, on the evening of Sunday 12 September 1915, reaching London late the following day. They found rooms at the Regent Palace Hotel, just off Piccadilly Circus. The hotel was still very new, the first establishment of its kind in the capital, a vast building reminiscent of a passenger liner, with hundreds of inexpensive bedrooms opening off long corridors. The boys had intended to go on to Downside next evening, but there was no train connection, so Wilfred rashly took them exploring round Whitehall in the dark, hoping to see a Zeppelin. All the lights were dimmed or out: London was bracing itself for air raids, Bloomsbury and the City having been badly hit a few nights before. Next morning tutor and pupils said goodbye at Paddington. Sad at losing his companions but determined to waste no time, Wilfred did some 'Enquiry Business', partly perhaps for Peyronnet but mainly about his own future. He went to the Artists' Rifles headquarters in Duke's Road on the northern edge of Bloomsbury, attested his willingness to serve and was examined by the kindly regimental doctor, who passed him fit.[30]

Wilfred was probably in Shrewsbury for most of the next month. His family must have been anxious about the dangers he was now facing, but they were in no doubt as to the rightness of his joining up. There had been an embarrassing contrast between his delay and the promptness of the Bulmans, Stanley Webb and many others who had long been in uniform. Loos was in progress, the worst battle yet, and the need for men was greater than ever. In the privacy of Mahim it must have been recognised that Wilfred was taking almost the last chance of volunteering. The authorities were not going to be able to rely on the voluntary principle for much longer, and it would be better to jump than be pushed.

Revisiting Alpenrose in mid-October, Wilfred went in to Reading to see Professor Morley, who invited him to tea, and Dr Rayner, who advised him to become a munitions worker like one of her former colleagues. Wilfred wrote to the colleague for information, but munitions work was unpleasant and entirely without glamour. He had made his choice, for the next few years at least. Long ago he had expected his future to be as a schoolmaster. The Timpanys had advised him to consider the civil service or journalism. Dr Rayner had suggested in 1912 that he should become a scientist, while Wigan had hoped he would enter the ministry. Perry had invited him to Mexico as an interpreter, Mme Léger had invited him to Canada in the same role and Langholz had urged him to buy a Berlitz school. Rowley had recommended him to try the consular service. Peyronnet had employed him as a commercial traveller, and had pressed him to take up a career in business.[31] Wilfred himself had hoped to teach, travel and write poetry. All those chances were now gone, except the poetry.

On the 20th Wilfred returned to the Artists' Rifles' headquarters in London, where he had to strip again and undergo a second medical, the doctor having forgotten to sign his form on the previous occasion. The Artists were still very selective. Three men were rejected in Wilfred's hearing, but the doctor had no doubts about him. Vision good at 6/6 in each eye, even though Watson's were still prescribing reading glasses; height five foot five inches; chest thirty-six-and-a-half inches; physical development 'fair'. Apparently nothing wrong with his heart. The height measurement would have been a disqualification in 1914, but the standard had been lowered since then. Next day, Thursday 21 October 1915, Wilfred returned to be sworn in, signing the routine Territorial Force undertaking to serve at home and abroad for four years. The recruiting officer, Captain C.J. Blomfield, asked him to read the oath:

I, Wilfred Edward Salter Owen, swear by Almighty God, that I will be faithful and bear true Allegiance to His Majesty King George the Fifth, His Heirs and Successors, and that I will, as in duty bound, honestly and faithfully defend His Majesty, His Heirs and Successors, in Person, Crown and Dignity against all enemies, according to the conditions of my service.

'Kiss the Book', Blomfield said, holding out a well-worn Bible that had probably never been opened, and Wilfred duly kissed it. One of the two men who were also volunteering gave it a gentle little kiss, the other 'a loud smacking one!!'. And soon afterwards Private Owen, TF, Number 4756,

28th London Regiment (Artists' Rifles), wrote home, scattering his breath-
less letter with exclamation marks and declaring, by mistake or design, 'I
am the British Army!'

Cadet

The Artists' Rifles

OCTOBER 1915–MAY 1916

Wilfred entered the British Army on 21 October 1915 under the auspices of the gods of war and the arts, Mars and Minerva. Their twin heads, the badge of the Artists' Rifles sculpted in Victorian terracotta, can still be seen above the door of the headquarters in Duke's Road. The regiment had begun as a Volunteer Corps for actual artists, and its founders had included Lord Leighton, Millais and other famous painters, as Wilfred was impressed to discover. The long line of recruits who passed through the door in Bloomsbury during the Great War included the poets Edward Thomas, Edward Shanks and W.J. Turner, the painters John and Paul Nash and many other cultured men. Nevertheless, the Artists prided themselves on being tough and highly efficient. They had sent a fighting battalion to France in August 1914, and had soon been given their special wartime role as an officer training unit. During the next four years over ten thousand Artists were trained, commissioned and dispersed throughout the army.[1]

Wilfred was at the head of a final surge of volunteers. On 19 October the Government's new director of recruiting, Lord Derby, had announced that all eligible men were to be canvassed personally in a last attempt to keep the voluntary principle going. The Derby Scheme was generally welcomed, H.G. Wells much preferring it to 'the vague Press ravings, the ridiculous placards, and the street-corner insults' of the recruiting campaign, but there could be little doubt that volunteering would soon be a thing of the past.[2] 'Look at the map,' Derby said grimly, and the front-line maps in the newspapers were indeed telling their own story, despite official optimism. On 28 October the King published a new appeal: 'The end is not in sight. More men and yet more men are wanted …'. The Artists were soon reporting a sharp increase in numbers. The 'best types', public school men in their twenties, had already joined, but 'quite good men' were coming forward, many of them released by banks and other big employers. Captain Blomfield, the Artists' recruiting officer, rather disapproved of latecomers. At twenty-two Wilfred was well above the minimum age (which was seventeen for Territorials, though they normally had to be older than that for active service), but so were many of his fellow recruits.

When Susan Owen had dreamed long before about the future of Sir Wilfred Salter-Owen, she can hardly have imagined that her baby would end up a soldier. At least one Salter had been a military man, but most had been in trade. Wilfred's size and strength hardly qualified him for front-line service, and his health had often given trouble, but he was not entirely unsuited to his new profession. He had been used to responsibility even as a child. As a trained teacher and competent amateur actor with a strong, deep voice, he would have no difficulty giving orders and instructing his men. He liked the thought of wearing uniform, having always enjoyed dressing up and playing new roles, and the streaks of grey in his hair that he had noticed at Dunsden might help to mitigate his otherwise youthful appearance. He was accurate with a gun, as he knew from target practice with his father and uncle. His inbred sense of class allowed him to adjust easily to the army's rigid hierarchy, and becoming one of His Majesty's officers would bring instant gentlemanly status. Soldiering still seemed a romantic adventure, earning almost universal approval, ensuring that his parents and others would no longer ask awkward questions about his future. And, as de Vigny had said, taking up arms might lead to poetry.

Newly enrolled Artists were assigned to the 2nd Battalion, the regiment's principal training unit, spending a few weeks in London learning the basics of drill and army routine before going to the battalion's camp at Romford. After nine weeks of hard work there, candidates for commissions would enter the School of Instruction for a month's even more intense study before being gazetted as second lieutenants – the most junior rank of officer – in whatever regiments they had applied for. In London they had to find their own lodgings, Wilfred choosing a French-speaking boarding house at 54 Tavistock Square, conveniently close to Duke's Road. This softened the transition from France to England, everything being French at Les Lilas, including cooking and conversation. Most of the other guests were Belgian ladies, refugees from Brussels. Bloomsbury was a polyglot district, the 'noisiest place in the world,' according to T.S. Eliot in 1914, '… given over to artists, musicians, hackwriters, Americans, Russians, French, Belgians, Italians, Spaniards, and Japanese, formerly Germans also … a delightfully seedy part of town'.[3] It was also given over to soldiers, the Artists having commandeered three squares for drilling purposes as well as two schools and a hotel. Wilfred had stayed in two Bloomsbury hotels earlier in the year, so he knew the area. He loved the dingy Georgian streets, unlit at night, and the squares, 'wadded with fog; skeletons of dismal trees behind the palings; but the usual west-end pervasion of ghostly aristocracy'. What would have seemed depressing in Manchester or Liverpool, he said, was romantic and antique in London. He remembered

Dickens had lived in Tavistock Square, although he probably had no idea that even in 1915 his near-neighbours included W.B. Yeats, Laurence Binyon and several members of the 'Bloomsbury Group'.

Immediately after swearing-in he was given an injection against typhoid and three days' sick leave – the doctor's description of possible after-effects was so graphic that one man fainted even before being touched by the needle. Wilfred soon felt as though a horse had got his arm between its teeth, but the free time was a civilised start to army service, and he made good use of it that evening by going to the Poetry Bookshop at 35 Devonshire Street,[4] only a few minutes walk away from his lodgings. Readings were held every Tuesday and Thursday at six. Harold Monro himself, tall, dark and sad-eyed, was probably in the little shop, welcoming visitors as usual. Wilfred went through to the yard and up a steep wooden staircase into what seemed to be an old stable loft, the only light coming from a pair of candles on the reader's desk. The effect was intentionally church-like. For half an hour the new soldier could rededicate himself to his true creed, forgetting the war and his aching arm, while Monro's assistant, Alida Klemantaski, read quietly from Emily Brontë and Christina Rossetti.

Wilfred attended a service at Westminster Abbey on Sunday 24 October, enjoying the music and sermon.[5] He had his first taste of drill next day, parading in civilian clothes, and on the Tuesday, his arm being fully recovered, he spent a whole day learning how to march, turn and stand to attention, finding the experience an odd mixture of boredom and entertainment. Discipline was fairly mild, the Artists' sergeants being good-natured, intelligent men, some with an excellent sense of humour, so he was spared the parade-ground bullies who made life miserable for many recruits. He began to feel awe, even devotion, in the presence of experienced NCOs and officers. 'If a Major-General approached me I think I should fall down dead.' He went to the Bookshop again, this time hearing Monro read from 'The City of Dreadful Night', a choice reflecting the slow, bitter loss of hope that the author of *Before Dawn* had been going through since the outbreak of war. Wilfred lingered to have a word with him afterwards, apparently mentioning Tailhade. Monro must have expressed interest, and Wilfred sent home for *Poèmes Aristophanesques*. Visiting the Bookshop and meeting its proprietor was good for morale, despite Monro's low spirits. The family in Shrewsbury kept up a stream of letters, aware that encouragement was needed. 'The enlisting was a *plunge*,' Wilfred admitted, 'and it *has* put my wits a little out of breath.'

By the middle of the week he was in uniform, having been issued with full kit. Would-be officers were expected to buy some things for themselves, and for the first time he came up against the absurdities of army life, discovering he had been given a toothbrush, for example, but not a belt.

He reluctantly accepted several remittances from home to supplement his allowance. Few economies were possible, as equipment had to be complete and in perfect order, with boots, buttons and badges polished daily. A route march up to Highgate, physical exercises in Cartwright Gardens and practising salutes on trees left him dog-tired but cheerful. He had never been in such a thoroughly masculine environment, and it was a relief to find he could cope. Everyone was willing to make friends, although he could see no way of deciding who to be friendly with except to choose men with pleasant expressions. Much of the conversation was about military details: how to massage one's new boots with castor oil, where the next posting would be, rumours, grouses, the next task. Almost without noticing, Wilfred and the others slipped into the military way of thinking, asking no questions, obeying orders and almost never talking about the long-term future.

One of the most striking features of Wilfred's letters from the day he enlisted in 1915 to his arrival at the front in 1917 is that he never refers to the conduct and progress of the war.[6] All through 1916 he makes no mention whatever of Verdun or the Somme, although he must have noticed the growing casualty lists and heard stories from men who had 'been out'. No doubt he wanted to keep his own mind and his mother's away from such things, and in July 1916 soldiers were ordered not to discuss the war, but his reticence also reflects the unspoken rules prevailing among the Artists. Edward Thomas noticed how no one in camp ever talked about the war for more than a moment or two.[7] Wilfred himself commented in March 1916 on the strangeness of army life: 'here we are prepared – or preparing – to lay down our lives for another, the highest moral act possible, according to the Highest Judge, and nothing of this is apparent between the jostle of discipline and jest'. Every now and then a senior officer would give a lecture on the war's aims and origins, but it was not done to mention horrors or failures, or even to dwell on successes. It was enough to be sure that Germany was bad and victory certain.

Wilfred was pleased to notice how old people smiled at his uniform and small boys gazed admiringly. He amused himself by looking sternly at men of his own age still in civilian dress, enjoying their embarrassed expressions. His working day lasted from half past nine in the morning to five in the evening ('Jolly reasonable!'), so he was able to go to the Bookshop again on 4 November, this time clumping self-consciously up the wooden stairs in his new boots, while the 'poetic ladies' in the audience turned to stare and Monro 'smiled sadly' to see that yet another young man had gone into khaki. Miss Klemantaski read from Rabindranath Tagore, 'without much insight into the Hindu spirit', Wilfred thought. His letters make no further mention of readings, but he no doubt went to more, and his browsings in the shop extended his knowledge of contemporary poetry.

He read some Yeats and bought Rupert Brooke's poems, A.E. Housman's *A Shropshire Lad* and Monro's latest book, *Children of Love*.

Monro's rueful smile made Wilfred suddenly aware of the true significance of uniform, and he thought of a poem in Monro's book about the typical soldier, David reborn as Tommy, heedless of danger even while old men plan the death of youth.

> *Happy boy, happy boy,*
> *David the immortal willed,*
> *Youth a thousand thousand times*
> *Slain, but not once killed,*
> *Swaggering again to-day*
> *In the old contemptuous way …*
>
> *Greybeards plotted. They were sad.*
> *Death was in their wrinkled eyes.*
> *At their tables, with their maps*
> *Plans and calculations, wise*
> *They all seemed; for well they knew*
> *How ungrudgingly Youth dies.* [8]

Companion poems portrayed the soldier as delirious with exhaustion during the Mons retreat, then as a corpse merging into the earth. Monro's irony and attempted realism, his anger against old men and his grief at the death of youth, made his work highly unusual for 1914–15 and Wilfred was to remember it.

Les Lilas had been an excellent place to stay during the first excitement of joining up, but its regular mealtimes were becoming tiresome, as was the noise, the proprietor being a retired opera singer. Wilfred came across an advertisement in the YMCA magazine: '20 Devonshire Street, Queen Square, WC. Bedrooms from 5/6. Board as required. Bed and breakfast, 2/6. Central, near tram, train and tube, terms moderate'. Twenty Devonshire Street was directly opposite the Bookshop. The district was the poorest part of Bloomsbury, the handsome old houses occupied by shopkeepers and craftsmen who sublet every available room. The tenant of No. 20, Arthur Middleton, ran what Wilfred described as a 'coffee shop', actually a cheap restaurant offering delicacies such as sheep's heart and toad-in-the-hole. The upper floors were spartan, with no bathroom, gas or electricity, but 5s 6d a week was indeed moderate (Les Lilas was 35s, full board) and there would be no difficulty about getting meals at odd times. Deciding to take a room, Wilfred gave notice at Les Lilas at the end of October, but no sooner had he done so than his batch of recruits were told they would have to leave London for Romford. He was to stay in his 'Poet's Room' in

Devonshire Street quite often in 1916, however, drafting poems and looking for inspiration across the narrow street to the symbol on the Bookshop's hanging sign, a torch flaming against a dark sky.[9]

~

On 15 November 1915, after a weekend at Alpenrose, Wilfred joined his company at Liverpool Street Station for the train to Gidea Park, Romford. Still a small market town well beyond the eastern outskirts of London, Romford was set among gently rolling fields and the estates of a few country mansions. A new garden suburb with its own station at Gidea Park had been completed early in 1911, advertising itself as 'Dreams Come True'. The Artists' camp, constructed four years later in the grounds of Hare Hall, next to the suburb, was also a model of its kind, planned and built by architects and engineers from the regiment. 'All very nicely set out here,' Wilfred reported as soon as he arrived. Designed to hold 1,400 men, the camp consisted of about forty long wooden huts in neat rows, divided by a central spine of services. Several larger huts contained the canteen, hospital, lecture room and sergeants' mess, and the YMCA had set up one of its usual refuges, providing refreshments and quiet reading rooms. The site was on the north side of Hare Hall park, near a little cluster of shops and pubs on the main Colchester road, with the centre of Romford only about twenty minutes' walk away. Just to the south of the huts stood the Hall itself, a handsome eighteenth-century house taken over as officers' quarters.

Everything was clean and tidy, but living conditions were austere. Wilfred was put into a hut with twenty-nine other men, and he must have found the lack of privacy trying. Each day began at six or earlier with physical exercises and a lecture, followed by at least seven hours of practical training, ending at about four in the afternoon, sometimes much later. There was often another lecture at eight, and each week one of the huts had to put on a 'concert'. Lights-out came early. The best policy was to be as keen and uncomplaining as possible. Wilfred said in his first week that he had been one of only three men out of the seven hundred in his half of the camp to take a cold shower in the morning. He was strong-minded if he kept that up, for the weather was freezing. Clutching an icy rifle all day was not pleasant.

The 2nd Battalion was the creation of its Commanding Officer, Lieutenant-Colonel William Shirley, a remarkable man.[10] Tall, lean, energetic, highly intelligent and occasionally ferocious, Shirley had retired from the Indian Army before the war and been appointed the first Director of Military Studies at Cambridge, returning to uniform in 1914. Wilfred heard him give a 'brilliant' lecture on the causes of the war, and must also have heard his introductory talk to new recruits, a powerful sermon on *moral* (or morale, to use the modern spelling), 'the most important factor in war'. Morale was indeed a moral quality for Shirley, and he had no compunction in using religious terms: 'now that you have entered upon the service of your Country, … you must proceed to serve her with all your heart and with all your soul and with all your mind and with all your strength.'[11] 'I believe in hard working and hard thinking, and a dashed deal of it,' Shirley said, and Wilfred would have been impressed by his long quotations from Ruskin on work, duty and 'creative war', an essential educational process for great nations.

'I exhort you', the Colonel went on, 'to go forth as the Champions of Right, not as the Avengers of Wrong.' He quoted the line from Horace that Wilfred already knew, 'Dulce et decorum est pro patria mori', but pointed out that living for one's country would often be more useful and more difficult than dying for it. Losing your own life unnecessarily was suicide, losing your men's was murder. An officer should always put his men's welfare before his own, while making himself their superior in all moral qualities, overcoming fear by work, smartness and comradeship ('the saving grace of the British Army'). The secret of success was to cultivate 'the spirit of the offensive' and above all the sense of duty. Shirley used another quotation that was to turn up in Wilfred's poetry and letters, Christ's saying, 'Greater love hath no man than this, that a man lay down his life for his friends.' Other nations might value glory (Wilfred would have remembered French rhetoric on that subject), but for a British soldier the finest thing was to be able to say like Nelson in the hour of death, 'Thank God I have done my duty.'

Shirley's unrelentingly high standards ensured that the work of the battalion was quasi-religious in its earnestness. The officer cadets were repeatedly told that their duty would be to lead and serve. Much emphasis was placed on 'care of the men': an officer had to know and understand his men, regularly check the state of their feet, boots and general cleanliness, and ensure they got their mail and decent food. The close relationship between a junior officer and his platoon, the crucial difference between the British and the continental armies, was vital to morale and would be the key to victory. Yet discipline was also crucial and there could be no slackening in the strict distinction between officers and Other Ranks, nor in the gentlemanly dress and conduct proper to officers. The experienced old soldiers in the camp were expected to advise recruits on such matters in private when necessary.

After the early-morning lecture the cadets breakfasted and collected packed lunches before parading at nine-thirty for a short burst of drill. They were then divided up into platoons, to be sent out across the park and neighbouring countryside for the day's work, sometimes marching for miles. Officers and NCOs taught them how to use weapons, plan an attack

126. - BORDEAUX. - La Porte Dijeaux

LES HAUTES-PYRÉNÉES
22. - BAGNÈRES-DE-BIGORRE. - LE CASINO

LABOUCHE FRÈRES, TOULOUSE.

Top left: Porte Dijeaux, Bordeaux. Wilfred's lodgings were a few doors down on the left.
Top right: Villa Lorenzo, Bagnères-de-Bigorre, *c.* 1914.
Bottom: The Casino and the outdoor stage, with a lecture or concert in progress, Bagnères, *c.* 1914.

Right: Wilfred and Mme Léger listening to one of Tailhade's lectures at the Casino, Bagnères, 22–23 August 1914.

Below: Wilfred being introduced to French literature by Laurent Tailhade in the villa garden, Bagnères, September 1914.

Opposite above: At the Châlet, Mérignac, summer 1915. Back row: Admiral Castéjas' daughter, Charles, Johnny, Bobbie, Wilfred, David. Front row: Mlle Puységur, a guest, Mlle Anne de la Touche, another guest and Admiral Castéjas' son.

Opposite below: Artists' Rifles officers and cadets arriving at Hare Hall camp, Romford, 1915-16.

Top left: The Poetry Bookshop, 35 Devonshire (now Boswell) Street, Bloomsbury. *Top right:* Lt-Col. William Shirley, founder and CO, 2nd Artists' Rifles. *Below:* Sentry duty, Hare Hall camp.

Opposite top: Wilfred's hut and its inmates, Hare Hall camp, November 1915. Cadet Owen is second from left, back row. The man standing immediately below him to his left is Herbert Briggs. *Opposite below:* Balgores House, Romford, in use as the Artists' Cadet School, *c.* 1916.

Belgorse Lane, Gic

Above: Second Lieutenant W.E.S. Owen, Manchester Regiment, newly commissioned. Photographed by John Gunston at Alpenrose, July 1916. *Opposite above:* Some of the officers of the 5th (Reserve) Battalion, Manchester Regiment, Witley camp, 1916. Wilfred is second from right, front row, sitting in front of Lt-Col. Ridge. *Opposite below:* Five Owens, dressed for a special occasion, probably soon after Harold's return from his last Merchant Navy voyage, September 1916. Harold wears the uniform of a PSNC cadet, Susan wears an Artists' Rifles badge as her neck brooch and Tom has a cigar.

Practice trenches dug by Artists' cadets near Romford, 1916.

British troops in captured enemy trenches at Serre, March 1917.

and construct and defend trenches. Wilfred found himself throwing bombs (hand grenades), firing machine guns, wielding a bayonet and taking his turn at every role from company commander to officer's servant. Occasionally he had to do a twenty-four-hour stint of guard duty on constant alert, forbidden even to remove his pack or boots. He learned to reconnoitre, read maps, select objectives and send signals. Everything that was taught had to be practised again and again – getting the details right in the front line might be a matter of life and death. A mapping notebook kept in 1916 by one of the cadets, William Robinson, shows the sort of tasks that were set.[12] Robinson makes notes on how to use a prismatic compass, how to find north without one and how to lead a march by the stars or in pitch darkness ('Do not halt men by night, as it puts the wind up them'). He plans a bivouac position for a brigade on the Romford–Brentwood road, noting the availability of water, fuel and fodder, and the facilities for defence ('Very poor'), and he designs a trench system round a local cross-roads. He draws panoramas, recording landscapes in simple planes as a guide for artillery. All the time he is developing a military eye for the Essex countryside, getting used to thinking of cottages as targets and defence points, woods as obstacles and shelter, tracks as routes for marching men and heavy guns. The back of his notebook contains notes of a lecture on 'The Attack'. 'Too long on defence destroys moral[e]': when in doubt, go on the offensive.

After less than a fortnight at Romford, Wilfred admitted that camping was beginning to be 'troublesome' now that the novelty was wearing off. He was clearly far from happy, depressed by bad weather, incessant work, poor food and constant discipline, and sometimes by the company he had to keep. A newspaper report in November said the battalion was 'democratic', meaning that private wealth counted for nothing, but Wilfred might have disagreed. Some of his colleagues came from much more impressive backgrounds than his own, and they were not averse to showing it. Among the characters mentioned in his Romford letters are a gilded youth with an income of two thousand a year, a seventeen-year-old know-all from an army family who was destined for the Guards (Wilfred called him the Scarlet Cockatoo), and a witty public school man whose sister knew Yeats and George Bernard Shaw. The society magazine, *The Tatler*, described the Artists as 'that Famous Training Corps' in November 1915, devoting a whole page to caricatures of the officers by an artist in the ranks. Wilfred cut the page out and sent it home.[13] One of the majors was a baronet, the doctor was a CMG and rumoured to have attended the King, and one of the subalterns, William Lee Hankey, was a respected painter. One of the map instructors, Lance-Corporal P.E. Thomas, was the well-known critic and writer on the countryside, Edward Thomas. Wilfred may well have been taught by him at some stage, either on Hampstead Heath in October or at Romford during the winter, when every platoon in the camp had to do a five-day mapping course, but neither Wilfred nor anyone else in the Artists had the least idea that Thomas had started writing poetry.

Wilfred never got to know any of the more distinguished people in the regiment, and he seems to have been ill at ease with upper-class recruits. His social mobility in France could not easily be repeated in England. Most of the cadets named in his letters came from backgrounds not unlike his own. Norris Jubb, the son of an engineer at a dyeworks, had studied at Huddersfield Technical College and the Royal College of Art. William Foster, whose father was a coal merchant in Poole, had started to train as a civil engineer. Hubert Crampton, ten years older than Wilfred, was a chartered accountant. Wilfred was pleased to meet a former Reading student, Ernest Denny, a would-be poet who was still in touch with Professor Morley.[14] One of the most interesting cadets was John Muff-Ford, formerly an art student in London and civil servant in South Africa, most recently an actor making good money.[15] He drew Wilfred's portrait and promised him a job after the war. 'He is a gentleman,' Wilfred said, 'and loves his profession. I wonder?'

The best companion proved to be Herbert Briggs, a nineteen-year-old who had joined up the day after Wilfred.[16] Briggs had earned a first in Matric and reached Intermediate chemistry at Leeds, and he hoped to return to university after the war. Wilfred described him as 'quite my best chum … a boy of admirable industry in work, inquiring mind, a hater of swank, malice, and all uncharitableness, and very Provincial'. Northern provincials were easier to get on with than self-assured southerners. When Briggs took him to the Romford baths, Wilfred reflected that danger and nakedness were the only forces that could obliterate social distinctions: 'neither Religion, nor Love, nor Charity, nor Community of Interests, nor Socialism, nor Conviviality can do it at all.'

At the end of November Wilfred managed to get a weekend in London. It was an easy journey by train and tube to the boarding house in Devonshire Street. He got a shilling seat at the opera for the Saturday night (*Cavalleria Rusticana* and *Pagliacci* were on at the old Shaftesbury Theatre), but what else he did during this and subsequent visits his letters do not say. The West End was crowded with soldiers on leave, having a good time while they had the chance, and civilians enjoying wartime's easy codes of behaviour. Wilfred may have returned to the East End, too, attracted to its romance as before, wandering through the streets of Limehouse and the rough slums of Shadwell on the river bank, where the water lapped at the foot of the old dock stairs.

Many of his precious hours in London must have been devoted to poetry. His current plan was for a collection of sonnets to be published as a Little Book of Georgian Verse, the series Leslie had told him about earlier in the year. Most of his sonnets, nearly all of them more or less in the style of Verlaine and Tailhade, seem to have been written in 1915–16. Leslie sent him 'a large packet of literatures' at the end of October 1915, probably poems by himself and a neighbour, Olwen Joergens, whom Wilfred had met at Alpenrose earlier that month. Aged about nineteen, dreamy but serious-minded, Olwen had managed to get her poems accepted as a Little Book, an achievement the cousins must have envied. An undated note among Wilfred's papers, apparently part of a draft preface or a letter to a publisher, says his sonnets have simplicity, 'unity of idea' and 'a solemn dignity in the treatment', and he suggests titles for a book: 'Certain Sonnets of Wilfred Owen', or 'Minor Poems – in Minor Keys – by a Minor' (he was not a minor, but Olwen was and it sounded good).

∿

The rigours of military life were made more tolerable in mid-December, when Wilfred happened to meet three Boy Scouts who were helping around the camp. He gave them tea and biscuits in the YMCA hut, and in return two of them asked him to their homes. It was a pleasure to have some youthful company again and to be welcomed into family life. Raymond Williams and Albert Harper, both aged thirteen and members of the 3rd Romford Scout Troop, lived near each other on the Emerson Park estate at Hornchurch, about a mile-and-a-half away. They had known the camp since May, when their troop had been given a guided tour. Ray, a quiet, shy boy, had won a war badge in April for devoting not less than three hours a day for a month to duties such as guarding bridges and carrying messages.[17] Wilfred had the boys to lunch several times in his hut, where their presence perhaps caused a little surprise, although he noticed it put a stop to swearing.

Home leave for Christmas seemed a possibility, then failed to materialise, so the Williamses asked him to supper on the 25th. He thus had two feasts on Christmas Day 1915, making up for the one he had missed in 1913. His hut held its own lunch first, having pooled extra pay to buy a couple of turkeys, as well as numerous plum puddings and other delicacies. It was agreed there should be no spirits at table, and no one got drunk, so Wilfred was in good shape when Ray called for him in the afternoon. Mr Williams, who was secretary and a deacon of the nearby Congregational church, had had a busy morning, but he and his wife and their four children proved delightful hosts, playing charades and Owen games with great enthusiasm. Wilfred discovered that the family was Welsh in origin, and he thought the surroundings of the house looked much like Monkmoor Road (though the gardens were in fact bigger than Mahim's and the houses more stylish). All cadets had to be back in camp by nine-fifteen, the usual time. As he walked back from Hornchurch he could hear the 'uproar' in the huts, and the noise went on for the rest of the evening.

Colonel Shirley, knowing that the war was becoming ever more serious, may not have been too pleased by the merrymaking. The recruiting boom was in the process of doubling the numbers under his command, so the camp was under considerable pressure and he could not risk trouble. When three men got drunk in January he put the local pubs and hotels permanently out of bounds, despite objections from Romford councillors. The camp was extended to take hundreds of new arrivals, and a patriotic landowner made two large houses, Gidea Hall and Balgores House, available as extra accommodation at no charge.[18] Despite appearances, though, the Derby Scheme had failed, and on 29 December the Cabinet at last decided on conscription.

Wilfred's turn for a week's leave came at the end of December, and he was able to see 1916 in at Mahim with his family. Only Harold was absent, now in another ship, the *Kenuta*, working along the Chilean coast. On the way back to Romford Wilfred paused in London for a meeting with Leslie, no doubt to talk about sonnets and Olwen's forthcoming book. The return to military discipline, coarse blankets and army food was an unpleasant shock, made worse by cold, wet weather. 'Rain, midnight rain, nothing but the wild rain / On this bleak hut, and solitude, and me,' Edward Thomas wrote early that January after lying awake in the camp, and Wilfred probably felt just as lonely. The rules had been tightened up, with the day's routine continuing for up to twelve hours, after which the evenings had to be spent preparing maps and reports for the next day. Soon after Wilfred got back from leave, the authorities asked for 500 volunteers for immediate active service. He wisely refused when his name was called, having not even started his rifle course, but it was a sobering moment.

Musketry training soon began on the firing range (no one used muskets any more, but the army liked to keep the old term), and at the end of January Wilfred decided to put in for a commission in the Manchester Regiment, as did Briggs, Jubb, Foster, Crampton and at least three other Artists of their intake. The regiment must have asked for new officers, and Wilfred may have felt he would be happier among northerners than in a southern unit. He filled in the forms, answering such questions as 'Are you of pure European descent?' and giving his height as five foot six (it was not uncommon for recruits to gain an inch or more during training). Finding time for a brief weekend in Shrewsbury, he took the papers with him and got the Vicar of St Julian's to sign the necessary certificate of good moral character. No doubt there was excitement and some apprehension at Mahim, but a commission was still some weeks away, and even then Wilfred would probably have to stay in England for months before being allowed into the firing line.

The return journey to camp on Sunday 30 January was interrupted by an air raid. As Wilfred tried to leave the Underground at Liverpool Street, he realised the station was blacked out and the subways unusually crowded. He was trapped with hundreds of people in the tunnels for nearly three hours, listening to the muffled thudding of the anti-aircraft guns, although in the end the Zeppelins failed to reach the City. He got back to camp very late after this unnerving experience, only to discover that his hut had been ruthlessly cleared and disinfected, several men having gone down with measles. The place reeked of carbolic, his bed had disappeared and his possessions had been left in chaos. 'It was the bitterest moment of many years,' he told Susan afterwards. Finding a few blankets, he rolled himself up on the floor, chilled to the bone. He was in quarantine for a fortnight, confined to camp and forbidden to use the YMCA or the canteen. Having already dated his commission papers for the 31st, he was told to wait for a few days in case measles developed. He and Susan had been suffering from colds over the weekend, and depression now made him feel really ill, but the impulse to collapse soon faded. The doctor passed him fit, the Major signed the forms on behalf of the Colonel, and Wilfred joined the category of men who had 'papers in'.

At the end of the week Mary wrote that Susan's cold had got alarmingly worse, and a letter from Tom brought less assurance than its author intended. A general came to inspect the battalion, and Wilfred thought the parade went very badly, although he was too worried to take much notice. He cheered up on the 9th at the sight of Susan's own handwriting on an envelope, and some days later she wrote again to say her illness had been diagnosed as congestion of the lungs, like his in 1913. Urging her to take her convalescence as gently as possible, he remembered how devotedly she had nursed him just three years before. That memory came to him every February, bringing with it 'a kind of sweet anguish', as he had told her in 1915, 'an ecstasy, (very difficult to describe, but something like the effect of a great music)'.[19]

Another spring observance soon followed. He slipped out of camp to visit the Williamses, carefully keeping his distance from the children. On the way back a string tied across the road alerted him to the presence of boys, so he chased the culprits, finding that one of them was none other than Bertie Harper, whom he hadn't seen for some time. Bertie came into camp next Sunday with his brother, Stanley, 'a Colinesque, adorable little creature of 10', to take Wilfred home for the evening, despite the lingering risk of infection. 'I had a very excellent good time indeed,' Wilfred reported, telling Susan that the children had taken to calling him 'Uncle'. 'Their affection – which has come up swiftly as the February flowers – seems without bounds and without restraint.' Exploring a nearby wood, they found a lesser celandine in flower amid masses of bluebell leaves. 'And we ate the Vernal Eucharist of Hawthorn leaf-buds. / These are the days when men's hearts (some men's) become as tender as the new green.'[20] He seems to have been given a standing invitation to visit the Harpers on Sundays and the Williamses on Saturdays.

Although still officially in quarantine, he was given leave to go to London twice to have some harmless lumps cauterised from the back of his throat at Bart's, and to have a tooth out. He may have taken the chance to meet his brother Harold, who had just docked from South America. Harold was invited to the camp. His memoirs contain two lengthy descriptions of Wilfred as a soldier, a pair of contrasting portraits. In the first, at Romford, Wilfred is disorganised and worried, looking wretchedly small and out of place in his ill-fitting tunic, only just able to hold his own among dozens of big, strong men. In the second he is a commissioned officer, sturdy, assured and impressively efficient. Harold heightens the contrasts as usual, but there must be truth in both pictures. He probably went to Romford on Saturday 19 February, by which time the hut was out of quarantine. According to *Journey from Obscurity*, Wilfred planned the day carefully. At lunch in the canteen he pushes through the crowd at the bar to get two large mugs of beer, an effort Harold recognises as a brave gesture of comradeship and rebellion. The brothers have never drunk together before, but now they are grown up at last, each having freed himself from their mother's dominance. They feel protective towards her all the same, Wilfred insisting she should not be told about the beer. Anxious about exams, he spends the afternoon studying, but Harold returns in the evening, Wilfred seemingly wanting him to experience the depressing harshness of the camp.

The rest of the story strains credulity a little. Wilfred causes amusement in the hut by meticulously shaving and washing, scrubbing what he calls the 'hated rifle-oil' from his fingers, operations that would more probably have taken place in the ablutions hut. Perhaps Harold really was invited in as a witness, but Wilfred's alleged loathing for rifle oil is one of many little touches worked into *Journey from Obscurity* to show the poet as a hater of war and weapons well before 1917. The brothers then walk miles to a town Harold later identifies as Ilford, where, after dinner in a hotel, he is surprised to be taken for another walk, this time with the waitress as well. Wilfred leads them to a secluded spot, then slips back to the hotel. Greatly embarrassed, Harold escorts the waitress home and returns to Wilfred, furiously upbraiding him for what Wilfred explains as an experiment in hospitality. Sailors always like female company, Wilfred says, so he has done his best to provide it. Harold explodes with lurid stories of Valparaiso brothels, all untrue, and then has to hurry his brother off to catch the last bus back to camp. Wilfred's cap and coat are awry, and he panics at the thought of military police, but Harold sorts him out, calms him down, restores brotherly affection and gets him safely on the bus in time to be back by midnight.

It is true that Romford hotels were out of bounds, so Ilford, five miles away, is not as unlikely a destination as it seems. If the Hare Hall gates really were open until midnight on a Saturday, perhaps only to men with late passes, the timing of the evening just about fits, and the sparse topographical details in Harold's narrative can all be found in Ilford. But the waitress is a stock figure in *Journey from Obscurity*, where Harold again and again finds himself alone with a girl in odd circumstances, always extricating himself before anything happens. Similarly, he shows Wilfred often coming close to talking about sex but always edging away again. Harold may have been as virginal as he portrays himself, but he exaggerates his brother's poetic ideals and 'monk-like austerity'. If Wilfred had no desire to spend time in the dark with a waitress, it was not merely because he preferred to sit in a hotel lounge reading a book. His motive in setting up the evening may in fact have been to tease Harold, who had perhaps boasted rather too much about South American whorehouses.[21]

～

On Wednesday 23 February 1916 the Artists of the November 1915 intake were ordered to London for a lecture course. They had been working alongside men in the School of Instruction for some time, so they assumed they were approaching the last stage in their training. Wilfred managed to get lodgings at the Poetry Bookshop itself, where several bedrooms were available to poets and artists at low rates (his predecessors had included Wilfrid Gibson, Jacob Epstein and T.E. Hulme). He had a brief word with Monro, asking him to comment on a batch of sonnets. Monro was always willing in theory to assist young poets in this way, although in practice he often seemed grudging, knowing all too well that the task was likely to be unrewarding. There seemed no chance of a proper conversation in any case, as Wilfred's days were filled with lectures about horses and bombs, and Monro was out every evening. The Swiss housekeeper, Marie Spati, was hospitable, doing the guest's laundry, taking soup up to his room and lingering to talk, no doubt delighted to find a fluent French speaker. Snow was falling and Wilfred was glad of the soup, even if he secretly resented the interruptions to the poems he must have been working on.

At some stage in 1916 Wilfred started drafting an ambitious poem about the war. Nothing now remains of it except a few rough jottings, with the title, 'An Imperial Elegy / Libretto for *Marche Funèbre*'. The Chopin he had played to Nénette at Bagnères, far away in another world, was running through his head again, and he seems to be trying to fit words to the music. He experiments with a line by Olwen Joergens, 'Afar off, afar off', writing it down twice with the stresses marked like a drumbeat, and then he works out a couplet about drummers and pipers. Another Joergens line, 'I looked and saw', from a visionary poem of hers about 1915, introduces his own vision: he sees not 'one corner of a foreign field' (an allusion to Rupert Brooke), but the trench line spanning Europe like a 'titan's grave'. He hears 'a voice crying' (a quotation from Isaiah) that this is 'the Path of Glory', a phrase that seems to have none of the irony of Gray's 'Elegy', where the paths of glory lead but to the grave. 'An Imperial Elegy' seems to have been planned as a conventionally heroic poem. Even so, it contains some of the essential elements in Wilfred's later work. He soars above immediate place and time, dismissing Brooke's egocentric viewpoint and surveying the entire battlefield like a Perseus-aviator. His allusions to the Titans, the very first war-makers, and to Isaiah illustrate the mythical, prophetic dimension he is reaching for. As in 'Strange Meeting' later, he has in mind some titanic conflict that is and is not the Great War. And he thinks of himself as an elegist. Even in 1918 he was to refer to his war poems as 'these elegies' and to think of publishing them as 'English Elegies'.

On the back of his notes for 'An Imperial Elegy' he writes some lines for what seems to be a Decadent love lyric, comparing a beautiful body to jewels and seasons, possibly trying to reflect a change in Chopin's music. Then he takes a second sheet and begins sketching out something very different again. Unfinished and confused, yet strangely familiar to anyone who has read the war poems, this fragment has often been regarded as draft work for 'Mental Cases' (1918), but it seems certain to be a 1916 manuscript, partly because it bears a marginal note of one of the training manuals he would have needed for his final courses at Romford, *How to Instruct in Aiming and Firing.*[22] Entitled 'Purgatorial Passions', but set in what seems to be hell rather than purgatory, it is a portrait of damned figures, leering with skull-like smiles, their fingers racked by some 'Wrong' they have committed. Their crimson, twitching eyes are sunk in 'blue chasms', sweat oozes from their hands and feet, and 'eternal terrors' stir their hair. It would be easy to read this with hindsight from 'Mental Cases', where much of the material is re-used, as a description of shellshocked soldiers, but Wilfred had neither the motive nor the experience to write about that subject in 1916. The word 'Passions' in his title points back to his earlier work, not forward to 1918.

Skull-smiles, tortured eyes, shaking fingers and similar details are conspicuous in the 'Perseus' fragments, especially 'The cultivated Rose', and even in Dunsden verse about hell, Despondency and the mermaid's statue. This recurrent, obsessive imagery grew from some of Wilfred's deepest feelings, and the 'Wrong' in 'Purgatorial Passions' seems likely to be sexual. However, some added lines mention Proserpine in the underworld, so perhaps the fragment was intended for 'Perseus'. If so, since he had already started developing 'Perseus' as a war poem, the damned figures can only be Germans. There were precedents, after all: popular ballads in 1914–15 had often described the torments of the Kaiser and his cronies in hell. Whatever Wilfred's intention was, the manuscript is striking evidence of the continuity of his 'poethood'. Much of the language and imagery of his 1917–18 poems was in place well before he knew the realities of the Western Front.

～

There was little time for poetry during Wilfred's stay in London. He visited Harold's ship in the East India Docks during a blizzard, and the two brothers met again a few days later, still in bitter weather, this time at the Bookshop, where Harold remembered being introduced to Monro.[23] This may have been the evening described in *Journey from Obscurity* when the brothers take refuge in a London cinema and Wilfred carefully removes puttees, boots and socks, then sits on the socks to dry them, unaware of the disturbance he is causing.[24] Harold sailed that night for Liverpool and was soon back at Mahim for a rest between voyages.

Wilfred's weekend was wrecked by guard duty at Duke's Road, and the ensuing weekdays were little better, with tedious lectures going on until late in the evening. After a few days his company was horrified to be suddenly told that their course still had six weeks to go, with intensive work and exams. 'There is only one consolation from this Delay, and that is a coward's,' Wilfred said. The change of plan was probably part of the army's current reorganisation of its officer training system. A dozen or more Officer Cadet Battalions were being established on the model of the 2nd Artists, which was itself about to be upgraded to become one of them. Edward Thomas's letters from Romford in March complain of enormous changes and a sharp increase in work (and it was now his hut's turn to be isolated by measles). Meanwhile, recruits were still coming in at head-quarters, some of them very young. Wilfred spotted the Dunsden schoolmaster's son, Ernie Hullcoop, who had been at school with Leslie.[25] A draft of men left for the front on the Thursday, and Wilfred's party marched with them to Waterloo with several bands playing, people gathering to give them a rousing send-off. The cadets were ordered out again in the evening for night operations on Hampstead Heath, where Wilfred had once walked in search of Keats. They marched up to the Heath and over it, no doubt making use of the regiment's practice trenches at Kenwood, and then they marched down to Bloomsbury again, getting back at breakfast-time, when they were told to parade in Regent's Park early on the Saturday, ready for the return journey to Romford.

Wilfred spread his things round his room at the Bookshop that Friday evening as a first step towards packing. He had given up hope of seeing his host, but at eleven o'clock there was a knock at the door and Monro entered amid the chaos, holding Wilfred's sonnets. 'So we sit down,' Wilfred told Susan, 'and I have the time of my life.' Monro was 'very struck' with the poems. He went through them in detail, pointing out what was 'fresh and clever, and what was second-hand and banal; and what Keatsian, and what "modern"', giving opinions that were quite unlike Professor Morley's, who had deplored some of the very phrases that were now being quoted with approval. Wilfred listened intently, realising his own critical standards were in need of radical revision. His later achievements were to owe more than is usually recognised to Monro's poems and advice. Even so, he thought Monro a 'peculiar being' and could not imagine becoming friendly with him, hoping only that they might have a business relationship, Monro being a publisher as well as a poet. When Wilfred asked whether the sonnets were good enough for a Little Book of Georgian Verse, Monro said they were far too good, and he seems to have promised to consider them for his own periodical, which he hoped to revive after the war. Then he very probably suggested going out, late though it was. He preferred not to drink alone, but he drank very heavily, sometimes in gay clubs. Wilfred got up next morning before anyone else in the house was stirring, but when he joined the parade in the park the officer in charge, Lee Hankey, gave him an hour's penal drill for having forgotten to put his belt on.[26]

Wilfred did not return to a hut at Romford, but to the Cadet School, formerly the School of Instruction, now based in Gidea Hall and Balgores House. His company was assigned to Balgores, a nineteenth-century mansion near the camp. The house had handsome, spacious rooms and extensive grounds with specimen trees, a lake and the inevitable practice trenches, but there was almost no furniture. The cadets had to sleep crowded together on the bedroom floors, and the house was miserably cold and uncomfortable, snow lying deep outside. But at least Balgores gave a first taste of life as an officer: the food was much better than in camp, and it was served by batmen at correctly laid tables. 'We expect the work to be strenuous,' Wilfred said, and so it was. He had to buy running clothes – he regarded them as a birthday present, because his parents paid for them – and training manuals. His room had to rouse itself at a quarter past five in the mornings 'to do our scraping, cleaning, washing, shaving, polishing, scrubbing, rubbing, brushing, oiling, sandpapering, folding, tying, tidying, cleaning up & clearing down, cleansing, ablutions, bucklings, foldings, etc. &c. Etc, and caetera'. There were 'eternal inspections, parades, inspections, punishment parades, & more inspections'. The Colonel drilled his charges on the golf course, cursing from the top of a mound or pursuing them, 'barking like a collie after straggling sheep', and when he left off a ferocious, foul-mouthed Guards sergeant took over. Evenings had to be spent on more preparation and cleaning, with lights-out at half past nine. Exams began in the second week. 'Now is the winter of the world,' Wilfred said on 18 March 1916, his twenty-third birthday, quoting from his sonnet, '1914'. 'But my life has come already to its month of March …'. The winter was in fact in retreat, 'the land freckled with snow half-thawed'[27] under warm sunshine.

'On the whole, I am fortunate to be where I am, and happy sometimes, as when I think it is a life pleasing to you & Father and the Fatherland,' Wilfred continued in his birthday letter. He was working out a new persona for himself. The Dunsden parish assistant, pale, earnest, ravaged by doubts, had given way to the sunburnt dandy in Bordeaux, and now the dandy had also gone, replaced by a disciplined soldier, fitter than the family could ever have imagined ('Father should indeed crow') and learned in every aspect of modern warfare. His hair, which had once flopped over his eyes like a poet's, was now half an inch long. He could keep pace with the rest of his company on long-distance runs, and in his exams he was getting full marks for drill and very good results in musketry and reconnaissance, coming top of his room. Yet the most bookish subject, military law, bored him as much as it bored most trainee officers. When he and others made mistakes they were kept in as a punishment and forced to study the textbooks all over again, a curious experience for an ex-teacher. He could see all this with detachment still, aware that his variable moods and 'relapses into solemnity' set him apart from the others.

His literary imagination was as active as ever, storing up imagery and noticing how odd the contrasts were in army life as men preparing to die spent their time joking, organising snowball fights and automatically obeying orders. At one minute they were scrubbing floors, at another making minutely detailed maps. While the fields echoed to the sound of gunfire, the almond trees were coming into bloom. He had been looking forward to a weekend in London on his birthday, but orders had come that all leave was cancelled. It was impossible to be one's own master. Sunday church parades were sometimes followed by digging trenches. One Sunday afternoon he hid himself away in the long greenhouse at Balgores to study the 'Assault with Fixed Bayonets', only to be ordered out again. Another contrast struck him when the Quayles failed to send a birthday present, at a time when his expenses were more than he could cope with unaided, yet when Monro's housekeeper forwarded his clean laundry she included a box of buns, biscuits and soup cubes, even with a screw of salt. There was no chance to visit the Williamses on Saturdays, but sometimes Sunday afternoons were free, allowing him to play with his Harper 'nephews' in the wood and help with their homework. He told his mother that the slight wound soldiering had inflicted on him was being 'repaired into a Pearl, a very goodly pearl, as befits / your solitary old Oyster'.

The war 'has but grazed us yet,' he said, but it came close on 31 March, just as the cadets were getting ready for bed. A series of violent explosions heralded the sudden appearance of a huge Zeppelin, dropping bombs and apparently heading straight for the camp. The sky was lit up by searchlight beams, while anti-aircraft shells burst far below and behind their target. Everyone in Balgores was ordered out on the parade ground, but the monster soon vanished behind a cloud. Wilfred thought the vapour was a screen put out by the Zeppelin itself. L.15 was in fact losing gas fast, having been hit after all, and the crew were unloading water ballast in a desperate attempt to get away. The wrecked airship was found off the Kent coast next morning.[28] Wilfred was as excited as any civilian by the spectacle of a Zeppelin under fire. He was enthralled, too, by a new drum and fife band in April, a 'thrilling affair'. The music and the 'gallant bearing of the twenty fifers … finally dazzled me with Military Glory. The fifers are worthy to rank with the demented violins that make Queen's Hall to spin round as a top, and with the Cathedral Choir that pierces thro' the heights of heaven. Sweetly sing the fifes as it were great charmed birds in Arabian forests. And the drums pulse fearfully-voluptuously, as great hearts in death.' The band was a sign of the battalion's improved status. Another was that the day was now measured by bugle calls, a sound that inspired Edward Thomas's poem, 'No One Cares Less than I', written at Romford in May.

The Colonel had been harrying the cadets because he knew a senior general was soon to inspect them. A 'terrible being' from the War Office duly arrived on 5 April, frightening everybody and snubbing one of the subalterns in front of Wilfred's company, but word came later that the visitor had been very pleased with what he had seen. Home leave was granted to half the School, giving Wilfred a weekend in Shrewsbury. The course drew to a close. He got through the final exams on 5 May without difficulty, answering every question and sending the papers home afterwards for his father's edification. Another brief leave followed, allowing successful candidates to get themselves measured for their new uniforms and buy necessities such as revolvers and Sam Browne belts. Wilfred went to one of the best military tailors, Pope & Bradley in Bond Street. Probably spending a night or two at 20 Devonshire Street, he toured the Academy summer exhibition as usual and saw a performance of *Hamlet*, revelling in 'the luxury of breathing LONDON'. He may have taken Ray or Bertie with him to the exhibition as a half-term treat. The sonnet 'To — ', dated with unusual precision 'London, 10 May 1916', describes Eros running between the poet and an unnamed friend along a sandy beach. Soon they will stumble, reaching adult knowledge, but as yet they still have the innocence of childhood.[29]

Wilfred was in London again a week later to have two more teeth extracted, a painful operation done without anaesthetic. There was still some routine work at Romford, where his company had moved to tents in

Hare Hall park, a pleasant change from the crowded bedrooms at Balgores. Thomas records that the weather was gloriously warm and still, with nightingales singing in the trees round the camp. The course ended at last on 19 May, and the prospective officers were sent away on 'LPG', Leave Pending Gazette. Wilfred went over to Hornchurch to say goodbye and was invited to stay the night with the Williamses. Next day he went on to Devonshire Street, and then travelled up to Shrewsbury. Harold was at sea again, Colin was working on a farm and Mary was probably still nursing. Wilfred had nearly a month in which to work on poems and be a solitary Oyster.

Second Lieutenant

5th Manchesters

JUNE–DECEMBER 1916

Wilfred spent most of his leave relaxing at Mahim, getting up at midday, walking Colin's new dog on the racecourse and reading poetry. He could be idle with a clear conscience, sure that his father would understand. On 3 June 1916 Private Owen was formally discharged from the Artists' Rifles, and next day even more formally commissioned as a second lieutenant in the Manchester Regiment, in due course receiving an impressive-looking document from the King. By 7 June the new officer was back in London, urging Pope & Bradley to hurry up with his uniform and trying to open an account with Cox's, the military bankers, who were doubtful about him because his name had not appeared in the *London Gazette*.[1] On Monday the 12th he reported to his new battalion, 3/5th Manchesters, at Witley Camp in the Surrey hills.[2]

Starting as an officer was in some ways harder to cope with than enlisting. Everything was strange, 'the country, the people, my dress, my duties, the dialect, the air, food, everything'. The camp was vast: Romford had been built for one large battalion, but there were enough huts on Witley and Milford Commons to take a dozen battalions with their attached units, in fact an entire division. The hutments were grouped in three areas, and Wilfred seems to have been in the largest, Witley North Camp, among ancient pine trees and above the lakes and open spaces of Thursley Common. It was a beautiful spot, although there was little chance to enjoy it. Soon after he arrived, at a moment when 'the men' were at leisure, he rashly walked down to Tin Town, as they called the cluster of temporary shops on the main road, 'and had to take *millions* of salutes'. The officers' quarters were set well apart, and for the first time he began to get the measure of the gulf fixed by the army between officers and Other Ranks. 'I am marooned on a Crag of Superiority in an ocean of Soldiers.'

The only people he knew were the handful of Artists from Romford, newly commissioned like himself. Briggs, who had arrived just ahead of him, introduced him to the Adjutant, who shook hands and left him to find his own way around. There were strict conventions that newcomers had to observe, such as leaving one's card on the mess table. Dinner was usually 'à la Grand Hotel', with enormous quantities of food, full regimental formalities and the band playing outside. Even the most junior subalterns had servants, whose sole job was to look after officers, run their errands and free them from the cleaning and polishing that had been such an annoyance at Romford. Wilfred set his man, a grandfather with sons at the front, to buying folding camp furniture – bed, chair, washstand – and generally organising a corner in a room occupied by three other officers. It was now possible to buy things without undue worry. Officer's pay meant that there was money to spare at last, and Wilfred was soon able to start sending cheques home, repaying the small sums his parents had been lending him since his enlistment. But with the money came innumerable duties. Life in the real army was a stern, intimidating business. He said he 'trod on knife edges' at first, remembering a metaphor from 'The Little Mermaid'.

The Manchesters were a typical infantry regiment, not particularly ancient or glamorous but with a history of hard fighting in many wars. They traced their origins back to two eighteenth-century regiments of foot, and their northern base and name to army reforms in 1881, when it had been decided that infantry units should have local identities. The two old regiments had become the 1st and 2nd Battalions of the new Manchester Regiment, part of the full-time ('Regular') army. They were still the regiment's core units in 1914–18, the 1st operating in the Middle East and the 2nd on the Western Front. Over forty additional battalions were raised before and during the Great War, some of them units in the reserve ('Territorial') army, others 'Service' or 'Pals' battalions of Kitchener volunteers. The 5th Manchesters was a Territorial battalion, actually based in Wigan and drawing many of its men from the coal-mining areas in and around that town. It is often referred to as a single unit, but it was in fact three in June 1916. The 1/5th, raised before the war, had been sent into action in 1914. It had soon spawned a 2/5th at home to provide it with reinforcements. The 3/5th, which Wilfred joined at Witley, was a home battalion, formed in Wigan in May 1915 to find and train recruits and retrain men who had come back wounded. From time to time the 3/5th would send drafts of men or officers to the front, where they were attached to fighting battalions.

The basic pattern of army organisation, familiar in theory from Romford lectures, now had to be experienced in practice. A typical battalion consisted of about eight or nine hundred men and some thirty officers commanded by a lieutenant-colonel, who was assisted by a senior major, a quartermaster, an adjutant and headquarters staff. Apart from troops assigned to headquarters and an assortment of cooks, drivers, armourers and specialists of one kind or another, most of the men were divided into four companies, usually commanded by captains, and each company was further divided into four platoons, commanded by subalterns (lieutenants or second lieutenants). Wilfred soon had his own platoon, probably about forty men, and his own staff, comprising a sergeant, a servant and two or three men who would act as scouts or runners. The platoon was organised into four sections, each under a corporal or lance-corporal. Some of the men were very young, some middle-aged, and those who had been in the trenches knew far more about war than their new commander did.

It was Wilfred's duty to oversee their training, demonstrating wherever possible that he was better at everything than they were. They had to be proficient in many things, from folding blankets and laying out kit for morning inspection to their three main tasks of marching, digging and killing. Above all they had to be expert in the use of arms, and every man was expected to be deadly with a rifle. Their other main weapons were the bomb, regarded as essential for clearing and 'mopping up' trenches; rifle-bombs, 'the howitzer of the infantry'; and the Lewis gun, a light, air-cooled machine gun capable of firing over forty rounds from a single magazine, in some circumstances worth another twenty-five rifles. The four sections would have to work as a team in attack and defence, and everything they did would depend on their commander. Wilfred knew all this and a great deal more from Romford and the training manuals. Even in rehearsal on the peaceful Surrey hillsides, his job seemed daunting.

~

His duties began as soon as he arrived, routine administration for the battalion and his company, and supervision of his platoon. Most of his men were 'hard-handed, hard-headed miners, dogged, loutish, ugly. (But I would trust them to advance under fire and to hold their trench;) blond, coarse, ungainly, strong, "unfatigueable", unlovely, Lancashire soldiers, Saxons to the bone.' Some who had been 'overseas' bore the scars of wounds, and it seemed absurd for a novice to be giving them orders. Wilfred felt guilty at his first kit inspection, when he sternly rebuked someone for lacking a toothbrush, only to find the man had lost belongings in the trenches (this may have been the germ for the 1917 poem, 'Inspection'). Private soldiers – their possessions inspected, their letters censored, their days regulated to the minute – had no privacy at all, but they had no responsibilities either; the army fed and clothed them, and saw to all their needs. It was the junior officers and NCOs who had to organise every-thing, hurrying from one duty to another, aware all the time that dozens, maybe hundreds of men were relying on their getting things right.

Wilfred was chosen to take a divisional exam in his first week to qualify him for active service, and he came second out of all the Manchester candidates, missing a distinction by only one mark. He took pride in doing his work well. Every morning the subalterns got up at a quarter to six, ready for strenuous physical training under the instruction of a deferential sergeant-major. They had to carry packs on morning parade and route marches, and there were endless forms and reports to deal with. Wilfred inspected his platoon (start at the feet and work upwards, the textbooks had said) and drilled them daily. Once he bawled 'Eyes Front' when he meant 'Eyes Left', but the sergeant pretended not to notice. Out on the sandy heathlands (he called them 'moors' in the northern way) he played his part in battalion and company manoeuvres, always remembering the British Army's insistence on the offensive spirit.

Hours were spent in digging. Wilfred knew how to construct a trench, and how to revet the lower stages with the timber sections that would be supplied by the engineers, and where to site latrines and Lewis guns, and why straight lines should always be avoided. A level parapet would be far too conspicuous, and a straight trench would give no protection from blast if a shell were to land in it. The platoon worked in the approved fashion, digging the forward fire bays, then joining them up with rear traverses, heaping the earth in front to make the parapet (the length of a rifle and bayonet, just over five feet, was enough to stop a Mauser bullet at close range) and at the back to make the parados, protection against shell-blast from behind. He and the sergeant drove the men to dig fast, because that might save their lives, but he felt ashamed to do it. There was exhilaration at the end of a long day, though, marching back to camp at the head of the platoon, keeping time with the company to 'a flourish of trumpets, and an everlasting roll of drums'. Gradually he began to notice 'the Intelligent, and the Smart' among his 'Lancashire Lads', not all of whom were loutish and unlovely after all.[3] They seemed touchingly open and trusting. Waiting with a leave party at Milford station one day, he wondered whether to distribute cigarettes, then thought better of it, only to be nonplussed when one of the youngest privates offered him some apples. 'Poor penniless school boy!' Wilfred thought, feeling sure no attempt was being made to curry favour. It was frustrating to have to keep up a strictly formal relation-ship. Even when he was out in the countryside with the platoon, patrols of military police were liable to gallop up at any minute, silently checking that discipline was being maintained.

No one was allowed out of camp without permission, but Wilfred was given leave to escape on Sundays, so he borrowed a rickety bicycle and rode through Godalming to Guildford, where it was a pleasure to be alone, wandering through the old streets or along the river bank, watching lazy civilians boating on the sunlit water. He found a teashop where he could settle in the bay window – 'a real old lattice Bay, no shams' – and survey the cobbled high street under its enormous clock. Thorpe's bookshop at the top of the street was another place to linger in, its cavernous, musty depths lined with treasures. He bought Edward Thomas's recent book on Keats, perhaps a sign that he had been aware of its author at Romford.[4] Returning to Witley he began to like the local countryside, curious though it seemed to a Salopian eye, 'neither mountain nor plain'. As he neared the camp the footpaths started to undulate with salutes, but being on a bicycle he was not obliged to respond.

In some places in the south of England, perhaps even at Witley, it was possible on still evenings to hear the low thunder rumbling across the sea from France in the last ten days of June 1916.[5] The Allied guns were firing their immense barrage, opening the way for the Big Push on the Somme that would break the enemy's defences at last. When the infantry went into action on 1 July, the 17th Manchesters scored one of the day's biggest successes by capturing the village of Montauban at the southern end of the British line. This achievement was no doubt celebrated in the mess at Witley when news of it came through, although experienced soldiers could soon see from maps in the newspapers that things had gone much less well further north. In front of Beaumont Hamel and Serre, the 'hinge' on which the whole advance was meant to turn, no ground had been gained at all. Lancashire and Yorkshire lads there, volunteer Pals' Battalions in battle for the first time, had suffered fearful casualties.

In the second week of July Wilfred was sent to Aldershot for a final musketry course. As an officer he would carry only a revolver in battle, but the authorities may have noticed that he was unusually competent with a rifle. At his first test he hit the bull's-eye with three of his five shots, an excellent start. He was temporarily attached to the 25th Middlesex and quartered with them in Talavera Barracks, a gloomy old building that had long been used by Regulars, and he thought that being in a real barracks in Aldershot, the army's traditional base, set the seal on his transformation into a soldier. It was an unpleasant place, with dirty shaving water and unappetising food, and until he found a single room he had to share with a colleague from Witley, a would-be High Church parson prone to making 'dogmatic, pig-headed, preachifying' conversation. The purpose of the course must have been to show new officers how to use the enormous ranges at Mytchett, east of the town, and after a fortnight's intensive work Wilfred was qualified to command firing parties.

There was time for a weekend at Alpenrose on 15–16 July. The new uniform was no doubt much admired, although the family would have been uncomfortably aware of the contrast between its wearer's heroic status and the questionable position of his civilian cousins, Gordon and Leslie.[6] Their sister Dorothy had written to Susan in praise of Wilfred's courage a few weeks before, and Susan had sent the letter to Wilfred, who replied that he was glad to have 'D.G.'s appreciation. There is no doubt about the craven-heartedness of *both her brothers*: at the same time I would rather my cousin Leslie did not perish, or become as the generality of men.'[7] Nothing would have been said about these matters at Alpenrose, but Uncle John arranged screens and lights in his studio and took one portrait after another of his nephew, profile and full-face, three-quarter length and close-up, with and without cap. In later years these photographs were to become ever more famous, until by the 1970s one was available as a National Portrait Gallery postcard, albeit attributed to Harold Owen. The attribution was corrected at Leslie's request, and the John Gunston portraits are now the standard image of the national war poet. Wilfred's dark eyes and faint Gioconda-like smile hint at what he was feeling that day at Alpenrose: pride in his new role, superiority over his cousins, and perhaps a little embarrassment.[8]

On the Sunday Wilfred revisited his past by attending morning service at Dunsden, where his uniform must have drawn every eye. The Vicar was his usual self, 'horrifyingly dismal' in church and genial afterwards in the porch, where he proclaimed, 'just in the Pulpit manner', that the war would be over very soon, an opinion widely held in those early weeks of the Somme fighting. Wilfred nodded and smiled to familiar faces, looking round for the one he most wanted to see, and there sure enough was Vivian, 'hovering behind the yew trees', wearing a straw hat with the ribbon of Reading School, one of the most prestigious secondary schools he and his mother could have hoped for. 'He looks well with his gay hatband, and melancholy brown eyes,' Wilfred told Susan, 'but his H's are a trifle uncertain still.'

$\sim$

Returning to Witley late on the following Saturday, after the end of the Aldershot course, Wilfred was startled to find he would have to lead his entire company to church parade next morning. It was a shock to be cast suddenly in the role of company commander, and to see the reason for it. Numerous officers, including three of the Artists, Jubb, Foster and Crampton, had been sent to France, and further drafts were being organised. The urgent need for reinforcements on the Somme must have been worrying everyone, with a consequent risk to morale. Presumably every company commander in the country had to do as Wilfred did at each daily parade: read aloud a War Office instruction that there should be no talk of war, even in private letters. He warned Susan that he might be sent overseas very soon. In the event, however, his superiors were to keep him in England until the end of the year, apparently valuing him as a capable instructor.

He was selected to attend some lectures on gas at which secret information was made available. Feeling sure that the knowledge would be useful, he familiarised himself with the subject and took his platoon out on the range to get them used to firing while wearing protective helmets. The thick, clumsy bags soaked in chemicals were grotesque headgear, and they made seeing and hearing difficult; one man let his rifle off by mistake, an offence for which Wilfred probably 'strafed' and 'crimed' him, negligent discharge being a serious offence. Military authority could only very rarely be laid aside. There was a field day when the battalion attacked a lake, and bathing was allowed afterwards, so Wilfred, typically, went exploring along the shore until he found a secluded corner inhabited by 'a solitary, mysterious kind of boy', who turned out to be the son of an aristocrat in the suite of the exiled King of Portugal. It was the sort of romantic encounter Wilfred delighted in, probably quite innocent but secret, strange and beautiful, all the more so for being hidden amongst army activity.

A day or two later he was up at four in the morning, having been detailed to take a party of about forty-five men to Mytchett for a musketry course. This time he would be teaching, not learning. A march of at least twelve miles in August was an unattractive prospect, though the early start would avoid the worst of the heat. His servant put the folding furniture into its bags and saw it safely stowed on a waggon. Men from throughout the division were going, so the column was a long one and the rear parties were choked with dust, but Wilfred was lucky enough to be put at the head, next to the officer commanding the whole expedition. 'March discipline is the ceremonial of war', according to the manuals: men had to march four abreast, hugging the side of the road and resting for ten minutes in every hour, and rest meant getting equipment off in thirty seconds and lying down, not wandering about. Singing on the march was encouraged, and NCOs were expected to consider it a disgrace if anyone in their section fell out. Wilfred's elderly servant fell out all the same, but there would have been a cart at the back for stragglers.

As soon as the sweating column arrived at the Mytchett huts Wilfred dutifully put his men's needs before his own, seeing to the Manchesters' billets and coping with incessant telephone calls and enquiries from NCOs (privates were not allowed to put requests to officers directly). 'I am most frightfully hard-worked,' he complained a few days later. 'It is one of the worst weeks I ever had in the army ... I am deaf with the 7 hours continual shooting, and stomach-achy with the fasting from food.' The time was coming, had he known it, when he would be able to look back on weeks like this as mere holidays. Meanwhile, the work was crucially important: 'The bullet beats the bomb and the bayonet', as the saying went, but the high command was worried that rifles were not being used well on the Somme. After each day on the range, the officers had to comment and criticise, distributing praise and blame.

Wilfred was glad of his grey hairs when, as sometimes happened, he had to reprimand his entire party, including the NCOs. When the Manchesters were detailed for guard, he drilled them for two hours in fixing bayonets, an art the newest recruits had not yet mastered. They had to make a good show or he would be in trouble himself. In return for his strictness the men watched his target pitilessly, but he scored better than they did, eventually qualifying as a first-class shot when most of them could only reach second or third. He did best at rapid fire, loosing off five rounds in thirty seconds and hitting two bulls and two inners. 'If allowed more time I do less well. It is an interesting part of my psychological "erraticness".' The men's psychology seemed equally erratic. In sunshine they were 'as dull and dogged as November', but in heavy rain they cheered up immensely. 'British troops are beyond my understanding,' Wilfred said, but he was beginning to admire them.

The course ended on Saturday 19 August, giving time for a night in Shrewsbury, although such a short break was merely unsettling. Saying goodbye to his mother on the following evening was painful, and he got in a panic at the station when he realised he had nothing to eat or drink, thereby annoying his father, who loved to show off sons in uniform but hated public discord. Wilfred sent apologies next day. The journey took him via Tamworth, and as he had an hour's wait there he went to look at the moonlit castle, remembering its appearance in *Marmion*. A suspicious policeman followed him all the way back to the station. He nearly missed his connection in London, but he crossed Waterloo Bridge as the dawn was breaking and the sight of the city skyline, silhouetted in purple against the orange east, made him forget all worries about trains and wars. He reported to the Adjutant in good time, and had to spend the morning practising with live Mills bombs, after which he was suddenly told to lecture on 'Discipline'. Discipline required him to obey, although he was by now desperately sleepy, so he took his obedience as the 'opening verse' for his talk and was pleased with the result. The old method of drawing a 'Message' from a verse worked just as well in the dedicated world of the army as it had done in a parish hall.

Wilfred had been told on first joining the battalion that all drafts were being sent to Egypt for Mesopotamia, but that had been before the Somme. Now the need was for more men and yet more men on the Western Front, and the Manchesters' home-based units were being thinned out so fast that on 1 September the 3/6th and 3/7th were amalgamated with the 3/5th to make a new 5th (Reserve) Battalion. The upheaval, part of a reorganisation of all the army's reserves, was immense, and Wilfred was disheartened when some of his men, as well as Briggs and other officers, were sent away to join other regiments.[9] The remaining Artists were soon sent overseas, and the casualty lists began to include names Wilfred knew. His luck held, however, and he was told by the Colonel, W.H. Ridge, that he would be on the staff of the 'New Battalion' as Second Muskets Officer, jointly responsible for the programme of rifle training. This was a real mark of approval. 'The C.O. appears to have found my work – or my person – not too offensive to him': hard work at Romford and a Pope & Bradley uniform were proving to be good investments.[10]

Wilfred said 'Thank you, sir' to the Colonel, but he was secretly hoping to apply for a very different job. Several officers had volunteered for the Royal Flying Corps, and he wanted to do the same. 'By Hermes, I will fly,' he told Susan on 27 August.

> I will yet swoop over Wrekin with the strength of a thousand Eagles, and all you shall see me light upon the Racecourse ...[11]
>
> Then I will publish my ode on the Swift.
>
> If I fall, I shall fall mightily. I shall be with Perseus and Icarus, whom I loved; and not with Fritz, whom I did not hate. To battle with the Super-Zeppelin ... would be chivalry more than Arthur dreamed of.[12]
>
> Zeppelin, the giant dragon, the child-slayer, I would happily die in any adventure against him ...
>
> But I am terrified of Fritz, the hideous, whom I do not hate.

Wilfred's poetic self, still youthful and romantic, was making a last struggle against the prosaic limitations of life in the infantry. Remembering his own and Leslie's attempts at epic, he could imagine himself even now as Perseus attacking the dragon. Zeppelins, child-slayers, were universally hated, because bombing civilians was still thought to be a supremely barbarous act, but the propagandists had not been able to make ordinary German soldiers seem equally detestable. 'Frightful Fritz' and 'Horrible Heinrich' could not really be blamed for the policies of their superiors. Wilfred went for an interview in London and was told that he might well be taken on as a trainee pilot if he could get his CO's support. Colonel Ridge sternly refused at first, saying Wilfred could not be spared, but over tea a day or two later he was 'frightfully decent' and promised to sign the forms. However, the application seems to have got nowhere, perhaps because the War Office already had enough volunteers.

If the attempt on the RFC achieved nothing else, it apparently revived Wilfred's poetic ambitions. Leslie Gunston once again proved to be a loyal collaborator; he too had applied to the RFC, hoping to get a 'Sedentary Flying Commission', but when both his and Wilfred's applications failed in September it seemed time to put aside the old subject of flight. Leslie roped in Olwen Joergens, and all three poets resolved to choose sonnet titles for each other. Sonnets would be easier for a busy officer to cope with than an endless epic on Perseus. One of the first titles was 'Purple', Wilfred's favourite colour, and his contribution, first drafted in September, sets out a familiar list: night skies, wine, passion, flowers, sunset, 'diamond dawn' and 'the veil of Venus, whose rose skin, / Mauve-marbled, purples Eros' mouth for sacred sin'. It would be impossible to guess from this lavish display of Decadent imagery that the sonnet's author was 'Muskets Two' in an infantry battalion, facing the possibility of being sent to the Somme.

Another agreed subject may have been 'Heaven', one of three titles, along with 'A New Heaven' and 'To a Comrade in Athens' (later Flanders), that Wilfred tried out for another September sonnet. A British naval force landed at Athens on 1 September, so the unnamed comrade, perhaps Briggs, may have hoped to be sent there, although in the event he must have gone to France or Flanders like everyone else. The poem proposes that the new heaven for a soldier to hope for, now that the old ones of religion, fairy tale and childhood have been lost, should be home. 'Let's die back to those hearths we died for.'

> *To us, rough knees of boys shall ache with rev'rence.*
> *Are not girls' [brows] breasts a clear, strong Acropole?*
> *– There our own mothers' tears shall heal us whole.*

There are several versions of these closing lines, all of them foreshadowing 'Anthem for Doomed Youth'. When Wilfred's spirits were low, he turned his thoughts homewards, thinking of Colin, knees rough from summer farmwork, and Mary's pale little face and Susan's consoling arms. Another year was to pass before that dream, too, was to fade like the others into outworn myth.

It may well be that some, perhaps most, of Wilfred's attempts at verse in 1916 have not been preserved. There are a few traces in his manuscripts of what seems to have been a poem about a handsome young man waiting on a quayside in summer, hoping to be picked up. Elements in this description were later to be used for 'Disabled', just as 'A New Heaven' was to be quarried for 'Anthem'.[13] In October he drafted two more sonnets, 'Music', another set subject, and 'Storm'. A manuscript perhaps also dating from the second half of the year shows him trying out a comparison between fierce sunlight and the sound of bugles and drums, memories of the rape of Danae, French military music and the Mérignac sun. Then come some strange lines about a youth sinking into a pond (another memory of himself in France), apparently an image of the pleasures of summer nights in Paris or London. At the top of this enigmatic sheet is a stanza from Swinburne's 'Laus Veneris', a poem about the once-saintly knight and poet, Tannhäuser, who was trapped in the mountain of love, a dark underworld peopled by tormented victims of unsatisfied desire.[14]

Wilfred was evidently still trying to write about the sort of subject matter he had worked with in the 'Perseus' fragments and 'Purgatorial Passions'.

His attempt at a poem about fiery sunlight and the sinister consequences of love may have got no further, but he rescued the metaphor of sunlight as music, reworking it into the opening lines of 'The End', another sonnet on an agreed subject. The summer day now becomes the Last Day, ending with a final sunset and the death of youth, themes common in Decadent poetry.

> After the blast of lightning from the east,
>   The flourish of loud clouds, the Chariot Throne;
> After the drums of time have rolled and ceased,
>   And by the bronze west long retreat is blown,
> Shall Life renew these bodies? Of a truth,
>   All death will he annul, all tears assuage?

Susan Owen later had the last two lines adapted for Wilfred's tombstone, with the omission of the final question mark, but the poem itself concludes that there will be no immortality. 'It is death,' the Earth says in answer to human questioning:

> 'Mine ancient scars shall not be glorified,
> Nor my titanic tears, the seas, be dried.'

Wilfred was not driven to that conclusion by the Somme, as is sometimes assumed. He had written that 'Science has looked, and sees no life but this' four years earlier, sitting in the dining room at Dunsden Vicarage.

~

'Harold came over yesterday afternoon in response to my telegram,' Wilfred reported to Susan on 13 September 1916, adding that Harold, who looked far healthier than in the winter, had accompanied him on his 'Afternoon Work' and then to supper in Guildford before staying the night in camp. Harold's version of the meeting is rather different: his memoirs say he arrived unannounced and stayed only a few hours, and Wilfred thought he looked ill.[15] Harold also claims to have been a Merchant Navy officer since at least 1914. He had in fact still been a cadet in March 1916, when he had signed on again soon after seeing Wilfred in Romford. Possibly he had been promoted after that at sea as a temporary measure, but a photograph taken in Shrewsbury, almost certainly in September 1916, shows him still in cadet's uniform. He had now decided to apply for the Royal Naval Air Service. If he had indeed served as an officer by the time he visited Witley, he and Wilfred were more nearly equals than they had ever been, both officers, both committed to the war effort and both dreaming of becoming airmen, and all those factors may have lowered the old barrier between them.

Harold recalls the meeting at Witley as exceptionally happy, 'the most splendid afternoon of our companionship', and he paints a golden image of it. Gone now is the anxious, disorganised cadet who had set up that ludicrous evening in Ilford with the waitress. Wilfred has become an idealised, faultless figure, an officer of 'quiet but superb quality', the quality being the result not of training but 'something innate and also indescribable'. He treats his servant, a boy to whom he has been teaching French, with exactly the right combination of kindness and authority (officers could choose their own servants, so Wilfred may well have replaced the grandfather). His relationship with the men is no less perfect, and they show warm admiration for him as they cluster round in the camp library, asking his advice about books. Wilfred is in charge of the library (his letters never mention it, however, nor does Harold suggest more likely places for a subaltern's Afternoon Work, such as rifle ranges and training grounds). As an elder brother, too, Wilfred's old patronising airs have vanished, to be replaced by the affectionate appreciation of a friend and equal.

Even Wilfred's appearance and equipment are impressive. His Sam Browne is 'richly lustrous', his shoes gleam, his uniform fits exactly. He has expensive leather dressing cases ('Swaine and Adeny,' Harold thinks to himself) and ivory-backed hairbrushes. He is first discovered shirtless, revealing a new and impressive physique, and from under the 'broad forehead' the 'deep-set dark-hued eyes' gaze serenely, dark grey eyes glazed with brown, or light brown overlaid with grey, Harold can never be certain which, but 'what I am never uncertain about is their depth of meaning'. Only the hair makes the younger brother wince, the once poetic locks now cropped horribly short, parted in the middle and plastered down with brilliantine.

Harold admits that after the war he had tried to suppress all photographs showing Wilfred's military hairstyle, and in so doing he gives a clue as to the source of some elements in his description. Writing half a century or so after 1916, he is thinking of John Gunston's portraits, with some help from Osbert Sitwell, who had described Wilfred's eyes as 'deep in colour, and dark in their meaning'.[16] Two other photographs probably helped to confirm Harold's two pictures of Wilfred as a soldier. One shows the new cadet at Romford, looking thin and awkward in the unlovely garb of a private. The other, taken at Witley in July 1916, shows the new officer, a compact, elegant little figure in tailor-made uniform, gazing steadily at the camera, determined to make a good impression. He wears gloves, unlike all but his most senior colleagues; his swagger stick is a riding crop, suggestive of good family; and his Sam Browne is of distinctly better quality than those of his neighbours. After months of training and effort, whether or not reinforced by the 'innate' quality of his Owen blood, Wilfred had indeed become a model officer.

～

Rumours had been going round of an impending move north, and when the actual destination was announced Wilfred wrote home delightedly, 'Oswestry!!!' The camp was reputed to be awful, the accommodation being only tents, so he was alone in being pleased.[17] The battalion set out in four early-morning trains on 22 September, an operation that must have caused many headaches for the subalterns. Wilfred had asked Susan to stay in Oswestry with some old friends, the Parrys (Mrs Parry was his god-mother), so that he could spend his evenings with her, and she appears to have done as he suggested. For the next month, based in his native town, he carried on with his musketry job, his mother met some of his fellow officers and perhaps saw him at work, and he had no need to write letters.

The tented camp was not suitable for winter occupation, so on 16 October the battalion was sent to the Lancashire coast, part of a large move by numerous battalions, including at least one entire division. This invasion by many thousands of men was welcomed as a boost to the local economy, although lodging-house keepers in Blackpool were soon com-plaining that the billeting rate of just over two shillings a man was not enough to house and feed a healthy young soldier. Officers were better provided for, as usual, and Wilfred soon wrote from 'cosy' lodgings at 168a Lord Street, the splendid boulevard at Southport. His kindly old landlady, Miss Sibbit, knew so little about military matters that she had thoughtfully dried out his gas helmet, thereby rendering it useless. He said Southport was the 'most unsatisfactory *sea-side* place in Europe', meaning the beach was so shallow that the sea was scarcely visible from the town, but conditions were far better than at Oswestry. On his first weekend he went to see the Quayles at Meols, pausing in his former home town, Birkenhead ('Can't think how We ever survived the place'). It was a disappointment at the end of the month to have to move into the Queen's Hotel on the Southport promenade, although the hotel was a good one and recently refurbished. He was put in a room with a second lieutenant named Ciceri, and the local newspaper duly announced in its regular lists of visitors that 'Lt Owens' and 'Lt Aceri' were at the Queen's, together with twenty-six other officers from the 5th Manchesters and numerous civilian guests.

No sooner had Wilfred joined this uncomfortably crowded combina-tion of family hotel and officers' mess than he was moved yet again, this time up the coast to Fleetwood in charge of another firing party. Arriving at Fleetwood on Sunday 5 November with similar parties from three other battalions, he marched his 120 men to the market hall and helped to send them off to billets. Sundays were the army's preferred day for travelling, and there was no point in apologising to Susan any more for Sabbath-breaking. The next few weeks turned out to be thoroughly enjoyable. In the space of five months Wilfred had risen from platoon to company commander, then to battalion staff, and now he was further promoted to brigade staff as officer in charge of the range firing point. This meant that officers and men from all four battalions in the brigade were under his orders when they were shooting. The commander of the entire detachment, Major T.R. Eaton of the Manchesters, 'an imposing warrior', treated him with every courtesy, even showing him a letter from the Brigadier-General which said, 'Owen should be of great assistance to you.' 'Didn't know he suspected my existence!' Wilfred said in justifiable astonishment. He handed over his battalion command to a junior, A.R. Rickard.

The OC Firing Point had two servants, one of them 'practically perfect', and quarters in what was termed an apartment at 111 Bold Street, a tall Victorian house in a tree-lined avenue, sharing with Arnold Rickard, who proved to be very congenial, 'not kin spiritually or literarily, but actually and personally and militarily we agree famously'.[18] Wilfred was reminded of the house-sharing partnership of Keats and Charles Browne. There was some social life: his letters mention a dance and a 'free and easy' theatre show, at which some of his men performed. He seems to have seen some Charlie Chaplin films, and he read an entertaining novel by H.G. Wells, probably *Kipps*. Some local friends of Susan's, the Averys, were hospitable, and Susan herself seems to have come over more than once, imploring her son to buy a trench coat, which he did in Blackpool, and helping him to do up its awkward buttons. One Sunday afternoon he sent her a postcard of the parish church, saying he had taken his 'little Family' there that morning.[19] It was almost like being in charge of 'the children' again at home. A national Mission of Hope and Repentance was in progress in the wake of the Somme; he said nothing about that, but wrote 'Local Colour!' on the card against a huge shop sign that said 'ASK FOR SLATTERY'S IRISH BREAKFAST BACON'.

He went to Blackpool twice, no doubt on the tram, which at that time had its northern terminus at the end of Bold Street. On his second visit the tram would have halted well before the centre of Blackpool, because the entire West Lancashire Reserve Division was on parade with all its transport, guns and a dozen bands.[20] The reporter for the *Fleetwood Chronicle* was deeply impressed by the tramp of feet and the forest of bayonets rising and falling, as some twenty thousand men marched along the promenade, eight abreast. Such events were no longer entertainment, the newspaper reflected, although a forgetful public had to be often reminded that the nation was in arms 'to save its honour, and to deliver a continent'. The jingo spirit was dead, and pageantry could wait until peacetime. 'We' were in the greatest war in history: 'the emphasis is on the personal pronoun. It is our work, our money, our blood, if needs be, that must win the war.' The Blackpool cinemas were showing the sensational new film of the Somme, the 'Greatest Historical Event that has ever yet been Picturised'.

The firing parties returned to Southport after a fortnight, to be replaced by others, while Wilfred and Eaton remained in post. Fleetwood had been an important musketry centre for a short time in the nineteenth century, and there were still some huts and two 800-yard ranges facing the sea at Rossall Point.[21] Some days were bright, the sun sparkling on the white-crested waves, but the firing point was desperately cold, exposed to the vicious wind. Wilfred had to stand in the same spot in his trench coat for six hours at a stretch, but he was unperturbed. He had felt deafened and hungry at Mytchett, but he had learned to cope with the noise since then and no longer had any qualms about eating on duty and shouting 'Sheesh Fire!!!' with a mouthful of crumbs. He and Eaton felt obliged to do some shooting themselves, and they scored very well, whereas some of the men could hardly hit the target at all. Wilfred told the lowest scorers he would never allow them near him at the front, but one of them was to save his life four months later.

Susan wrote that Leslie had managed to get a poem into print, a little Swinburnian love lyric in the YMCA magazine, but Wilfred was determined to be unimpressed, having still not reached print himself.[22] He said his own work would be rejected as blasphemous by the magazine. 'Young Men' no longer existed, anyhow, and 'quite right too. We are youths, lads, fellows, pals, chaps, comrades, boys, blokes if you will, but not your Young Men.' He had learned the language and spirit of comradeship. He looked out the 'Ballad of Peace and War', the poem about heroic comradeship and sacrifice that he had written at Mérignac. If infantrymen could not emulate Perseus, they could do better still, and he changed the title to 'Ballad of Kings and Christs', organising the lines as a dialogue between women and dead soldiers. In answer to questions from the dead, the women insist that Britain is safe for children and old people because 'your dear cheeks are bloody ... ye are our Kings / And Christs'. The dead do not disagree. Wilfred could still believe that 'every lad was seraph-clad / Who wore his own bright blood'.[23] Not every patriotic poet would have been quite so ready to imagine blood, but imagery of dying soldiers as angels, Arthurs and Christs was standard stuff. He never quite lost this way of thinking, but in a final attempt at the ballad, probably written in 1918, the dead at last contradict the women.

Only one thing went wrong at Fleetwood. Tom had unwisely mentioned that a pair of Zeiss binoculars had been handed in at Shrewsbury station, and Wilfred had persuaded him to send them up to Fleetwood. An urgent telegram soon arrived on the range to say the owner had been found, and by that stage Wilfred had apparently damaged the case. In sending the package home he diplomatically enclosed a card to his father, quoting the General's approving remark in the hope that Tom would be mollified.[24] Tom was not mollified: he had to pay an exorbitant price for repairs, and narrowly missed getting into serious trouble. 'I knew Father would strafe me about the mutilated Case,' Wilfred commented resignedly afterwards. The incident perhaps cast a small shadow over celebrations of his parents' Silver Wedding on 8 December, even in his absence.[25]

$\sim$

On 4 December Wilfred wrote from the Queen's Hotel at Southport. He was in low spirits.[26] His Fleetwood posting was over, and he was no longer under Eaton but another major, a 'snotty, acid, scot, impatient, irritated wretch'. The subalterns now had to set out early every morning for a three-mile march to the range, all leave had been stopped for some reason and there were rumours of work being extended to seven days a week. Wilfred's throat trouble had flared up again. The hotel was in the teeth of the wind, and he had been given an unattractive little room on the top floor. He grumbled at not being visited by his family. But none of this was at the root of his depression. 'Am I getting fed up with England?' Most of the officers in the Queen's had 'been out' by now and many wore gold stripes on their sleeves, showing that they had been wounded. One of the Artists, Jubb, was already back, recovering from a rifle-grenade injury. Wilfred must have felt uncomfortable at being a fit and competent man in a cushy home job. He had put his name down for Egypt, but the draft had been cancelled. He had also spoken to Colonel Ridge about applying to the RFC again. Ridge had been very nice about it, promising to speak to the Brigadier-General, but the General perhaps replied that the army could not afford to lose a highly-trained officer whose expertise in musketry would be of no use in the air.

The circumstances of Wilfred's departure from Southport, like those of his departures from Dunsden and Bagnères, and from Scarborough in 1918, will never be known except for a few dates. Two faded typewritten notes from the Adjutant are still among his papers. The first is dated 11 December 1916: 'Please note that you are placed under orders to proceed overseas. You will proceed on your final leave today, returning on the 16th inst.'[27] The strain of those five days at Mahim can only be guessed at. There was no chance of staying on for Christmas. All too soon Wilfred was back at Southport, undergoing the usual medical check, paying his mess bill and getting his servant to pack his valise, the capacious travelling bag that all officers took to the front. On the 24th the Adjutant sent further instructions and a railway pass. Wilfred was to report to the Assistant Embarkation

Officer at Folkestone by 9 p.m. on the 29th. 'You will be attached to the Lancashire Fusiliers.' The Averys may have provided a Christmas meal on the 25th, and just possibly Susan came to stay with them for a night or two.

Wilfred's next surviving letter was written on the 28th from a 'magnificent' room in the vast Hotel Metropole at Folkestone.[28] He had already come near to being killed. Travelling down to London in the guard's van on a crowded train, he had been woken up with a violent shock when some loose timber on a passing goods waggon had smashed into the roof above his head, a bad start to the coming ordeal and an omen of the shellburst that was to precipitate his eventual neurasthenia. He was met at Charing Cross by Harold, now uniformed as a trainee airman in the RNAS. 'It was a fine thing to see him,' Wilfred said. 'He is translated utterly from the being he was five years ago.' Harold joined the train for the short distance to London Bridge, then he too had to say goodbye. Wilfred was told at Folkestone that a boat would leave at eleven-thirty next morning. He was lucky enough to get talking to a Canadian doctor who was due to make the same crossing, and they agreed to take their last chance of luxury by sharing a room at the Metropole. There, among the palm trees, deep carpets and 'golden flunkeys', Wilfred did his best to relax. The pageboys, apparitions dazzlingly unlike the clumsily-uniformed Tommies he had been used to, looked as though they had been 'melted into their clothes'.

Seventh Hell

Serre and Beaumont Hamel

JANUARY–MARCH 1917

The British war effort was now colossal and highly organised, the manifestation of an unprecedented, single-minded resolve. In disembarking at Calais on 29 December 1916 Wilfred would have felt more than just excitement and fear.[1] There was a grim sense of common purpose in the activity he saw around him, even though soldiers seemed to be milling about everywhere. Moreover coming back to France had a special significance for him personally, because it was here less than two years earlier, inspired by Tailhade's example and the danger to *la patrie* and the language of the poets, that he had made his decision to enlist. This return journey was 'The Only Way'. He had kept his word.

He took a train down the coast to the enormous base camp at Étaples among the windswept dunes and pinewoods, where drafts bound for the front were required to remain for a few days of intensive training as a final preparation for the rigours of the trenches. Thinking about the place a year later, Wilfred remembered it as a 'vast, dreadful encampment', 'a kind of paddock where the beasts are kept … before the shambles', but that is the voice of his late 1917 self, the friend of Siegfried Sassoon and bitter critic of the war. When he was there at the start of the year he described Étaples much more mildly as 'a sort of Hotel Camp'. Conditions were quite good for officers. He had a tent to himself and a helpful servant. Meals in the officers' mess were cooked by a former chef to the Duke of Connaught and presided over by a baronet.[2] Even so, it was hard not to dread the future.

As 1916 passed into 1917, Wilfred lay awake in his tent, listening to the bitter wind blowing in from the sea and the carousings of Scots troops keeping Hogmanay, and wondered what his chances were of reaching 1918. He had already seen a sight that was to haunt him afterwards, the look on men's faces, a 'look of set doggedness', as he described it that January; his later self recalled it as 'not despair, or terror,' but 'more terrible than terror, … a blindfold look, and without expression, like a dead rabbit's'. There was no hope or enthusiasm any more, only a strange, numb determination.

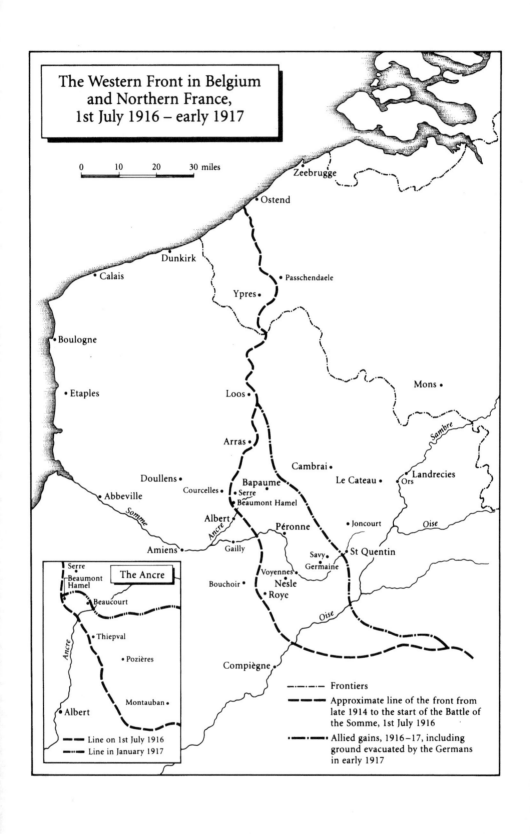

The Western Front in Belgium and Northern France, 1st July 1916 – early 1917

0   10   20   30 miles

Zeebrugge
• Ostend
Dunkirk
• Calais
• Passchendaele
Ypres •
• Boulogne
• Etaples
Loos •
Mons •
Arras •
Sambre
Cambrai •
Landrecies
Doullens •
Le Cateau •   • Ors
Courcelles •   Bapaume
Serre
• Abbeville   Beaumont Hamel
Albert
Péronne
Somme
Ancre
• Joncourt   *Oise*
Amiens •   Gailly
Savy •   St Quentin
Germaine •

The Ancre

Serre
Beaumont Hamel
Beaucourt
Bouchoir •
Voyennes •
Nesle
• Roye
Ancre
• Thiepval
Oise
• Pozières
Compiègne •
Montauban •
• Albert

Line on 1st July 1916
Line in January 1917

—·—·— Frontiers

— — — Approximate line of the front from late 1914 to the start of the Battle of the Somme, 1st July 1916

—·■—·■ Allied gains, 1916–17, including ground evacuated by the Germans in early 1917

But no one talked of giving up, and not just because any such talk would have risked severe punishment. They would keep going, come what may, and he would have to do the same.[3]

One reason for the pause at Étaples was that the authorities there had the job of finally allocating soldiers to units in the field. While Wilfred waited for orders he took part in training exercises like everyone else, and was even slightly wounded on 1 January, rather to his satisfaction, when a bomb splinter grazed his thumb. That afternoon he was instructed to join not the Lancashire Fusiliers, as he had been told at Southport, but the 2nd Manchesters. 'I have come off mighty well,' he told Susan, delighted to be going to his own regiment. He put it down to luck that he had been chosen, apparently alone among the officers newly arrived from the 5th, although inwardly he may have suspected he had been recommended as a promising man. 'There is a fine heroic feeling about being in France, and I am in perfect spirits,' he said after receiving the order, adding hopefully that he didn't think it was the real front he was going to. The heroic feeling soon evaporated. His new battalion was not much more than forty miles away, but the French railways were in crisis, choked with far more traffic than they could cope with, and the journey took him well over twenty-four hours, with many tips to porters for carrying his bags from one train to another. He was stranded at least once and had to get himself and others invited into a sergeants' mess to ask for much-needed food and beer. By the time he reached the Manchesters at Halloy-lès-Pernois, a village south-west of Doullens, he was wet and exhausted.[4]

His pleasure at being attached to one of his own regiment's two Regular battalions must have been mixed with trepidation. The 2nd Manchesters had been in action since August 1914, at Ypres and on the Somme, gaining a well-deserved reputation as tough, dependable fighters who could be put into the line wherever it most needed strengthening, and they were just about to go into action again after a six-week 'rest'. Their previous show, as they would have called it, had been in November 1916 at Serre, in the final operations of the Somme campaign. By then almost all the original objectives had been gained, including, on 13 November, the ruined village of Beaumont Hamel, near Serre, but Serre itself at the northernmost end of the battle front was still holding out behind impregnable defences. The Manchesters had run into appalling difficulties. Heavy snow had fallen, vital supplies of bombs had failed to arrive and the guides had got lost in the communication trenches. The leading companies had reached the German second line on an exposed ridge, only to be surrounded and virtually wiped out, the active strength being reduced to six officers and 150 men. By the time Wilfred joined, the battalion was practically a new unit, rebuilt with large drafts from England, but it still had a core of experienced officers, men not likely to make allowances for newcomers.[5]

The CO, Lieutenant-Colonel Noel Luxmoore, was a surprising man to find in charge of a Manchester battalion, being a native of Devon and an Old Etonian. He had served for years with the Devonshire Regiment, losing a leg in the South African war, and had been given command of the 2nd Manchesters in 1915, leading them through some of their worst ordeals. He was said to be a fire-eater, adored by troops but a terror to subalterns, and Wilfred later put him on a level with Keats, Christ and Elijah in a famous letter to Sassoon.[6] The Colonel allocated Wilfred to A Company under Captain H.R. Crichton-Green, whom Wilfred described as 'a gentle-man *and an original*' (meaning Green had been in the original BEF). Green put the newcomer in command of No. 2 Platoon, although Wilfred soon managed to take over No. 3 instead because he 'liked the look of the men'. He was the third most senior officer in the company, after Green and Lieutenant Arthur Heydon. The latter, a chartered accountant from Stockport, had joined the ranks in August 1914 and been wounded in the arm at Gallipoli before being commissioned. In 1916 he had served as Assistant Adjutant at Witley and Oswestry, where Wilfred had known and liked him, and he had been in the Queen's Hotel at Southport, too, so he must have been another recent arrival at Halloy.

Conditions in billets were wretched. If Wilfred had brought ivory-backed hairbrushes and Swaine & Adeny cases with him, they must have seemed ludicrously out of place. After the luxuries of the Metropole and the Étaples mess, he had been 'let down, gently, into the real thing, Mud'. By 4 January it had penetrated his sleeping bag and even his pyjamas, thanks to a careless servant. He had at first chosen a servant who was reputed to be good with a bayonet, as servants had to be their officers' bodyguards in battle, but the man was in the bombing section and so not available. The substitute seems to have been less satisfactory. Wilfred had to sleep on a stone floor in a cottage, sharing a room with three other officers next to the foul-mouthed band, 'the roughest set of knaves I have ever been herded with' (this first use of the cattle metaphor was clearly not inspired by feelings of pity). No one could wash, or get warm and dry. 'Everything is makeshift.' Food was served in old tins. All the officers wore a harassed look Wilfred had never seen before and could not imagine seeing in England, except in jails. Worse still was the troops' unconcealed depression. 'We feel the weight of them hanging on us.' They were like the 'expressionless lumps' in Bairnsfather cartoons, and even men who had been in Wilfred's detachment at Fleetwood could hardly smile a greeting, glad though they seemed to be to see him. Everyone knew what lay ahead. Regulations prohibited all mention of place-names in letters, but Wilfred had agreed with Susan that if he used the word 'mistletoe' the first letters of the following lines would form a word. He used the code for the first time on 4 January, and the letters read 's o m m e'.[7]

A thousand-strong battalion must have seemed daunting to a new subaltern as it readied itself for battle, but it was only a small part of a huge machine from the General Staff's point of view, even with its supporting units of engineers, signallers and trench mortar men. Four such battalions made a brigade, three brigades a division; and the division, not the battalion, was the basic fighting force, capable of firing 120,000 rifle rounds and 1,000 shells a minute, as well as thousands of rounds from machine and Lewis guns.[8] There were fifty-six British infantry divisions and five of cavalry in France and Belgium at the beginning of 1917, over one-and-a-half million men in all. Two or three divisions made a corps, two or three corps an army. The Manchesters were with 1st Dorsets, 15th Highland Light Infantry (HLT), and 5/6th Royal Scots in 14th Brigade, 32nd Division, V Corps, Fifth Army (General Sir Hubert Gough). In war on such a scale, private soldiers could know almost nothing of what was going on. Subalterns were a little better informed, and Wilfred's horizons had to extend at least as far as the brigade, because the four battalions in it would be regularly relieving each other in the line. The larger picture was known only to generals far to the rear, and they in turn had only limited knowledge of actual movements in the smoke and confusion of the front. The Somme, as yet the largest battle ever fought, had been beyond anyone's final control.

V Corps had been out of the line for some time, and was now due to take its turn in action. The 14th Brigade set out for the front on 6 January 1917, following the broken lanes to tents at Beauval, south of Doullens, the men suffering badly under their heavy loads in rain and sleet. Wilfred was heavily loaded, too, although he managed to get a horse for part of the way. He seems to have been quick to master the front-line art of borrowing and scrounging. Arriving at Beauval he saw to his platoon as he had been trained to do, then found his own tent, and while he was spreading his damp sleeping bag on a stretcher borrowed from the doctor he heard the guns for the first time, 'a sound not without a certain sublimity'. The Manchesters paused for a day while other units went ahead in heavy rain to take up forward positions. After a three-hour inspection in the morning, when platoon commanders had to read Trench Standing Orders to their men, there was little for the troops to do but sing the favourite song of the moment, 'The Roses round the door / Makes me love Mother more' ('I don't disagree,' Wilfred said) and write letters, all of which had to be censored by the subalterns. Wilfred read dozens of these compositions, with their gloomy forebodings, dreams of peace and hollow assurances that the writer was 'in the pink'. In the afternoon he went into the village, writing his own letter in a café. 'I have no Fancies and no Feelings,' he told Susan. 'Positively they went numb with my feet.'

The battalion moved further east at noon on 8 January, into the uplands above the Ancre valley, past wide fields scattered with camouflaged guns and through little villages that had been used as bases for battalion after battalion throughout the Somme fighting. They travelled in buses to Bertrancourt and then marched to the ruins of Courcelles, relieving the 15th HLI as brigade reserve. That was a relief for the Scotsmen only in the army sense; they had to go into the line, where they came under heavy fire as the enemy guns answered a British barrage. 'There is a terrific Strafe on,' Wilfred wrote from Courcelles on the 9th. 'Our artillery are doing a 48 hours bombardment. / At night it is like a stupendous thunderstorm, for the flashes are quite as bright as lightning.' A letter from his mother reached him, the first to do so since he had arrived in France, and he thought how wrong it seemed for her handwriting to come into 'such a Gehenna as this'. His latest servant, 'new chosen and faithful', a former chemist's assistant, found him a hut with a real four-legged chair in it and got a fire going in the stove, but rest was scarcely possible because a howitzer was firing nearby. Every concussion made Wilfred's 'pharmacopæia, all my boots, candle, and nerves take a smart jump upwards' and a rain of dust fell from the ceiling.⁹ When he went to watch the battery in action and get used to the noise, the Major in charge was pleased to have a visitor and astonished him by giving him a book of poems to read 'as if it were the natural thing to do!!' But Wilfred could read nothing except Susan's letters. He asked for more, and for cigarettes, chocolate, lamp refills and a balaclava to wear at night. 'There is nothing in all this inferno but mud and thunder.'

Preparations were now almost complete. The battalion sent working parties up the line to deliver rations and help repair wire and trenches, while the officers held frequent meetings, poring over maps and orders. One of the last rituals, like some nightmare sacrament, was for the troops to anoint their feet with whale oil as a precaution against trench foot, a circulatory trouble caused by standing for hours in cold water. Wilfred went round his platoon with a candle to see that the job was done properly, remembering how the lecturers at Romford had stressed the importance of healthy feet. He had by now equipped himself with the steel helmet, leather jerkin, gauntlets and thigh-length rubber waders that everyone had to wear, so that when he and other officers went up to reconnoitre the positions they were to occupy they looked like Cromwellian troopers, as he told Susan. They were shelled on the way, but shells falling wide were no great physical danger, merely burying themselves in the heavy clay of Picardy and sending up spectacular fountains of earth. Often the worst danger was psychological, the incessant noise and vibration threatening to break even the steadiest nerves in the end. When he emerged from the long, winding communication trench he had his first sight of the front, probably through a periscope. It was a scene worse than he had ever thought possible, the tidy trench diagrams of the training manuals reducing themselves at last to a chaos of split sandbags, shattered timber and mud.

A plan had been drawn up for all four companies to go forward when the battalion's turn came to relieve the 15th HLI on 12 January, but the generals must have decided there was no risk of a German attack, so C and D Companies were allowed to remain in the comparative safety of Courcelles. A and B assembled in the afternoon, the men drawing their gumboots from the brigade store, and as the light began to fail the column set out for the line. Ahead of them to the east the Germans were firing another heavy barrage, soon matched by the British guns. Wilfred had written home again, using the mistletoe code to tell Susan his destination: 's e r r e'. The Manchesters were returning to the sector where they had been butchered in November. 'I cannot do a better thing or be in a righter place,' Wilfred said, echoing Sydney Carton in *A Tale of Two Cities*. He asked Susan to 'annoy Gordon Gunston for my wicked pleasure', but no civilian optician, prescribing glasses in a Holborn shop, could begin to imagine Serre.

The village itself was – or had been, for there was virtually nothing left of it above ground – tiny, a score or so of houses on the road from Mailly-Maillet to Puisieux; but in a landscape of high, gently undulating ground Serre had the supreme advantage of being on the top of a rise, commanding the surrounding countryside and approachable only up long, shelterless slopes. Ten heavy machine guns, skilfully placed amid a maze of barbed wire, deep trenches and concrete bunkers, had kept the place inviolate despite ferocious attacks in the previous July and November. To the west of the village, the triple line of British trenches – front, support, reserve – ran roughly north–south on a line first established by a French victory in 1915. The support trenches were still in use, albeit in appalling condition, but the original front line, shelled and flooded more or less out of existence, had been replaced by a chain of outposts in shell craters and any other protection that could be found. The maps show most landmarks as 'obliterated' or 'destroyed'.

To the south the Allied front had been pushed forward from the 1916 Somme battle line, and after the capture of Beaumont Hamel and Beaucourt in November, Serre had been left in a right angle where the new line ballooned out eastwards from the old. Taking the village would be an essential preliminary to any larger offensive in the spring. Ground conditions were so bad – worse than at any other time or place on the Western Front, according to the official historian – that an immediate attack could not be contemplated, but limited operations were beginning with the aim of improving local positions and worrying the enemy. The forty-eight-hour bombardment that Wilfred had seen and heard had been fired all along the Fifth Army's front, partly to mislead the Germans into expecting an all-out offensive and partly to cover a much smaller move by units on the right of V Corps. In two days of severe fighting, 10–11 January, 7th

Division had taken Munich Trench and other positions on high ground above Beaumont Hamel, at last gaining full observation of Serre and its hinterland.

The firing ahead of A Company on the 12th must have been a German attempt to prevent the new positions from being consolidated. The noise slackened as the company plodded on, the men burdened with arms, packs and tools, their rubber boots slithering on the uneven ground. Snow had fallen the day before, followed by more rain. They marched along the remains of a road under sporadic shelling for what Wilfred reckoned was three miles, probably to Colincamps, then went almost as far again along a communication trench, never out of water and sometimes up to their knees in liquid mud.[10] The trench took them to the remains of La Signy Farm, below which, criss-crossed by dissolving trenches and churned up by eighteen months of shellfire, what had once been fields sloped down to No Man's Land and the German line.[11]

The enemy had been battering communication trenches on the slope for two days to prevent troops moving up, and no repairs had been possible, so the last part of the journey had to be in the open, through 'an octopus of sucking clay' up to five feet deep, past craters where a fall meant death by drowning. Some men got stuck, losing waders, equipment and even clothes before they could be freed. As A Company stumbled forward in pitch darkness, B came up behind them to occupy support and reserve positions in dugouts at the farm and in Basin Wood, an old chalk-pit where wounded men cowered under steel shelters, waiting to be evacuated. Crichton-Green and Heydon set up company headquarters and positioned about two-and-a-half platoons in the second line. Wilfred had to go on with the rest: he had been put in charge of the outpost line.

As he told Susan later, he found himself not at the front but in front of it. In keeping with the spirit of the offensive, officers were expected to regard No Man's Land as British territory, pushing their advance posts as close to the enemy as possible and sending out frequent night patrols. The 14th Brigade was now in the northern arm of the right angle southwest of Serre, looking down at a strongpoint known as the Quadrilateral, the object of relentless attacks from two directions. When the French had driven the Germans off the slope in front of La Signy Farm in 1915, the Quadrilateral had been left as a vulnerable projection in the German line, so the Germans had turned weakness into strength by developing it into a

(See map opposite.) Trench Map 57D NE 3 & 4 (detail), showing the front at Serre in November 1916. No Man's Land (N) runs north–south between the British lines on the west and the German lines on the east. There are already two mine craters outside the Quadrilateral (Q). This map was secret, confined to Brigade HQ, because it shows the British trenches in detail. Officers had to memorise the maze, then lead their men through it.

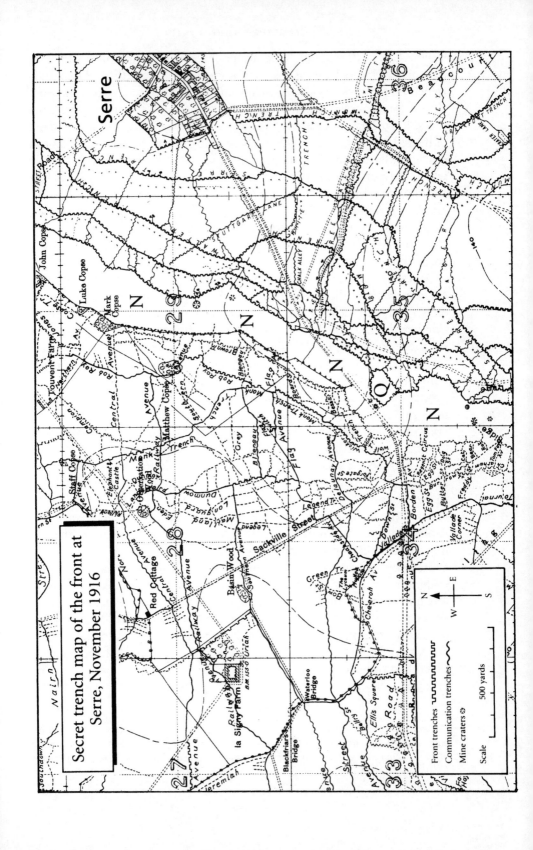

Secret trench map of the front at Serre, November 1916

Front trenches ⊔⊔⊔⊔⊔
Communication trenches ∿∿
Mine craters ⊛

Scale   500 yards

heavily fortified redoubt, able to pour enfilading fire into attackers crossing No Man's Land. It was now at the very point of the right angle. A trench map drawn up a week before the Manchesters arrived shows that British forces, pressing down from captured enemy positions on Redan Ridge above Beaumont Hamel, had begun to break into the southern flank of the redoubt, while three mine craters, one of them very recent, had been blown under its western parapet. There seems to be no record of exactly where Wilfred's outposts were. C and D Companies soon afterwards had to hold a post behind an abandoned tank on the road leading to Serre and another in one of the three craters, but recent patrols had gone further, advancing into the Quadrilateral itself or into trenches very near it. The 15th HLI were actually holding several dugouts somewhere within the enemy line.

At about ten o'clock that Friday evening, 12 January 1917, Wilfred and his party reached the first of these positions, 'Three quarters dead, I mean each of us 3/4 dead' after their exhausting march. As the Scotsmen clambered out of the dugout, their faces showing all too clearly what their successors could expect, Wilfred detailed twenty-five of his men to replace them, left sentries at the low doorway and took another eighteen men, his bombing section, to relieve the occupants of a second dugout 150 yards further on. He was doing as he had been taught, for sentries always had to be posted and bombers always led a platoon attack, although in reality the bombers' main task would be to warn the others if enemy troops appeared (a similar post further up the line that day was captured, with several men taken prisoner or killed). Wilfred was responsible for at least two more posts on the left, but a junior subaltern was in immediate charge of them, so there was nothing else to do but return to the main party and wait. 'The Outpost line will be held at all cost,' battalion orders had said, 'even if the flanks be turned and it must be distinctly understood by all ranks that on no account must any retirement take place from any line.'[12]

Had the dugout been of British construction it might have collapsed under the bombardment, but the Germans had dug in for a long, defensive war and some of their refuges were thirty feet or more below ground under massively reinforced roofs. The worst dangers for Wilfred and his men were from flooding or a direct hit on the entrance, which naturally faced away from the British line and therefore towards the enemy artillery. There had been two entrances, but one had already been blown in. The other, a steep, narrow tunnel rising perhaps as high as a house, was the

(See map opposite.) January 1917: No Man's Land (N) west of Serre is where it had been for many months, but further south the British have overrun the German line and reached the edge of the Quadrilateral (Q). The 2nd Manchesters occupied positions in the section of the line EF, then moved up to GH on Redan Ridge.

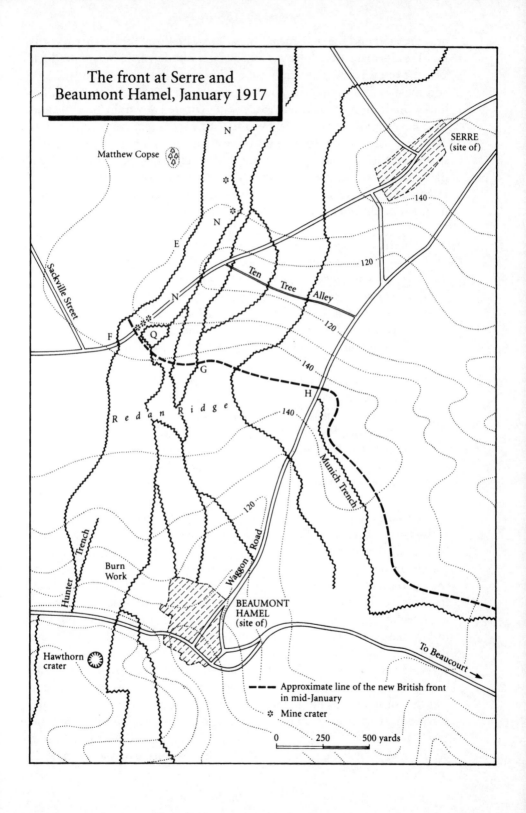

The front at Serre and Beaumont Hamel, January 1917

SERRE
(site of)

Matthew Copse

N

N

E

N

140

120

Ten Tree Alley

120

F

Q

G

140

H

_R e d a n   R i d g e_

140

Munich Trench

120

Hunter Trench

Burn Work

120

Waggon Road

BEAUMONT
HAMEL
(site of)

Hawthorn
crater

To Beaucourt →

- - - Approximate line of the new British front
in mid-January

❋ Mine crater

0   250   500 yards

Sackville Street

only air shaft and the only means of escape. The Royal Scots' diary records that the Germans were 'firing blind' at their old defences, but Wilfred felt sure the fire was being carefully aimed. For the whole of Saturday the 13th and most of the Sunday, he and the others remained close-packed in the low-roofed, stinking chamber, while water trickled down the stairway and rose slowly above their knees. Even the strongest men shook uncontrollably, and occasionally someone would vomit or foul himself, helpless in shame and fear. From time to time Wilfred changed the sentries, telling them to shelter halfway down the steps when the shelling was at its most intense. Over a year later, in 'The Sentry', he went back to the worst moment of all, when a shell landed near the doorway.

> Buffeting eyes and breath, snuffing the candles,
> And thud! flump! thud! down the steep steps came thumping
> And sploshing in the flood, deluging muck,
> The sentry's body; then, his rifle, handles
> Of old Boche bombs, and mud in ruck on ruck.
> We dredged it up, for dead, until he whined,
> 'O sir – my eyes, – I'm blind, – I'm blind, – I'm blind!'
> Coaxing, I held a flame against his lids
> And said if he could see the least blurred light
> He was not blind; in time they'd get all right.
> 'I can't,' he sobbed. Eyeballs, huge-bulged like squids',
> Watch my dreams still, – yet I forgot him there
> In posting Next for duty, and sending a scout
> To beg a stretcher somewhere, and flound'ring about
> To other posts under the shrieking air.

That January weekend in 1917 brought huge disillusion to Wilfred, but it also confirmed some of his deepest certainties. The spirit of the offensive had resulted in nothing but the passive suffering so often experienced by troops on the Western Front, and he admitted to Susan afterwards, as in the poem, that he had been tempted to let himself drown. Despondency had tried to drown him before, dragging him down in 'sucking, slimy fen' at Dunsden. Nevertheless there was work to do, as usual. He had referred to his charges at Mytchett and Fleetwood as his 'little family', and in the dugout he had to act as a father, ordering, encouraging, consoling – and carrying responsibility and guilt, for he had led them there and posted the sentry. The man had instinctively called to him, not to anyone else, and it was the commander's job to look into the terrible eyes. Hundreds of other subalterns had been through similar experiences and feelings on the Western Front. As Colonel Shirley had pointed out, an officer had to stay alive for as long as he could and do his duty, a duty that was in the end based on Christ-like love. 'Those fifty hours were the agony of my happy life,' Wilfred told Susan, thinking of Christ's 'agony' in the garden. Love had always been a strange compound for him, 'paternity, fraternity and amativeness all in one' as he had put it four years earlier in trying to describe his feelings for the Dunsden children, and in his dreams and poems he had foreseen that love's supreme revelation would be a Decadent vision of beauty and horror, tormented 'phantasms' with terrifying eyes, trembling convulsively in some twilit underworld. Now he had entered 'hell's low sorrowful secrecy' in reality, and the scene of damnation in 'Purgatorial Passions' was being acted out by living men under his own leadership.

At about six on the Sunday evening, 'when, I suppose, you would be going to church', as he commented to Susan, he climbed the littered stairs, thinking of her slowly making her way up Wyle Cop to St Julian's. The shelling had quietened down again, so he was 'mercifully helped to do my duty and crawl, wade, climb and flounder over No Man's Land to visit my other post. It took me half an hour to move about 150 yards. / I was chiefly annoyed by our own machine guns from behind. The seeng-seeng-seeng of the bullets reminded me of Mary's canary. On the whole I can support the canary better.' Later that night the outposts were relieved, although A Company was in the front line for another day. The subaltern on the left came out 'completely prostrated', a hospital case, and the officer who took Wilfred's place for the remaining day was so shaken that he left three Lewis guns behind, an offence Wilfred thought would incur a court-martial.[13] By contrast, Wilfred himself had earned what Shirley had defined as the highest prize a British officer could hope for, the right to say, 'Thank God I have done my duty.' He had kept his nerve and successfully extricated all his men and weapons. The sentry had been his only casualty, and he had saved the man's life by keeping him below ground, whereas the sentries on the left, including the bomber he had first chosen as servant, had been blown to nothing. Colonel Luxmoore could have reflected that young Owen had done rather well.

Just before midnight on the Monday the HLI relieved the Manchesters, who trudged wearily back to Courcelles. Heavy snow was falling, and conditions in billets were more unpleasant than ever. The officers huddled together in a shattered farmhouse, where Wilfred's bed was a rabbit-wire hammock next to a gaping hole in the wall. Melting snow dripped through the broken roof on to his blanket as he tried to sleep. Later that day he wrote home, telling Susan something of what he had been through. 'I can see no excuse for deceiving you about these last 4 days. I have suffered seventh hell.' He was not much concerned to spare her feelings, partly because he needed her sympathy and partly because he wanted people at home to know what soldiers were having to endure. In much the same spirit he had announced to her from Bordeaux in 1913, 'I must not conceal from you my malady', and had sent Harold details of the army hospital in 1914 'to educate you to the actualities of the war'. Earlier still he had told Mary about the sufferings of the poor at Dunsden, saying, 'Why am I telling you these dreadful things? Simply to let them educate you, as they are educating me, in the Book of Life.' Teacher and evangelist still, he felt driven to speak out, even though the rules and conventions governing a soldier's conduct required him to keep silent. He asked Susan to have portions of his letter typed for Leslie and others.

C and D Companies relieved the HLI on the Wednesday, while A and B remained in reserve, but being in reserve did not mean being safe or idle. Working parties had to be sent up in the usual way, often remaining in the line for hours under fire. Sudden, severe frost had set in, hardening the ground so that movement was much easier and digging possible, though very laborious. When Wilfred accompanied a party on the Thursday, he lost his way in darkness and snow, giving himself a nasty fright by walking into tear gas. Trying to describe the landscape, he could only grasp at traditional metaphors that became hopelessly inadequate even as he wrote them down: hell, Inferno, Purgatorio, Gehenna, the Slough of Despond, Sodom and Gomorrah, the ruins of Babylon, nothing anyone had ever seen or imagined could be as desolate as the wasteland in front of Serre. So he began searching for the new images that he would later use in 'The Show', personifying No Man's Land as a body or a terrible face, 'pockmarked like a body of foulest disease and its odour is the breath of cancer … No Man's Land under snow is like the face of the moon chaotic, craterridden, uninhabitable, awful, the abode of madness.' People wanted to call the place England because the British controlled it: 'I would as soon call my House (!) Krupp Villa, or my child Chlorina-Phosgena.'

The anger that would fuel his later poetry was already beginning to build up, after only three weeks in France. He told Susan the troops were cursing 'our distinguished countryman', presumably meaning Lloyd George, the new Prime Minister. The Somme films that were still causing excitement at home were the laughing-stock of the army, Wilfred said, as were the model trenches on display in Kensington.[14] 'The people of England needn't hope. They must agitate. But they are not yet agitated even.' These comments do not mean that he had suddenly turned against the war, as modern readers sometimes assume, but rather that he was taking up the attitudes of a hardened soldier, scorning civilian complacency now that he had acquired the secret knowledge that could only come from battle experience. He did not say what the people of England should agitate for. Lloyd George had won popular support by calling for the fight to be 'to a finish – to a knock-out', and the battalion may well have been cursing him for their being pushed too far ahead. On the other hand, one of the bitterest grievances among soldiers was that shirkers were not being rounded up fast enough, and Wilfred may once again have been thinking of the Gunston brothers. Explaining the vehemence of his letter, he said he had written 'in the exuberance of having already done "a Bit"'. Having emerged from the dugout with honour and apparently unscathed, like a probationer knight getting through a rite of passage, he had cause for exuberance.

~

Wilfred was under the impression that the battalion was about to go back for a long rest, but he soon discovered his mistake. The 32nd Division was extending its right front to relieve its neighbour, and 14th Brigade was merely to be transferred from one dangerous point in the line to another not far away. Leaving Courcelles on the afternoon of the 21st, the Manchesters marched westwards to Bus-lès-Artois, getting out of the way of incoming troops, and then returned southeastwards, keeping well to the rear of the angle in the line. They spent the night of the 22nd in a transit camp near Beaussart, and next day entered the former German stronghold of Beaumont Hamel, deep in its hollow above the Ancre.

It seems from Wilfred's letters that A Company was once again the first to go into the line. They would have marched up Waggon Road, a steep, shell-damaged track leading north out of the village. It was a sunken lane for part of the way, with shell craters and German dugouts in the banks, but as it reached the hilltop it flattened out, and anyone who took a step too far was silhouetted against the sky, instantly visible from Serre across the open fields. The company crawled forward as far as they could go and lay still, acutely aware that the least movement on the snow-covered ground might be seen by German periscopes. Their position was 'almost wusser' than the dugout, as Wilfred said afterwards. He had apparently not seen any corpses during his first 'tour' of the trenches, although he had felt and smelled them in the dark, but now they were everywhere, frozen in hideous attitudes. 'Very bad for the men,' the officers would have said, such sights being profoundly damaging to morale. Worse still, some of the men may have recognised 'half-known faces', for it had been on this same hilltop that the 2nd Manchesters had suffered near-annihilation in the previous November.

A Company was on the eastern spur of Redan Ridge, straddling the former German line, their position running west from Waggon Road for about 600 yards just above the 140-metre contour, halfway between Beaumont Hamel and Serre. Below them to their left, partly out of sight, the British line turned its right angle round the Quadrilateral and joined the trenches they had just occupied. To their right it swung back through another right angle along the newly captured Munich Trench, facing enemy-held trenches in the valley below. The company was thus open to shelling from east as well as north. Directly ahead to the north, only a few metres higher than their own ridge, was Serre, seemingly a short walk away over level ground, but between them and the village, Waggon Road dropped down into a shallow, hidden valley, the dip concealing a formidable barrier, a double trench known as Ten Tree Alley and at least two machine gun posts.

A few old communication trenches ran east–west across the ridge, but they seem to have been unusable. Wilfred and his platoon had no shelter whatever except the slight rise in the ground ahead of them. They lay out on the 'burning snow' under a lethal wind, unable to move by daylight and unable even to drink because their water cans were frozen. He managed to sleep for a while, but when he woke up he thought he was dead and in hell.

> The marvel is that we did not all die of cold. As a matter of fact, only one of my party actually froze to death before he could be got back, but I am not able to tell how many have ended in hospital. I had no real casualties from shelling, though for 10 minutes every hour whizz-bangs fell a few yards short of us. Showers of soil rained on us, but no fragments of shell could find us.
>
> I had lost my gloves in a dug-out, but I found 1 mitten on the Field; I had my Trench Coat (without lining but with a Jerkin underneath.) My feet ached until they could ache no more, and so they temporarily died. I was kept warm by the ardour of Life within me. I forgot hunger in the hunger for Life. The intensity of your Love reached me and kept me living. I thought of you and Mary without a break all the time. I cannot say I felt any fear. We were all half-crazed by the buffeting of the High Explosives. I think the most unpleasant reflection that weighed on me was the impossibility of getting back any wounded, a total impossibility all day, and frightfully difficult by night.
>
> We were marooned on a frozen desert.
>
> There is not a sign of life on the horizon and a thousand signs of death.
>
> Not a blade of grass, not an insect; once or twice a day the shadow of a big hawk, scenting carrion.

The battalion diary confirms that one unnamed Other Rank did die from exposure that January; he may be the subject of Wilfred's 1918 poem 'Futility', just as the whole platoon is the subject of 'Exposure'.

Despairing though those two 1918 poems are, the last week of January 1917 was not entirely without hope. The enemy's artillery was as aggressive as ever, but his infantry seemed curiously thin on the ground, and the month was a comparatively safe one for the battalion, with total casualties of only eight killed, twelve wounded and two missing, far lower than in the previous November. The authorities could reckon things were not going too badly, and even Wilfred would not have described the war as futile when he was actually on Redan Ridge. His letters give no indication that any progress was made, but the division was in fact inching its way over the crest of the hill, establishing new posts in the ruined enemy defences. The Ancre valley lay behind them, with places made famous by the 1916 fighting – Beaumont Hamel, the Hawthorn crater, 'Y' Ravine, the dreadful heights of Thiepval – all now in British hands. The optimism that had preceded the Big Push now seemed absurd, but the past six months had brought what just might be the beginnings of victory, hard though it was to believe that the world could survive such a winter or that there could be any purpose, human or divine, in recent events. Over a year later Wilfred fumbled to explain his men's endurance:

> Since we believe not otherwise can kind fires burn;
> Nor ever suns smile true on child, or field, or fruit.
> For God's invincible spring our love is made afraid;
> Therefore, not loath, we lie out here; therefore were born,
> For love of God seems dying.

That stanza from 'Exposure' attempts to portray the men's state of mind. They think of home and the people they love, of England in spring, and the Christian themes of the redeemer born to die, his agony in the garden and cry from the Cross, a pattern of sacrifice and renewal remembered, maybe only dimly, from church parades and school. Something like that probably did motivate Wilfred and his platoon on the burning snow. They held their ground.

They remained on the ridge for two days and nights before making their way back to support positions in deep dugouts, where they were able to drink at last and thaw out. Wilfred said the dugouts were warm like mines. There were many such shelters under Beaumont Hamel, old chalk quarries the Germans had made astonishingly comfortable, with electric light, pictures on the walls and even a four-poster bed or two for senior officers. Battalion headquarters and reserves were in Burn Work, a former enemy strongpoint (*Werk*) that had been a deadly obstacle in the previous July, and the company was probably there on the 27th when all the Manchesters were sent back for four days' rest at Bertrancourt.

One of Susan's parcels was waiting for Wilfred at Bertrancourt. She had made him the woollen 'sleeping helmet' he had asked for, so he put it on under his steel helmet two days later when he had to go up with his platoon and Heydon on a working party. The men were still shaken after their torments in the dugout, and some of them had puttees wrapped round their feet because frostbite had prevented them from getting their boots on. The officers had to make them trudge the five miles or so back to the ridge to dig the frozen ground. The corpses were still there, grinning and unchanged. Luckily there was very little shelling, and the platoon got back safely at about two in the morning, Wilfred noticing how even the lamest men could somehow keep going on the homeward journey. He had suffered slight frostbite himself – or trench foot or perhaps a combination of both – and had developed a heavy cold, but his worst trouble was dysentery, caught, he believed, from eating snow to quench his thirst. He insisted it really was dysentery, but he left the details to Susan's imagination.[15]

Advance patrols by the Royal Scots on the 28th reported that no contact could be made with the enemy, who seemed to be far back on the slopes behind Serre. Divisional headquarters must have begun planning an attack immediately, for an enemy withdrawal could not be allowed to go unpursued. Colonel Luxmoore happened to be due for a month's leave from 1 February, so he was about to hand over his command to the senior Major, J.F. Dempster, whom Wilfred loathed – very probably as a result of unpleasant personal experience – as an arrogant snob. At this moment, with offensive action imminent under the leadership of the 'horrid old Major', an instruction came through from Division that an officer should be sent to the Advanced Horse Transport Depot at Abbeville for a month's special training. It was presumably Luxmoore who chose Wilfred, perhaps thinking the new subaltern was not only efficient and quick to learn but also in need of a rest after two brief but exceptionally punishing stints in the line. Maybe, too, the Colonel had noticed that Dempster and Wilfred did not get on. The other subalterns and even the captains made no secret of their envy at Wilfred's good fortune, and he himself must have had great difficulty in hiding his relief. When he received the Assistant Adjutant's typed order on the 30th, he wrote a line from Tagore on the back of it: 'When I go from hence, let this be my parting word, that what I have seen is unsurpassable.'

~

By the time the Manchesters returned to the line on the last day of January, Wilfred had moved off in the opposite direction and hailed a lorry, not caring where it went, watching with delight as the landscape changed, the shell craters becoming scarcer until they disappeared altogether. Once out of the fighting zone he hitched rides on five buses and by evening arrived at a small town, perhaps Doullens, where he spent the night and was able to soak in a hot bath for the first time since leaving England. He reached Abbeville next day. His servant had apparently travelled with him, carrying the heavy valise, no doubt as pleased as his master to be so far from the guns. The course started on 2 February and by the 4th Wilfred was writing to Susan in high spirits. 'Me in Transports? Aren't *you*?'

In spite of the near-impossibility of finding fuel, and cold so intense that blankets were stiff with frost in the mornings, the officers on the course were determined to enjoy their month's reprieve. They had all been drawn from the same area of the front and knew they were likely to go back to it. Making their servants labour at cleaning and polishing, they became 'desperate nuts in dress', some even brightening up their khaki by sporting violet silk handkerchiefs, an ignoble use for such a poetic colour, Wilfred thought. After weeks of washing in nothing better than handfuls of snow, he bathed and shaved meticulously, turning himself out as smartly as anyone. His cold and dysentery, if it had been dysentery, vanished. He was young, fit and still exuberant. 'I tell you,' he wrote to Mary, 'these days are the best I've ever had in the army.'

He knew how to be sociable when he wanted to be, and that side of his character flourished in the ephemeral comradeship of the transport school. He could shine as a French speaker and as a capable horseman, and within a few days the others elected him Mess President, which meant he had to take the chair at meals, order provisions, keep the key of the whisky cupboard and make sure everyone paid their bills.[16] Having been at ease in the saddle since childhood gallops with Alec Paton, he could cope with having to ride round and round for hours, performing circus tricks without reins or stirrups. Learning about animal diseases was less pleasant – he put scent on his handkerchief to help drown the smell. Sometimes he had to drive a four-horse waggon, and in the afternoons there were long rides through the frozen countryside, on one occasion passing the field of Crécy. Once a horse bolted under him, but he managed to hold on, despite being badly shaken.

He told Susan where he was by the simple expedient of sending her a postcard of Abbeville with no signature or message except the letters 'O.A.S.' (on active service). Years before at school he had made a study of the town, so the cathedral and old streets were pleasantly familiar.[17] Drink and women were conspicuously available, had he wanted either, but he knew about the temptations of French towns and assured his mother he was being a 'very good boy'. At first he shared a room and apparently a bed (though nothing can be read into that, as such sharing was necessarily very common) with a young Scots officer, but soon moved to better quarters because the man was inclined to roll in drunk at midnight. Letters came from family and friends, many of them in response to dozens of field postcards Wilfred had fired off from the front. Alfred Kemp wrote from Watford, where he was now a curate, and Bobbie de la Touche from Stonyhurst, where he and his brothers were now all at school together; Bobbie said their aunt had taken charge of a hospital for Belgian refugees in Surbiton. Tom Owen wrote several times with 'spirited approbation', praise his son found both moving and embarrassing. More parcels arrived from Susan, full of chocolate, cigarettes, disinfectant, the familiar gingerbread and far too many socks.

At the end of the month Susan wrote that Harold had managed to crash a plane on one of his first training flights as a navy pilot, although he had escaped without injury, much to her relief. Wilfred sent him brotherly sympathy, mixing it with patronising advice and condescending remarks, probably comparing sailors' supposedly comfortable lives with the horrors of Beaumont Hamel and Serre. Re-reading this letter many years later, Harold reached for his ink pot and painted out words, lines and even whole pages, leaving the manuscript as vivid evidence of the resentment Wilfred had so often aroused in him. What remains of the letter shows that Wilfred was still interested in the sensations of flying, and that both he and his brother had developed insomnia.

Wilfred had not emerged from the front line unscathed after all. His 'unsurpassable' experiences there were to disturb his sleep for the rest of his life. His mother had decided against having his letters typed, thinking it would be rather pretentious, but she had shown some of them to the Gunstons. She told Wilfred that her sister had commented on the 'awful *distaste*' underlying his descriptions, and he said his aunt was right.

> I suppose I can endure cold, and fatigue, and the face-to-face death, as well as another; but extra for me there is the universal pervasion of *Ugliness*. Hideous landscapes, vile noises, foul language and nothing but foul, even from one's own mouth (for all are devil ridden), everything unnatural, broken, blasted; the distortion of the dead, whose unburiable bodies sit outside the dug-outs all day, all night, the most execrable sights on earth. In poetry we call them the most glorious. But to sit with them all day, all night … and a week later to come back and find them still sitting there, in motionless groups, THAT is what saps the 'soldierly spirit' …

Ugliness was extra for him because his poetic creed had set beauty as the supreme goal. That high standard had made the horrors harder to bear than they might have been for most men, but it had also enabled him to judge clearly. He now knew beyond doubt that death in war was not glorious, and if other poets said it was they were either ignorant or dishonest. To later generations, trained by Wilfred's poems among other things, that may not seem an original insight, but in early 1917 it was at odds with nearly all the poetry that was being published.

He said he was writing down his experiences for the sake of future reminders of 'how incomparable is an innocent and quiet life, at home, of work creative or humdrum, with books or without books, moneyed or moneyless, in sunshine or fog, but under an inoffensive sky, that does not shriek all night with flights of shells'. The gap between the front line and home was already beginning to seem impassable. He had thought of Susan and Mary all the time while lying on the snow, but his references to Mary's canary and Susan going to church have a hint of irony. When the family asked for souvenirs, he said England was going to need an 'anti-souvenir'. He was annoyed by photographs of smiling Tommies in the *Daily Mirror*, and by a comment from the Bishop of London, a celebrated recruiting preacher, that it was disgraceful for young men to be interested in lace (one of the bravest officers on the transport course was a lace-designer in civil life). All this might seem to suggest that Wilfred was already planning to write poems that would be an 'anti-souvenir' for England, but there is in fact no sign that he wrote, or even thought of writing, any of his characteristic war poems before August 1917. He had not yet met Sassoon.

When he told Susan he was 'settling down to a little verse once more' at Abbeville in February, the verse was not about his recent experiences but about sonnet subjects agreed with Leslie and Olwen. He had already written 'The End' in Olwen's apocalyptic style, and now he wrote on a title set by Leslie, 'Golden Hair', composing a catalogue of golden delights in the sort of style Leslie favoured. Then he tackled another of Olwen's subjects, 'Happiness', and that proved more demanding. He thought of a recent unhappy letter from Harold, and of the distance that the war had opened up between their current life and the consolations that had once been available from home. He could try to convince himself, as he tried to convince Harold, that their mother could still give them comfort, but he knew the link was broken.

> *… the old happiness is unreturning.*
> *Boys have no grief so grievous as youth's yearning;*
> *Boys have no sadness sadder than our hope.*

Six months later, he said that these lines from the first draft of 'Happiness' had been his first mature work, and that the maturity had come from Beaumont Hamel.

~

While Wilfred was travelling to Abbeville at the end of January, the 2nd Manchesters were going back into action on the Beaumont Hamel spur. During the next two weeks they and other battalions pushed down into the dip in the ground ahead, the 'Valley of Death' as some called it, capturing Ten Tree Alley and what was left of the Quadrilateral in fierce fighting. That success took them to the foot of the final slope up to Serre, opening the way for a full-scale assault on the village itself, so plans were drawn up for a March offensive. The battle would not be possible before then, and the Manchesters would not be involved in it, because the line was about to be reorganised. The Commander-in-Chief, Sir Douglas Haig, had agreed to relieve the French by extending the British front southwards, an operation requiring enormous troop movements for a month or more. The 32nd Division was to be transferred to IV Corps in General Sir Henry Rawlinson's Fourth Army, with the task of holding the extreme British right on the Amiens–Roye road. On 13 February, as a thaw set in and the land once again turned to mud, the 2nd Manchesters started a long march south to their new position, occasionally pausing for a few days' training. Their route led them through the outskirts of Amiens, then towards Roye, and on 25 February they took over French dugouts at Bouchoir. Meanwhile, astonishing news had been arriving from their former fighting grounds north of the Ancre. There had already been puzzling signs of local German absences, and in mid-February the generals began to realise that a much larger withdrawal was taking place. On the 24th three patrols from the 21st Manchesters walked unopposed into Serre. The stronghold that had cost so many lives was captured at last without a shot being fired.

13

To the Hindenburg Line
St Quentin

MARCH–APRIL 1917

Wilfred's course at Abbeville ended in late February, and the journey to rejoin the 2nd Manchesters took him several days. On 1 March he reported to battalion headquarters in a French-built dugout at Bouchoir, on the Amiens–Roye road. The course had prepared him to be Transport Officer, a job that would often have kept him out of the front line, but unfortunately he was not needed in that role. Colonel Luxmoore, newly returned from leave, made him a platoon commander as before, this time in B Company. The 2nd Manchesters were in a relatively undamaged sector, very different from Serre, 'a glorious part of the Line,' Wilfred told Susan, 'new to us, and indeed, to the English (sh!). Most comfortable dug-outs, grass fields, woods, sunshine quiet.' In his next letter he said his dugout was decorated with mistletoe, and the left-hand margin of his letter duly spelled out a message: 's o f l i n e j o i n i n g f r e n c h'. Despite his optimism, everyone was making the usual complaints about French standards, having found the front-line trenches in a poor state and the bedding straw infested with lice. Nor were the Germans as relaxed as they seemed. Going up with a digging party on his first night, he scrambled over the parapet to get to the head of his men and was very nearly killed by a sniper. Someone hissed 'Get down, Sir!' just in time, and he recognised one of the poorest marksmen in his 'little family' at Fleetwood. Next day there was a gas alarm, followed by a tremendous barrage, the officers in the dugout making the routine joke to each other that there seemed to be a war on.

B Company was well run by its captain, Sebastian Sorrell, whom Wilfred discovered to be a fellow poet and aesthete, alert to words and quick to check foul language, 'one of the few young men who live up to my principle: that Amusement is never an excuse for "immorality", but that Passion may be so.' Obscenity had been rife in A Company and Wilfred had joined in with the rest, but the new regime was welcome. He was 'ever so happy' to be with Sorrell, who evidently talked to him about literature

225

and ideas, on one occasion giving him a choice between going on a fatigue party or writing a sonnet. Sorrell had been a private secretary before the war, living in Kensington with his mother. He was now under considerable strain after two years of continuous service, during which he had suffered a slight wound and a recent spell in hospital with fever.[1] Perhaps he was gay; at any rate he seems to have become Wilfred's closest friend in the battalion.

The days were filled with endless working parties, helping to bring the defences up to British requirements. The French were just as committed to an offensive policy as their ally, but they were less inclined to concentrate troops in the front areas, so there was an immediate need for stronger forward positions, the land being flat and shelterless. Several of the men had been under Wilfred's command in 1916, and he remembered how he had made them dig trenches on Thursley Common in the days when he was still a very new officer. The brigade was relieved on 8 March, withdrawing a few miles to ruined houses at Beaufort, where a training programme was badly interrupted by renewed icy weather and demands for yet more working parties. Wilfred was rather pleased to be posted nearer the line, probably at Le Quesnoy, in charge of a party excavating new dugouts. The job allowed some relaxation, being well away from headquarters. He complained that he had run out of reading matter, except for the magazines Susan was sending him – *Punch*, as enjoyable as ever, and the YMCA journal, which he despised for its 'war impressions' by ignorant civilians – but somewhere in Bouchoir he picked up a battered copy of Elizabeth Barrett Browning.

The front-line villages were not safe places to walk about in. One night, either in Bouchoir or Le Quesnoy, stumbling about in pitch darkness in search of a sick man, Wilfred fell into a fifteen-foot hole, probably a ruined cellar, hitting the back of his head on the way down. Half blind with nausea, he lost his watch and apparently his revolver, as well as all sense of the passage of time, and he could do little more than light a candle. He seems to have been entombed for at least a day and a night, perhaps more, but a letter describing the incident has been lost. With hindsight one can see that this fall was the beginning of his neurasthenia, and the end of his 'exuberance' at being an officer who had done his honourable bit and survived. Somehow he climbed out of the hole or was rescued. By the time he reported to the doctors he had no worse symptom than a bad headache, so they diagnosed slight concussion and passed him fit for duty.[2] The battalion had returned to the firing line and he had to follow, risking sniper fire by walking in the open because he felt too weak to plough through the mud in the communication trench.

He must have found the troops in a state of uncharacteristic excitement. Rumours had been going round for some time that the German retreat in the north was spreading southwards, and mysterious fires could now be seen behind the enemy lines. Patrols sent forward on 15 March reported trenches occupied as normal, but by next day it was clear that something very unusual was happening and divisional headquarters began sending out a flurry of orders and counter-orders. In the middle of all this, Wilfred was suddenly, violently sick. His concussion had caught up with him, bringing muscular pains and a high fever. He was sent back to a Casualty Collecting Point in a 'shanty' somewhere in the rear and from there to a Casualty Clearing Station (CCS).[3] Thus, for the second time, he was fated to miss dramatic events. On 17 March, when Manchester patrols were penetrating the German third line without opposition, and French troops on their right were marching triumphantly into Roye, and away to the north the British were entering Bapaume, Wilfred was being driven through peaceful back areas to the comfort of a hospital bed.

~

His concussion left him confused for some time, so much so that his birthday on 18 March passed without his even noticing it until the day after. It must have been thanks to his servant that all his possessions arrived with him, together with a lot of mud and the servant himself.[4] Casualty Clearing Station No. 13, a large collection of huts and tents in fields near Gailly, east of Amiens, could hold six hundred patients or more.[5] An exceptionally large intake of 275 men arrived on the same day as Wilfred, many of them victims of the weather, suffering from ailments such as trench foot and influenza (only seventeen of them were wounded), but at first he was aware of little more than his own ward and its ten or so occupants. Occasionally the nursing sister looked in to give shrill orders, her heels clacking irritatingly on the floor. He preferred the deferential calm of the male orderlies, smart young soldiers who did most of the work. The ward would have been exclusively for officers, of whom there were rarely more than a dozen in the entire hospital, and the standard of care seems to have been high.

He was kept in bed for several days. When he got up, snow was falling and he joined the other patients in a morose circle round the stove, thinking how dull they all looked. No mail reached him, and there was nothing to do except read Elizabeth Barrett Browning, although one of the sisters brought him a few novels, 'about as palatable as warm water to a starving jaguar', and he managed to find an exercise book to write and draw in. Stung – or as he put it in a pararhyme, 'winded … yea, wounded' – by a comment in Mrs Browning's *Aurora Leigh* that too many people waste their youth in writing tame verse instead of setting up home and doing something useful, he spent a day planning an ideal bungalow for himself, deciding that after the war he would devote half his time to keeping pigs and half to poetry. Having dealt with Mrs Browning's objection, he began work on a new sonnet. Colin had demanded souvenirs, so Wilfred imagined sending him one of the identity discs that all soldiers had to wear on a string round their necks:

> But let my death be memoried on this disc.
> Wear it, sweet friend. Inscribe no date nor deed.
> But let thy heart-beat kiss it night and day,
> Until the name grow vague and wear away.[6]

While Wilfred was convalescing at the CCS, dreaming of pigs and sonnets, the Allied advance was continuing amid rising hopes. There were two great causes for renewed confidence: one that the Germans were retreating on a ninety-mile front, the other that they had declared unrestricted submarine warfare, a move certain to bring the United States into the war. In 32nd Division, now hastily adapting itself to a war of movement, elation was mingled with bewilderment and suspicion, the divisional chaplain writing in his diary of 'these tremendous days' and wondering what on earth Germany was planning.[7] For there clearly *was* a plan: the withdrawal had all the signs of careful organisation, with villages destroyed, trees felled across highways and huge craters blown at every crossroads. The whole thing just might be a trap, luring the Allies out of their defences into a devastated terrain where they would be easy targets.

Anxious generals reconnoitred the ground and conferred with their staffs, fearful of risking lives yet determined to stay close on the enemy's heels. Here and there the Germans turned to fight a rearguard action, but there was little resistance on 32nd Division's front. The 15th Highland Light Infantry marched into Nesle behind their pipe band, to the cheers of liberated civilians, and the Manchesters followed. The Dorsets built a bridge across the Somme east of the town. While a screen of cavalry and cyclists went ahead, the infantry constructed defences along the Somme river and canal in case of attack. The Manchesters laboured at Voyennes for some days, digging trenches, putting up wire and filling craters. By 25 March they were on the east bank, holding the bridgehead at Buny. The men had to be repeatedly warned not to stray ahead too far, and to watch out for mines and the innumerable booby traps that had been left under anything that might look interesting or useful. The thoroughness of the destruction seemed to confirm the old 1914–15 stories of German barbarism. All domestic animals had disappeared – rumour had it that the dogs had been slaughtered and sent back to Germany for sausages – and countrymen among the troops noticed with disgust that even the fruit trees had been fatally ringbarked. The thought that the Germans might be heading for defeat, and that they seemed to deserve it, did much to improve morale.

At about the same time that the Manchesters were crossing the Somme, Wilfred was strolling along the towpath far to the rear, only vaguely aware of what was happening in the east. He was now fit enough to be allowed out in the afternoons, the weather having turned sunny. The CCS was well placed next to the Somme and a railhead, so that casualties could be transported by both rail and water, and the poplar-lined canal, with the river winding lazily alongside it, was a relaxing place to be. He was amused to see British sergeant-majors captaining tugs, and khaki-clad corporals steering the strings of big hospital barges, squeezing them through the lock at the tiny hamlet of Gailly.

On the 24th he went some miles further east by hitching a ride in a Daimler ambulance, stopping to talk to a party of children and old women, refugees who had just been evacuated from the newly-captured area. A boy told him the Germans had taken all males over fifteen, 'left 5 days bread rations for the remainder, set fire to almost every building, choked up the wells with farmyard refuse and disappeared'. The guns were growling far ahead, and Wilfred felt he ought to be there, doing his bit for France. He scrounged another lift next day, a Sunday, this time in the opposite direction, to Corbie, where he bought a new watch and attended evening service. Corbie had once been an important religious centre, and the big church still had a collection of sacred relics, a display of Roman Catholicism that brought out all his old prejudices. Propping his cap and stick against 'a piece of the true Cross', he contemplated the statues, 'St John in bathing-costume looking ruefully at another saint in a gold dressing gown', and the acolytes, 'scarlet urchins holding candles and chewing, – probably the grease'.

If he learned nothing in the church, he was learning a good deal in the ward, where two of the patients, the observer and pilot from a crashed plane, were being treated for terrible injuries. The pilot had 'both arms broken, abdominal injuries, both eyes contused, nose cut, teeth knocked in and skull fractured'. The poem 'A Terre', drafted at the end of the year, may be based on memories of him: 'Sit on the bed. I'm blind, and three parts shell ...'. Wilfred had discovered in Bordeaux in 1914 that he could cope with hospital horrors better than most people, so he helped to look after the pilot at night, and the more he did so the more he was impressed by the devoted skill of the sister. His attitude had changed considerably since he first arrived: the patients were no longer uninteresting, the sisters no longer tiresome, and the immediacy of suffering brought out a selfless tenderness in him. 'Constitutionally I am better able to do Service in a hospital than in the trenches,' he told Susan. 'But I suppose we all think that.' Service in the trenches was what he had volunteered for, however, and the doctors soon told him to get back to it. He left the CCS on 30 March, going first to Amiens, where he bought a new revolver and sent a postcard home. Then he spent four days slowly 'caravanning' along the congested roads towards the battalion, less than fifty miles away.

~

There was likely to be hard fighting ahead, and the enemy retreat was no longer a mystery. The Germans had begun constructing a new defence line in the previous autumn, using all their strategic and industrial skills, having realised their old positions were not strong enough to withstand another offensive like the Somme. The new 'Hindenburg Line', as the British were beginning to call it, was not a conventional triple line of trenches but a complex system four or five miles deep, strengthened with enormous belts of barbed wire, deep tunnels and hidden concrete pill-boxes. Putting this huge obstacle in place was a gigantic labour, and the outpost and rear areas had been far from complete when, in late January 1917, the German High Command had decided to order the withdrawal for mid-March, earlier than had been intended. French villagers were rounded up as slave labour, but the work was still unfinished when the Allied pursuit started. The French had high hopes of a breakthrough, although General Rawlinson was less sanguine, knowing it would be a long time before he could get enough forces into the line.

The British extreme right moved north-east as the chase continued, perhaps because the French were determined to capture St Quentin, the first big prize ahead, so that the junction between the two Allies was slightly to the north-west of the city by the time the advance patrols came within sight of the cathedral. This huge medieval building, dominating the countryside for miles around, was an ideal observation post for the enemy, and the shelling that greeted the advancing troops showed that the Germans had reached their stopping-point. St Quentin had been made into an immense bastion, massively protected with guns and wire. The villages on the slopes to the west of it had been flattened, and the little hills and woods among the fields were full of machine-gun nests. The Fourth Army, with 32nd Division and 2nd Manchesters still next to the French, was about to enter the outpost zone of the Hindenburg Line.

As Wilfred travelled slowly east from Amiens, held up by the strains which the advance was putting on communication lines, there was more than enough time to dread what was coming and, worse still, to dread fear itself. He had recovered from the cellar fall, but his nerve was beginning to be unreliable and he knew it. He had missed death too often – on the train to Folkestone, in the German dugout, on the snow at Beaumont Hamel, in the cellar and many times under shell and sniper fire – and his luck could not hold much longer. He must have reflected, too, that everything he had done in France so far had been rendered futile by the enemy retreat, although it was said, and was indeed true, that the pressure on Serre in

January had been a crucial factor in the German decision to withdraw. By the second day of his journey he was 'in blues as deep as the Prussian Blue'.

Fortunately his sense of purpose was strongly revived on the last night, when he found shelter with a refugee family named Lemaire.[8] Charming and of 'good class socially', they were thrilled to meet an English officer who could speak French, and they took turns to hug and kiss him with Gallic enthusiasm until he felt like some great-hearted god, a hero of the liberation. One of the five children, André, became a 'sudden great friend', impressing him deeply by having done 'more damage to the Boche when his fiery soul was under their hated domineering than I ever managed to do'. André, who cannot have been more than fourteen, claimed to have thrown hundreds of bombs, as well as wrecking a staff car by stretching a wire across the road. Meeting the Lemaires revived Wilfred's affection for France and French people, and his belief that the war was worth fighting. By the time he reached battalion headquarters at Germaine next day, 3 April 1917, he could tell Susan he was no longer in the blues but 'in the pink'.

Fear could not be overcome so easily. He began his letter home by explaining his shaky handwriting as the result of having cut his finger on a tin of lobster, but a few lines later he admitted his long rest had shaken his nerve.[9] 'Without Your letters I should give in,' he said, adding in a rush of emotion that what he was fighting for was not his motherland, a good land, nor, after all, his mother tongue, but his mother. He had been longing for letters, none having reached him at Gailly, but none had got through to the battalion either, a bitter disappointment. He promised to send some souvenirs to Colin. 'Ah my poor angel! He wants to be with me. He would not live three weeks in this sector of Hades.' The blues were evidently returning in the grim atmosphere of headquarters, where the authorities may well have commented sharply on the time it had taken Wilfred to get back from the CCS. He was informed that he had just missed an extraordinary 'stunt' and that a counter-attack was expected at any time; he should get himself into the line immediately, reporting to A Company under Captain Green, not B under Sorrell.

Once again Wilfred had missed events that were to be put into history books. Had he reached the line a day earlier, on 2 April, he would have been in time for one of the battalion's greatest exploits. The 32nd Division had started operations against the Hindenburg Line outposts on 1 April, when two brigades had taken Savy Wood and village. A little railway ran through the wood, partly on an embankment and partly in a cutting. Early next day under incessant shellfire, 14th Brigade had advanced to the embankment, from there launching a rapid charge northwards, parallel to the main German front. While the 1st Dorsets went ahead on the left to capture Holnon, and the 15th HLI protected the right flank, all four

Manchester companies headed up the centre. The enemy had destroyed most of the woods and all the buildings, leaving almost no cover, and much of the ground was in view from the cathedral, but the outposts were held by raw recruits, no match for an experienced Regular battalion. Many of the defenders fled when they saw the Manchesters coming, only to be shot down as they ran.

D Company on the left captured the ruins of Francilly-Selency, driving out enemy machine-gunners. Just beyond the village, C Company and part of B (though not Sorrell, who was with the reserves at Savy) ran into a gun battery, taking it at bayonet point in a dramatic flanking attack. On the right, A Company under Heydon (Green was also with the reserves) was badly cut up by machine-gun fire from a quarry, but they captured the quarry none the less and the hill beyond it, known thereafter as Manchester Hill in honour of the day's triumphs. Selency was also taken, and when all was done the brigade joined up with others who had fought their way round the west side of Holnon Wood, thereby encircling the wood so that it, too, could be cleared. The Manchesters' tally on that 2 April was eight machine guns, six of them captured by A Company, plenty of small arms and equipment, seventeen Germans taken prisoner and many more killed, and above all the battery of six field guns, with its seven ammunition and signalling waggons. The haul was one of the greatest made by any battalion until the last weeks of the war, and the British Army had seen nothing so spectacular since 1914. For a brief moment soldiers had been engaged in the sort of action they might have hoped for: fast movement and hand-to-hand fighting against a visible, panic-stricken enemy who had left splendid trophies and innumerable souvenirs.

The price had been heavy, with many casualties, including two officers whom Wilfred knew well, Second Lieutenant Hubert Gaukroger of B Company, killed, and Arthur Heydon, in agony with a smashed thigh joint and not expected to live.[10] The weather had been very bad throughout, with rain and sleet. A private in the battalion, George Dixon, recorded in his diary that he and others were trapped in a crater in driving snow for three days after the attack, several men drowning in the dissolving clay.[11] The captured battery proved impossible to extricate until the night of the 3rd, when a divisional officer, Major F.W. Lumsden, managed to get all six guns out under heavy fire with help from the 15th HLI, an achievement that earned him a VC and instant promotion, although it took away some of the glory from the Manchesters.

Wilfred fought against his feelings as he trudged across open fields towards the firing on 3 April. Had he been in action the day before and still with B Company, he might have helped capture the guns, perhaps winning himself a medal, but he had missed it all and he knew he was in for plenty of ironic remarks. Men he had known in A and B Companies were dead or

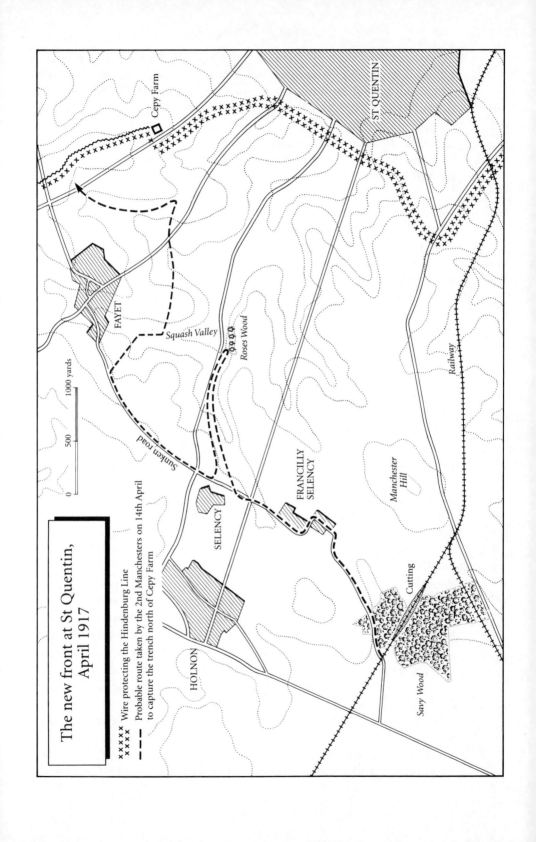

The new front at St Quentin,
April 1917

××××× Wire protecting the Hindenburg Line
××××
– – – Probable route taken by the 2nd Manchesters on 14th April
to capture the trench north of Cepy Farm

Cepy Farm

ST QUENTIN

FAYET

Squash Valley

Roses Wood

1000 yards

500

0

Sunken road

SELENCY

FRANCILLY
SELENCY

Manchester
Hill

Railway

HOLNON

Cutting

Savy Wood

injured, and the news of Heydon was especially distressing. It was up-setting, too, not to be with Sorrell any more. The landscape was still unscarred by trenches, and primroses were coming up in the woods in spite of the weather, but directly ahead lay St Quentin, '*the* town on which the hopes of all England are now turned', and there seemed to be every sign that a major battle was looming.

In the event, though, the Germans did not counter-attack. Their long-term plan was to fight a defensive war in France and Flanders until they had pacified their eastern front, and it was not yet in their interests to engage in offensive operations at St Quentin. They accepted the loss of their outposts and kept up a slow, steady shelling on their easily observed enemy. Wilfred caught up with A Company and the rest of the battalion on the eastern slopes of Manchester Hill, where they were feverishly digging and wiring, helping to construct a new defence line for the division in the wake of the previous day's successes. The men were exhausted after the forced marches of the pursuit and the murderous fight for the hill, and only two officers were left in the company, including Green. Wilfred had to keep awake day and night, being much fresher than the others. He could see French troops probing towards the city through the vast fields of wire that protected it. 'I kept alive on brandy, the fear of death, and the glorious prospect of the cathedral Town just below us, glittering with the morning. With glasses I could easily make out the general architecture of the cathedral: so I have told you how near we have got.'

Heavy snow fell all day on the 4th, then thawed slightly, while the men rested in the relative safety of the railway bank in Savy Wood, the only real shelter in the area until spotter planes flew over next day and directed heavy shelling on it.[12] There were still some Germans west of the Hindenburg wire, so Wilfred was ordered to locate one of their positions and estimate their strength. Taking a night patrol forward, he deliberately made a noise, drawing fire from at least two machine guns and several rifles. On another night, setting up an advanced post, he and his party were detected and shelled, the man next to him getting a 'beautiful round hole deep in his biceps', beautiful because it was a blighty wound, not dangerous but serious enough to warrant treatment in England. Wilfred was to reflect later on the strange notion of beauty that this involved. The poem he tried to write about the incident includes the information, historical or not, that the wound turned gangrenous, so that the man never reached home after all.[13] Wilfred himself was hit by nothing worse than blast and a spent fragment of shrapnel. Once he hung his Blackpool trench coat on a bush and a splinter promptly tore a hole right through it, but he seemed to have a charmed life.

The Manchesters were relieved on the night of 6 April. Perhaps it was now, as they trudged towards their distant rest, 'all of us half dead with fatigue & some quite, poor lads', that Wilfred's platoon was overtaken by gas, the incident described in 'Dulce et Decorum Est' when one man, too slow with his helmet, chokes to death.

> *Dim, through the misty panes and thick green light,*
> *As under a green sea, I saw him drowning.*

The survivors reached the village of Beauvois at three in the morning. The servants took their officers' valises into a cellar that had recently been cleared of mangel-wurzels, while the officers themselves saw to the men. By the time Wilfred stumbled wearily down the cellar steps there were blankets neatly laid out on the floor and, at last, a letter and parcel from home. Snuggling down, more or less dry and warm for the first time in four days, he began opening the parcel and fell asleep. Captain Green warmly approved of Mary's gingerbread next morning. Susan had been ill again, this time with measles. 'O darling Mother you can't think how you could secure my peace of mind by being able to tell me you are well,' Wilfred wrote back, sadly aware he was never going to get that kind of assurance. He said he was in perfect health himself, despite near-death from nerves and cold, and he made no mention of horrors.

What was left of A Company had to be pulled together after its losses. Green was busy for hours at headquarters, fighting to get medals for the men, and the other officer went sick, so most of the training work fell to Wilfred. Rather as in the early days at Witley, he felt uncomfortable at having to give orders to 'these heroes', some of whom were being recommended for high awards. He had hoped to revisit the Lemaires, but there was no time for that even though it was Easter weekend. On Easter Day, when the officers were having tea in their cellar with something like Sunday serenity, the calm was shattered by machine-gun fire. Wilfred rushed out just in time to see a German plane come 'shuddering down the sky', hit by a French fighter over Villeveque.[14] He ran across the fields, feeling the frostbite still in his feet, and took a bloodstained handkerchief as a souvenir from the pilot's horribly broken body. He sent the trophy and a bit of the plane's wooden fuselage to Colin, saying he wanted the handkerchief kept for himself.

Morale was high after the successes of 2 April, despite the strain of the past few days. The engineers had just put up a bath-house for the division, big enough for two battalions to be put through the showers in a day, so the men were sent off in batches, coming back in clean, lice-free clothes. News came through that the United States had finally declared war on Germany. The Battle of Arras began on the 9th (Edward Thomas was killed in the first hour, and Siegfried Sassoon encountered a German corpse in one of the Hindenburg Line tunnels), and the advance there looked promising. For a wild moment the French convinced themselves that St Quentin was being evacuated, having seen fires in the city. They were proposing to attack it on the 10th. Rawlinson instructed 32nd Division to support them, although he was still sceptical because his reserves had not caught up and the French were reluctant to shell the town. British trench-mortar men had been amusing themselves by firing the captured guns and scoring several hits on the cathedral, a game that must have upset their ally, until the authorities intervened and ordered the guns to be towed away to base.

Wilfred had expected to go into action on the 10th, but the French attack was postponed. The battalion moved on the 12th, becoming brigade reserve at Savy, ready to occupy the city's western suburbs in the event of a French success. The brigade commander went on leave that day, Colonel Luxmoore replacing him for a few hours until the replacement arrived, the former Major Lumsden, now Brigadier-General Lumsden, VC. Heavy snow fell in the afternoon, making observation virtually impossible, and waterproof sheets were issued to the men. Long before dawn next morning the Manchesters took up their assembly positions while all available guns fired an hour-long barrage on the Hindenburg Line, the prelude to a brave but futile French assault. St Quentin with its industry and communications was crucial to the new German defence system; there was no possibility of capturing it without massive reinforcements and months of preparation. A second attack failed just as badly in the evening, by which time the Manchesters had already been ordered back to Savy.

While 14th Brigade had been moving forward to cover the French, the other two brigades in the division had been preparing to capture strongpoints north of Selency, places from which the enemy could have enfiladed any French advance. It seemed sensible to go ahead with these attacks, in conformity with Rawlinson's stated aim of clearing German outposts and taking ground from which the Hindenburg Line could be observed and shelled. So, very early on 14 April, 97th Brigade swept through the village of Fayet, taking several hundred prisoners. When news of that success reached headquarters, one of 14th Brigade's battalions, the 1st Dorsets, was abruptly ordered to take Cepy Farm, an isolated group of buildings on a ridge just east of Fayet. Caught by surprise, the German garrison withdrew from the farm, blowing it up as they did so, and the Dorsets dug in round it, not realising they had entered a death trap.

General Lumsden, keen to do well in his first brigade command, had been too optimistic. The area had not yet been fully mapped, and he may not have realised that Cepy Farm was no mere outpost but an integral part of the Hindenburg front line, dominating the northern approaches to St Quentin. The Germans could not afford to lose such a vital position, and their batteries soon started raining shells on it, causing many casualties. Meanwhile 97th Brigade had run into difficulties north of Fayet, and there were signs of an imminent enemy attack from the north-east, so the Dorsets were dangerously exposed. In mid-morning an urgent order reached the Manchesters, most of whom were now in reserve in Savy Wood, to rescue the situation by moving up into the gap between 97th Brigade and the farm. Luxmoore got on his horse and took the battalion northward through Francilly, keeping to low ground, until the scouts rounded a steep bluff at Roses Wood and found themselves looking straight at the cathedral. Visibility was exceptionally good: after weeks of bad weather the landscape was bright under a cloudless sky and strong wind.[15] The order from Brigade had been far from clear, specifying an assembly point about half a mile ahead but not explaining what the ultimate objective was. It was obvious that the next half-mile was within sight of the enemy, so the Colonel rode off to headquarters to ask for clarification and to explain that the battalion would have to take a long way round.

Brigade and battalion diaries are not entirely consistent about what happened next, but it seems a fair guess that there was a sharp exchange between the two commanders, Colonel Luxmoore perhaps resentful at Lumsden's promotion and annoyed at being given unsatisfactory orders, and General Lumsden exasperated to be told that the Manchesters were not in position and that they were going to be late.[16] According to the brigade diary, the Colonel was told to 'find his battalion at once and proceed with the attack at all costs', and there is no mention of a detour. The objective was a trench running north of Cepy Farm, a serious danger to the Dorsets if the enemy were to attack down it. Luxmoore could not argue, but he had no intention of leading his men into certain destruction, so he sent them in a loop, down a sunken road towards Fayet and into a sheltered spot marked on later maps as 'Squash Valley', while he himself rode ahead to reconnoitre.

Wilfred's letters, and one of his poems, give a little information about his own part in the day's events. He says the battalion was rushed into action, and clearly the whole affair was unplanned and confusing. Somewhere along the sunken road an alarm was raised that Germans had been seen, and there was a 'tremendous scurry' as everyone tore off rifle covers, fixed bayonets and readied ammunition, only to be faced with one solitary German 'haring along towards us, with his head down and his arms stretched out in front of him, as if he were going to take a high dive through the earth'. He became the Manchesters' only prisoner for the day. Reaching the valley, the battalion rested out of the wind, feeling the warmth of the sun and waiting for the order to attack, many of the men lying down to eat their midday rations.

> Halted against the shade of a last hill,
> They fed, and eased of pack-loads, were at ease;
> And leaning on the nearest chest or knees
> Carelessly slept.

But Wilfred and others seem to have remained on their feet, gazing at the 'stark blank sky' beyond the hill, 'Knowing their feet had come to the end of the world'.

The next stage of the advance had to be over the ridge, and for a short distance the battalion would after all be in full view from the cathedral. The normal procedure in 1917–18 would have been to advance in small groups, widely separated, but the men were heavily burdened and time was short, so the companies lined up in straight lines or 'waves', the attack formation that had been used on the first day of the Somme. As they climbed the slope, the sun ceased to be a friend. Wilfred's company had to go first.

> *So, soon they topped the hill, and raced together*
> *Over an open stretch of herb and heather*
> *Exposed. And instantly the whole sky burned*
> *With fury against them; earth set sudden cups*
> *In thousands for their blood; and the green slope*
> *Chasmed and deepened sheer to infinite space.*

Wilfred's last poem, 'Spring Offensive', is based on his experience of that hurricane barrage at Fayet, although he changed some of the details. The soldiers in the poem race over the hill in May, but in reality the month was April and the battalion walked. Running would have invited chaos. As he told Colin afterwards,

> There was an extraordinary exultation in the act of slowly walking forward, showing ourselves openly.
> There was no bugle and no drum for which I was very sorry. I kept up a kind of chanting sing-song: Keep the Line straight!
> Not so fast on the left!
> Steady on the Left!
> Not so fast!
> Then we were caught in a Tornado of Shells. The various 'waves' were all broken up and we carried on like a crowd moving off a cricket-field. When I looked back and saw the ground all crawling and wormy with wounded bodies, I felt no horror at all but only an immense exultation at having got through the Barrage.

This description is probably a little more accurate than Luxmoore's, whose report on the action says that the ranks moved through the shelling as though on parade, each wave keeping its distance and every carrier keeping his load. 'By the Grace of God alone,' the Colonel wrote, 'only thirty men were lost in this barrage.' Only eight of the thirty were actually killed, which was indeed a near-miracle. There was shelter again at the foot of the slope, allowing the battalion to get its breath back and regroup.[17]

Luxmoore now rejoined his officers to report on his findings. The Dorsets and 97th Brigade were still under severe pressure, and as it was now two o'clock, an hour later than Lumsden had wanted, there was no time to be lost. Orders were that the battalion should assemble at Cepy Farm and capture the northward trench by charging up it in waves, a fine notion in theory, but in practice the ground in front of the farm was under constant machine-gun fire from St Quentin. It would be much safer to advance under cover in the valley below, parallel to the trench, and then launch a sudden frontal attack. A Company was still in the lead. The outcome was a faintly absurd anticlimax. The trench turned out to be unwired, only a foot deep in places, and held by a single company who fled as the Manchesters approached. Much more serious trouble came from snipers in the rear, apparently hidden in a wood on the edge of Fayet.[18] They gave the battalion a bad time for the next four hours, according to Wilfred, forcing him and others to keep close to the ground in the shallow parts of the trench. Even so, he admitted afterwards that he had 'rather enjoyed the evening after the Stunt, being only a few hundred yards from the Town … and having come through the fire so miraculously: and being, moreover, well fed on the Bosche's untouched repast!! It was curious and troubling to pick up his letters where he had left off writing in the middle of a word!'[19] At eight o'clock that evening the battalion handed their trench over to 97th Brigade and made their way back to Savy, leaving one company as support for the Dorsets and one in Roses Wood.

The Manchesters had been the heroes of 32nd Division on 2 April, but at Fayet on the 14th they were only minor players and their contribution was not very glorious. They seem to have received no thanks for capturing the trench, although it was very close to, possibly even part of, the Hindenburg Line itself.[20] Luxmoore sent round a message next day congratulating the battalion on the way it had got through the barrage, saying the 'leadership of the officers was excellent, and the conduct of the men beyond praise', but it may not have been coincidence that he was replaced as battalion commander only a fortnight later.

From the generals' point of view the battalion had carried out a bit of incidental support work while in reserve, but things seemed rather different to the men involved, and there was clearly some resentment at what followed. 'The reward we got for all this,' Wilfred told Susan, 'was to remain in the Line 12 days. For twelve days I did not wash my face, nor take off my boots, nor sleep a deep sleep. For twelve days we lay in holes, where at any moment a shell might put us out.' He corrected the number of days to nine in a subsequent letter, but even nine days was an exceptionally long time to be in action. Reinforcements were simply not yet available. Wilfred was at one with the troops in blaming shirkers. 'I think that the terribly long time we stayed unrelieved was unavoidable; yet it makes us feel bitterly towards those in England who might relieve us, and will not.' Bitterness notwithstanding, 14th Brigade obeyed orders, the four battalions relieving each other when they could, although there was only the railway cutting to retire to. At least one relief had to be abandoned when the guides got lost in the dark. As yet there were no dugouts or communication trenches, nor any guns powerful enough to suppress the enemy artillery. The Manchesters were spread out between Roses Wood and Manchester Hill, the men labouring night and day, digging and connecting trenches and constructing a double belt of wire, often in rain and under shellfire. Occasionally there was time for souvenir-hunting (Wilfred took some 'Loot' for Colin from a dead German's pocket and unbuckled a bugle for himself), but no one could rest. The bombardment on Cepy Farm reached such a pitch of ferocity that the place had to be abandoned. Other positions were held, being in truth no great threat to the Germans, who completed their front-line defences and felt safe enough behind the most elaborate barrier that human ingenuity had ever devised.

It was during these nine days, 13–21 April 1917, that Wilfred's nerve finally gave way. After many escapes from shells and bullets, he was asleep one wet night on the railway bank in Savy Wood when a big shell exploded a few yards from his head, blowing him into the air. He was briefly unconscious, later referring to 'coming-to after the Embankment-Shell-Shock'. He told his mother he had spent most of the following days in the cutting, sheltering 'in a hole just big enough to lie in, and covered with corrugated iron. My brother officer of B Coy, 2/Lt Gaukroger lay opposite in a similar hole. But he was covered with earth, and no relief will ever relieve him, nor will his Rest be a 9 days-Rest.' Gaukroger, who had been killed on 2 April, lay 'in various places round about'. He had presumably been buried in the cutting and later horribly disinterred by a shell.[21] Wilfred was not completely incapacitated. According to a now-lost letter, it was his duty to leave the cutting at 'about midnight to flounder across to the French and knock at the door of the company H.Q. and ask if all was well, to be answered by a grunt'.[22] Nevertheless, an officer ought not to have been sheltering alone for so long, leaving his men leaderless. There may be a memory of Savy Wood in the closing lines of Wilfred's late-1917 poem, 'The Show', where he describes his platoon as a worm which 'half had hid / Its bruises in the earth, but crawled no further' and himself as the worm's newly-severed head.

The relief was thorough when it came, the entire 32nd Division being withdrawn to become Corps Reserve for several weeks, with headquarters at Voyennes. The Manchesters left the line in the early hours of the 22nd, making an eight-mile march to safe billets in cellars at Quivières. Wilfred had recovered well enough to go with them. His cellar may have been the church crypt, where the packed-up saints lay serried and a statue of the Virgin was crowned with an old tin hat, as described in his poem, 'Le Christianisme'. 'We are now doing what is called a Rest,' he told Susan a few days later, although the programme of training was anything but restful. Reveille was sounded at 6.15 a.m., soon followed by parades, drill, physical training and bayonet practice. The afternoons were filled with organised sports and games, and after tea at five there were lectures and map classes until a hot meal at eight. Lights-out for the men came an hour later, while the officers stayed up for another hour or so to attend what Wilfred called a 'Pow-Wow'. Any spare time he could find had to be devoted to censoring letters and dealing with enquiries about missing men. Exasperating though the constant activity was, it paid off for men who were still fit, as the authorities knew it would, and the troops were soon in high spirits. Messages poured in from Haig, Rawlinson and others, praising the Division for its 'gallantry and dash', and a series of inspections was planned to honour 14th Brigade. Rugby matches were held against the French, bands played and spring weather came at last. And Wilfred struggled to behave normally, trying to forget that he was still dizzy from the shell-blast and sick with the memory of Gaukroger's shattered remains.

His morale suffered another blow on the 23rd, when Sorrell was sent away to the CCS with severe shock, having been twice blown up and buried while on a working party. No one could doubt his courage, and he was successfully recommended for a Military Cross.[23] If it was reassuring for Wilfred to see that shock need not always be a disgrace, it must have been disheartening to lose a good friend and kindred spirit. How long he was able to keep going after Sorrell's departure is not clear, but the interval was not to his advantage. Officers who collapsed immediately after a shell-burst were more likely to get credit than those who managed to continue working for a while. Delayed shock was very common, but it could look like funk. Wilfred's letters give no sign that he was on parade for the inspection by General Lumsden on the 27th, or for the grander inspection by the divisional General three days later, when medals were distributed. One of his 1918 letters mentions his having spent three nights in hospital at Nesle, so he may have been sent there at this time, the doctors perhaps suspecting a recurrence of his concussion. However, he was certainly with the battalion on 1 May.

The parade on 30 April was probably the last occasion on which Colonel Luxmoore rode at the head of the 2nd Manchesters. He had led the battalion for over two years and now, whether at his own request or Lumsden's or for some quite different reason, he was about to leave for a staff posting. On 1 May the odious Major Dempster took temporary command as acting Lieutenant-Colonel, and on that same day, according to Wilfred's army file, Second Lieutenant Owen was 'observed to be shaky and tremulous, and his conduct and manner were peculiar, and his memory was confused'.[24] The observer may well have been Dempster himself. It would have been a tense moment, the new CO conscious of needing to assert his authority in the absence of his much-admired, much-feared predecessor, and Wilfred on the edge of breakdown, bereft of Sorrell's support and Luxmoore's leadership. Wilfred seems to have thought the battalion was going into action again, although the officers were in fact planning nothing more than a big practice attack. He may have said something that revealed confusion and apprehension. Whatever happened, it seems that Dempster made some cutting remark, implying Wilfred was a coward.[25] Only a few words perhaps, and perhaps more cruel than they were meant to be, barked out by a man under strain, but they seem to have hit Wilfred very hard. He was sent to the Medical Officer, and next day wrote home from 13 CCS, the familiar hospital at Gailly. In his absence, the battalion carried out its attack exercise under Dempster's critical eye and continued training, with special attention to the 'Attack in Open Warfare'. But there was to be no more open warfare in the St Quentin sector until the catastrophic German breakthrough in March 1918.

14

Mental Case

Gailly and Craiglockhart

MAY–AUGUST 1917

When Wilfred's poems were published after the war, several reviewers said his nerve had failed on the battlefield, a comment that allowed some of his first readers, Henry Newbolt for example, to dismiss his book as the work of a 'broken man'. His supporters responded by doing all they could to deflect attention from his breakdown, knowing the authority of the poems would be badly undermined if the war generation were able to think of them as the self-pitying complaints of a coward. This reticence has persisted until recent times, even though the reason for it has long since disappeared. Wilfred's life and work form a record of high courage, needing no defence, and his shell-shock has to be recognised as an essential stage in his becoming, as John Middleton Murry was to call him, the poet of the war. Shell-shock gave him seventeen months of safety, time in which to think and write, and he was told that purposeful activity was the best of all cures. By great good fortune he came under the care of two exceptionally skilled doctors, who made him face up to his front-line experience in all its horror. He was encouraged to work towards controlling his memories, relating them to his personality and earlier life, because that was the only way he could become a whole man again. The treatment worked: to use one of his favourite metaphors, he looked into the eyes of the Gorgon and was not turned to stone. In due course the nightmares that might have destroyed him were objectified into poetry.

~

At first he suppressed his recent memories, writing long, cheery letters home that hardly give an inkling of the trauma he was going through, although Susan must have seen that his light tone was often forced. For a while sheer relief at getting away from the fighting predominated over all his other feelings, at least by day. There was a happy moment as he was getting into an ambulance on the way to Gailly, when he was asked for his name by a dignified corporal who turned out to be one of his

243

contemporaries at the Shrewsbury Technical, Fred Hartop. Astonishing nearby Tommies by greeting each other with more enthusiasm than was usual between an officer and an NCO, they exchanged news of old friends at the PTC and memories of the 'years that were better than these, or any years to come'. Hartop was still reading books they had all studied together, so Wilfred eagerly borrowed some.

The Casualty Clearing Station at Gailly was now a specialist hospital. It had been designated a centre for shell-shock back in March, and the first cases had begun arriving while Wilfred had been there. By the time of his second visit almost all the patients, twenty or so officers (including some Frenchmen) and about four hundred Other Ranks, were suffering from mental rather than physical troubles. The huge incidence of shock during the Somme had forced the authorities to revise their earlier opinion that the condition only affected 'degenerates', the poorest mental and physical types. New terminology had been introduced, 'neurasthenia' being the preferred label for all but the most serious cases, and new hospitals had been set up at home so that shock cases would not have to be sent to existing asylums.[1] Even so, plenty of people, army doctors included, would still have regarded men at 13 CCS as malingerers and cowards, as Wilfred well knew. The first poem he wrote after meeting Sassoon in the summer, 'The Dead-Beat', is based on an actual incident, when a member of his platoon had collapsed, unable to respond to orders even at revolver point; next day the Medical Officer had said, 'That dirt / You sent me down last night's just died. So glad!'[2]

Two or three of the officers at the CCS and perhaps a dozen of the men were SIW (self-inflicted wound) cases, self-evidently cowards by the standards of the time, having shot themselves in their hands or feet rather than remain in the trenches. The great majority, though, were in the grip of demons they could not control. Some patients had lost the use of their limbs, some were mute or gibbering, and many had severe stutters and unsteady legs. Some were terrible to watch, as Wilfred was to recall in 'Mental Cases' later:

> *Wading sloughs of flesh these helpless wander,*
> *Treading blood from lungs that had loved laughter.*
> *Always they must see these things and hear them,*
> *Batter of guns and shatter of flying muscles,*
> *Carnage incomparable, and human squander,*
> *Rucked too thick for these men's extrication.*

Men in that state would have been hidden away from other patients as much as possible, but no one could have been in any doubt as to what sort of hospital the CCS now was.

The small band of officers, comfortably segregated from the Other Ranks, kept up a spirit of *bonhomie*. They were all in the same predicament, and happy at least to be warm, clean and free from responsibilities. Wilfred was soon saying he liked them all as good fellows, even as 'socially-possible' friends for the future. Two days after he arrived the weather turned hot, allowing him and the others to sunbathe in the surrounding fields, sharing dreams of farming after the war. The orderlies put bowls of yellow flowers round the ward, a detail he was to use in his poem, 'Conscious'. Another poem written later, 'Hospital Barge', is based on memories of the Somme Canal, including a trip he made in a steam tug down to Corbie in blazing sunshine, imagining himself as King Arthur being carried in the barge to Avalon. 'But the Saxon is not broken,' he added in the letter which describes this Arthurian idyll. The guns were still thundering in the east.

One of Wilfred's fellow patients asked him to translate some letters into French, having no doubt seen how easily he chatted to the French patients, and in return he was given a letter of introduction to Erskine Macdonald, publisher of the Little Books of Georgian Verse.[3] That set Wilfred thinking again about the possibility of getting himself published in the series. He unearthed the notebook he had used during his previous stay at the CCS and made notes for a book of sonnets, this time to be entitled 'Sonatas in Silence' and printed in the same type as *Before Dawn*. The Decadent-sounding title and Monro's chosen typeface would certainly have reaffirmed some allegiances, but he had forgotten Monro's advice about the Little Books. He set to work on one of the subjects he had agreed with Leslie and Olwen, 'Sunrise', producing an absurdly elaborate sonnet full of Tailhadesque sound effects:

> *Loomed a pale Pearl more marvellous than the Moon's,*
> *Who thereby waned yet wanner than she was,*
> *Because of the pallor of the Pearl of dawn, – because*
> *Her Pearl was whiter than the wan, worn Moon's.*[4]

Wilfred revealed little about his state even to his mother, beyond explaining that he had been shaky and prone to headaches traceable to his concussion. '*Some* of us have been sent down here as a little mad,' he said on 4 May. 'Possibly I am among them.' But he went no further, and he asked Susan not to tell anyone he was in hospital again. The less said about being an unwounded casualty the better. Most of the clues as to his condition are actually in his poetry. Among the commonest symptoms of shell-shock were uncontrollable trembling, a rapid pulse, profuse sweating, especially from palms and scalp, and a sense of suffocation. He already knew these troubles, all of which had figured in his work for 'Perseus' and other pre-1917 verse, and they probably returned to plague him after Savy Wood. It was a characteristic of shell-shock, according to experts at the time, that it struck its victims where they were most vulnerable, so that, for example, a man who had always been liable to go 'weak at the knees' under stress might lose the power of locomotion altogether. Wilfred's worst symptom was violent dreams. His earlier 'phantasms', visions of 'bloodiness and stains of shadowy crimes', came back in wartime guise, infinitely more dreadful than before. Worst of all were the faces, among them those of the gassed man ('In all my dreams ... He plunges at me') and the sentry in the dugout ('Eyeballs, huge-bulged like squids' / Watch my dreams still').[5] Like many of the other patients, Wilfred must often have woken screaming in the night.

In the early days of the war, shock cases had been sent directly to hospitals in Britain, but doctors had soon discovered that treatment needed to be immediate. Shell-shock centres were sited as near the front as possible, so that casualties could be attended to within twenty-four hours, as Wilfred was. The senior neurologist at Gailly, William Brown, an eminent man in his field, treated several thousand patients there, reckoning that with proper rest and treatment over two-thirds of them could be sent back to the line within a fortnight. The more serious cases might need up to three months, while a small minority needed even more. Wilfred remained under Brown's observation for a month, then spent five months in hospitals at home and a further nine on light duties. He was clearly a very sick man. Yet he was not as ill as some. Sorrell had already been sent to England, and was to be in a bad way for years afterwards.[6] Brown must have decided very quickly about Sorrell, but he was less sure about Wilfred, perhaps seeing his remarkable inner resilience. There must have been a possibility during that month at Gailly that Wilfred would after all be declared fit and sent back to the battalion.

He described Brown as 'a kind of wizard, who mesmerises when he likes'. The doctor required patients to talk about their experiences, as many of them were deeply reluctant to do, and hypnosis was a useful means of uncovering buried memories. The essential first stage in recovery was to identify the moment of failure, the breaking point that each man most wanted to hide. Brown often induced the process known as abreaction, making men live through their ordeal again until the original event recreated itself so vividly in their minds that they would sometimes fling themselves howling to the floor. It may be that Wilfred's habitual interest in his own mental processes allowed him to talk more freely than most, without any need for hypnosis or abreaction. Only a week after arriving at the CCS he was able to tell Mary that the cause of his collapse had not been the blast on the railway bank but sheltering near Gaukroger's remains, an insight he must have reached with Brown's help. The next step was to trace his nightmares back into his past. After a few weeks of these consultations, Wilfred would have known more about himself than he had ever done before.

Recovery was a slow, unsteady business, with the possibility of permanent breakdown never far away. Wilfred diverted himself by tinkering with sonnets, reading comic novels and composing long, facetious letters home, filling pages with pseudo-biblical nonsense and long parodies of the litany, an army form and a medical chart. Anything to occupy time and keep horrors at bay. Dorothy Gunston wrote another of her exalted letters, praising his heroism. She and others at home need never know what had happened. When he was fit again he would have a chance to redeem himself, perhaps with a different unit. He told his mother he didn't care if he were sent to some other battalion than the 2nd Manchesters, now that Sorrell and Luxmoore had gone and the 'horrid old Major' had taken over.

When he did allow himself to reflect on the war, his first thoughts were about religion, a subject he had said almost nothing about in his letters since Dunsden. His mock-biblical letter of mid-May showed him how many texts were stored away in his mind, and he told Susan he was becoming

> more and more Christian as I walk the unchristian ways of Christendom. Already I have comprehended a light which never will filter into the dogma of any national church: namely that one of Christ's essential commands was: Passivity at any price! Suffer dishonour and disgrace; but never resort to arms. Be bullied, be outraged, be killed; but do not kill. It may be a chimerical and an ignominious principle, but there it is. It can only be ignored: and I think pulpit professionals are ignoring it very skilfully and successfully indeed.

His anger against Wigan and the Keswick preachers in 1912, and his sympathy with the village boys and the scar-backed mining lad, were now reviving on a much larger scale. He was scornful of 'pulpit professionals' such as the Wood brothers, and of Fritz Wood's having renamed himself Frederick, and of the Bishop of London and all the other civilians who were proclaiming that God was on the British side.

> And am I not myself a conscientious objector with a very seared conscience? ...
> Christ is literally in no man's land. There men often hear His voice: Greater love hath no man than this, that a man lay down his life – for a friend.
> Is it spoken in English only and French?
> I do not believe so.
> Thus you see how pure Christianity will not fit in with pure patriotism.

Wilfred's misquotation, '– for a friend' instead of the biblical 'for his friends', is deliberate. The plural had allowed propagandists to exploit Christ's saying, using it to imply that any soldier who died in battle was a modern saviour, a redeemer helping to atone for the sins of the whole nation and in the process earning himself a place in heaven. There was even a myth that the Germans had crucified a Canadian soldier, a story accepted by many people including Colonel Shirley, who had referred to it in his introductory lecture at Romford. The idea of the soldier-Christ provided subject matter for innumerable poems, paintings and stories during the war. Among the leading proponents of it were the tabloid journalist, Horatio Bottomley, and the best-selling poet, John Oxenham. When Susan sent Wilfred one of Oxenham's little volumes, Wilfred told her bluntly that most of the poems were worthless and that Oxenham held 'the Moslem doctrine – preached by Horatio Bottomley, but not by the Nazarene – of salvation by *death in war*'. Nevertheless, Wilfred had used the soldier-Christ image himself in the 'Ballad of Kings and Christs', and it remained attractive. By altering 'friends' to 'a friend' he could bring the saying down to the individual level, where it still seemed to make sense.

He said one of the causes of the war had been '*selective ignorance*' by Church leaders who had chosen to overlook the inconvenient bits of their creed, but by changing a scriptural text to suit his own thinking he was tacitly admitting that he, too, had to be selective. Composing his facetious army form, he gave his religion as 'Primitive Christian' and his aim in war as 'Extinction of Militarism *beginning* with Prussian', two ideals that seemed irreconcilable. A soldier had to ignore the commandment 'Passivity at any price!' because Prussian militarism could only be extinguished by military means. Wilfred thought H.G. Wells's latest book, *God the Invisible King*, was absurd because it argued that God was working out a divine purpose through the war, but he would still have assented to Wells's 1914 declaration that the Allies were fighting a 'war that will end war'.[7] 'Sonnet on Seeing a Piece of Our Heavy Artillery Brought into Action', perhaps drafted at the CCS, expresses the Wellsian idea:

> *Sway steep against them, and for years rehearse*
> *Huge imprecations like a blasting charm!*
> *Reach at that Arrogance which needs thy harm,*
> *And beat it down before its sins grow worse.*
> *Spend our resentment, cannon, – yea, disburse*
> *Our gold in shapes of flame, our breaths in storm ...*

As the *Fleetwood Chronicle* had said in 1916, it was 'our work, our money, our blood, if needs be, that must win the war'. 'But when thy spell be cast complete and whole,' Wilfred ended his sonnet to the gun, 'May God curse thee, and cut thee from our soul!' Only when German 'Arrogance' had been destroyed could British militarism also become a thing of the past.

The conclusions Wilfred had thus far reached about religion and war were not unusual for a subaltern who had been in the trenches in early 1917. He could well have heard similar ideas from his fellow patients. War was a hideous, unchristian business, and the churchmen who were trying to pretend otherwise were lying. People at home had to wake up to what conditions were really like, just as they had to wake up to the realities of human life in general. Wilfred praised the realism of Wells's *The Passionate Friends*, a novel about sexual relationships. Similarly, he said the description he had sent to Colin about going over the top was a 'wholesome bit of realism'. It was important to clear young Colin's head of heroic illusions, and to make Susan see that Oxenham's type of religion was fatuous. Tom Owen's patriotic views, 'Father's ethics' as Wilfred called them in a letter to Mary, needed challenging, too. Even so, almost everyone in the army thought there was no alternative to battering away at the enemy, and as long as Wilfred thought the same he would not be able to get beyond the ideas in his 'Artillery' sonnet.

~

The recent advance meant that 13 CCS was now too far from the front as a shell-shock centre. The staff spent a week packing up all their equipment, even the mugs and ashtrays, before departing to a site nearer the line, and the huts, beds and patients at Gailly were handed over to an entirely new team on 23 May, when the place was renamed 41st Stationary Hospital.[8] In the middle of this upheaval, Wilfred developed a temperature and had to spend a few days in bed, in a ward without chairs, screens or even medicines. A new batch of officers arrived, keeping up a louder show of jollity at night than he could stand, but fortunately an artillery colonel summoned the sister, 'a wretched trembling maiden just out of England'. 'Look! Madam!' the Colonel thundered, flapping his pyjama sleeves in fury, 'Is this a hospital or is it a – – – ???' Wilfred told the story to Mary, who was also a nurse, when he wrote to her for her twenty-first birthday at the end of the month. 'Enough of those who profess and call themselves Sisters. I have a real sister, and I want her with me!' He ended his letter affectionately with his 'very dearest wishes for the best years of my darling sister. May they be without cloud or ruffle of storm. May they each be long years, that is to say, full, and may they be full of good, filled from Heaven. You will speak for me when you look up to God; and I will stand by you and for you as long as we move among men.'

The chaos in the hospital was infuriating while it lasted, but things soon improved. By early June Wilfred was working on a long, pseudo-medieval ballad about the Lady Yolande and her love for a beautiful pageboy. He described his mood as 'highest variety of jinks', his appearance as 'sun-boiled lobster' and his health as 'quite restored'. He said he had found a 'chum' and they were clearly enjoying themselves. His time at Gailly was almost up, however. On the 6th he and other patients were driven to the railhead for evacuation, only to be told that the ambulance train had no accommodation for officers. 'The O.C. Train a min*ute* doctor, with many papers and much pince-nez, refused to let us board: especially as a Major who was with us expressed himself thus: "Aw I decline. I *eb*solutely decline, to travel in a coach where there are – haw – *Men!*" '⁹ German patients were put into the train instead, while some British stretcher cases were left lying in the sun on the platform. Wilfred and the other officers were driven back to the hospital, to be greeted with ironic applause. Another attempt four days later was more successful, and Wilfred was soon at No. 1 General Hospital, Étretat, near Le Havre, admiring the magnificent coastal scenery and being looked after by Americans. On 16 June, after crossing to Southampton on a luxury liner with a cabin to himself, he was sent to the Welsh Hospital at Netley.

The main building at Netley, facing Southampton Water, was a vast affair that he referred to ironically as a 'Bungalow', but 'the Welsh' was a group of huts round the back. Time dragged, pleasant though it was to be among Welsh people. The nurses were evidently unsure about his condition, keeping him in bed for a day until he could be seen by a specialist. Leslie Gunston, who was doing his bit by working in a YMCA hut at Hazeley Down near Winchester, came for an afternoon, afterwards writing to Susan to report on the invalid. An official report was made on 25 June, when Wilfred was interviewed by a Medical Board. He explained the history of his shock, starting with his concussion in March. The Board noted there was now 'little abnormality to be observed but he seems to be of a highly strung temperament. He has slept well while here.' The doctors would have known that such cases were liable to relapse if sent back into action too soon, and they decided Wilfred should be transferred to Craiglockhart Hospital, just outside Edinburgh, for special observation and treatment. They graded him as unfit even for home service for three months and for active service for another six, the longest period they were allowed to recommend.

Wilfred had hoped for three weeks' leave in Shrewsbury, but the doctors ordered him to set out for Edinburgh as soon as the interview was over. He could manage nothing better than a brief pause in London, where he bought himself a new cap and made his usual summer visit to the Academy exhibition, finding the pictures disappointing. One of them was a heroic scene by the propaganda artist, Caton Woodville, showing the Manchesters capturing the guns at Francilly, a painful reminder of the action he had missed by one day. The gap between civilian illusions and front-line realities, and between heroic acclaim and his own collapse, was going to be hard to bear. He comforted himself by making for the Shamrock Tea Rooms, an agreeably exclusive haven where there was 'the usual deaf old lady and her Companion holding forth upon the new curate. I happen to know,' he added, 'that a few stories higher in the same building is an Opium Den. I have not investigated. But I know. That's London.' He loved to have secrets. But then came another reminder of the recent past. Strolling down New Bond Street to order new trousers at Pope & Bradley, he had the misfortune to run into the 'last person on earth or under the earth' he wished to meet. It was Dempster. The temporary Colonel pretended to be affable, but he must have remembered their previous encounter well enough.

The overnight train from King's Cross reached Edinburgh in time for Wilfred to have an enormous breakfast in the North British Hotel and walk the length of Princes Street, remembering his tour of the city with John Bulman in 1912. Of the three young men who had helped Nelly Bulman entertain the Owens at Kelso, only John was left; his brother Bill and their sister's fiancé, Walter Forrest, had both been killed, the former at Gallipoli in 1915 and the latter only recently, in April at Gaza. It was best not to reflect too much on such things. Wilfred took a taxi for the two-and-a-half miles to Craiglockhart on the western edge of the city.

~

Craiglockhart War Hospital for Neurasthenic Officers had been established in the autumn of 1916, as part of the army's effort to cope with the thirty thousand cases of shell-shock that had resulted from the Somme. Until then the place had been a hydropathic hotel, opened in 1880 and advertising itself as a going concern right up to the moment of closure, so the patients inherited not only a huge building with about three hundred rooms and a dozen acres of grounds, but also numerous amenities and quantities of furniture and equipment. The building was tall and imposing, designed to command immense views towards the Firth of Forth and distant mountains. The grounds contained a bowling green, tennis courts, a cricket pitch and a half-mile cycle track, as well as the scant remains of a medieval castle. Despite all its attractions, however, the Hydro had never prospered, perhaps because it faced northwestwards into the wind and rain. By 1917 it was badly in need of refurbishment.

Wilfred's heart sank as he entered the tiled lobby and looked down the long, gloomy corridors swarming with patients and nurses. He was recognised by several people, presumably men he had known at Gailly, good companions there perhaps, but now only embarrassing evidence of shared failure. Most of them seemed healthy enough, apart from the usual stammers and sudden, nervous movements. The Craiglockhart authorities were doing their best to make the place seem more like a convalescent home than a mental hospital, and the most serious cases had been sent elsewhere.[10] Even so, rather too many people seemed to be hanging about aimlessly, with vacant eyes and unsteady legs. Wilfred reported to the office, where he was registered as 'Neurasthenia' like almost everyone else and given an appointment with one of the Medical Officers, Dr Brock, next morning. The corridors got darker and narrower as he went upstairs. He seems to have had a room to himself, but if it had a view or any other advantages he says nothing about them in his letters. The lock had been removed from the door. He wrote home, then went out to explore.

One encouraging find was a reading room, stocked with new books from a lending library in Edinburgh as well as with the Hydro's old collection of novels and encyclopaedias. The vast lounge was less appealing, peopled by bridge players and men dozing in leather-covered armchairs. There was a big recreation room with a proscenium stage, a room set up as a cinema, and even a little swimming pool and Turkish bath, although the gadgetry which the Hydro had installed for fashionable water-cures was apparently not in use. The noticeboards in the hall advertised numerous activities, from language classes to model yacht racing. Outside, beyond the sports pitches, there were allotments and a hen run where the Gardening and Poultry Keeping Association was raising vegetables and chicks. Patients were obviously expected to keep busy, yet everything seemed to be voluntary. Military discipline was unobtrusive; some men were even wearing nothing but bathing costumes borrowed from the pool, a practice that soon had to be forbidden by an edict in the hospital magazine, The Hydra. The CO, Major Bryce, was so unsoldierly that he sometimes forgot to wear his cap, answering salutes with an absent-minded bow, but The Hydra said he was 'an absolute brick'.[11]

The relaxed atmosphere of Craiglockhart did not outlast the daylight. Many of the patients had good reason to fear the dark. They kept themselves awake as long as possible, smoking incessantly despite admonitions from the staff, and when sleep finally overcame them they were in the trenches again. Wilfred put his revolver beside him out of habit on his first night, but in the morning it had gone, removed by a nurse on her rounds; weapons could not be permitted in a hospital full of violent dreams. The corridors at night were frightening, echoing to sudden shouts and hurrying feet, and some patients could hardly bear to walk down them even by day. Wilfred says little in his letters about his own dreams, but he clearly had some terrifying 'Barrage'd Nights', paralysed in the dugout by the sentry's eyes, or walking slowly through the shellfire at Fayet, or struggling half-stifled in his gas mask while dying men stared piteously at him, crying for the help he could not give. Only a few days after he arrived he wrote to Leslie that he had sat up reading until three in the morning. Later he described himself as 'one of the weary who don't want rest' and was glad when the nurses gave up trying to cajole him into turning his light off.

~

On the morning of 27 June 1917 Arthur Brock and Wilfred faced one another for the first time across the doctor's table: the little subaltern still nervy, with an occasional stammer in his warm, deep voice, his carefully-brushed hair streaked with grey and his face burned by sunshine and harsh weather; and the tall, angular doctor, impractical, humourless, a temporary captain in the RAMC but obviously no soldier, his sharp nose, long bluish hands and high voice somehow suggestive of Arctic regions.[12] The two men could hardly have been more different, yet either by luck or good judgement the army had sent Wilfred to precisely the right doctor. There were three other Medical Officers at the hospital, a popular American major named Ruggles, a Lieutenant McIntyre, who was prone to remarking in a thick Glaswegian accent that most of the patients needed nothing more than a good dose, and the famous anthropologist, W.H.R. Rivers, but each doctor supervised his own patients and had little or no contact with those of his colleagues. Brock's theories and methods were unique.

Enough evidence survives to show how Brock worked, although his meticulous diary and all his wartime case notes were thrown away after his death, a sad loss to the history of psychiatry as well as to Owen biography. His post-war letters to Susan Owen have also disappeared, except for one comment, quoted by Edmund Blunden, that Wilfred was 'a very out-standing figure, both in intellect and in character'.[13] That high praise suggests that the match between doctor and patient worked both ways. Brock was pleased to have a receptive listener, already sympathetic to his way of thinking. As for Wilfred, who had always longed to be at university, consultations with the doctor were the nearest he would ever get to experiencing scholarly tutorials. He even seems to have had a fellow student, Charles Mayes, a nineteen-year-old artillery subaltern who had been at Craiglockhart since March. Brock liked patients to work in pairs, each as the other's doctor, so Wilfred and Mayes often took part in activities together.

Brock was a farmer's son, with values rooted in what he believed to be the best way of life, that of the sturdy Scottish countrymen he had known in his youth. A right relationship with the environment was the key to health. He had studied in Edinburgh, Vienna and elsewhere in Europe, not only qualifying as a doctor but also mastering several languages and becoming learned in a prodigious range of subjects from the classics to anthropology. He had recently published a translation of one of the writers he most admired, the ancient Greek doctor Galen, who had argued that a physician should treat the whole man. It was central to all Brock's ideas that the organism could only exist, and only be understood, in terms of its relationship to its environment, a relationship that was its *function* or work. Neurasthenia was a failure of function, a dissociation between organism and environment. The illness that was being treated at Craiglockhart was merely an extreme form of the neurasthenia that had affected all Western society in the years before 1914, when people had lost touch with nature and the shape and significance of their cities. The body politic had been diseased. Similarly, many of the diseases of the human body had social origins, so that drugs and 'mechanical' methods of doctoring were bound to fail.

The way back to wholeness, as Brock explained in his post-war book and many articles, was for people to grasp their environment mentally and then to work on it, studying their landscape, towns and language. Botany, geology, civics, philology, literature and the arts should all be within the province of the healthy individual. That meant strenuous effort. Craiglockhart had been built for rest cures, catering for people suffering from what Brock called ergophobia, fear of effort, but his method of treatment was the work-cure, or as he called it, ergotherapy.[14] And here the doctor gestured with long, cold fingers to a picture on the wall that must already have caught Wilfred's attention, an engraving of a classical sculpture, two muscular figures wrestling with each other. Brock was scornful of notions of art for art's sake, believing that art should serve social ends, and he had pinned up the picture as a teaching aid. The losing wrestler being held up in the air was the son of earth and sea, Antaeus, who had been invincible as long as he had kept contact with his mother, the Earth. His opponent, Hercules, had discovered his secret and lifted him off the ground, killing him easily. The neurasthenic, likewise, would be crushed to death by the war machine unless he could quickly reconnect himself to his environment.

Brock explained that bad dreams were expressions of failure, guilt and loss of self-confidence. He drew a parallel between the hideous, pursuing apparitions that peopled many war dreams and the evil spirits of folklore. There was much psychological truth in the old stories: the goblins who turned milk sour or made ewes sterile would only torment inefficient farmers. Self-respect and hard work were the best ways of ensuring peaceful nights. In his one published mention of Wilfred after the war, Brock said that every work of imagination was

a projection into sensory form of the artist's deepest personal experiences. Dante's *Vision of Hell* is an imagery of his own moral struggles; so also with Bunyan's *Pilgrim's Progress*, Mrs Shelley's *Frankenstein*, the gruesome paintings of Wiertz, etc. In the powerful war-poems of Wilfred Owen we read the heroic testimony of one who having in the most literal sense 'faced the phantoms of the mind' had *all* but laid them ere the last call came; they still appear in his poetry but he fears them no longer.[15]

From the doctor's professional point of view Wilfred's poems were interesting not so much for what they said about war as for their proof that ergotherapy had '*all but*' succeeded. Brock probably recognised the horrors in the poems as some of the dreams Wilfred had told him about in 1917.

The doctor was inclined to talk at great length about his ideas, and not all his patients were appreciative. 'We hear', one of them remarked wearily in *The Hydra*, 'a certain stoical MO has discovered an organism entirely without environment.' However, Wilfred, who had been thrown off the earth by the shell in Savy Wood, saw the point of ergotherapy at once. Miss Wright and Miss Jones at the Technical had taught him earth sciences alongside poetry about, in Wordsworth's phrase, 'the ennobling inter-change' of action between mind and nature, and at Reading Dr Rayner and Professor Morley had taught him science and language while encouraging him to read and write poetry. Unlike officers whose schooling had been, in theory at least, superior to his own, he had not been reared on the classics or trained to see the arts and sciences as two separate cultures. He would have noticed with pleasure how Brock could illustrate a medical point by quoting Tennyson or Dante.

Even so, the first stage of ergotherapy could not be attained through tutorials. It was common for men in shock to long for their mothers, and Wilfred was desperate to see Susan again. 'I am not able to settle down here without seeing Mother,' he confessed to Mrs Bulman on 1 July, writing to thank her for sending an emissary with a gift of strawberries and cream. 'I feel a sort of reserve and suspense about everything I do.' He met Blanche Bulman in town, worked on his ballad, drafted a sonnet or two, and went to a church service ('It gave me the indigoes, not half'),[16] but he could not make the kind of effort the doctor was demanding. 'I have made no friends in this place, and the impulse is not in me to walk abroad and find them,' he told Susan. '*Oh Mother!*' Brock would have understood. It was no doubt with his approval that Susan made arrangements to visit Edinburgh.

Wilfred's letter to Nelly Bulman is a rare example of how he wrote to people outside his immediate family. It was not an easy letter to compose, given her recent losses, but she had nevertheless written to him encouragingly at the front. He managed his words well. 'I have endured unnameable tortures in France,' he told her, 'but I know that I have not suffered by this war as you have and are suffering. I felt your sympathy with me out there; but now, my dear Auntie Nelly, it is all on my part.' He had been less tactful, quite unintentionally, when her friend had arrived with the strawberries; an orderly had said, 'Young Lady to see you, Sir,' whereupon Wilfred had replied listlessly, 'I don't think, but what's it like?', not knowing the lady was just round the corner.

A few days more, and Susan arrived. Wilfred met her in the Caledonian Hotel, and as she glided up to him, raising her veil, he felt the sort of 'exultation' he had experienced on getting through the barrage at Fayet. For a brief moment he was a 'Mother's Boy' again. Having not seen her for over six months, he noticed her grey hair, 'the ashes of all your Sacrifices: for Father, for me, and for all of us'. Somehow the moment was a release, as the organism made its first vital reconnection with its environment.

Susan's network of friends extended to Edinburgh, so she was able to stay with a family named Newboult at Summerside Place, Leith. Wilfred thought they were very dull, resenting having to spend time in their company instead of having his mother to himself, but he made friends with their seven-year-old son Arthur, later taking him to the zoo, buying him his first penknife and writing two poems about his innocent, classical beauty. Susan toured the city with Wilfred and visited the hospital, attending a Saturday concert. He seems to have introduced her to Brock, who liked to meet patients' families, and to Mayes and some of 'Dr Brock's Ladies,' friends of the doctor's who were willing to help with ergo-therapeutic activities. She went on to stay with Mrs Bulman at Yetholm, where Wilfred soon wrote to her, saying he was 'full of activities now'. He promised her lunch in town and 'an hour on the Tower' when she came back to Edinburgh on her way home.

There was no need to explain his treatment in letters. Susan had heard all about ergotherapy in conversation with him, and probably with Brock as well, so she knew what the 'Tower' was and why Brock had just set Wilfred an essay on it. A visit to the Outlook Tower at the top of the Royal Mile was essential to understanding what Brock was trying to do. The building, a medieval tower house rising among grimy tenements, belonged to the Edinburgh professor, town planner and polymath, Patrick Geddes, who had equipped it as a centre for sociological studies. A small band of his disciples, including some of Dr Brock's ladies, were just managing to keep it open in wartime. It was another teaching aid, organised as a spiritual journey, the visitor first climbing to the roof to view the city through a Victorian *camera obscura*, then descending through a series of exhibitions that widened out from Edinburgh through Scotland, Language, Europe and finally the World, with the opportunity, which Wilfred took, of pausing in a little room set aside for meditation. All this was a practical illustration of Geddes's creed, summed up in his formula, 'Place – Work – Folk': the purpose of the tower was to relate folk to their place by encouraging them to participate in what he called 'Regional Survey'.[17]

Brock had been a follower of Geddes for years before the war, giving lectures at the Tower on Bergson, one of his favourite philosophers, and taking natural history expeditions into the Pentlands. He was also chairman of the Tower's Open Spaces Committee, working to establish gardens in the poorer parts of the city. His own formula, 'organism – function – environment,' was a biologist's version of Geddes's, and he saw his holistic method of diagnosis as a kind of Regional Survey of each patient. Similarly, Regional Survey was the patient's core task in ergotherapy. 'I perceived that this Tower was a symbol,' Wilfred said, reading his essay aloud to the doctor as though to a tutor, 'an Allegory, not a historic structure but a poetic form.' It was a military work, too, 'the rallying point of a defence to whose aid we are summoned'. By being next to a slum and open to all, it had the power to disarm its enemy, the 'spirit of exclusiveness'. 'The Tower is suggestive of the great Method [of] Philosophical Thinking which is Correlation or Coordination.'[18] Wilfred had made an excellent start, responding to the Tower in his own way as the poet, soldier and teacher he was, bringing together his own knowledge and personality just as Brock and Geddes would have wanted.

Another of his first assignments was to tour a foundry and then do some practical metalwork, hammering out a copper bowl, but Brock always tried to set work suited to a patient's special interests and the next task was to write a poem about Antaeus.[19] Wilfred thought of composing a sonnet, until the project took on a life of its own, becoming a blank verse narrative that vividly expressed its author's sense of returning energy.

> As pythons shudder, bridling-in their spite
> So trembled that Antaeus with held strength,
> While Heracles, – the thews and cordage of his thighs
> Straitened and strained beyond the utmost stretch
> From quivering heel to haunch like sweating hawsers –
> But only staggered backward.

Hercules is baffled until his young friend Hylas tells him Antaeus's secret. That development of the story hardly illustrated ergotherapy, but Brock seems to have approved of the poem.

The doctor may have encouraged his patient to continue working on technique, having perhaps noticed the pararhyme of 'thews / thighs' and other conspicuous sound effects. During the next few weeks Wilfred wrote 'Song of Songs' and probably the very similar poem, 'From My Diary, July 1914', a reminiscence of Bagnères and the last days of peace. The method of end-rhyming in these two poems – 'laugh / leaf / life', 'Bees / Boys', 'Flashes / Fleshes' – was new in English, so much so that reviewers after the war floundered to find a word for it. 'Pararhyme', as Edmund Blunden named it in 1931, was Wilfred's invention as a regular rhyme scheme. Critics have suggested many sources for it, from ancient Welsh verse to recent French experiments, but no fully pararhymed poem earlier than Wilfred's has yet been discovered. Robert Graves believed Wilfred had got the idea from him, and there certainly is a partly pararhymed poem in Graves's first book.[20] However, there is no evidence Wilfred had read any Graves before writing 'Song of Songs'. He may well have worked out the system for himself, having been interested in musical effects ever since Bordeaux. Pararhyme soon turned out to be ideally suited to elegiac war poetry, but he first used it for two love lyrics in a style that looked back to France and Tailhade.

> Leaves
>> Murmuring by myriads in the shimmering trees.
> Lives
>> Wakening with wonder in the Pyrenees.[21]

The careful crafting evident in 'From My Diary' and 'Song of Songs' suggests that they, like the copper bowl, were products of ergotherapy.

Brock's treatment was not limited to directing patients into outward activities. He recognised the importance of analysis, though he thought Freud had over-emphasised sex, and he worked with his patients to release the 'phantoms of the mind'. It would have been consistent with his methods if he had advised Wilfred to use poetry as a way of understanding those phantoms, perhaps starting with non-military subjects. Two of Wilfred's most explicitly confessional poems seem to have been written, or at any rate worked on, during the early stages of the work-cure. The unfinished 'Lines to a Beauty Seen in Limehouse' (first entitled 'A Vision in Whitechapel') is about a young Londoner Wilfred had seen in the slums of the East End, presumably in 1915–16, a 'half-god' sitting bare-kneed like a marble idol awaiting human sacrifices, his lips bright with 'mine own blood in dreams that woke me faint'. This sado-masochistic image is a clue to the content of those dreams of 'bloodiness and stains of shadowy crimes' that Wilfred had suffered from well before the war. There are comparable clues throughout his verse. The notebook he had used at the CCS, for example, contains a convoluted image about searching for beauty in sweet wounds made by the flames of love, flames extinguished by his own spurting blood.[22] In the Limehouse fragment the poet's imagination sidles against the half-god's smooth knees and vermilion lips, but his admiring glance, offered like incense, is met with only the faintest acknowledgement.

> And shall the dust of this foul city
> Darken thy marble cheek? Fools call thee pretty,
> Who art the eternal beauty of [the years]

> *Which I would wash with [perfumes] and [with] tears.*
> *Tonight, shall thy mouth's petals give their bloom*
> *To soiled pillows in tattered room*
> *And shall they touch thy fingers, who not feel,*
> *Nor see, nor care for beauty: whom thy heel*
> *Could crush, if I might tell thee how.*

The youth will take his pleasures with his kind, 'Where love is easy, where I cannot go', and the poet is held back by 'the old fear of beauty' as well as by social class.

In 'Has your soul sipped', the poet claims to have been witness of 'a strange sweetness', sweeter than anything that could be imagined, sweeter than sun, moon, rose, nightingale, love, death, the end of all wars, martyrdom: the sweetest of all experiences has been to see the smile on 'a boy's murdered mouth'.

> *But with the bitter blood*
> *And the death-smell*
> *All his life's sweetness bled*
> *Into a smile.*

Had Wilfred written that in Bordeaux in 1914–15, it could be seen as mere Decadent affectation, a list of standard properties leading to a deliberately shocking conclusion, but the only manuscript appears to belong to early August 1917.[23] Had it been written a few weeks later, after he had met Sassoon, it could just about be read as some sort of moral statement about war and 'greater love'. But there is no such ulterior purpose, nor protest, nor irony in 'Has your soul sipped'. The poem means what it says. Wilfred had seen a young man bleeding to death, and the sight had been supremely beautiful. Late Romantic poets, especially Swinburne, had often written about bleeding mouths as symbols of passionate excess, and the image had a strong sexual significance for Wilfred, as the Limehouse fragment shows. Somewhere on Redan Ridge or in the fields between Savy and Fayet, the poetic quest for strange beauty and exquisite sensation had found a kind of fulfilment.

While slowly gaining control over his inner visions, Wilfred devoted his days to ergotherapeutic pursuits, which ranged from German lessons at the Berlitz School in Edinburgh to regular swimming in the public baths. He told Susan, in language learned from Brock, that swimming never failed to give him 'a Greek feeling of energy and elemental life'. As yet, Brock's principal means of reconnecting patients with their environment had been to get them gardening, and he had been the driving spirit behind the allotments, but there were better methods. It may have been as a result of discussions with Wilfred that the doctor got together some of the more thoughtful patients on 13 July to start a club for Regional Survey. 'I am one of the founders of a real learned society,' Wilfred wrote proudly to Leslie, remembering their old Astronomical, Geological and Botanical Society. No sooner had his scientific interests been catered for by the foundation of the new Field Club than he was given literary work as well by being made editor of *The Hydra*, a distinction that must also have pleased him, although the job proved as demanding of his time and effort as Brock no doubt intended.

Almost every day now brought a meeting or an expedition. On 27 July the Field and Camera Clubs made a joint exploration of the Almond estuary. Next day Wilfred appeared in the Saturday concert, with a walk-on part in the trial scene from *The Merchant of Venice*. Two of the patients, J.L. Isaacson, a former member of the Benson Company,[24] and J.W.G. Pockett, were professional actors, as were their wives, so theatrical standards at the hospital were higher than might have been expected, even though Mrs Isaacson as Portia forgot her lines.[25] On the Monday Wilfred lectured to the Field Club on 'Do Plants Think?', arguing that they do because plants, like people, must interact with their environment. The subsequent report in *The Hydra* said the lecturer had gone to the limits of modern research (much of Wilfred's material had really been gleaned long before, from volumes of *Cassell's Popular Science* at Alpenrose). Being well versed in how to keep an audience interested, he drew lively diagrams on the blackboard and made jokes about plants showing exaggerated reflexes or doing no work, like some Craiglockhart patients. He ended with a stirring passage from Mrs Browning that he had read at Gailly, about every common bush being afire with God. Warm applause and a long question-and-answer session followed, and for a moment he felt the same sort of 'exultation' he had felt at Fayet and at his recent meeting with his mother. 'My swotting & pottering of the good old Matric. days, and my laborious escapes from Dunsden Vicarage to Reading College have been well crowned tonight,' he told Susan, quoting some 'exquisite' words from the Bible, 'To him that overcometh, I will give the bright and morning star.'[26]

The Officers' Club, the body that co-ordinated hospital activities, held its monthly general meeting on 3 August, and Wilfred, now on the committee by right of his editorship, successfully proposed that *The Hydra* should be free to patients. No doubt he had the support of Mayes, who was treasurer. When the magazine came out on the Saturday, Wilfred 'plunked' the free copies outside the breakfast-room door where officers could help themselves. Freed from responsibilities for a while, he took the tram into town next day for a solitary walk on Salisbury Crags, looking down on Holyrood, 'a floating mirage in gold mist'. On the Monday there was another Field Club lecture. On the Tuesday he had a long talk with a fellow patient, J.B. Salmond, a professional journalist in civil life, who had some promising ideas for improving the magazine. That evening Pockett offered Wilfred a speaking part as 'a fashionable young fellow' in a full-length play, *Lucky Durham*, to be performed over two Saturday evenings.[27]

Wilfred could take some pride in his progress. With his physical and mental energies fully revived, he had achieved the sort of social position he had briefly held at the transport school in February, becoming, as he said, 'one of the ones' in the hospital. He felt 'delightfully at ease' during the play, enjoying being on stage with four real actors, at least one of them a Bensonian. He was also able to hold his own in matters of botany and geology when he accompanied Brock and a handful of Field Club members on a long walk through the Pentlands. In all his varied activities he was making a conscious effort to connect himself with everything he saw around him.

> I am a sick man in hospital, by night; a poet, for quarter of an hour after breakfast; I am whatever and whoever I see while going down to Edinburgh on the tram: greengrocer, policeman, shopping lady, errand boy, paper-boy, blind man, crippled Tommy, bank-clerk, carter, all of these in half an hour; next a German student in earnest; then I either peer over bookstalls in back-streets, or do a bit of a dash down Princes Street, – according as I have taken weak tea or strong coffee for breakfast.

He was almost ready to begin his *annus mirabilis*. Identifying himself with other people was not only an ergotherapeutic discipline but also what poets had to do. Keats had said that a poet should be 'continually inform- ing and filling some other body', and Shelley had argued that it was through exercise of the poetic imagination that people could learn morality and love, putting themselves 'in the place of another and of many others', making the pains and pleasures of humanity their own.[28] Wilfred wrote a little poem, 'Six O'Clock in Princes Street', imagining how he could join the happy crowds in town or, as he watched a melancholy newsboy,

> *be you in the gutter where you stand,*
> *Pale rain-flawed phantom of the place,*
> *With news of all the nations in your hand,*
> *And all their sorrows in your face.*

But his old ambition to be a meteor-poet, flying above the ordinary world, meant he had to follow his own course, not keeping step with the crowd but following 'gleams unsafe, untrue', 'tiring after beauty through star- crowds'. Critics have pointed out the echoes in 'Six O'Clock' of Yeats, Tennyson, Cowper, Wordsworth, Keats and Shakespeare. Wilfred wanted above all to be with the poets.

'A quarter of an hour after breakfast' and vague notions of following 'gleams' were not going to get him very far in mid-1917. He still had not found his subject, although he was instinctively moving very close to it. The most intense, most passionate experience of his life had been war. When he read in a biography that Tennyson had always been a great child, he commented, 'So should I have been, but for Beaumont Hamel.'[29] He was pleased when Susan said she was thinking of making bandages for the wounded instead of sending Bibles to Africa:

> Leave Black Sambo ignorant of Heaven. White men are in Hell. Aye, leave him ignorant of the civilization that sends us there, and the religious men that say it is good to be in that Hell ... Send an English Testament to his Grace of Canterbury, and let it consist of that one sentence, at which he winks his eyes:
>
> 'Ye have heard that it *hath* been said: An eye for an eye, and a tooth for a tooth:
>
> But I say that ye resist not evil, but whosoever shall smite thee on thy right cheek, turn to him the other also.'
>
> And if his reply be 'Most unsuitable for the present distressing moment, my dear lady! But I trust that in God's good time ... etc.' – *then there is only one possible conclusion*, that there are no more Christians at the present moment than there were at the end of the first century.
>
> While I wear my star and eat my rations, I continue to take care of my Other Cheek; and, thinking of the eyes I have seen made sightless, and the bleeding lads' cheeks I have wiped, I say: Vengeance is mine, I, Owen, will repay.[30]

The handwriting of this letter, scribbled late at night on 10 August 1917, slants awkwardly across the page, and around the phrase 'made sightless' there are marks that could be blots or tears.

The Bible said, 'Vengeance is mine; I will repay, saith the Lord'. But wearing a second lieutenant's star and taking army pay meant usurping the divine prerogative, and when Wilfred thought of the dying men he had tended, and their blinded eyes and bleeding mouths, he was willing to go on fighting, damnable though the work was.[31] There could be no Christian defence of the fighting, not even the idea of 'greater love' that he had put forward at Gailly. He said the notion that 'men are laying down their lives for a friend' (as in March, he kept the last word singular) now seemed 'a distorted view to hold in a general way', so he resolved not to publish his 'Ballad of Kings and Christs'.

He could not escape the war. Even when he was watching Edinburgh life from the tram window, he was conscious of the distinctive blue armband that declared him to be a hospital patient. Men wearing those armbands were subject to special regulations, such as not being allowed into pubs. Local people tended to stare and glance away uneasily, aware that patients from up the hill were rumoured to be lunatics.[32] He was still 'a sick man in hospital, by night'. 'Got up rather late this morning,' he told Susan on the 15th, 'having had some very bellicose dreams of late'. And in the same letter:

I have just been reading Siegfried Sassoon, and am feeling at a very high pitch of emotion. Nothing like his trench life sketches has ever been written or ever will be written. Shakespere reads vapid after these. Not of course because Sassoon is a greater artist, but because of the subjects, I mean. I think if I had the choice of making friends with Tennyson or with Sassoon I should go to Sassoon.

15

Disciple
Craiglockhart

AUGUST–NOVEMBER 1917

'He is here you know,' Wilfred told Susan on 15 August 1917, 'because he wrote a letter to the Higher Command which was too plain-spoken. They promptly sent him over here!' The authorities had indeed reacted promptly to Sassoon's letter by labelling him neurasthenic and sending him to the hospital on 23 July before his action became public knowledge. A week later his statement was read out in Parliament by a pacifist MP and widely reported, at which point all Craiglockhart must have started talking about the newcomer. Wilfred may not have realised at first that Sassoon was a poet. It was not until Saturday the 18th that he screwed up enough courage to introduce himself, equipped with several copies of Sassoon's latest book, *The Old Huntsman and Other Poems*, so that he could ask for autographs, much as he had called on Miss Coleridge in 1910.[1]

Sassoon was sitting on his bed cleaning golf clubs, the sun blazing on his purple dressing gown. He was six years older than his visitor, one rank higher and obviously upper middle class. Wilfred's first impression was of a handsome, 'very tall and stately' man with a general air of boredom.[2] Gazing vaguely somewhere above Wilfred's head, Sassoon noticed that 'little Owen', as he often referred to him later, had a slight neurasthenic stammer and was 'perceptibly provincial' (years afterwards, irritated by an enquirer, he said Wilfred had spoken with a grammar school accent and had been 'embarrassing').[3] It would have surprised both poets to know that they had each spent more or less the same amount of time in the front line, and that Wilfred's experiences there had been far worse than Sassoon's. Sassoon was ashamed to be trapped in the hospital with men he regarded in the typical army way as 'degenerate-looking', 'wash-outs and shattered heroes'.[4] He had been suffering from hallucinations and night-mares himself, and believed he had come very close to a breakdown. Having been persuaded by friends, including Robert Graves and Robert Ross, not to pursue his protest, he was beginning to realise he could be seen as a washout himself, not only by his civilian backers, who were sadly disappointed in him, but also by his fellow soldiers, who were fighting on in France while he was safe at home.[5]

Sassoon's good looks and some at least of his psychological difficulties came from his parentage, English on his mother's side and Middle-Eastern Jewish on his father's. The Sassoons were a fabulously wealthy dynasty, relatively new to England and very conscious of being a clan, but Sassoon's father had been a black sheep, earning the family's disapproval by marrying a gentile and then leaving her for another woman. Siegfried had grown up a curiously solitary child, despite being the second of three brothers. By the age of eleven he was writing verse, with the encouragement of his mother, whom he adored. After completing less than half his time at Marlborough, and then leaving Cambridge without taking a degree, he had devoted himself to fox-hunting and cricket. Just before the war, uncertain whether his sporting or his poetic self was the more important, he had started making literary friends in London, notably those two encouragers of young poets, Robert Ross and Edward Marsh. He had also corresponded with the homosexual guru Edward Carpenter, having realised he was himself, in Carpenter's word, 'Uranian'. He dreamed of finding the perfect lover, but told Carpenter he was '*unspotted*'.

War ended Sassoon's indecision. He joined up in the ranks on 1 August 1914, embarking on a military career that was to be as uneven as his progress through school and university. His poem 'Absolution', written in mid-1915, expresses his heroic, sacrificial feelings as one of the 'happy legion' made wise by war. He never suppressed the poem, knowing it was a true record: part of him always longed for heroic martyrdom, and he believed war *had* made him wise, ending his old, aimless life and deepening his understanding of humanity.[6] Sent to France in November 1915 as a subaltern in the Royal Welch Fusiliers, he met another Fusilier poet, Robert Graves, and was briefly in the trenches. 'The Redeemer', his first trench poem, compared a weary Tommy to Christ. The image was more than a little hackneyed by that stage in the war, but the closing lines struck a confidently Brooke-like note: 'But in my heart I knew that I had seen / The suffering spirit of a world washed clean'.

Sassoon saw the front again early in 1916, when he had to visit the trenches as Transport Officer, the relatively safe job that had eluded Wilfred. His first sceptical war poem, 'In the Pink', was written that February. In March he was in action for two weeks and sent Marsh a new ending for 'The Redeemer', this time using colloquial language: 'And someone flung his burden in the muck, / Mumbling: "O Christ Almighty, now I'm stuck!"'[7] The death of his beloved friend David Thomas a few days later inspired him to a bout of anti-German fury. Briefly in the line again in May, he won a Military Cross for leading a futile raid. When his battalion followed up the southern successes on the Somme on 4 July, his company was held in reserve, but he disobeyed orders by going ahead and clearing an enemy trench single-handed. He was kept out of the next engagement, perhaps because he had shown himself to be unreliable, and soon afterwards he went down with trench fever. By early August 1916 he was convalescing in Oxford, where Ross took him to meet Lady Ottoline Morrell at Garsington Manor. Garsington was a centre for pacifists, so Sassoon encountered opinions about the war that he had never heard before.

He did not see action again until April 1917, when he took part in the Battle of Arras for a few days and got into the Hindenburg Line tunnels before a bullet in the shoulder sent him home once more. The lack of awareness that he found in England, the arguments he had heard at Garsington and his memories of corpses at Arras all made him think of protesting. Lady Ottoline introduced him to two leading pacifists, Bertrand Russell and John Middleton Murry, with whose help he composed his famous statement, declaring that the conflict was being 'deliberately prolonged by those who have the power to end it'. 'I believe that this War, upon which I entered as a war of defence and liberation, has now become a war of aggression and conquest.' If the politicians had stated their aims at the start, he said, those aims would now be attainable by negotiation. Claiming to be speaking on behalf of all soldiers, he stressed he was not protesting against the military conduct of the war but against political deception; and he hoped his action would help to break down the complacency with which 'the majority of those at home regard the continuance of agonies which they do not share, and which they have not sufficient imagination to realise'.

Sassoon's ideas had come from civilians, not soldiers. Most of his friends in the army were appalled by his action, but civilian opponents of the war believed not only that peace could be achieved through diplomacy, but also that the British and French governments were keeping the war going in the hope of grabbing colonies and destroying the enemy. The political realities were not quite so straightforward. Politicians had certainly become keen to collect territory, but the liberation of Belgium was still a principal aim. In Germany, peace moves had begun in the Reichstag, but power lay with the generals, who were unlikely to be interested in mere talking at a time when Russia and France were weakening and the first American troops were only just starting to arrive in Britain. Almost no one in Britain, probably not even Sassoon, was willing to contemplate a German victory. He had no chance of finding much support, either at home or in the army. The Passchendaele offensive began on 31 July, the day his statement appeared in *The Times*. The fighting was going to go on until one side or the other faced defeat.

It was easy for the Under-Secretary for War, questioned in the Commons, to explain that this 'extremely gallant officer' was ill and that members should not exploit 'a young man in such a state of mind'. Sassoon was spared a court-martial, much to his friends' relief. At Craiglockhart he was assigned to Dr Rivers, who decided that he seemed fit in mind and body with no sign of neurasthenia. Sassoon admitted he would not object to the continuation of the war if there were a reasonable chance of a quick result. So the new patient was neither mentally ill nor a pacifist, although he was badly in need of a rest. Luckily he took to Rivers at once, and when they were not conferring he was free to play golf on a course some miles away or go for long walks, thereby avoiding hospital activities. He began putting his feelings about the war into poetry again. It is a nice irony that the official attempt to silence him actually launched him, and consequently Wilfred, into a period of intense creativity.

~

The first meeting between the two poets came at a good time for Wilfred. He had dumped bundles of his third *Hydra* outside the breakfast room that morning and was due to appear in the second part of *Lucky Durham* in the evening. With his health and self-respect well on the way to recovery, he was ready for what was to be in effect the final stage of his cure. Sassoon proved to be the ideal doctor, not insistent like Brock but helpful almost without noticing, providing exactly the right sort of advice, confidences and in due course contacts. When Wilfred called again on 21 August, Sassoon enlisted his help in deciphering a letter from H.G. Wells, and then politely asked to see some of his work. Wilfred sat up that night assembling all the presentable poems he could find, even adding to them by drafting a first 'trench life sketch' in Sassoon's manner, 'The Dead-Beat', appropriately about a victim of shell-shock.[8] Sassoon looked through the pile next day, pointing out inconsistencies in 'The Dead-Beat', deploring some of the old sonnets, praising 'Antaeus' and warmly admiring the musical qualities of 'Song of Songs'. He advised against early publishing, but added as Wilfred was leaving, 'Sweat your guts out writing poetry!'

Wilfred's ideas about life and poetry went through a profound change during the next few weeks as he listened to Sassoon. He looked back through all his old work, asking Leslie and Susan to send all the manuscripts they could find. Susan even had to break into a locked cupboard, with strict instructions not to read anything she found there. Wilfred told Sassoon about the arrangement with Leslie and Olwen, and wrote one more sonnet on an agreed subject, 'Beauty' (later 'My Shy Hand'). Shown this and the companion efforts by the other two collaborators, Sassoon wrote a poem himself on the same subject, even echoing some of Wilfred's phrases, but he was sceptical.[9] Leslie was gathering his own poems for a book, so Wilfred produced some of them, proud to have a cousin who was about to appear in print, but the response was unexpected and embarrassing. 'Sassoon considers E.L. Gunston not only flatulent, but hopeless,' Wilfred reported to Susan. And with that, abruptly, the old partnership with Leslie came to an end. His poems could now be seen for what they were, bloodless imitation-Swinburne, a 'river of dreams,' to use one of his own lines, 'soft as a slow song, slow with a sigh'.

'Nothing great was said of anything but a definite experience,' Wilfred said later of his cousin's book.[10] That was the first lesson to be learned from Sassoon, as is evident from notes written for Leslie on the first draft of 'The Dead-Beat', 'True – in the incidental' and 'Those are the very words!'. 'My dear,' Wilfred told Mary, recommending Sassoon's book, 'except in one or two of my letters, (ahem!) you will find nothing so perfectly truthfully descriptive of war ... *Now* you see why I have always extolled Poetry.'[11] The principle that poetry had to be true to experience was fairly new to Sassoon himself, whose early verse had been hopelessly ethereal, but Marsh and others had urged him to keep his eye on the object and deal with definite ideas. He passed the advice on to Wilfred with a convert's zeal, even though he sometimes still forgot it in his own work.

The second lesson was that even the most painful war experience could be material for poetry. Wilfred thought the finest poem in *The Old Huntsman* was 'The Death-Bed', an elegiac description of a young soldier dying in a hospital ward. Sassoon agreed. He had recently told a Uranian acquaintance, John Gambril Nicholson, that such poems had 'the *best* part of me in them, the quest for beauty and compassion and friendship'.[12] 'Beauty is truth, truth beauty': as admirers of Keats, both Sassoon and Wilfred could understand that a poem like 'The Death-Bed' could be beautiful because of its truth of feeling and experience, despite its subject matter. Wilfred was later to express a similar idea in a famous sentence: 'The poetry is in the pity.' Sending a copy of *The Old Huntsman* to his father with a friendly letter, he said 'The Death-Bed' was 'a piece of perfect art'. He praised the poem again to Mary, also singling out 'The Redeemer', saying he had wanted to write such a poem every week for the past three years.

Another discovery could not be mentioned in letters home. The two poets would soon have realised they shared the same sexual orientation. Sassoon was still avoiding sexual activity as something unclean, so Wilfred probably said little about wanderings in the East End, although he wrote home for Tailhade's poems. Sassoon may well have explained Carpenter's ideas about love between men: beauty, compassion and friendship were central Uranian values, and Carpenter believed that Uranian men tended to be musical and artistic, fond of children, liable to strong emotions, and quick to pity. Wilfred would have recognised an ideal version of himself, and the recognition would have been enormously reassuring. His sexual nature, far from being shameful or a handicap, could be very much to his advantage as a poet, and at last he could talk about it. His confidence was not merely restored at Craiglockhart but greatly increased.

Members of a 2nd Manchesters working party taking a break among the shell craters near Serre, January 1917.

Below: Troops clearing a mined road in Nesle after the German withdrawal, March 1917.

Above: St Quentin cathedral seen from the new front line near Manchester Hill, 24 April 1917.
Below: The buildings and grounds of Craiglockhart War Hospital, from the air.

Opposite, top left: Captain Arthur Brock, RAMC, in his room at Craiglockhart. *Top right: The Hydra,* as it looked during Wilfred's editorship. *Bottom left:* Siegfried Sassoon. *Bottom right:* Nancy Nicholson in landgirl's costume, with her new husband, Robert Graves, 1918.

The HYDRA

Journal of the Craiglockhart War Hospital

No. 8   AUGUST 4TH, 1917   PRICE 6D

CONTENTS

H. & J. Pillans & Wilson, Printers, Edinburgh.

Wilfred with Arthur Newboult, at Leith, Edinburgh, July 1917.

Charles Scott Moncrieff

Robert Ross

Above: Osbert Sitwell
Right: Harold Monro

Above: North Bay, Scarborough, showing the Clarence Gardens Hotel, 1918.
Below: The parade ground, Burniston barracks (now demolished), Scarborough.

Above left: The last photograph of Wilfred, taken at Hastings, late August 1918; 'badly printed,' his mother wrote later, '. . . but looking at a little distance it is *him* . . .'
Above right: Second Lieutenant John Foulkes, Manchester Regiment.
Below: Wire and the unfinished German front trench, Beaurevoir-Fonsomme line, October 1918.

Above: 'Swiss Cottage' (Moulin Grison Farm), Joncourt, and the German front trench after the battle. Photographed by the Australians, 5 October 1918.
Below: The Sambre-Oise canal near Ors after the crossing, November 1918.

When the conversation ranged into wider social matters and the war, Carpenter would have been relevant again as an advocate of the simple life, preaching doctrines not unlike those of Brock, who admired his work. Wilfred would have asked about Wells, the prophet of internationalism and war to end war. Sassoon knew many other authors. He was reading Goldsworthy Lowes Dickinson's new book, *The Choice Before Us*, which argued for internationalism and a League of Nations.[13] Dickinson pointed out that militarist civilians were already discussing 'the next war', whereas soldiers were discovering war's 'futility', phrases that Wilfred was to use as poem titles. Wilfred thought of writing a three-act play set in a federated Europe in the year 2000, with the aim of exposing war to 'the criticism of reason'.[14] Meanwhile the truth of war had to be told. Sassoon lent him books, one of which was *Under Fire*, the English translation of Henri Barbusse's *Le Feu*, the most harrowing description of trench warfare yet published (there are clear traces of *Under Fire* in Wilfred's subsequent poems). Another writer who must have been discussed, and who was to be a significant influence on Wilfred's work, especially on 'Strange Meeting', was Bertrand Russell. Russell's two 1916 books, *Justice in War-Time* and *Principles of Social Reconstruction*, outlined some of the ideas on which Sassoon's protest had been based.

~

During September Wilfred worked on another sonnet, putting it through at least seven drafts and repeatedly asking for Sassoon's advice. 'Anthem for Doomed Youth', a mirror of its author's poethood up to mid-1917, is the work of a Romantic, Decadent and still patriotic poet who is just beginning to absorb new ways of thinking.

> *What passing-bells for these who die as cattle?*
> *Only the monstrous anger of the guns.*
> *Only the stuttering rifles' rapid rattle*
> *Can patter out their hasty orisons.*
> *No mockeries now for them; no prayers nor bells;*
> *Nor any voice of mourning save the choirs, –*
> *The shrill, demented choirs of wailing shells;*
> *And bugles calling for them from sad shires.*
>
> *What candles may be held to speed them all?*
> *Not in the hands of boys, but in their eyes*
> *Shall shine the holy glimmers of goodbyes.*
> *The pallor of girls' brows shall be their pall;*
> *Their flowers the tenderness of patient minds,*
> *And each slow dusk a drawing-down of blinds.*[15]

Part of this is a reworking of the 1916 sonnet, 'A New Heaven', but much of the imagery has its origins in Wilfred's earlier life. As in 'A New Heaven' he thinks of his family. The Keatsian language reaffirms his early Romantic allegiances, and the image of pale brows hints at the Decadence and that strange 1914 poem, 'Long ages past'. The bells echo those of All Souls' Night in Bordeaux, and the 'mockeries' of religious ritual recall Wilfred's responses to the double funeral at Dunsden and to that other funeral in Bordeaux, when he had been impressed by the candles and solemn music. In politics as in religion he had been both sceptic and believer, and if the cynicism of 'cattle' and 'mockeries' repeats the angry disbelief he had shown at Dunsden, some of the other language in the poem comes from patriotic literature. The last line elaborates on Laurence Binyon's famous 1914 elegy, 'For the Fallen': 'At the going down of the sun … / We will remember them.' The second line borrows a conspicuous adjective from Beatrix Brice's 'To the Vanguard', a 1916 poem that was as well-known during the war as it is forgotten today: according to Brice, the army was best honoured not by rituals at home but by 'the voice of *monstrous* guns / Fed by the sweat, served by the life of England'. More conspicuously still, Wilfred borrowed from a sentence in an immensely popular novel, Ian Hay's *The First Hundred Thousand*, the story of a Kitchener battalion in 1914–15: 'a hurried outburst of rifle fire; a machine-gun begins to *patter* out a *stuttering* malediction.'[16]

Sassoon realised that the first draft of 'Anthem' could be read as a statement in support of the war. Just as Wilfred's 'Heavy Artillery' sonnet had described a gun hurling 'malison' (Hay's 'malediction') at an enemy that had to be beaten down, so the first attempt at 'Anthem' said that 'the monstrous/solemn anger of our guns' was the only possible response to the slaughter of (British) troops. Sassoon tried to neutralise the anti-German implication by changing 'our' to 'the' and choosing 'monstrous' in preference to 'solemn'. Wilfred then introduced the cattle simile, and replaced the funeral rites with 'mockeries'. But these and other alterations were not enough to disguise the ennobling language of the poem. Wilfred still had to move away from his urge to seek shelter at home, and from the patriotic commitment to military victory that had kept him going all through his training and even at the front.

Conversations between the two poets continued throughout September and October. Sassoon took things slowly, avoiding talk of horrors for fear of unsettling Wilfred's nerves, so the usual army reticence prevailed for a while.[17] Full understanding, when it came, changed Wilfred's poetry as nothing else had ever done. He had been horrified by conditions at Serre back in January, saying the people of England must agitate, but there had been no point in agitating if the war had to be fought. In a war of defence and liberation, or even better a war to end war, protest would merely weaken morale. If on the other hand the real aims were now aggression and conquest, and if peace could be achieved by negotiation, poets should be speaking out on behalf of all soldiers. Poetry was the best medium. It could get past the censor as prose could not, and half-a-dozen lines in a magazine could have more impact than a lengthy article. The aim should be to strike at the civilian conscience, so that pressure would be brought to bear on the politicians. Dr Brock now seemed absolutely right to argue that art should have a social purpose. By the autumn of 1917, for the first time, Wilfred had purpose enough.

His revived enthusiasm for poetry made him less keen than he had been to take on other ergotherapeutic work. Editing *The Hydra* became a chore, although he took the chance to publish new work by Sassoon and even some, anonymously, by himself. His editorial of 1 September quoted eight lines he had written for 'The Dead-Beat', satirising civilian complacency, and the same number included not only Sassoon's 'Dreamers' but also 'Song of Songs', the first of Wilfred's poems ever to appear in print. Wilfred told Susan that Sassoon was sending copies of the magazine to 'Personages', but in the copy that went to Lady Ottoline Morrell Sassoon wrote under 'Song of Songs': 'The man who wrote this brings me quantities & I have to say kind things. He will improve, I think!'[18]

~

Happily ignorant of Sassoon's real opinion of his verse so far, Wilfred lived some of the 'fullest-happiest' days of the year. Life was sociable in town, as well as in the hospital. Mayes introduced him to two families who were sharing a large house in St Bernard's Crescent, a majestic Georgian terrace in the Edinburgh New Town. The Grays and Steinthals were 'modern' people of a sort Wilfred had hardly met before, except perhaps in the Légers' house in Bordeaux, and he was amazed by their drawing room, with its 'black carpetless floor, white walls, solitary superb picture, grand piano, Empire sofa and so on'. The two wives wore short hair and fashionable, artistic clothes. He was to get to know them well: Maria Steinthal, a 'mighty clever' German sculptress who had studied under Maillol and other modern masters, and Mary Gray, an intelligent, witty but overemotional woman who became very fond of Wilfred, perhaps too fond. He said the husbands were less effusive than their wives. Leonard Gray, a captain in the Royal Scots, had returned to Edinburgh to manage a family-owned foundry, now a munitions works, probably the one that Wilfred had toured in July. Francis Steinthal, 'a History Honoursman at Oxford' as Wilfred could not resist describing him to Susan, was a former schoolmaster and rugby international, now a captain in the Royal Fusiliers.[19] Wilfred went to several 'perfect little' dinners at St Bernard's Crescent, evenings of 'extraordinary fellowship in All the Arts'. The ladies enthused over 'Song of Songs' and other poems, and lent him lots of books.

After one of these occasions Wilfred and Mayes got back to Craiglockhart very late, giving themselves away by scrunching across the gravel. At midnight a nurse knocked on Wilfred's door: "'Dr Brock will see you at once Mr Owen!" I went: in pyjamas and perspiration. He said a lady in Edinburgh expected me to lunch today to show me around the Slum Gardens. Goodnight! I retired in stupor.' Brock wanted Wilfred to re-connect himself to society at all levels. The gardens were the Open Spaces organised by the Outlook Tower, and the lady was a Miss Wyer, who duly gave Wilfred lunch at her and her sister's 'palatial' house in Rothesay Place before taking him into some of the city's roughest quarters to see little pockets of green among the tenements. Afterwards he went back to the house for tea, discovering with astonishment that the ladies, keen Tower supporters, shared his 'almost secret' views on art, politics, ethics and many other matters.

Following the Open Spaces tour, Mrs Gray started taking him slum-visiting, presumably at Brock's request. They went to see an Italian opera singer who had fallen on hard times. She said later that they visited the family often, Wilfred soon becoming adored by the children, but his letters only mention the first call, when the old man was out and Mrs Gray got stared at everywhere for her outlandish clothes and expensive rings. After another little dinner, Wilfred and his hosts shared a taxi up to the hospital, taking a wreath to present to Mayes, who was in the play that evening. Either the play or the presentation, or both, left Mayes so overwrought that when he came into Wilfred's room next morning he was mute, staring with appealing eyes and making strange gestures, much to Wilfred's alarm. Keen actor and debater though Mayes was (he played Sir Toby Belch a fortnight later), he was still far from cured.[20] Wilfred himself was still suffering from 'disastrous dreams', although they were decreasing and becoming civilian in character, 'motor accidents and so on'. He knew his friends in town were not being merely sociable. Once when he went to see the Newboults and played a favourite game with Arthur, whirling him round in the air, the family dog got so excited that it bit the boy on the wrist, and Arthur's sister remembered years later how the parents had been much less concerned about their son than about their guest, who had been distraught.[21] For much of the time Wilfred seemed perfectly normal, but there was always the risk that he might relapse, as Mayes sometimes did.

Mary Gray's charitable efforts were directed as much towards Wilfred as towards the slum-dwellers, but she was clearly baffled by his response. Writing about him after the war she heaped praise on him as the embodi-ment of 'pity for suffering humanity', yet went on to say he had been reserved to a degree that some people had found 'almost inhuman'. She had been 'in trouble' herself (her husband was unfaithful, and she may have been showing the first signs of the mental illness that was later to incapacitate her), but she felt sure Wilfred had sympathised, even though he had said nothing. Read in conjunction with his letters, her memoir seems to owe more to what she wanted to see in him than what was actually there, but she clearly felt a need to defend him against the sort of criticism that was later to be made by his brother, that he had been strangely unfeeling on an individual level. But perhaps there was a particular reason for Wilfred's reserve towards Mary Gray: she may have fallen in love with him. She respected his silence, however, seeing it as a symptom of shell-shock. He was fighting hard to regain his confidence, she thought, and he never despaired, even when 'in the grip of his painful delusion, the belief in his commanding officer's regarding him as a coward'.[22]

Through the Grays, Wilfred met Henry Lintott, painter of the picture in their drawing room, and another eminent Scottish artist, John Duncan, soon becoming friendly with the two families, including, as usual, the children.[23] When the Berlitz German course ended, he was offered lessons by another of the Grays' acquaintances, the university librarian Frank Nicholson. It had probably been Brock who had first advised Wilfred to learn German, knowing he was good at French and hoping to make him think of Germans as something other than 'the Bosche'. Maria Steinthal no doubt gave further encouragement. Wilfred thought the language a 'vile' one to learn, but Nicholson later recalled that he had picked up enough to start reading a German novel, albeit with plenty of help. After one of their sessions Wilfred talked about pararhyme over tea in a café, defending his new method with engaging confidence, like 'a child insisting, half humorously and half defiantly' that he was in the right. Nicholson was charmed by him, remembering his youth and 'comeliness' and his 'dark and vivid eyes', expressive of his personality. 'There was something at once clear-cut and fluid about the features, and his figure had the elegant compactness of a small boy's together with the robuster development of the young man's.' According to Nicholson, Wilfred was collecting photographs of wounds and mutilations to show to people who glorified war: 'he put his hand to his breast-pocket to show me them, but suddenly thought better of it and refrained.' There is no other evidence for those photographs, although some critics have made much of them. Nicholson may have misunderstood: Wilfred, who later referred to 'A Terre' as a 'photograph', perhaps had new poems in his pocket.[24]

Dr Brock was still busy finding work for patients. Having set up the Field Club for 'synoptic seeing' (seeing the world as a whole), he started a Boys' Training Club for 'synergic action' (practical work in the community). Most members of the new club were asked to work with Scouts or to teach subjects such as map-reading, first-aid or drill, usually in the nearest school, Tynecastle. Wilfred alone chose to teach literature. On 25 September he met his Tynecastle class of thirty-nine boys and their young teacher, Mrs Fullerton, wife of an army doctor. The boys were on their best behaviour, thrilled to be taught by a uniformed officer, and lessons were a great success. Wilfred read *Hiawatha* with them, and R.L. Stevenson's *St Ives*, parts of which are set in the Craiglockhart area, and he got them to talk about the war, finding to his satisfaction that some of them were already interested in the idea of internationalism.

On the same day that he taught his first lesson at Tynecastle, he was called before a medical board again, exactly three months after being boarded at Netley. No doubt with advice from Brock, the panel of three doctors agreed that the patient should remain at Craiglockhart for another month, after which he would be fit for light duties and home service for three months and then for general service.

Time now being short, Wilfred withdrew as far as he could from hospital affairs, although he agreed to lecture to the Field Club on 'Soil'. He had already turned down further offers of acting, as well as a suggestion that he might start a French class. Someone, probably Mayes, had persuaded him to join the Debating Society Committee, but his letters never mention it.[25] He must have been relieved when the Officers' Club decided *The Hydra* should be suspended for a month, so that it could be relaunched in a new format in November. He was to remain as assistant editor, but the bulk of the redesigning was to be done by J.B. Salmond, whose professional expertise did indeed transform the magazine. Wilfred's last two numbers, published on 15 and 29 September, contain Sassoon's 'The Rear-Guard' and 'Wirers', as well as two contributions by the editor, a comic pseudo-medieval account of Craiglockhart by 'Sir Wilfred de Salope, Knight' and an unsigned sonnet, 'The Next War', with an epigraph that referred to both Sassoon and Robert Graves. The sonnet reflects its author's pride in being able to associate with such battle-hardened poets:

> Out there, we've walked quite friendly up to Death;
> Sat down and eaten with him, cool and bland, – ...
>
> Oh, Death was never enemy of ours!
> We laughed at him, we leagued with him, old chum.[26]

Wilfred was careful not to print anything too critical of the war in *The Hydra*. The patriotic, blatantly anti-German tone adopted by many of his contributors, and their arch comments about girls, must have become increasingly distasteful, but he sometimes had to write in the same way himself when pages needed filling.[27] There was no point in upsetting patients by being controversial.

He tried to spend as much time as possible either writing or in Sassoon's company. His letters describe a September evening that was probably typical:

> ... Sassoon called me in to him; and having condemned some of my poems, amended others, and rejoiced over a few, he read me his very last works, which are superb beyond anything in his Book. Last night he wrote a piece which is the most exquisitely painful war poem of any language or time. I don't tell him so, or that I am not worthy to light his pipe. I simply sit tight and tell him where I think he goes wrong. He is going to alter one passage of this very poem for me.[28]

Next day Wilfred went to Sassoon's golf club, where his 'discipleship was put to a severe fleshly trial': having rashly had no breakfast in the expectation of a large lunch at the club, he was kept waiting for hours by his host, who would never break off a game for anyone. But Sassoon came in eventually, and after lunch they walked to the Observatory for tea with the Astronomer Royal, who knew Rivers and Brock. On another occasion Sassoon took Wilfred to tea with Lady Margaret Sackville, a pacifist poet and former president of the Poetry Society.[29]

Wilfred was more than a disciple. He was in love, although it was love mixed with a good deal of hero-worship. His excitement was impossible to conceal in letters, and it seems to have caused unease at home. Susan asked some 'searching' questions, to which her son replied that Sassoon, whom he liked equally as man, friend and poet, was 'already a *closer* friend than, say, Leslie', 'intensely sympathetic, with me about every vital question on the planet or off it'. 'We have followed parallel trenches all our lives, and have more friends in common, authors I mean, than most people can boast of in a lifetime.' That was not quite true, given Sassoon's veneration for poets Wilfred scarcely knew, such as Hardy and Vaughan, but the two men had enough in common to be able to talk freely on most vital questions, even the most intimate. It was not only Sassoon's love of literature but also his Uranianism that made him seem such a sympathetic friend.

In a society that regarded homosexual love as unspeakably wicked, Uranian poets had to be secret, outwardly conforming where they could, inwardly knowing themselves to be 'eccentric, lone, / Lawless', as Wilfred had half-foreseen in 'O World of many worlds'. Being outsiders, they were more likely than other people to see society's faults, and being 'intensely sympathetic', easily moved by others' suffering, they were more likely to be driven to protest. The two poets knew they were far ahead of society in general, both in feeling pity for doomed youth and in seeing the need to speak out. Their compassion for the troops was no less valid for its strong sexual element. With Sassoon's help, Wilfred was able to deal with the most difficult problem of all in the process of integrating himself with the world he lived in. His sexuality could be central to his writing, without being visible to people who might disapprove of it. His poetry, like his friend's, would be driven by love for men, an entirely honourable motive that could be openly stated yet at the same time kept hidden. But for the time being he was in no position to take a public stand. As a shell-shock case with a questionable record of courage, he would be ignored as a failure and a pacifist. 'I hate washy pacifists as temperamentally as I hate whiskied prussianists,' he explained to Susan. 'Therefore I feel I must first get some reputation of gallantry before I could successfully and usefully declare my principles.'

By early October he was writing in earnest. His manuscripts are often impossible to date accurately, but it seems likely that most of his Sassoonish poems were at least begun in these last weeks at Craiglockhart.[30] 'I send you my two best war Poems,' he had written to Susan on 25 September. 'Sassoon supplied the title "Anthem": just what I meant it to be.' Then, only a week later: 'I ... send you my most lurid war episode.' Whatever this poem was, its tone and content were clearly unlike those of 'Anthem for Doomed Youth'. The next poem was more lurid still. 'Here is a gas poem, done yesterday,' he wrote on the 9th. 'The famous Latin tag means of course *It is sweet and meet to die for one's country. Sweet*! And *decorous!*'[31]

> *If in some smothering dreams you too could pace*
> *Behind the wagon that we flung him in, …*
> *My friend, you would not tell with such high zest*
> *To children ardent for some desperate glory,*
> *The old Lie: Dulce et decorum est*
> *Pro patria mori.*

Then came 'Disabled', completed by the 13th. On the 21st: 'I wrote quite six poems last week, chiefly in Edinburgh; and when I read them to S.S. over a private tea in his room this afternoon, he came round from his first advice of deferred publishing, and said I must hurry up & get what is ready typed', advice that Wilfred ignored for the time being. The six unnamed poems may have included 'The Chances', 'Conscious', 'Inspection', 'The Letter' and 'At a Calvary near the Ancre', but he was also writing lyrics: 'Winter Song', addressed to Arthur Newboult, is dated 18 October. Other poems were germinating: a sheet of rough notes made at Craiglockhart includes early work for 'S.I.W.' and 'The Sentry', as well as for a satire on Edinburgh civilians that never got finished.[32]

Wilfred was exploring a new style, as well as new ideas. He had experimented with it in 1911, after reading Harold Monro's *Before Dawn*, but had not pursued it very far. Monro had advised him in 1916 to be more modern and less Keatsian. Edward Marsh had given similar advice to Sassoon, some of whose poems were about to appear in the third volume of Marsh's famous anthology, *Georgian Poetry*, to be published by Monro from the Poetry Bookshop. The Georgians, led originally by John Masefield, Wilfrid Gibson and Rupert Brooke, had turned away from Victorian rhetoric, preferring to write about real life in plain language, and Wilfred's new poems took up their methods in earnest. He used actual incidents, direct speech and army slang, making his lines concise and energetic. However, it would have been a denial of all that ergotherapy stood for if he had abandoned his past work: in poetry, as in everything else, his task was integration. His two most interesting Craiglockhart poems, 'Dulce et Decorum Est' and 'Disabled', are rooted in work done before he knew Sassoon.[33] Both describe beautiful youths who are now in hell. The gas victim is said in a preliminary draft to have had a head 'like a bud, / Fresh as a country rose', and he writhes in torment like the sufferers in 'The cultivated Rose' and 'Purgatorial Passions'. The casualty in 'Disabled', who had looked 'a god in kilts', is a mutilated version of the bare-kneed 'half-god' in 'Lines to a Beauty seen in Limehouse'. Wilfred's apprenticeship as a Romantic and Decadent had not been wasted.

On 13 October Robert Graves came to see Sassoon, who was due to play golf, and Wilfred was deputed to meet the visitor's taxi and accompany him to the clubhouse at Baberton. If Wilfred did confide in Graves about affairs with young men in Bordeaux, as Graves claimed long afterwards, it can only have been during that rainy afternoon, waiting for Sassoon. Graves does seem to have heard some confidences, either from Wilfred or Sassoon: he says in the first edition of his autobiography that Wilfred 'had had a bad time ... in France; and ... it had preyed on his mind that he had been accused of cowardice by his commanding officer. He was in a very shaky condition.'[34] When the Owen family objected to this reference to the cowardice story, Graves inserted 'unjustly' before 'accused'; in some later editions, he replaced the whole statement with a comment that Wilfred had been an 'idealistic homosexual', a change that can hardly have pleased Harold. Perhaps Wilfred did feel able to talk openly to someone he knew to be Sassoon's close friend, and Sassoon may have told him that Graves had difficulties of his own about both courage and idealistic homosexuality. Whatever was said, Wilfred feared afterwards he had made a poor impression. Later in the day, though, Sassoon showed 'Disabled' to Graves, who soon wrote warmly to its author, saying it was 'a damn fine poem'. 'I am so glad you like Owen's poem,' Sassoon wrote to Graves on the 19th. 'I will tell him to send you on any decent stuff he does. His work is very unequal, and you can help him a great deal.'[35]

Sassoon was more unhappy than ever about his own predicament. Lady Ottoline was still hoping he would maintain his stand against the war. He pointed out that the poems he was publishing in *The Nation* and *The Cambridge Magazine* made his opinions very clear. Graves, whose later reputation as an opponent of the war has little basis in anything he wrote at the time, thought that even the poems were achieving nothing useful; he told Edmund Gosse on 24 October that Sassoon 'thinks he is best employed by writing poems which will make people find the war so hateful that they'll stop it at once at whatever cost. I don't. I think that I'll do more good by keeping up my brother soldiers' morale as far as I can.'[36] Sassoon regarded that sort of attitude as cowardly acquiescence. As several of his Craiglockhart poems record, he was tortured by guilt at the thought of soldiers still fighting, struggling through the mud towards Passchendaele. He felt he had to join them, yet that would mean abandoning his protest. Ordered to appear before a board on 23 October, Sassoon told Wilfred he didn't know what to do, and in the event he failed to attend, much to Dr Rivers's fury.

~

Wilfred's last fortnight at Craiglockhart was busy and encouraging. Miss Wyer took him to the village of Colinton, where they called on a childhood friend of Stevenson. He revisited the Lintotts, and met Mrs Gray's mother and sister. Mrs Steinthal painted his portrait, an 'impressionistic' oil that Wilfred liked, and her mother-in-law did a small watercolour which he thought a failure.[37] One Saturday he went out into the country to have tea with an eminent judge, Lord Guthrie, at Swanston Cottage, a house that figures in Stevenson's *St Ives*. Guthrie dismayed him by asking him to embark on some historical research in the Advocates' Library, but this last bout of ergotherapy hardly had time to get started. Classes at Tynecastle continued to go well, and Wilfred took Mrs Fullerton and four of the boys into the Pentlands to see Swanston Cottage. Writing to Sassoon later about this outing, he described how he and the boys had walked back to the tram terminus singing, shouting, whistling and dancing under the stars until they all fell silent, watching meteors, knowing 'we loved one another as no men love for long. / Which, if the Bridge-players Craig & Lockhart could have seen, they would have called down the wrath of Jahveh, and buried us under the fires of the City you wot of.' That reference to Sodom and the intolerant bridge players gives a clue to some of the things the two poets had talked about during the previous two months.

Wilfred spent all day with Sassoon on 26 October, 'Breakfast, Lunch, Tea and Dinner', mostly at the Conservative Club in Princes Street. After dinner Sassoon read aloud from a book of astonishingly bad verse, recently presented to him by its author, Aylmer Strong: 'When Captain Cook first sniff'd the wattle, / And Love columbus'd Aristotle …'. The two friends' helpless laughter disturbed the club's usual hush.[38] Next day Wilfred heard he was to be boarded again, now that his month was up, and this time Brock thought he would be discharged. 'I am rather upset about it,' Wilfred told Susan. 'Especially as I am so happy with Sassoon … I am seriously beginning to have aching sensations at being rooted up from this pleasant Region.' The language derives from ergotherapy: 'Region' from Regional Survey, 'rooted up' from his Antaeus poem (in which Antaeus is 'Rooted … up' by Hercules). He assured Susan her little finger had power to 'break all the charm of Edinburgh, and all the love that it has thrown about me', but for the rest of his life he was to think of Edinburgh as the place he would most like to return to. That afternoon Mrs Fullerton held a farewell party at her flat for Wilfred and the Tynecastle class. She said she had never enjoyed a party so much, and he said he could almost agree. Sassoon, who called at his room in the evening, was annoyed to hear of the impending Medical Board, promising to raise the matter with Rivers. Next day, the sky being still clear, he took Wilfred to the Observatory again, and they looked at the moon through the great telescope.

The Board met on 30 October. Its report does not survive, but its findings are summarised in a brief note in Wilfred's file. He was discharged from the hospital and given three weeks' leave, after which he was to report to his reserve unit. That seems to be all he was told. Privately, his previous Board had thought he would be fit for general service by February 1918, but this time the doctors agreed he should be assigned to 'Light duty of a clerical nature' for four months, and they added that he was permanently unfit for overseas service, even with a labour or garrison battalion. There is no clue as to whether this surprising decision really means he was less well than he had been a month earlier, or whether the Board was influenced by special pleading from Brock and possibly Rivers. Had Wilfred known he was not to be sent into action again he would have been overwhelmed with relief, mixed with some humiliation. As it was, he only knew that he would soon be back in camp somewhere, subject to discipline and hard work once again.

He had to leave Craiglockhart that day. No doubt he said goodbye to Mayes, who was due to be discharged himself in a few days' time, and to Brock, who must have been secretly delighted not to have to go through what he regarded as the army doctor's worst ordeal, the pain of having to send a man back to active service. Wilfred had promised to spend a night or two at St Bernard's Crescent so that Mrs Steinthal could finish his portrait. He may in fact have spent four nights there, because Sassoon recalled a final dinner with him on 3 November, exactly a year before Wilfred's death. When Sassoon left to get back to the hospital, he handed over a sealed envelope, and Wilfred sat alone in a corner on the club stairs to open it, imagining he had been entrusted with some great personal secret. It contained the address of Sassoon's friend and mentor, Robert Ross, together with a ten-pound note and a characteristic message, 'Why *shouldn't* you enjoy your leave? Don't mention this again or I'll be very angry. S.S.'[39] Wilfred groaned aloud at being tipped like a schoolboy, went upstairs to write a letter that became too emotional to send, and left to catch the midnight train.

For all his protestations to Susan that he wanted to spend his leave in Shrewsbury, Wilfred was actually there for less than half his three weeks. Arriving at Mahim on 4 November, he wrote to Sassoon next day, using silly phrases from Strong's book ('a gourd, a Gothic vacuum', 'Smile the penny!', 'grame') to lighten the intensity of what he wanted to say.

> Smile the penny! This Fact [the ten-pound note] has not intensified my feelings for you by the least – the least *grame*. Know that since mid-September, when you still regarded me as a tiresome little knocker on your door, I held you as Keats + Christ + Elijah + my Colonel + my father-confessor + Amenophis IV in profile.
>
> What's that mathematically?
>
> In effect it is this: that I love you, dispassionately, so much, so very much, dear Fellow, that the blasting little smile you wear on reading this can't hurt me in the least.
>
> If you consider what the above Names have severally done for me, you will know what you are doing. And you have *fixed* my Life – however short. You did not light me: I was always a mad comet; but you have fixed me. I spun round you a satellite for a month, but I shall swing out soon, a dark star in the orbit where you will blaze. It is some consolation to know that Jupiter himself sometimes swims out of Ken![40]

In thinking of himself as a satellite, soon to become an independent star, Wilfred was remembering the recent Observatory visit and his old prophecy in 'O World of many worlds' that he would become a meteor, 'Warning the earth of wider ways unknown'.[41] Sassoon had no doubt been shown the poem, so he would have understood the allusion. The declaration of love in the letter must have embarrassed him, as Wilfred knew it would. Subsequent letters were even more outspoken, so much so that Sassoon burned several of them years later rather than show them to Harold Owen, an action for which Harold actually thanked him.[42]

Gazing across the racecourse to Haughmond from the familiar window, Wilfred longed to be back with his friend. Like many men on leave, he was finding home hard to cope with. 'I am spending happy enough days with my Mother,' he told Sassoon, 'but I can't get sociable with my Father without going back on myself over ten years of thought.' He probably spent much of his time in his room, reading and writing. The ten-pound note enabled him to order several copies of Graves's forthcoming book, as well as a new biography of Keats: 'damn it,' he wrote to Sassoon, echoing the message he had read on the club staircase, 'I'm to enjoy my leave!'

Mary's canary was chirping as annoyingly as ever, as though the machine guns at Serre had never existed, but all the Owens were committed to the war effort in one way or another. Tom was doing his bit by helping to keep the railway going; his patriotic opinions would have conflicted with Wilfred's new ideas at every turn. Mary was still working as a nurse, and Susan was presumably still making bandages. Colin, now seventeen and still full of romantic illusions, was dreaming of becoming an airman, as his two elder brothers had dreamed in their turn, but he got no encouragement from Wilfred, who had seen what could happen to airmen. Harold was away at sea; his brief flying career had ended in the spring after a second crash, so he had joined the Royal Naval Reserve as a midshipman. His autobiography says almost nothing about his war experiences, except that he disliked talking about them.[43] They were probably less eventful than Wilfred's, beginning with a year or more of routine patrols in northern waters.

After a mere four nights at home, Wilfred left for London. His first call was to his old haunt, the Poetry Bookshop, where he was amazed to be recognised by Alida Klemantaski. Once again he stayed at the Regent Palace Hotel, which had become one of the West End's main gathering places now that pubs were closing early under wartime licensing laws. The big public rooms on the ground floor were crowded for most of the night with soldiers and civilians, drinking, dancing and in many cases looking for sex. Wilfred later advised Susan not to let Colin stay there.

Next day, 9 November, Wilfred went to the Reform Club in Pall Mall for lunch with Robert Ross, who proved to be as friendly and hospitable as Sassoon had said he would be. Within minutes the new poet's initiation into London literary society had begun. Ross led the way to a table and they sat down next to someone who looked like 'an upstart rodent' but turned out to be Arnold Bennett. Another man joined them, his threatening eyes and huge moustache reminding Wilfred of bayonets seen over sandbags, and Ross introduced H.G. Wells. Wells at once recognised Wilfred's name, having heard of him from the editor of *The Nation*, to which Sassoon had sent 'Anthem for Doomed Youth'.[44] The three club members often had lunch together, so the conversation was relaxed, the awed guest even managing to join in the banter. Over coffee, when they were joined by the editor of the *Daily News*, Wells kept Wilfred spellbound for an hour with talk of political secrets. Afterwards Wilfred went to Gidea

Park, presumably to see his old friends the Williamses and Harpers. He met Ross again next day for dinner at the club, followed by an evening at Ross's flat in Mayfair.

Ross was forty-eight, although his bald head and sad, tired eyes made him look older. His big scarab ring and jade-green cigarette-holder were redolent of the 1890s, and he was indeed an Aesthete of the Oscar Wilde era, well-known as a connoisseur and former art dealer. In fact, 'Robbie, with the face of Puck and the heart of an angel' had almost certainly been Wilde's first male lover.[45] He had remained loyal during Wilde's trials and exile, and had done all he could as literary executor to restore the disgraced man's reputation. His efforts had resulted in persistent attacks from Lord Alfred Douglas, who was no longer Wilde's rose-lipped Bosie, poet of the love that dared not speak its name, but a self-appointed, vindictive guardian of public morals. Douglas had forced Ross to sue for libel in 1914 by describing him as 'the High Priest of all the sodomites in London', and had then triumphantly produced fourteen witnesses. Ross had withdrawn, but no police prosecution had followed as it had done for Wilde, partly because Ross had friends in the Liberal Government, including Asquith himself. But now in 1917, with Asquith no longer in power, Ross was vulnerable and knew it. He loathed the war and had encouraged Sassoon, to whom he was devoted, to satirise it, but he had been appalled by Sassoon's protest, knowing how destructive publicity could be.

Ross's flat at 40 Half Moon Street was in a house kept as 'residential chambers' by the redoubtable Nellie Burton, formerly his mother's maid. Burton, as she was always called, looked after him and let spare rooms to single gentlemen, many of whom were his friends. Wilfred would have stayed there himself, had a room been available. It was taken for granted that most residents and guests were, in the language of the time, 'so', but Burton expected them to behave (when one young man shot himself in the bathroom after the war to avoid scandal, she complained that he should have done it in the park). Ross's flat itself was magnificent, with a large drawing room recently decorated in dull gold as a protest against war economies. Old master paintings and antique bookcases lined the walls, and in the evenings the long table was set with biscuits, Turkish delight, brandy and cigarettes for any friends who happened to call. In the safety of the golden room, men could tell stories and express opinions that they might have kept to themselves elsewhere. Wilfred stayed talking until one in the morning. Some of the conversation seems to have been about his poems. 'I and my work are a success,' he told Susan afterwards, and Sassoon wrote to Graves that 'Little Owen went to see Robbie in town and made a very good impression ... I am sure he will be a very good poet some day, and he is a very loveable creature.'[46]

Getting up late next morning, Wilfred remained in London until the afternoon to hear a concert at the Queen's Hall, after which he went down to Winchester to see Leslie, who was still working at the Hazeley Down YMCA.[47] Wilfred stayed for three nights, longer than he had intended, sleeping on a camp bed and helping to serve coffee to the troops, the first time he had been among Other Ranks for almost six months. The cousins spent a whole afternoon exploring the cathedral. They had much to talk about. Leslie was worried about his current girlfriend, who was not writing to him. Wilfred, full of stories of Sassoon and Ross, seems to have revealed his own preferences for the first time. 'I left you the key to many of my poems, which you will guard from rust or soilure,' he wrote to Leslie a few days later.[48]

As Wilfred walked back alone to Winchester, crossing the long backs of the downs, he thought of the troops at the camp, and other men he had known on Redan Ridge and on the slopes above St Quentin, until the hollows seemed to fill with corpses. On the train to London, he found himself sitting opposite the jingoist editor of *John Bull,* Horatio Bottomley, famous for his assurances to the British public that men killed in war were already on the streets of heaven in glory.[49] Wilfred began drafting 'Asleep', an elegy for any dead soldier, as it were an answer to Bottomleyism.

> *Whether his deeper sleep lie shaded by the shaking*
> *Of great wings, and the thoughts that hung the stars, …*
> *Who knows? Who hopes? Who troubles? Let it pass!*
> *He sleeps. He sleeps less tremulous, less cold,*
> *Than we who wake, and waking say Alas!*

Pausing in London, Wilfred again visited the Bookshop, this time seeing Monro, with whom he had 'a good chat'. He bought *Georgian Poetry 1916–1917,* just published, containing poems by Sassoon and Graves as well as by Monro himself. Copies of Graves's new book, *Fairies and Fusiliers,* actually arrived while Wilfred was there. When a woman customer started asking about Sassoon, Monro was 'as reticent as his books', but he and Wilfred exchanged 'delicious winks'. It was the sort of moment Wilfred loved: he was 'one of the ones'.[50] Later, however, he was chagrined to discover that Sassoon had been in town that very day to take part in a poetry reading for charity with other poets, including Robert Nichols.

Knowing nothing of this event at the time, Wilfred returned to Shrewsbury for the last six days of his leave. Sassoon had wanted him to visit Garsington to meet Lady Ottoline and her pacifist friends, but that would have meant an even longer absence from home. On 20 November, exactly three weeks after leaving Craiglockhart, Wilfred left to rejoin his old unit, now based at Scarborough on the Yorkshire coast.

16

Major Domo

Scarborough

NOVEMBER 1917–MARCH 1918

Wilfred's journey to Scarborough was broken by a long wait in York, where he arrived at three in the morning on 21 November to find the station hotel full, without even a couch available. He trudged round the town knocking at other hotels, but could get no response, and the silent streets with their closed shutters and doors seemed an image of civilian indifference. At seven he caught the morning train to Scarborough and was soon amid scenery familiar from childhood holidays. He reported to the barracks at Burniston on the cliffs just north of the town, only to be told that the officers were quartered elsewhere.

The 5th (Reserve) Manchesters had been at Southport when Wilfred had left them at the end of 1916, but in the following summer they had moved to Scarborough, adding coastal guard duties to their usual tasks of training recruits and retraining convalescents. Scarborough had been the target of a notorious enemy bombardment in December 1914, when four German warships had steamed round the South Bay, firing hundreds of shells into the town, causing panic and numerous casualties. The town had also been shelled for ten minutes by a submarine in September 1917, and rumours abounded of spies landing from submarines, so there was a strong army presence in the area. At least one suspect was shot while Wilfred was there, and the seafront was barricaded with barbed wire, sandbags and sentry posts. The 'men' of the battalion, many of them now 'A4s', boys under eighteen too young to be sent overseas, were at the barracks, while the seventy or eighty officers were a ten-minute walk away at the Clarence Gardens Hotel.

Scarborough is divided into two bays by a steep ridge, with the old town on its southern flank and a ruined castle on its eastern spur, high above the sea. The shops and cafés on the South Bay, where the Owens had once been photographed on ponies, were mostly closed in wartime November and some still bore the signs of the 1914 shelling, but the little harbour was busy with fishing boats. The North Bay, quieter and more sedate, stretched round from the castle in a long crescent of Victorian boarding houses; on the cliff edge at the far end stood the Clarence Gardens (now the Clifton) Hotel, drawing attention to itself with a large corner turret. Wilfred said the hotel was well furnished and commodious, better than the Queen's at Southport. To anyone who had been on the Western Front it was gloriously comfortable, and the officers were making the most of it. There was a guest night on the evening Wilfred arrived, followed by a mess dance the evening after, with sumptuous meals and plenty to drink, even though the country was desperately short of food.

He soon knew everything about conditions at the Clarence Gardens. To his complete surprise he was put in charge of domestic arrangements, not at all the sort of light duties he had been expecting, and before he had a moment to think he was immersed in minor administration. There was no time to be homesick.

> I have to control the Household, which consists of some dozen Batmen, 4 Mess Orderlies, 4 Buglers, the Cook, (a fat woman of great skill,) two female kitcheners, and various charwomen!
>
> They need driving. You should see me scooting the buglers round the dining-room on their knees with dustpan and brush! You should hear me rate the Charwoman for leaving the Lavatory-Basins unclean.

He described himself to his mother and to Sassoon as 'Major Domo', but he probably had no official title, the job being a very junior one. Nominally he was answerable to the President of the Mess Committee (PMC), a kindly doctor named Mather whom he had known at Witley, and to a 'Food Specialist', but in practice he was on his own, unnoticed when he did well and the object of incessant queries and complaints when anything went wrong.[1] He was responsible for supplies of food, fuel, wine and tobacco, as well the allocation and inspection of rooms, and he had to supervise prisoners on their daily exercise, taking care to keep to the landward side of an especially large former sergeant-major. Every evening he had to ensure that the dozens of windows were thoroughly blacked out, as the hotel was an easy target from the sea. There were innumerable letters to write and accounts to check, and when drafts of officers were sent out to France he had to spend hours working out individual mess bills. Nevertheless he soon began to enjoy himself, reckoning he had an 'hereditary aptitude' for such work, descended as he was from many shopkeepers and tradesmen. 'I am well pleased with this job,' he told Susan within a week of arriving.

'I sit alone at last,' Wilfred wrote to Sassoon on 27 November after a busy day, 'and therefore with you, my dear Siegfried. For which name, as much as for anything in any envelope of your sealing, I give thanks and rejoice.' Sassoon had written suggesting they should be on first-name terms, a sign of close friendship.[2] 'The 5th have taken over a big Hotel, of which I am Major Domo,' Wilfred went on. 'I boss cooks, housemaids, charwomen, chamber-maids, mess orderlies – and drummers ... / There is no one here whose mind is Truth, or whose body Keats's synonym for Truth. / I'll mind my business, I'm a good worm.' (The dash was meant to be noticed: drummers were boys. The last sentence is a line from Graves's 'The Caterpillar', a poem in *Fairies and Fusiliers*.) One of the results of Wilfred's job was that he had very little contact with the troops and not much even with his fellow subalterns. Instead he had sole command of his little team of servants, soon deciding that the men and boys were much more teachable than the women. Several of the orderlies were recovering from neurasthenia. The bar-corporal had been in hospital in Edinburgh, where he had apparently been nursed by Blanche Bulman.[3] Wilfred chose one of the worst shock cases as his own servant, although the youth had to be given a rest after a month.

During the day the Major Domo was often hidden in the 'uncertain privacy' of his office. In his free time he could withdraw to his bedroom in preference to joining the other officers in the hotel lounges, where the air was thick with tobacco smoke and the tables occupied by bridge players. He had one of the best rooms in the hotel, lit by a five-windowed bay in the corner tower, probably on the first floor.[4] The furniture was ugly but comfortable, with a good bed, and there was even the luxury of a fireplace with enough coal for an evening fire. When the responsibilities of lunch were over and the coffee had earned general approval, he would escape to his tower window and sit looking down at the sea. There were days that winter when the sun shone so dazzlingly that he half-closed the blinds and could imagine himself back in the villa at Bagnères. On other days there was nothing outside but fog, or the wind blew until the air was crystal clear and the bay white with foam. He was free to organise his time to suit his work, being excused all parades by special order of the Colonel and allowed to come and go as he liked. Best of all, there seemed to be no need to worry about the future. Someone in authority must have hinted at the decision of his last Medical Board: 'I *think* I am marked Permanent Home Service,' he told Susan on 23 November. Confident that he was going to survive after all, he began going to antiques auctions, hoping to find furniture for the cottage he was going to live in after the war.

Yet the Scarborough posting was not altogether happy. Wilfred was touched at first by being warmly greeted by officers and NCOs who had heard a rumour that he was dead. It may well be, though, that the false story was soon replaced by a more accurate one, that he had lost his nerve under fire. He must have been unpleasantly conscious of the undistinguished end to his period in the line, and embarrassed to be given what was in effect a civilian job with no military duties. He made few friends in the battalion and none in the town. His Southport flatmate, Arnold Rickard, was in Scarborough but in hospital, having just broken open a severe leg wound during an unwise game of football. Another old acquaintance, Lieutenant Roland Bate, a former Artist who had been in the same hut as Wilfred at Romford, noticed how withdrawn and unsmiling Wilfred was. Bate was unsure whether to put this down to shyness or snobbery, but he decided on snobbery fifty years later when he read Wilfred's scathing comments about the Scarborough subalterns in the *Collected Letters.*[5]

Bate was not entirely mistaken. Many recently commissioned officers were 'temporary gentlemen', working-class men promoted to a social level they could never have aspired to in peacetime. They were inclined to show off their new status, and other officers tended to despise them. Wilfred thought the newcomers were snobs themselves. 'I am pestered by these new officers, who are in the first flush of commissionhood, and need to be suppressed,' he told his mother. Then he added, 'I shall soon be putting up another pip.' A second pip, the badge of a full lieutenant, would have been welcome proof of seniority, and he was due for it after eighteen months of service. But the expected promotion never came through. Not until the day after Wilfred's death in November 1918 did the War Office finally announce that he had indeed been promoted with effect from December 1917. To be left with only one pip among so many juniors was another humiliation. He kept aloof, and Bate was probably not the only officer who thought him a rather feeble specimen.

Certainly the CO was openly contemptuous, bullying Wilfred in public, according to Bate. Lieutenant-Colonel Spencer Mitchell was a 'dug-out', a retired officer who had been recalled in 1914. Now in his late fifties, he had lost two sons in the war and had held commands in the line. Many of his current subordinates were recovering from serious wounds, so he was not likely to feel much respect for neurasthenia. He must have been at least partly responsible for delaying Wilfred's promotion. Wilfred described him as 'a terrible old "Regular"', unpopular, bad-tempered and exacting, liable to explode if his bathwater were cold or his plates too hot. To be fair to Mitchell, though, being in charge of a thousand or more young soldiers amid the distractions of a resort town inevitably required stern discipline. Some men who served under him remembered him later as a 'villain', others as vigorous, highly efficient and even inspiring; one said that recruits were lucky to be with 'such an essentially sympathetic, though seemingly rugged, commander'.[6] Wilfred saw little of the sympathy. Luckily the Colonel was at his worst early in the day, and dealings with him could usually be postponed until the evenings. The other senior officers were much more agreeable. Major Frank, who embodied his surname, was 'so courteous & pleasant to all that I knew he valued War Poetry before he told me so!' No doubt Frank had read and admired Sassoon, as had Captain Mather, who had the additional distinction of being the son of a Ruskin biographer.

~

'War Poetry', and not just poetry, had become Wilfred's highest priority. He was worried at first that his official duties would interfere with his real work, but he found that once dinner had been cleared away and the last orderlies issued with passes to get them back into the barracks, he could be sure of being undisturbed in his room. Replacing his uniform with the more appropriate garb of purple slippers and a warm dressing gown, 'my enchanter's fleece', he could draw up an armchair to his fire and become a poet.

A reminder of the sort of poetry he had left behind came very soon, when a parcel arrived containing several copies of *The Nymph and Other Poems* by E. Leslie Gunston. The new book was dedicated to Wilfred 'with affection', and many of the poems were familiar: elegies to Swinburne and the aviator Gustav Hamel, sonnets on agreed subjects such as 'Purple' ('Rich, radiant, royal, rapturous and romantic!': Leslie enjoyed alliteration) and 'Golden Hair', and lyrics in praise of summer and the sea. There were two patriotic pieces, 'A Hymn of Love to England' and a salute to the navy. The dominant theme was young love, with frequent references to pure but alluring maidens whom the poet longed to kiss. 'Her lips! Red as the dawn of doubtful days ... / O! I must taste their sweet beyond all praise.' Wilfred liked the simile, but as he leafed through the book he grew more and more impatient with the sentiment, knowing very well that his cousin had no more kissed a girl than seen the trenches.

'I congratulate you on the Binding & Type,' he wrote to Leslie, trying to be kind, but he felt obliged to say that the poems would have 'enriched themselves with time', and that 'every poem, and every figure of speech should be a *matter of experience.*' 'I don't like the "Hymn of Love to England", naturally, at this period when I am composing "Hymns of Hate".' Wilfred sent a copy of *The Nymph* to Sassoon with some apologetic comments. To Susan he was blunt, saying the book was 'a mere orgy of kissing': the poems were not founded on 'a single act or fact', which was pitiable from a human point of view, though no doubt admirable from a Pauline one.[7]

This confident verdict was Georgian as well as Sassoonish. Wilfred was reading Edward Marsh's anthology and beginning to think of himself as a Georgian poet. He already knew three contributors to the anthology, and had read the work of the group's original leader, Rupert Brooke. In December he studied books by two pioneers of the Georgian style, John Masefield and Wilfrid Gibson. Gibson's *Battle* (1915), with its brief, simple poems about the psychological experience of ordinary soldiers, had been the first book of its kind, providing a model for subsequent work by the anthology's trio of young soldier-poets, Sassoon, Graves and Robert Nichols. The Georgians were still widely regarded as the spearhead of what Brooke had called 'the New Poetry', and to be recognised as one of them would be a high distinction. Wilfred was interested to hear that Sassoon was forging a friendship with Nichols after meeting him at the charity reading in November. Sassoon had left Craiglockhart and was expecting to go abroad, so he thought Nichols might stand in for him as Wilfred's mentor and friend. Meanwhile Graves tried to interest Marsh: 'I have a new poet for you, just discovered, one Wilfred Owen ... the real thing; when we've educated him a trifle more. R.N. and S.S. and myself are doing it.'[8]

Wilfred read Nichols's *Ardours and Endurances*, which had been a huge success earlier in the year, but in the event he never heard from its author. Perhaps that was just as well. He hardly needed more educating, and he could see that Nichols's poems were sadly 'self-concerned & *vaniteux*'. Poets often seemed very unlike their work, so it was amusing to hear from Sassoon that Nichols seemed every bit as self-concerned in person as in his poems (he had been embarrassingly over-emotional at the reading). That seemed an instructive contrast to the character of true poets. 'I thought he must efface himself in a room,' Wilfred remarked to Sassoon, 'even as you who write so acid are so – unsoured; and me, who write so big, am so minuscule.' Similarly, Graves was 'a big, rather plain fellow, the last man on earth apparently capable of the extraordinary, delicate fancies in his books', as Wilfred had commented to Susan in October.[9] Little Owen, un-distinguished as a soldier and scarcely noticed even in a reserve battalion, need have no qualms about writing big.

Sassoon had been discharged from Craiglockhart on 26 November, having come to an agreement with his military superiors that he would not protest again, provided he could return to active service immediately without the usual period of light duties. If that was a defeat for him, it was also a tacit admission by the authorities that he had never really been a shell-shock case. His conscience, patiently worked on by Dr Rivers, had persuaded him that his only honourable course was to return to leading men in the field, caring for their needs as he had been trained to do. He was also driven by his instinct for martyrdom: having failed to be a martyr on the home front he was once again keen to risk his life in the sort of escapades that had earned him the name of 'Mad Jack' in 1916. That alarmed Wilfred, who had no such impulse, and he sent Sassoon an appeal in verse, without much hope that it would succeed. Graves had already written a poem to Sassoon describing the pleasures of life after the war; if those lines were not enough 'to bring you to your senses, Mad Jack', Wilfred wrote, 'what can *my* drivel effect to keep you from France?'

The 'drivel' must have been the little-known poem, 'Earth's wheels', long regarded as nothing more than preliminary work for 'Strange Meeting' but actually a poem in its own right.

> *Earth's wheels run oiled with blood. Forget we that,*
> *Let us turn back to beauty and to thought.*
> *Better break ranks than trek away from progress ...*
>
> *We two will stay behind and keep our troth ...*
>
> *Then when their blood has clogged the chariot wheels*
> *We will go up and wash them from deep wells,*
> *Even the wells we dug too deep for war.*[10]

Wilfred has to fall back here on biblical and Shelleyan language for the first time since meeting Sassoon, the Georgian style being hardly suited to such an elevated declaration of poetic intent. Nevertheless he uses his invention of pararhyme, and develops ideas that come as much from Bertrand Russell and H.G. Wells as from Shelley. Russell wanted wise people to stand aside from the cycle of violence until war exhausted itself, when they would be needed to reconstruct society. Wells had called for 'devoted men and women ready to give their whole lives, with a quasi-religious enthusiasm, to this great task of peace establishment'. Reflecting on the state of the world in the last weeks of 1917, Wilfred believed that he and Sassoon should follow that call and 'stay behind', witnessing to beauty and truth until the war machine choked itself to a halt. Then they would help refresh the human spirit from what Shelley had called the 'deepest wells of passion or of thought / Wrought by wise poets in the waste of years'.[11] But Sassoon reported to his regimental depot near Liverpool and waited to be sent overseas. Wilfred would have to stay behind on his own.

Wilfred worked hard. At the end of November he wrote a poem he referred to as 'Vision', probably an early version of 'The Show', the bleakest of all his evocations of the battlefield, seeing it from the air like an aviator and using images he had tried out in letters from the front. On Sunday 2 December, when his fire smoked in the wind, he was able to finish 'an important poem ... in the right atmosphere'. He drafted three more poems that same afternoon, and planned to get up at dawn next day to 'do a dawn piece which I've had in mind since those dismal hours at York, 3 to 7 a.m.!' (no doubt a first attempt at 'Exposure', with its memory of York: 'Shutters and doors all closed: on us the doors are closed'). During the next few days he wrote 'Wild with all Regrets', later to be revised as 'A Terre', a monologue in the colloquial style of Masefield's notorious 1911 poem, *The Everlasting Mercy*, and during the following weekend he composed the last of his many sonnets, 'Hospital Barge', after 'a Saturday night revel in "The Passing of Arthur".[12] 'Wild with all Regrets', like 'Earth's wheels' and 'Vision', was written in pararhyme. 'If simplicity, if imaginativeness, if sympathy, if resonance of vowels, make poetry I have not succeeded,' he wrote to Sassoon. 'But if you say "Here is poetry", it will be so for me. What do you think of my Vowel-rime stunt … ?'

Wilfred's mention of Tennyson's poem about the death of King Arthur is one of many clues that he was reading, or in most cases re-reading, famous elegies. In December he bought a translation of the elegies by Bion and Moschus that had been Shelley's model for *Adonais*. There are traces in his 1918 poems of Milton's 'Lycidas', Gray's 'Elegy Written in a Country Churchyard', Tennyson's *In Memoriam*, Wilde's *Ballad of Reading Gaol* and elegies by Arnold, Housman and Hardy.[13] When he came to plan a book of war poems in the spring of 1918, he referred to its contents as 'these elegies'. His critics have sometimes argued that elegy is a false response to war, because it offers consolation. They forget that it has often included protest, usually at lack of pity. Milton attacks priests in 'Lycidas', Shelley savages critics in *Adonais*, and Wilde's *Ballad* denounces official cruelty. Wilfred himself said his own poems were 'in no sense consolatory', at least to his own generation. As Douglas Kerr has pointed out, the disbelief – even lack of interest – in an afterlife that Wilfred had so firmly stated in late Dunsden verse is carried through into the war poems, where the pity is for living soldiers, not for dead ones. Elegy's traditional consolations of heaven or 'becoming one with nature' are treated as more or less irrelevant. The elegiac tradition was there to be used, and Wilfred developed it in a way that was both radical and comfortless.

∼

Probably no one in the Clarence Gardens Hotel had the least idea that the Major Domo was spending his evenings writing poetry, even though he sometimes talked about 'War Poetry' to colleagues like Frank and Mather. Life during the day was 'a mixture of wind, sand, crumbs on carpets, telephones, signatures, clean sheets, shortage of meat, and too many money sums. But I like it.' Even in a hotel there were opportunities for seeing to his men's needs. The drummers were being overworked, so he hired several maids to help out. But when he was asked if he would do some teaching as part of an attempt to educate the A4s, he decided he would not lecture on military subjects, suspecting that the scheme was 'a Jesuitical movement to catch 'em young, & prepare them for the Eucharist of their own blood'.

Mrs Fullerton, the teacher at Tynecastle School, wrote to say she was about to leave: if Wilfred were ever to see her with the class again it would have to be very soon. Much to his surprise he had no difficulty in getting permission to go up to Edinburgh for a few days, and on Wednesday 19

December he set out again for York, this time finding better luck at the station hotel, where the dinner was excellent. The onward train was delayed, eventually reaching Edinburgh after six in the morning, so once again he breakfasted at the North British Hotel before going out to Craiglockhart. Dr Brock's first word on seeing him was, typically, 'Antaeus!': Wilfred's poem was wanted for *The Hydra*. If that was flattering, greetings from other people were less so, many patients assuming the former inmate had been sent back as a relapsed case. However, a glorious welcome awaited him at Tynecastle, where the boys were busy making Christmas cards to send him – his address was actually on the blackboard. They gave him his present, a hundred cigarettes. 'It was most touching, for I had given most of them nothing – beyond *Hiawatha*.' He played with them for a while in the wigwam they had built. Farewells, when they came, must have been made in a roar of cheering and a desperate effort on his part to smile and keep his voice steady. He could have stayed at St Bernard's Crescent, but chose instead to find lodgings of his own, perhaps not wanting to risk time alone with Mary Gray. He dined with the Grays and Mrs Steinthal on the Friday, and left for Scarborough next morning. He was never to see any of his Edinburgh friends again.

His mother was probably hurt that he had not devoted his first leave from Scarborough to her, especially as there was now no chance of his getting home for Christmas, and to add to his embarrassment his sudden visit to Edinburgh had prevented him from finding presents for the family.[14] The nearest he was able to get to a Christmas celebration was tea on the 24th with an old friend from his childhood, Cousin May Davies, who was still in charge of a private school in Scarborough.[15] Another lady at the tea party, a Miss Bennett, offered to give him German lessons, so that he could continue the studies he had begun in Edinburgh. Christmas itself was 'very mopish': Colonel Mitchell 'held an orderly Room for punishments in the morning – a thing forbidden in King's Regulations on Christmas Day – and strafed right & left, above & below.' The Major Domo may well have been a target for the strafing.

The mail brought consolations, including a big parcel from home and 'crowds' of cards. From Bordeaux came a four-volume anthology of French poets killed in the war, edited by Carlos Larronde, the poet Wilfred had met in 1915. The books were a present from Pierre Berthaud, who was working as an interpreter in an American YMCA, thanks, he said, to the English Wilfred had taught him. He had inscribed the first volume 'en témoignage de notre constante communion d'idées et de notre fraternelle amitié'. Johnny and Bobbie de la Touche sent cards with pictures of monkeys and the motto, 'Times change, & we with Time, but not in the ways of Friendship'. 'So they are unchanged,' Wilfred said, '– from the old shallow waggery, and the old deep affection.' But the most gratifying message was a warm-hearted and completely unexpected letter from Robert Graves, who had just been shown Wilfred's latest poems by Sassoon. 'Don't make any mistake, Owen,' Graves wrote; 'you are a damned fine poet already & are going to be more so ... you have found a new method ... those assonances instead of rhymes are fine – ... Puff out your chest a little, Owen, & be big – for you've more right than most of us ... You must help S.S. and R.N. and R.G. to revolutionize English Poetry – So outlive this War.'

Graves promised to pass the poems on to Nichols, and he also sent them to Edward Marsh, saying they showed Wilfred's 'powers and deficiencies – Too Sassoonish in places: Sassons is to him a god of the highest rank'. When Marsh replied that the poems seemed very uneven, Graves agreed, 'but he can see and feel, and the rest will be added unto him in time'. Graves was quite sure, then and later, that Wilfred's talent was indeed 'the real thing'.[16] Wilfred was enormously encouraged to have won such generous approval. 'They believe in me, these Georgians,' he told Leslie on 30 December, adding rather tactlessly that Sassoon had made no comment on *The Nymph*, having perhaps taken offence at the patriotic poems. 'Remember Poetry with him is become a mere vehicle of propaganda.'

That comment suggests Wilfred was beginning to have second thoughts about Sassoon's work, partly as a result of Graves's letter. Graves disapproved of using poetry for propaganda. He had recently told Sassoon to 'cheer up' and stop sending him 'corpse poems', and he said much the same to Wilfred: 'For God's sake cheer up and write more optimistically ... a poet should have a spirit above wars.' Wilfred seems to have been prompted to compose a reply in verse: 'I, too, have ... sailed my spirit surging light and clear / Past the entanglement where hopes lay strewn.' The new poem was originally entitled 'The Unsaid' and then 'Apologia lectorem pro Poema Disconsolatia Mea' ('A defence to the reader of my disconsolate poem' – or Wilfred may have meant 'poetry'. 'Poema' should in any case have been 'Poemate': he may have been hoping to impress his public-school friends, but his Latin let him down). 'Apologia' explains that writing optimistically about war might lead civilians to believe that soldiers were well content in the trenches. 'If there be a bright side to war, it is a crime to exhibit it,' Wilfred wrote on a draft of 'Apologia', misquoting Barbusse.[17] Nevertheless, the 'unsaid' truth was that love, beauty and 'exultation' (the word Wilfred had twice used of his feelings after getting through the Fayet barrage) could be found at the front. The love was not the sentimental kind represented in one of Leslie's poems as 'the binding ... of lips, the binding of eyes', but the comradeship Graves had described in a poem addressed to Sassoon ('By wire and wood and stake we're bound, / ... by the wet bond of blood'). Wilfred took up both images: love among soldiers was not 'the binding of fair lips', but 'wound with war's hard wire whose stakes are strong; / Bound with the bandage of the arm that drips'.

War poetry was going to have to be more than a mere vehicle for propaganda. Somehow it would have to deal with the unsaid truths of battlefield experience, but writing optimistically risked justifying war and reinforcing civilian complacency. Most of Graves's poems, dazzling though they were, did not face up to horrors. His attitude, like Charles Sorley's, whose poetry he much admired, was the product of a classical, public-school education. Wilfred came from a different tradition, and although he rejected Leslie's 'old song' he remained true to the Romantic poets he had believed in since his years at the PTC and to the Decadents he had read in France. Beauty could be found in horror and death, pleasure and pain being sometimes scarcely distinguishable: poets had a secret knowledge that set them apart, and there were parallels between that mysterious fellowship and the bond between soldiers. It ought to be possible to find a new mode for war poetry, neither Graves's cool stoicism nor Sassoon's tormented satire.

~

On 31 December 1917 Wilfred wrote to Susan, remembering the old Evangelical custom of looking back over the year and counting one's blessings. One great blessing was friends. 'I never found one false, or that did not surpass me in some virtue.'

> And so I have come to the true measure of man.
>
> I am not dissatisfied with my years. Everything has been done in bouts:
>
> Bouts of awful labour at Shrewsbury & Bordeaux; bouts of amazing pleasure in the Pyrenees, and play at Craiglockhart; bouts of religion at Dunsden; bouts of horrible danger on the Somme; bouts of poetry always; of your affection always; of sympathy for the oppressed always.
>
> I go out of this year a Poet, my dear Mother, as which I did not enter it. I am held peer by the Georgians; I am a poet's poet.
>
> I am started. The tugs have left me; I feel the great swelling of the open sea taking my galleon.

And then his mind went back to the previous New Year's Eve, when he had been at Étaples, 'a kind of paddock' it now seemed, 'where the beasts are kept a few days before the shambles', and he remembered the dreadful look on all the faces, 'a blindfold look, and without expression, like a dead rabbit's'.

> It will never be painted, and no actor will ever seize it. And to describe it, I think I must go back and be with them.
>
> We are sending seven officers straight out tomorrow.

I have not said what I am thinking this night, but next December I will surely do so.

I know what you are thinking, and you know me   Wilfred.[18]

'I think I must go back and be with them.' Perhaps he was only thinking of a staff job at Étaples, but more probably he meant he ought to return to the trenches. He was under the mistaken impression that Sassoon had just been sent to France, and officers were regularly being sent out from the hotel. Sooner or later he would come up against the same choice he had met in Southport a year earlier, not that it had really been a choice. A fit officer could not honourably stay at home for long, just as a poet could not honourably speak out before getting 'some reputation of gallantry'. He was still not entirely fit, however, and things were quiet on the Western Front. As if to illustrate his convalescent state, his left foot and leg broke out in blisters, a legacy from Redan Ridge. He took on a new servant, a 'secondary-school-educated youth' who had fought at Beaumont Hamel and Serre 'and all those places, if they can be called places'. The man had been badly wounded in the leg and still wore his shell-torn boots. Master and servant limped about the hotel, Sassoon was sent to the relative safety of Ireland and then Palestine, and the call from the front grew fainter.

~

Wilfred would have liked to give six hours a day to his 'art' ('For it is an art, & will need the closest industry'), but three hours a week was now about all he could manage. Writing home late at night on 5 January 1918, he said he had been working on hotel business without even a meal break from seven in the morning until nine at night, preparing the 1917 accounts for the auditors and dealing with other chores. *John Bull* had just attacked the battalion's officers for allowing the men a mere quarter of an hour for breakfast. Colonel Mitchell asked Wilfred what he should do about this 'lie', and Wilfred suggested prosecution, but there may have been a grain of truth in the story. A café was hastily opened for the men, with Wilfred in charge of its staff, which consisted of a sergeant, a 'baby-corporal', a pastry-cook and 'various fatigue urchins'. The first job was to order the filthy mugs to be cleaned out with acid, the Major Domo nervously drinking out of most of them afterwards in case his order poisoned the battalion.

When there was time for writing, it had to be used intensively. If the creative process is painful, as many writers have testified, it was exceptionally so for a war poet still recovering from neurasthenia. Wilfred had learned during months of therapy that the way to deal with memories of Beaumont Hamel and Serre was to face up to them, a harsh discipline that coincided with the labour of composition. 'I confess I *bring on* what few war dreams I now have, entirely by *willingly* considering war of an evening. I do so because I have my duty to perform towards War.' He had not forgotten Colonel Shirley's exhortation that one should do one's duty, whatever the cost. When an invitation arrived to Graves's wedding, Wilfred said that going was 'a kind of duty' both to himself and Graves. Hard work, self-sacrifice, loyalty to one's fellows: these were poetic as much as military duties. By contrast, the sort of poeticising that Leslie liked was absurdly undemanding. A reviewer of Leslie's book in the *Times Literary Supplement* said he rhymed with ease but without originality or power, and Wilfred agreed. He warned Leslie not to become 'a lagoon, salved from the ebbing tide of the Victorian Age', and offered to lend him *Georgian Poetry*.

In mid-January the newspapers carried harrowing reports of a colliery explosion at Halmerend, near Stoke-on-Trent. Over 140 men and boys had been killed. Wilfred stared into his fire, remembering his old interest in geology.

> *I listened for a tale of leaves*
> *And smothered ferns, …*
>
> *But the coals were murmuring of their mine,*
> *And moans down there*
> *Of boys that slept wry sleep, and men*
> *Writhing for air.*
>
> *I saw white bones in the cinder-shard,*
> *Bones without number.*

The miners became soldiers, digging pits of war, and by the end of the poem he was one of them.

> *The centuries will burn rich loads*
> *With which we groaned,*
> *Whose warmth shall lull their dreaming lids,*
> *While songs are crooned;*
> *But they will not dream of us poor lads*
> *Lost in the ground.*[19]

'Miners' wrote itself in half an hour. He sent it off at once to *The Nation*, one of the few periodicals willing to print criticism of the war. The editor accepted it, no doubt impressed by its topicality and the remarkable originality of its sound effects. When it was published Leslie complained that the rhymes offended his musical ear. Wilfred was secretly amused, but he replied amiably, welcoming his cousin's frankness: 'I suppose I am doing in poetry what the advanced composers are doing in music. I am not satisfied with either.'

Graves's wedding was on the 23rd. Wilfred applied for leave and sent a present of eleven apostle spoons (no doubt a trophy from an antiques auction), with a note explaining that the twelfth spoon was awaiting execution after being court-martialled for cowardice. Susan complained that once again he was going away without visiting home, so he felt obliged to call in at Mahim for the night of the 22nd, an inconvenient detour that resulted in a rushed journey next morning to London, where Ross had again invited him to lunch at the Reform Club. He hired a bathroom at Paddington for a last-minute shave and bath, only to be summoned to his taxi before he could get into the water. He said later he had got to the club on time, but lunch evidently had to be a hasty affair. After exchanging a few words with Wells, who was at another table, he hurried out with Ross to hail a cab for the short distance to St James's, Piccadilly.

Wilfred's arrival at the church as Ross's sole companion may have caused some people to murmur that dear Robbie had found yet another handsome young man, but Wilfred thoroughly enjoyed himself, just as he had enjoyed being befriended by Tailhade in 1914. Graves was already in the front pew, in full-dress uniform with spurs and sword. His bride was Nancy Nicholson, the daughter of a well-known society painter, so the guests included artists and bohemians, some of whom struck Wilfred as surprisingly dowdy. Nancy arrived in a blue-check dress and a furious temper, having just discovered what sort of vows she would have to make. Afterwards, at the reception in her father's flat nearby, she horrified her mother-in-law by grabbing a bottle of champagne and marching off to change into her land-girl's costume. Wilfred was pleased to identify a few celebrities, including the caricaturists George Belcher and Max Beerbohm. He had hoped to meet Robert Nichols, but Nichols was absent, as were Sassoon, who was on a gas course in Ireland, and Monro, Graves's first publisher, who had just been sent to the Northern Command Depot at Ripon. However, Wilfred was introduced to several interesting people as, gratifyingly, 'Mr Owen, Poet' or 'Owen, the poet'. He seems to have talked to William Heinemann, publisher of the latest books by Sassoon and Graves, hearing Heinemann's worries about the outspokenness of Sassoon's new work, and he certainly met two of Graves's most helpful advisers, Edward Marsh and Charles Scott Moncrieff. When the party ended he went back to the Reform, where he had been invited to dinner by Ross's friend, Roderick Meiklejohn.

～

The start to a memorable evening was probably rather dull. Wilfred did not discover until afterwards that his host at dinner was a senior controller in the Treasury and a former private secretary to Asquith. Meiklejohn was devoted to Sassoon, whom he had visited at Craiglockhart, but conversation with him was usually 'slightly dreary', according to Sassoon, like 'talking to the family solicitor'. Even so, shy and respectable though he was, Meiklejohn was known to enjoy the company of young men.[20] He was a regular visitor (later a resident) at 40 Half Moon Street, and he took Wilfred back to Ross's flat there after dinner. Wilfred stayed for hours, talking with Ross and 'two Critics'. One of the critics (occasional reviewers would have been a more accurate term) was Scott Moncrieff, the other probably Ross's old friend and former colleague, William More Adey, who had been one of Wilde's close associates. Graves had hoped that 'Owen, the poet' would make some useful contacts at the wedding, but he was unhappy with the result later. The day that saw Graves finally commit himself to hetero-sexuality, after years of thinking of himself as an idealistic Uranian, also saw Wilfred accepted as a member of Ross's circle, at the heart of what was soon to be attacked in the press as the 'Oscar Wilde cult'.

Scott Moncrieff later recalled his first meeting with Wilfred:

It was in January, 1918, at the crowded wedding of another poet, that I first saw him. I had been provisionally released from hospital a few days earlier, and had spent all that day, ineffectively, at a Police Court. I was too sore at first, in mind and body, to regard very closely the quiet little person who stood beside me in a room from which I longed only to escape. But that evening I met him again after dinner, and found that we had already become, in some way, intimate friends.

Scott Moncrieff always liked to leave clues in his writing: that apparently unnecessary mention of a police court would have reminded anyone in the know that Ross's former secretary, Christopher Millard, had just been arrested for a homosexual offence. Scott Moncrieff must have volunteered to appear as a character witness, a brave thing to do at the time. He further reminds readers of his article that he had been wounded in action, thereby portraying himself as a hero on two fronts, against prejudice at home and Germany abroad. Sassoon, who detested him, grumbled later that the article was written entirely for its author's self-advertisement.[21] Being one of those in the know, Sassoon could also see – resentfully – that Scott Moncrieff's claim to have become Wilfred's 'intimate friend' was another clue. On Scott Moncrieff's side, if not on Wilfred's, the intimate friendship was in fact a love affair.

Four years older than Wilfred, Charles Scott Moncrieff – ScoMo to his friends, of whom he had relatively few, being a sharp-tempered, difficult man – was a handsome, scholarly captain in the King's Own Scottish Borderers with an unimpeachable war record despite frail health. A reservist before 1914, he had been mobilised immediately, and his army file records a history of war-related illness: rheumatism and frostbite in 1914, trench fever and hospital in 1916, gastritis, jaundice and tonsillitis in 1917. His fighting career had come to an end at Arras in April 1917, where he had won the Military Cross for continuing to direct and encourage his company after being severely wounded. A shell bursting close behind him had torn into his left leg, shattering bones in several places, and a bullet had hit him in the thigh. Months of hospital had followed. He had been given a job at the War Office a week before Graves's wedding at his own 'urgent' request, but he was still under treatment and his leg was in a calliper. Nevertheless he remained a firm believer in the war effort, writing heroic, patriotic verse quite unlike Sassoon's, whose war poems he had deplored in a review.

Scott Moncrieff's attitude to warfare on the home front was also very different from Sassoon's. Sassoon had protested against the war, but on sexual matters he was reticent and still 'unspotted'. Scott Moncrieff, by contrast, regarded risk-taking as a fine art, and he was as openly gay as anyone at that time could dare to be. Even as a boy he had got into trouble at Winchester for publishing a homosexual story, and he delighted in exchanging learnedly obscene verse and parodies with his friends. As an undergraduate at Edinburgh in 1907 he had met Millard, one of his first lovers, and Millard had introduced him to Ross. It was typical of Scott Moncrieff to speak up in court for a friend who had already been in prison once and seemed certain to be going there again.

Wilfred must have heard anxious discussion at Half Moon Street about Millard's likely fate and its implications. If the press were to get hold of the story, the names of Ross and Oscar Wilde would be bound to be dragged in. Millard's principal task as Ross's secretary had been to compile a bibliography of Wilde's works, thereby enabling Ross as literary executor to establish control of copyright. And that raised another worry: unwisely, Ross had just given permission for a performance of Wilde's *Salome*, a play many people regarded as indecent. With the war at an apparent stalemate, public opinion was becoming dangerously volatile and rumours were growing that some hidden force was at work, corrupting government and betraying the armies. The usual victims were likely to be blamed: spies, foreigners, Jews, homosexuals. Lord Alfred Douglas and those who thought like him had been given their chance.

When the conversation in the golden room turned to other matters, the visitor may have been persuaded to read his latest poem, 'Miners'. Much impressed, Ross offered to look through all Wilfred's war poems to see whether they might make a book. Scott Moncrieff, who delighted in literary ingenuities, was fascinated by the pararhyme in 'Miners'. He no doubt engaged Wilfred in bookish conversation about ancient forms of rhyming; fortunately Wilfred knew a little about Welsh and Old English. The gathering did not disperse until two in the morning. Once again

Burton can have had no rooms to spare: Wilfred had booked himself into the Imperial Hotel, where he had stayed in 1915. At ten next morning he caught a train to Scarborough.

~

'Miners' was published in *The Nation* on 26 January. It gained its author two guineas, 'my first proud earnings', and he sent one of them to Susan, telling her to spend it on coal fires ('only poetic justice! Stoke up!'). On the 30th he attended another Medical Board, three months after the last one at Craiglockhart. The doctors decided he should remain on light duties for another three months and then go to the Northern Command Depot for fitness training. Comments made at the interview may have led him to suspect, rightly, that he was no longer to be marked 'Permanent Home Service'. He 'put up' the blue chevron he was entitled to as an officer who had served overseas during the previous year, but there was still no sign of his lieutenant's pip.

He wrote home on 11 February 1918 about his future. Something he said must later have worried his brother, who tore away part of the first page, so that the letter now begins:

> and with plenty to sing about. 'But few have the courage, or the consistency, to go their own way, to their own ends.'
> It all depends what manner of opening I, or my friends, can wedge open for me in England, that is, London.[22]

Since New Year's Eve Wilfred had been thinking that the right thing to do as both poet and officer would be to emulate Sassoon by going back to be with the troops. Now someone, probably Scott Moncrieff, had written to say that a poet with plenty to sing about should go his own way rather than conform to army expectations. The Wildean creed of individualism corresponded with Wilfred's old ambition to be a lawless meteor, but hoping for a safe London posting was nevertheless a major change of direction, and long afterwards Harold Owen may have thought it looked like shirking. The Medical Board's decision and advice from new friends had persuaded Wilfred that the wisest course would be, after all, to 'stay behind'. Something could surely be arranged. Ross and Meiklejohn ought to be able to exert influence, and Scott Moncrieff, who was working at the War Office and related to a senior general, had access to officials and confidential files.

The missing part of Wilfred's letter probably also told Susan about a new friend in Scarborough, Philip Bainbrigge, to whom he had been given an introduction by Scott Moncrieff.[23] Bainbrigge turned out to be excellent company. Tall, thin and short-sighted, the son of a West End clergyman, he was far from soldierly, but he was widely read and had a great sense of humour. He had attested at the last moment under the Derby Scheme and had been called up for home service in 1917. After trying in vain to get into the same regiment as Scott Moncrieff, who had been his friend and probably lover for years, he had ended up as a subaltern in the Welsh Regiment and was now attached to the 5th Lancashire Fusiliers. In civilian life he had been a master at Shrewsbury, the public school Wilfred had often gazed at enviously. Later in 1918 he mentioned Wilfred in a letter to Edward Dent, a Cambridge don who knew many of Ross's friends, including Sassoon. Bainbrigge said that Wilfred, who was 'simpatico', wrote rather well and had enjoyed some poems that Bainbrigge had been able to repeat to him.[24] Dent would have understood the implication: most of Bainbrigge's poems were what Scott Moncrieff later described as ballads of a 'private kind'. The recitations seem to have had an immediate effect on Wilfred, who was always inclined to imitate a newly encountered poet. Continuing his February letter, he told his mother he had written 'profusely' during the previous week, but not on topical matters.

Several of Wilfred's more or less 'private' poems seem likely to date from this period.[25] 'I am the ghost of Shadwell Stair', based on Wilde's 'Impression du Matin' (Wilfred seems to have been familiarising himself with Wilde, reading books by and about him),[26] describes a 'ghost' lingering at Shadwell Dock Stair, a place Wilfred would have known from his East End walks in 1915 and perhaps later. When the dock sirens announce the dawn like an urban cock-crow, the ghost is 'lain' with another ghost. Wilfred sent this mysterious poem to Scott Moncrieff, who translated it into French in the summer of 1918 and implied that the first ghost was Wilfred himself. The second ghost is perhaps meant to be understood as a rent-boy picked up on the stairs.[27] Another poem, 'Reunion', is about a relationship, apparently both sexual and illicit: 'I needed, you ceded'; 'we were two … against the town's taboo' and then 'one' against 'the anger of the sun'. 'Men drove us and clove us', but the pair are now reunited and no longer alone: 'We shall be many / Against the enemy'. Whether the relationship was fiction or not, the poem's sense of solidarity against society and the world was typical of Half Moon Street.

Wilfred's manuscripts also include three ballads of a private kind, all written on Clarence Gardens paper: 'The Rime of the Youthful Mariner', 'Page Eglantine' and 'Who is the god of Canongate'. All three have homo-sexual implications, although the first is no longer intelligible. The third seems to be about rent-boys in Canongate (Edinburgh) and Covent Garden (London), collectively represented as a 'little god' who walks the pavements barefoot. This 'lily-lad' is visited up 'secret stairs' by men who 'lift their lusts and let them spill'. Draft work includes the phrase 'Bow Street cases': Wilde and others had appeared before magistrates at Bow

Street. The strange ghosts and deities in these 1918 coded poems seem more accessible than their predecessors, the 'half-god' in Limehouse, the 'rain-flawed phantom' in Princes Street, the god Eros in several sonnets and the 'phantasms' Wilfred had seen in dreams. Maybe he had by now been up secret stairs in London and Edinburgh, or perhaps he had just heard stories at Half Moon Street and from Bainbrigge. There is no evidence either way, except for the growing confidence of his poems, together with his repeated insistence that poetry should be based on experience, and a single, incautious mention to Leslie of '*mon petit ami*' in Scarborough. The *ami* may perhaps have been the 'little Scot' referred to in a few letters to Susan, apparently a young soldier on Wilfred's staff at the hotel, but there is no clue as to the innocence or otherwise of the friendship.[28]

Secrecy was essential. Talking to Bainbrigge in an oyster bar they took to frequenting in Scarborough, Wilfred would have heard about the extraordinary allegation recently made by an extreme right-wing MP, Noel Pemberton Billing, that the German secret service had a Black Book listing 47,000 prominent British people who practised vices 'all decent men thought had perished in Sodom and Lesbos'. The forthcoming production of *Salome*, authorised by Ross, was advertised in *The Times* on 10 February, and on the 16th Pemberton Billing suggested that the audience would surely include some of the 47,000. The actress who was to play the name part, Maud Allan, and her producer, J.T. Grein, an unfortunately Germanic name, decided to start a libel action. Ross and his friends were going to have to keep their heads down.[29]

~

The London visit and conversations with Bainbrigge, as well as Graves's advice against writing like Sassoon, all seem to have combined to distract Wilfred from the poetic task he had set himself. He lost his sense of urgency for a while. Apart from a first draft of 'The Last Laugh', no new war poems are mentioned in his letters between late January and late March 1918. Even more surprisingly, Sassoon seems not to have heard from him at all during the first half of the year.[30] Wilfred apparently reverted to working on old sonnets, arranging fair copies of twenty of them in a numbered sequence as though once again hoping to get them published. He even drifted back into his old partnership with Leslie, joining him in entering a *Bookman* competition for lyrics and ballads. 'Song of Songs' won a consolation prize, rather to its author's embarrassment, and he was also listed as a runner-up in the ballad section (if he had sent one of his recent private ballads to the magazine he must have been relieved it was not printed).[31]

He was still keeping out of the social life of the battalion. A habitué of

Ross's golden room had little in common with the temporary gentlemen in the Clarence Gardens Hotel. He was friendly with real gentlemen now: Bainbrigge was Eton and Cambridge, Scott Moncrieff Winchester and Edinburgh, Sassoon Marlborough and Cambridge, Graves Charterhouse and destined for Oxford. Less than a year ago Wilfred had only been able to dream of moving in such circles. He had been reading H.A. Vachell's sentimental novel, *The Hill*, the story of a passionate friendship between two boys at Harrow. 'Lovely and melancholy reading it is for me,' he told his mother, consoling himself that there had been a hill in his own life, too, at Broxton, 'whose bluebells it may be, more than Greek iambics, fitted me for my job'. At the end of the book one of the boys, handsome, talented but morally weak, redeems himself by becoming an officer in the South African war: his company halts at the foot of a hill in 'a storm of bullets', the 'word' is given to attack, fire comes from invisible foes, and the young officer, running as though 'racing for a goal', leads the charge, dying at the highest point of the hill, 'smiling at death'. Wilfred must have been moved: there are echoes from that brief scene in his last completed poem, 'Spring Offensive'.[32]

He had only two friends in the battalion. One was a fat, bespectacled painter, Second Lieutenant W.M. Claus, who knew and revered the name of Robert Ross. After an entertaining evening with Claus exploring the moonlit alleys of the old town, Wilfred reflected that revelling in fresh air and 'miles of glorious eighteenth-century' was a much better way of getting drunk than wasting time and money in the officers' bar.[33] The other friend was Lieutenant Henry Priestley, who had recently become President of the Mess Committee. 'Uncle Henry', as he was affectionately known, was a popular figure, but he was especially close to the Major Domo, his chief assistant, who was lucky to gain such a well-placed ally. Roland Bate remembered how Wilfred became the PMC's shadow, sheltering from the Colonel's bad temper. In private, however, unseen by Bate and other unsympathetic colleagues, Wilfred could relax over tea in Priestley's room and be himself, enjoying his host's fine china and sharing thoughts about life after the war. 'Priestley bought some wonderful large Ranunculi this morning,' Susan was told in February, 'and they are so fine that nothing would do but he must buy a fine bowl to set them in. So we are winning at least the "Warness" of War.'

Priestley had been a manufacturer in Bradford, according to his army file, and he clearly had money of his own. Like Wilfred, though ten years older, he was a single man and an Artist, having enlisted at Duke's Road in July 1915, and he had been at the front in 1917, but his service had been interrupted by poor health. Tall and thin like Bainbrigge, he was evidently something of an aesthete, and he seems to have been responsible for Wilfred's new-found enthusiasm for antiques, taking him to a 'secret' shop and helping him to bargain. Wilfred had never spent much money on himself before, but he could afford to do so now and he made a number of purchases, including a heavy Jacobean chest and a little bronze statuette of Mercury, naked and winged. Priestley also bought at least one object on his behalf in the spring, a massive oak chest of drawers made up from Jacobean fragments.[34] Buying oak meant there was no need to compete with Priestley, who preferred walnut, and Wilfred could amuse himself by being supercilious about his friend's 'finds'. Uncle Henry was clearly a congenial companion, and he seems to have been a regular at the oyster bar: Wilfred said later that 'Priestley has spent pounds on me (oysters etc.)'.[35]

Despite these civilian pleasures, the 'Warness of War' was rapidly closing in. Things were looking 'stupefyingly catastrophic' on the Eastern Front, Bainbrigge remarking in the oyster bar on 22 February that civilisation seemed on the edge of collapse. Peace negotiations between Germany and revolutionary Russia had broken down, and Germany was capturing vast tracts of central Europe. As soon as that victory was complete, German troops could be brought back for a final assault in the west. In Scarborough, leave for officers was sharply reduced, and Wilfred was warned that he might soon be sent to a camp for physical training, to get fit for 'serious warfare'. He tried to hope for the best. Perhaps he would not be passed by the doctors. He asked his mother if Owen Owen, an eminent schools inspector the family had known in Oswestry, could get him an 'Education Job'.[36] Scott Moncrieff was still hoping to find him a job through the War Office.

On 9 March the order came through that Wilfred was to report to the Northern Command Depot at Ripon. The recommendation of his last Medical Board, that he should remain on light duties until the end of April, had evidently been overruled. 'Not a bad idea even if I be demobilized!' he told Susan, trying to sound optimistic. He applied for a few days' leave, but was refused. Priestley was away, Claus was 'spy-hunting' somewhere and Bainbrigge, marked down for overseas service at last, had been sent on what was probably embarkation leave. Wilfred sent off a big box of books and winter clothes to Shrewsbury, packed his military kit and on Tuesday 12 March set out for Ripon on the other side of Yorkshire. 'Farewell Books, Sonnets, Letters, friends, fires, oysters, antique-shops. Training again!'

17

Getting Fit

Ripon

MARCH–JUNE 1918

The Northern Command Depot at Ripon was one of the largest army camps in the country. Built on green fields to the west of the town in 1915, it had become a city in itself, larger and busier than the one it half-encircled. It had its own power station and branch railway, twenty-six miles of roads, forty-eight miles of sewers, and innumerable bakeries and kitchens catering for over thirty thousand men. When Wilfred arrived at the railhead on 12 March 1918 he would have been cheered to see the nearby Garrison Theatre, with posters advertising a performance of *The Merry Wives of Windsor* by his beloved Benson Company, but there was little else to be pleased about. He had not seen military activity on such a scale in England since 1916. Thousands of anxious young conscripts were learning how to kill, and wounded men were being made fit again for home duties or the trenches. Here and there squads of mutilees were exercising what was left of their arms and legs. As soon as he had found his own quarters among the endless lines of long wooden huts, Wilfred sent a postcard home: 'An awful Camp – huts – dirty blankets – in fact WAR once more.'

His hut held thirteen other officers, '13 too many. Most of them are privates & sergeants in masquerade (as were half the officers at Clarence Gdns.) I'd prefer to be among honest privates than these snobs.' The hut seems to have been in the South Camp on Hellwath Common, an open plateau with a fine view of the cathedral towers a mile or so away.[1] He made for them as soon as time allowed next day, and was just going in at the west door when he had the good luck to meet an old friend from Craiglockhart, Leslie Isaacson, who was once again a full-time Bensonian. The two former patients had tea together, and Wilfred was invited to visit the theatre, where the actors gave him a warm welcome. He seems to have been asked to come back and meet the Bensons themselves, but to his bitter disappointment he was prevented from going by a sudden bout of fever.

Sweating under muddy, bloodstained blankets in an isolation hut, he was afraid his 1913 illness had returned, until the doctor assured him he had caught an infection that often struck down newcomers to the camp. Wilfred wondered later whether it had in fact been the influenza that was just beginning to ravage the world, but whatever it was it only lasted a few days. He blamed it on his 'extreme disgust' at the camp and the vile food, knowing himself well enough by now to understand that his ailments had often been associated with low morale. Sent back to his own hut on the 17th, a Sunday, he showed his real state of health by going for a long day's walk, setting out into parkland beyond the camp and unexpectedly finding himself in one of the most spectacular man-made landscapes in England, the sequence of water-gardens that leads to the ruins of Fountains Abbey. Further on he came to Fountains Hall ('a glorious house … Almost worth fighting for!') and climbed up to How Hill Tower, an eighteenth-century folly with two tiny cottages attached. He persuaded a cottager to give him tea and absorbed the magnificent view, wondering whether he might rent one of the houses as a secret workshop, but the hill was too far from camp.

The camp regime was not demanding by army standards, despite Wilfred's initial disgust. It had seemed much harsher to Harold Monro, who had been there a month or two earlier, but Monro had never done any fighting and could see no sense in army methods. He had even tried to argue a political case against the war in the mess, with the inevitable result that he had been ostracised as a suspected pacifist and coward. Wilfred knew better than to draw attention to himself by challenging the opinions of the average subaltern. He politely declined a seat at the card tables, kept quiet about his front-line record and was glad of the blue chevron on his sleeve. Since his official purpose at Ripon was to get fit, he resolved to give up alcohol and tobacco and took to getting up at seven for a shower. From nine to three every day he had to do physical exercises and attend lectures, but the rest of his time was free. 'I shall not know what to do unless I can get a Room where I can use my big spectacles to advantage.'

He spent the afternoon of his twenty-fifth birthday in the cathedral, perhaps praying to the God he had never quite ceased to believe in. Next day he went to Harrogate, which was dull, and on the 20th he walked a few miles to visit some friends of the Gunstons, who were duller still. 'Mrs Aslin can click the piano quite quickly: … I wonder these people buy pianos at all, when a good typewriter is so much cheaper, and makes almost the same noise.' Wilfred wrote that on the morning of Thursday 21 March, a day that would be remembered as the most ominous in the war. Even as he was amusing himself by being unkind about Mrs Aslin, events were taking place in France that were to claim many thousands of lives, including in the end his own. The German offensive had begun.

The enemy had crossed the Hindenburg Line at daybreak in huge numbers under cover of fog, racing up from St Quentin through the defences Wilfred had helped to build. Manchester Hill, once again held by a Manchester battalion, had resisted uselessly for a few hours. The Fifth Army, undermanned and massively outnumbered, was falling back in chaos, losing whole battalions. During the next few weeks the daily casualty rate rose to higher levels than at any other time in the war. All the places Wilfred knew, Savy, Germaine, Quivières, then Voyennes and Nesle, were overwhelmed, and soon even the site of the CCS at Gailly was in German hands. On the 26th the Germans crossed the Ancre, recapturing Serre, their old stronghold. 'It is specially cruel for me to hear of all *we* gained by St Quentin having been lost,' Wilfred said. 'They are dying again at Beaumont Hamel, which already in 1916 was cobbled with skulls.' The newspapers put as favourable a gloss on things as they could, but there was no disguising the fact that a major retreat was in progress.

After two slack months, Wilfred's creative energy came flooding back. Within a day or two he had found a room in a cottage at 7 Borrage Lane ('close to camp: the very thing') where he could work on the poetry that now urgently needed writing.[2] He would have seen the cottage on the pleasantest route he could take into town. Borrage Lane could be reached by following steps down from the common to a footbridge over the Laver, a 'happy little stream' that flowed alongside the lane past paddocks, nursery gardens, a few old houses and one miniature terrace. The occupant of No. 7, a house in the terrace, was no doubt only too pleased to earn a little

Houses in Borrage Lane, Ripon. Wilfred's retreat was under the skylight.

307

money by letting him use the front room during his free time. He kept his new base secret from everyone in camp.

His duty as an officer would now require him to return to France, and the tone of his letters changes with that recognition. There was no longer any chance for peace negotiations nor any point in protesting. Germany had imposed crushing peace terms on Russia and was clearly intent on military victory. 'What did I say about America?' Wilfred lamented. 'Why did I denounce them?' His last Craiglockhart poem, 'Soldier's Dream', had satirised the Americans for ensuring that the war would continue, but now they seemed the best long-term hope for peace. Meanwhile the need for reinforcements was so great that even the A4s at Scarborough were being sent to the front. 'I think less of leaving the Army: and more of getting fit,' Wilfred wrote to Mary, and to Colin: 'I don't think there is the least probability of demobilization now. On the contrary, I am trying to get fit.' 'All the joy of this good weather is for me haunted by the vision of the lands about St Quentin crawling with wounded,' he told Leslie. 'I must buck up and get fit!' For the moment he forgot the possibility that Scott Moncrieff might yet be able to find him a home posting.

The fine spring weather and peaceful Yorkshire countryside made a poignant contrast to what was happening at the front. Priestley sent some beautiful flowers from Scarborough. Walking along Borrage Lane, 'my lane', to the cottage, Wilfred noticed how all the lesser celandines came into bloom together. He had studied the flower for Matric in 1911, and would have known that Wordsworth had written three poems about it. One of its characteristics is to open in sunshine and close in bad weather, an excellent example of a 'thinking' plant, an organism responding to its environment. For a poet, too, spring was a time for response and growth: 'as trees in Spring produce a new ring of tissue,' Wilfred had written from Mérignac in April 1915, 'so does every poet put forth a fresh, and lasting outlay of stuff at the same season.' Children outside the cottage were making such a noise playing soldiers that he moved up into the attic, a cavernous room occupying the whole space under the roof, lit by a single skylight. This 'jolly Retreat' proved to be an ideal place in which to 'contemplate the inwardness of war, and behave in an owlish manner generally'. Drinking tea brought up to him by his landlady, and occasionally allowing himself half a cigarette, he embarked on his last and most creative spring.

~

Wordsworth had said that the poet is the rock of defence for human nature, and he had claimed that all good poetry arises from 'the spontaneous overflow of powerful feelings', allied to long and deep thought. The emotion is 'recollected in tranquillity' until it recreates itself in the mind and a poem begins to grow. Wilfred knew that the recollecting and thinking had to be done, but it was going to be a dangerous business. In all the history of English poetry, there can have been few braver, more extraordinary undertakings than his at Ripon. His double duty was now clear: as an officer, he had to return to the front; as a poet, he had to write about it. By day he trained for the fighting that would probably kill him, and in the warm spring evenings he walked down a quiet country lane to his secret retreat, a windowless room where he could open his 'inward eye' to the experiences that had almost driven him mad a year earlier. There was pleasure in it, as Wordsworth had promised, the pleasure of being driven by the poetic impulse and using a fast-developing talent to the full, but there was also terror. Alone and with no support, Wilfred summoned up the phantoms of the mind, and as they gathered in the shadowy corners of the room he forced them to show themselves and obey his will.

'The enormity of the present Battle numbs me,' he told Susan. The numbness would have to be an essential element in his poetic method. Borrowing form and language from Wordsworth's 'Immortality' ode, a poem about the loss of imagination, he wrote 'Insensibility', describing the unimaginative state of the battle-hardened soldier.[3] 'We wise' – poets, officers –

> who with a thought besmirch
> Blood over all our soul,
> How should we see our task
> But through his blunt and lashless eyes?

Understanding the look on soldiers' faces, 'more terrible than terror … like a dead rabbit's', was crucial. Insensibility could be a means of control rather than denial, allowing strong feelings to emerge in a poem without destroying the writer. It was nevertheless a crime for non-combatants to be insensible, and Wilfred ended his ode with an angry, Shelleyan denunciation of civilian 'dullards'. 'By choice they made themselves immune / To pity.' He had moved far beyond Sassoonish satire. By Easter Sunday, 31 March 1918, he had written one new poem in his attic, planned another and revised much of his existing work. Between then and his leaving Ripon in early June, he seems to have composed or revised virtually all his war poems, except the two or three that were written later. His manuscripts, many of them fair copies heavily overlaid with alterations, bear witness to his passionate industry. New work at Borrage Lane almost certainly included 'Greater Love', 'Arms and the Boy', 'The Send-Off', 'Strange Meeting', 'Mental Cases' and 'Futility'. 'Wild with All Regrets' was recast as 'A Terre'. 'Exposure' was completed. The new poems were markedly different from those of 1917, being more expansive, more elegiac, and applicable to any nation in any war, yet they were still securely rooted in personal experience.

The earliest known Ripon manuscript is the fragment 'As bronze may be much beautified', dated Good Friday at Borrage Lane and written on the back of one of the old sonnets that Wilfred had been working on at Scarborough. 'Greater Love', also first drafted on the backs of sonnets, was probably another Easter poem. Here, as in the fragment, he shows his intense feeling for the young bodies that were being destroyed at the front, but he always had doubts about 'Greater Love'. Despite having wanted to write on the soldier-Christ theme since 1914, he had recognised even in 1917 that the image was 'a distorted view to hold in a general way'. 'God so loved the world that he gave his only begotten son' was the Church's Easter message, but Wilfred changed it in a letter home: 'God so hated the world that He gave several millions of English-begotten sons, that whosoever believeth in them should not perish, but have a comfortable life.' News had just come through that a long-range gun had been shelling Paris, hitting a church during the Good Friday service: 'pretty work,' Wilfred said.

I wonder how many a *frau, fraulein knabe und madchen* Colin will kill in his time?

Johnny de la Touche leaves school this term, I hear, and goes to prepare for the Indian Army.

He must be a creature of killable age by now.

Thoughts of Colin, Johnny and the children playing soldiers in the lane probably lie behind 'Arms and the Boy'. Another Ripon poem, 'The Send-Off', also seems to reflect its local origin: Wilfred must often have seen drafts of soldiers being marched away from the 'upland camp' on Hellwath Common to the railway on the first stage of their journey to France. 'Down the close darkening lanes they sang their way / To the siding-shed …' The men go 'secretly, like wrongs hushed-up', their uniforms decorated with white spring flowers, emblems of good luck and death, the ambivalent gift of women (or 'we mourners' or 'cowards' in draft work) who have seen them pass. Seven drafts or part-drafts of the poem survive, recording their author's detailed attention to every word. Some phrases came to him instantly, some had to be 'long "waited" for', some were the result of hard labour, yet such is his mature skill that it is impossible to guess from the final version which lines caused him the most difficulty.

Wilfred's deepest response to the March 1918 disaster is 'Strange Meeting'. The poem is a vision, full of literary references, but also an intensely personal war dream, close to the nightmares he must often have suffered. Many earlier poets had told stories of a living man descending into the underworld, finding a cave full of sleeping warriors, or meeting a dead spirit who tells the 'truth untold' about the life that has been lost. Wilfred is remembering strange meetings in classical mythology, Dante, Spenser, Keats, Shelley and elsewhere, including Monro's latest book, *Strange Meetings* (the poem's title is probably taken from Shelley, as Dennis Welland suggested long ago, but it may also be a gesture to Monro, a poet to whom Wilfred had been indebted since 1911). Yet Wilfred had also entered the underworld himself, in sleep at least since Dunsden and later in reality, in the German dugout, the ruined cellar, the hole 'just big enough to lie in' at Savy Wood and the haunted corridors at Craiglockhart.

Among the thousands of poems written during the Great War, there are very few about the poet-soldier meeting his dead victim, fewer still in which the two men talk to each other, and perhaps none except 'Strange Meeting' in which the killer stands his ground, accepting the truth of what he has done. No other 1914–18 poet went as far as Wilfred into the 'inwardness of war'. The journey took him into his own mind, and the figure of the Other, the strange friend with 'fixed eyes' and tortured face, brings together many of his dreams: the bulging eyes of the sentry at Serre, the 'white eyes writhing' of the gassed man, the frozen eyes of 'half-known faces' on Redan Ridge, and behind these and other wartime horrors the petrifying stare of the Gorgon-Despondency at Dunsden, the blind 'wide eyes' of the mermaid's statue (a phrase repeated in draft work for 'Exposure': 'their wide eyes are ice'), the 'phantasms' of 1913 and the agonised descriptions of hell in 'Perseus'. Poetry – and ergotherapy – required the poet to look steadily at terror, and as he did so, like Keats under the blind gaze of Moneta, he was granted the vision he sought.

The deliberate universalising of 'Strange Meeting' prevents the poem from being read as purely biographical. Wilfred would have known literary examples of men meeting their doubles, an encounter that was often believed to be fatal, but the poem is an elegy not just for himself but for all poets and visionaries lost in war, and for the healing powers they could have used for the benefit of the world. The Other's speech incorporates a version of 'Earth's wheels', the exhortation Wilfred had addressed to Sassoon at the end of 1917, but the tenses are altered from 'will' to 'would have'. The change in the war has destroyed any hope that poets could keep out of the fighting to tell 'the truth untold … the pity of war, the pity war distilled'; instead, the two men have killed each other, and when they meet in hell the killing is re-enacted. Once again the Other's face is twisted in the staring smile of agony, and he raises his hands as if to parry or bless. The weapon that had killed him the day before had been a frown ('so you frowned … through me') as well as a sword or bayonet, and now it is his own expression ('his dead smile') that tells the killer that the place is hell. Wilde had written in *The Ballad of Reading Gaol* that 'each man kills the thing he loves, … / Some do it with a bitter look', lines that Wilfred had partly quoted in what seems to be preliminary work for 'Strange Meeting'. The destructive force in war does not derive from weapons. The killer is himself killed with a look, knowing that the 'pity of war' will die with him. His strange friend and former enemy, seeing he is dead, invites him to sleep as a lover might, a seemingly peaceful close that is not in fact peaceful at all, for sleep in this cave of the damned is 'encumbered' with dreams.

~

Wilfred knew his chances of survival would be slight if he were to be sent back to France, but for a moment in early April 1918 he seemed to be in much less danger than his brother Harold, who was expecting to be sent on a top-secret naval mission (actually the Zeebrugge raid, for which Harold was not in the end chosen). Wilfred was granted forty-eight hours' leave, and on about 9 April he arrived at Mahim for what was to be a last family reunion. All six Owens were present: Tom, weary and anxious but trying to be his old cheery self; Susan, motherly and worried, urging everyone to eat the special meal she and Mary had laboured over; Mary, tiny and silent; Colin, who had left school and was doing farmwork until July, when he would be eighteen and old enough to join the RAF; Harold, still a midshipman;[4] and Wilfred. When supper was over, the two eldest brothers were left alone to talk. It was their last chance to be open with each other.

Harold's account of the ensuing conversation, added to *Journey from Obscurity* at a late stage, is designed to deal with speculation that his brother might have been homosexual.[5] Wilfred's dedication was like that of a Roman Catholic priest, according to Harold, and it required celibacy. The conversation begins with Wilfred as the ideal war poet, saying he intends to return to the front even though he knows he will be killed: 'it's the only place that I can make my protest from' (he was in fact delighted to be promised a home posting a few weeks later). The two brothers then move on cautiously to talking about sex, Wilfred readily admitting that he likes women 'very much'. Harold expresses puzzlement about homosexuality, and Wilfred replies in astonishment that by chance he, too, had intended to raise 'this disgusting subject', hoping that 'with your seafaring experience you might know more about this sort of thing than I do'. 'However,' Wilfred goes on, 'we obviously can't help each other so let's talk of other things.' Neither brother can find much else to say.

Harold's record of this dialogue does not quite tally with a panic-stricken letter he had earlier written to Edmund Blunden, begging for help in suppressing rumours about Wilfred. Harold says in the letter that he is sure Wilfred was never a 'homo-sexualist'. In the course of a long 'academic' discussion of the subject during their last evening together, he had 'taxed' Wilfred about it and Wilfred had denied personal involvement, saying he was only interested '(again academically)' because he wondered why clever men so often seemed to find homosexuality attractive.[6]

Both versions of the story suggest that Harold had missed the point. Wilfred probably wanted to exchange confidences. Sassoon had come out to a younger brother before the war, finding to his relief that the brother was also gay. Unfortunately Harold's knowledge of homosexuality was limited to sights that had shocked him in school lavatories and the crew quarters of his ships, and his revulsion would have been clear to Wilfred, who promptly changed the subject. Wilfred must have been disappointed, and Harold remembers him as nervy and reclusive next morning, avoiding their father. In all the years that followed, Harold was never able to cope with the thought that Wilfred had not been heterosexual. Nevertheless their last evening together was not quite as reticent as he later believed. 'Harold has had some terrific adventures,' Wilfred told Leslie Gunston, 'but chiefly on land: & not connected with the war.'

While the brothers were at Mahim, a renewed German offensive was breaking out in France, alarmingly near the coast. On 11 April Haig issued his famous 'backs to the wall' order, urging the exhausted troops to fight on. They did fight on, taking enormous casualties and filling gaps in the line with makeshift forces, but it seemed to people at home that defeat was imminent. Wilfred returned to Ripon and continued his training. He had already been moved up from the sixth, lowest class of fitness, and his accurate responses to trick orders from the drill sergeant convinced him that his mind had fully recovered from shell-shock. However, the doctors were not yet convinced about his physical state. 'There is no doubt,' he told Leslie, '– from the elaborate soundings to which I'm subjected – that my heart is shock-affected.' Leslie, saved from military service by his own suspected heart defect, had just got an enviable job as a trainee architect, and Wilfred could not resist making the occasional dig at his conscience.

Having started by loathing the camp, Wilfred soon found ways of enjoying it. There were comfortable chairs in the common-room hut and sometimes a trio playing 'most lovely music'. Priestley, Bainbrigge and the Grays had all given him introductions to local friends of theirs, and the young Scots private whom he had befriended in Scarborough had told him to call on two kindly old ladies who would give 'a mighty good tea to anything in khaki'. But the war was ever-present. The Ripon streets echoed incessantly to the noise of bands, tramping feet, horses, and the wheels of limbers and heavy guns. One fine Saturday Wilfred walked miles to Aldborough to see the Roman remains, and he thought sadly of visits to Uriconium with Stanley Webb, who had recently been killed in action.

Hidden in his attic, he sometimes worked on lyrics as a change from war poems. 'A Tear Song', an ironic little ballad in Wilde's manner, probably dates from Ripon, as does an elaborately-rhymed 'Ode' for an unnamed poet. A rough fragment beginning 'O true to the old equities' describes a youth who feels within his shoes the breeze of winged sandals, an allusion to the sandals worn by Perseus. Wilfred still hoped to finish 'Perseus': the title is among four 'Projects' that he listed on 5 May. The other three projects are to write blank verse plays on old Welsh themes, using Irish and English plays by Yeats and Tennyson as models; 'Idyls in Prose'; and 'Collected Poems, 1919'. Apart from the last, these were old-fashioned schemes to be thinking about in 1918; he was still unaware of Modernist poetry.[7]

By early May Wilfred had reached the third division of fitness. He now had well over twenty finished war poems, enough for a small book, and leave was available, so he decided to take them to London. This time Nellie Burton had a vacancy at 40 Half Moon Street: Wilfred was able to occupy a whole flat above Ross's for three nights, from Thursday 16 May, for a mere 7s 6d including breakfast. He had a 'glorious' time on the Friday, lunching with Ross at the Reform and spending all afternoon at the War Office with Scott Moncrieff, who was more confident than ever about a home posting, having recently arranged for Graves to be given a safe job training cadets in Wales. If Wilfred felt any twinges of conscience at such a prospect, his mind was soon put at ease. He had done his bit for the war effort, his London friends would have told him, and his duty now was to stay at home and write. With a 'glorious' sense of relief, he agreed to let his name be put forward for an instructorship as soon as his course was over. He had a future after all.

The new poems had a 'magnificent' reception in Ross's golden room that evening, and it was agreed that Wilfred should send typescripts to Heinemann, an ingenious scheme because Heinemann would certainly send them to Ross for an opinion. The newest poem of all, 'The Deranged', soon to become 'Mental Cases', was sensational. Someone suggested it should be sent to *The English Review*, but More Adey disagreed, saying the *Review* should not be encouraged. Wilfred told Susan afterwards that five years earlier this would have turned his head, but now celebrity was the last thing he wanted. '*Fame is the recognition of one's peers.*' Such recognition was beginning. He had the 'silent and immortal' friendship of Sassoon and Graves, and Scott Moncrieff had recently mentioned him in a review alongside them, Nichols and Osbert Sitwell as one of 'Our younger fame'.

Sitwell was a friend of Sassoon's and had started writing satires against the war, so Ross telephoned him to come round, warning him that the visitor was rather shy. Sitwell took to Wilfred at once, remembering him later as a sturdy, youthful-looking figure, with deep eyes set wide apart under a broad forehead, 'tawny, rather sanguine skin', an eager yet bashful manner and a ready smile. Wilfred's provincial origin was no doubt as obvious to Sitwell, Old Etonian and heir to a baronetcy, as it had been to Sassoon. However, the former Technical student was treated as a friend and equal by everyone at Half Moon Street, and he had more invitations to meals than he could manage. One invitation that he was able to accept seems to have been from Osbert, to meet the other two Sitwells, Edith and Sacheverell.[8] Wilfred's next letters glow with elation: he was beginning to be recognised by his peers, his poems were going to be published and he was going to survive the war.

There may have been another factor in Wilfred's excitement. His letters record nothing of how he spent the rest of his weekend, except that in two days and nights he only got three hours sleep. He had found on two previous occasions that conversation in the golden room tended to continue into the small hours, and this time, as he only had to go upstairs to bed, he could safely enjoy his host's brandy. Long afterwards Graves recalled having been told by Ross that Scott Moncrieff had once got Wilfred drunk and seduced him, to Wilfred's subsequent distress. Certainly Scott Moncrieff was not slow to exploit opportunities, and he was strongly attracted to Wilfred. He was a frequent visitor at Half Moon Street, and his current lodgings were in Arlington Street, just across Piccadilly. On Sunday 19 May he presented Wilfred with a cryptic sonnet, later writing at least two more: all three poems seem to imply a brief sexual relationship that had somehow failed.

The first sonnet, a manuscript in Scott Moncrieff's hand with the date neatly added by Wilfred, contains an apology:

> *Blame not my eyes that, from their high aim lowered*
> *Yet saw there more than other eyes may see:*
> *Nor blame head heart hands feet that, overpowered*
> *Fell at thy feet to draw thy heart to me.*
> *Blame not me all that all was found unworthy ...*

The second sonnet, written within three weeks of Wilfred's London visit, assures its unnamed subject that he has kept his honour despite having been in 'an honest House of Shame'; 'we' had killed friendship to make way for love, and had slept together, weary, in the new-dug grave, but 'with the dawn you rose, and clean escaped, / Strode honourably homeward'. The third sonnet refers mysteriously to 'shame' and 'scandal'. Rumours about whatever had happened may have got round among Ross's friends, and perhaps Ross did indeed pass the story on to Graves.[9]

Writing to Wilfred on 26 May, Scott Moncrieff explained that the poems were not only 'vivisection really – you and me', flowing from the 'fount of passion', but also an attempt to test a theory about Shakespeare's sonnets.

Wilde had argued brilliantly that Shakespeare had been in love with, and rejected by, the sonnets' 'onlie begetter', 'Mr W.H.', and Scott Moncrieff seems to have felt that he himself was now in much the same predicament with 'Mr W.O.' (as he later called Wilfred). According to Wilde, Shakespeare's aim had been to immortalise his young friend, even though they could not be lovers. More modestly, Scott Moncrieff hoped his own sonnets would live by reflecting Wilfred's future fame. 'Part of thy praise, shall these my dumb rhymes live / In thee, themselves as life without thee vain?' Wilfred probably enjoyed the flattery. The fact that he kept the first sonnet and dated it suggests he may not have been quite as displeased by Scott Moncrieff's advances as Graves later believed.

It may be, though, that there was an element of shame in Wilfred's feelings as he travelled back to Ripon on the evening of 19 May. There was another heavy air raid on London that night, causing over two hundred casualties; it would in fact be the last, but no one in Britain yet had any idea that the war might be turning in the Allies' favour. It was not quite honourable to be using a friend to wangle a safe job. Moreover, Scott Moncrieff's motives were not quite honourable either, as Wilfred perhaps now had good cause to know. On the other hand, there could be years of productive work ahead. Scott Moncrieff had promised life and fame, and Wilfred had himself argued in 1914–15 and again to Sassoon in December 1917 that a poet was more useful to the nation alive than dead. In any case, the Nation at Home, as it was often called, hardly seemed worth fighting for. The performance of *Salome* had taken place the day after Haig's 'backs to the wall' order, the worst possible moment. Pemberton Billing's newspaper, *The Vigilante*, had inevitably reported Millard's conviction for homosexuality, and had published verses by Lord Alfred Douglas attacking Ross. The actress Maud Allan's libel action, launched at Bow Street on 6 April, was due to be heard on 29 May, and it was attracting immense, spiteful public interest. Wilfred must have shared in the feelings of disgust and apprehension at Half Moon Street.

Nothing could be done on Wilfred's behalf at the War Office until he was certified fit, so he was pleased to be moved up to the second division soon after his return to camp. Graves wrote to Sassoon on the 23rd that Scott Moncrieff was going to send Wilfred to Wales, and three days later Scott Moncrieff himself told Wilfred that a job might be going at a cadet school in Oxford.

~

Wilfred started planning a book, although he took it slowly, remembering his cousin's rashness. In answer to hopeful enquiries from home, he said he was determined not to hurry into print, explaining that he took himself 'solemnly' now, and that he was writing so much better than a year ago that for every poem he added to the end of his list he took one away from the beginning of it. One of his lists shows him putting his poems into a carefully designed sequence, giving each one a 'motive'. The scheme would have made the book unique, the only collection of 1914–18 verse designed as a course of re-education, taking the reader from 'Protest' and anger to 'Cheerfulness' (of the troops) and 'Description', and then through 'Grief' to 'Philosophy' or meditation. The end result was intended to be pity, 'the pity of war, the [one thing] war distilled', for the aim of poetry, as Shelley had said, was to make people share imaginatively in the experience of others and to pity them. Without such fellow-feeling there could be no reform.

Wilfred roughed out some notes for a preface. Prefaces to books of war poetry had usually made grand statements about heroes and national glory, offering traditional consolations, but Wilfred's would be different. 'This book is not about heroes,' he began. 'English Poetry is not yet fit to speak of them ... Above all' – and here he was thinking of the sort of poetry he had often enjoyed writing with Leslie – 'I am not concerned with Poetry. My subject is War and the pity of War. The Poetry is in the pity ... Yet these elegies are to this generation in no sense consolatory. They may be to the next ... All a poet can do today is warn [children]. That is why the true [War] Poet must be truthful.' It was characteristic of him to choose children as his audience. He would not tell the war generation and its parents what they wanted to hear, but the future might listen to his poems, which were both warnings and elegies.

He thought of calling his book 'English Elegies' or 'With Lightning and with Music', a quotation from Shelley's elegy for Keats. He was as much a disciple of the great Romantics as he had ever been. His poems would be as shocking as lightning and as beautiful as music, albeit the music of 'the advanced composers', and they would endure, like Keats's Grecian Urn, to tell the truth. Nevertheless he needed a less archaic-sounding title, and he settled on a bleakly modern one, 'Disabled and Other Poems'. Then, thinking back over the friendships and allegiances that had helped to shape his poethood, he made a note of people he would send the book to: Leslie, Dr Rayner, Tailhade, Sassoon, Graves, the Poetry Bookshop; Mrs Gray, Dr Brock, Mrs Fullerton, Miss Wyer, Lady Margaret Sackville and the Astronomer Royal in Edinburgh; Bainbrigge, Meiklejohn, Wells, Bennett; Johnny de la Touche; Nichols, Yeats, John Drinkwater.[10] But his plan would have to incubate for a while. He would have plenty of time to write in Oxford.

Two of the last poems to be finished in the Ripon attic were probably 'Futility' and 'Mental Cases'. The latter, 'my terrific poem' as Wilfred described it on 25 May, vividly illustrates how his wartime work grew out of his earlier poetry and reading. 'Mental Cases' no doubt contains memories of actual shell-shock victims, but its portrait of madmen, 'purgatorial shadows', is closely based on 'Purgatorial Passions', the description of hell that he had probably drafted in 1916. The imagery of fixed skull-smiles and dreadful eyes also derives from the 'Perseus' fragments and earlier poems and nightmares. Some of the new lines added at Ripon are as Decadent as anything in Wilfred's 1914–16 work. The simile of dawn breaking open 'like a wound that bleeds afresh' would have been admired by Tailhade and by the young Rupert Brooke, who had written to a Decadent poet in 1907 about sunsets being like a 'suppurating sore … opened afresh'.[11] As in 'Strange Meeting', Wilfred prevents 'Mental Cases' from referring exclusively to 1914–18 by giving the poem a Dantesque framework. Once again a living visitor enters hell and asks questions, this time as though entering a hospital ward rather than a dugout. In the Cary translation of the *Inferno* that both Keats and Wilfred knew, Dante asks Virgil, 'Instructor! who / Are these by the black air so scourg'd?' and in 'Mental Cases' the questioner asks, 'Who are these? Why sit they here in twilight?' The poem's authority is rooted in the long Western tradition of moral epic, as well as in Wilfred's own experience. There is no arguing with the guide's final answer to the visitor's opening question:

> *– Thus their hands are plucking at each other;*
> *Picking at the rope-knouts of their scourging;*
> *Snatching after us who smote them, brother,*
> *Pawing us who dealt them war and madness.*

'Brother' because the two speakers are perhaps to be understood as fellow soldiers and poets, as in 'Strange Meeting', but the word strikes at the reader's conscience.

~

May ended with a burst of magnificent weather, and Wilfred wrote home for a tennis racket. 'This is the pleasantest camp I know.' He went bathing in the River Ure, where an over-enthusiastic Artist cadet dived into shallow water, cutting his head open, and Wilfred sent him off to hospital in a cab.[12] Another youngster to be befriended was a drummer named George. Wilfred's account of him to Susan is now, predictably, 'missing', but George came from Dunsden and may well have been in the 1911–12 Scripture Union class. Meeting him must have been a moving experience. They talked for hours, sharing old memories.

Wilfred went into town to get presents for his sister and father, whose joint birthday was on 30 May, but he could not decide on anything, so he sent 'congratulations to dear Father' and asked Susan to do the shopping. Then he sent a letter and a pound note to Mary, explaining he had no idea what she was interested in 'beyond Mother'. She needed 'some tie to Mother Earth', he told her, thinking of Antaeus, and if she thought that was a pagan suggestion she should say so. That led him on to his current notion of religion, which

> consists in a sort of beautiful and Christ-like Intervention between the disputing parties Paul of Tarsus and the ruined but skilful silversmiths of Ephesus. Very gently I should make some clever remark which should send the silversmiths contentedly back to their beautiful work, and give Paul a contract for as many tents as the army required for subjugating the Gauls, and exiling the soldiery.

It was better to design a church, Wilfred added, than to sit in it once a week. All this upset Mary, so he had to write again a few days later to apologise.

And then, in a brief postscript dated 4 June, he hurriedly announced that he had been graded fit by a Medical Board and ordered back to his unit. 'He has considerably improved since the last Board,' the doctors noted in their report. 'There is now no disability. Report forthwith to O.C. 5th Res Bn Manchester Regt Scarborough. Railway Warrant issued.' There was time for little more than one brief leave-taking. 'Drummer George of Dunsden *wept* when I said goodbye,' Wilfred told Susan afterwards. '(I had seen him 3 times!) This you must not tell *anybody*. Such things are not for this generation of vipers.'

18

Normal Again

Scarborough

JUNE–AUGUST 1918

'Gratified to know you are normal again,' Tom Owen wrote from Shrewsbury on hearing that Wilfred had been passed fit. Wilfred winced, but he too could feel some satisfaction. More than a year after he had sheltered in Savy Wood among the remains of Second Lieutenant Gaukroger, he was free at last from the stigma of being an apparently unwounded convalescent. However, the pleasures of convalescence were also at an end. When he got back to Scarborough on 5 June he found that the officers had moved back to the barracks at Burniston, where there was now almost enough room for them as a result of the crisis in France. Colonel Mitchell had decreed that all fit officers should occupy tents. From now on, except for a few brief intervals, Wilfred's life would be the comfortless one of a serving soldier.

'Had a rather pleasant *arrival*.' Priestley had been given a flat in the seaward-facing villa that housed the officers' mess, of which he was still President, and he welcomed his former assistant with a private tea – 'fine China tea, – in priceless porcelain'.[1] Wilfred had left him negotiating for antiques, and the latest bargain, the chest of drawers, was waiting to be admired by its new owner. Many of the officers who had been at the Clarence Gardens were now in France, and Wilfred was perhaps secretly relieved not to have to see them again. Unfortunately some of his orderlies and drummers had gone as well, their jobs now being done by WAACs.[2] Everyone was at full stretch. There would be no chance for visits to antique shops or the oyster bar, and Priestley could offer little help except to put the apartment at his disposal whenever time allowed.

Wilfred's tent was on the cinder-surfaced parade ground, a yard or two from the main gate, so it was full of gritty dust. Reveille was at six, and duties were incessant until the evening, 'after which we are too tired to move'. 'I cannot keep alive here long,' he wrote miserably to Susan on 6 June. 'Here one does not live at all. One eats, (badly) sleeps, (well) and works like a demented piece of clockwork.' The war still seemed to be heading for disaster (the Cabinet was even considering a British withdrawal from France). Trained recruits were desperately needed and the Colonel was driving his officers hard. But Wilfred felt sure of getting a safe job fairly soon. Not even bothering to unpack his books and papers, he informed the War Office that he was now fit, and Scott Moncrieff duly recommended him to the authorities as an instructor.

As at Ripon, the shock of camp life quickly wore off, and within a few days Wilfred's letters were sounding more cheerful. He was far senior to the other second lieutenants, so Priestley managed to get him moved to the only single tent, 'with long grass & buttercups all round to act as dust-screens'. For the next few weeks he was assigned to familiar duties on the firing range, thanks to a lieutenant who remembered his expertise at Fleetwood in 1916. 'Today [has] been Revolver Shooting,' Wilfred wrote on 21 June, '& it may be a final proof of my normality (for Father's satisfaction) that I shot better than most.' When not on the range he had to spend hours putting his platoon through its basic training, supervising drill, checking kits and giving simple lessons in map-reading and other essentials.

New recruits, mostly teenagers, arrived from the Lancashire mill towns, 'awful specimens, almost green-pale'. If Wilfred and his NCOs worked efficiently, the newcomers would soon turn into 'mahogany swashbucklers' like the men who had finished their training. He chose as his servant 'a Herefordshire gardener's-boy, with the garden still lying in loamy beds about his ears'. It was pleasing to find a few 'Shropshire lads', too, and to see that they and some Welshmen were 'indeed, look you, I am prout to say, the muscle, as well as the voice, look you, of the company'. When the influenza epidemic reached the barracks, Wilfred was unaffected, even though the boys dropped on parade like flies and every spare space seemed 'carpeted with huddled blanketed forms'. He went for a cross-country run ('Have seldom enjoyed any exercise so much') and wrote a little poem about it. The easiest way to socialise with the troops was to play games, when all distinctions of rank were temporarily suspended. He refereed a football match and played cricket 'with the lads'.

His fitness doomed him. Encouraging messages continued to come from the War Office for a while. Oxford ceased to be a possibility, but he was told he might be sent for training at the School of Instruction at Berkhamsted, and then as an instructor to the Artists' Rifles or its rival battalion, the Inns of Court. But on 21 June, and again three days later, he said he had heard no more. After that, his surviving letters make no further mention of a home posting, although he must have told his mother something of what had happened. The General Staff had approved Scott Moncrieff's recommendation, but the Adjutant-General's department had rejected it on the grounds that all fit men were needed at the front.[3] Scott Moncrieff no doubt tried to be reassuring. 'I shall likely be here another month,' Wilfred wrote home on the 24th, '– unless drafted out, which is *not* probable'. Perhaps it was only coincidence that his war dreams began again, caused, he said, by the flapping of the tent canvas all night or 'the hideous faces of the Advancing Revolver Targets I fired at last week'.

~

There was no time to copy out poems for typing, nor to complete plans for a book, and Ross was too distracted to be of any help. The Pemberton Billing trial had been held amid extensive publicity during Wilfred's last days at Ripon. Alfred Douglas had repeatedly insulted Ross from the witness box, calling him a sodomite, and had described Wilde as 'the greatest force for evil for 350 years'. The jury had found for Billing, who was greeted as a hero by cheering crowds, and on the day Wilfred arrived at the barracks the newspapers were rejoicing at a great moral victory. Ross remarked bitterly that the public was kicking Oscar's corpse to make up for German successes. He was deeply distressed, and friends were anxious for his health. Wilfred would not have felt able to remind him of the plot to send 'Disabled and Other Poems' to Heinemann.

Fortunately there were other possibilities for publication. On 15 June 'Futility' and 'Hospital Barge' appeared in *The Nation*, and on the same day a letter came from the Sitwells asking for contributions to the forthcoming volume of Edith's anthology, *Wheels*. The Sitwells had been impressed by a draft of 'Mental Cases', shown to them by Scott Moncrieff. Wilfred happened to have a rare free morning, so he retreated to Priestley's rooms and unpacked his manuscripts after all. Then he went into town to look for *Wheels*, having never seen any poetry by the Sitwells. The main bookshop regarded the anthology as unsaleable even though the Sitwells had a house in Scarborough and were well-known locally, but Wilfred insisted so strongly on ordering a copy that the assistant caused heads to turn by exclaiming she was sure he was 'Osbert himself'. 'No, Madam,' Wilfred replied smugly; 'the book is by a friend of mine, Miss Sitwell.'

Osbert sent a little epigram about Clemenceau, the French Prime Minister, being satisfied with the crucifixion (Clemenceau was often reported as being satisfied with events at the front). 'I rehearsed your very fine epigram upon our Mess President – rather a friend of mine,' Wilfred replied, self-consciously adopting the casual yet sophisticated tone of a Half Moon Street regular. 'He did not immediately recognize Jesus. The rest of the Mess would not of course know the name of Monsieur Clemenceau … May I send [the epigram] to a French youth who might translate and circulate it where it would be appreciated?' Having thus presented himself as a friend of the Mess President, the only other cultured officer in camp, and of an equally cultured French correspondent (presumably Pierre Berthaud), Wilfred composed a famous paragraph, an elaborate Wildean conceit, taking his cue from the epigram.

For 14 hours yesterday I was at work – teaching Christ to lift his cross by numbers, and how to adjust his crown; and not to imagine he thirst till after the last halt; I attended his Supper to see that there were no complaints; and inspected his feet to see that they should be worthy of the nails. I see to it that he is dumb and stands to attention before his accusers. With a piece of silver I buy him every day, and with maps I make him familiar with the topography of Golgotha.

Wheels 1917 was Wilfred's introduction to Modernist poetry. Intended as a counter-blast to *Georgian Poetry*, it was the first English avant-garde anthology. The contributors, led by the three Sitwells, were in open revolt not only against conventional techniques and subjects but also against the war. Unlike Wilfred, they were evidently aware of recent work by T.S. Eliot and others, and they had picked up the fashion for street imagery: 'the sad houses sleep', 'Places to scribble our names on, seats, lamp-posts and walls', 'The weathercocks fly helter-skelter'. Keen as always to learn from a new style, Wilfred made his first and only attempt at a Modernist poem, although he was never able to finish it.

> The roads also have their wistful rest
> When the weathercocks perch still & roost ...
> The old houses muse of the old days ...
>   And the dead scribble on walls ...

That 'also' may imply a link with 'The Kind Ghosts', a late-July poem about a woman sleeping in a palace built out of the corpses of young men.

> She sleeps on soft, last breaths; but no ghost looms
> Out of the stillness of her palace wall,
> Her wall of boys on boys and dooms on dooms.
>
> She dreams of golden gardens and sweet glooms,
> Not marvelling why her roses never fall
> Nor what red mouths were torn to make their blooms.

With its ornate sound effects, carefully marked in the manuscript, and its ghastly flowers, 'The Kind Ghosts' is more Decadent than Modernist, but it is in the mood of *Wheels*. The sleeping woman, presumably Britannia, the Nation at Home, embodies something of Susan Owen, resting at home while her sons risk death to keep her safe. Colin Owen had just been accepted by the RAF, to Wilfred's regret, and Harold, promoted at last to the lowest possible officer rank, Acting Sub-Lieutenant, was about to be sent to a ship off the coast of South Africa. Susan's passivity and un-questioning respectability seemed to symbolise the current condition of England.

Wilfred's sense of belonging to a secret brotherhood deepened during his last months at Scarborough. Devoted though he still was to his parents, he knew there was much he could never tell them. As a soldier he was cut off from all civilians, and in the battalion perhaps only Priestley knew he wrote poetry. Maybe Priestley also knew and understood about Half Moon Street, but such matters had to be kept the closest secret of all. It was a relief to exchange letters with Scott Moncrieff, who understood nearly everything.

Scott Moncrieff had been prompted by Wilfred's use of pararhyme to start translating one of the great medieval war poems, the heroic *Song of Roland*, with its Old French assonances. He sent the opening verses to Wilfred with a long dedication to 'Mr W.O … my master in assonance … that you may cover the faults in my handiwork with the protection of your name'. 'Any success I may have had,' Scott Moncrieff later wrote of the translation, '… was entirely due to Owen's example, criticism and encouragement.' Wilfred clearly deserves some credit for Scott Moncrieff's brilliant career as a translator, which began with *Roland* and culminated in the 1920s with a celebrated version of Proust. In return, the *Roland* translation may have influenced Wilfred, making him think of writing about heroes, a subject he had rejected in his Ripon preface on the grounds that English poetry was 'not yet fit to speak of them'. Not *yet* – but he began to imagine a poem that might be adequate to the courage of the men who were still holding the line, noting down two possible titles: 'Attack', 'Spring Offensive'.[4] The *Roland* dedication expressed the hope that the ancient *chanson* would teach modern British soldiers to 'rely upon our own resources, and to fight uncomplaining when support is witheld from us; to live … honourably and to die gallantly'. If that was a salute to the armies in France, it was also a message to Wilfred, who was facing the ever-growing likelihood of being drafted overseas.

Word came at last from Sassoon, who was once again in France, having been sent back from Palestine with thousands of other reinforcements after the March crisis. His latest book, *Counter-Attack*, mostly poems Wilfred had seen at Craiglockhart, was due out at any minute. Two letters from him arrived at the end of June, apparently the first time either poet had heard from the other since 1917. He was so far out of touch with Wilfred's whereabouts that he had addressed one of the letters to Craiglockhart, whence it had twice been forwarded to Dublin after some other Owen. 'Have you met Wilfred Owen, my little friend, whose verses were in the *Nation* recently?' he wrote to Osbert Sitwell in July. 'He is so nice and shy, and fervent about poetry, which he is quite good at, and will do *very well* some day.'[5] Sassoon had still not got the measure of Wilfred's poetry, but Wilfred was delighted to hear from him and wrote back as soon as possible, doing his best to sound cheerful because Sassoon sounded gloomy.

Sassoon had enclosed a little poem, 'Testament', in effect an acknowledgement that the German onslaught had made further protest useless. 'For the last time I say – War is not glorious, / Though lads march out superb and fall victorious … / O my heart, / Be still; you have cried your cry; you have played your part.'[6] Wilfred had no intention of telling his own heart to be still: if Sassoon had fallen silent, that was all the more reason for another poet to keep writing. Yet Sassoon was as right as ever that war was not glorious, however superb the lads were. 'Spring Offensive' was going to be a difficult project.

Work continued relentlessly.

I dare not go out in the evening (we are not free till 8.30 or 9 p.m.) for fear of getting to bed late, which would mean disastrous inability to get up on the Bugle. For the same reason I dare not begin to read earnestly or write earnestly in the evening. I am haunted by bugles and startled by drums and perturbed by the tramp of feet every moment of the daylight hours.

A ship was torpedoed offshore, but Wilfred was only too glad not to be called out '(such is the spirit of the Army)'. On top of his routine duties he had to attend a gas course for a week, with an exam on the Saturday morning. That afternoon he had to pay the coast patrols, so he scrounged a lift on a motorbike, and felt envious of the patrol officers. 'They complain of Loneliness. My stars!' All he could hope for was a few hours of free time on Sunday afternoons and, very occasionally, a hasty treat of tea and perhaps strawberries in Priestley's rooms. Now that he was taking a full share of responsibilities, it was absurd that he was still only a second lieutenant. Priestley and others must have wondered whether there had been a mistake somewhere. 'I still wear one pip,' Wilfred said in mid-July, 'because nobody knows whether I am Lieut. or not.' But no promotion came through.

When the Battalion Messing Officer went on leave for ten days, the former Major Domo was the obvious man to replace him. Wilfred became 'responsible to the Colonel & my conscience for the feeding of a thousand "souls". (I wish men's Souls were as hungry as these Bodies.)' His team this time was mostly female, 'a dozen brawny W.A.A.C.s' as day cooks, with three men for night work and a couple of boys to stoke the ovens. Two skilled corporals dealt with orders and the complex business of rationing, a task made worse when an order came through that boys under nineteen should get extra meat and bread. Wilfred had to battle desperately against dirt and disorder, even putting on overalls himself to whitewash the cookhouse, which stank sickeningly in the hot weather. Needing to appear all-powerful and all-knowing, he kept up bursts of strafing, hearing his voice take on the tone his mother used when she scolded her servant at Mahim, but the women were unused to army discipline and tended to weep or run away, making him fiercer than ever. 'I'd like to smack 'is brown face forrim,' one of them said when his back was turned.

While Wilfred slaved to feed the battalion, his mother took one of her periodic holidays with the Gunstons at Alpenrose. Urging her to speak out against the war while she was there, he recommended Sassoon's new book as salutary reading for Leslie. Leslie and his brother Gordon were still civilians, and Wilfred still disapproved. He could not bring himself to send good wishes to Gordon, who had been engaged for over a year and was soon to be married.[7] It is not clear whether Wilfred ever visited Alpenrose in 1918, although there is a family memory of his being there at some stage in the war and lighting up a cigarette, whereupon he was told to go and smoke in the garden. His aunt's moral principles, which evidently did not extend to shaming her sons into khaki, were less easy to tolerate than they had been. Susan may have said little to her strong-minded sister, but she was coming round to Wilfred's way of thinking about the war.

Just as Wilfred's stint as Messing Officer was ending, Priestley was ordered into hospital for kidney treatment. Wilfred's antiques had to be packed up and sent to Shrewsbury. The last of Priestley's many kindnesses was to arrange for him to take on the mess presidency. It was highly unusual for a second lieutenant to do a job that was more often reserved for a major, but Colonel Mitchell was away and no one seems to have objected. Wilfred was not altogether keen, because he would still have to command WAACs, but for a few days he enjoyed the luxury of living in Priestley's flat and cycling into town in the mornings to choose wine and food for the officers' table. Then the Colonel returned, and the temporary PMC was ordered back to a tent and musketry duty.

～

On his final day in the flat, 26 July, Wilfred heard from someone in London that Sassoon was in hospital there, having been shot by a British sniper. That changed everything. If Sassoon was at home and no longer able to speak for the troops, another poet would have to stand in for him. That night, listening to the sea and the sounds of the camp from Priestley's window, Wilfred made up his mind at last.

> For leaning out last midnight on my sill,
> I heard the sighs of men, that have no skill
> To speak of their distress, no, nor the will!
> A voice I know. And this time I must go.[8]

Sassoon had gone out on one of his 'Mad Jack' adventures on 13 July, crawling across No Man's Land to throw bombs at an enemy machine gun. Returning towards British lines and feeling pleased with himself, he had paused in a sheltered hollow, stood up, taken off his helmet and been shot in the head. One of his own men had mistaken him for a German. He had been sent home to the American Red Cross Hospital at Lancaster Gate in London, where a stream of talkative visitors – Marsh, Ross, Meiklejohn, Nichols, Sitwell – had proved almost too much for him. He was ashamed to be safe, with no more than a minor wound, and he wrote an unhappy letter to Wilfred, who sent it to Susan on about the 30th with a covering note:

> I send you a precious letter, from the Greatest friend I have.
>
> I was inoculated again on Sat. but it was Siegfried's condition and not my own that made me so wretched. This time surely he has done with war ...
>
> Now must I throw my little candle on his torch, and go out again.
>
> There are rumours of a large draft of officers shortly.[9]

That sounds as though Wilfred had decided to return to France of his own free will, but he must have known by this time that the Adjutant-General's department had marked him for overseas service. The precise circumstances of his being sent to France in 1918, as in 1916, will probably never be known. He told Scott Moncrieff he was keen to go, a state of mind that was undoubtedly a result of the news from London. He would do his duty, and do it with high morale because it was a poet's duty as well as a soldier's. He asked for his name to be put on the draft.

With Priestley gone and the future hugely changed, Wilfred could find nothing to enjoy in Scarborough. On Thursday 8 August he reported 'another black week, alarms calling us out at 4 in the morning, & since Sat. continuous Rain, so that my tent floor was half under water for 2 days'. On the 9th there was a mock alarm at three in the morning, after which he had to spend all day on the range. On the Saturday another boat was torpedoed in the bay, with only ten lives saved. 'I wish the Bosche would have the pluck to come right in & make a clean sweep of the Pleasure Boats, and the promenaders on the Spa, and all the stinking Leeds & Bradford War-profiteers now reading *John Bull* on Scarborough Sands.'[10] That bitter comment was no doubt the sort of thing Wilfred had heard from Priestley, who had been a Bradford businessman himself, but it was also prompted by an order just received from Northern Command in York that Second Lieutenant Owen should 'join the British Armies in France', reporting to the embarkation authorities at Folkestone on 17 August.[11] 'I am glad,' he told Susan. 'That is I am much gladder to be going out again than afraid.' Echoing Sassoon's poem, he explained that he would be 'better able to cry my outcry, playing my part'. He was instructed to attend a medical with the rest of the draft on the Sunday morning, after which he would be free to go home for a week on draft leave.

At least things were now looking less ominous at the front. If 8 August brought the end of a 'black week' for Wilfred, it also brought what Ludendorff later called 'the black day of the German army'. The Allies had been regaining the initiative in France since July. Strongly reinforced with men and guns and making use of newly developed tactics, the British line had recovered from its March retreat. The Battle of Amiens, the four-day assault that began on 8 August, pushed the enemy eight miles back across the plains east of the town. On the left the Gailly area was retaken, despite heavy fire from the hills north of the river, and on the right Canadian troops advanced down the Amiens-Roye road, reaching villages where Wilfred had fought in March 1917.

Sassoon had just written to say he was to be moved from Lancaster Gate in a week's time to a nursing home at Lennel, near Berwick-on-Tweed. 'How far is it from Scarborough?' he asked. 'Overtures are already beginning to make me exchange pride & clean soul for safety & the rest of it. But I am too feeble to be able to think it out at all. I only feel angry with everyone except those who are being tortured at the war.'[12] Wilfred, having finally rejected 'safety and the rest of it', was gearing himself up for the medical and what would follow. He wrote home with his mind 'a cobweb of lines radiating to Shrewsbury, London, Hastings [where Colin had just been posted], Berwick, London, Shrewsbury, Berwick, Edinburgh, Portsmouth [where Harold was about to embark] …'. 'All I feel sure of is my excellent little servant Jones, who'll pack my stuffs in quarter of an hour, night or day.' Officers changed servants fairly often: Jones may or may not have been the Herefordshire gardener's boy whom Wilfred had mentioned in June. If he was the same man, it is odd that Wilfred later described him to Sassoon as having 'lived in London, a Londoner', a curiously phrased remark, just possibly a Half Moon Street code. Jones was to prove an ideal companion, thoroughly dependable and sympathetic. He and Wilfred talked a good deal during the next few weeks, and by the end of August there can have been little that either man did not know about the other.

The medical on Sunday 11 August had an unexpected outcome, as Wilfred told Scott Moncrieff that evening. 'I was struck off the draft by the M.O. this morning. He won't pass my cardiac valves … Yes, I got myself put on the draft list of 22 officers, but couldn't work it this time.'[13] Like the doctors at Ripon and Dr Gandy in 1912, the Medical Officer had heard a heart murmur, and Wilfred was suddenly safe again. Scott Moncrieff immediately revived the attempt to get him an instructorship. Leave had been granted, and Wilfred was due for it even though he was no longer on the draft. He probably arrived at Mahim that Sunday evening, to the delight of his parents and Mary. Harold had left for South Africa, but there was still just time to see Sassoon. By the Wednesday Wilfred was in

London, where Scott Moncrieff gave him a copy of Sacheverell Sitwell's latest poems, perhaps at the Poetry Bookshop. Wilfred dined with Meiklejohn at the Reform Club in the evening, no doubt going on to Half Moon Street, where Burton may once again have provided a room and breakfast.

Thursday 15 August was gloriously relaxed and civilised. Wilfred was reunited with Sassoon, who was now well enough to be allowed out of hospital by day, and they spent the afternoon in Chelsea, where Osbert Sitwell took them to call on the distinguished harpsichordist Violet Gordon Woodhouse. She gave them a private concert for two hours, Sitwell later recalling how Wilfred had sat 'dazed with happiness' at the brilliance of her playing. Tea at Sitwell's house in Swan Walk followed, culminating, according to Sassoon, 'in – was it raspberries and cream? – and ices of incredibly creamy quality'. Then the three poets walked over to the walled Physic Garden and sat among the shrubs and flowers under a cloudless sky. Wilfred seems to have mentioned the help he was being given at the War Office. Sitwell and Sassoon were no doubt glad to hear that Scott Moncrieff was being useful, although Sitwell liked him no more than Sassoon did. Wilfred and Sassoon went on together, first to the Reform for dinner with Meiklejohn and then to Lancaster Gate, taking leave of one another on the hospital steps.[14] Wilfred apparently said something about wanting to go out again. Sassoon replied that it might be good for his poetry, but threatened to stab him in the leg if necessary to stop him going. Soon afterwards Sassoon wrote to Marsh that 'someone' had intervened to keep Wilfred at home. 'Great relief to me.'[15]

Back at Shrewsbury on the Friday for one more night, Wilfred took his mother to task for her constant ill-health. There seemed to be nothing seriously wrong except worry, so there was no reason for her to be as lethargic as the rest of the Nation at Home. He made the splendidly subversive suggestion that she should take to drinking claret or at least tonic wine, and she agreed to try, although the idea must have appalled her. He got back to barracks by nine on the Saturday evening and was able to catch up on lost sleep before getting up for church parade next morning. Sunday put him in arrears again, because he had to be a patrol officer, sleeping for only half an hour in his clothes. He said he enjoyed the duty, but his frostbitten feet started causing trouble and he could scarcely walk next day. His letter to Susan on the Monday evening is full of emotion.

... I am quite wretched tonight, missing you so much. Oh so much!

Taking the world as it really is, not everybody of my years can boast, (or as many would say, confess) that their Mother is absolute in their affections.

But I believe it will always be so with me, always.

He enclosed money for half-a-dozen bottles of wine, telling her to eat, drink and be merry, 'for tomorrow we live, and the day after tomorrow *live, live, live*. Even in Scarborough I must live; though I feel dead to all these people.'

> Strange how suddenly my toes went wrong! It is the old frostbite 'playing on' me again as Jones says. Because I said I was sad, little Jones is prattling to me now, & I am talking volubly while I write.
> I am also thinking wildly and crying a little for only you to hear.

The strong feeling in this letter sounds like more than simple homesickness. Something seems to have happened, and the return of Wilfred's lameness, like that of his war dreams in June, was perhaps not coincidence. He may have heard that day from Scott Moncrieff, whose renewed attempt at rescue had failed disastrously. The Military Secretary's department had ruled that an officer sent home after apparently losing his nerve under fire did not deserve privileged treatment. 'The case was put more briefly,' Scott Moncrieff wrote later, 'but in words which do not look well in print.' If a copy of the official letter was sent to Colonel Mitchell, he would have been furious to discover that Wilfred had apparently been trying to get a safe job through the back door – and frostbite in August looked suspiciously like malingering. Mitchell may have had a word with the doctor. Wilfred was required to attend another medical, and this time, despite his feet and heart, he was judged to be fit for active service. On Monday 26 August he was instructed by the Adjutant to report to Folkestone in five days' time.

Wilfred settled his mess bill that Monday with the new PMC, a Major Fletcher, and must have left Scarborough the same day for draft leave at home. There had been very little time to work on poetry since Ripon. He looked through his 1917–18 manuscripts while he was at Mahim and scribbled what improvements he could, managing to send a few poems to the Sitwells for *Wheels*.[16] His mother would have to try to get his work published if he did not come back. He filled a sack with other papers that he had no wish for her or anyone else to see, telling her to burn its contents unread in the event of his death. He had always been inclined to leave things until the last minute, and he was clearly very tense and rushed. All soldiers bound for the front were advised to make wills, but he forgot to make one and even forgot to pack one of his identity discs. Somehow he got his luggage together, and by the Friday he and his mother were with Colin at Hastings, where all three were photographed together.[17] When the time came to say goodbye, Wilfred looked towards France and repeated the line from Tagore that he had quoted after first coming out of the trenches in 1917: 'When I go from hence, let this be my parting word, that what I have seen is unsurpassable'. Nothing else is recorded about that last farewell. Wilfred returned to London alone, having arranged for Scott Moncrieff to meet him.

'So, on a summer evening, I saw him for the last time,' Scott Moncrieff remembered afterwards. 'He had been to Hastings, where a Royal visit enormously delayed his returning train, and it was late when at last I met him at Victoria. I was sickened by the failure to keep him in England, and savage with my own unhealed wounds ...'. Wilfred found a trolley and wheeled his luggage to a hotel he had in mind, but the place was full. The ensuing search for a room evidently annoyed his companion. 'If I was harsh with him,' Scott Moncrieff wrote, 'may I be forgiven, as we tramped wearily round the overflowing hotels.' In the end a vacancy was found at an officers' club in Eaton Square that Scott Moncrieff knew,

and we sat down to a strange supper in the Queen Mary Hut ... After a few intense hours of books and talk in my lodging, I escorted him to his. As we reached it, he discovered that he had left his stick behind, but insisted that it was too late now to return. I left him on the doorstep and went home to find, not only the stick but his pocket-book with, I suppose, all his money, on my table. I went back with them, but I hope he was already asleep.

Scott Moncrieff, quirky and sharp-tempered, was not the ideal friend to meet after the strain of parting from Susan and Colin. If he suggested that he and Wilfred should spend the night together instead of tramping round the hotels, the suggestion may not have been well received. He had tempted Wilfred before, perhaps sexually in the spring and then by encouraging him to hope for a safe job. It was an awkward last evening in London, with what seems to have been a hurried ending. Part of Wilfred's subsequent letter to Susan is 'missing'.

Wilfred got up at five-thirty next morning to be sure of catching the train he had been ordered to take, the seven-thirty from Victoria. He was astonished and pleased to meet Major Fletcher, who had been unexpectedly 'pushed off' from Scarborough only a day after his own departure. At Folkestone they reported to the embarkation officer, who told them the boat would leave at three in the afternoon. Wilfred went to get a shave, a last luxury, and then took the chance to go for a swim. He expected to be depressed, as he told Sassoon next day.

But I was too happy, or the Sun was too supreme. Moreover there issued from the sea distraction, in the shape, Shape I say, but lay no stress on that, of a Harrow boy, of superb intellect & refinement; intellect because he hates war more than Germans; refinement because of the way he spoke of my Going, and of the Sun, and of the Sea there; and the way he spoke of Everything. In fact the way he spoke –

That final vision of England was repeated almost verbatim to Susan with the prudent omission of the word 'Shape'. It shows Wilfred as a man of his time, as sentimental and class-conscious as H.A. Vachell or Ian Hay, novelists he enjoyed, yet his poetic imagination is at work, moving his subject into a different dimension. The boy 'issues' from the sea like a figure in classical myth, born full-grown from the waves, a modern Antaeus, the son of Sea and Earth. Wilfred described him to Susan as 'the best piece of Nation left in England'. There was a future still for the Nation at Home, and some at least of the next generation would understand.

19

Through the Hindenburg Line

France

SEPTEMBER–OCTOBER 1918

Wilfred was sent on from Boulogne to the familiar base camp at Étaples. He wrote at once to his mother, and then to Sassoon, who was still under the illusion that Wilfred was safely in England.

Goodbye –
 dear Siegfried –
I'm much nearer to you here than in Scarborough, and am by so much happier.

 I have been incoherent ever since I tried to say goodbye on the steps of Lancaster Gate. But everything is clear now: & I'm in hasty retreat towards the Front. Battle is easier here; and therefore you will stay and endure old men & women to the End, and wage the bitterer war and more hopeless.

 When you write, please address to Mahim,

Monkmoor Rd.
Shrewsbury.

What more is there to say that you will not better understand unsaid.

Your W.E.O.

The next day, 1 September, being a Sunday, Wilfred took a tram to the seaside, where he found 'nothing to do'. He wrote again to Sassoon, telling him about the Harrow boy at Folkestone. He was determined to keep his spirits up, and his letters were resolutely cheerful. 'Serenity Shelley never dreamed of crowns me,' he told Sassoon. 'Will it last when I shall have gone into Caverns & Abysmals such as he never reserved for his worst daemons?' He was at Étaples for a week, sleeping in a dormitory hut, exercising troops by day and finding congenial company in his free time. The place seemed much more habitable in warm September sunshine than it had done in the vicious winter of 1916-17. The regime for Other Ranks had been relaxed a little, too, after a brief mutiny in September 1917, although the troops were

333

still kept under wary control, herded at night into enormous compounds behind barbed wire. Wilfred described himself to Susan as once again 'a cattle driver', and to Sassoon as 'a Herdsman; and a Shepherd of sheep that do not know my voice'. Actually the daily routine was much like Scarborough, except for the convoys of wounded on the roads.

In one respect, in fact, Étaples was all too like Scarborough. Wilfred had caught up with a number of junior officers who had been drafted out from the barracks before him. They were likely to know rather too much about his recent history, and it was perhaps in order to avoid them that he sought out a quiet YMCA hut at the station and made friends with the civilian in charge, 'an extraordinary hunch-backed little Irishman, of very pleasant manners'. Conal O'Riordan, whose name Wilfred vaguely knew, was a novelist and playwright, a friend of Yeats, Synge and other famous writers, and a former director of the Abbey Theatre in Dublin. Despite being middle-aged and badly crippled from a boyhood riding accident, he had volunteered for overseas work, braving air raids and watching over hundreds of young officers as they slept under his roof for a few hours before he woke them for their trains. He said later that he remembered Wilfred more vividly than any other officer he had met in France. There could have been 'no cheerier companion or blither soul than charming young Wilfred Owen'. 'I can see so clearly his charming face, a child's, despite the tiny moustache, smiling at me in the sunlight or under the rays of the swinging lamp he would light for me when I drew the curtains at evenfall.'[1]

According to Wilfred, who visited O'Riordan daily, they talked 'not books, but life & people, as is the way between Authors'. O'Riordan thought Wilfred's conversation ranged from 'the most beauteous and humane wisdom to … comprehensible but not the less unbalanced and intellectually indefensible folly'. The 'folly' was Wilfred's belief that the Germans were no more to blame for the war than the Allies, if as much, a view O'Riordan deplored as dangerous heresy. It was certainly dangerous for a subaltern, and Wilfred had already remarked half-jokingly to Sassoon that he might end up in front of a firing squad if he talked in his sleep or wrote poems in the dugouts. O'Riordan pointed out that he himself as an Irishman had little reason to sympathise with the British Government, but he had felt duty-bound to help in the fight against 'the crazy beast Hohenzollernism'. Germany had a cult of killing, he said, whereas recent British violence in Ireland was the result of 'conceited incompetence' rather than bloodlust. He thought he detected some yielding on his guest's part, but Wilfred would not have wanted to push the argument too far. They were able to agree wholeheartedly that killing and newspaper propaganda were hateful, and Wilfred thought it best not to produce his poems, although he talked openly to O'Riordan about everything else.

No 'cheerier companion or blither soul'. Roland Bate, who was convinced Wilfred had never smiled at Scarborough, would have been incredulous. 'You would not know me for the poet of sorrows,' Wilfred told Susan. He was remembered as convivial by another man he met at Étaples, Lieutenant Murray McClymont, to whom he was apparently introduced as a poet. Three poems by McClymont had appeared in *Soldier Poets: More Songs by the Fighting Men* (1917), a popular anthology from the publisher of the Little Books of Georgian Verse. The two soldier-poets chatted in the sunshine and then had dinner together, talking about Sassoon. Afterwards they stumbled around the camp in the blackout, having perhaps had a little too much to drink. Next day, 7 September, McClymont gave Wilfred a copy of the anthology with a humorous inscription.[2]

Wilfred had hoped to get himself attached to a Welsh regiment, partly perhaps in emulation of Sassoon and Graves and partly because of his own Welsh blood. Wales was the land of soldiers as well as poets. However, he was told to rejoin his previous unit, the 2nd Manchesters, and think himself lucky. He was not as pleased as he had been in 1917, but at least he would get away from the 'Scarborough mob', who were being sent to other battalions. The 2nd Manchesters seemed the best Lancashire unit available, and few if any of its current officers would remember his failure at Savy Wood. He was instructed to proceed to Amiens, taking a detachment of troops with him. As the men were forming up with their herdsman on the afternoon of the 8th, a private rushed out from the crowd to shake Wilfred's hand, and with some difficulty, for the man now looked middle-aged, Wilfred recognised a former drummer from Southport. It seemed a good omen, putting the draft in confident mood, reinforced by O'Riordan's smiling farewell at the station. The men behaved excellently, even when they reached Amiens in pitch darkness with no idea where to go, and after some delay Wilfred delivered them to their billets and found his own.

Amiens had been within range of enemy artillery in the spring – Wilfred blamed Haig for the damage, not altogether justly – and the civilian population had been evacuated. Wilfred was allocated to a good room in a large house, where the windows had lost their glass but kept their 'valuable hand-lace-curtains'. His bed was a table, for which a helpful Scot found a mattress, and he shared the room with another second lieutenant, Frederick Potts. A small man like Wilfred and five years younger, Potts had been conscripted in 1917 as a cadet, having already trained in the OTC at Manchester Grammar School and then at Manchester University, where he had been studying chemistry. A blighty wound in early March 1918 had sent him home, but he was now fit again. He proved to be intelligent, well-informed and easy for Wilfred to get on with.[3]

The next week was spent reading, sleeping, talking and 'gathering roses from bewildered gardens'. The only drawback was the absence of letters, which were all being sent direct to the battalion. It was 'huge fun' looting for furniture and kicking about the rubble, looking for souvenirs. Wilfred found plenty of French books and picked up a 'delightful wee lace-surplice' near the cathedral. Potts chose a toby jug 'in very bad taste'. Wilfred said it was scarcely possible to feel pity for the wrecked houses, which were 'all in bad style', or for the French soldiers who had once lived in them and who were now probably among 'the Unreturning'. He took a joy-ride in a tank and revisited the Somme canal where he had once taken another joy-ride on a hospital barge. He sent a facetiously amended field postcard to the 'Rt. Rev.' O'Riordan, and wrote letters from an Australian YMCA, where he was recognised again, this time by a private who had shared the torment of the railway banks in Savy Wood. It was reassuring to hear that the man had not been through a worse time since. Wilfred told Susan that whatever lay ahead could not be as terrible as those experiences in 1917. Meanwhile she was not to reveal to friends and relations that he was having an 'amusing little holiday'. One of his letters is headed 'Not to be hawked about', in contrast to his early 1917 letters, which he had wanted to be typed and circulated. She could tell his brothers, but them only, how 'peculiarly unreluctant' he was to be back with 'the Nation' and away from 'all that the Gunstons typify'.

~

The newly arrived officers were spared the nuisance of having to travel up to the front. On Saturday 14 September their battalion 'embussed' at Tertry behind the combat zone and came back for a rest at La Neuville, just across the Ancre from Corbie, where Wilfred had been a sceptical observer at a church service in March 1917. The great church at Corbie was roofless now and the civilians had gone, but the area was safe again. Wilfred had to supervise guides and help prepare billets, including quarters for the Brigadier-General. Watching the troops march in, he was pleased to be recognised by at least two more men, 'strangely enough the very two I most hoped had survived'. There were plenty of familiar faces among the NCOs, but if he saw any of the officers he had been with in 1917 his letters do not mention them.

On the Sunday morning Wilfred, Potts and four others, including Second Lieutenant John Foulkes and Major Joseph Murphy, MC, formally joined (or in the case of Wilfred and Murphy rejoined) the strength. Wilfred and Foulkes were given platoons in D Company under Captain Hugh Somerville, MC, who turned out to be both likeable and literary-minded. Somerville was a native of Edinburgh and had read English for three years at Edinburgh University, where he thought he had known Scott Moncrieff. He had joined up as a sergeant in November 1914 and had then been commissioned, becoming a company commander in July 1916, so he was an old hand. Wilfred automatically became his second-in-command as the most senior second lieutenant.

The 2nd Manchesters had been in and out of the line in many places since Wilfred had left them in May 1917. They were now once again part of General Rawlinson's Fourth Army, although it was not the Fourth Army of 1916-17 but what had been Gough's Fifth Army, renamed and rebuilt after its March retreat and transformed into the most aggressive, successful force on the entire Allied front.[4] The battalion was still in 32nd Division (Major-General T.S. Lambert), which had recently been transferred to IX Corps within the Fourth Army, but the division's battalions had been reshuffled in the spring, when all brigades had been reduced from four battalions to three. The Manchesters had been moved from 14th Brigade to 96th (Brigadier-General A.C. Girdwood) alongside the 15th and 16th Lancashire Fusiliers, two battalions of volunteer 'Pals' from Salford. They had been fighting hard just south of the Amiens-St Quentin road since the Battle of Amiens in early August, advancing rapidly from one village to another as far as the Villeveque area, only a few miles from Savy Wood and Manchester Hill. Wilfred said the current CO, Lieutenant-Colonel Gordon Robertson, DSO and bar, was an 'agreeable non-ferocious gentleman' who let his officers get on with their work without interference.

The authorities may have felt Robertson was rather too non-ferocious, in fact, for they had brought in a celebrated guards officer, Lieutenant, now Major, J.N. Marshall, as second-in-command. This 'Mad Major', or 'Terrible Major' as Wilfred called him, was the most 'arrant utterly soldierly soldier' Wilfred had ever come across. 'Bold, robust, dashing, unscrupulous, cruel, jovial, immoral, vast-chested, handsome-headed, of free, coarse speech', recently wounded for the tenth time and awarded a bar to his MC, Marshall happened to be at battalion headquarters when Wilfred went in to pester the orderlies for letters, and an icy offer of help was enough to send the newly joined subaltern scuttling out of the room. Nevertheless Marshall was a kindly man at heart, hugely admired by men and officers for his humanity as well as his extraordinary courage, and it may have been thanks to him that eight letters were 'mysteriously' delivered to Wilfred at dinner.

The battalion remained at La Neuville for ten days. Sunday and Monday were devoted to the usual 'general clean-up' of billets, kits and equipment, and of the men themselves, who were sent off to the divisional bath-house for showers and fresh clothes. The officers reconnoitred the training area, and from the Tuesday onwards the four companies took turns at drill, musketry, Lewis gun and bombing practice, physical exercises and games. Every now and then there was a surprise gas drill, and the Divisional Gas Officer gave two lectures and demonstrations. Numerous medals were awarded for the recent fighting, including a bar to Somerville's MC. The Adjutant decided that Wilfred as an experienced man was worth a specialist job, so he made him the battalion's Bombing Officer, even though Wilfred had no specialist knowledge in the subject.

On 22 September Wilfred wrote to Sassoon, enclosing three poems. One was a final version of 'The Sentry', a description of that first and worst front-line experience in the German dugout at Serre. 'I try not to remember these things now', the poem said, but Wilfred had often tried to remember during the previous year, and almost all his war poems had been based on deliberate recollecting. Another of the three poems was not a memory, however: 'Smile, Smile, Smile' had been inspired by recent newspaper reports of speeches by the Minister of Labour and the French premier, Clemenceau. Both politicians had acknowledged the debt owed to the men in the ranks, but in language that revealed how patronising and ignorant civilians still were. *The Times* had reported Clemenceau as declaring that 'the greatest glory will be to those splendid *poilus* [common soldiers], who will see confirmed by history the titles of nobility which they themselves have earned'. Their only desire was to complete 'the great work which will assure them of immortality.' Wilfred quoted from the speech in his poem, amending the phrasing a little so that he could introduce the word 'nation', developing the contrast he had already referred to in letters between the Nation at Home and the Nation Overseas. 'Head to limp head, the sunk-eyed wounded' scan the newspapers, where politicians declare that

> '
> …
> *The greatest glory will be theirs who fought,*
> *Who kept this nation in integrity.'*
> *Nation? – The half-limbed readers did not chafe*
> *But smiled at one another curiously*
> *Like secret men who know their secret safe.*
> *(This is the thing they know and never speak,*
> *That England one by one had fled to France,*
> *Not many elsewhere now, save under France.)*

Optimistic reports in newspapers were often accompanied by pictures of smiling wounded.[5]

> *And people in whose voice real feeling rings*
> *Say: How they smile! They're happy now, poor things.*

'Smile, Smile, Smile' is its author's last Sassoonish satire, and he hoped it would drive Sassoon into protesting again, but its stress on secret knowledge is typical of Wilfred alone.

The third poem sent to Sassoon was a part-draft of 'Spring Offensive' with the message, 'Is this worth going on with? I don't want to write anything to which a soldier would say No Compris!' Sassoon must have replied encouragingly, and Wilfred later found time to add a closing stanza. 'Spring Offensive' incorporates memories of the hurricane barrage at Fayet in April 1917, although some of the details are altered to resonate with literary tradition. Long ago, in his early enthusiasm for Keats, Wilfred had hoped for a vision like those granted to 'old dreamers on May Morn', and his last finished poem is set in a May, Shropshire-like landscape, where Wordsworthian nature is a moral teacher. Buttercups and brambles offer benediction and love, but the offensive is against the spring as well as in it. When the soldiers attack – organisms turning against their environment, Antaeus attacking his mother the Earth – nature responds with necessary fury until the air is once again cool and peaceful. The soldiers are heroes, but their heroism is not the absurdly naïve value admired by story tellers such as H.A. Vachell. Civilian pieties are brushed aside in the last stanza. Only soldiers who have entered hell as living men can know the truth, and they keep their secret.

> *Some say God caught them even before they fell.*
>
> *But what say such as from existence' brink*
> *Ventured but drave too swift to sink,*
> *The few who rushed in the body to enter hell,*
> *And there out-fiending all its fiends and flames*
> *With superhuman inhumanities,*
> *Long-famous glories, immemorial shames –*
> *And crawling slowly back, have by degrees*
> *Regained cool peaceful air in wonder –*
> *Why speak not they of comrades that went under?*

That stanza with its final question, probably the last poetry Wilfred ever wrote, is a pencil addition to the manuscript. If it was written in October, as it may well have been, it contains memories not only of the 1917 barrage at Fayet, but also of the catastrophic charge of the 16th Lancashire Fusiliers at Joncourt on 2 October 1918, a disaster that Wilfred had to watch at close quarters.

～

The rest period soon came to an end. On 24 September the Manchesters 'embussed' on the road between Corbie and Villers-Bretonneux, the area where the German advance had finally been brought to a halt in the spring. After lurching for three or four hours along the Roman road that leads due east from Amiens across the wide plains towards St Quentin, the buses reached Tertry again, where bivouacs were waiting. Three more days of training followed, the troops rehearsing how to move from marching column to small groups and back again, an essential drill in open warfare when a company might suddenly have to clear a road or avoid shellfire. The old routines of 'digging in' were no longer needed. General Girdwood came to watch on the 26th, complimenting the battalion on its recent work at the front. Senior officers often talked about 'work'. Wilfred could have reflected on how the Vicar of Dunsden had often used the word, too, meaning the Lord's work, a war against evil in which victory depended on commitment and morale. Soldiers, like poets and parish assistants, were a kind of priesthood, dedicated, selfless, set apart, a band of brothers.

Sitting on straw in his 'tamboo', a corrugated iron shelter, Wilfred wrote home on the 28th. The surrounding countryside had been wrecked by the German withdrawal in 1917 and again by more recent fighting, and autumn weather was closing in, but he kept up his jovial tone. He had all the necessities that could be wanted, he said, clean air, enough water to wash in, letters, plenty of plain food, and 'an intellectual gentleman for Captain; 3 bright & merry boys for my corporals; & stout grizzled old soldiers in my platoon'. The other D Company officers had taken to calling him 'The Ghost', possibly a nickname that had followed him from Scarborough, where he had been greeted at first as a man risen from the dead and had then become elusive, Priestley's shadow. If his letters are any guide, he was not elusive now. More than at any other time in his life, he wrote appreciatively about the people around him and enjoyed their comradeship.

Wilfred's closest colleague, John Foulkes, recorded some memories twelve years later. A qualified elementary teacher like Wilfred, Foulkes was a native of Warrington, where his father worked as a wire-drawer. He was ten months younger than Wilfred, but had joined up ten months earlier, reaching the rank of sergeant before being selected for officer training in 1917. 'Plenty of confidence and Power of Command,' his superiors had decided. 'A very good man. Well above average. Should make an excellent officer.' Excellent officer though he undoubtedly was, the factory worker's son who had come up through the ranks regarded Wilfred as a genuine gentleman, not a temporary one like himself: 'a thorough gentleman. Ever courteous to all ranks – willing and eager to help anybody.' The role that Wilfred had always aspired to had become natural to him at last. But he was not like other officers. 'I always suspected him of having an extra soft spot for Tommy,' Foulkes wrote, 'although he never allowed it to interfere with discipline. Whilst seeming to thoroughly understand the soldier's attitude in most things he himself seemed to me to have a curious lack of growl …'.[6] If Foulkes had any idea why Wilfred had a soft spot for Tommy, he did not say so in his memoir. He certainly had no idea Wilfred was a poet, although he did overhear him discussing Sassoon with Somerville at Corbie.

Just possibly Foulkes noticed that there was one Tommy for whom Wilfred had a special affection. Little Jones was once again Wilfred's servant, as he had been in Scarborough. Wilfred makes no mention of him until early October, but they must have been together at least by the time the battalion reached Tertry. There is no way of knowing how Jones had arrived, whether he had been sent to La Neuville with a draft from the barracks or travelled with his officer from England.[7] Nor can it be known how close the relationship was. Even the mildest personal friendship between platoon commander and private would have had to be concealed. Within the mystery of being a poet and the mastery of being an officer lay that further secret, and Wilfred had to keep it safe.

～

The war was now well into the period later known as the Hundred Days or the Advance to Victory, but few people even in the Fourth Army could have guessed that the end was little more than six weeks away. The Germans had fallen back on the Hindenburg Line, from which they had never yet been dislodged. They were cunning in defence, they had many divisions in the field and their gunners were as active as ever. Their huge, ingenious barrier had gained the extra protection of the former British trenches, although these were already being retaken (the French captured Manchester Hill on the 26th). The outworks of the Hindenburg Line itself were still inviolate behind vast thickets of wire, and in the valley beyond lay the main line, an intricate network of concrete fortifications on the east bank of the St Quentin Canal, itself a moat that could be raked by machine guns. If attacking troops achieved the seemingly impossible feat of getting through, they would enter the first field of fire, some two miles of open valleys and uplands where they would often be hidden from their own artillery but in full view of the enemy. Then came the trenches of the support line, connected by tunnels to the front so that reinforcements could be moved up unseen and used if necessary to attack invaders from the rear. Beyond the support defences was a second battle zone, three miles deep, and finally the reserve line, with heavy guns hidden behind the hills and machine gun posts commanding the ridges.

Nevertheless the Fourth Army had some grounds for confidence. British arms and tactical skills had improved enormously since 1916. Surprise had become an essential weapon, and attacks were launched at unpredictable times instead of at dawn, the hour that had become traditional in the trenches. The artillery was far more powerful and accurate, the RAF had air supremacy, and tanks were now numerous, if still unreliable. By sheer good luck a secret plan of the Hindenburg Line had been captured, so that

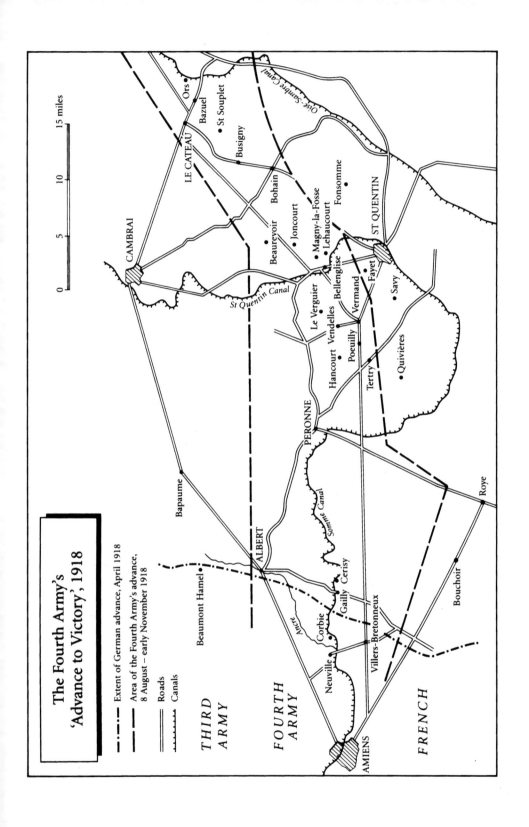

The Fourth Army's 'Advance to Victory', 1918

- —·—·— Extent of German advance, April 1918
- — — — Area of the Fourth Army's advance, 8 August – early November 1918
- ══════ Roads
- ⌐⌐⌐⌐⌐ Canals

0   5   10   15 miles

THIRD
ARMY

FOURTH
ARMY

FRENCH

Bapaume

Beaumont Hamel

ALBERT

Ancre

Corbie
Neuville
Gailly Cerisy
Villers-Bretonneux

AMIENS

Bouchoir

Roye

Somme Canal

PERONNE

Hancourt
Poeuilly
Tertry
Quivières

Le Verguier
Vendelles
Vermand
Fayet
Savy

CAMBRAI

St Quentin Canal

Beaurevoir
Joncourt
Magny-la-Fosse
Lehaucourt
Bellenglise

Bohain
Fonsomme

ST QUENTIN

LE CATEAU

Ors
Bazuel
St Souplet
Busigny

Oise–Sambre Canal

the British commanders knew its details and would be able to target vulnerable points such as the tunnel entrances. Had the commanders known all that their German counterparts knew, they would have been more confident still. There were plenty of enemy divisions, but they were so badly undermanned that the Allies actually had considerably greater manpower. The support and reserve Hindenburg systems were still unfinished, even after two years of labour. Threats of famine and revolution were growing at home. Above all – and this was becoming obvious to both sides – ordinary German soldiers were losing heart, allowing themselves to be captured in ever-increasing numbers.

'The forthcoming news should be of intense interest to you,' Wilfred said in his letter from the tamboo on 28 September, giving his mother gentle warning that a battle was about to begin, but he made himself sound reassuringly snug and secure, ending his letter on a homely note as Jones appeared at the shelter entrance. 'Here is my lunch; roast beef & baked potatoes! I'm hungry!'

Nothing in the letter gave any hint of what was already happening. Late on the 26th, 1,600 guns had opened up with one of the most intense barrages ever fired on the Western Front. The generals had decided on an all-out attack on the Hindenburg Line before the enemy had time to settle in. There was no chance of surprise in such a massive operation. For an appalling six-and-a-half hours mustard gas had fallen on German command centres, batteries and other key points. Next morning the shells had changed to high explosive, aimed to destroy as much wire and concrete as possible, and the guns were still roaring as Wilfred wrote his letter on the 28th. To the south the French were gathering for an assault on St Quentin, the prize they had longed to regain since 1914. The junction between themselves and the British had been nudged a little to the left of its 1917 position, to just north of Fayet, so that IX Corps on the extreme British right was facing a dangerous stretch of the canal. On IX Corps' left a joint Australian-American corps, Rawlinson's spearhead troops, had been given the crucial task of advancing over the canal tunnel north of Riqueval, the only place where tanks could cross.

On the afternoon of the 28th, not long after Wilfred and the rest of his battalion had written their last letters and eaten their last hot meal, 32nd Division started to move. From now on all progress would have to be on foot. The 96th Brigade brought up the rear as reserve, setting out on the first and shortest of its route marches in the evening, observing the familiar discipline of 500 yards between battalions, 100 between companies, ten minutes rest each hour. The Manchesters moved off at 7.38 p.m. Avoiding the crowded roads by following lanes and a field track, they reached bivouacs near Vendelles at nine-fifty. The guns continued firing all that night.

The attack by IX Corps early next morning was led by three Staffordshire battalions in 46th Division. The artillery was now fairly efficient at clearing wire, and the Staffordshires got through what was left of the entanglements without much difficulty. The next obstacle was a deep, near-impregnable canal cutting, where the enemy was not expecting trouble. Aided by fog, and wearing life-jackets sent up from the Channel ferries, the attacking troops scrambled down into the cutting and were up the far side almost before the enemy knew they were there. German pioneers hastily trying to blow up the bridge at Riqueval were killed before they could fire the charges. Keeping close behind a dense creeping barrage, a protective curtain of shells moving steadily ahead of them, the Staffordshires poured through the defences. By mid-afternoon the entire divisional front had been captured, with the extraordinary total of 4,200 prisoners, seventy guns and hundreds of machine guns and trench mortars, at a cost of 800 British casualties. This achievement, perhaps the greatest in a single day by any British division in 1914–18, was undoubtedly made possible by the enemy's failing commitment. Despite the many scientific and tactical innovations since 1915, morale was still, as Colonel Shirley had prophesied, 'the most important factor in war'. Later that day the Kaiser was advised by his generals to seek an armistice.

Not everything had gone well for the Fourth Army. The inexperienced Americans had rushed bravely into battle over the canal tunnel, but the Germans had been expecting them and the position was very strongly defended. The attackers fell back with stories of comrades still trapped in the field, so the supporting Australians had to go forward without the usual cover of a barrage. Severe casualties resulted. The tanks eventually started getting through, but the delay meant that IX Corps had to advance without adequate support on the left.

In late afternoon 32nd Division began 'leap-frogging' through the victorious 46th, taking over the lead. Safe at the back, the Manchesters suffered no casualties at all that day. They passed the ruined village of Le Verguier, crossed the canal on pontoon bridges somewhere between Riqueval bridge and Bellenglise, and spent the night in captured trenches in the Hindenburg support line just west of Magny-la-Fosse. Next day, 30 September, the Manchesters and Lancashire Fusiliers in 96th Brigade advanced through the lethal countryside between the support and reserve lines, doing their own leap-frogging through other brigades to reach the divisional front. Here and there machine guns had to be dealt with. Twenty Other Ranks and three officers among the Manchesters were wounded. Magny was in a sheltered hollow, but a party of Lancashire Fusiliers (LF) seem to have strayed too far over the ridge to the north, coming into the sights of a machine gun in the valley below, firing from a hidden block-house on the edge of Joncourt. The dead lie there still in a little cemetery

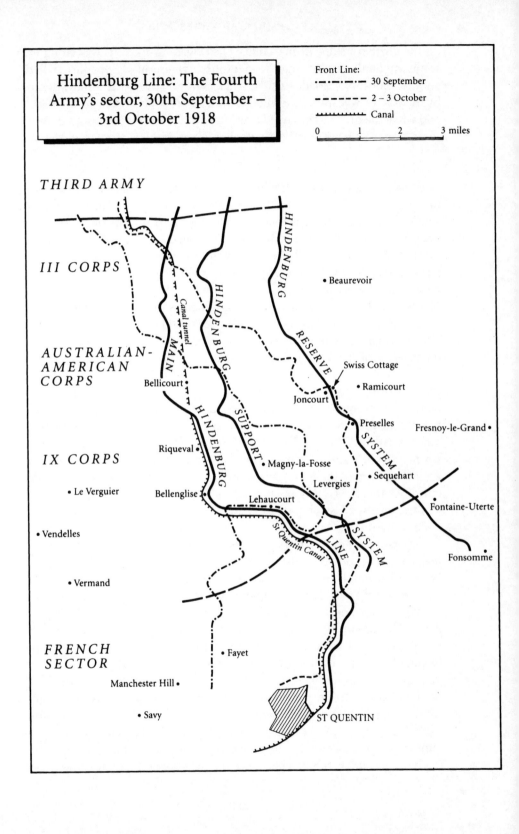

Hindenburg Line: The Fourth Army's sector, 30th September – 3rd October 1918

Front Line:
-·-·-·- 30 September
------- 2 – 3 October
⊣⊣⊣⊣⊣⊣ Canal

0   1   2   3 miles

THIRD ARMY

III CORPS

AUSTRALIAN-
AMERICAN
CORPS

IX CORPS

FRENCH
SECTOR

HINDENBURG

HINDENBURG

HINDENBURG

HINDENBURG

Canal tunnel

MAIN

SUPPORT

RESERVE

SYSTEM

LINE

SYSTEM

St Quentin Canal

• Beaurevoir

Swiss Cottage

Bellicourt •

Joncourt

• Ramicourt

• Preselles

Fresnoy-le-Grand •

Riqueval •

• Magny-la-Fosse

Levergies

• Sequehart

Bellenglise •

Lehaucourt

• Le Verguier

Fontaine-Uterte •

• Vendelles

Fonsomme •

• Vermand

• Fayet

Manchester Hill •

• Savy

ST QUENTIN

on the northern slope of the ridge.[8] The brigade worked its way along the southern flank of the ridge to a point just south of Joncourt, where another blockhouse made further progress impossible. After a vain attempt by the 15th LF to capture the village, the brigade took shelter for the night, and while the officers conferred over maps and orders, the troops, many of them teenagers new to battle, slept where they could on the damp ground.

~

The brigade had kept roughly in step with another on its right, but it was uncomfortably far ahead of the Australian–American corps on the left. The most immediate danger was enfilading fire from Joncourt, so it was agreed that 15th LF would attack the village again next morning. Once the southern blockhouse had been taken the Manchesters would be able to tackle a far more daunting objective, the Hindenburg reserve line itself, known in this sector as the Beaurevoir-Fonsomme line. The German planners had made good use of high ground east of Joncourt, a long ridge protected on the south by a wood at Preselles and on the north by Moulin Grison Farm, renamed Swiss Cottage by the British map-makers, a quadrangle of brick buildings round a yard. An unfinished but thickly wired trench ran up the ridge from the farm and along the summit to the wood, connecting twenty or more little pillboxes, each consisting of a platform for a machine gun, with a chamber underneath just big enough to hold the gun and its team during a barrage.[9] There were also numerous pits for riflemen. Behind this line, on the reverse of the slope, was a stronger trench and a light railway for bringing up supplies. Further on again, sheltered in the folds of the hills, lay the heavy guns. And beyond the gun lines there was only open country. The Hindenburg reserve system was the enemy's last prepared defence. Were it to fail, the way would be open to Berlin.

Orders from headquarters were coolly resolute. 'The 32nd Division will break the Beaurevoir–Fonsomme line tomorrow not later than 4 p.m.' Four tanks would co-operate with the infantry. Planes, which now carried wireless, would patrol overhead, directing the gunners. If a plane sounded a klaxon, troops on the ground would show their positions by sending up flares. The Manchester officers worked out their plan of attack in conformity with divisional arrangements. A frontal charge up the hill would be suicidal, but the contour map showed a way of advancing from the right flank with less climbing and at least some shelter from the guns that were no doubt concealed in the wood at Preselles.[10] If the artillery could cut the wire, the leading companies, which were to be C and D, ought to be able to rush through and fight their way up the trench. The enemy machine-gunners would be kept in their bunkers until the last minute by the creeping barrage, and as the 'creeper' moved ahead the emplacements could be

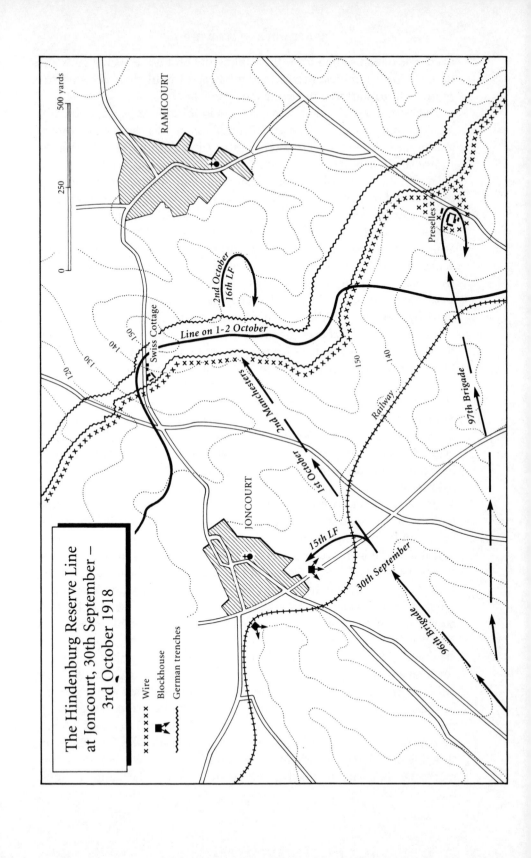

The Hindenburg Reserve Line
at Joncourt, 30th September –
3rd October 1918

xxxxxxx Wire

▞ Blockhouse

⌇⌇⌇ German trenches

RAMICOURT

500 yards

250

0

Swiss Cottage

2nd October
16th LF

Line on 1-2 October

2nd Manchesters

1st October

15th LF

30th September

96th Brigade

97th Brigade

Preselles

Railway

JONCOURT

120 130 140 150

150 140

overcome one at a time from the flank with good use of Lewis guns and bombs. Forty minutes after zero the barrage would stop, allowing five more tanks to start moving along the enemy line.

During the night some of the Germans in Joncourt escaped up the hill. Next morning, 1 October, the Lancashire Fusiliers silenced the blockhouse and pushed through the southern part of the village to join up with the Australians, who were attacking from the west. The assault on the ridge was delayed until the last minute in the hope that the Australians would take the rest of Joncourt, but they were held up, leaving a dangerous gap to the northeast between the village and the ridge. D Company was to lead the Manchesters' charge, and Wilfred as second-in-command to Somerville had to time zero hour on his watch. Jones kept close to him, acutely aware that a servant's duty in battle was to protect his officer at any cost. The artillery put down a strong barrage of high explosive, shrapnel and smoke, and at exactly four o'clock Wilfred gave the signal for the whistles to blow. By then, three of the tanks had already been put out of action.

The advance was soon brought to a stop, probably by uncut wire and the loss of the tanks, and D Company seems to have had to take cover in a hurry. Little Jones, perhaps even at the moment of trying to shelter Wilfred, was shot through the head. For the next half-hour the two friends lay next to each other on the hillside, Jones bleeding profusely but alive, his head resting on Wilfred's shoulder. No Decadent poet could have imagined a more strange, intense and dreadful intimacy. 'Catalogue? Photograph?' Wilfred wrote to Sassoon afterwards. 'Can you photograph the crimson-hot iron as it cools from the smelting? That is what Jones's blood looked like, and felt like. My senses are charred.'

At 4.40 p.m. the barrage fell silent, as arranged, and the five supporting tanks went into action. One of the three damaged tanks also got going again, and D Company was now able to move. Jones and the other casualties, who included Somerville, hit in the thigh, had to be left for the stretcher-bearers. Wilfred took command, and as he stood up, his tunic soaked in Jones's blood, he perhaps felt the sort of battle madness that had briefly driven Sassoon after the death of David Thomas in 1916. He told Susan later that the only word he could find to describe his experiences was 'SHEER'.[11] 'It passed the limits of my Abhorrence. I lost all my earthly faculties, and fought like an angel.' Accompanied by a 'seraphic' boy lance-corporal as his company sergeant-major, the angel led D Company up the hill to swift victory. The defenders were vulnerable on their gun platforms in the face of a determined charge, and before long they were giving themselves up all along the line. Wilfred himself claimed to have captured 'scores' of prisoners and 'a few' machine guns with the seraph's help, shooting only one man with his revolver at thirty yards, a final proof of his marksmanship, and taking the rest 'with a smile'. The battalion took twenty-four machine guns and over two hundred prisoners altogether.

While D Company worked north towards Swiss Cottage, C Company under Lieutenant Benjamin Cobley pushed south along the shallow trench towards Preselles. The left, northern half of the front was under the command of Captain Leonard Taylor, MC, while Major Murphy commanded the right. At six o'clock Cobley sent a runner back to battalion headquarters with a message that all his company's objectives had been gained, with one officer wounded. He asked for more Lewis gun ammunition and warned that the enemy appeared to be massing for a counterattack. Forty drums of ammunition were sent up to each company, as well as all available officers. Colonel Robertson himself arrived to take overall command (he was later awarded a second bar to his DSO for his courage and 'the magnificent way he handled his battalion' during the battle). He asked for further help, and a company of 15th LF was ordered up. For a while the right flank seemed secure as the neighbouring brigade fought its way through to Preselles. Further south, French troops were entering St Quentin at last.

D Company apparently reached Swiss Cottage fairly soon, but the Germans launched a ferocious counter-attack through the gap northeast of Joncourt, recapturing the farm and thereby not only threatening the Manchesters' positions on the ridge but also dominating the slope behind them. Wilfred ordered Foulkes to take a party down with Lewis guns to retake the farm, and then, seeing that covering fire was urgently needed, he and the seraph ran to two of the machine guns they had captured and turned them on the enemy. Wilfred's gun was in an isolated position and he must have been in full view, but he kept firing, clearing the way for Foulkes. This contribution to the 'long-famous glories, immemorial shames' of war was to earn Wilfred his Military Cross. Had he not used the machine gun, 96th Brigade might have been driven off Joncourt ridge, and the Fourth Army's fight for the Hindenburg reserve line might have been even harder than it was. If he took lives, he also saved them, but he might not have allowed that as an excuse.

Visible to the enemy, Wilfred was also seen by his own side, and his exploit may well have raised cheers from the British line. Foulkes and his men were able to rush an enemy machine gun, killing its crew and securing the farm. He and Wilfred were immediately recommended for awards by Captain Taylor, who said Wilfred had shown 'great coolness throughout': 'his energetic devotion to duty is worthy of the highest praise'. The final version of the citation, published among hundreds of others in the obscure recesses of the *London Gazette* in 1919, records that Wilfred had 'inflicted considerable losses on the enemy'. Few of his admirers during the next half-century can have known about that. When Harold Owen came to edit his brother's letters he found an official copy of the citation, but the wording seemed unacceptable. The great poet of pity could not be thought, could not even be imagined, to have won a medal by slaughtering Germans. Someone, presumably Harold himself, typed out a new version, making it look as much like the original as possible but replacing 'inflicted considerable losses on the enemy' with 'took a number of prisoners', a phrase that was duly printed in the *Collected Letters*.[12]

The recapture of Swiss Cottage was completed by 7 p.m., and 'OC D Coy' dictated a confident note for a runner to take to headquarters: 'All objectives gained Swiss Cottage is now ours 13 prisoners taken there C Coy getting into touch on our right There is no one up on our left Enemy withdrawn Full report following.'[13] Cobley reported nearly three hours later that C Company was holding its sector of the front trench with the Lancashire Fusiliers on the right, while A Company had come up in support. 'Situation quiet.' During the next half-hour C Company moved forward to occupy the German support trench on the east side of the ridge, and D Company probably did the same. Taylor reported that Foulkes, who had been 'working splendidly', had tried to push north from Swiss Cottage but had run into strong resistance. A post was being established there to await the Australians. Wilfred set up D Company's headquarters in a pillbox, where, as he told Sassoon later, he held 'a most glorious brief peace talk', perhaps with the seraph.[14] A letter from Scott Moncrieff arrived, impressive testimony to the army's postal service.

The quiet did not last. The Germans knew exactly where their former defences were, and their shelling, mingled with gas, soon became frighteningly accurate. The pillbox became a death trap and probably had to be abandoned, as did the entire support trench, the companies crawling back to the unfinished, foot-deep front trench on the western slope. Wilfred noticed how a former guardsman next to him shook violently at every shellburst, but his own nerves held steady. Early on 2 October Taylor sent word that a small counter-attack had been beaten off at 2 a.m., but he was expecting more: things were looking serious, with the enemy apparently beginning to penetrate on the right. He was ready to fire SOS flares for artillery help. The Germans had in fact retaken Preselles, and the Manchesters were now exposed on three sides. Taylor rallied his men with 'an utter disregard' for his own safety, and they successfully resisted another counter-attack. Foulkes and his platoon fought desperately at Swiss Cottage, losing their positions more than once but regaining them.

The enemy regrouped, and Taylor began to sound worried: 'This front position is impossible. All officers hit and considerable casualties. Have sent up S.O.S. 3/4 of an hour ago with no result. The enemy has worked forward. Swiss Cottage is in the air & practically surrounded. We are now holding on to the enemy front line. Can you do any thing please.' A few officers, including Wilfred and Foulkes, were in fact still unwounded, but casualties were rapidly increasing. Taylor soon wrote again: 'The enemy is extremely active & looks very much like a counter-attack. Cant you get a barrage down before dawn from the line we have withdrawn from onwards. We have no answer to the SOS and its very disconcerting if we are to hold on to the last.' Murphy on the right was equally alarmed: 'The enemy are shoving forward on us. I am afraid of strong attacks at dawn. May I have strong reinforcements at once. We have no one behind us.' The expected assault came on the right, and the barrage must have fallen just in time. The line nearly gave way on A Company's front, where all the officers had become casualties, but the Company-Sergeant-Major, Charles Mutters, led a ferocious resistance, killing many Germans. Cobley worked with 'tireless energy' to hold C Company's line, and in due course the attack evaporated.

In the pause that followed, the 16th LF came up to the ridge. They had been given the hopelessly unrealistic task of capturing the next village, Ramicourt. Meanwhile the divisional commander, General Lambert, had sent congratulations to all ranks of the Manchesters. Hoping for a break-through, he said the day's operations might lead to 'one of the greatest successes of the War, maybe', and he noted that the Manchesters had been 'the only men in the Division who did their task and held it'. 'May I be allowed,' Colonel Robertson added in circulating the message, 'to offer my sincere thanks to all for their work, and the honour they have again added to the Battalion's credit which is so dear to us all.'[15]

The 16th LF went forward at 8.30 a.m. Several hundred of them were shot down instantly, including their CO, Lieutenant-Colonel A. Stone. Taylor soon had to report that the survivors had only got a few yards before being forced back into the shallow trench alongside the Manchesters. There was no success that day, despite Lambert's hopes. The three battalions were pinned down in the trench in wet, penetratingly cold weather. They were all but surrounded, with the left half of the front under enfilading fire from high ground beyond Swiss Cottage and the right shelled from the wood at Preselles. (Hence Wilfred's *double entendre* to Sassoon afterwards: 'I desire no more *exposed flanks* of any sort for a long time.') Even retreat was almost impossible, with the western slope of the hill open to fire from the north. All day the wounded groaned from No Man's Land. Three of Wilfred's stretcher-bearers were hit one after the other. 'I had to order no one to show himself after that, but remembering my own duty, and remembering also my forefathers the agile Welshmen of the Mountains I scrambled out myself & felt an exhilaration in baffling the Machine Guns by quick bounds from cover to cover.' There may have been moments, when Wilfred was crawling about on the eastern side of the ridge among the dead and dying, that he was ahead of anyone else in all the Allied armies, but there was little he could do. The wounded could not be got back, and food, water and ammunition were all running low.

That night officers and men lay in the mud, soaked to the bone, 'utterly despondent'. A party of Lancashire Fusiliers risked death to bring up rations. Wilfred felt the cold biting into him, but even as memories of Redan Ridge began to threaten his self-control a lance-corporal next to him produced a blanket '(not supposed to be carried)' and spread half of it over him. The 'warmth came like the rising of the May-day sun. So I was saved from the nearest approach to the excruciation of my First Campaign.' After hours of shelling, gas and probably more counter-attacks, the brigade was relieved by units of 46th Division, and at 5 a.m. on 3 October Wilfred led his company out 'by the stars, through an air mysterious with faint gas'. Exhausted and disoriented like everyone else, he imagined it was five in the evening for a while, but his knowledge of astronomy stood him in good stead. 'This is where I admired his work in leading his remnants, in the middle of the night, back to safety,' Foulkes wrote. 'I remember feeling how glad I was that it was not my job to know how to get out. I was content to follow him with the utmost confidence in his leadership.' By breakfast-time the battalion was in shelter on the east bank of the St Quentin Canal near Lehaucourt. Well before they got there the firing on Joncourt ridge had begun again. With support on the flanks at last, the fresh troops of 46th Division were able to push forward into Ramicourt, although the opposition was still very strong. It would be another two days before the last of the Hindenburg defences could be broken.

Wilfred headed his first letter after the battle '4th (or 5th) October 1918 / In the Field / Strictly Private'. He was probably writing at Lehaucourt on the 4th. 'My nerves are in perfect order,' he told his mother, and all the evidence suggests this was true, even though he had seen men killed and horribly wounded. Then he made a famous statement. 'I came out in order to help these boys – directly by leading them as well as an officer can; indirectly, by watching their sufferings that I may speak of them as well as a pleader can. I have done the first.' He had done the second, too, without fully realising it, and his distinction as an officer would reinforce his authority as a poet. Writing to Scott Moncrieff a few days later he said he was glad to have been recommended for an MC, because it would give him confidence in dealing with civilians.[16]

Manchester casualties had been heavy. Only four men had been killed in the first day's fighting on the ridge, but seventy-eight had been wounded and seven had disappeared, captured or blown to pieces. The officers, leading from the front, had lost seven wounded, including Potts, who had been hit in the arm by a machine-gun bullet. Once the companies had taken shelter there had been no more officer casualties, but twenty-three Other Ranks had been killed and another seventy wounded. Some of these had been caught by gas, having failed to get their helmets on in time despite all the drills. Twenty more men and one officer were found to be missing by the time the battalion reached safety. One of the wounded officers, Reginald Gregg, soon died. Wilfred had heard him talk proudly in Scarborough of his little daughter. 'I suppose the child will be told she should be proud of Daddie, now.'[17]

Perhaps no one will ever know what happened to Jones. A Private Thomas Jones, killed on 1 October, is buried in the British cemetery at the foot of Joncourt ridge, but the surname was a common one in the battalion. Wilfred as company commander was responsible for writing casualty reports, and he would have known if 'little Jones', his own servant, had died.[18] A week after coming out of the line he said that Jones had been 'happily wounded'. The context of that phrase, in a letter to Sassoon, is revealing. Wilfred first mentions O'Riordan.

> It was easy, & as I reflect, inevitable to tell him [O'Riordan] everything about oneself.
> I have nothing to tell you except that I'm rather glad my servant was happily wounded: & so away from me. He had lived in London, a Londoner.

'I have nothing to tell *you*' – because Sassoon already knew Wilfred's other secrets – except that it was as well that the servant, 'a Londoner', was safe but no longer around. Wilfred could now keep his feelings to himself, although he was already thinking of using them for poetry. 'Of whose blood lies yet crimson on my shoulder,' he told Susan, 'where his head was – and where so lately yours was – I must not now write.'

> It is all over for a long time. We are marching steadily *back*.
> Moreover
> The War is nearing an end.
> Still,
>   Wilfred and more than Wilfred

The Final Battle

France

OCTOBER–NOVEMBER 1918

On the afternoon of Friday 4 October the battalion returned to bivouacs at Vendelles, and by the following afternoon they were at Hancourt, near Tertry, their starting point. They camped at Hancourt for twelve days. On the Sunday, after church parades and a congratulatory speech from General Lambert, the officers and drums of the Manchesters joined the depleted ranks of the 16th Lancashire Fusiliers for the funeral of Colonel Stone, whose body had been brought back from Joncourt ridge. The Colonel's grave is still in the British cemetery at Hancourt, where Wilfred once stood to attention as the rifle volley echoed across the untended fields. After the ceremony the officers got back to work, preparing training programmes and dealing with the aftermath of battle, while the men were once again marched off to the bath-house.

As commander of D Company with the acting rank of captain, Wilfred completed his casualty reports and wrote personally to the parents of all his dead and missing men.[1] 'I'm frightfully busy (as O.C.D.),' he told Scott Moncrieff, 'and many glorious Cries of the blood still lying on my clothes will have to be stifled.' Then he added cryptically, 'I find I never wrote a letter with so much difficulty as this. Perhaps I am tired after writing to so many relations of casualties. Or perhaps from other causes.'[2] Remembering 'Insensibility', he let his brain grow dull, as he told Sassoon. 'I shall feel again as soon as I dare, but now I must not. I don't take the cigarette out of my mouth when I write Deceased over their letters. / But one day I will write Deceased over many books.' Exercises, drills and football occupied the days. The front was advancing again and there would be a long trudge back to it, so three route marches were organised. Wilfred asked Susan not to send him old, darned socks, but new ones, Maddox's best at half-a-crown a pair. He was delighted one day when Foulkes happened to quote a line of Keats – 'Owen's face shone with wonder and delight,' Foulkes remembered, 'and from that time I fancied he regarded me with real affection.' They shared a ramshackle iron shelter, Wilfred making it a little less bleak by putting up a picture of Sassoon. The men were entertained one evening by the Pedlars, 32nd Division's team of comedians, a dozen men in pierrot costume, some in drag. Reinforcements arrived. Major Marshall, who had missed the fighting, returned from leave and was immediately transferred to the 16th LF as Acting Lieutenant-Colonel in place of Stone. Colonel Robertson went on leave, handing over command of the Manchesters to Major Murphy.

Wilfred could not but enjoy being in charge of his 'glorious little company'. He wrote to his father with 'soldierly braggadoccio', knowing how pleased Tom would be.[3] The temporary captain was apparently allowed to ride a horse, and he held a daily 'orderly room' at which he issued praise and punishment and heard complaints. At first he had Foulkes and one other as his junior officers, and then two more. The Sergeant-Major was an old acquaintance, having been a corporal in the dugout at Serre ('He remembers it …'). When more men arrived from Scarborough, Wilfred recognised several former drummers, boys who had not only been his waiters at Clarence Gardens but also members of his company at the barracks. Much to his delight, they were put in his company again. 'Some of them look pretty scared already, poor victims.' He did his best to cheer them up, and came across some appreciative comments in their letters. 'Mr Owen is my Coy. Commander,' one man wrote home, 'and his such a desent chap.' 'Do you know that little officer called Owen who was at Scarborough,' wrote another; 'he is commanding my Company, and he is a *toff* I can tell you. No na-poo. Compree?' Wilfred translated the trench slang as 'a fine fellow, no nonsense about him' and added, 'I record this because it is more pleasing than military medals with many bars.' He was not allowed to give the company the most obvious reassurance of all, that the war might end any day: instead he had to read out an order from General Rawlinson that 'Peace talk in any form is to cease in the Fourth Army'. The authorities were worried that enemy calls for peace might weaken morale before a final result could be secured.[4]

Scott Moncrieff wrote with news of two deaths. His old friend Philip Bainbrigge had died of wounds on 18 September, and Robert Ross had died of a sudden heart attack on 5 October, exhausted by the strain of the Pemberton Billing affair. Wilfred was especially sad to hear about Ross, who had been immensely kind to him. Susan sent an obituary from *The Times* which said that friendship had been the chief business of Ross's life, and Wilfred thought that was 'marvellously true of him, and kind, considering the *Times* was never his friend'. Scott Moncrieff had got himself to Amiens with the job of guiding famous war correspondents. He hoped to drive over to see Wilfred at Hancourt before long.

Wilfred's brief command ended on 14 October, when a senior lieutenant, R.W. Carroll, rejoined and was put in charge of D Company. Wilfred had to revert to being a second lieutenant, exchanging the iron shelter for a tent. More officers joined the battalion, some returning from leave or hospital, others arriving newly commissioned from England. Most of the latter were far from being toffs. Wilfred disliked them, predictably enough, confiding to Susan that he would like to send them away to get a secondary education and train as corporals. Perhaps he withdrew a little into himself: Foulkes often noticed him sitting alone, reading a volume of Swinburne. The book, a copy of *Poems and Ballads*, was the only poetry Wilfred had chosen to keep with him. He had bought it in August, sticking a postcard of old Scarborough in it to remind him of England.[5]

Swinburne had been the last great voice of the Victorian age, the age that had bred the war, and his sombre music seemed the right accompaniment to the death throes of the old world. Many phrases were familiar, reminding Wilfred of his own work: 'sweeter than all sweet', 'blood-sacrifice', 'ache of purple pulses', eyelids on eyes 'like fire on fire', 'fields unfurrowed and unsown'. 'Shall this dust gather flesh hereafter?' – and Swinburne answered his own question: 'there is no God found stronger than death; and death is a sleep'. Wilfred had given a similar answer in 'The End', 'Asleep', 'Strange Meeting' and other poems. His early scepticism had been learned from books and from Dunsden, but his later experience of what Swinburne called 'the mystery of the cruelty of things' had brought him knowledge far exceeding that of any nineteenth-century poet. He had descended into one of the many mouths of hell at Serre. He had seen the unsurpassable sweetness of the smile on a boy's murdered mouth, perhaps at Beaumont Hamel, and had felt the searing heat of Jones's blood on Joncourt ridge. 'My senses are charred,' he said, borrowing the word from Swinburne, but the stains on his uniform were 'glorious Cries' and in due course they would have to be made into poems.[6]

He was only twenty-five, and his post-war future had never looked so promising. With friends like Sassoon, the Sitwells, Monro and Scott Moncrieff he would be able to earn a living from reviewing and other literary work, with no need to endure the slavery of elementary teaching. He would base himself in 'the Cardiac Region' of London well away from home, furnishing a couple of rooms as cheaply as he could with army kit.[7] If he prospered he would do as Monro and other writers did and rent a country cottage, filling it with books and antiques. Now that his military record was no longer an embarrassment, he would be able to speak out freely for the war's survivors and all who were going to need help in the hard times ahead. New ways of writing were developing and he would absorb them into his poetry, just as he had absorbed the work of the Romantics and Victorians, Monro, Tailhade, Sassoon, the Sitwells and many others. He would become – had already become – a voice for his own time.

He could be ever more confident that his poems were going to speak for ordinary soldiers. The army's state of mind was rapidly changing, and no orders from any general could put a stop to 'peace talk'. Now that the Hindenburg Line had been cleared, officers and men alike were beginning to suspect, as Sassoon and his civilian friends had done in 1917, that the politicians were keeping the war going for their own ends, while duping the Nation at Home with propaganda. Lieutenant Carroll had come back from London 'utterly disgusted with England's indifference to the real meaning of the war as we understand it'. By 'we' Wilfred meant 'every officer & man left, of the legions who have suffered and are dust'.[8] At long last the troops were cursing the newspaper they had always regarded as their champion, Bottomley's *John Bull*, which was howling for all-out victory. The battalion celebrated news that Germany had accepted American peace proposals, Wilfred joining in the singing. When Mary Owen wrote with what was meant to be the encouraging remark that the war would surely be over by summer 1919, her brother replied that Christmas was 'the Limit of our Extreme Patience'. He was glad to hear that Susan was reading Tolstoy the great pacifist (there was a volume of Tolstoy's stories with an informative preface on his shelves) and that she was finding the courage to speak against the war. 'I am paralysed when I try to write to Leslie,' he told her, listening to men coughing from the effects of the gas he had led them through: 'so many of these boys are *so much less* fit than he!'[9]

~

However much ordinary soldiers, Wilfred among them, might long for peace, the truth was that the Germans were still putting up strong resistance, hoping even now that something might be gained by fighting on. On 17 October they made a stand on the River Selle, and the Fourth Army was soon in trouble, having not realised the enemy had brought up reinforcements. The 32nd Division was ordered to follow up in case help was needed. The Manchesters set out that morning, 'in a hurry' according to Wilfred, for a march of over eleven miles from one ruined village to another along the muddy roads. Poeuilly – Vermand – Vadencourt – somewhere an hour's break for what orders firmly called 'dinner' – a new bridge over the St Quentin Canal at Bellenglise, the village littered with wreckage – and in early afternoon Lehaucourt again, where the wind stank of dead horses. The guns were rumbling incessantly on the eastern horizon. It was impossible not to hope the noise would stop at any minute, 'but it still goes on,' Wilfred said, 'a gigantic carpet-beating'. The front was pushed across the Selle next day, so the Manchesters were able to rest their feet at Lehaucourt for a while, Wilfred occupying an entrance to one of the deep Hindenburg tunnels. The march began again on the 20th, this time with no meal break: Levergies – Sequehart – Fontaine-Uterte – Fresnoy-le-Grand – and Bohain-en-Vermandois. Wilfred had the painful task of organising and goading the stragglers at the rear, and probably also of deciding who could ride in the horse ambulance that followed. 'Will is the best medicine,' he said afterwards, advising his mother on how to deal with her ailments.

Liberated eleven days earlier, Bohain had been the first inhabited town reached by the advance. Hundreds of bewildered, half-starved women and children were doing what they could to provide a welcome. They were a pitiful sight, cowed after four years of occupation and frightened by the recent shelling, but they had brought a flag out of hiding and Bohain was French again. The place was relatively intact, apart from damage done by British shells and huge craters blown at every crossroads by the retreating Germans. Wilfred was billeted in a kitchen and put to questioning the locals, being much more fluent in French than most of his colleagues. Another clean-up was organised, and some last-minute training. General Lambert distributed medal ribbons to the many Other Ranks who had distinguished themselves on the Hindenburg Line.

Communications were becoming ever more difficult, hampered by distance, delayed-action mines and the onset of winter rain, but letters were still getting through, much to Wilfred's astonishment and pleasure. His mother was ill again, but this time he refused to be anxious in return. 'How happily I think of you always in bed,' he told her. She should have all his 'Articles of Vertue' brought in to represent him: carpets, candlesticks, pictures, tables, the Jacobean chest – 'have them all in'.[10] He could not hope for leave before the New Year, 'even were Prussianism removed from London & Berlin and Peace happened before Christmas', but when he did come home he would walk to Haughmond with her, and while she rested on the top he would run round the Wrekin to warm his frostbitten feet. Susan, who had difficulty even in getting up Wyle Cop, was never really likely to climb Haughmond, but the imagery is telling. After years of struggling to escape from her confining embrace, Wilfred was now in control. Even in his absence he could surround her with his possessions, make her speak against the war and perhaps even drink wine. When he came home, he would heal himself with his own energy, not with her nursing.

He assured her he would not reach the front for a 'considerable time', long enough for 'the British Government & its accomplices to save their Nations'. On the afternoon of 22 October the battalion moved on a few miles to Busigny in territory captured by the Americans a fortnight earlier. The Americans and Australians had now been withdrawn, reducing the Fourth Army to two undermanned corps, XIII and IX. The Manchesters spent a week at Busigny, training and clearing roads. Eighty-five reinforcements arrived, and the General came to inspect them.

On the 25th Wilfred wrote to Leslie Gunston, who had just had a poem, 'Les Morts', published in *The Nation*. It had been inspired by a civilian cemetery he passed every morning on his way to work, but Wilfred assumed it referred to the war and promised to tell Sassoon. After a little more name-dropping, Wilfred went on:

> You must not imagine when you hear we are 'resting' that we lie in bed smoking. We work or are on duty *always*. And last night my dreams were troubled by fairly close shelling. I believe only civilians in the village were killed (Thank God). In this house where I stay five healthy girls died of fright when *our* guns shelled the place last fortnight. You & I have always been open with each other: and therefore I must say that I feel sorry that you are neither in the flesh with Us nor in the spirit against war. You know why I could find no word of greeting for Gordon (on the occasion of his marriage.)[11]

Wilfred said he had seen no sign of German atrocities, despite the reports Leslie had been reading in the right-wing press.[12] The local girls had been respectfully treated. Nevertheless they were delighted to be free, and Wilfred was being singled out by two of them in his billet for kisses and chatter, much to the envy of the other subalterns, who had held a mock court-martial on him.[13] 'The dramatic irony was too killing, considering certain other things, not possible to tell in a letter,' he told Leslie. One of Foulkes's letters had recently been opened by the base censor, so Wilfred could not risk saying more, but Leslie would be able to guess what the 'other things' might be. The trust between the cousins had survived the strains of war.

On the 29th, still at Busigny, Wilfred told Susan that the battalion was about to move on again, though '*not* to fight'. He said the local civilians, 'wretched, dirty crawling community' though they were, were suffering even more than the soldiers. People in the Allied countries who had pre-vented a peaceful enemy withdrawal were 'sacrificing aged French peasants and charming French children to our guns. Shells made by women in Birmingham are at this moment burying little children alive not very far from here.' He had come a long way since writing in the first draft of 'Anthem for Doomed Youth' that 'our guns' could provide war's only adequate 'priest-words'.

The battalion assembled at midday and marched to St Souplet, keeping off the road wherever possible to make way for wheeled traffic. The vast arable lands of Picardy were now far behind them, and the scenery was much more like home – winding lanes, dense hedges and little meadows, a terrain giving many advantages to the enemy. Next day one more parcel arrived from Susan, with the right sort of socks this time, and no sooner had Wilfred opened it than the order came to move into the line. The Manchesters followed field tracks, pausing for an evening meal just west of

Bazuel. They had marched more than forty miles since leaving Hancourt. When darkness fell they took over front-line positions from a Shropshire unit. Wilfred and his new servant, Private Roberts, one of his Scarborough men, spent part of the night crouching in a draughty tamboo, eating chocolate from Susan's parcel. They were in a forest, though the trees had long since been felled for trench props. D Company's headquarters and Wilfred's platoon established themselves in what the maps called the Forester's House, one of the few buildings on the road through the wood. The brick-lined cellar was relatively safe.

～

Colonel Marshall, commanding the 16th LF, was asked by 32nd Division's staff to reconnoitre the divisional front. It was an unusual request, but Marshall was no ordinary commander. Scrambling through the tangle of stumps and undergrowth he could see that two of 96th Brigade's battalions, his own and the 2nd Manchesters on their right, were on a slope leading down to fields and the Oise–Sambre Canal, a ribbon of water about a mile away and some forty feet wide, with drainage ditches on either side that the Germans had flooded. The enemy was strongly established on the east side. The canal banks, raised three or four feet above the surrounding ground, might give some protection to attackers and defenders alike, but there would be no other shelter. On the right of the Manchesters, 14th Brigade was facing the little village of Ors and boggy ground south of it along the canal. Ors bridge was broken, but the Germans still had some alarm posts and machine guns west of the canal. Northwards, where the canal turned sharply east to skirt the Happegarbes Spur, the enemy was still on the west bank in force. The spur looked insignificant enough, scarcely even a hill, but it gave command of the canal down to Ors and beyond, and it would have to be captured by 96th Brigade's remaining battalion, the 15th LF, before any crossings could be attempted. Beyond the canal, in front of 16th LF and the Manchesters, paddocks and orchards sloped gently up to La Motte Farm. Picturesque though the scene was, despite a fast-growing crop of shell-craters, Marshall's practised eye took in fortifications round the farm, as well as a worrying number of camou-flaged machine guns and infantry positions near the canal. Equally worrying was the rising ground itself, enabling German observers to watch

(See map opposite.) Ors: the battle plan. Crossing points were to be at A (16th Lancashire Fusiliers), B (2nd Manchesters) and C (1st Dorsets). The grids show the two creeping barrages that were to shelter the advancing infantry. The 'creeper' in front of A and B was to fall on the east bank for 5 minutes from zero hour (5.45 a.m.), then lift 300 yards and remain stationary for 30 minutes before starting to move forward at a rate of 100 yards every 6 minutes. The unexplained gap between the two areas selected for bombardment may have allowed the Germans to bring up field guns during the battle.

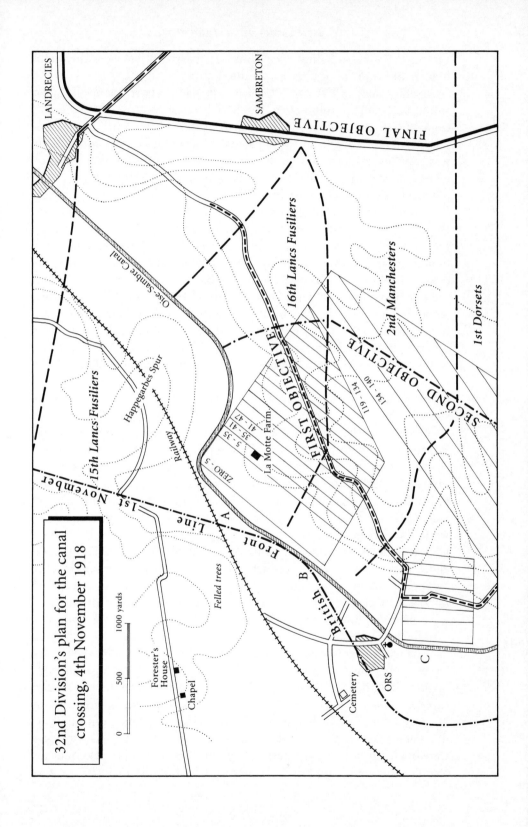

32nd Division's plan for the canal crossing, 4th November 1918

LANDRECIES

SAMBRETON

FINAL OBJECTIVE

16th Lancs Fusiliers

2nd Manchesters

1st Dorsets

Oise-Sambre Canal

SECOND OBJECTIVE

FIRST OBJECTIVE

Happegarbes Spur

15th Lancs Fusiliers

Railway

La Motte Farm

119 - 134

134 - 140

41 - 47

35 - 41

5 - 35

ZERO - 5

1st November

Front Line

A

B

C

British

Felled trees

Forester's House

Chapel

Cemetery

ORS

0   500   1000 yards

the canal banks and direct the guns and mortars that were no doubt hidden and ready on the reverse of the slope.

A senior staff officer came to hear Marshall's report. Marshall said it would be 'virtually impossible' for 96th Brigade to cross. His adjutant, Captain G.A. Potts, never forgot the staff officer's reply: 'You will find that the weight of the artillery behind you will blot out all the opposition.' Potts was appalled, knowing very well that experience on the Somme and elsewhere had shown such optimism to be almost always misplaced.[14] He and Marshall had worked hard to stiffen their battalion's morale after its disastrous charge on Joncourt ridge, and now they would have to pretend that all would be well on the canal. It must have been obvious to everyone that all would not be well. 218 Field Company, Royal Engineers, allocated to 96th Brigade, was dangerously short of time and materials. At first the plan was to build four bridges for the two battalions that were to cross, but the engineers' commander, Major Arnold Waters, decided that only two would be possible. The two front battalions in 14th Brigade could be no better provided for. The army always preferred to allow generous margins for error, but a single bridge for a whole battalion allowed no margin at all.

Prospects for the battle looked very much better elsewhere on the Fourth Army's front. Dozens of infantry assault bridges were being prepared, with many more for tanks and lorries. Of the two divisions on IX Corps' front, the 1st had been luckier than the 32nd. The 1st Division had been ahead in the advance and had found a German supply dump at Bohain. Central control of bridging supplies having been more or less abandoned by this stage in the war, the engineers had helped themselves to numerous steel floats and any other materials that might be needed, and the division had reached the canal with ample time to reconnoitre and get ready. The 32nd Division, arriving later, had done much less well. There would be enough timber, but three of the division's four bridges would have to ride on kerosene tins, light but all too sinkable. The fourth, allocated to the Manchesters, which as a Regular battalion perhaps had the best chance of crossing, would be on cork floats. Cork – sheets of it bound into large blocks with wire netting – was almost unsinkable, but the floats were probably waterlogged after use on the Selle, and wet cork was extremely heavy.[15]

During the next few days the sappers worked feverishly with the help of a pioneer battalion, 16th Highland Light Infantry, fixing each pair of cork floats to long poles to form a 'pier'. Up to eight men would be needed to carry each pier up to the canal and launch it, probably under fire. Lengths of specially made duckboard and a simple rope handrail would then be fitted across the piers to form a narrow walkway.[16] Smaller plank bridges were made for crossing the drainage ditches, and rafts were also built for ferrying men and supplies across the canal while the main bridge was being put in place. Meanwhile the gunners kept up a busy, irregular shelling to keep the enemy nervous, and the infantry made their own preparations, taping out the ground and rehearsing every detail of the coming action. Secrecy was crucial. 'Every officer and man who is seen helps the enemy,' orders said. The best chance lay in catching the already demoralised Germans off their guard.

On the evening of 31 October Wilfred wrote to his mother from the 'Smoky Cellar of the Forester's House'. As so often, his letter was designed to reassure. Saying nothing about the impending attack, he kept his mind on the present, describing the high-spirited fellowship around him, a band of brothers, in the world yet not of it, secret men who knew their secret safe.

The Forester's House, nears Ors

So thick is the smoke in this cellar that I can hardly see by a candle 12 ins. away, and so thick are the inmates that I can hardly write for pokes, nudges & jolts. On my left the Coy. Commander snores on a bench: other officers repose on wire beds behind me. At my right hand, Kellett, a delightful servant of A Coy. in *The Old Days* radiates joy & contentment from pink cheeks and baby eyes. He laughs with a signaller, to whose left ear is glued the Receiver; but whose eyes rolling with gaiety show that he is listening with his right ear to a merry corporal, who appears at this distance away (some three feet) nothing [but] a gleam of white teeth & a wheeze of jokes.

Splashing my hand, an old soldier with a walrus moustache peels & drops potatoes into the pot. By him, Keyes, my cook, chops wood; another feeds the smoke with the damp wood.

It is a great life. I am more oblivious than alas! yourself, dear Mother, of the ghastly glimmering of the guns outside, & the hollow crashing of the shells.

There is no danger down here, or if any, it will be well over before you read these lines.

I hope you are as warm as I am; as serene in your room as I am here; and that you think of me never in bed as resignedly as I think of you always in bed. Of this I am certain you could not be visited by a band of friends half so fine as surround me here.

Ever Wilfred x

November the first was a quiet day, with neither side showing itself. On the 2nd the 15th LF cleared the Happegarbes Spur, only to be driven back with severe casualties. The enemy was clearly determined to hold the canal line at any cost. The Manchesters nevertheless 'exterminated' the last German post on their stretch of the west bank that evening, with the capture of four survivors and three machine guns. The 15th LF took the spur for the second time on the 3rd, but once again their losses were heavy and it was decided to vacate the position until the main attack. For miles along the canal that evening the Fourth Army's units rested as comfortably as they could.[17] The mood in the smoky cellar was perhaps a little more sombre than it had been. 'The shadow of the morrow weighed on men.'[18]

Zero hour was set for 5.45 next morning, Monday 4 November. The two leading Manchester companies, of which Wilfred's was one, were to assemble well back from the canal to avoid the opening barrage. The shells would fall as a dense, deep curtain on the far bank for five minutes, then lift three hundred yards to higher ground in front of La Motte Farm, remaining there for thirty minutes. More than five minutes might break down the bank and make the whole enterprise impossible. At the moment of the first lift the companies would dash forward to give covering fire while the bridge was built, and before the allotted half-hour was out they would be over the canal, ready to follow the barrage as it started to creep across the fields. The staff officer's confidence had clearly counted for more than Marshall's warnings. Nevertheless Division was aware of the risks, recognising that there was a 'very large concentration' of enemy troops and machine guns close to the far bank. Orders stressed that 'surprise and complete superiority of fire' would be essential.

The first part of the plan worked perfectly. The Manchesters gathered in a lane about a quarter of a mile from the canal, Private Roberts keeping close to Wilfred as Jones had done before. As soon as the barrage lifted the two front companies ran forward and lined the bank. Helped by fog, smoke and darkness they had achieved the surprise they wanted, and by the time the enemy was able to put down an answering barrage it fell harmlessly behind them. The pioneers struggled up with the heavy floats, and as each pier was dropped into the water the engineers hooked a length of duckboard into place and began fixing poles from one pier to another to give extra stability.

But Marshall had been right. Very soon the defenders on the east bank opened up with ferocious machine gun and trench mortar fire, after a while adding shrapnel and gas. The attackers answered with rifles, Lewis guns, machine guns and a few mortars. As the bridge grew across the water, the fog began to clear. Thirty of the forty-two engineers became casualties. Seeing the need for stronger cover, Second Lieutenant James Kirk mounted a Lewis gun on a raft and paddled across until he could shoot at close range. When he ran out of ammunition, more was sent out to him. A sapper named Archibald went out on the bridge to finish it, and other men joined him, but all were hit or gassed. Major Waters, who by this stage had no officers left, coolly walked over to complete the fastenings himself. His bridge had been built in thirty minutes, almost as planned. He returned and led two platoons of Manchesters across. Kirk was hit for the third time and killed. Then a shell smashed the bridge. The barrage seems to have been called back, but it could not be brought close enough to the canal now that some Manchesters were on the east bank. Officers and men on the west bank started desperate efforts to repair the bridge.

Two men from Wilfred's platoon who went to see his mother afterwards told her how he had patted them and said, 'Well done' and 'You are doing well, my boy'. ('So *well I* can picture that encouraging "pat" of his,' Susan wrote to Sassoon. 'I know his "boys" loved him – no one could help loving him.') Ten minutes later, according to Susan, while '*helping* his men to get some planks across', Wilfred was hit and killed. Foulkes, who did not see what happened, having become a casualty himself with an ankle wound, told a journalist a few years after the war that Wilfred had been 'on a raft and in the teeth of a murderous enemy fire'. A story became current later that Wilfred had been on the bank, but it seems likely that he had in fact taken to a raft with men and planks. Antaeus had lost contact with the ground. Soon afterwards the attack was called off, and the surviving Manchesters took shelter behind the bank, sending double runners north and south to find out what had happened at the other bridges.[19]

On the left the 16th LF had come under heavy fire from well-hidden machine guns. Colonel Marshall had stood on the bank to direct his men, careless of his own safety, but the engineers had been unable to anchor the bridge to the far bank. Two-and-a-half hours after zero he reported that two attempts to cross had failed, and that his companies were dug in on the west bank. He asked for ammunition and stretcher-bearers, and said he could make another attempt at night if he could have more bridging materials, but a daylight crossing was impossible unless enemy machine guns could be eliminated. Something then happened to make him change his mind. Perhaps headquarters sent a sharp reply, or perhaps the bridge was finally anchored. Calling for men to follow him, Marshall started to cross and was shot in the head. According to an obituarist, he fell smiling in the death he had wanted, that of a 'soldier and gentleman'.[20]

The runners who had gone south came back with better news. The Germans had beaten back two attempts to cross at Ors lock, but they had failed to notice the engineers building a bridge for the 1st Dorsets just beyond the village. The Dorsets and 5/6th Royal Scots were now on the far bank, and at about 8.30 a.m. the 2nd Manchesters and 16th LF were sent to join them. Meanwhile the 15th LF had cleared the spur for the third time and reached the canal. No bridge had been planned for them, so they turned north and crossed at the next town, Landrecies. By the following morning all 32nd Division's original objectives had been gained. Victoria Crosses were later awarded to Marshall, Kirk, Waters and Archibald. The 96th Brigade had been the only unit to suffer badly: elsewhere the Fourth Army's many crossings had succeeded with relatively few losses. The war's last battle was an overwhelming victory, and its outcome finally persuaded the German leadership to seek an immediate armistice.

On 5 November, the day after Wilfred was killed, the *London Gazette* reported that he was to be a full Lieutenant, with effect from 4 December 1917.[21] The long-delayed promotion had come through too late, and for months it went unnoticed. On the 8th the battalion diary noted that Wilfred, Foulkes and three other officers had been awarded the MC. On the same day Colonel Marshall was buried in the village cemetery at Ors in the presence of Major-General Lambert of 32nd Division, Brigadier-General Girdwood of 96th Brigade and representatives from the brigade's three battalions. Marshall's grave was set apart from the rest as a mark of honour. The other dead were buried nearby, possibly on the same day. The generals may have paid their respects to James Kirk, but they probably took little notice of a wooden cross bearing the name of Second Lieutenant W.E.S. Owen. Three days later, on 11 November, the war ended, and on that same day a telegram arrived at Mahim to say that Wilfred was dead.[22]

Epilogue

It is something of a miracle that none of Wilfred's war poems were lost after his death. His mother's systems of storage seem to have been chaotic, and she often sent irreplaceable manuscripts to editors by ordinary mail. She gave some drafts away to friends, and even considered donating one to a charity auction. Even so, there is no evidence that any complete poems went missing, except for a few minor pieces that survive only as copies made by Leslie Gunston.[1] Wilfred himself had no doubt thrown away many rough drafts and early verse over the years. What went into the sack that he instructed Susan to burn ('it was like burning my heart,' she said later) can only be guessed at, but after her death Harold found remarkably few letters *to* his brother, even though Wilfred had maintained an extensive correspondence.[2] Wilfred had been in too much of a hurry to sort through his papers and may well have hurled letters indiscriminately into the sack, perhaps knowing that a few of them, from Scott Moncrieff for example, could have shocked his family and even caused trouble for their authors.

It is strange to reflect that at the time of his death Wilfred was almost completely unknown. There are now memorials to him in his three home towns, Oswestry, Birkenhead and Shrewsbury, and even in Manchester Cathedral and beside the lock at Gailly. The Wilfred Owen Association, based in Shrewsbury, has flourished for over a decade, with hundreds of members at home and abroad. But only five of Wilfred's poems reached print in his lifetime – 'Song of Songs' in *The Hydra* and *The Bookman*, 'The Next War' in *The Hydra*, and 'Miners', 'Futility' and 'Hospital Barge' in *The Nation* – and only the last three attracted any attention. He had been asked to contribute to *Wheels*, so his mother wrote to Osbert Sitwell and as a result seven poems appeared in the 1919 volume of the anthology, meeting with warm approval from reviewers. Edith Sitwell then prepared a small edition of Wilfred's war poems, although her strong feelings and lack of scholarly experience led to a good many misreadings. Before she had finished, Sassoon, who had belatedly heard of Wilfred's death, insisted on taking over the project, saying Wilfred would have wanted him to be editor. *Poems by Wilfred Owen* was published by Chatto & Windus in 1920.[3] Sassoon's introduction said that any record of Wilfred's life would be 'irrelevant and unseemly': the poems should speak for themselves. This stern discouragement to any attempt at biography was followed by silence for over a decade, except for little-noticed comments by Scott Moncrieff and Graves, who between them revealed that Wilfred's courage had been doubted by the military authorities.

With the revival of interest in the war and 'war books' in the late 1920s, Edmund Blunden was commissioned by Chatto & Windus to produce a new, enlarged edition of the poems, with notes and a long memoir. Blunden gathered reminiscences from a few people who had known Wilfred in 1917–18, but most of his information came from Susan Owen. She supplied quotations from the letters, holding back most of the originals because she felt they were too personal. When Blunden submitted his typescript for the family's approval, she asked him not to quote a mention of beer in one of the letters ('not quite "Wilfred"'); Tom asked for the omission of a reference to 'the British Government & its accomplices' in a late 1918 letter ('too political'); and Harold was emphatic that nothing should be said about the cowardice question. Blunden himself presented Wilfred as a typical junior officer of the Great War, heroic, selfless and long-suffering. Invaluable though the memoir was, it had the effect of enshrining an idealised version of its subject. Blunden's edition came out in 1931, and little more was said about Wilfred's life for over thirty years. Sassoon had the principal manuscripts bound in two red leather volumes, and they were bought for the British Museum.

~

Tom Owen retired in 1925, having never become Superintendent of the Joint Railways. He moved with his wife and daughter to a Somerset vicarage, sharing the house with Susan's cousin, the Reverend William Davies. House-sharing was not a success, however, and the three Owens soon found a new home, with the aid of John Gunston: 193 Peppard Road, Emmer Green, not far from Dunsden and Alpenrose. They named the house 'Wilmot'. Tom died in 1931 and was buried at Dunsden by Herbert Wigan, who was still the local vicar. Susan, who died in 1942, and Mary, who died in 1956, are also buried in the churchyard, as is Wigan himself.

Harold Owen left the Royal Navy after the war in poor health and could find no permanent employment. His tribulations are described in *After-math* (Oxford University Press, 1970), his fourth volume of autobiography. In 1927, happily, he married Phyllis de Pass, who had money of her own, and Harold was now able to fulfil the old family ambition by becoming a country gentleman. He and Phyllis lived in Oxfordshire, again not very far from Dunsden, in a house designed for them by Leslie Gunston. Harold is said by some to have become a snob, but others remember him and his wife as a charming, devoted couple, friendly and welcoming to everybody. They had no children. Harold had taken up painting again after the war, but could never gain much recognition. In the end he burned almost all his work. The few pictures that survive reflect a tormented imagination and a striking, if not fully realised talent. He devoted his last years to writing his memoirs. *Journey from Obscurity* (3 vols, OUP, 1963-5) was generally well received, and Harold was at last able to feel that he had produced work that would endure as long as Wilfred's. He died in November 1971.

The youngest of the three Owen brothers, Colin, became a senior probation officer in Kenya. He married and had three sons, the eldest of whom, Peter Owen, is Wilfred's next of kin and the genial, highly effective President of the Wilfred Owen Association.

Leslie Gunston became an architect, designing schools for the Bedfordshire education authority. He also designed the Reading war memorial. He died in 1988.

~

Wilfred's books and papers, including the verse manuscripts that had not gone to the British Museum, passed to Harold on Susan's death. Living all his life in Wilfred's shadow, Harold longed to prove that he had been his brother's most understanding friend. He was also anxious that the world should see a 'true' version of Wilfred, and he responded to the first signs of academic interest by ruling that only 'members of the family' could interpret his brother correctly. After hoping for years to edit the poems, he had to recognise that the task was beyond him, and he eventually agreed that C. Day Lewis should produce a new edition. *The Collected Poems of Wilfred Owen* (Chatto & Windus, 1963) included many poems that had not been seen before, but Day Lewis chose to reprint Blunden's memoir as an appendix rather than add to the biographical record.

It may have been in deference to Harold's wishes that the 1963 edition did not go far beyond Blunden. Harold wanted to write his own life of Wilfred, a plan that finally evolved into *Journey from Obscurity*. Writing did not come easily to him, but he persevered and his artistic skills were useful. In a preface that remained unpublished for many years, he said that the only way he could describe Wilfred was by 'painting' him as 'a reflection of myself and the others'; he went on to qualify the statement, but it gives an insight into his method.[4]

Harold refused all offers of publication for Wilfred's letters until his own portrait of Wilfred was in print, and he censored the letters. Various motives drove him: acute class-consciousness, resentment at Wilfred's slighting references to himself, an urge to shield his brother, and a desperate anxiety to suppress anything that might assist rumours that Wilfred had been gay. Fortunately his editor at Oxford University Press, John Bell, had shown much tact and understanding in getting the typescript of *Journey from Obscurity* into a fit state for publication, and it was agreed that he and Harold would co-edit the letters. The resulting *Wilfred Owen: Collected Letters* (OUP, 1967) was a fine achievement. Some at least of Harold's inhibitions were overcome. He supplied new, if not always accurate, information and allowed obliterated passages to be restored as far as possible. People mentioned by Wilfred were traced and their memories recorded, and many allusions in the letters were explained.

For many years Wilfred was regarded as a fairly minor poet, although his work had been appearing in anthologies since 1919. Histories of literature often ignored him altogether. The 1960s and Vietnam changed all that. It was no coincidence that the Day Lewis edition, Harold's memoirs, the letters and the first academic book about Wilfred, Dennis Welland's *Wilfred Owen: A Critical Study* (Chatto & Windus, 1960), all appeared in that turbulent decade. Benjamin Britten's use of the poems in his *War Requiem* (1962) caused a surge of interest. Wilfred was at last beginning to be a nationally known poet. The moment had clearly come for an 'official' biography. John Bell's colleague at Oxford University Press, Jon Stallworthy, was appointed to write the life and edit the complete poems. That maintained a tradition, for Jon Stallworthy, like Day Lewis, Blunden, Sassoon and Edith Sitwell before him, was a poet.

Phyllis and Harold Owen had unfortunately sent the manuscript letters to auction after the publication of the *Collected Letters* (they were bought by the University of Texas), but in 1975 Phyllis gave all Wilfred's books and remaining papers, together with a large collection of photographs, family relics and her late husband's papers, to the English Faculty Library at Oxford, where they form the Owen Collection.

Jon Stallworthy's *Wilfred Owen: A Biography* (OUP) came out in 1974 to great acclaim. After more than half a century Wilfred's life was described clearly and objectively, with new material and many illustrations. In due course, however, the book came to be seen as incomplete. Important areas of Wilfred's life were not discussed. He emerged as rather innocent and still somewhat idealised, not yet quite free from the controls that had been imposed by his brother'.

Professor Stallworthy's edition of the *Complete Poems and Fragments* was published in two volumes jointly by Oxford and Chatto in 1983. It contains virtually all Wilfred's known verse and reproduces many of his manuscripts (in type, not facsimile) so that his revisions can be followed. Although, inevitably, some work remains to be done, the abridged paperback version has become the standard text.[5]

I hope the present book has taken Owen biography a stage further. It is not, of course, definitive. There will be additions, amendments and new interpretations – and maybe in some attic, in Edinburgh perhaps or Bordeaux, a bundle of Wilfred's letters, tied in faded purple ribbon, still waits to be discovered.

Appendix A:
The Salter Family

Wilfred Owen's maternal ancestry can easily be traced back to the late seventeenth century and one Richard Sallter of Little Ness, near Baschurch, a village halfway between Oswestry and Shrewsbury. Establishing links beyond that might be difficult, but there had been de Selfacs, le Salters, Sallters and Salters in Oswestry since the thirteenth century or earlier, their name and wealth originating from the brine springs of Shropshire and Cheshire.[1] In fact a survey of 1393 lists so many of them that there were probably numerous unrelated families, and local historians who discussed the subject in the 1890s and later were rash to assume connections. It seems almost certain, however, that Wilfred was descended from prosperous traders who had lived in or near Oswestry at least since the early Middle Ages.

Richard Sallter's son, Joseph Salter (1726–1800), married Jane Jackson of Ellesmere and lived in Llwyd's Mansion, the picturesque Tudor house still standing in the centre of Oswestry. A churchwarden and leading citizen of his time, Joseph worked primarily as a watchmaker, but also as a banker and general dealer, and he seems to have been the town's first printer. The eldest of his four sons, Robert, another watchmaker, was an author, probably the only one in the family until Wilfred. Robert's one book, *The Modern Angler*, a series of letters on fishing, was published in 1800 by his youngest brother, Jackson, who had taken up their father's trade of printing. Joseph's second son, Richard, was a captain in the Shropshire militia, but after Waterloo he advised his son, another Jackson, that there was no future in soldiering, so the young man settled down to become Oswestry's leading printer, stationer and bookseller, serving as mayor in 1866–7. One of Jackson junior's many cousins, Samuel Salter, followed a similar career in Welshpool, becoming that town's printer and in 1882–3 its mayor. The Salter tribe thus included at least four printer-booksellers, as well as an author, so Wilfred had a bookish, if not literary, ancestry.

Joseph Salter's third son, Thomas (1761–1838), Wilfred's great-great-grandfather, a timber merchant in Oswestry, married Elizabeth Moody, a publican's daughter, and had at least fourteen children. Their eldest son, Edward Salter, the builder of Plas Wilmot,[2] was born in Church Street,

Oswestry, on 4 November 1797 (exactly a hundred and twenty-one years before his great-grandson's death on the Sambre Canal). Edward trained as a joiner, no doubt under the supervision of his father the timber merchant, and at an early age went to Chester to make his fortune, returning to Oswestry in 1820 to marry a local girl, Mary Cross Simpson. The young couple set up their home within the ancient walls of Chester, and their first child Mary was born there in 1821, to be followed by Edward two years later (he lived for only eighteen months), Harriett in 1825, another Edward in the following year and Francis in 1829. The walled town was not a healthy place to live, as the old burial registers testify. Edward senior's health began to fail. He decided to move to the country, having either inherited or bought a 'garden' on the edge of his native town, in an area where Salters had owned land for centuries. He made arrangements with Oswestry carriers and tradesmen, recording the details in a little notebook and getting his father and sisters to witness contracts for bricks, stone and timber. Work began on Plas Wilmot in the summer of 1829, but Edward did not live to see the house completed. On 10 January 1830, in a savagely cold winter, he died in St Martin's parish, Chester, 'after a long illness', aged only thirty-two. When his will was proved in April he was recorded as 'Edward Salter, gentleman',[3] not as a joiner.

Edward's widow lived at Plas Wilmot until her death in 1842, when the estate passed to her eldest daughter, Mary Salter, Wilfred's grandmother. Mary's sister and two brothers married within weeks of each other in 1848. Harriett married a physician, Charles Whatmough of Whitchurch; Edward junior married Jane Munday of Dublin; and Francis, described as a 'surgeon' despite his early age, married Mary Bennion. Edward junior had a curiously unsettled career. He seems to have started as a schoolmaster in Somerset, but in 1852 he was ordained in Chester Cathedral. He took up a curacy in Dukinfield, moving on very soon. He officiated at the marriage of his sister Mary to Edward Shaw in 1857 at Gisburne, Yorkshire. Later he appears as chaplain of Penzance prison and head of the local school.[4] His career of teacher-becoming-parson must have been known to his niece, Susan Owen, and it became her hope for Wilfred after the loss of Plas Wilmot.

During Susan's childhood, the principal male Salter in Oswestry was Jackson junior, the printer and bookseller, a redoubtable local character, honest, sturdy and sharp-tongued. He kept a shop and subscription library at 31 Church Street. He was active on the town council for many years, and it was fitting that when he died in 1886 his place as an alderman was taken by Susan's father, Edward Shaw. Jackson's grave can still be seen near the porch of St Oswald's.

Appendix B:
The Accusation of Cowardice

The question of Wilfred's alleged cowardice has a long history of being suppressed, skated over, forgotten or, much less often, wildly exaggerated. It first surfaced when Charles Scott Moncrieff said in a 1920 article that Wilfred had been ordered back to France in August 1918 because he had come home in 1917 'in a state which hinted at loss of moral [morale] under shellfire'. Correspondence seen by Scott Moncrieff it the War Office in 1918 had put the matter 'more briefly, but in words which do not look well in print'. Several reviewers picked up the story, Robert Nichols saying that Wilfred had been found unfit to command troops and John Middleton Murry saying that Wilfred had been sent home 'because his nerve had failed'. When Edith Sitwell issued an angry denial on behalf of the Owen family and Sassoon, Scott Moncrieff went public again to repeat that military officialdom in 1918 had certainly regarded Wilfred as having suffered 'shock and a consequent weakening of his *moral*' in 1917.[1]

Scott Moncrieff's statements refer only to the authorities' reasoning in 1918, when every fit man was needed at the front. There is nothing now in Wilfred's army file that even hints at any loss of morale. The Medical Board in June 1917 decided he was suffering from neurasthenia caused by his cellar fall in March and the shell-blast in April. The Board noted – as it was required to do in case he later applied for a wound gratuity – that the injury was not his fault. The 1918 decision may have been based on nothing more than a general ruling that men who had fully recovered from nervous collapse should not be exempted from active service.

An entirely separate story emerged in 1929, when Robert Graves said in the first edition of his autobiography, *Goodbye to All That*, that it had preyed on Wilfred's mind at Craiglockhart that he had been 'accused of cowardice by his commanding officer'. (Later printings read 'unjustly accused'.) This statement seems to be supported by Wilfred's friend in Edinburgh, Mary Gray, writing about Wilfred to Edmund Blunden in 1930. She said Wilfred had never despaired, 'even in the grip of his painful delusion, the belief in his commanding officer's regarding him as a coward'. Blunden had probably told Mrs Gray about Graves's book (he had certainly mentioned it to another of his contributors, John Foulkes) –

hence her use of the definite article ('*the* belief') – but she seems to be remembering something Wilfred had told her. The original draft of Blunden's 1931 memoir of Wilfred included her comment, as well as a dismissal of Graves's 'callous mis-statement', but when Wilfred's parents read the typescript they asked Blunden to omit all reference to the cowardice question. This request was made on strong advice from Harold Owen, who first wanted to sue Graves and then decided that silence was a better policy. Susan also asked Blunden not to tell the Gunstons, saying she was especially anxious they should not know about the story. Her letters to both Blunden and Sassoon imply that Graves's allegation came as a surprise to her.

Sassoon objected to Graves's statement, telling Blunden that the cowardice accusation was 'only an indefinite idea which worried O' and protesting to Graves that the accusation had seemed a 'negligible affair' because Wilfred had said little about it.[2]

That seems to be all the evidence. One has to conclude, I think, that there was some kind of accusation, and that Sassoon knew about it (and perhaps had even mentioned it to Graves in 1917). I have suggested in Chapter Thirteen above that the commanding officer in question was not Colonel Luxmoore, whom Wilfred continued to hold in high esteem, but the newly promoted Acting Colonel Dempster, whom Wilfred detested. There is no sign that Dempster ever wrote anything down, nor that the authorities in 1918 had any knowledge of whatever he may have said, but even a passing remark would have been shattering to Wilfred, who had set himself high standards. The least hint that an officer had been 'windy' was profoundly insulting during the war and for a long time after it.

Attitudes are very different now. During the recent campaign to get pardons for men executed for cowardice in 1914–18, it was sometimes said that Wilfred himself had been in danger of court-martial and execution. There are no grounds whatever for that sort of speculation. Many senior officers were suspicious of 'neurasthenia' (even Sassoon thought most of the Craiglockhart patients were 'degenerates'), but by 1917 the condition was widely recognised as genuine and needing medical care. Wilfred was never in the slightest danger of being court-martialled. Except for his delayed promotion, he seems to have been treated rather well, whatever Dempster – and perhaps Colonel Mitchell at Scarborough – may have said about him.

Appendix C:
Military Cross Citations

The *London Gazette* (supplement, 30 July 1919) gives official citations for awards to officers who had given outstanding service in the battle for Joncourt ridge. Names from the 2nd Battalion, Manchester Regiment, include Lt-Col G. McM. Robertson (second bar to DSO), Maj. J.L. Murphy (DSO), Capt. L. Taylor (bar to MC), and Lt B.R. Cobley, 2/Lts B. Burrows, F. Johnson, J. Foulkes, W.E.S. Owen and Sgt-Maj. C.W. Mutters (all MC). A typed copy of Wilfred's citation, embossed with a War Office stamp and identical to the Gazette version, is in a scrapbook kept by Tom Owen (OEF):

> For conspicuous gallantry and devotion to duty in the attack on the Fonsomme Line on 1st/2nd Oct. 1918. On the Company Commander becoming a casualty, he assumed command and shewed fine leadership and resisted a heavy counter attack. He personally manipulated a captured enemy M.G. from an isolated position and inflicted considerable losses on the enemy.
> Throughout he behaved most gallantly.

A very similar typed copy, lacking the War Office stamp, survives among Harold Owen's papers. It has a different penultimate sentence:

> He personally captured an enemy Machine Gun in an isolated position and took a number of prisoners.

It seems likely that this version of the citation was produced by Harold Owen for use in the *Collected Letters*, where it is quoted in a footnote (p. 580). Both typescripts are reproduced in *Wilfred Owen: The Last Year* (p. 174).

Captain Taylor roughed out immediate recommendations for Wilfred and Foulkes, almost certainly in the field. In 1940 Taylor's widow gave these notes to a friend to pass on to Foulkes, whose daughter still owns them. The handwriting and signature match those of the messages Taylor sent back to headquarters during the battle.

The Adjt   PEDE
I beg to make the following recommend[ations]

2 Lt Foulkes for conspicuous Gallantry upon shewing great initiative.
After the final objective had been taken the left flank was subject to
heavy MG fire from Swiss Cottage; Lt Foulkes made a great effort to get
to this place according to Coy. orders. the first attempt failed & by the
aid of an enemy MG capture & LG [Lewis guns] 2 Lt Foulkes took a
party of 1 Sgt and 6 ORs down to the Cottage[?] surrounding & capturing 1 officer and 12 ORs & MG. He then pushed through the farmstead
& tried to work north along the Fonsomme line but found it strongly
held so returned to establish posts round the Cottage. This officer
shewed remark[able] courage which gave great confidence to the men
and ensured the success of the patrol.

2 Lt Owen: who when the Coy. Cdr was wounded took comd of the coy.
realising the position to[ok] steps to guard the left flank as this was very
much in the air. the enemy shortly after the Objective had been taken
attempted to counter attack from Swiss Cottage with two platoon[s]. 2
Lt Owen got [?two] captured MGs into action. The enemy was forced to
retire. later during the night 2 Lt Owen was in charge of Swiss Cottage
posts when the enemy attempt[ed] a further attack this also being
repulsed.
   This officer shewed great coolness throughout the operation and the
enemys attempts to drive us out and his energetic devotion to duty is
worthy of the highest praise.

L. Taylor Capt.

Appendix D:
Harold Owen's Voyages

The facts of Harold Owen's seagoing career are far from clear in *Journey from Obscurity*. He gives the impression that he was a 'hard-case officer' well before the outbreak of war, and that he had been sent to sea at a cruelly young age, perhaps even as early as 1910. He implies at one point that all his Merchant Navy voyages were before August 1914, or at least before his eighteenth birthday in September 1915.[1] He earns the complimentary rank of Fourth Officer in 1913, and is promoted to Third not long before August 1914. After completing his memoirs, however, Harold made a list of the ships he remembered serving in. The ships' names make it possible to trace him in logs and crew agreements.[2] These official documents show that many of his dates are inaccurate, and that he was still not an officer when he signed up for his sixth and last merchant voyage in March 1916.

Harold's first voyage was to Calcutta as a cadet (apprentice officer) in the SS *Montgomeryshire*, renamed *Bengali* in 1913, owners T. & J. Brocklebank, Liverpool. The agreement shows him joining on 14 March 1913, but the log is missing so there is no record of his heatstroke. He describes going home overland from Tilbury, and the ship did indeed call in at Tilbury before returning to Liverpool, where he signed off on 26 July.[3]

Harold says his second voyage, his first to South America, began in summer 1913,[4] a date repeated in *Collected Letters* (*CL*) footnotes, but there are clear indications in Wilfred's letters that Harold was in fact still at home at Christmas 1913 and for over three months after that. On 6 March 1914 Wilfred writes from Bordeaux expressing astonishment to Susan that Harold 'has not "made a move", neither by acceptance by the Line nor by rejection by Papa. It makes me mad. Your accounts of his occupations made me furious; (it was quite like being at home.)' This is a unique insight into how the family – or at any rate Wilfred and Susan – thought about Harold. He destroyed many references to himself in the letters, but he let this one stand, except for obliterating the word 'Line', because he was convinced his 'occupations' in March 1914 had been adventures in distant ports.

In April 1914 Wilfred wrote more kindly, congratulating Harold on 'eventually getting on La *Esmeraldas* – prettier name ... than "Carcoodoodledoo"'. Harold had been taken on as a cadet by the Pacific Steam Navigation Company, at one time the biggest shipping line in the world. He had presumably expected to sail in the PSNC's ship *Corcovado*, but in the event he joined the *Esmeraldas* on 22 April, first stop Le Havre, second South America a month later. As he rightly remembers in *Journey from Obscurity*, the ship was off Montevideo when war was declared. The *Esmeraldas* reached Liverpool on 6 September 1914. Harold describes her as a decaying 'rat ship', but she was in fact fairly new and the PSNC fleet was maintained to high standards.

Harold's list of ships includes six PSNC vessels, but his name only occurs in documents for two of them. He may well have spent short periods in the others while in South American waters. Typically there would be a call at Glasgow or Barry, then a French or Spanish port before the long crossing to Tierra del Fuego and the Straits of Magellan. The crew, consisting of a master, usually three (not four) officers, a purser, one or two cadets and about seventy British sailors, would be augmented by thirty or forty coast labourers picked up on arrival in Chile, men Harold portrays with unconcealed disgust. The ship would make rapid stops at thirty or more Chilean and Peruvian ports before dropping the labourers and heading for home, pausing in London for at least a week. The round trip took about five months, and after a break of ten days or so the cycle would begin again.

Logs record frequent disasters. A hatch falls on a labourer, a cadet loses part of a finger in a block, someone steps into a pail of boiling tea, a trimmer gets into a fight with the cook. Men are often fined or even put in irons for being drunk on board. One goes mad and has to be put in a straitjacket; another has hallucinations, convinced the firemen are plotting to throw him overboard. Invalids have to be left behind, and sometimes men jump ship, abandoning their scanty possessions. But Cadet Owen is mentioned only once, when he goes to a doctor for sore lips in Mejillones in December 1914.

Two British cruisers were sunk off the Chilean coast in November 1914. Harold's third voyage, in the *Esmeraldas* from 13 October 1914 to 3 (London) and 20 (Liverpool) March 1915, took the safe outward route of Spain, Havana and the new Panama Canal. The cargo was apparently human, hundreds of poor migrants, and Harold describes the crowded hold in a scene strongly reminiscent of Conrad's *Typhoon*. The last of von Spee's ships was not disposed of until March 1915, but the *Esmeraldas* made her usual calls and returned home by the southern route. 'What a relief to know that Harold is landed!' Wilfred wrote on 13 March.

When Harold returned to the ship in early April he found that she had been commandeered for transport duties in the Mediterranean. The log notes that he was transferred to another PSNC ship on 7 April. An exclamation by Wilfred on 15 March, 'What a chagrin for Harold and for Father!', is assumed by a *CL* footnote to refer to Harold's disappointment that 'no officer under 21' was allowed to be sent to Gallipoli, but Wilfred's comment perhaps meant something else. Harold may have done an officer's job during his latest voyage, only to be told in London that the rank was not going to be confirmed. Despite the *CL* footnote, he remained a cadet. Hence Wilfred's otherwise incomprehensible remark on 10 April that Perseus had been a sailor-lad and a hero, though never wearing epaulets and gold braid.

It is not clear which ship Harold was transferred to, but he must have made a fourth voyage in April–September 1915. His fifth, from 27 September 1915 to 28 February 1916, was in the SS *Kenuta*. The crew agreement notes his pay, £1 13s 6d a month, less than the cook's boy. Apprentices were paid with experience rather than money. The ship returned to London on 14 February, remaining for twelve days in the docks, where Wilfred seems to have visited her.[5] Harold spent a day at Romford and Ilford (the evening with the waitress), and the two brothers met again a few days later in London, when Wilfred was staying at the Poetry Bookshop.

The *Kenuta* sailed again on 28 March 1916. Unlike any of Harold's other recorded merchant voyages, this one included a stop at the Falklands, so that may give the date, 30 July 1916, for his dramatic story of being marooned for a night in a hulk, an experience *Journey from Obscurity* places in January 1914. According to his list of ships he became Third Officer in the *Kenuta*. Maybe he was temporarily promoted at sea. The crew agreement for this final voyage shows him as still an apprentice, but the log fails to mention him at all, conceivably a clue that his rank changed during the trip. 'Excellent news of dear old W.H.O.,' Wilfred said on 12 August. The ship must have paused in London as usual, enabling Harold to visit Wilfred at Witley on about 12 September, the occasion he remembers with such pleasure in *Journey from Obscurity*.

After a brief career as a trainee pilot with the Royal Naval Air Service from October 1916 to March 1917, Harold became a midshipman in the Royal Naval Reserve in April 1917. He later believed he had been appointed Sub-Lieutenant on 8 March 1918, but his promotion, like Wilfred's, was in fact backdated, probably from August 1918, when he was sent to join HMS *Astraea* off South Africa. The details may become clear when his RNR file, if it survives, is made available.

Harold describes entering his cabin on the *Astraea* soon after the Armistice and seeing Wilfred sitting there, smiling 'his sweetest and most endearing dark smile'.[6] Some people express incredulity at this incident, others find it completely convincing. As with so many of Harold's stories, there is no way of knowing the truth.

Sources and Abbreviations

The following abbreviations are used in the Notes and Appendices. The list includes principal sources; other sources are given in the Notes.

BCL   Birkenhead Central Library.

CL   *Wilfred Owen: Collected Letters*, ed. Harold Owen and John Bell (1967).

CPF   *Wilfred Owen: The Complete Poems and Fragments*, ed. Jon Stallworthy, 2 vols (1983).

CRO   Cheshire Record Office, Chester.

CSM   Charles Scott Moncrieff.

CUL   Cambridge University Library.

DK   Douglas Kerr, *Wilfred Owen's Voices: Language and Community* (1993).

DW   Dennis Welland, *Wilfred Owen: A Critical Study* (revised and enlarged edn, 1978).

EB   Edmund Blunden or his edition of *The Poems of Wilfred Owen* (1931).

HO   Harold Owen (brother).

HRC   Harry Ransom Humanities Research Center, University of Texas at Austin.

IBI   *In Broken Images: Selected Letters of Robert Graves 1914–1946*, ed. Paul O'Prey (1982).

IWM   Imperial War Museum.

JFO   Harold Owen, *Journey from Obscurity*, 3 vols (1963–5).

JMW   Jean Moorcroft Wilson, *Siegfried Sassoon: The Making of a War Poet* (1998).

KS   Kenneth Simcox, *Wilfred Owen: Anthem for a Doomed Youth* (1987).

L   denotes one of WO's letters, followed by its number in *CL/SL*. Where a letter number is followed by n (e.g., L98n), the reference is to an editorial footnote in *CL*.

*L   denotes one of WO's letters as amended or added to in OL.

LG   E. Leslie Gunston (first cousin).

MO   Mary Owen (sister).

M/G   Helen McPhail and Philip Guest, *On the Trail of the Poets of the Great War: Wilfred Owen* (1998).

OEF   Wilfred Owen Collection, English Faculty Library, Oxford. OEF followed by a number indicates a MS or other item in the collection.

OG   Dominic Hibberd, 'Wilfred Owen and the Georgians', *Review of English Studies* 30 (February 1979), 28–40.

OL   Dominic Hibberd, 'Wilfred Owen's letters: some additions, amendments and notes', *The Library* 4 (September 1982), 273–87.

OS   Osbert Sitwell, *Noble Essences* (1950).

OTP   Dominic Hibberd, *Owen the Poet* (1986).

PGW   *Poetry of the Great War: An Anthology*, ed. Dominic Hibberd and John Onions (1986).

PRO   Public Record Office, Kew.

RG   Robert Graves.
SL   *Wilfred Owen: Selected Letters*, ed. John Bell (second edn, 1998).
SO   Susan Owen (mother).
SRC   Shropshire Records and Research Centre, Shrewsbury.
SS   Siegfried Sassoon.
SSD   Siegfried Sassoon, *Diaries 1915-1918*, ed. Rupert Hart-Davis (1983).
SSJ   Siegfried Sassoon, *Siegfried's Journey* (1945).
TLY   Dominic Hibberd, *Wilfred Owen: The Last Year 1917-1918* (1992).
TO   Tom Owen (father).
WO   Wilfred Owen.
WOB   Jon Stallworthy, *Wilfred Owen: A Biography* (1974).
WPO   *Wilfred Owen: War Poems and Others*, ed. Dominic Hibberd (1973).

OWEN MANUSCRIPTS
The main collections of WO's MSS are in the British Library (verse), HRC (letters) and OEF (verse, notes, miscellaneous items, WO's books, family photographs and relics, HO's papers).

LITERARY HISTORY AND CRITICISM
See *OTP* for a detailed bibliography. Since 1986 there have been several short books about WO other than those listed above, including Helen McPhail, *Portrait of Wilfred Owen: poet and soldier*, and Merryn Williams, *Wilfred Owen* (both 1993).

MILITARY HISTORY
PRO has a wealth of original material, including trench maps, officers' individual files (not all these survive or are as yet available) and the war diaries kept by all units from battalions up to armies while on active service. Less than ten years ago Ministry of Defence officials were insisting that WO's own file had not survived, but it is now in a special class in PRO, alongside files for such luminaries as Kitchener and the Kaiser. The unfortunate result is that it is already suffering from overuse. Documents in it can be viewed on a website that also shows many of the manuscripts, *The Hydra* and other material: http://info.ox.ac.uk/jtap/. Another useful site is www.wilfred.owen.association.mcmail.com. Manchester Regiment archives are at Stalybridge (Tameside Local Studies Library). Local studies libraries in Godalming (for Witley) and Romford have maps of home camps. George Derbyshire, 'A Wigan Military Chronicle', an unpublished history of the 5th Manchesters, is in the Wigan Metro Archives at Leigh; vol. 3 (1957) contains a limited amount of information about the 3/5th or Reserve Battalion.
    Published works most frequently referred to in the Notes:

History of the Great War [the 'official history']: *Military Operations, France and Belgium,
    1917*, vol. 1, comp. Cyril Falls (1940), and *1918*, vol. 5, comp. J.E. Edmonds (1947).
Latter, J.C., *The History of the Lancashire Fusiliers 1914-1918* (1949).
Montgomery, A.A., *The Story of the Fourth Army in the Battles of the Hundred Days*
    (1920).
[Whinyates, R., ed.,] *Artillery and Trench Mortar Memories: 32nd Division* (1932).
Wylly, H.C., *History of the Manchester Regiment* (1925).

    Other military histories that I have found particularly useful include: Malcolm Brown, *The Imperial War Museum Book of 1918: Year of Victory* (1998); Paddy Griffith, *Battle Tactics on the Western Front: The British Army's Art of Attack, 1916-18* (1994); J.P. Harris and Niall Barr, *Amiens to the Armistice: The BEF in the Hundred Days Campaign* (1998); Gary

Sheffield, *Forgotten Victory / The First World War: Myths and Realities* (2001); Ben Shephard, *A War of Nerves* (2000); and volumes in the Battleground Europe series: Nigel Cave, *Beaumont Hamel* (1994); Jack Horsfall and Nigel Cave, *Serre* (1996); Helen McPhail and Philip Guest, *St Quentin* (2000); Peter Oldham, *The Hindenburg Line* (1997).

Notes

INTRODUCTION (PAGES XVII–XIX)

1   Patric Dickinson, 'Wilfred Owen', BBC Third Programme talk, 17 August 1953 (scripts in OEF and HRC). The fragments quoted by Dickinson are not in *CPF*.

CHAPTER 1: FROM PLAS WILMOT TO WILMOT HOUSE (PAGES 10–13)

1   'Salter–Owen': cp. Mostyn–Owen, the name of the Oswestry landed family.
2   It is perhaps not correct to say WO was named after Edward Salter, or for that matter after Edward's son, another Edward, a clergyman. WO's second name was probably in honour of his grandfather Edward Shaw, just as HO was christened William after their other grandfather.
3   E. Harward Salter of Ellesmere to HO, 7 April 1964 (OEF 12:134). Miss Salter seems to have been a granddaughter of Jackson Salter, the Oswestry printer. For the Salter family, see Appendix A.
4   The only source for Mary Shaw's being known as May is *JFO*. I have used the name to avoid confusion.
5   *Oswestry and Border Counties Advertizer*, 8 January 1873. See also 20 January 1897 (Shaw's obituary) and 2 December 1891 (his wife's death).
6   He was employing eleven men at the time of the 1851 census.
7   Press cutting kept by HO, n.d. (OEF 29:1).
8   It remains a mystery that two girls from Oswestry should have married Londoners, although Oswestry had become an important railway centre and the Shaws seem to have had a wide network of acquaintances.
9   L176.
10 Colin Dymott tells me that a T. Owen played football for the Oswestry White Stars in the 1870s and was even selected to play for Wales in 1879. Ceri Stennett (historian, Football Wales) adds that this Owen, like TO, died in October 1931; on the other hand, a T. Owen played for Oswestry in 1882, when TO was in India. There were certainly several T. Owens in Oswestry and Shrewsbury in this period. It may never be possible to be sure that TO played for Wales, but it does seem likely that he sometimes played in the same teams as Edward Gough Shaw.
11 Great-Uncle Charles Salter, died 1869.
12 L258.
13 L663 [forefathers]. *JFO* III, 9 [cry]. DW, 107, 161 [MO's letter].
14 *WOB*, 4, says William and Martha (her correct name) moved in with William's parents at Nixson's Row, but the 1861 census shows the parents at 90 Welsh Row and the young couple at 86. Presumably TO was born at 86 (his birth certificate merely says Welsh Row).
15 *JFO/WOB* give TO as the youngest of the four children, and the others in order of age as

'May', 'Emily' and 'Anne'. The family tree in *CL*, 17, names Emily as Emma. HO probably confused his Owen aunts with his maternal ones, May and Emma Shaw. The names and sequence were in fact Ann ('Annie'), Tom, Edith Charlotte and Emily ('Emmie') Eliza.

16 Elizabeth Owen tells me that Mary Ragge, who knew the Owens in Shrewsbury, remembered TO often talking to his children about nature and the stars.

17 *WOB*, 4, gives TO's employer in Oswestry as the Great Western, but I can find no trace of him in GWR registers. He joined the Joint Railways in 1884 on a recommendation from Cambrian. His career thereafter can be traced in LNW & GW Railways Joint Committee staff registers (PRO, CRO).

18 HO, rarely sure about numbers, says more than once that TO was in India for four years. *WOB*, 5–7, accepts the story in *JFO* I, 6–7 but discovers the wedding was in 1891, so assumes TO was away until then. TO is indeed listed in the 1884 *Times of India Calendar and Bombay Directory*, but not in later volumes (nor ever, I think, in the directory's lists of the GIPR Volunteer Corps, although he may have joined as a cadet). He was a witness at his sister Edith's wedding in Shrewsbury in 1888. The 1891 census shows him as 'Railway Accountant' living at 2 Hawthorn Villas with William ('Commercial Traveller drapery'), Martha and the youngest sister, Emily.

19 Jeremy Ward has discovered that Taylor's home and shop were at 74, now 104, Heaton Moor Road, Stockport. The premises are still occupied by a newsagent. *CL* describes Taylor as a bookseller, but street directories also list him as a newsagent and stationer.

20 Despite its name, the society met in the town centre and was not especially literary.

21 A birthday book (OEF) SO was given in 1882 contains the signatures of Tom, William, Martha, Edith and Emmie Owen. Edith uses her maiden name, so the signatures must have been written between 1884, when Tom returned from India, and 1888, when Edith was married.

22 *JFO/WOB* state that both May and Richard Loughrey died young as a result of working in the East End. May's illness could have been caused by slum conditions, but the addition of her husband's death is an example of HO's myth-making tendency. Richard remained in practice at 146 Mile End Road at least until 1909.

23 *JFO* I, 85.

24 Not (*JFO/CL/WOB*) 1895. MO and TO shared birthdays on 30 May; WO and SO had birthdays one day apart.

25 The original sale catalogue (cp. *CL*, 1) has disappeared. Photographs of it are in OEF.

26 *JFO* I, 124–5.

27 L1. Cp. *CL*, 1.

CHAPTER 2: SCHOOLBOY (PAGES 14–34)

1 Information about Birkenhead from the Institute's records, including its magazine *The Visor* and directors' minutes, and local directories and newspapers (BCL). TO was charged 17s, half the full fee, for WO's first term in 1900. *WOB*, 19, 28, mistakenly gives the year as 1899 and the date of HO's entry (actually April 1904) as October 1903.

2 *JFO* I, 85–6.

3 *JFO* I, 13, 19.

4 HO puts TO's salary at not more than £90 in 1900–3. It actually reached that figure in 1889, going up by small increments to £150 (March 1900), £165 (October 1901), £180 (January 1904), £190 (January 1906). All but one of the other staff at Woodside earned under £100. For comparison, masters' salaries at the Institute ranged from £80 to £150; Miss Farrell, WO's first teacher there, earned £105, and in 1903 the new head started on £250.

5   Christ Church Sunday School register (CRO) gives WO's address in November 1902 as 14 Willmer Road and HO's a year later as 51 Milton Road. The March 1901 census shows all six Owens and a maid at 7 Elm Grove. Street directories show TO at Elm Grove 1901–2, Willmer Road 1903, Milton Road 1904–7. The sequence and dates in *WOB* (Willmer 1898, Elm later in 1898, Milton from winter 1898–9) are presumably based on the table in *CL*, 9, which must itself be based on HO's erratic memories. A blue plaque placed on the Elm Grove house in October 2001 gives the date 1900–3, but 1900–2 seems more likely.

6   L226.

7   L50.

8   WO's prize, *Nursery Songs and Rhymes of England*, now belongs to Peter Owen. Speech Day was held in March 1901, having been delayed by the death of Queen Victoria.

9   The connection between Robson and the Owens has hitherto gone unnoticed, probably because WO refers to him only as 'the Canon' (L74, 110, 118, 125).

10   Robson, *Christian Life: A booklet for the young* (1911).

11   2 Kings 4.26, Isa. 43.1, 2 Tim. 2.12, Isa. 66.13.

12   L118, 125. The preacher was E.W. Moore.

13   *JFO* I, 131–2. Despite his later cynicism, HO is listed with MO and Colin among the successful entrants to a 'Bible Searcher' quiz in *The Christian* as late as 15 August 1912.

14   SO to Paton, 27 May [1919] (photocopies, HRC and BCL).

15   L3, 14. *JFO* I, 44, 150–1, 49.

16   Sunday School register (CRO). *JFO* I, 61. *JFO* I, 40, is mistaken in saying TO became a churchwarden.

17   L139.

18   David Gunston, 'Tea with a poet's mother', *The Lady* (6 November 1990), 900–1.

19   This paragraph owes much to Elizabeth Owen, who also suggests SO may have had a miscarriage between the births of WO and MO.

20   L281.

21   L122, 99, 273 [furniture].

22   Two experts, Sally Roberton and Pamela Bowen, have kindly looked at examples of HO's adult writing and confirmed that he does indeed seem to have been dyslexic.

23   L162. *JFO* I, 15. Information from June Calder and others.

24   *JFO* I, 25.

25   *JFO* I, 103. L593. *OTP*, 2, 8.

26   *JFO* I, 12.

27   Mary Walczak to HO, 5 October [1965] (OEF 13:16).

28   L162.

29   *Oswestry Advertiser*, 22 July 1931.

30   *JFO* I, 77–8. Bäckman, *Tradition Transformed: Studies in the Poetry of Wilfred Owen* (Lund, 1979), 101–2.

31   *JFO* I, 107–12. May (Mary), born Oswestry 1863, was a niece of Edward Shaw. Her brother was a clergyman, probably the only one in the family during WO's lifetime, but WO is unlikely to have met him. Revd William Davies was a missionary in India, 1887–94, then had an Isle of Man parish until 1923. TO and SO shared a house with him briefly after TO retired.

32   *JFO* I, 85. The parenthesis is worth savouring.

33   A.R. Entwisle to HO, 10 November 1964 (OEF 12:187). Entwisle met the unnamed master in a Liverpool bookshop.

34   *JFO* I, 37.

35   *JFO* I, 96. The Christ Church register records HO as having 'No school yet' when he

started Sunday School in November 1903. His memories of Birkenhead perhaps really belong to Shrewsbury: his stories of the two towns have obvious similarities (e.g., in each place he attends three schools, fighting bullies in the first, and is educated for a time at home). Another inaccuracy in his Birkenhead story concerns his friend 'Matheson', who lives on the edge of town, well away from the Owens' area. The Mathiesons (school register) or Mathisons (street directories) actually lived in Circular Road, a stone's throw from the Institute.

36 F.E. Smith, the future Lord Birkenhead, had lived in Clifton Road, the grandest road in Higher Tranmere, and had been a pupil at Galloway's, according to *The Visor* (Summer 1935, 135).

37 I guess the minimum entrance age was six and a half, hence HO's joining in mid-year. There were rarely more than one or two boys under seven in the school.

38 Brothers qualified for discounts. In spring 1904 TO paid £2 11s 6d for WO in the Junior School, including a discount of 2s 6d, and £1 12s 6d for HO in the Prep, including a discount of 1s 6d. Discounted fees for the two Owens continued to be paid every term until 1907. HO was clearly mistaken in remembering that his parents preferred to spend money on WO's education rather than his own.

39 Scholarship certificate (OEF 3:425) dated 1905. The scholarships for 1904 were awarded at the March 1905 Speech Day; those for 1905 were presumably awarded in 1906, although the press report does not mention them.

40 Williams, letter to the Institute, 3 December 1960 (BCL). HO could not remember ever walking to or from school with WO, but Williams recalled walking along Derby Road with both brothers.

41 *JFO* I, 86, 92. L214 [Wulfie], 175.

42 Paton to Joseph Cohen, 7 February 1954 (HRC). *JFO* I, 110. See also Paton's contribution to T.J. Walsh, comp., *A Tribute to Wilfred Owen* (Birkenhead Institute, 1964).

43 *WOB*, 34, drawing on Eric's recollections.

44 Library opened, June 1965. HO was unable to attend the ceremony, but letters from him and the prize book are in BCL.

CHAPTER 3: PUPIL-TEACHER (PAGES 35–61)

1 L557.

2 OEF 410.

3 *Shrewsbury Chronicle*, 31 January, 18 June 1908. Also 6 February 1909 (a dinner when TO was vice-chairman).

4 SRC 3465/xxxviii/15. WO may have started at the Technical a little before his birthday: an exercise in a chemistry notebook he had used at Birkenhead is dated 13 March 1907. *How to become a teacher in a Public Elementary School* (1912) and other Board of Education publications explain the pupil-teacher system.

5 TO's salary went up from £190 to £230 in 1907, but all his children were now of school age.

6 KS (1987), 85 [Williams]. Reminiscences by A.J. Wright, Roy Jones and others who knew the Owens in Shrewsbury: unsigned TS annotated by HO (OEF 29:6).

7 KS, 83. A.J. Wright recalled that WO played Buzfuz.

8 L23, misdated 1907 in *CL*.

9 *L24.

10 L258.

11 L195n gives this date, though William's name remains until 1910 in Shrewsbury directories, where he is described as 'clothier's manager', 1900–10.

12 *L26, L31 [blessings].

13 L221, 480. WO's name is on the St Julian's war memorial as a member of the congregation.

14 L37 and information from David Gunston.

15 13 Bertram Drive. The view and garden are less extensive now than in 1908. The Quayles were there until 1941.

16 Cp. L46 ['glaring'].

17 Unpublished letter, 1993 (copy, OEF 29:13).

18 L593.

19 WO first used the image of the sun 'blessing all the field and air with gold' in 1914–15 without any mention of boots or feet ('A Palinode'). HO's annotated copy of EB is in OEF. For many years he hoped to edit the poems himself.

20 *JFO* I, 186–99. HO later claimed he had not read WO's letters before writing *JFO*, but he quotes here from a lost letter about Tarr and uses phrases from other letters.

21 L95, 74. King's Scholarships had been replaced by a different scheme in 1907, but the name seems to have persisted.

22 *List of persons who have passed the preliminary examination for the Elementary School Teacher's Certificate* (Board of Education, 1911) gives candidates' results and schools.

23 WO said in 1914 that he had been working for money since the age of sixteen (L258, end).

24 KS identifies HO's three Shrewsbury schools. The first must be the Lancasterian near the station: the head, with 'a dash of French blood' (*JFO* I, 126), was T.G. Robin, a Channel Islander who also taught French at the Technical. The second is Allatt's, the only charity foundation in the town: several of HO's correspondents remembered him there, though they were puzzled by his alleged fight with the head, J.W. Jepson, who was highly respected. L78n confirms that the third school was Wyle Cop (the site is now a car park near the Lion Hotel).

25 The later chapters of *JFO* I misdate events by a year or more, ending at autumn 1911. *JFO* II corrects the error by starting in late 1912, discarding a year without comment. KS, 78, was first to find the Council minute.

26 L91 [amiable], 141 [palmy], 66 [Wyle–Copic].

27 L295 [Lightbown is the correct spelling], 258 [crushing], 80 [object lesson].

28 The editor was Robert Bridges.

29 Cp. Keats, 'Sonnet Written in the Cottage where Burns was born'. See *OTP*, 3.

30 *CPF*, 385.

31 L80. Dr J. Wilbur Chapman and Mr Charles M. Alexander spoke to large audiences, 22 April–4 May 1911, amid scenes of remarkable fervour. Cp. L111 [Alexander].

32 HO's version of the deal (*JFO* I, 256), including the alleged offer of tuition, has been generally believed. Had any tuition occurred, Wilfred would have mentioned it; had it been promised but not provided, he would have complained bitterly. Wigan later offered to teach him Greek, but Wilfred seems to have declined.

33 L74.

34 His choice shows that he thought of Matric as a route away from teacher training college. College applicants had to have a pass in geography.

35 L90, 103.

36 *CPF*, 409, where the fragment and WO's Hampstead visit are mistakenly ascribed to 1912.

37 L258. As far as I can discover, *OTP* and other commentaries are mistaken in assuming that WO's failure to get a first prevented him from going to university. But he certainly regretted his 'mere Pass' (L258).

38 Mary Ragge (n.17 above) recalled being proud to be seen in public with WO in his finery.

CHAPTER 4: PARISH ASSISTANT (PAGES 62–83)

1 L146.

2 An octogenarian, A. Webb, told Christine Bland in 1995 that Wigan had been president of the football, cricket and lads' clubs and had always supported teams by attending matches.

3 Information about Dunsden and Vicarage from parish records and the Sonning Parish Magazine, to which Wigan contributed a regular report. See also Brian R. Law, *Eye and Dunsden: two centuries of change* (2001).

4 When Wigan eventually inherited the Luddesdown patronage from his mother, he gave it to the (Evangelical) Church Pastoral Aid Society. For his career, see L83n, 98n; *The Bloxhamist* (February and July 1900, March 1902); and church, Radley and Oxford registers.

5 Lewty went to South Africa in December 1911, presumably to become a missionary.

6 Labels from Poynder's, Golder's and Smith's show that many of WO's textbooks were bought in Reading.

7 L279n.

8 This suggestion is Jean Eastwood's. The well-head survives, though not in its original position.

9 The hall was certainly next to the green, not (*WOB*, 70) attached to the Vicarage. It was renamed the 'Mission Hall' in April 1914. Later it had to be propped up with buttresses, in the end becoming a ruin. No trace of it now remains, although villagers still remember it.

10 L105. Many years later a villager could still quote the carol (KS, 31).

11 For an example, see *CPF*, 16, where the poem is identified as a chorus at my suggestion.

12 L146. Hullcoop (correct spelling) was remembered by A. Webb as a harsh disciplinarian, often using the cane. Some pupils had to walk miles to school, but latecomers had to stand with their hands above their heads for five minutes.

13 *CPF*, 396. *CPF*'s suggestion that this fragment may describe Wigan derives from me (OG, 29), but I now think I was mistaken: the details don't fit.

14 L111, written in late January.

15 The miniature organ now in Dunsden church may be the one Wigan bought in 1912.

16 WO mentions 'wasted hours' (L106) in a sketch for a poem about his angrily beating heart (*CPF*, 394–5), written on the back of some notices for a lantern lecture by a missionary from Korea. He had exhausted himself delivering these notices.

17 *CL* prints the March–April letters slightly out of sequence. I think the correct order is: L123 (16 February), L126 (11 March), L127 (16 March), L128 (19 March), L129 (23 March), L125 (Thursday 28 March), L130 (3 April), L124 (Good Friday, 5 *April*), L131 (12 April).

18 Opinions differ as to whether the Montagues lived in the other semi or in the separate Oak Villa on the other side.

19 Vivian Rampton (1899–1977) and Milly Montague were childhood sweethearts later, until he saw her walking out with another boy. Vivian took a job with the Westminster Bank after leaving school. He was conscripted in 1917, but the war was over before he saw action. He then joined the Hong Kong and Shanghai Bank and was stationed in Malacca for five years, after which he moved to the Eastern Bank in London, eventually becoming Secretary. He married and had three children. His daughter Mary Townsend remembers him as an excellent father – and as an 'above average' piano player. It seems almost certain he never realised that Mr Owen of Dunsden and the famous war poet were one and the same man.

20 The refurnishing of the Vicarage is unexplained. Wigan may have inherited some antiques.

21 *OTP*, 14.
22 Kendrick School for Boys, absorbed into Reading School in 1915.
23 L132, dated 16 April, actually written on 17th (the day of the eclipse mentioned in the letter). WO's college application form (Reading University Library) is dated 17 April 1912. Classes began on the 18th and ended on 2 June. The fee was £3 13s 6d.
24 L133. For the literary allusions in this letter and WO's quotation from Laurie Magnus, *Introduction to Poetry*, see *OTP*, 14, 210 n.17. See also DK on Magnus.
25 'Written on a June Night (1911)'. Despite the title, this unfinished poem seems to have been started in spring 1912.
26 A copy of the 1920 edition of WO's poems recently seen by Vanessa Davis has an unsigned note on the flyleaf apparently by Dr Rayner, recording that WO often visited her house; she thought more highly of his abilities than his English tutor (presumably Edith Morley) did, and she saw him for the last time in 1917.
27 It was agreed that the lavatories should be whitewashed and a rotten fence replaced. The minute book survives at Dunsden, with entries in WO's hand for 2 July and 15 October 1912. The entry for 14 January 1913 was begun by him but completed by Wigan.

CHAPTER 5: APOSTATE (PAGES 84–98)

 1 L146–7. *JFO* places the Kelso holiday in 1911, thereby missing the connection between WO's exhaustion and Dunsden.
 2 The 1912 Convention is very fully reported in *The Life of Faith*, *The Christian* and *The Keswick Week 1912*. See also *The Keswick Convention: its message, its method and its men* (1907).
 3 Rough note written in 1917 for a letter (OL, 286–7). See also L185 [Coniston] and *CPF*, 31.
 4 L142 [Honours 1914], 157–8 [payment for UCC course]. Set books for Intermediate 1914 included *Faerie Queene* II, *Tempest* (ed. Weekes), *Dr Faustus* and Albert S. Cook, *A First Book in Old English*. Copies of these and two other Old English textbooks, all bought in Reading, are still in WO's library.
 5 For the literary allusions in the letter, see my 'Images of darkness in the poems of Wilfred Owen', *Durham University Journal* 56 (March 1974), 156–62.
 6 *L82. The printed version of this September 1912 letter (ascribed to June 1911 in *CL*) accidentally omits WO's opening sentence, in which he says he is spending several hours a day on parish food and clothing accounts.
 7 Texts used by WO and LG are in OEF. Other readers were Emma and Vera Gunston, Herbert Billing and Flora Poole, but not SO or MO.
 8 The accident was reported in great detail in Reading newspapers. I also draw on Wigan's comments in the parish magazine.
 9 Arthur Clyde Henderson Black (1872–1948) left Dunsden in 1913 apparently in poor health, but he went on to the London College of Divinity in 1915 and eventually became a vicar in Sussex.
10 Beeches are a feature of the Chilterns.
11 *CPF*, 437–8.
12 Morley to Roland Duthoy, quoted *WOB*, 75. Information about Morley from obituaries and her unpublished autobiography (Reading University Library). L167 implies that WO first met her in late November or early December not (*WOB*, 75) June.
13 KS, 51.
14 L172. *CL* dates this letter 4 January, but MS bears no date; internal evidence suggests later in the month. Mnemosyne: goddess of memory, cp. Keats, *Hyperion* (WO may mean that Wigan had forgotten the 'furor').

15 WO seems to have taken the opportunity to visit Kemp in Highbury (L485).
16 Monro echo: OG, 30.

CHAPTER 6: ESCAPE (PAGES 99–107)

1 L205, 214, 239 ('to-night': *c.* 24 February).
2 *OTP*, 25.
3 Betty Egan to HO, 16 August 1963 (OEF 12:90).
4 *Rules as to the issue of Certificates for Teachers of Art* (Board of Education, 1912). The new age limit would have made no difference to HO. The existing rules prevented students from beginning the two-year pupil-teacher course until the August after their sixteenth birthday; his birthday was in September, so he would not have been able to qualify until just before age nineteen in any case. For HO's 1912 exams, see KS, 78.
5 *JFO* II, 61. For HO's Merchant Navy career, see Appendix D.
6 Annie was now living in the house to which her husband had retired and where he had died in August 1912: La Vallée, 48 Sherwell Lane, a large end-house in Belle Vue Crescent.
7 L185n.
8 *CPF*, 71–4. I see no evidence for the dates *CPF* ascribes to the second poem, but a Dunsden start certainly seems probable.
9 *L193. *JFO* I, 251–2.
10 SO's suggestion of France: L74. WO was longing to escape there while at Dunsden (L82, September 1912).
11 One of these archaeologists was Mortimer Wheeler.
12 L195. There seems no evidence that WO fell ill again after this Meols visit (*WOB*, 93). The confusion arises from *JFO*, where HO forgets that the summer intervened between WO's post-Dunsden illness and France.

CHAPTER 7: PROFESSOR OF ENGLISH (PAGES 108–26)

1 L244, 253, 330. Details in the surviving Bordeaux letters are sometimes easy to miss. HO's assertion that WO received funds from home has usually been accepted, for example, yet comments in the letters show that WO refused offers of parental help.
2 Entrance at the side in the Rue du Temple.
3 Information about Bordeaux from local newspapers, especially *Le Petite Gironde* and *La Vie Bordelaise*, and volumes of the *Annuaire de la Gironde* (annual directory). WO says Perry spoke bad French and worse English (L199) but gives no clue as to his origins. In effect the *ballon* seems to have been a miniature Zeppelin. It received enthusiastic reviews. The first public performance on Friday the 19th was thinly attended because Poincaré was in town and there was a great firework display, but numbers soon went up.
4 L202 [band], 324 [river]. Park: the *jardin public*, the English-style park in the city centre. The only source for the Sir Thomas story is *JFO* III, 52–6. HO does not seem to have invented it, although one may doubt his defensive details (e.g., that the title originated from WO's friends, not from WO himself). WO's letters give no evidence whatever for HO's claim that TO's visit was prompted by news that WO was ill and attending hospital as an out-patient.
5 Dr Aumont: not (*WOB*, 97–8) the same man as Maurice Aumont. The 1913 *Annuaire* lists both of them and a G. Aumont, an insurance inspector, at 14 Cours du Chapeau Rouge.
6 The two friends from the *Union* were presumably Protestant, hence their giggling. One of them may have been Raoul Lem. L404 confirms that WO ate alone.

7   WO suggested facetiously that Colin, about to become a Scout, should be able to detect invading Germans (L213).

8   *L242. Notes in *CL* that HO was at sea in winter 1913–14 are contradicted by WO's letters. See Appendix D.

9   L312. (L311–13, three postcards, belong to 1914, not 1915 as in *CL*.)

10   *L238. The reference to HO is further evidence that he was still at home. He later painted out the last lines of this passage, but they can still be deciphered.

11   A note in SO's Bible shows her choosing five texts for special prayer that day.

12   L245n.

13   HO describes Raoul as effeminate, with 'great moist eyes' (*JFO* III, 63).

14   Houses WO visited included 12 Rue St Louis, now Paul Berthelot (Lem), 23 Rue de la Franchise (Berthaud), 54 Rue Leberthon (Bizardel) and 110 Chemin de Passac, now Gallieni (Peyronnet).

15   The PSNC was in fact now based in Liverpool.

16   Helen McPhail suggests this parallel between the lilac and the ambivalent spring flowers in 'The Send-Off'.

17   *CPF*, 467–70, prints this fragment as two separate pieces, but they clearly belong together. I see no grounds for a 'probable' 1915 date. *CPF*'s wording and word order also need amending (e.g., 'us heal' and 'rough' should be 'no heat' and 'soul').

18   The two widows, Martha Owen and her daughter Annie Taylor, soon moved in together. Martha was to outlive her grandson: she died at Babbacombe in November 1921.

19   WO's route back from Bizardel's house probably took him past the great medieval church of Ste Eulalie.

CHAPTER 8: TRÈS-JOLI GARÇON (PAGES 127–40)

1   Charles, not (L265n) Alfred.

2   L538.

3   The Tuesday events, known as the *Mardis de Madame*, are mentioned in *La Vie Bordelaise*. WO says Léger ran an experimental theatre, but I have found no record of it.

4   L279n.

5   L516.

6   He was a rarity in Bagnères. Most of the 365 foreign visitors there in June 1914 were Spanish; only four were British.

7   L302 [language], 298 [mother-tongue].

8   For Tailhade, see Paul Cardeilhac, 'Laurent Tailhade pamphlétaire, satirique et poète maudit de la Bigorre', *Bulletin de la Société Ramond* (Bagnères, 1959–62), 88–108; Gilles Picq, introduction to Tailhade's *Plaidoyer pour Dreyfus* (Paris, 1952); *OTP*, ch. 3 and notes; Malcolm Pittock, 'Wilfred Owen, Tailhade, Tolstoy, and Pacifism', *Review of English Studies* (May 1998), 154–66. Some sources say Tailhade renounced anarchism after his prison sentence, but he seems to have remained a rebel. P. d'Elissagarey, 'Un duel avec Laurent Tailhade', *Bulletin de la Société Ramond* (1966–8), 70–5, tells the story of his fifteenth duel. My translation of his speech at the Casino is based on a report in *L'Avenir*.

9   OL, 286. The punctuation is probably SO's.

10   Tailhade to WO, 1 April 1915 (OEF 469–70).

11   Renan, *Recollections of My Youth*, tr. C.R.B. Pitman (1929), 344.

12   *CPF*, 435, and MS have 'crown' for 'crowd', a slip of WO's pen. Tailhade's word is 'plèbe'. 'Moon-white': WO's adjective, embellishing Tailhade's 'blancs'.

13   *CPF*, 433, 437–8. I emend the text of these two quotations from MS.

14   *CPF*, 259–60.

15   *Poèmes Élégiaques*, 179.

16   *OTP*, 193–4. For Albine's unfinished novel, see Jean Loisy, *De la mort à l'espérance* (Paris, 1952).

CHAPTER 9: FREELANCE (PAGES 141–65)

1   L288. HO could not resist adding a footnote that he had been in 'submarine waters at this time'. He was in fact at home when WO wrote (see Appendix D).

2   *JFO* says WO actually went to La Rochelle, but WO's letters seem to contradict this.

3   KS, 41.

4   *JFO* III, 63.

5   André: L292 (October 1914), 375 (August 1915). Only in the second of these references to the boy does WO mention his name. Silence about it in 1914 concealed the fact, deliberately or not, that André's mother and WO's landlady at Rue Desfourniel (correct spelling) were both named Veuve (Widow) Martin. The two women were not one and the same, but they may have been related. Wilfred found the Desfourniel room remarkably quickly; perhaps André helped him.

6   *OTP*, 199.

7   L305n.

8   L303. WO misdates this letter December for January.

9   L304 [redeemers], 307 [Scarborough], 308 [happenings].

10   In late January WO mentions arranging credits at Alexandria and Cairo. In April Tailhade believed WO might be going to Egypt or even India. On *c.* 25 March WO asks LG not to 'spread news of my Travel', but this might refer to an otherwise unrecorded visit to Paris to see LG and his father (a Gunston family sketchbook shows that the two Gunstons were there, 27 March–3 April).

11   *L319. See also L330.

12   For the 'Perseus' fragments, not all of which are identified as such in *CPF*, see *OTP*, 42–53.

13   But Garros had invented a new weapon, a gun that could be fired forward through the propeller by the pilot.

14   L363 [strokes], 367 [sorrowfully], 302 [pretty], 328 [China], 316n.

15   L308. *WOB*, 118, seems mistaken in assuming the Christmas acolytes were the de la Touche boys. The Easter date was, of course, 1915, not (*CPF*, 109) 1914.

16   L340 [stuff], 303 [seraphic], 339 [woods], 340 [Perseus].

17   L339 (this letter, MS undated, seems *c.* 20 April, not early in the month).

18   L370 [composer].

19   The content of this ballad implies 1915, but I see no evidence for *CPF*'s assertion that the poem was written in London in October–November.

20   Now the Waverley House Hotel, Southampton Row.

21   L349 [happy], 362 [nerves].

22   L361 [Morley]. WO apparently heard about Morley's current feminist campaign for mixed recreation clubs (L362). L360 postscript implies that he visited Dunsden. Information about Wigan's marriage from the parish magazine and local memories. Cuthbert Wigan and Trevor Lingley assisted at the service, which was held in a leading Evangelical church in Bristol.

23   L352. Card to Johnny: OL, 287.

24   This phrase comes from Flaubert's *Madame Bovary*, a book WO had no doubt read on Tailhade's advice. It reappears in a 1917 fragment and leads to the passing-bells in

'Anthem'. See *OTP*, 212 n.34, 112. 'A Palinode' has features in common with the 'Ballad of the Morose Afternoon'.

25 WO did not (*WOB*, 121) soon move to another room, but simply made a small correction to his address (L357, opening sentence).

26 L365, 376. *CL* prints at least three postcards out of sequence in this period: L367 is postmarked 23 August, not July; L376 seems July, not August; L377 is late June, not August.

27 Or perhaps the lines date from 1916, when WO certainly saw a Zeppelin.

28 *CPF*, 76, where the two halves of the poem, previously regarded as two separate works, are reunited at my suggestion. See OL, 287.

29 On a part-draft of 'Impromptu' sent to LG, WO comments approvingly on something called 'The Weaver'. This was a poem in Mona Douglas, *Manx Song and Maiden Song* (June 1915), the first of the Little Books.

30 WO's army file records that his first medical was on 15 September 1915.

31 Science, religion, business: see L309.

CHAPTER 10: CADET (PAGES 166–85)

1 See S.S. Higham, ed., *The Regimental Roll of Honour and War Record of the Artists' Rifles* (1922); H.A.R. May, *Memories of the Artists' Rifles* (1929); C.J. Blomfield, *Once an Artist, Always an Artist* (1921). The original suggestion of a Volunteer Corps for artists came from Edward Stirling, a friend of Carlyle's. The Corps was formed in 1860 at a time when volunteers were being raised all over the country in response to a perceived threat from France. Later, when Germany began to look dangerous, the Volunteers were reorganised as the Territorial Force.

Army names and numbers can be confusing. By 1914 the Artists' Rifles was officially 28th Battalion, London Regiment, and its own three battalions were 1/28th, 2/28th, 3/28th. Nevertheless Higham and May refer to what was technically a battalion within the London Regiment as a regiment in its own right, as WO does on occasions. The army fought by battalions, not by regiments, and it was common for soldiers to refer to their own battalion as 'the regiment'. 1/28th was the Artists' only active service battalion. 2/28th was formed soon after the war started, and 3/28th at the end of 1914. In 1915 2/28th was absorbed into the other two, whereupon 3/28th was renumbered 2/28th and then reclassified as 2nd Artists' Rifles OTC (*Times*, 12 October 1915) just before WO joined. The CO (Commanding Officer) of this 2nd, formerly 3rd, battalion was William Shirley, not (L404n) W.C. Horsley. Until 1916 the Artists were one of only two mobilised officer training units, the other being the Inns of Court OTC.

2 *Times Recruiting Supplement*, 3 November 1915. See also articles on the Artists, *Times*, 14 September, 5 November.

3 Eliot, *Letters*, ed. Valerie Eliot (1988), I, 56.

4 Now Boswell Street, off Queen Square. For a description of the 'Poetry House' see my *Harold Monro: Poet of the New Age* (2001).

5 The 'dazzlingly fine' anthem was 'Thou wilt keep him in perfect peace' by Charles Jekyll; the preacher was Canon W.H. Carnegie.

6 Another marked feature of WO's letters during his training is that many of them are very brief and often dated only with the day of the week. Most of the dates given in *CL* were supplied by HO, frequently inaccurately. So, e.g., WO writes only 'Wednesday' and HO adds '10 February 1916', but 10 February 1916 was a Thursday. In this case and many others HO seems to be copying the postmark from an envelope he then threw away; WO would have written the letter at night and posted it next morning. Sometimes, though, HO is out by much more than a day. Among others, L389 is probably 12

November, not 2; L418 must be 5 February; L428 precedes L426. Many other corrections are listed by Paul Norgate in *SL*, Appendix C.

7   Thomas, *Collected Poems*, ed. R.G. Thomas (1981 edn), 156. See also his *Selected Letters*, ed. R.G. Thomas (1995), and Eleanor Farjeon, *Edward Thomas: The Last Four Years*, ed. Anne Harvey (1997).

8   L388. The poem is the first in Monro's quartet, 'Youth in Arms', written in autumn 1914.

9   L388, 436 (where the address is given as 21, either WO's error or a misprint; 21 was a greengrocer's). *WOB*, 129, seems mistaken in saying WO actually moved in at Devonshire Street in October 1915 (see L390). L436n says WO kept the room for some months, if not for the whole of 1916. He certainly mentions escaping from camp to his 'Poet's Room' in March 1916 (L425) and asks SO to write to him c/o Middleton in May, but he may not have had a permanent booking. He chose to stay at the Bookshop itself in February.

10 Born William Scharlieb in 1866, Shirley had changed his name in 1914. His father had been a colonel and magistrate in India, and his mother (Dame) Mary Scharlieb was famous as the first woman gynaecologist.

11 William Shirley, *Moral: the most important factor in war* (1916). Cp. the greatest of all Christian commandments, 'Thou shalt love the Lord thy God with all thy heart, and with all thy soul, and with all thy mind, and with all thy strength'.

12 Essex Record Office.

13 *Tatler* (17 November 1915), 217. The 3 November number has a photograph of the officers.

14 Miss Morley thought Denny a more promising student than Wilfred. He was killed in 1917, but some of his poems were eventually published (*Triumphant Laughter*, 1978).

15 Born Hans Waldemar Schenk, Ford had changed his name in 1914. When he applied for a commission at the end of 1915 (with the support of Col. Shirley, formerly Scharlieb), he was told that men of enemy parentage had to fight in the ranks before they could become officers. It was to take Ford more than a year to overcome this ruling, and even then he was only allowed to serve in South Africa.

16 Herbert Bradley Briggs was wounded near Bullecourt in August 1918 but survived to return to Leeds and graduate BSc in 1921, MSc in 1922. He became a chemist with ICI after the war. His father, a manufacturer of washing machines in Leeds, died when Herbert was two, and his mother had to struggle to find university fees.

17 *Romford Times*, 12 May, 28 April 1915. Information about Romford, Hornchurch, the Williams and Harper families, Briggs and the Artists from Danny Wigley. Albert Charles Williams, a commercial clerk, and his wife lived at The Croft (now 29) Ernest Road, Emerson Park. Edward Williams and Stanley Harper, younger brothers of the two Scouts, joined a newly formed 6th Romford Troop in 1917. Ray's elder sister, Molly, later married another Artist who used to visit the house, Austin Bullock; her daughter, Mrs Mary Knight, still has Mrs Williams's birthday book, in which WO has written his name and address.

18 *Romford Times*, 9 February, 26 January 1916.

19 L323.

20 Walter and Jessie Harper lived at Cheshunt in Isabel Road (now 22 Burnthouse Avenue), a substantial seven-bedroomed villa next to the Congregational church in Emerson Park; they were probably church members like the Williamses. Mr Harper, an insurance inspector, served as a special constable in 1916–19. The wood must have been Burnthouse Wood just across the road, then still a wild area on the banks of a little river.

21 *JFO* III, 141–51, 262 [Ilford], 146 [austerity]. The suggestion that WO was in fact playing

a practical joke comes from Danny Wigley, who has made a meticulous study of the possible facts and fictions of HO's story.

22 The manual title is not the only evidence for dating 'Purgatorial Passions' and the Elegy. The handwriting and the Brooke and Joergens quotations are likely to be pre-1917, and the drums and pipes may derive from the new drum and fife band in April 1916. *CPF*, 454, ascribes both MSS to between September 1915 and early summer 1916, but WO did not enlist until October 1915 and did not start musketry until January 1916. He would not have needed to know how to *instruct* until later still.

23 *JFO* III, 262.

24 *JFO* III, 132–6; cp. L105 [socks].

25 Hullcoop was commissioned from the Artists into the Royal West Surreys, December 1916.

26 L553. I assume the Regent's Park parade was on 4 March 1916.

27 Edward Thomas, 'Thaw', March 1915.

28 Charles Thomas Perfect, *Hornchurch during the Great War* (1920), 121–2. The crew survived.

29 If Ray was the companion, the outing could have been a treat for his birthday (1 May). But Bertie is perhaps more likely, as his family seem to have had cultural interests. The sonnet describes the sort of scene popular among Academicians of the day; WO may have been thinking of a painting in the exhibition. *WOB* believes 'To —' 'almost certainly' refers to the de la Touche boys, but there is no evidence WO saw any of the four brothers after 1915.

CHAPTER 11: SECOND LIEUTENANT (PAGES 186–202)

1 WO, Crampton and T.A. Doran are listed together in the *Gazette*, 8 June 1916, 5726.

2 *CL* misdates many of WO's letters from camp (see ch. 10 n.6 above), usually by a day or two. Among others, L438 must be 12 June, not 18th; L439 must be Saturday 17th, not 19th; L443 is probably 10 or 11 July, not Friday 7th; L447 must be 31 June, not 23rd; L448 is August, not July, written from Mytchett later than L450.

3 'Lancashire Lads': a widely used phrase in the ranks and elsewhere (cp. 'laads', L442). WO could be deliberately echoing Housman's *A Shropshire Lad* (a phrase he elsewhere applies to Colin), but he was writing to Colin (L441) and would not have intended any homosexual implication, despite claims to the contrary by some recent critics.

4 WO's copy of Thomas's book, published May 1916, is inscribed 'Witley Camp', so was not (*WOB*, 130) bought in Essex. I assume Wilfred found it at Thorpe's, a shop he certainly went to; the place was still a delight in my childhood half a century later.

5 A correspondent in the *Surrey Advertiser*, 8 July 1916, reported hearing the guns from Leith Hill.

6 Gordon's son, the late David Gunston, once suggested to me that as an optician Gordon might have been engaged in secret work on rangefinding devices, but he offered no evidence. He had earlier said that both his father and LG had 'lain low' during the war. If Gordon had been doing secret work, he would have worn an 'On Government Service' badge and WO would have known that he did so.

7 Passage omitted from L442.

8 I owe this reading of the portraits to Danny Wigley.

9 Gary Sheffield tells me that moving men into other units was deliberate policy from July 1916. Until then 'pals' had often volunteered for the same battalion, with the result that the Somme casualties had caused great distress in home communities.

10 Acting Lt-Col. W. Hughes Ridge had commanded the 3/5th Manchesters since June 1915, having been in the Volunteers for years before the war.

11 Gustav Hamel had given a flying display from the Shrewsbury racecourse before the war.

12 Southeast England was dreading the new Super-Zeppelin, capable of flying far higher than planes.

13 See *OTP*, 79–82.

14 *CPF*, 323–5. In my opinion this fragment should be regarded as work for a poem that has not survived or was never completed, not as work for 'The End'. See *OTP*, 63–5.

15 L459 (dated 'Wednesday', so 13, not 15, September). *JFO* III, 151–8.

16 OS, 103.

17 The huge camp at Park Hall had many huts, but they must have been occupied by other units.

18 Slightly younger than WO, Rickard was the son of a Wesleyan minister in Barbados and had been educated at Kingswood School, Bath. He had joined up in the ranks in 1914 and had served in Gallipoli.

19 Mr and Mrs Hugh Avery lived at 'Maisonette', 143 Southbank Road. I have not discovered how SO knew them. For the coat, see L471, 503. WO also used the phrase 'little family' at Mytchett (L450).

20 The 5th Manchesters were in the East Lancs Reserve Division.

21 Two target mounds can still be seen on the golf course. The firing point must have been on the site of the modern road, Knowsley Gate.

22 LG, 'L'Amour', *YM* (10 November 1916). See *OTP*, 123. WO said it would be better to send his own poems to 'Helen Bowick' for recitation. Ellen Bowick had given recitals to the Abbey Foregate Literary Society in Shrewsbury, as had Ernest Denny (not the Romford cadet of that name). SO apparently did send some poems to Denny, who politely declined to use them (L471, 487).

23 *CPF*, 508–9. The 'Kings and Christs' drafts are undated, but see L471.

24 L466n says the case suffered in transit, but WO's letter implies that he was responsible. L469 is a card addressed to 'T. Owen, Esq.', not to SO.

25 WO thought of clubbing with HO to buy a silver teapot, jug and basin, but a year later he sent a teapot from Scarborough, where he had learned to bargain for antiques. The 1916 present was presumably something cheaper (L472, 575).

26 L473. WO dates this letter 'Monday'. HO adds 9 December, actually a Saturday. Other letters show that WO was at Fleetwood for four weeks from very early November; he would have been back at Southport by Monday 4 December.

27 OEF 447.

28 L474, dated 29 December by HO, but actually written on the 28th. WO was ordered to embark on the 29th and clearly did so; his order was stamped that day by the authorities at Calais.

CHAPTER 12: SEVENTH HELL (PAGES 203–24)

1 Calais because a ship had run aground at Boulogne, blocking the harbour entrance.

2 Lt-Col. Sir Percy Cunynghame, 10th Bt, a former diplomat.

3 There seems no reason to believe that WO must 'surely be wrong' (*WOB*, 297 n.4) in remembering he was at Étaples on 31 December 1916.

4 Wylly (the Manchesters' historian) and others confuse this Halloy with the one east of Doullens.

5 T.S. Eliot's brother-in-law, Maurice Haigh Wood, was a subaltern in the 2nd Manchesters, but he seems not to have been in France at the same times as WO.

6 L557. Luxmoore: PRO WO76/31, ff. 63, 68. Philip Guest draws my attention to Whinyates, 669: Luxmoore was apparently nicknamed 'Corky' because of his artificial leg.

7   See my 'Concealed messages in Wilfred Owen's trench letters', *Notes & Queries* (December 1980), reprinted as Appendix B in *SL*.

8   John Keegan, *The First World War* (1998), 22.

9   One of the characters in Frederic Manning's great novel, *The Middle Parts of Fortune* (1929), describes Courcelles as 'lousy with guns'.

10 The army called such progress 'marching', although, as WO said, there was no 'Left-Right-Left' discipline to it. Communication trenches began at Colincamps. The distance from Courcelles to the front as the crow flies was barely three miles, but the sinuous trench no doubt made it twice that.

11 It has never been pointed out, I think, that *The Middle Parts of Fortune* ends with a scene in exactly the same positions that the Manchesters occupied. Using his own experience of the assault on Serre in November 1916, Manning places his fictional battalion in reserve at Courcelles, then in the line with forward HQ in Legend Trench (also used by the Manchesters) and the front companies in Monk Trench (see map). The principal character, Bourne, takes part in a raid on what seems to be the Quadrilateral and is killed returning through No Man's Land; his body is carried through Monk and Delaunay trenches. Manning would have had no idea that some of WO's poems describe this same sector.

12 Order dated 17 January 1917, the day C and D went in (battalion war diary, PRO WO95/2392). I assume a similar order was issued to A and B. WO said after he came out that the battalion was never going to go back to the dugout; hence, perhaps, the lack of any reference to it in the order to C and D. The order expects four companies to go forward, but the diary is clear that only two did on both occasions, one in the line and one in support. Despite the confident map in M/G, I do not think there is enough evidence to prove an exact position for the dugout.

13 I have not found any record of such a court-martial; WO may have heard a false rumour. There is some doubt about the date of the relief: the Manchesters' diary says they were back in billets by 2.30 p.m. on the 15th, but I think that has to be an error. According to 14th Brigade's diary and orders, the Manchesters were relieved on the night of 15/16th. Reliefs had to take place in darkness, and according to 32nd Division's location reports the Manchesters were still in the line at 6 a.m. on the 15th (there is no report for the 16th). The HLI diary is less clear but seems to confirm that the Manchesters were relieved at about midnight on 15/16th.

14 The Somme films actually impressed many soldiers, despite WO's scorn.

15 The official historian says that many soldiers made themselves ill by drinking melted ice in January 1917, but at least the frost put a stop to trench foot; he does not mention frostbite. Wilfred's feet were still giving trouble in 1918.

16 WO said he was 'honoured' to be President: the job was not an unwelcome chore, as some commentators have described it.

17 L482: 'Quite 10 years ago I made a study of this town & Cathedral, in the Treasury'. The old Treasury building survives in Abbeville; WO's 'in' is probably an error for 'and'. I assume he refers to a school project, but he could have visited Abbeville in 1908–9 on holiday with TO. WO's 1917 postcard from the town is with his letters (HRC).

CHAPTER 13: TO THE HINDENBURG LINE (PAGES 225–42)

1   Sorrell's army file records him as single, RC, born in 1888 to British parents in Buenos Aires and educated there. No trace has been found of his poetry.

2   WO's file says the fall was into a well at Bouchoir. EB quotes from the lost letter, apparently dated 14 March from Le Quesnoy, in which WO says the fall into 'a kind of well' had happened the night before, but subsequent letters describe the hole as a deep cellar and imply that he had been in it for twenty-four hours or more (L494–5).

3   L494n identifies the shanty as the military hospital at Nesle, but as Philip Guest has pointed out, Allied troops did not enter Nesle until 18 March. The route for a casualty was collecting point – clearing station – base hospital – home.

4   WO names the servant as Pte Heath, but does not say whether Heath remained at Gailly.

5   13 CCS war diary (PRO WO95/562).

6   Each man had to wear two discs (not three as in *WPO*, 114). If he was killed, one was buried with him, the other sent to army records.

7   Whinyates, 184.

8   WO identifies the place only as 'V', probably Voyennes, near Nesle. The Germans had concentrated civilians in those two places. *CL* suggests Villers-Bretonneux, but that seems too near Amiens.

9   L502. WO dated this letter 4 March, perhaps a sign of nerves; it must in fact have been written on 3 April. Elsewhere he says he spent four days travelling from the CCS to the battalion and another four in the line. The battalion was relieved on the night of 6 April (not 8th, as in *CL* and Wylly), so WO must have left Gailly on 30 March and reached the battalion on 3 April, spending 3–6 April inclusive in the line.

10 Heydon in fact survived, though his fighting days were over. He was given a job in the Ministry of Munitions.

11 The late Martin Taylor drew my attention to Dixon's diary (IWM).

12 The winter of 1916–17 was one of only two periods in the war when the Germans had air superiority.

13 'Beauty', *CPF*, 490.

14 The divisional padre also saw the crash (Whinyates, 196). Helen McPhail tells me the plane was an Albatross, piloted by Lt Roland Nauck (Patrick Richard, *Quand leurs ailes se brisaient*, 2000).

15 Most sources imply that April 1917 was a period of unrelieved bad weather, but Fourth Army's diary records the 14th as a rare moment of clear sunshine. I have mistakenly said elsewhere that the sunlight in 'Spring Offensive' is not a factual memory.

16 Lumsden, educated at Bristol Grammar School, belonged to the Royal Marine Artillery, not the infantry. He had been promoted from Major through Colonel to Brigadier-General in one go, on the back of an exploit by the Manchesters. Col. Luxmoore, Old Etonian and long-serving infantryman, may well have had difficulty in treating him with due respect. Lumsden was killed in action in 1918.

17 The CO's report is with the battalion diary. Wylly ignores the day's operations entirely, apart from quoting Luxmoore on the men's courage during the barrage (which Wylly places at Savy Wood, thereby misleading later commentators into regarding WO's mentions of Fayet as evidence of mental confusion). Wylly's silence suggests the day was not remembered as a great success.

18 Possibly a case of 'friendly fire'. WO says (L506) that the snipers were German, but they may in fact have been British: the wood seems to have been captured by this stage.

19 L506. WO regularly refers to the enemy as the 'Bo(s)che' or 'Hun', as most soldiers did. The modern notion that such terms were mainly used by propagandists seems questionable.

20 Maps in use at the time are marked 'Suspected trench' north of the farm, but the line is not fully shown. The trench may have been taken back by the Germans, or it may have been incorporated into the new British line, which ran remarkably close to the enemy wire here in 1918. Maps made in 1918 show a 'Dancourt Trench' at or near this point, but the name and possibly the trench itself date from May–December 1917, when the area was occupied by the French.

21 Hubert Gaukroger, born Manchester, fruit grower at Honeybourne before the war, enlisted in ranks, Worcesters, August 1914. Commissioned, Manchesters, 1915. Buried 'in the vicinity of Savy', according to an official letter in his file, and later moved to the war cemetery outside the village. Dixon's diary records that some men were killed on the railway bank when the attack started on 2 April.

22 EB, 22. I assume the quotation is from one of WO's letters. It appears to refer to nights after his shell-shock.

23 *London Gazette*, 4 June 1917, 5484, reports Sorrell's award. I have not found the citation.

24 Medical Board report, 25 June 1917. This is the only description of WO's symptoms in his file.

25 Dempster took over signing the battalion diary from Luxmoore on 1 May, so I assume that was the day on which effective command was transferred. WO's continued respect for Luxmoore and dislike for Dempster suggests that it was Dempster who made the cowardice accusation. See Appendix B.

CHAPTER 14: MENTAL CASE (PAGES 243–63)

1 I have used the terms neurasthenia and shell-shock more or less indiscriminately, as WO did, but doctors at the time distinguished between them. Neurasthenia meant a state of nervous exhaustion, with symptoms such as depression, loss of self-respect, insomnia and violent dreams. Shell-shock was more serious, a complete breakdown. Specialists regarded the word 'shell-shock' as inaccurate – many breakdowns were not directly caused by shelling – but it remained in popular use.

2 MS of first draft, *TLY*, 41. WO noted that these were the doctor's very words, although 'dirt' may be a euphemism.

3 The introducer must have been less familiar with the publisher than he pretended. Macdonald did not in fact exist, the name being an alias for Galloway Kyle, the unscrupulous Director of the Poetry Society.

4 L509n. Cp. LG, 'The moon shone pale as a pearl' (*The Nymph*, 9).

5 'Dulce et Decorum Est', 'The Sentry'. WO had always been susceptible to eyes: Rampton's were 'melancholy', André Martin's 'beautiful', Nénette's 'her chief feature' (L283), M. Lèger's 'deep, dark' (L278), M. Poitou's 'dark and terrible' (L250), and eyes seen in paintings were 'thrilling' (*L82) or movingly 'sad' (L549).

6 Sorrell had a serious relapse in October 1917 and spent some time in a mental hospital. He was fit enough to be sent to Italy in 1918, but he was suffering from insomnia and hypertension by 1919, when his file ends.

7 L512. WO must be referring here to *God the Invisible King*, published 10 May 1917. He had apparently read only an extract from a review.

8 13 CCS, presumably including Brown, went to Tincourt, east of Péronne.

9 This major was surely not (*WOB*, 187n) Dempster.

10 A few patients' files from Craiglockhart recently came to light at the Rivers Clinic, Royal Edinburgh Hospital, all of serious cases who would have needed treatment even in peacetime. Some of these officers protested furiously at losing their freedom when sent on to asylums and clinics. Craiglockhart was an open hospital for men who were expected to recover. *TLY*, 19, is mistaken in suggesting WO would have seen severe 'mental cases' there.

11 When William Brown, the specialist from 13 CCS, took over Craiglockhart in July 1918, he was appalled at the 'hopelessly drifting and inefficient way' the place was run. Among his many reforms was to sack the matron, Margaret MacBean, because she was failing to control patients and ensure food hygiene (PRO WO399/5084 – I am grateful to Margaret Hall for this reference).

12 Arthur John Brock (1879–1949): in addition to sources given in *OTP*, 195–6, and *TLY*, I draw on unsigned, undated notes made for Sassoon by a former member of the hospital staff (IWM).

13 EB, 29. If Brock's letters referred to the cowardice question, they would have been destroyed by HO.

14 I have mistakenly said elsewhere that the term 'ergotherapy' was Brock's own coinage. Actually it was in use on the Continent well before 1914; he had probably come across it while studying in the German-speaking countries. He regarded Germany as the most neurasthenic nation of all, given over to specialisms and mechanical ways of doing things, but many of his ideas had German origins. His originality lay in linking notions of occupational therapy with the theories and practice of the Outlook Tower.

15 A.J. Brock, *Health and Conduct* (1923), 171–2.

16 *L532.

17 The *camera* can still be visited. The word 'sociology' has changed its meaning since Geddes's day, but his ideas have been influential in such matters as town planning. *OTP* lists some of the many studies of Geddes. See also Vernon Lee, *The Tower of Mirrors* (1914). The National Library of Scotland has Tower records, Geddes MSS and Brock's minutes of the Open Spaces Committee. Keele University Library has associated material.

18 The guidebook, *A First Visit to the Outlook Tower* (c. 1910), explained that 'to fully and truly observe and understand our region we must seek the help of all the specialists, from astronomer to historian, from physician to poet'.

19 'The Wrestlers', *CPF*, 520–5 (where the long endnote cites and largely derives from my 'A Sociological Cure for Shellshock: Dr Brock and Wilfred Owen', *Sociological Review*, May 1977, 377–86).

20 *IBI*, 317.

21 The next lines refer to 'Bards' cutting hay, perhaps a memory of getting in the haycrop with M. Léger.

22 *CPF*, 460–1.

23 The surviving manuscript (EB, 56, quotes another) is written on a type of paper WO otherwise only used for the Limehouse fragment and four letters between 30 July and 10 August 1917. The strict pararhymes suggest the period of 'Song of Songs' and 'From My Diary'.

24 2/Lt John Leslie Isaacson had transferred from the Royal Garrison Artillery to the Royal Flying Corps in 1916 and had collapsed with nervous strain after a long flight in May 1917. In January 1918 he was allowed to resign from the army as permanently unfit.

25 Knowing SO's suspicion of actresses, Wilfred assured her the two ladies were 'model wives ... model women'.

26 WO misquotes from Rev. 2.7, 2.28 and 22.16.

27 Wilson Barrett, *Lucky Durham* (1905). I have never found a copy; Samuel French, the theatre publishers, tell me none may survive.

28 Keats to Wodehouse, 27 October 1818. Shelley, *Defence of Poetry* (1821).

29 'Tennyson is like a great child, simple and very self-absorbed': Coventry Patmore, quoted in A.C. Benson, *Tennyson* (1912), 79.

30 *L539. WO wrote 'lads' cheeks', I think, not 'lad's cheeks' as in *CL*.

31 Rom. 12.19. As in some late Dunsden poems WO subverts a biblical text to defy Church authority. He had criticised Church leaders earlier in 1917; at that stage he had still blamed Germany for the war, and in my opinion he is still doing so here: he will 'repay' by continuing to fight. By 10 August he could have been reading SS, but I do not think his comment about vengeance can bear a Sassoonish interpretation.

32 There was a large asylum, Craig House, near Craiglockhart. The armbands are a running joke in *The Hydra*. A poem in a 1918 number, marked by Brock for WO's attention, also refers to distinctive tabs and says that patients were stared at in Princes Street: 'all people think us mad'.

CHAPTER 15: DISCIPLE (PAGES 264–83)

1   *TLY* mistakenly suggests WO first met SS on Thursday 16 August. L540 (Wednesday 15 August) has a postscript dated 'Friday aft.' which gives no sign the meeting has yet taken place. L541 (22 August) says WO first called on SS 'one morning last week', which makes Saturday the 18th the only possibility.

2   L541 to LG describes SS's head as 'chisel'd', a teasing allusion to a phrase of LG's ('a white chiselled nose', *The Nymph*, 33).

3   Peter Parker, *The Old Lie* (1987), 193n.

4   *SSD*, 183, 189.

5   My account of Sassoon's military career is indebted to JMW.

6   SS to E.J. Dent, 5 April 1916 (CUL), defends the poem as true to what SS still feels.

7   *PGW*, 199 n.64.

8   First draft reproduced, *TLY*, 41. The title was no doubt suggested by SS's 'The Death-Bed'.

9   *OTP*, 107–8. WO's poem was written before SS's, not (*WOB*, 212) after: see L548.

10 CL omits this and the previous comment on LG's book from L546, 569. See *TLY*, 42, 72.

11 *L544.

12 *OTP*, 97, 218 n.6.

13 JMW, 574 nn.17, 18. SS's copy of *The Choice Before Us* is inscribed 'Sept. 10, 1917'.

14 *TLY*, 50.

15 This is the accepted final version of the poem, although *CPF* ignores what seems to be a later (but not better) draft (reproduced, *TLY*, 51). Another draft, given by HO to Benjamin Britten and first reproduced in the *Daily Telegraph*, 7 November 1998, uses the Keatsian word 'wailful' ('wailful choir', 'Ode to a Nightingale').

16 My italics. For Brice, see *PGW*, 112, 201. Hay (1915), 276. WO read one of Hay's comic novels at Gailly with enthusiasm (L509, 517). Cp. also phrasing in another popular wartime novel, John Buchan's *Greenmantle* (October 1916), ch. 16: 'the *voice* of the great guns ... their *solemn litany*, with a *minute's interval* between each' (WO's first draft begins 'What minute bells'). *WPO*, 119, suggests the Binyon echo and another from Yeats, both of which are repeated in *CPF*. *CPF*, 488, states that 'Anthem' was 'triggered' by a passage in *Poems of Today* (1916), but I am not convinced.

17 *OTP*, 104–5.

18 *OTP*, 106, 218 n.22.

19 Foundry: Miller & Co., London Road. Leonard Gray (1893–1969): see *Who Was Who*. Served on many public bodies. Interested in the garden city movement and no doubt knew Brock. Married Mary Rachel Scott, June 1916; the marriage broke up in 1929 after persistent infidelity on his part. Mary eventually became permanently insane. Francis Steinthal (b.1886): gained a third in modern history at Oxford. Married Maria Zimmern in Württemburg, 1913. Played rugby for Oxford and England and taught at Durham School before the war. Held up in his army career by his German name, but worked his way up from the ranks. Changed his name to Petrie, 1919.

20 Mayes was never fit enough again for active service; in 1918 he had a job in the Ministry of Munitions.

21 Mary Newboult to John Bell, 26 February 1967 (Oxford University Press archive, partly reproduced, *CL*, 594).

22 Years ago, asked about WO's homosexuality, LG told me WO had written to him in confidence from Edinburgh with a story that showed WO was by no means 'immune to female charms'. LG would say no more. Mrs Gray's memoir, partly quoted in EB, is among EB's papers (HRC). Cowardice: see Appendix B.

23 The Lintotts and Duncans also lived in St Bernard's Crescent. Stephen MacDonald tells me the Lintotts had an autograph MS of SS's 'The Glory of Women', perhaps given to them by WO.

24 Nicholson's memoir: EB, 133–5.

25 *TLY*, 35. Several autumn 1917 letters are missing.

26 *Hydra*, 29 September 1917.

27 WO edited six numbers (*OTP*, 206). He is obviously the author of 'The Counter Attack: a story full of morals' (21 July), an archly comic piece about meeting two of the nurses in town and accompanying them on an embarrassing shopping expedition in search of silk stockings; the French phrases and schoolmasterly asides are very typical. Whatever did he think of 'Little Pierre' (15 September), a story of a French refugee boy and an evil German soldier? The sentiments would have appalled SS, but WO had met two refugee boys in France and had been moved by their stories of German atrocities.

28 L546. SS thought the poem was 'Dreamers', but that had already appeared in *The Hydra. OTP*, 106, suggests the last stanza of 'Prelude: The Troops', but see JMW, 413, 573 n.100.

29 DW, 157–8.

30 *TLY*, 195–201, lists all WO's war poems with the most accurate dates I can provide.

31 L552. *CL* dates this letter '?16 October', but events mentioned in it and in later letters show that it must have been written 9–10 October. A draft of 'Dulce' is dated 8 October.

32 In an interesting article, 'Shell-shock and Poetry: Wilfred Owen at Craiglockhart Hospital', *English* (Spring 1987), Paul Norgate suggests that the 'quite six poems' were lyrics, but the six poems he names are hardly strong enough to have made Sassoon recommend early publishing. Norgate, like *CPF*, seems to me a little too confident about poem dates.

33 For the origins of these two poems, see *OTP*, 112–15.

34 SS protested to RG in 1930 about this description of WO, pointing out that RG had only met WO twice, once at Craiglockhart and once at RG's wedding (*IBI*, 206–7). In an unpublished letter to EB, 1 March 1930, SS says something had indeed been preying on WO's mind – the memory of seeing a friend [Gaukroger] blown to bits – but at Craiglockhart WO had looked healthy, cheerful and not at all shaky. See Appendix B and *OTP*, 76, 199.

35 *SSD*, 191.

36 RG to Edmund Gosse, 24 October 1917 (Brotherton Library, Leeds).

37 The portrait was later destroyed by SO, a regrettable loss. WO thought the watercolour a failure. The National Portrait Gallery has a photograph of a small watercolour said to be of him, but it is scarcely a likeness.

38 *WOB, TLY* and others accept SS's date of 3 November for this hilarious evening, but he seems in fact to have confused two evenings, one on 26 October, when he inscribed and dated the absurd book (Aylmer Strong, *A Human Voice*, 1917), the other on 3 November, when WO was due to catch a late train (*SSJ*, 64–5). Cp. L555, dated 29 October by SO but evidently written on the 27th.

39 OEF 3:452. *TLY*, 56.

40 WO had visited the Royal Scottish Museum's Egyptian collection, which includes a carving of Amenophis IV (Akhenaten) in profile.

41 L557n.

42 JMW, 572 n.82. *TLY*, 207, n.6.

43 *JFO* III, 126.

44 L559, 583. One draft of 'Anthem' is marked 'Nation'.

45 Wilde's phrase, quoted, Richard Ellmann, *Oscar Wilde* (1987), 538.

46 *SSD*, 196. 'You had better make him [WO] the third in your triangle,' SS told RG, who had been talking of forming a working trio with SS and Nichols. SS's slightly patronising attitude to WO suggests he was slower than RG to recognise WO's talent. For Ross and his circle, see Maureen Borland, *Wilde's Devoted Friend* (1990); *SSJ*; OS; *OTP*, 196–7. The two parts of L559 describing WO's first two meetings with Ross are printed in reverse order in *CL*.

47 The concert included works by Beethoven, Wagner and Elgar, but the piece WO wanted to hear was no doubt 'Le Nil' by Leroux, the composer he had met in Paris. The conductor was Henry Wood.

48 For the 22 words omitted from L561, see *TLY*, 64.

49 *TLY*, 61–2.

50 For some reason it has become commonplace to assume that these winks about SS implied an understanding between WO and Monro that all three poets were gay. There are no grounds for this. Monro had probably not yet met SS. WO would not have given away confidences, nor hinted at them in a letter home.

CHAPTER 16: MAJOR DOMO (PAGES 284–304)

1 *CL* guesses WO was 'Camp Commandant', but H.R. Bate told me that the job was much too lowly to merit such a title. A Camp Commandant in 1914–18 was a senior figure.

2 Among men, Christian names were normally reserved for family members and very close friends. WO was still addressing even CSM by surname in October 1918.

3 L567. The man had been 'at Bangower, & Blanche has written to him since!' Bangour War Hospital was near Edinburgh (the patients in autumn 1917 included Ivor Gurney).

4 My guess in *TLY* that WO's room was on the top floor (because he liked attics) was clearly mistaken: he says he used to sit in the turret and look down on the sea, but as Peter Owen has pointed out, the window-sills in the top-floor room are too high for that to be possible. The first floor, within easiest reach of the office, seems the most likely.

5 H. Roland Bate, 'Sixty Years After', TS with MS additions (IWM). Bate had thought of WO at Romford as 'harmlessly coddled in his own nervous and precious shyness', but by 1917-18 WO seemed to have 'acquired a positive attitude of aloof superiority'. Bate, who became a priest, disapproved of the pessimism of WO's poems and retained a poor opinion of the man. He was exasperated by what he regarded as the 'idolised' portrait of WO in *WOB*. Faced with evidence of WO's capacity for laughter and courage, Bate could only suggest that both were the result of whisky, a notion he repeated to me when I met him a decade or so ago.

6 George Derbyshire, historian of the 5th Manchesters, to Joseph Cohen, several letters, 1953–5 (HRC).

7 L569. Passage omitted from *CL*; quoted in full, *TLY*, 72.

8 *OTP*, 120.

9 'plain': WO originally wrote 'ugly'.

10 From a version published in *The Athenaeum* (13 August 1920).

11 Russell, Wells, Shelley: *OTP*, 130–2.

12 One draft entitled 'Hospital Barge at Cerisy' (the village next to Gailly). In a letter quoted in EB, 124, now lost, WO describes the poem as 'Sunday morning's effort'; final draft actually dated 8 December, a Saturday.

13 *OTP*, 140–2. DK, 277–95, adds elegies by Swinburne and SS to my list. DK's discussion of WO as elegist could hardly be bettered.

14 WO had sent a silver teapot (it survives), but this may have been a belated Silver Wedding present. See ch.11 n.25 above.

15 Cousin May must have gone away soon afterwards, for WO saw no more of her. She reappears in later Scarborough directories, sharing an address with a Miss Monument, whom WO probably met (the curious name appears in draft work for his poem, 'Schoolmistress').

16 *OTP*, 120.

17 'It would be a crime to exhibit the fine side of war, even if there were one!' (Barbusse, *Under Fire*, 1929 edn, 342). For the echoes of RG and LG in 'Apologia', see DW, 67, and *OTP*, 121–3. The final draft of the poem is dated November 1917, but it reads like a response to RG's December letter (*CL*, 595–6).

18 L578. Spacing of the last line as in MS.

19 *Nation*, 26 January 1918.

20 Meiklejohn: see JMW, 307-8, and Anthony Powell, *The Strangers All Are Gone* (1982), 42.

21 SS to SO, 20 February [1921] (OEF).

22 L588. The surviving fragment of this letter is dated '11 Feb 1918 HO'. I have not identified the quotation; WO had just had a letter from CSM.

23 Philip Gillespie Bainbrigge (1890–1918). For an example of his 'private' verse, see Timothy d'Arch Smith, *Love in Earnest* (1970), 148–50. See also Martin Taylor, ed., *Lads* (1989), 69. Bainbrigge's father was a prebendary of St Paul's and Vicar of St Thomas, Regent Street, London.

24 Bainbrigge to Dent, 19 June 1918 (CUL, Add MS 7973/B/7).

25 For dates of these poems, see *TLY*, 198. Of the two drafts of 'Reunion', one is impossible to date; the other is on a type of paper WO was using in December 1917–March 1918.

26 WO owned copies of Wilde's poems and of Robert Sherard, *Oscar Wilde*, and he read Sherard's *The Real Oscar Wilde* in December 1917. L593 (22 February 1918) contains a misquotation from *De Profundis*, although WO is careful not to identify the source (*OTP*, 223 n.16).

27 CSM's translation, sent to Marsh after the war, identifies the first ghost as 'petit fantassin' (little infantryman), presumably 'little Owen' himself. See *OTP*, 155. Douglas Kerr suggests WO's nickname of 'The Ghost' (L661) may have originated in Scarborough, where people had heard he was dead. The implications of the Shadwell poem were lost on a later generation; it was even read by Ian Parsons, chairman of Chatto & Windus, at a Dunsden memorial service as an example of WO's lyric style.

28 *petit ami*: L608, from Ripon. The *ami* had just written to WO, signing off with the phrase 'Yours to a cinder'. For 'Scottie', see L588, 607, 632.

29 For a lively but unfortunately not always reliable account of the Pemberton Billing affair, see Philip Hoare, *Wilde's Last Stand: Decadence, Conspiracy and the First World War* (1997).

30 SS to RG, 28 June 1918 (CUL Add. 954/5/50: microfilm MS 11285), complains that WO hasn't written since December. This may seem scarcely credible, but there is no contrary evidence in WO's letters.

31 *OTP*, 223 n.13.

32 Cp. phrases in 'Spring Offensive': 'Halted against the shade of a last hill', 'surf of bullets', 'the little word', 'raced', 'O larger shone that smile'.

33 Claus: see *TLY*, 206 n.11.

34 LG told me the statuette was probably bought in Scarborough, not (as I had first gathered from him, OTP, pl. 6) Bordeaux. WO also mentions candlesticks and a table. I assume the teaspoons and teapot were other Scarborough finds.

35 L603.

36 Owen Owen. I assume WO's two mentions of this name (L480, 595) refer to the distinguished Welsh inspector (and certainly not to Owen Glendower, as one recent critic has suggested!). Apparently no relation to TO, this Owen Owen had been head of Oswestry High School in the 1880s and had married a daughter of John Jones, Edward Shaw's successor as mayor.

CHAPTER 17: GETTING FIT (PAGES 305–19)

1 For the site of the hut, and other references to Ripon sources, see *TLY*. Officers' huts would have been secluded from the others, as usual.

2 WO took the room between his letters of 21 and 23 March, so he must have been responding to the crisis. Ripon directories show a Miss Burton living at 7 (now 24) Borrage Lane in 1902–6; she may still have been there in 1918. He seems to have continued to sleep in camp, the cottage base functioning as a study, not as a bedroom. Borrage (from 'burgherage', not the herb) is the modern spelling, but Borage was sometimes used in WO's day.

3 For the dates of 'Insensibility' and other poems that I ascribe to Ripon, see *TLY*, 198–201.

4 *TLY* mistakenly has HO as an officer on this occasion, failing to note that *JFO* III, 166, has him as a midshipman. See Appendix D for his promotion.

5 *JFO* III, 162–9. John Bell tells me the passage was a late addition to the book.

6 HO to EB, 16 October 1950 (HRC).

7 'Projects': OEF 2:409 (reproduced, *TLY*, 116).

8 Sir Sacheverell told me years ago that he had met WO (he started our conversation by remarking, 'Of course you know he was homosexual, poor thing'). L634 shows that WO also met Edith ('a friend of mine').

9 CSM's sonnets: see *OTP*, 198–9; *TLY*, 118–9. First sonnet and part of a 26 May letter to WO from CSM: OEF 3:460–1. Two more sonnets (*New Witness*, 7 June 1918, 10 January 1919) contain echoes of WO's Shadwell poem and 'To Eros'. 'House of Shame': a phrase from Wilde's *Ballad of Reading Gaol*.

10 WO (or SS) had recruited a poem, 'Reciprocity', from Drinkwater for *The Hydra* (MS in OEF). WO later asked for Drinkwater's *Tides*, which includes the poem, as a Christmas present. Perhaps he also knew Drinkwater's one-act play, *X=O* (1917), a possible source for 'Strange Meeting': one side of Drinkwater's equation is a pair of Greek soldiers, a poet and a would-be social reformer, and the other is a near-identical pair of Trojans. In darkness and ignorance, the Greek reformer kills the Trojan artist, and the Trojan reformer kills the Greek poet.

11 *OTP*, 31. WO could not have known of Brooke's letter (to St John Lucas), but bleeding sunsets and sunrises were a stock feature of Decadent literature.

12 According to *The Ripon Advertiser*, this or a very similar accident actually proved fatal, an outcome WO probably never knew.

CHAPTER 18: NORMAL AGAIN (PAGES 320–32)

1 The villa (photograph, *TLY*, 137) was demolished in the 1990s with the rest of the barracks. It was just to the rear and south of the other buildings.

2 Members of the Women's Army Auxiliary Corps.

3 WO's army file contains no information about the period between his last medical at Ripon and his death. The only source for the story of his being sent back to France remains his (clearly incomplete) letters and CSM's articles (see Appendix B).

4   These two titles appear in a list WO seems to have drawn up while considering which poems to send to *Wheels* (CPF, 540). 'Spring Offensive' was completed in France but probably started in Scarborough.

5   OS, 98.

6   *PGW*, 166, 208.

7   Gordon was married on 4 September 1918. His daughter Marjorie remembers that her mother disliked WO.

8   'The Calls'. I can't prove the date of this poem. The only MS is on a type of paper used at Ripon, but WO could have had some sheets left. The news about SS seems to have reached him on Friday 26 July while he was still in the flat, and he had few chances in 1918 to lean on a sill (the Ripon cottage only had a skylight). But 'sill' may be no more than a convenient rhyme word.

9   The inoculation was presumably a first step towards being drafted.

10   'Stinking' was a banned word in the Owen family, and HO marks it in MS for deletion. In L637, where *CL* reads 'smell of the Cookhouse', WO's word was undoubtedly 'stink', but it has been torn out of the MS, not quite completely.

11   Order dated 9 August from York, received Saturday 10 August at Scarborough. This and the 26 August order reproduced, *TLY*, 142, 149.

12   The only extant letter from SS to WO, 8 August 1918 (OEF 3:453; reproduced, *TLY*, 140).

13   Quoted, CSM (1921).

14   *SSJ*, 71–2; OS, 108–9. This Chelsea afternoon is the only incident in WO's life recorded in two autobiographies. CSM was not (*WOB*, 267) present. I have had to guess at some chronology. OS says the afternoon was a July Saturday, but the month was certainly August. *TLY* opts for Saturday 17 August, failing to notice that SS left for Lennel that day according to his diary. L644 records that WO reached barracks by 9 p.m. on the 17th. He could hardly have done that after a relaxed tea in Chelsea, where OS says he could not bring himself to leave in time for his train. I guess the Chelsea day was Thursday 15 August, and that WO actually left not for a train to Scarborough but with SS for dinner at the Reform, afterwards accompanying SS to the hospital (where they parted: L648). The Reform Club librarian, Simon Blundell, told me when I was researching for *TLY* that a club guest book records SS and WO dining there with Meiklejohn on the 15th, and he has since found evidence that WO was also Meiklejohn's dinner guest on the 14th. It thus seems probable that WO spent the Wednesday and Thursday nights in London, perhaps at Half Moon Street, returning to Shrewsbury on the Friday and from there to camp on the Saturday. The fact that his subsequent letters to SO make no mention of the London visit suggests he had already been able to tell her about it in person.

15   *SSJ* comments that the day was SS's only chance for 'intimate talk' with WO in 1918, so I assume he made his stabbing threat then (L649n). SS's letter to Marsh (Berg Collection, NY) is dated 'Thursday', but it may actually have been written on the Friday; SS says he will be leaving for Lennel next day (see previous note).

16   I think *CPF* ascribes too many final drafts to the second half of 1918. Only the most hurried amendments are likely to be post-Ripon, some perhaps dating from those last few days at Mahim. The poems WO sent for *Wheels* must have arrived too late: none appeared in the 1918 volume.

17   *OTP*, 162.

CHAPTER 19: THROUGH THE HINDENBURG LINE (PAGES 333–53)

1   Conal O'Riordan, 'The Poets are Cheerful!', *John O'London's Weekly* (6 June 1941), 225–6; 'One More Fortunate', *Martial Medley*, ed. Eric Partridge (1931), 357–61,

2 *WOB*, 269–70. Given WO's reluctance to be known to other soldiers as a poet, McClymont's memory of their introduction seems slightly improbable.

3 Jeremy Ward tells me that Potts became a chemistry teacher after the war, gaining a first-class London external degree in 1927 and serving from that year until his death in 1960 as senior chemistry master, North Edge (later Abbeydale) GS, Sheffield.

4 Rawlinson's original Fourth Army, in which WO had served on the Ancre, had suffered so badly in the Somme battles that it had been wound up in 1917 and Rawlinson had been given a home posting. He returned to France in late March 1918 to take over Gough's Fifth Army, which was renamed the Fourth.

5 WO may have been thinking of a recent photograph in the *Sketch*: see *OTP*, pl. 14 and 181–2.

6 John Foulkes, unsigned memoir, written for and partially quoted in EB. MS in EB's papers (HRC). Like Potts and Somerville, Foulkes was a schoolmaster after the war. He became head of a secondary modern school in Stockport and died in 1967.

7 *TLY* guesses that Jones and WO travelled together, but there is no evidence in WO's letters.

8 Uplands Cemetery, a curiously exposed site, is in direct view from a blockhouse on the now-disused railway on the western edge of Joncourt. I assume the site was chosen because men died there, although many of the Lancashire Fusiliers buried there were no doubt killed later in the day during the attack on the village.

9 Most of these pillboxes are now below ground level, but they were clearly not like the two strong blockhouses that can still be seen in Joncourt (nor like the German command bunker at La Baraque, illustrated and misleadingly captioned in *TLY*, 170). The pillboxes on the ridge appear to have been small flat-topped cubes, entered from the side or in at least one case through a trapdoor in the roof. Villagers today explain them as gun platforms.

10 Montgomery, map 10, shows a line of attack aiming at a point roughly halfway between Swiss Cottage and the elbow in the German line. 96th Bde diary records that the Manchesters first captured the elbow itself, the highest point in the line, then worked north to Swiss Cottage and south to the next bend, just short of Preselles.

11 The word came from headlines: 'ADVANCE BY SHEER FIGHTING', 'SHEER FIGHTING' (*Daily Mail*, 19 September and 3 October 1918).

12 MC citations: see Appendix C.

13 Manchester Regt archives, Stalybridge, preserve this and a dozen or so other pencil notes scrawled amid the fighting, many lacking a time or date. The standard of writing suggests most were dictated to runners. The only note from OC (Officer Commanding) D Coy is not in WO's hand, but it must have been written after Foulkes had captured thirteen (actually eighteen) prisoners, an action that certainly happened after WO had taken command. In reconstructing the sequence of events I have used these notes, also battalion, brigade and division diaries, Montgomery, Latter and other sources, including Taylor's two draft citations (see Appendix C) – and some guesswork, for the details are sometimes scarcely possible to reconcile.

14 WO said SS would have been '*en pamoisons*' (in a swoon) at the 'peace talk' in the pillbox. The tone of this comment may imply that the talk had been with an attractive young soldier (cp. DK, 212), either British or German, but the reference is also to a recent general order banning all 'peace talk' (see next chapter).

15 Souvenir copies of the message were made later. One belonging to Foulkes is reproduced in M/G, 93.

16 DW, 158.

17 Lt R. Gregg, 6th Manchesters, died of wounds 1 October 1918 aged thirty-eight, buried

at Uplands. He had one child, Mollie, aged ten. He has been confused even in army files with Reginald Arthur Gregg (L449), 5th Manchesters, who joined up as an Artist aged seventeen and survived the war.

18 *WOB*, 280, assumes Jones died, but there is no evidence for that. It seems highly unlikely WO could have been misinformed. He clearly thought Jones had been sent 'away' to hospital and home, describing him as 'wounded' and 'happily wounded' (L663–4). If Jones did in fact die, Philip Guest has found that only two 2nd Manchesters of that name died in the last two months of the war. Pte Thomas Jones – died 1 October, buried at Joncourt, apparently a single man (no age given) – had enlisted in Wigan so almost certainly came from the 5th Manchesters, a Wigan battalion; he could have been in Scarborough with WO. Pte Arthur Jones, a married man aged thirty-four, died 3 October in hospital at Rouen (other Manchester casualties were also sent to Rouen); it is possible that this Jones was wounded on the 1st and that news of his death took time to reach his unit.

CHAPTER 20: THE FINAL BATTLE (PAGES 354–66)

1 The Artists' Rifles *Roll of Honour*, which shows the highest rank attained whether permanent or acting, lists WO as Captain.
2 DW, 158.
3 The letter to TO has not survived, but see the end of L667.
4 Rawlinson's order, 7 October 1918, reproduced, *TLY*, 176.
5 *Poems and Ballads (First Series)*, Golden Pine edn (*TLY*, 151).
6 'lest the kiss / Leave my lips charred', Swinburne, 'Laus Veneris'.
7 L611.
8 WO quotes from SS's 'Prelude: The Troops'. He still regarded SS as the supreme spokesman. WO's last letters are unusually full of political comments: his convictions seem to reflect, and to be strengthened by, the mood around him.
9 *CL* omits this sentence from L667.
10 Cp. 'The Kind Ghosts', in which a woman sleeps in a richly furnished palace, undisturbed by doomed youth. 'Quiet their blood lies in her crimson rooms' (cp. 'Her little chambers drip with flower-like red', 'Laus Veneris').
11 *L671. Amendments and an addition from MS.
12 WO's experience was not altogether typical. Two other poets, Richard Aldington and Herbert Read, both knew of atrocities in the last stages of the war.
13 'Until last night though I have been reading Swinburne, I had begun to forget what a kiss was' – another dig at LG, who had perhaps still not kissed a girl.
14 Papers of Capt. Gordon Alan Potts, MC (IWM). This collection includes orders for the 1918 attack, Potts's reminiscences and some Marshall-related material. (G.A. Potts was no relation to WO's friend in Amiens.) Revisionist historians have recently – and rightly – been drawing attention to the army's success in learning from the Somme offensives, but the staff officer seems to have learned very little.
15 The content of these two paragraphs and other details in this chapter: © Vince Connolly, 'The final battle: the 4th Army crossing of the Sambre-Oise Canal, 4th November 1918', a paper read at the IWM as part of the 'Mars in the Ascendant' conference, August 2001.
16 For the probable bridge structure, see *TLY*, 182-3, 210-11.
17 Roland Bate, now attached to the 9th Royal Sussex, also took part in the attack. He had become friendly with a Royal Sussex signals officer, Richard Aldington. The events at the end of Aldington's *Death of a Hero* (1929) seem to be partly based on Bate's experiences (see David Wilkinson, '"Dying at the word of command": The last days of

Richard Aldington's war', in *Richard Aldington*, ed. A. Blayek and C. Zilboorg, 1994, 7–18). It seems unlikely (*WOB*, 298 n.6) that Aldington had WO in mind.

18 A line from a Craiglockhart fragment (CPF, 487).

19 SO to SS, 10 September n.y. [?1920] (Columbia). Foulkes: undated cutting from a Warrington newspaper [1920s] now in the possession of his daughter. Foulkes's original memoir of WO, written for EB, states that Foulkes had been told WO had been 'actually crossing the Canal'. EB replaced this with a sentence of his own, saying WO had been 'at the water's edge'. The notion that WO was killed on the bank seems to derive from this alteration by EB, who may have been using information from SO. SO had eye-witness evidence from the two soldiers who came to see her. On the other hand, her letter to SS seems consistent with Foulkes's story, and there is no contrary evidence in her letters to EB. On balance, I think Foulkes was probably right. 32nd Division's diary mentions 'repeated' attempts to repair the bridge.

20 Potts papers (IWM) include two pencil messages sent by Marshall from the canal bank at 0722 and 0815. The first says the bridge was adrift, but another attempt would be possible if more floats could be sent. The second, with its element of 'I told you so', may well have annoyed Division. Battalion, brigade and division HQ were in touch by wireless, as had not been the case in earlier battles, so a swift reply could have been sent to Marshall's HQ not far from the canal.

21 *Gazette*, 12977: 'to be Lieutenant, next above Lt. T.A. Doran. 4th Dec. 1917.' This backdated promotion, which must have brought back-pay with it, restored WO to his original position in the 5th Manchesters, immediately above Doran. It was long overdue: by October 1918 he had been third among more than eighty second lieutenants in the 5th, and all those junior to him had been commissioned in 1917–18.

22 It seems almost certain that WO never knew about his promotion or that his recommendation for a MC had been successful. Elizabeth Owen tells me his medal ribbon appears never to have been stitched to a tunic; it was probably sent to the family after his death. TO was still unsure about WO's final rank in January 1919 and had to write to the War Office to enquire. Foulkes returned to Ors soon after the war and took photographs, later giving copies to the Owens (*TLY*, 191). The temporary cross was inscribed '2nd Lieut', with no 'MC'. The stone that later replaced it is marked 'LIEUTENANT W.E.S OWEN MC' and has a misquotation from 'The End' chosen by SO: 'SHALL LIFE RENEW / THESE BODIES? / OF A TRUTH / ALL DEATH WILL HE ANNUL. W.O.' SO's letters to SS confirm that the telegram arrived on 11 November.

EPILOGUE (PAGES 367–71)

1 I discovered these poems when LG lent me a bundle of old copies he had made from WO's MSS.

2 Writing to EB in 1947, HO commented on the absence of letters to WO and speculated that SO had destroyed them. WO kept in touch with plenty of people beyond his immediate family: when he rejoined the 2nd Manchesters in September 1918, for example, ten letters were awaiting him, only two of them from SO.

3 A facsimile, ed. Martin Taylor, was published by the Imperial War Museum in 1990.

4 Harold Owen, *Dear Old Wolf*, ed. John Bell (The Backwater Press, privately printed, 1996).

5 CPF is, of course, a great improvement on earlier editions, but I have some reservations. A few early fragments and later drafts have been overlooked, wording needs amendment in places, especially in the fragments, and the reproductions of WO's rough work sometimes obscure his intentions. Some footnotes are not quite on the mark, and many of the dates ascribed to poems seem to me questionable: often no

evidence is given, or watermarks are relied on exclusively (though not consistently) as proof of first composition. The fact that a manuscript was probably written at the same time as letters with the same watermark does not mean that there were no earlier drafts.

APPENDIX A: THE SALTER FAMILY (PAGES 372–3)

1 For early Salters, see indexes to *Bye-gones, relating to Wales and the Border Counties* (reprinted articles from *The Oswestry and Border Counties Advertizer*), various dates; also 'Salter of Welshpool', *Montgomeryshire Collections* XXIV (1890), 341–6, and Isaac Watkin, *Oswestry* (1920), 107, 214–5. These sources sometimes seem to confuse the generations; I have had to do a little guessing. I have found no evidence for HO's belief that SO had some Celtic blood, although 'The Salters of Shropshire' by 'Salopian', *Shropshire Magazine* (July 1968), 28–9, claims, without solid proof, that Joseph Salter was descended from Welsh princes.

2 Plas: house. Oswestry being near the border, many local place-names are Welsh. Wilmot: probably a Mr Wilmot had once owned land in the area. A correspondent to the Oswestry newspaper in 1878, noting that the name was common to several local houses, recalled that a recently demolished cottage had been inscribed 'M.I.W. 1696'.

3 SO gave Edward's notebook to a later inhabitant of Plas Wilmot; it is now in the Oswestry public library. Edward's will, now apparently lost, is listed in *Index to wills and admons formerly preserved in the Probate Registry Chester, 1826-1830* (1972), 176. His death is noted in *The Chester Courant*, 12 January 1830. Other details from church registers.

4 A list of Edward senior's descendants, probably made by his eldest daughter and still owned by the family, names Edward junior as both Edward and Edwin; this list is clearly the source for the slightly inaccurate details in *WOB*. Edward junior's ordination papers (CRO) show that he had no qualifications but was accepted as a 'Literate Person'. His referees testified he had given good service to secondary schools in the Bath area. He never appears in Crockford's, but the *Clergy List* includes an 'E. Salter', presumably the same man.

APPENDIX B: THE ACCUSATION OF COWARDICE (PAGES 374–5)

1 CSM's reminiscences of WO are in his article, 'The Poets There Are. III – Wilfred Owen', *New Witness*, 10 December 1920, 574–5, and his subsequent letter, 'Wilfred Owen', *Nation & Athenaeum*, 26 March 1921, 909–10.

2 SO's letters to EB and Mary Gray's memoir: EB's papers, HRC. SO's letters to SS: Columbia University. Replies to her: OEF. See also *OTP*, 76–7, and *IBI*, 206–7.

APPENDIX D: HAROLD OWEN'S VOYAGES (PAGES 378–80)

1 *JFO* II, 286, 282.

2 Not all these documents survive. Those that do are at PRO; National Maritime Museum, Greenwich; and Memorial University, St John's, Newfoundland. HO's list of ships belongs to Peter Owen.

3 HO evidently did some checking between writing *JFO* and helping to edit *CL*. In contrast to the erratic chronology in *JFO*, *CL* 182n gives the date of his first voyage as 13 March 1913, no doubt the day he left home.

4 *JFO* II, 266.

5 *JFO* III, 262.

6 *JFO* III, 198-9.

Index

pupil-teacher, 37–41, 51–2, 53–4, 58;
delights in 'Fine Language', 39;
encounters Romantic poets, 39–40, 54,
see Keats, John, Shelley, Percy,
Wordsworth, William; with the
Gunstons at Alpenrose, 43–6, and the
Taylors in Torquay, 42, 46–7, 50–1; and
girls, 47–8; enjoys museum and
Haughmond, 48–9; his response to
nature, 49; takes correspondence
courses, 54, 65, 80, 88; his future
undecided, 56; passes Matric, 59, 60–1;
as parish assistant, 57, 61, 62, 65–8,
69–71, 73–83; assailed by religious
doubts, 72, 74–5, 77–8, 85–7; friendship
with Vivian Rampton, 76, 79; registers
for botany classes, 80, 82; health, 81,
82, 84; holiday at Kelso, 84–5; at
Keswick Convention, 85–7, 89; falls off
his bicycle, 88–9; inner conflict
becomes unbearable, 93, 94–5; 'furor'
and departure from Dunsden, 95–8;
illness and 'phantasies', 99–100; fails
scholarship, 101, 104–5, 106
1913–1916: goes to Bordeaux, 107, 108;
teaches at Berlitz School, 108, 109–10,
112; a music-hall engagement, 110;
pretends his father is titled, 111–12;
postpones second attempt at
scholarship, 112, 119; loneliness and
illness, 112–14; thoughts of buying
Berlitz franchise, 116; winter in
Bordeaux, 115–17; his 21st birthday, 118;
friendship with Pierre Berthaud,
118–19; the Henriette episode, 120–3;
feels 'the call of art', 124; becomes
Mme Léger's tutor, 125, 126, 127–9, 130;
and declaration of war, 130–2;
friendship with Tailhade and his
influence, 132–4, 135, 136, 137–8, 139,
140, 147; returns to Bordeaux with
Légers, 140, 141–2; watches surgical
operations, 142; finds pupils, 142, 143,
144–5, 146–7; first thoughts of
enlisting, 147, 150; with the de la
Touches, 147–50, 154–5; ambition as a
poet, 151–2; illnesses, 154, 156; with
Tailhade in Paris, 156; in London,
157–8; revisits East End, 158–9; returns
to the de la Touches, 159–63; enlists in
Artists' Rifles, 163, 164–5; training in
Bloomsbury, 166–7, 168–9; visits
Poetry Bookshop, 168, 169–70; at
Romford camp, 171–4, 175–6; invites
Boy Scouts to lunch, 175; Christmas

with the Williamses, 175; applies for
Manchester Regiment, 176; in London
air raid, 177; in quarantine, 177; games
with 'nephews', 177–8, 183; and
Harold's visit, 178–9; in London,
staying at Poetry Bookshop, 179, 181;
Monro goes through his poems, 181–2;
at Cadet School, Romford, 182–5; on
leave at Mahim, 185, 186;
commissioned in Manchester
Regiment, 186; at Witley Camp, 186–9,
190, 191–2; Sundays in Guildford,
189–90; on musketry courses, 190,
192–3, 200; applies to RFC, 194, 201; on
'New Battalion' staff, 194; visited by
Harold, 196–7; at Blackpool and
Fleetwood, 198–200; at Southport, 198,
201; ordered to France, 201–2; nearly
killed on train, 202
1917–1918: at Étaples base camp, 203, 205;
joins 2nd Manchesters, 205, 206;
encodes messages to mother, 206, 209,
225; at the front, 207–10, 212, 214–15,
217–20; anger and disillusionment,
214, 216–17, 222–3; sent on training
course at Abbeville, 220–1, 223; rejoins
2nd Manchesters, 225; friendship with
Sorrell, 225–6; back at the front,
225–6; fall and concussion, 226–7; at
CSS, Gailly, 227–8, 229; returns to the
front, 230–2, 234–6; gets souvenirs for
Colin, 235, 240; in action, 237–8,
239–40; shocked by shell explosion,
240–1; probably accused of cowardice,
242, 243, 374–5; treated at Gailly, 242,
243–50; sent to Netley Hospital, 250;
transferred to Craiglockhart Hospital,
250; treatment, 251–5, 256–8; his
mother's visit, 255, 256; takes German
lessons, 259, 273, 292; meetings and
expeditions, 260, 261; edits *The Hydra*,
260, 274; acts in plays, 260, 261, 267;
makes progress, 261; friendship with
Sassoon, 264, 267–9, 270, 271, 275–6,
278–81; meets the Grays and the
Steinthals, 271–3; teaches at Tynecastle
School, 273–4, 278; meeting with
Graves, 277; discharged for 'light
duties', 279; brief visit home, 280–1;
lunches with Robert Ross, 281–2;
misses Sassoon, 283; posted to
Scarborough as 'Major Domo', 284,
285–7; delayed promotion, 287, 300,
325, 366; gives 'War Poetry' highest
priority, 288; as a Georgian poet,

Poem	Motive	Doubtful
Miners	How the Future will forget ~~Unrecognition of~~ the dead in war.	Protest	Greater Love / A Penderer Du / Greater Love / Identity Disc / ~~See~~ Heaven. / Soldier Dream / The Seed. / ~~After the Blast~~
Arms & the Boy. } Sonnet 7. }	The unnaturalness of weapons.	Protest	
The Chances } Aliens }	Madness.	Protest	
Letter	Heroic Lies.		
Inspection } Last Word } Dulce et Decorum } Dead Beat	Inhumanity of war Indifference at Home		
Parable	Willingness of old to sacrifice young.		
S. I. W.	The insufferability of war.		
Draft.	Mentality of Troops + Vastness of Losses: with reflections on Civilians.		
The Show.	Horrible beastliness of war		
⚥ Next War:	Cheerfulness + Description. + Reflection.		
Apology:	"		
Nothing happens: } The Light	Description.		
Conscious } C de } Anthem }	Grief		
Hospital Barge } ~~Futility~~ } Strange Meeting	Foolishness of War.		
Killed Asleep : À Terre: ~~Conscious~~ The Women & the Slain }	The Soul of Soldiers	Philosophy.